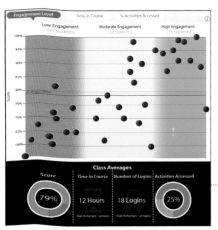

# DEVELOPING & ADMINISTERING

## a CHILD CARE AND EDUCATION PROGRAM

### 9TH EDITION

Dorothy June Sciarra
*Professor Emerita,
University of Cincinnati*

Ellen M. Lynch
*Associate Professor,
University of Cincinnati*

Shauna M. Adams
*Associate Professor,
University of Dayton*

Anne G. Dorsey
*Professor Emerita,
University of Cincinnati*

CENGAGE
Learning

Australia • Brazil • Japan • Korea • Mexico • Singapore • Spain • United Kingdom • United States

**CENGAGE Learning**

**Developing and Administering a Child Care and Education Program, Ninth Edition**
Dorothy June Sciarra, Ellen Lynch, Shauna Adams, and Anne Dorsey

Product Director: Marta E. Lee-Perriard

Product Manager: Mark Kerr

Content Developer: Kate Scheinman

Product Assistant: Julia Catalano

Marketing Manager: Chris Sosa

Content Project Manager: Samen Iqbal

Art Director: Marissa Falco

Manufacturing Planner: Doug Bertke

IP Analyst: Jennifer Nonenmacher

IP Project Manager: Brittani Morgan

Production Service/Project Manager: Lynn Lustberg, MPS

Photo Researcher: Sundar, Lumina Datamatics, Ltd.

Text Researcher: Sharmila Srinivasan, Lumina Datamatics, Ltd.

Copy Editor: Julie McNamee

Cover and Text Designer: CMB Design

Cover Image: by Jenna Williams

Compositor: MPS Limited.

Library of Congress Control Number: 2014939783

Student Edition:

ISBN-13: 978-1-305-08808-5

Loose-leaf Edition:

ISBN-13: 978-1-305-49690-3

**Cengage Learning**
20 Channel Center Street
Boston, MA 02210
USA

Cengage Learning is a leading provider of customized learning solutions with office locations around the globe, including Singapore, the United Kingdom, Australia, Mexico, Brazil, and Japan. Locate your local office at **www.cengage.com/global**.

Cengage Learning products are represented in Canada by Nelson Education, Ltd.

To learn more about Cengage Learning Solutions, visit **www.cengage.com**.

Purchase any of our products at your local college store or at our preferred online store www.cengagebrain.com.

Unless otherwise noted, all photos are ©Cengage Learning or from the Bombeck Family Learning Center.

Printed in the United States of America
Print Number: 01   Print Year: 2014

Photo by Sharon Civitello

students and colleagues alike. Her knowledge of theory and evidence-based classroom practice were unparalleled.

Over the years, Anne served professional organizations tirelessly. She was a member of the National Association for the Education of Young Children (NAEYC) Ethics Panel and the Professional Practice Panel. She was also a long-term board member of the Ohio Association for the Education of Young Children (OAEYC). As a member of the NCATE Board of Examiners, Anne visited many colleges and universities evaluating teacher education programs seeking accreditation. As a supporter of the National Association of Early Childhood Teacher Educators (NAECTE), she served as secretary, program chair, and president. Moreover, she facilitated the development of the *Journal of Early Childhood Teacher Education* from its early beginnings as a newsletter to its current status as a highly regarded publication.

Anne received numerous awards throughout her career, including the NAECTE Outstanding Early Childhood Teacher Educator Award of 1999. Additionally, she was honored with the coveted *Cincinnati Enquirer* Woman of the Year in 1991 for promoting the discipline of early childhood education, for her untiring advocacy for children, and for influencing so many individuals in their choice of career path. Anne also received the OAEYC Outstanding Teacher Educator Award.

Following her retirement, Anne maintained extensive writing and consulting schedules that included working with early education programs committed to conducting appropriate assessment of children's development. She was also a devoted volunteer for her church. This invaluable work continued until the time of her passing.

To us, her coauthors, Anne was a beloved colleague, teacher, mentor, role model, friend, and woman of faith. And we are confident that her legacy will live on in those of us who had the good fortune to know her.

We will miss her greatly.

*D.J.S., E.M.L., and S.M.A.*

We dedicate this edition of our text to the memory of our beloved coauthor, Anne G. Dorsey, who passed from us far too soon on March 25, 2014, in Cincinnati, Ohio.

Anne was first and foremost a loving and loyal wife to her husband, Bob, for 57 years. She was a devoted mother to Andrew, Peter, and Kurk, and sister to Susan. She was a proud grandmother of six grandchildren.

Anne was Professor Emerita and former program chair of early childhood education at the University of Cincinnati. As a faculty member, she served as an outstanding role model of ethical practice and professionalism for

**To my colleagues and former students** who continue to offer support and inspiration to me, and also to my coauthor and dear friend, Anne G. Dorsey, without whom this edition as well as all the previous editions could not have been written

*D.J.S.*

---

**In memory of my parents, Jean and Rex,** whose lives were a model of strength and faith; to my husband, Dennis, whose unending patience and thoughtfulness never cease to amaze and support me; to my children Heather and Josh, who fueled my personal and professional interest in childhood; to Kaitlyn and Taylor, whose spirits continue to change my life so powerfully, absolutely, and unexpectedly; and to my coauthors whose knowledge of early childhood education and commitment to ethical practice are unparalleled.

*E.M.L.*

---

**To Stan,** my husband, partner, and best friend, who inspires me to see the glass as half full—without your love and support I would be truly lost. To my daughters, Meredith and Jillian, who add much joy to my life—thank you for allowing me to share your stories in my teaching and my writing. To my colleagues and the teachers, staff, children, and families of the Bombeck Family Learning Center, whose work inspired my contributions to this book. To my coauthors—thank you for allowing me to add my voice to your sagacious work.

*S.M.A.*

---

**To Robert Frost,** without whom I may never have met Robert W. Dorsey.

*A.G.D.*

# BRIEF CONTENTS

# CONTENTS

# CHAPTER 10
Recruiting Children   194

# CHAPTER 11
Supporting Quality Curriculum 220

# CHAPTER 16
Marketing the Program  338

# PREFACE

The ninth edition of our text *Developing and Administering a Child Care and Education Program* focuses on honoring our past while we embrace the future. In the midst of this revision, our writing team and the field of early childhood suffered a tremendous loss at the passing of one of the original authors, Anne Dorsey. Anne's contributions to the field serve as the foundation for this work, and we strive to honor her in this and all future revisions. In her memory, we will continue to strive to provide the best and most current information for you and your students. Our goal is to provide professors of early childhood education and their students an understanding of the need for well-prepared directors who come to their role with a background in child development, appreciation of how learning occurs, and knowledge of basic business practices—particularly those involving finance and staff and client relations.

## STATE OF THE DIRECTORSHIP

As more attention is given to the importance of the early years of child development and learning, additional scrutiny of early childhood programs is occurring. Educators, legislators, funders, program administrators, staff, and parents all want the best for children. But, of course, wanting the best, knowing what children need, and being able to provide it doesn't come easily. Yet strong standards for directors of programs for young children are not fully developed in many areas. Progress is evident based on the work of individuals such as Paula Jorde Bloom, who for many years has written about leadership and provided programs in support of directors' development. Roger and Bonnie Neugebauer have for more than 30 years provided bimonthly information specifically for directors in their *Exchange* publication. Most states have Quality Rating and Improvement Systems (QRIS) and have established early learning and development standards.

We recognize that one book alone will not prepare directors for their role. Our goal is to help future teachers and directors understand the importance of the director's role for early childhood staff, children, their families, and the community. We hope that our text will also help those who are designing director licensure move more quickly to that goal.

## OUR AUDIENCE

The ninth edition of *Developing and Administering a Child Care and Education Program* was written for college students interested in early childhood education. They may be preparing to be teachers of young children or they may be planning ahead to become administrators. Our intention is to depict the role of director, whether starting a new center or administering one already in operation. When teachers understand this role, they are more likely to recognize why their director has certain expectations of teachers, and what teachers' responsibilities are as they plan and implement a flexible, interesting program for the young children in their group. Students in associate, baccalaureate, and masters programs need this information. As they study these chapters, they begin to realize that in an early childhood education career, the roles of the director are varied and interdependent.

## CONCEPTUAL APPROACH

When the director is competent to engage in a wide range of human interactions as well as in managing the center's business components, the center will function well. When the director's background in one or both of these components is weak, the center is likely to close, or even more disturbing, the program will continue in a way that is not productive for the children it serves.

Above all, we see the director as a well-prepared, ethical person who is authoritative and dedicated to meeting the needs of young children and their families. We emphasize adopting and using the National Association for the Education of Young Children's Statement of Commitment, Code of Ethical Conduct, and the Supplement for Early Childhood Program Administrators whenever puzzling situations arise that may be of an ethical nature. We see the director's responsibility as educating staff and families about the Code and how it can be used appropriately.

## USING THE TEXT

Within the chapters, we include boxes that illustrate the points discussed in that section of the chapter. Called "Director's Corner," these vignettes clarify the material with examples described from a director's experiences. Throughout the text are features called "Reflections," which are designed to give readers an opportunity to pause and consider their understanding of the points being made in the text. These boxes often relate to an experience a student may have had. Each chapter ends with a summary followed by one or more activities labeled "Try It Out!" in which directions for individual, partner, or small group activities are included.

Appendices in our book provide a wealth of updated lists for both instructors and students. These include sources of materials, equipment, and supplies; early childhood professional organizations; early childhood periodicals, and information sources; and copies of many NAEYC standards.

When presenting material from *Developing and Administering a Child Care and Education Program*, instructors may choose to follow the existing order of chapters, or they may decide to depart from that order. Every chapter is self-contained, so either approach works well. Some instructors use the content as the basis of lectures, adding examples from their own experiences or inviting local directors to meet with the class to discuss a particular topic. Others assign students to interview directors on topics addressed in the text.

Many students enrolled in an administration class are involved in or will have completed an early childhood field experience. Many may be working in early childhood programs. Because the focus of college-level students may be primarily on the classroom, instructors may have students reflect on those experiences to determine how a director influences a program. For example, in your center, how does the director's work affect the health, safety, and nutrition of the children?

Some instructors use the Reflections feature found throughout the text as a starting point for class discussions or as a topic for writing assignments. The Director's Corner feature, which presents quotes from directors on the chapter topic, can also be used this way. Other instructors use the Try It Out! exercises to stimulate discussion or reflection on personal experiences or feelings. These activities may take the form of role-playing, debates, or other authentic problem-solving activities.

Most students are comfortable with the reading level of our book. Terms that may be new are explained in context. *Developing and Administering a Child Care and Education Program* lends itself well to related field experiences. Advanced students may be assigned as interns to work with directors, much as student teachers work with mentor teachers. Other instructors may assign students to form teams to create their own center on paper. This assignment may include creating an imaginary site, a mission statement, a funding plan, a tuition schedule, a budget, a marketing plan, a staffing plan, a policy and procedures manual, and a salary schedule. The assignment may be limited to one or more of these components. Instructors may assign students to write a paper or prepare a class presentation on one of the topics discussed in the text, using related resources listed in the appendices or at the end of each chapter.

## WHAT'S NEW IN THIS EDITION—AN OVERVIEW

The ninth edition of *Developing and Administering a Child Care and Education Program* presents completely updated and expanded content. Here are some of the major revisions to both the text as a whole as well as those for each chapter:

The learning objectives correlated to the main sections in each chapter show students what they need to know to process and understand the information in the chapter. After completing the chapter, students should be able to demonstrate how they can use and apply their new knowledge and skills.

New and improved coverage of NAEYC standards includes a chapter-opening list of standards to help students identify where key standards are addressed in the chapter. These callouts and the standards correlation chart help students make connections between what they are learning in the textbook and the standards. The standards and guidelines provided are the following: (a) NAEYC Program Administrator Definitions and Competencies that outline the skills and knowledge administrators need in the areas of management and early childhood education; (b) NAEYC Standards for Early Childhood Professional Preparation Programs that present the core knowledge that should be addressed in programs that educate early childhood educators; and (c) NAEYC Accreditation Standards for Early Childhood Programs that identify the criteria by which quality programs for young children are measured.

Downloadable and often customizable, TeachSource Digital Downloads are practical and professional resources that allow students to immediately implement and apply this textbook's content in the field. The student downloads these tools and keeps them forever, enabling preservice teachers to begin building their library of practical, professional resources. Look for the TeachSource Digital Downloads label that identifies these items.

The TeachSource Video Vignettes feature footage from the classroom to help students relate key chapter content to real-life scenarios. Critical-thinking questions provide opportunities for in-class or online discussion and reflection.

In an effort to reflect our changing field, two new features have been added:

■ The "Making the Case" feature provides specific examples that demonstrate how a director might explain new and emerging emphases in the field in order to facilitate change. "Making the Case" boxes highlight more controversial issues in the field or those topics that should be of concern to the contemporary administrator.

- "Working Smart with Technology" boxes present information related to the use of technology in today's early childhood program. This feature was designed to bridge the divide between students who are digital natives and those for whom technology is an emerging skill.

These two new features can serve as catalysts for class discussion or as prompts for writing assignments.

Updated references have been included for every chapter.

Summaries were rewritten to directly relate to expanded/updated learning objectives.

New marginal Diversity icons highlight coverage of diversity in the broadest sense.

New and updated Try It Out! Activities appear at the end of the chapters.

New and updated Director's Resources, many of which are also Digital Downloads, offer students authentic examples of materials such as forms, surveys, evaluations, and handbooks that have been used by effective directors. Many of the Director's Resources are used to complete the end of the chapter Try It Out! activities.

## Key Revisions and Additions to Each Chapter

### Chapter 1—The Effective Director

- Additional focus on the need for computer literacy in managing today's programs and the importance of understanding the administrative roles played by directors

### Chapter 2—Assessing Community Need and Establishing a Program

- Additional information on the importance of advocacy
- New information on using online surveys to complete needs assessments

### Chapter 3—Licensing and Certification

- Updated information regarding licensing and accreditation of programs
- Updated information related to Quality Rating and Improvement Systems
- Updated and expanded information about the various types of credentialing and credentialing bodies
- Inclusion of a new Director's Resource related to developing a plan of operation for a new child care program

### Chapter 4—Organizing Center Structure and Working with a Board

- Additional focus on the use of technology to communicate with the board and its committees
- New information related to the benefits of diverse board membership

- Updated information on orientation of new board members
- Inclusion of a new Director's Resource related to completing articles of incorporation

### Chapter 5—Handling Financial Matters

- Updated information about the importance of staff input in establishing budget priorities
- New information on using technology supported budgeting tools
- Updated figures on wages based on national comparisons
- New information about the Affordable Care Act

### Chapter 6—Funding the Program

- Additional information related to seeking funding beyond what is needed for a current year's operation
- Updated information on employer-supported child care and on government funding of early care and education
- New information on establishing an integrated system of child care

### Chapter 7—Developing a Center Facility

- New information on planning centers based on universal design
- Inclusion of a new Director's Resource related to the way in which a program's mission and goals might impact the planning of an early childhood facility

### Chapter 8—Equipping the Center

- Expanded information related to technology needs in equipping the center and digital literacy
- Updated information related to equipment list resources
- Updated information related to playground safety concerns
- New information related to safety concerns for infants and toddlers
- Expanded information on purchasing equipment for children with disabilities

### Chapter 9—Staffing the Center

- New information related to growing leadership from within
- New information related to using LinkedIn and other web-based systems to recruit and manage the hiring process
- New example of a program handbook included as a Director's Resource
- New example of a staffing schedule included as a Director's Resource
- New example of a performance valuation included as a Director's Resource

## Chapter 10—Recruiting Children

- New information about including children with special needs

- Expanded information about creating a quality website to recruit children and families

## Chapter 11—Supporting Quality Curriculum

- Expanded information on the theoretical basis for quality curriculum

- Expanded information about the role of the director as a curriculum mentor

- Expanded information about the effective use of technology with young children

## Chapter 12—Managing the Food and the Health and Safety Programs

- New information challenging students to consider how food is used in their program

- New information related to the national Farm to School movement

- Expanded information on how technology can be used to manage the food program and maintain the health and safety of children and staff

- Updated information on legal issues related to health and safety in early childhood programs

## Chapter 13—Working with Families, Volunteers, and the Community

- New information about comprehensive communication systems

- New information about communicating with families through web-based portfolios

- Inclusion of a new Director's Resource related to evaluating of the program's family engagement system

## Chapter 14—Providing for Personal and Professional Staff Development

- Expanded information on job-embedded professional development

- New information on online professional development

## Chapter 15—Evaluating Center Components

- New information on developing assessment policies for programs

- Expanded information on the use of portfolio assessment with children

- New information on the use of electronic portfolios in evaluating children's progress

- Updated information on cultural competence self-assessments in early childhood programs

- Inclusion of a new Director's Resource related to annual staff performance reviews

## Chapter 16—Marketing the Program

- New focus on word-of-mouth marketing

- Expanded information on using social media

- Updated information on marketing the program to digital natives

- New section on the characteristics of a quality child care center website

- Updated references to support website development

## Appendices A through H

- Completely updated

# ANCILLARY MATERIAL

## MindTap

MindTap for Sciarra, Lynch, Adams, and Dorsey DEVELOPING AND ADMINISTERING A CHILD CARE AND EDUCATION PROGRAM 9e represents a new approach to teaching and learning. A highly personalized, fully customizable learning platform, MindTap helps students elevate their thinking by guiding them to do the following:

- Know, remember, and understand concepts critical to becoming a great teacher.

- Apply concepts, create tools, and demonstrate performance and competency in key areas in the course.

- Prepare artifacts for the portfolio and eventual state licensure, to launch a successful teaching career.

- Develop the habits to become a reflective practitioner.

As students move through each chapter's Learning Path, they engage in a scaffolded learning experience, designed to move them up Bloom's Revised Taxonomy, from lower- to higher-order thinking skills. The Learning Path enables preservice students to develop these skills and gain confidence by:

- Engaging them with chapter topics and activating their prior knowledge by watching and answering questions about TeachSource videos of teachers teaching and children learning in real classrooms

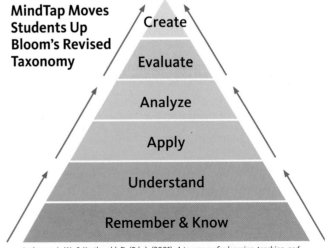

**MindTap Moves Students Up Bloom's Revised Taxonomy**

Create
Evaluate
Analyze
Apply
Understand
Remember & Know

Anderson, L. W., & Krathwohl, D. (Eds.). (2001). *A taxonomy for learning, teaching, and assessing: A revision of Bloom's taxonomy of educational objectives.* New York: Longman.

- Checking their comprehension and understanding through *Did You Get It?* assessments, with varied question types that are auto-graded for instant feedback

- Applying concepts through mini case scenarios— students analyze typical teaching and learning situations and create a reasoned response to the issue(s) presented in the scenario

- Reflecting about and justifying the choices they made within the teaching scenario problem

MindTap helps instructors facilitate better outcomes by evaluating how future teachers plan and teach lessons in ways that make content clear and help diverse students learn, assessing the effectiveness of their teaching practice, and adjusting teaching as needed. The Student Progress App makes grades visible in real time so students and instructors always have access to current standings in the class.

MindTap for Sciarra, Lynch, Adams, Dorsey, DEVELOPING AND ADMINISTERING A CHILD CARE AND EDUCATION PROGRAM 9e helps instructors easily set their course because it integrates into the existing Learning Management System and saves instructors time by allowing them to fully customize any aspect of the Learning Path. Instructors can change the order of the student learning activities, hide activities they don't want for the course, and—most importantly—add any content they do want (e.g., YouTube videos, Google docs, links to state education standards). Learn more at http://www.cengage.com/mindtap.

## PowerPoint® Lecture Slides

These vibrant Microsoft® PowerPoint lecture slides for each chapter assist you with your lecture by providing concept coverage using images, figures, and tables directly from the textbook!

## Online Instructor's Manual with Test Bank

An online Instructor's Manual accompanies this book and contains information to assist the instructor in designing the course, including sample syllabi, discussion questions, teaching and learning activities, field experiences, learning objectives, and additional online resources. For assessment support, the updated test bank includes true/false, multiple-choice, matching, short-answer, and essay questions for each chapter.

## Cognero

Cengage Learning Testing Powered by Cognero is a flexible online system that allows you to author, edit, and manage test bank content from multiple Cengage Learning solutions; create multiple test versions in an instant; and deliver tests from your Learning Management System, your classroom, or wherever you want.

## ABOUT THE AUTHORS

**Dorothy June Sciarra** continues to be an active early childhood educator in a diverse variety of situations. She has served as director of the child development laboratory center at the University of Cincinnati, serving children and families from a wide range of backgrounds. Her work as director set the standard throughout the area for taking a stand for appropriate practice whether or not it was popular. Teachers who worked with her understood their responsibility to the children and families and developed a clear understanding of early childhood education under her guidance.

Dr. Sciarra's work as professor of child development/early childhood education has been highly praised. Former students still talk about her child development courses and her deep understanding of childhood. Dr. Sciarra served as department head with responsibility for early childhood associate, bachelor's, and master's degree programs and pioneered a system for career development as capable students were enabled to move seamlessly from the CDA to the associate and then on to the baccalaureate degree level. She has been involved in several community early childhood efforts, including board membership on the University of Cincinnati Early Learning Center. She is active in 4C, a Child Care Aware Agency (formerly National Association of Child Care Resource and Referral Agency), and has participated tirelessly on many of its agency training committees. Dr. Sciarra is a recipient of the 4C Early Childhood Award and was the first recipient of the Ohio Association for the Education of Young Children's Early Childhood Teacher Educator Award. In 2007, 4C again recognized Dr. Sciarra's work at a statewide luncheon where it was announced that the 4C library would be named in her honor. Dr. Sciarra has mentored many early childhood educators, including co-author Anne Dorsey. Together they also wrote *Leaders and Supervisors in Child Care Programs,* published by Thomson Delmar Learning. In 2010, Dr. Sciarra and Professor Dorsey were honored with the United Way Impact Award for their work in promoting appropriate early childhood education.

**Ellen M. Lynch** is associate professor of early childhood education at the University of Cincinnati. Her doctorate is in special education with a focus on early childhood special education. She has been active in local and state early childhood organizations, including the Ohio Association for the Education of Young Children (OAEYC), for which she served as chair of the Children with Special Needs Committee; the state Board of Directors; and the Division for Early Childhood of the Council for Exceptional Children. Additionally, she served as president of the Ohio Coalition of Associate Degree Early Childhood Programs. Dr. Lynch's current scholarly interests include engaging in the scholarship of teaching and learning

(SoTL) and exploring the use of technology to support learning among preservice teachers. She is both an editor and reviewer for several problem-based learning journals. She has presented widely at local, state, national, and international levels on a variety of aspects of teaching young children, teacher education, and best practices for teaching in higher education.

**Shauna M. Adams** is an associate professor of early childhood at the University of Dayton, where she also serves as the executive director of the Center for Early Learning. Dr. Adams has taught graduate and undergraduate students in such courses as child development, preschool methods, primary methods, and early childhood advocacy, research, and leadership. In her role as the director of the Center for Early Learning, Dr. Adams promotes opportunities for the Bombeck Family Learning Center to serve preservice and in-service early childhood professionals as a demonstration school and forum for professional development. She also advocates for children and families by serving on local and state committees that support quality early care and education and serves the University's mission by providing support for Catholic Early Childhood programming.

After teaching special education in public schools for 10 years, Dr. Adams became a school psychologist, working with children in preschool and the primary grades. She earned her doctorate in Early Childhood and Special Education from the University of Cincinnati. Dr. Adams became immersed in early care and education through her work with the Bombeck Family Learning Center and has established partnerships with Head Start, Public School Preschool, Early Care and Education, and a variety of agencies that support young children and families. Additionally, Dr. Adams worked with community partners to develop the University of Dayton's online Early Childhood Leadership and Advocacy programs, which were designed to address the need for leadership in early childhood while also supporting the early childhood career lattice. She is also the lead author of the *ACCESS Curriculum* and has produced a number of articles, conducted presentations, developed websites, and pursued other outlets to share this curriculum with the field of early care and education.

**Anne G. Dorsey** began her ECE career working in the Child Life Department at Cincinnati Children's Hospital. Three sons later, she taught both preschool and college courses while attending graduate school. When she received a full-time faculty position, Dr. Dorothy June Sciarra convinced her that she should be her coauthor and, years later, that she should become leader of the lab school and the ECE college programs. Professor Dorsey's interests in the broader community were based on her belief that working together, the University of Cincinnati child development and early childhood education program could benefit from collaboration with local agencies such as United Way, 4C, and Cincinnati Association for the Education of Young Children. Agencies could also benefit from the collaboration with faculty and college students.

Locally, Professor Dorsey served on the Committee of Management of YMCA Child Development and continues to serve on the UC Early Learning Center Board, the Promoting Resilient Children Advisory Board, and the SPARK Advisory Board of the Children's Home. She was a member of the NAEYC Ethics Panel, the NAEYC Professional Practice Panel, and the Ohio Association for the Education of Young Children Board. Professor Dorsey visited many colleges and universities as a member of the National Council for Accreditation of Teacher Education Board of Examiners. As a strong supporter of the National Association of Early Childhood Teacher Educators, she served as secretary, program chair, president, and editor of the *Journal of Early Childhood Teacher Education* in its very early format, and served as president of the NAECTE Foundation. She received the OAEYC Teacher Education Award and the NAECTE Outstanding Early Childhood Teacher Educator Award. Traveling with her husband, she has visited 24 countries over the years and focused on early childhood education in each country, except, of course, Antarctica, where she waded among hundreds of penguins and their young. Professor Emeritus Dorsey enjoyed volunteering as data manager for NAECTE and as an assessor of kindergarten and preschool children for the schools and for the United Way Collaborative Partners Committee, of which she was a member. Her favorite child comment came from a preschooler whom she had assessed several times during the child's years in an early learning center. "Well Anne, I guess we won't see each other anymore; I'm going to kindergarten!"

## ACKNOWLEDGMENTS

Our book is the result of continuous support from friends and colleagues who have helped us immeasurably, even when they didn't realize the contributions they were making. We particularly want to thank the directors, many of whom are former students, who helped us understand their day-to-day work from a wide variety of situations and perspectives. Special thanks go to Kathleen Bryan, who explained the popular year-long Developing Early Childhood Leaders Program. We are indebted to the teachers, staff, children, and families of the University of Dayton's Bombeck Family Learning Center who shared their practice so that it might be captured in photographs and used in real-life examples. We particularly want to thank Ashley Smith (director) and Joy Comingore (curriculum specialist) of the Bombeck Center for their inspiration and willingness to share their perspectives of the quickly changing field. Special thanks goes to Caroline Davis, Leah Lauver, and Deborah Poppaw who organized photo shoots, and to our photographers, Jenna Williams, who took many of the new photographs, including the cover shot, and Jessica Pike and Meredith Adams, whose work included the photographs taken for the eighth edition. We also appreciate the guidance and encouragement given to us by our Cengage editor, Kate Scheinman.

We also would like to express our gratitude to the following reviewers, who offered numerous, valuable suggestions:

Jeanne Barker, Tallahassee Community College

Yvonne Beirne, North Shore Community College

Jo Ann Burnside, Richard J. Daley College

Deb Farrer, California University of Pennsylvania

Colleen Fawcett, Palm Beach State College

Lisa Godwin, Central Piedmont Community College

Jill Harrison, Delta College

Joanny Iaccino, Los Angeles Valley College

Willie Jones, Tougaloo College

Janiece Kneppe, Red Rocks Community College

Debra Lawrence, Chestnut Hill College

Mary Lowe, College of the Albemarle

Maureen O'Neil, Tallahassee Community College

John Ronghua Ouyang, University of North Florida

Beatrice Paul, Salem State University

Donald Roberts, Cochise College

Joan Robison, Cloud County Community College

We hope our readers will find here the technical information they need to direct a viable program. Our greater desire is that they will recognize the significance of the leadership role of the director and the challenge and personal satisfaction derived from creating and implementing an excellent early care and education program for young children and their families.

*Dorothy June Sciarra, Ellen M. Lynch, Shauna M. Adams,*
*and Anne G. Dorsey*

## Learning Objectives

After reading this chapter, you should be able to:

**1-1** Identify the diverse stakeholders to whom administrators are responsible.

**1-2** Explain the purpose of the NAEYC Code of Ethical Conduct and Supplement for Early Childhood Program Administrators.

**1-3** List four subsystems that are included within the early childhood program system.

**1-4** Compare and contrast administrative styles and roles.

**1-5** Identify the responsibilities that directors have as managers of a center.

**1-6** Describe the role of curriculum leader, and identify the issues that must be considered in planning and implementing program curriculum.

**1-7** Discuss the knowledge and skills that program administrators must possess to be successful leaders.

**1-8** Describe tools that enable the director to blend program management and people leadership.

*The successful director and center personnel work to learn to build their organization in a way that is satisfying to them and to their clients, and that creates a true system of learning.*

## Standards Addressed in this Chapter

**naeyc**

Accreditation Standard 1 – Relationships

Accreditation Standard 10 – Leadership and Management

Administrator Competencies – Management Knowledge and Skills 1, 3, 5, 8, 9, 10

Administrator Competencies – Early Childhood Knowledge and Skills 6, 10

Professional Preparation Standard 6 – Becoming a Professional

Learning about the management and leadership of early childhood programs is important for staff and for current and prospective directors. The role of administrator requires knowledge and skills in early childhood education and development as well as in business practices. With expertise in both of these areas, whether demonstrated by an individual or by a team, the program is likely to be successful for children, families, staff, and investors.

An effective director of an early childhood education center is involved in all the jobs that will be described in this text, from enrolling children to evaluating staff, from budgeting to taking inventory, and from maintaining a physical plant to bandaging a child's scraped knee. The director's job includes doing or overseeing all aspects of program management and leadership. To do any one of these tasks, a director must have skills and knowledge; to do all of them requires stamina, understanding, and organization; and to do all of them effectively demands exceptional interpersonal skills as emphasized throughout this text. These characteristics and abilities enable the director to bring the best to parents, children, staff members, board members, and the community. In turn, serving as a model of these skills encourages those same people to give their best to the center. The effective director realizes that an early childhood education center can never be a one-person operation. A network of caring and learning together transcends the day-to-day chores and makes being part of a center worthwhile.

# 1-1 MAKING A COMMITMENT TO DIVERSE STAKEHOLDERS

When you agree to become a director, you take on a tremendous responsibility to a very diverse group of stakeholders, including the following:

- children enrolled in the center (and those seeking enrollment)

- families of those children

- all center personnel (and those who apply for positions)

- the center's board, funders, and other agencies and administrators to whom you report or with whom you interact

- the community

- yourself

How can you possibly make a commitment to all of these individuals and groups? Perhaps you believed that you would be responsible for seeing that the teachers at your center did what they were supposed to do. Perhaps you thought there might be a problem with one or two of them, but you felt confident to handle that type of

situation. Maybe you thought there would be one or two parents who expected special treatment, or a child who frequently hurt other children. And maybe you thought, "Sure, I can handle that."

Being an administrator entails much more than *handling* people and situations. The director must recognize that her constituency consists of the six components just listed. She must become familiar enough with all of them to know what is important to each.

You may be wondering why the director's constituency includes those *applying* for enrollment or positions at the center. Policies, procedures, and interactions in *every* aspect of the organization's work are included. Therefore, although the director may not have an opening for a child or may find that a job applicant is not appropriate for the role, she is expected to treat each of them in accordance with the center's philosophy.

# 1-2 MEETING CHALLENGING SITUATIONS BASED ON ETHICAL PRINCIPLES

Any individual who assumes responsibility must recognize that challenges will arise. Some of these are easily met, but often there is no clear-cut solution. As you ponder what to do in such situations, you may wonder, "Is this a policy issue, one for which I, as director, should take action and maintain the policy, or are there other factors that make this a moral or an ethical issue?"

You can expect to be challenged by ethical issues as you work to meet the needs of a wide range of constituents. Fortunately, you have valuable tools at your fingertips: The National Association for the Education of Young Children (NAEYC) Code of Ethical Conduct and the Statement of Commitment as well as the Supplement to the Code for Early Childhood Program Administrators (NAEYC, 2011; 2006) are on the NAEYC website and are included in Appendix A, parts 1 and 2. Becoming familiar with the Code and the Supplement now will help you when you are faced with a dilemma.

Both the Code and the Supplement begin with statements of core values. All individuals who work with young children should be expected to commit to holding and acting on those values. For example, directors should value and be committed to the belief that "the well-being of the children in our care is our primary responsibility, above our obligations to other constituents" (NAEYC, 2006).

Both the Code and the Supplement contain ideals, which "reflect the aspirations of practitioners," and principles, which "guide conduct and assist practitioners in resolving ethical dilemmas" (NAEYC, 2006). For example, one ideal maintains that administrators "design programs and policies inclusive of and responsive to diverse families." A related principle suggests that directors "shall work to create a respectful environment for and a working relationship with all families, regardless of family members' sex, race, national origin, immigration status, preferred home language, religious belief or affiliation, age, marital status/family structure, disability, or sexual orientation." Note that the documents do not purport to provide specific answers; rather, they serve as guides for decision makers who are facing unique situations.

After the director is familiar with the Code and the Supplement, she can begin to help staff and families understand their importance. Distributing copies to staff and families as part of their handbooks and then holding discussion sessions enables everyone to become familiar with why the center espouses the use of the Code and the Supplement. In the dialogue with others, be sure to include the importance of *reflecting* on an ethical dilemma and seeking guidance from a trusted professional when needed. As in all other aspects of early childhood work, confidentiality is essential.

---

### REFLECTION

After you have read and thought about the Code of Ethical Content: Supplement for Early Childhood Program Administrators, reflect on situations you think would be most challenging for you. Have you encountered any ethical dilemmas for which using the Code might have been helpful?

---

## 1-3 CONSIDERING THE CENTER'S SYSTEMS AND SUBSYSTEMS

Leaders of new or redeveloping businesses **naeyc** often begin their work by calling personnel together to create a vision. But the vision can only be achieved when everyone in the organization is committed to it. Often most people do not realize that all businesses, whether operated to design and sell automobiles or to support children's well-being, operate as systems. We know that each of our bodies is a system, and we are usually well aware when something goes wrong with our bodily system. We know, too, that this system is composed of many systems: the digestive system, the respiratory system, and so forth. We can see patterns emerging. For example, a pattern of overeating and lack of exercise affects one or more systems and can lead to obesity. Most of us are becoming more aware of environmental systems as well. Destroying the habitats of various species can lead to their extinction. To work effectively in any business, including the early childhood education business, we must recognize that each of us plays a role in that system. Each of us must engage in systems thinking.

Senge defines systems thinking as "a conceptual framework, a body of knowledge and tools that has been developed over the past 50 years, to make the full patterns clearer, and to help us see how to change them effectively" (2006, p. 7). A body of knowledge and tools for working together exists in each early childhood program. New members join that program with many of the beliefs, theories, and practices common to the field, but they must grow together with their colleagues to create the unique system that enables their program to function successfully.

Because each early childhood program operates as a system, whether the system is visible or not, the director and staff must work together to recognize the characteristics of that system. Periodically, a review must be conducted of the overall system on which a program's operation is based that answers questions such as these: Who are we as a center? What is it that makes us the XYZ Center? What premises do we hold that guide us in our work? Are those premises valid? Are some of the center's operating methods still in place simply out of habit? Today, some centers are curtailing or eliminating independent playtime for preschoolers and substituting group instruction. Center personnel need to discuss the reasons for these actions and ensure that such changes support the center's vision.

---

### DIRECTOR'S CORNER

"We have six centers within our corporation, widely spread over the local area. Each center has its own identity. The populations we serve at each site differ. However, everyone who works here shares the same basic beliefs about children's learning and development."

"I meet with the six directors as a group every month. We all look forward to that, and each of us benefits. Each of the directors is at a different stage in her development as a director, yet as a group, we share our thinking and support one another. Each director goes back to her center and has a meeting with her staff. Together they learn how to create the kind of program that we and they believe is supportive of children and families."

"Several schools and companies have asked us to create and operate centers at their sites. We're choosing carefully where we'll expand and under what circumstances. We must follow the principles that we have agreed on in order to operate."

—*Executive director, not-for-profit, multisite corporation*

## 1-3a Subsystems in Early Childhood Programs

The system for an early childhood center consists of a number of subsystems. Some of these subsystems, which will be addressed in other chapters, include the finance system, the systems for securing and managing facilities and equipment, and the personnel system. The subsystems each make a contribution to the whole, and together they create a whole that is greater than the sum of the parts.

Those who create systems base them on what they believe to be important. For example, presumably you have a system for planning curriculum. As center personnel gather to review curriculum, you may find that a teacher says, "We have always had our own way of doing things. Let's just leave it at that." However, in systems thinking, the willingness of each group member to meet and share thinking, to be open to each other's ideas, and to be willing to search for the best solution enables the group to learn together. Establishing such group openness takes time, a willingness on the part of the leader to be open also, and a commitment to implementing the plan to which the group agrees.

*The director and staff find ways to support each child's development and to help each child learn.*

In an early childhood education center, several key systems are external to the organization and beyond the direct control of center personnel. Consider that diverse family systems affect the center's operation. Family members want what is best for their children. Family members interact with other systems, such as those at their place of employment. Those systems affect family members' ability to participate at the center and how the center views the role of families. For example, family members may not be free to attend conferences and programs at the center.

The regulatory system, whether required (such as licensing) or optional (such as accreditation or a state quality program), is another external system that interfaces with early childhood programs. Regulatory systems have different requirements, some of which may coincide with the way the center wants to function and some of which may not.

An important aspect of the director's role in working with the overall system and the related subsystems is emphasis on establishing an understanding among all personnel (including the director) that they are colleagues rather than a hierarchy. This process is challenging because the difference in daily responsibilities is quite apparent and necessary. However, when all personnel have developed trust in one another, they can learn to suspend the hierarchy for the sake of discussion. The challenge is to learn how to learn together (Senge, 2006).

## 1-4 ADMINISTRATIVE STYLES AND ROLES

Although all directors are responsible for administering a program, their administrative styles are unique and, therefore, the outcomes of their programs differ. Some of the differences are based on the roles assigned to the directors, while others are based on their personalities, knowledge, skills, and attitudes. Their effectiveness in supporting the development of a "we" feeling—group spirit—is a key factor in the success of the

---

### MAKING THE CASE FOR *QUALIFIED ADMINISTRATORS*

Becoming a successful administrator of an early childhood program requires a complex set of skills and abilities. Understanding yourself and others, as well as your roles and responsibilities, is key to your ability to direct a program for young children. Preparation for an administrative position is vital! Reflect on the following questions:

**1.** What abilities do you possess that will enable you to address the many roles you will fill as a director?

**2.** What educational preparation and experience are required in your state to become an administrator of an early childhood program? How do these compare to the competencies identified in the NAEYC Program Administrator Definition and Competencies? (See Appendix C.)

organization. Each member of the team must be ready to work in a way that contributes to the overall organization. Other early childhood programs may follow trends—real or imagined—such as, "Kindergarten teachers expect us to have these children prepared to read, knowing how to print all the letters, and able to sit and complete worksheets for a half hour or more." Although that may be the case in some schools, many kindergarten teachers see each child as an individual and work with the child accordingly. The administrator plays an important part in helping teachers, children, and families recognize the role of the present system and how it relates to future systems in kindergartens and above.

## 1-4a Styles

Individuals who head an organization often start out using a managerial approach. They determine what has to be done, how it is to be done, and who should do it. The assigned staff member is expected to report back to the manager when the task is completed or at intervals along the way. If that does not happen, the manager takes responsibility for checking up on the staff member and commenting on the staff member's work or lack of success. This style may be appropriate when many staff members are relatively new in the field and have little background to draw upon. Even in that situation, however, when given opportunities, staff members often exceed expectations. Or they may begin to feel like a cog in a wheel, going round and round and never really having an opportunity to be involved.

Other managers use a more laissez-faire approach, leaving much of the decision making to the staff. Little or no overall structure may leave staff members with no support for decisions they make and confused about how the many independent decisions fit together. The administrator's interest may be directed more toward building outside relations for the benefit of the center. Although building relations beyond a business locale is essential, building a knowledgeable staff who understands the vision and goals cannot be minimized. This approach certainly does not support the development of a center-wide system, although staff may develop an effective system on their own. There is such a variety of managerial styles that it is impossible to describe each one.

Some directors are natural leaders rather than managers. Others, over time and with mentoring, reading, and studying, become leaders. As the leader, the director looks to the staff for ideas, initiative, and implementation. Certainly, the leader does not turn over the running of the center to any staff member who steps forward. Rather, the leader supports and encourages staff to become part of the team that will help the center and its programs thrive. Directors realize that they must balance day-to-day reality with the vision that the center's stakeholders have

*Children make room to learn together. Do we?*

prepared. The director whose leadership skills include the ability to accept and welcome ideas from others demonstrates competence and confidence. (To read more about becoming a leader, see Bruno, 2012; Carter, 2014; Covey, 2004; McCrea, 2002; Sciarra & Dorsey, 2002.)

### DIRECTOR'S CORNER

"I had no idea how complex my role as director would be. Such a wide variety of people seem to need me immediately for such a wide variety of reasons. Meeting them all would probably be impossible (and maybe not even wise), but at the end of the day—most days—I know the challenges have been worthwhile. All it takes is one little pair of arms hugging me or one teacher smiling and saying on her way out, 'See you tomorrow, Chris!' "

—*Director, large suburban preschool*

## 1-4b Roles

If all the directors of centers in one state or county were to gather and discuss their roles, the job descriptions would undoubtedly cover a very wide range of categories. Some directors teach, perhaps spending half of every day in their own classrooms. Others never teach but are responsible for several centers; they travel between the centers, keeping abreast of two or more sets of circumstances, staff members, children, families, equipment lists, and so forth. Some may be responsible to an industry, a corporate system, a public school principal, or a parent cooperative association, while others are proprietors and owners.

Some directors make all the policy and procedure decisions; others are in settings where some policy is set by a school system or corporate management team. In other situations, every procedural detail is administered by a board. A director in a large center may have an assistant director, secretary, receptionist, and a cook; however, a director of a small center often does all the record keeping, supervising, telephone answering, and meal preparation. Directors work with half-day programs, full-day programs, or even 24-hour care programs. The programs may offer care for infants and toddlers, or for older children, both before and after school. Sick child care or care of children with major special needs also may be provided.

The financial plan may involve proprietary or agency operations and may or may not be organized to make a profit. Program goals range from providing a safe place where children are cared for to furnishing total developmental services for children, including medical and dental care; social services; screening and therapy; and activities that promote intellectual, motor, emotional, social, and moral development.

Both the program clients' expectations and the community's expectations affect the center director's role. Some communities appreciate a director who actively participates in the affairs of their community council, in lobbying for legislative reform, and in helping to preserve the cultural backgrounds of the children. Others prefer a director who focuses strictly on center business or on preparing children to deal with the demands of elementary school. Directors must blend their personal philosophies with those of the community to achieve a balance. This blending can occur only if a potential director and a board explore each other's philosophies before agreeing on the responsibility for administering a particular program. If the philosophies of the director and those of

the center truly are incompatible, one or the other must be changed.

Sometimes, the director is confronted with a conflict between the two roles. The job description and the expectations of the people connected with the center may dictate that the director be present to greet teachers, parents, and children each day and to bid them good-bye each evening. In between, the director may be expected to be present in case an emergency arises. Simultaneously, however, obligations to the profession and to the community must be met. The director may be asked to speak at a luncheon meeting of a community group that is ready to make a contribution to the center, to attend a board meeting of a local professional association, or to provide information at a session called by the diagnostic clinic to plan for one of the children with special needs who attends the early childhood education center.

Directors, especially those with experience, also have a responsibility to serve as child advocates. Although the NAEYC Code of Ethical Conduct calls on all who work with young children to "acknowledge an obligation to serve as a voice for children everywhere" (NAEYC, 2011), directors are more likely to have opportunities to see the broader picture of events in the community and beyond. They can keep informed about important legislative issues and about conditions affecting children and families by reading professional journals and newsletters and by being knowledgeable about local and national news.

Many advocates are working for an all-encompassing system of early childhood programs. For example, when you type "NAEYC" in a search engine, you will

*Directors perform many roles, including observing staff and greeting families.*

receive a list of NAEYC sites with wide-ranging information about the organization. You can also subscribe to online mailing lists such as Exchange Everyday, sponsored by Child Care Exchange, and updates from the Children's Defense Fund. Share your findings with others interested in early childhood, and you will quickly find dozens of sources of related information. As with any website, however, it is important to check legitimacy.

Because directors are leaders and models, not only in their own centers but also throughout the community, staff, parents, and others often look to them for information about advocacy issues. Some directors may post information for staff and parents; others may make a concerted effort to involve people in an action plan. Some may write letters to editors or to legislators, while others may testify before various governmental groups. In determining participation in advocacy efforts, each director must weigh the responsibility to be an advocate against the responsibility to the center, as well as consider personal time.

Although many directors work more than a 40-hour week, it is unreasonable and unwise to expect them to devote evening and weekend hours to their jobs on a regular basis. Directors who spend too much time on the job may become physically and emotionally exhausted, leading to ineffectiveness. As models for staff members, directors must demonstrate a balance of personal and center needs. As you study this text, you may wonder how directors do it all. Knowledge, disposition, organization, and support all contribute to their success.

## 1-4c Personal Qualities

Directors may become enmeshed in unreasonable workloads because they have become personally involved in the center's work. An effective director should be involved closely with the activities of the center while maintaining distance, which is a difficult combination to attain. The primary reason for the difficulty in achieving this balance is that good directors assume their roles largely because they care about people. Caring is apparent when the director assumes the role of learner as well as teacher and stays abreast of current research while providing this information to staff when it is relevant. Caring is demonstrated by paying attention to detail, such as spelling an unusual name correctly, ordering the special food a teacher would like for a project, and seeing that each board and staff member is notified of an early childhood lecture being held in the community. Caring is regarding the operation of the center in a serious manner, yet maintaining a sense of humor.

For some people, caring is shown in an exuberant manner with lots of enthusiastic conversation, hugging, and facial animation. Others who are just as caring are quiet, seem somewhat reserved, and perhaps move into relationships more slowly. Directors may have other combinations of personal qualities, but the genuine and essential ability to care is the one that makes the difference.

An interesting aspect of caring is that it may be misunderstood. Because they are concerned for others, directors sometimes may have to adjust the style in which they relate to the diverse people with whom they interact. For example, some individuals may be uncomfortable with being touched; if the director unknowingly puts an arm around people who feel this way, they may be annoyed or insulted and be unable to accept the care and concern that is intended.

Being a caring person in the face of all the responsibilities of directing a center can be difficult. At times, a director may feel overwhelmed. The caring director is constantly helping others by listening and providing emotional support for both children and adults, and the director may well need people to respond in kind. Those individuals who become effective directors usually enjoy giving to others; they seem to thrive on it. However, because they are seen at the center as the source of so much giving, they must seek sustenance from either the caring network at the center or a relative or friend outside the center. Even those people who freely and happily give of themselves need, at times, to receive support and encouragement through recognition and understanding.

Directing can be stressful because the director, although surrounded by people, is in a very real sense an isolate. She has no peers in the center and, no matter how loved and respected, is "the boss." This feeling can prevail even when all personnel, including the director, have come together to form a learning system. Overdoing the caring component of the director's role can be damaging to staff, children, and families. The director's role is to support others, rather than to oversee and manage their comfort. Furthermore, the director is still ultimately responsible to the owner, the board, the main office, funders, and others.

Confiding in one particular staff member would be inappropriate because some of the information with which the director works cannot be shared with anyone at the center. Some directors have established a network of other directors. They meet, perhaps monthly, for a relaxing lunch and conversation. There is reassurance in knowing that other directors have to report child abuse, experience staff turnover, have too many forms to fill out, and have considered quitting. As a group, directors can create ways to solve problems, to support one another, and to heighten community awareness regarding the needs of young children and their caregivers while maintaining confidentiality.

Directors realize they have the power to create healthy, supportive communities for children, families, and staff, but they also recognize that their early childhood training and classroom experiences have not prepared them to carry the vast array of responsibilities of running a center. Until relatively recently, little attention was paid to credentialing directors. Depending on the size, scope, and type of program, directors find they have duties as varied and complex as those of major corporate leaders. Yet they have had little or no preparation and often have no opportunity to prepare for the job. Limited mentoring is available.

---

### DIRECTOR'S CORNER

"Although I had been assistant director at the center, my role did not go beyond visiting the classrooms to see that all was well. When our director and her family moved to another state, I was offered the director's position. Little did I know how much I had to learn! Where is there a copy of the budget? Do we have enough money? What is expected of me? Do we have to pay taxes? What if someone doesn't pay tuition? Uh, oh, my computer isn't working. How can I get it fixed?"

NOTE TO SELF: 1. BEGIN CREATING A CENTER MANUAL.
2. RECRUIT AND TRAIN ASSISTANT DIRECTOR."

—*Director, nonprofit center*

---

To be effective leaders, directors must ensure that their own needs are met. Being a martyr, even a cheerful martyr, who never takes vacation or sick days, may lead staff to feel somewhat guilty when they recognize and meet their own needs. Competent directors serve as models of balance.

*Directors and staff work together to welcome children and families.*

## 1-5  MANAGING THE PROGRAM

Although directors may have a broad range of roles that bring a variety of personal qualities to these roles, every director is responsible for program maintenance. Completing this task, whatever its parameters, is possible only when the director is skilled and knowledgeable. Throughout this text, the information essential to doing the work of a center director is discussed. This information, when combined with some teaching and administrative experience, should help you meet the responsibilities that are required for appropriate program maintenance and enhancement. As with every other professional role, directors need to continue learning and developing. A list of typical responsibilities is included here.

Depending on the organizational structure of your center, some of these responsibilities may be carried out by other personnel. However, the director is responsible for ensuring that they are carried out appropriately.

1. Develop goals and objectives in relation to the center's philosophy, placing emphasis on the needs of clients.

2. Develop and maintain knowledge of standards created by professional and regulatory groups. Ensure that standards are being addressed appropriately throughout the center.

3. Work with staff to plan a curriculum to meet the objectives of the center.

4. Visit each classroom frequently, preferably daily.

5. Develop a positive working relationship with the board of directors and its committees, placing emphasis on communicating the center's accomplishments and needs to the board.

6. Establish policies for center operation, or become familiar with policies established by the center board, parent corporation, board of education, or other sponsor.

7. Draw up procedures for implementation of policies.

8. Prepare and maintain a manual for board and staff members.

9. Work with licensing agents to meet applicable licensing regulations.

10. Provide adequate insurance coverage.

11. Comply with all local, state, and federal laws relating to the center's operation.

12. Establish and operate within a workable budget.

13. Keep accurate financial records.

14. Pay bills and prepare payroll.

15. Collect tuition.

16. Write proposals and seek other funds for operation of the center.

17. Locate and maintain suitable physical facilities for the center's program.

18. Order and maintain equipment.

19. Develop and maintain a marketing plan.

20. Enroll and group the children.

21. Employ appropriate staff.

22. Provide staff orientation.

23. Coach the staff.

24. Develop knowledge levels and skills of the staff members so that upward mobility within the profession is feasible.

25. Evaluate the program, the staff members, and the children's progress.

26. Develop an effective communication system among staff members through regular staff meetings, conferences, and informal conversations.

27. Provide in-service training for staff and volunteers.

28. Fill roles of other staff members in emergency situations.

29. Plan and implement a family program that is responsive to needs and interests.

30. Explain the center's program to the community.

31. Participate in professional organizations.

32. Become an advocate for children.

33. Continue professional development through reading and attending pertinent courses such as workshops, conferences, and lectures.

Successful program maintenance requires that the director be organized. Just as the director expects teachers to have a plan for the year, month, week, and day, so too must the director have plans. Whether the plans are on a handheld device or on paper, they must be followed to a reasonable degree. Document organization is also essential. Although some paper forms are necessary, computerized systems often simplify documentation. If backed up and stored appropriately, they can be easy to locate, use, and modify. At the same time, discarding items that are no longer needed will make it easier to find working documents.

As you read other chapters of this text, you will notice the many types of files directors are expected to keep, including policy manuals, staff records, child records, financial data, as well as numerous others. Most, if not all of these, can be made available online if access is restricted to those who have a right to see them. As with all important documents, it is essential to have a backup copy in a safe place. You will find additional information

## Working Smart with Technology

### Computer Literacy

Today's successful director must be computer literate. Like nearly every other business, the management of child care centers can be greatly enhanced and somewhat simplified through the use of technology. Directors can use technology to organize, store, and complete paperwork; manage finances; apply for center licensing; communicate with parents, staff, and board members; provide staff development resources; and complete online educational opportunities. For additional information related to the use of technology in today's early childhood programs, check issues of the *Young Children* journal and *Exchange* magazine.

*Today's directors must be familiar with the ways in which technology can be used to simplify, organize, and complete numerous tasks.*

about essential documents on the child care licensing website for your state.

## 1-6 SERVING AS CURRICULUM LEADER

An important responsibility of a director is that of curriculum leader. Early childhood teacher preparation programs have at least one course devoted to curriculum. Directors who do not have an adequate early childhood background should expect to complete at least one course in early childhood curriculum. A section in an administration textbook and course will not suffice, however, because directors as well as teachers must continue to develop their understanding of curriculum and its relation to child development. Read Chapter 11 on the director's role in leading curriculum to learn more about the importance of this topic.

Numerous books are available to help with updating curriculum information. Directors must assume responsibility for becoming familiar with curriculum for the young child, including its sources, goals, and implementation approaches (see the Director's Library in Appendix H for suggested reading).

The director is responsible for instituting and maintaining a high-quality curriculum. Consulting with the teachers is expected, but the director must ensure that the goals and philosophy of the program are reflected in the curriculum. Directors who employ new teachers or teachers with little or no background in child development and early childhood education will need to provide detailed coaching (Curtis, Humbarger & Mann, 2011; Skiffington, Washburn & Elliott, 2011).

The director must recognize that a curriculum claiming to have already done all the planning and provided all the necessary materials is highly unlikely to be effective. Such programs are usually costly. They may also be unaesthetic, with "art" that should not appear in classrooms. Most important, it is impossible for the best teacher to plan every day's curriculum a year in advance. Such a plan cannot take into account the changing needs of the children. Nor can such a plan address the children's specific cultures, individual backgrounds, or current interests. In short, a preplanned commercial curriculum should be examined carefully to determine whether it addresses the outcomes and uses a theoretical base that fits your organization's mission and that will be significant for children's learning. Recall that when developmentally appropriate practice was first being discussed, hundreds of manufacturers labeled their products, books, and curriculum kits "developmentally appropriate." Today, with the emphasis on research or evidence-based curricula, curricula are being labeled "research based." Before adopting a curriculum on the strength of that claim, make sure you see the research. Find out who the subjects were, what was done, and what the results were. Determine whether the results relate to your center's mission and goals.

Carter and Curtis (2010) remind directors of the importance of having a vision that goes beyond a high score on a state or national evaluation or getting new equipment. They encourage directors to envision how the program and experiences of staff and children *could* be. Directors can help staff, children, and families go beyond "cookie cutter" environments, equipment, and activities. But first, the director and staff must reflect, read, and believe in the goal of becoming what they would really like to be, going beyond today's criteria for success. Because directors can get mired down in day-to-day tasks, turning to resources that focus on *what should be* can renew their delight in the roles of director, staff member, and child.

## 1-7  LEADING PEOPLE

Directors sometimes acquire program management skills and stop there, failing to realize the importance of the skills of leading people. Centers can and do run, at least for a while, without people leadership; however, centers that lack program management quickly close their doors. People leadership and enrichment are at the very heart of a worthwhile early childhood education program. Without it, program quality begins to disintegrate, and staff turnover may become a major problem.

Directors can enhance their effectiveness at leading a diverse group of people by developing an understanding of their own interpersonal styles. They also will benefit from studying various approaches to leadership, analyzing their own administrative styles, and determining their strengths and weaknesses in these areas. Most directors have had limited opportunities to acquire this information because they often move into administrative roles due to their effectiveness as teachers. Fortunately, many seminars, books, videos, and DVDs are available to enable directors to learn about interpersonal styles and management approaches.

Many agencies, such as Child Care Aware® of America (formerly the National Association of Child Care and Resource and Referral Association), offer coaching programs for teachers and directors. Coaching has also become an important component of the Quality Rating Improvement Systems (QRIS) in many states that seek to improve the quality of early childhood programs (Smith, Robbins, Schneider, Kreader & Ong, 2012). Typically, the director or teacher is observed, followed by discussion with the coach. Although many athletic teams have provided this service for their players for years, it is relatively new in early childhood centers.

The professional director understands that the role involves leadership as well as management. Beginning directors usually have to grow into the leadership role, but with motivation and support, they can acquire the characteristics that will help them develop the entire center's organization as a learning system. Their major contribution will be creating and supporting a team whose members work effectively, efficiently, and positively with one another and with clients. For more information on this topic, see Bruno (2012).

The center's board of directors may be willing to fund some training opportunities for the director, particularly if board members understand and use this type of information. Possibly, a board member could furnish training or related materials.

## 1-7a  Addressing Conflict Resolution

Another option is to provide total staff or joint board–staff coaching in an approach such as conflict resolution. This approach to professional development, if well done, leads to confirming the director's role as leader, while establishing the responsibility of each staff member for the success of the center's program. The sessions can also emphasize the responsibility of the director to see that staff members are involved in decision making and that their ideas are valued and accepted.

However, satisfaction obviously does not mean that everyone's demands will be met. For example, a teacher may be unhappy about working with a particular assistant whom she regards as lazy. When the teacher approaches the assistant with directions about what is to be done, the assistant does not complete the assigned tasks. In such a case, the director can facilitate a discussion between the teacher and assistant. However, had the teacher and assistant been coached in conflict resolution, they might have solved the problem themselves. This situation certainly does not preclude the director from making a decision about retaining the assistant. However, helping a teaching team learn to work together is often more productive than terminating someone and bringing in a new person. The decision to terminate should only be made when the director is convinced that termination is in the best interest of the children and staff.

Because conflict in any organization is inevitable, preparing people to address it in a straightforward, rational manner can lead to satisfaction. Such an approach also goes a long way to eliminating gossip, dissension, and rumors. Everyone connected with the center—directors, board, staff, families, and children—realizes that their ideas will be respected. They begin to recognize that when disagreements occur, a people-centered approach to a solution is possible. The director does not have to be the judge in most situations. Individuals are empowered to work together to solve problems.

The basic ideas include bringing together the people who are experiencing conflict. This may be two individuals, the staff and director, or any other combination. When the people who are concerned are together, have them each state what the problem is. Depending on the situation, it may be helpful to write the results of each step for everyone involved to see. If two teachers want to use the playground at 10:00 a.m., and there is room for only one group of children at a time, the problem is stated as a question: "How can playground time be scheduled to everyone's satisfaction?" (Notice how similar this is to the problem of two children wanting the same toy at the same time.)

Next, brainstorm solutions. All solutions are presented for consideration. No comments about a potential solution are appropriate at this point.

Examine the suggestions one at a time, eliminating any with which either party disagrees. Continue until a solution that is agreeable to each is reached. Agree to try the solution for a set period of time and to renegotiate at the end of that time if necessary.

In summary, the process is as follows:

1. State the problem.
2. Generate solutions.
3. Select a solution agreeable to all.
4. Implement the planned solution.
5. Check after an agreed-upon time to determine whether the solution is working.
6. If it is not working, return to step 1, and continue the process.

The staff and board members who agree to commit to a conflict-resolution type of philosophy use the concept that their customers (children and families) are their first priority as a starting point. By extension, one of the director's priorities must be staff satisfaction, and the board's priority must be a successful outcome for the operation of the center. This approach works well when everyone understands it and accepts this basic principle.

Directors who are quite comfortable with an authoritarian role may find it difficult or impossible to relinquish that role, just as teachers who are convinced that a teacher-directed approach is the only appropriate way to work with children may be unable to provide choices for children. Directors willing to invest time and effort in learning about management usually find they are far more able to lead the staff and clients in ways that are more satisfying to everyone and that the responsibility for the smooth running of the center no longer rests primarily with one person.

The staff-oriented director plans time each day to visit each classroom, greet each staff member, and acknowledge their efforts and successes. She coaches and supports them as they develop new understandings and skills, and she provides honest, sensitive feedback. The staff-oriented director remembers and relates to events and incidents that are significant to staff, children, and families. It may be as simple as commenting to a teacher about how well she managed a frightened child during a thunderstorm by describing specifically the effective approach the teacher used. Perhaps the director stops to greet a child who is proudly bringing his rabbit to school for a visit. Maybe the director telephones a father to thank him for organizing a book fair to benefit the center.

Tending to the personal and professional development of the people associated with a center's program is seminal to the program's success. The manner in which the director carries out people-support tasks is a major contributing factor in program maintenance and vice versa. There is a delicate balance between successfully dealing with the mechanics of efficient program operation and simultaneously creating a caring environment for adults and children.

### Leadership Practices in Child Development Centers: Personnel System

This video provides an overview of the many roles that directors of early childhood programs must play. As you view this video, *Leadership Practices in Child Development Centers*, reflect on the following questions:

1. What strategies does this director use to ensure that morale among staff members is maintained?

2. What are the characteristics of a successful director?

A director can exhibit human relations skills, care for others, ask for their ideas and opinions, encourage them to try new methods, and provide positive feedback. But if that same director does not have the skills and knowledge to accomplish the huge amount of work required of an administrator, the program cannot succeed. Similarly, the director who is task-oriented, skilled, and knowledgeable may conduct a center that provides services but never really addresses or satisfies people's needs. Obviously, the director must combine work-orientation skills with communication skills. If skills in either area are lacking, precious time will be wasted doing jobs or rebuilding relationships. Meanwhile, the children will not receive the excellent care they deserve.

Throughout this text, you will read many more details about both program management and leadership, which are required of all directors. You will begin by learning to manage a range of circumstances and tasks. Gradually, as you work at being a manager, if you are committed to developing your abilities and those of the staff, you will find yourself analyzing situations that occur in a child development program. As you reflect on what you do, why you do it, and the outcomes of your decisions, you will be creating new knowledge and understanding for yourself—something that no text or instructor can give you. You will be well on your way to moving from the role of manager to the role of leader.

Realizing that you may be feeling overwhelmed at the magnitude of the director's job, we turn now to a discussion of management tools to help you manage a challenging role.

## 1-8 MANAGEMENT TOOLS

Every director has a limited amount of time in which to do numerous tasks and develop many relationships. This work can be accomplished most effectively if the director is well organized. Then, when the inevitable unexpected event occurs, the director will be in a stable position to withstand the demands of the crisis. For example, the director whose financial records are in order may not have extra cash available to replace a broken water heater but at least is better prepared to adjust other budget categories to provide the funds. The disorganized director may not even know the income and expenses anticipated within the next few months in order to adjust the budget to meet the financial crisis. An efficient director can comfortably take time to listen to a group of excited children who burst into the office describing all the worms they found on the sidewalk. But a disorganized administrator may be too busy planning menus that are already overdue. Obviously, administration will not always run smoothly for any director; however, the director who knows about appropriate techniques and uses them is certainly better prepared to cope effectively with the hubbub that often is evident in a child care center.

The use of several management tools can enable directors to administer programs effectively. Key tools for beginning directors include policies and procedures manuals and time-use skills.

### 1-8a Policies and Procedures Manual

A manual containing all the center's policies and procedures facilitates the administrator's job. Generally, when there is a board involved, the board members make the policies, and the director develops the procedures for implementation of those policies. For example, the board may establish a policy to admit any child between the ages of 3 and 5 who can profit from the center's program. The director then establishes the procedures necessary to accomplish the child's enrollment such as plans for informing the community, distributing and receiving enrollment forms, and notifying parents that their child has been accepted or that the center is full. The director also designs the necessary forms and includes copies in the manual.

When procedures are overly detailed or cover self-explanatory material, they become burdensome and even may be neglected or circumvented by staff members. For example, teachers may be required to fill out a lengthy form to request permission to purchase something for which they will be reimbursed; they also might be required to fill out another form after having purchased the item. At this point, some teachers may decide not to bother with purchasing needed items for their classrooms. They can carry their reaction one step further by disregarding the otherwise accepted procedures for using materials from the central storeroom. Naturally, some established procedures will be unpopular with the staff, but if directors are open about why the procedures are important, and if they are careful about limiting the number of procedures to be followed, they will find that staff members are willing to comply.

Staff input prior to the establishment of procedures is common, although the director still may need to make some independent decisions. When directors focus on their own need for power instead of on establishing procedures to ensure an operation runs smoothly, it becomes impossible for the staff to feel respected. Staff members for whom every procedure is spelled out have no freedom. How, then, can they be expected to offer freedom to the children with whom they work?

## Other Contents of the Manual

In addition to policies and procedures, the manual contains the center's bylaws, job descriptions, salary schedules, and information about the center such as philosophy, goals, sponsorship, funding, and perhaps a brief history. Each of these should be dated with the adoptive date. If the manual is large, a table of contents and an index are essential. Placing all materials in a loose-leaf binder enables staff members to add and delete pages as necessary. Each staff and board member receives a manual when first joining the center. It is the holder's responsibility to keep the manual up to date and to return it to the center when vacating the board or staff position.

## 1-8b Using Technology

Taking advantage of current technology can be a major time-saver and organizer. Directors who are not already comfortable using computers will find that the initial learning period may be time-consuming. After gaining some confidence in their use, however, the benefits will accrue.

One question often encountered when applying for financial assistance is "How will your company's financial records be maintained?" Financial record keeping and report generation are essential and time-consuming components of the director's role. Completing these tasks using software saves time and promotes accuracy after the data are properly entered. Available software can provide computations for payroll deductions, billing, attendance, inventory, and a range of additional tasks. Most directors have access to a computer and use it for word processing tasks, but many do not use other components that can be helpful. You may choose to contract with a specialty business for payroll, fiscal reporting, and other functions, and yet you may find it reasonable to manage child information on paper. Nonetheless, analyzing staff time in terms of cost plus the cost of contracted services compared with software cost and reduced staff time to generate comparable information may be surprising. Admittedly, the initial learning time will increase costs. Another important consideration is the professional appearance of computer-generated reports.

---

### REFLECTION

Imagine you have planned to spend the evening writing a term paper that is due the following day. A friend telephones. He is terribly upset about his wife's illness. Think about what you might do.

Now imagine that at 3:00 p.m., you, as an early childhood center director, are greeted by a teacher who is leaving for the day and wants to talk about her husband who has just lost his job. You had planned to spend the rest of the afternoon working on the major equipment order that is needed for a board committee report the following morning. You may choose one of the following:

- Listen to the teacher.
- Tell the teacher you do not have time to listen because of the report you must prepare.
- Schedule time the following afternoon to listen to the teacher.
- Choose some other plan.

Any of these choices may be appropriate; the director must make the best choice. But the directors who always find themselves too busy to listen and those who always find themselves spending so much time listening that they must work all evening must analyze why their scheduling problems recur. Think about your own reaction to this situation.

---

To find a software company that fits your center's needs, perform an online search for "child care software." Read information provided by various purveyors, and then contact them to ask for a demonstration. You can also check professional journals for reviews of child care software. *Child Care Information Exchange* and *Young Children* are potential sources, as are other directors who are experienced users of business software. At regional and national conferences, ask for demonstrations of software packages. Take a list of questions with you, and jot down the answers and your impressions.

Consider which features you would like and which are essential. Ask whether you can buy components if you do not want or need a comprehensive package. Many software companies will offer a complimentary trial disc or access to an online trial.

Your staff may also benefit when you add computer technology to your center. Aside from paperwork (child records, assessments, and curriculum planning) that they may be able to complete more easily and professionally on a computer, they may also use the computer for continuing education courses. The director can set up a calendar of tasks to be completed, appointments, and so forth. Explore these and other uses and packages thoroughly before buying.

## 1-8c Time-Use Skills

Some directors study time management as a tool to use in allocating available time wisely. The board may provide tuition or released time for a director to attend a time-management course or seminar. Several time-management techniques can be acquired easily and put to immediate use.

### Analyzing Use of Time

As a beginning, directors can analyze how they spend their time by writing down in detail everything they do for several days and how much time is spent on each task. The next step is to make a judgment about which activities have not been enjoyed, have not been done well, or have not been related either to the personal goals of the director or the goals of the center. When time is frittered away on such activities, less time is available to invest in other, more productive activities. The individual alone can decide which activity should take priority. In some businesses, listening to a client discuss an emotional problem is considered a waste of the administrator's time. In early childhood education, with its focus on children and families, time that the director spends listening may be the most effective use of the available administrative time.

Voice mail, email, and other computer communication approaches help the director keep in touch while controlling the use of time. However, directors must be careful to avoid communicating with families and staff solely through technology. The sensitive director is alert to the need for a live, human contact and a handwritten note in some situations.

Although some of the director's tasks may not be appealing, they may need to be done. A director can, at least, recognize how much time must be devoted to undesirable tasks; then this amount of time can be put into perspective. The director also may decide to devise ways to make tasks more manageable. Of course, if the majority of tasks seem undesirable, the director may choose to change jobs.

### Grouping and Assigning Tasks

The director who needs to economize on time also may decide to make an effort to read and answer all mail, place outgoing telephone calls, and record financial transactions at a specified time each day. Directors who allocate time for these types of chores and establish the policy that they are not to be disturbed during that time will probably have more time for meeting people's needs during the rest of the day.

Directors also should consider which jobs they must do and which jobs they can delegate. For example, could the janitor let the director know on a regular basis what supplies are needed instead of the director checking on supplies? Perhaps the receptionist can be trained to respond to the general calls for information about the center instead of involving the director in a routine conversation about when the center is open and the age range of children the center serves.

When the center's operation is reasonably under control, additional staff members can be prepared to fill the director's role in her absence, thereby allowing the director to move into the wider community on occasion. It is not appropriate to insist that other staff people do the director's work, but it is appropriate to coach them to assume the role of director temporarily. In this way, both parties can benefit professionally.

### Planning a Time Line

One of the ways a director develops efficiency is through the development of a time line. Jobs that must be done on a regular basis are scheduled, and then the director completes them according to the schedule.

This simple concept curtails procrastination by helping the director recognize that when she postpones a job scheduled for this week because it is distasteful, time and energy are spent thinking about it anyway. Because the job must be completed eventually, no time is saved by waiting until next week; nor does the job become easier. In fact, the director then may be in the uncomfortable position of having to apologize.

*The director checks in daily with teachers and children.*

Each director must develop a time line based on the personal responsibilities unique to the type of program and the clients' needs. No matter which jobs and time frames are included, writing a time line gives the director and others a clear picture of the work to be done. The time line can be flexible when circumstances warrant, but the basic goal is to adhere to the plan so that regularly scheduled tasks will be completed, and time will be made available for working with people.

Throughout this book, you will learn how important the director's interpersonal relationships are and how they set the tone for the center. Now, as you prepare to learn more about the director's role, you will see this theme reemphasized. It may seem impossible that a director really could focus on establishing a "we" feeling when most of the chapters present an almost overwhelming set of director responsibilities. Nonetheless, directors who know what is involved in the job, who work to acquire the necessary knowledge and skills, and who use a managerial approach that reflects an understanding of the needs of staff and clients are found in nearly every community.

These competent and successful directors know that being a director is exhausting,
and frequently challenging,
sometimes frightening,
never boring,
sometimes lonely,
many times hectic,
and, yes, even fun.

They also know that being a director—*a really good director*—

*The director ensures that the physical plant is well maintained.*

a leader,
a manager,
a model,
a coach,
and a supporter
is hard work and time-consuming.

And being a director just often enough is deeply satisfying,
even exhilarating,
and richly rewarding!

## SUMMARY

Effective directors of early childhood programs combine skills, knowledge, and caring to accomplish the following:

- Understand their responsibility to a wide variety of stakeholders.

- Be familiar with the NAEYC Code of Ethics, which provides important guidelines for professional decision making and practice.

- Recognize that early childhood programs operate as complex systems and that the director and staff must work together to identify the characteristics and interworking of systems and subsystems.

- Be aware that although directors fill a variety of roles in countless styles, no effective director can let either the management and operation of the center or the care of and communication with people occupy an inappropriate proportion of time.

- Identify and be able to perform the numerous responsibilities that directors have as managers of a center.

- Understand that the director is responsible for instituting and maintaining high-quality curriculum and ensuring that teachers are able to appropriately implement the curriculum.

- Be aware that performing one's role as a leader of people can require a significant amount of skill, time, and energy, but this must be balanced with the management of the program.

- Use a wide variety of tools that support both program management and people leadership.

# TRY IT OUT!

1. Discuss with a classmate the personal qualities you possess that might impact your ability to successfully manage an early childhood program. Which of these qualities might prove useful as a director? Which qualities might present challenges to being an effective manager or leader?

2. Discuss the kind of director you would like to be with three members of your class. Review the director's responsibilities as described in the chapter. On which of the director's roles would you like to spend the most time? Which of the roles would you find more challenging? Why would this be the case? Compare and contrast your ideas with those of your classmates.

3. If you were the director, which of the tasks in the director's responsibilities could you assign to someone else? Why would it be appropriate to do so?

# REFERENCES

Bruno, H. E. (2012). *What you need to lead an early childhood program: Emotional intelligence in practice.* Washington, DC: NAEYC.

Carter, M. (2014). Leadership for sustainable organizations. *Exchange, 215*, 8–12.

Carter, M., & Curtis, D. (2010). *The visionary director: A handbook for dreaming, organizing, and improvising in your center.* St. Paul, MN: Redleaf Press.

Covey, S. (2004). *The 8th habit: From effectiveness to greatness.* Rochester, NY: Free Press.

Curtis, R. R., Humbarger, J. A., & Mann, T. E. (2011). Ten tips for coaching adults: An emotionally healthy approach. *Young Children, 66*(1), 51–54.

McCrea, N. (2002). Learn leading for authenticity. *Child Care Information Exchange, 147*, 10–14.

National Association for the Education of Young Children. (2006). *Code of ethical conduct and statement of commitment: Supplement for early childhood program administrators.* Washington, DC: Author.

National Association for the Education of Young Children. (2011). *Code of ethical conduct and statement of commitment: Guidelines for responsible behavior in early childhood education.* Washington, DC: Author.

Sciarra, D. J., & Dorsey, A. G. (2002). *Leaders and supervisors in child care programs.* Clifton Park, NY: Thomson Delmar Learning.

Senge, P. M. (2006). *The fifth discipline: The art and practice of the learning organization.* New York: Doubleday.

Skiffington, S., Washburn, S., & Elliott, K. (2011). Instructional coaching: Helping preschool teachers reach their full potential. *Young Children, 66*(3), 12–19.

Smith, S., Robbins, T., Schneider, W., Kreader, J. L., & Ong C. (2012). *Coaching and quality assistance in Quality Rating Improvement Systems: Approaches used by TA providers to improve quality in early care and education programs and home-based settings.* New York: National Center for Children in Poverty. Retrieved from http://www.nccp.org /publications/pub_1047.html.

# 2 ASSESSING COMMUNITY NEED *and* ESTABLISHING *a* PROGRAM

## Learning Objectives

After reading this chapter, you should be able to:

**2-1** Identify information that will help determine the types of child services needed now and in the future.

**2-2** Develop a mission statement that reflects the program's core values.

**2-3** Determine the various types of child care needed by families in the region.

**2-4** Identify where the standards of quality practice can be located and how they should be used when determining the program's core values.

*The decision to start a program is best conceived when the voices of multiple stakeholders are heard.*

## Standards Addressed in this Chapter

Accreditation Standard 8 – Community Relationships

Administrator Competencies – Management Knowledge and Skills 2, 6, 7, 9, 10

Administrators Competencies – Early Childhood Knowledge and Skills 1, 6, 10

Professional Preparation Standard 2 – Building Family and Community Relationships

Professional Preparation Standard 3 – Observing, Documenting, and Assessing to Support Young Children and Families

Professional Preparation Standard 6 – Becoming a Professional

---

Creating a new program is an exciting challenge that requires abundant creativity and energy and can be overwhelmingly complex. The process requires program planners to consider multiple factors in a stream of ever-changing priorities. Planners need to be agile decision makers and problem solvers, considering the priority of the day and shifting to the next important decision as needed in order to get a complete picture of both program and community needs. Clearly, there must be a need for the program. And there must be some driving force in the community, whether an individual or a group, that will generate the creative energy to

- examine the need
- develop the program mission and values statements
- decide about the type of program that will fit the need and available resources

These three major activities will be taking place simultaneously, and each will influence the program that is developed.

The driving force for developing the program might be an early childhood educator with a desire to open a center, or it might be a group of parents who have an interest in providing child care services for their children. Sometimes community agencies choose to expand their services to include child care. Perhaps there is a need for an expansion of both employer- and public-school–sponsored child care programs. These are a few of the common catalysts for developing a program, and as the need for care continues to increase, it is important to be aware of new forces that impact how a program might be sponsored. The planners, whether an individual, an agency, or a corporation, must be prepared to carry out all preliminary tasks until a director is hired, including dealing with funding issues, undertaking public relations campaigns, and carrying out the needs assessment.

Program sponsors examine what services can be delivered realistically without diluting quality. Usually, setting up a program that will be responsive to every demand and meet all needs is unrealistic. The same can be said for expecting to start a new program and have it fully enrolled immediately. Bringing a new program up to full enrollment can take several years to accomplish. It is better to begin on a small scale, carefully weighing the assured need against the services that can be delivered under the existing financial and resource constraints. Overextending by trying to meet everyone's needs or by providing a large-scale operation that overtaxes the resources is dangerous. Problems also arise when the need is overestimated, and a program is set up that is under-enrolled. In either case, program quality diminishes, and children become the victims of impoverished environments. Then, families do not trust the program to deliver the promised services, and it is doomed to failure.

---

**DIRECTOR'S CORNER**

"I projected it would take us three years to reach capacity in this new center, which is licensed for 115 children. We are now at the beginning of the third year of operation and we are about two-thirds full—so my prediction was on target."

—*Director/owner, franchised center*

---

## 2-1  ASSESSING THE NEED

To ensure that the planned program is properly scaled to meet both the size and the nature of the community need, it is important to do a needs assessment during the preliminary planning period. The needs assessment can begin before or after a director is designated or hired, but it must be completed before any financial or program planning begins. The purpose of the needs assessment is to determine the number of families and children that will use a child care service and the type of services desired by those who will use it.

## 2-1a  What Must You Know about Need?

The first step in the needs assessment process is to determine what you need to know. After that has been decided, procedures for collecting the data can be worked out. In some situations, there may be a group of stakeholders—persons who have an interest in the success of the program and how it is configured. This group can be helpful in informing the fact-gathering process, but they cannot replace more comprehensive data collection.

### Number of Families and Children

One way to start the needs assessment is to determine the number of potential families and children that you could serve. It is useless to go beyond the earliest planning stage unless families are available who will use the service. Simply assessing the *number* of children is not sufficient because number alone does not determine interest or need. If you currently are running a program for preschool children but get many calls for infant/toddler or school-aged child care, you are alerted to a need to expand your program offerings. However, between the time you assemble your waiting lists and accomplish the program expansion, many of those families on your list will have made other child care arrangements. One quick and informal way to decide whether to proceed with a needs assessment is to find out if other centers in the vicinity have waiting lists.

Some planners overestimate the number of families who need child care and fail to consider how many of those families will use or pay for center-based care if it is provided. Although the numbers of preschoolers in child care whose mothers work outside the home has increased sharply over the past five decades, determining who cares for the children of these working families is difficult. As of 2008, "more than 60 percent of children under age six and 70 percent of school-age children in 44 states and the District of Columbia have all parents in the labor force" (Children's Defense Fund, 2014, p. F-3). However, many of these children are with friends or family members, thus making it difficult to determine how many of these working parents would choose center-based care or family child care homes for their children if it became available to them.

One resource for planners is the Early Childhood Longitudinal Study, Birth Cohort (ECLS-K), sponsored by the U.S. Department of Education's National Center for Education Statistics, a Center of the Institute of Education Sciences (Denton, Flanagan, & McPhee, 2009). This study collected national data on the early home and educational experiences of children from infancy to kindergarten entry. Table 2-1 shows a picture of the type of care and education that 4-year-olds use during the year prior to kindergarten in the United States.

**TABLE 2-1** Primary type of nonparental care arrangement prior to kindergarten entry

|  | Number of children (in thousands) | Percentage distribution of children |
| --- | --- | --- |
| No regular nonparental arrangement[1] | 699 | 20.9 |
| Home-based care | 711 | 21.2 |
| Relative care | 499 | 14.9 |
| Nonrelative care | 212 | 6.3 |
| Center-based care | 1850 | 55.3 |
| Multiple arrangements[2] | 84 | 2.5 |

[1]This refers to the type of nonparental care in which the child spent the most hours.
[2]"Multiple arrangements" refers to children who spent an equal amount of time in each of two or more arrangements.

*Source: U.S. Department of Education, National Center for Education Statistics, Early Childhood Longitudinal Study, Kindergarten Class of 2010–11 (ECLS-K:2011).*

## Socioeconomic Level of Families

Many families may be interested in child care services but are unable to pay enough to cover the cost of the services they choose or need. For example: "In 2011 center-based care for infants was more expensive than public college in 35 states and the District of Columbia, and 4-year-old child care was more expensive than college in 25 states and the District of Columbia" (Children's Defense Fund, 2014, p. 63). When families are unable to pay the high cost of quality child care outside the home, operators cannot depend on tuition but must seek outside sources of funding if planned programs are to succeed. It is important to know how many families that express a need for assistance actually qualify for state or federal subsidy. When families

**▶❚❚ TeachSource Video Vignette**

### PreK Funding Cuts

This video provides an overview of the importance of the impact of state and national policy on the availability of PreK for all children. View the video vignette entitled, *PreK Funding Cuts*. Reflect on the following questions:

1. Why is it important to know what is happening at the state and national level in terms policy, funding, and legislation related to early childhood?

2. How do state and national policies impact local need?

---

## MAKING THE CASE FOR *ADVOCACY*

As the need for quality early care and education has become widely accepted by both major political parties in the United States, it finally seems possible for all young children to have access to rich learning and development experiences prior to starting school. Although external support is important, there is also a need for those in the field to inform advocacy. Well-intentioned advocates who do not know the complexities of the field can support decisions that, in the end, do more harm than good or spend limited resources in ways that do not support children and families effectively. Decisions about how to fund early childhood are made quickly and require a commitment from early childhood leaders to inform the decisions that are being made. To support effective advocacy, directors need to

1. Seek out ways to become more politically connected and aware of trends in the field. Become a member of email distribution lists such as those associated with the U.S. Department of Education, the National Child Care Resource and Referral Association, the National Institute for Early Education Research, and other organizations that inform the field.

2. Be aware of the local champions for early care and education. Know the local organizations that are advocating for young children and stay connected with them. These organizations will notify stakeholders when there is a call to action.

are able to pay, determining what they are willing to pay for center-based or home-based care is important. It is reasonable to expect that many families can afford to pay up to ten percent of their total income for child care. However, low-income families could be forced to pay as much as 25 percent of their income for child care.

## Ages of Children to Be Served

The ages of participating children affect all program planning considerations and can make a considerable difference in the cost of delivering the service. Determine the number of families who expect to have infants or toddlers participate in the group care program outside the home. Although early childhood education programs have traditionally served 3- and 4-year-old children, the increase in the number of one-parent families and the number of working mothers has increased the demand for infant/toddler care for before and after school as well as for year-round programs for school-aged children. Therefore, when doing the needs assessment, inquire not only about 3- and 4-year-olds who may need care but also about older children and those under age 3.

## Type of Service the Families Prefer

In assessing the need for a program, one of the first things you must find out is whether families prefer full-day child care or a half-day program. Working families must have full-day care, and they often will need it for children ranging in age from birth through school age.

While the demand for half-day programs has decreased because of families with all parents in the workforce, those families that choose half-day programs may use a program for toddlers and 3- and 4-year-olds (sometimes called preschoolers) but may prefer to keep infants at home. These families might select a five-day program for preschoolers but often prefer a two- or three-day program for toddlers. Parents who want to become involved in the program may choose to place their children in a cooperative child care program. Other parents may not have the time or the interest in becoming directly involved in the school program.

In some situations, family child care homes may be more suitable than a center-based program because they can serve a broad range of needs, can be available for emergency care, and can provide evening and weekend care. The family child care home involves parents taking their children to someone else's home and paying for child care on an hourly, daily, or weekly basis. These arrangements usually are made individually, although there is often some regulation of the number of children for whom care can be provided in a given home. In a few cases, satellite programs are set up involving the coordination of family child care homes by a child care center staff member or an employer. Parents make arrangements through the child care center or the employer referral service for placement of their children in an affiliated family child care home. They make payments to the center or make use of this employer benefit. The center or employer, in turn, pays the caregiver and provides the parents with some assurance that the home and the caregiver have been evaluated and that placement for the child will be found if the caregiver becomes unable to provide the service due to illness or other reasons. When the need for care is immediate and critical, it may be useful to locate and organize a few child care homes while the planning and financing of a center-based program is under way.

## 2-1b How Do You Find Out about Need?

After you have determined the kind of data necessary to substantiate the need for a program, you are ready to decide how to collect the data. Some information for long-range planning can be obtained from census figures, chambers of commerce, or data on births from the health department. However, planners in most communities have access to information from their Child Care Resource and Referral (CCR&R) agency. These agencies are funded through Child Care and Development Block Grants issued to the states through the U.S. Department of Health and Human Services and were created to support families and providers who are interested in affordable and quality child care. CCR&Rs provide technical assistance for a variety of child care providers, including family child care, center-based programs, and after-school programs. They support programs that serve infants, toddlers, preschoolers, and school agers. Many CCR&R agencies will generate zip-code–specific program planning reports that can include the number and type of child care slots available as well as the number of children by age in an area. Child Care Aware of America (formerly the National Association for Child Care Resource and Referral Agencies [NACCRRA]) serves as a professional organization and useful resource for child care. It is important to be connected with the CCR&R that supports your area.

Although the CCR&R agency should be the first stop for data collection, other detailed information needed for decision making will likely need to be obtained to answer all necessary questions.

Data must be collected, recorded, compiled, and analyzed so that the need for the program can be explained to anyone who is involved in initial planning, including members of a sponsoring group or funding agency. The data collection process might be formal and wide in scope to cover a broad potential population, or it can be informal and confined to a very small group of parents and community representatives. Possible methods of collecting needs assessment data include mailed questionnaires; telephone or online surveys; or informal, small group meetings.

## Working Smart with Technology

### *Online Surveys*

Online survey development tools, such as Kwik Survey, Survey Monkey, and Survey Gizmo, can provide opportunities for directors to send out surveys to a broad audience. Because online surveys are easy to access and can be returned by clicking the submit button, the return rates are often much higher than pencil-and-paper surveys that have to be returned by mail. Online surveys are easy to develop and can include a variety of multiple-choice, true and false, and open answers and can include demographic questions. Most free online survey development tools limit the number of questions that can be included. Surveys that limit the number of questions to 10 are more likely to be returned. Another benefit of using online surveys is that they typically include a tool that allows the user to create charts and graphs , which can be useful when presenting survey results to stakeholders.

Photograph by Tara Koenig

*Using online survey development tools can help directors gain insight from a variety of stakeholders quickly and inexpensively. When individuals can access surveys anytime, anywhere, the return rate is much higher.*

## Use of Questionnaires

When a large group of potential clients is sampled, it is wise to develop a questionnaire that can be completed online or that can be returned in an enclosed, addressed, and stamped envelope. Questionnaires provide specific data that can be recorded, compiled, and analyzed. These data are usually quite accurate; however, some families may indicate interest in child care and then no longer need it or decide not to use the child care when it becomes available. In some communities, the use of online survey tools such as Survey Monkey or Kwik Survey might be appropriate. Many online tools are free, easy to use, and can design surveys that collect both open-ended and forced-choice data.

The use of online surveys can reduce the cost and also increase the percentage of returns. The task of developing a good questionnaire or survey can be challenging, and getting the survey into the hands of the right group of people requires some thoughtful consideration. Those who determine that a traditional paper-and-pencil survey is best for their project will need to plan for the cost of mailing the survey with an enclosed addressed and stamped envelope in order to increase the number of returns. They should plan on a lack of response and realize that unreturned questionnaires often create more questions because it isn't clear whether those families are not interested in the service or whether they are interested but have neglected to return the questionnaire.

### DIRECTOR'S CORNER

"At the beginning of our planning process, we worked with our neighborhood elementary school and received permission to sponsor a booth at the school's fall open house. The booth included some information on the importance of quality child care and some enticing trinkets that brought children to the booth with their families in tow. We asked visitors to fill out an interest survey and provided both a pencil-and-paper version and an online version of the survey using a laptop computer. We were somewhat surprised to see how many people preferred to use the computer to complete the survey, and many took a card with a link to the survey website with them so that others not at the open house could complete the survey. We were also able to talk with the principal who offered to include a link to our survey and a short article in the school's electronic newsletter, which generated a lot of interest and greatly increased the number of completed surveys. When it came time to compile the data, we were able to input our pencil-and-paper data into the online version. The online survey automatically analyzed our results and presented our data in a series of colorful and easy-to-understand charts and graphs, which we used as we presented our findings to potential funders."

—*Director, private nonprofit centerr*

Whether using a pencil-and-paper or online version, developing good surveys or questionnaires can be difficult. The questionnaire must be brief and understandable by the recipient, and the items included also must be carefully selected to provide precisely the data that are important to the needs assessment for any given program. Therefore, if you are involved in drafting a questionnaire, it is imperative to analyze the potential audience first so that items are covered in terms the audience understands and that it is family friendly; then you must be sure to include inquiries about *all* the information you need while keeping the form brief.

Before planning the location, type, and size of the program, and ages of children to be served, it is helpful to ask for the following information:

- number of adults in the household
- number of those adults employed
- number and ages of all children in the household
- number of children cared for outside the home
- number and ages of children with special needs
- estimate of family income
- estimate of how much is or could be spent on child care
- days and hours child care is needed
- preferred location of child care
- whether the family will use the proposed child care center when it becomes available

## Use of Telephone Surveys

In the past, the use of telephone surveys was a viable option for collecting data. Today, telemarketing has come under public scrutiny with many households opting out of being called at home by signing up for the National Do Not Call Registry. Although it is unlikely that conducting a needs assessment survey would fall under the Do Not Call Registry guidelines, the public's annoyance with telemarketing calls is clear, and many families use caller ID to screen their calls. Many families also rely on cell phones versus land lines, which makes acquiring lists of accurate phone numbers challenging. When an existing phone list is available, and a telephone survey is determined as the option of choice, be prepared for a time-consuming and costly task, especially if you expect to include a large number of families. One way to reduce both cost and time is to call a sample of the large potential population to obtain fairly accurate information about the total group without calling each family. If you are involved in an extensive needs assessment program, you should consult a marketing specialist about appropriate sampling techniques. On the other hand, if you have access to a group of volunteers who can do some telephoning, and the population to be contacted is small, calling prospective families may

yield accurate data, provided that the questioning is conducted uniformly and that the data collected are what you need to know.

To ensure uniformity, telephone surveys also must use a questionnaire. The survey caller verbally asks the questions and fills in the questionnaire. The same considerations that apply to mailed or online questionnaires apply to those used in telephone surveys: understandable wording, complete coverage of data, and brevity.

### REFLECTION

Think for a moment about being called by someone doing a telephone survey. What was your reaction to the call? Was the call at a convenient time, or did it interrupt your study time or dinner? Did the caller get to the point quickly or waste your time, inquiring about your health or if you were having a good day? What led you to agree to participate in the survey or decline and hang up? Recalling your reaction to a telephone survey can help you gain insights into how parents might respond to a needs assessment telephone survey.

Now consider an online survey that you have taken. How did this experience compare to the telephone survey? Did you complete the online survey at a time that was convenient to you? During which experience were you more likely to provide complete and accurate information?

## Small Group Meetings

Holding informal group discussions with families who express interest in having their children participate in a program is a good way to obtain information about need. Small group meetings are practical when the potential client population is defined (for example, church members, apartment complex dwellers, employees of a particular company) or when the size of the community or neighborhood limits the number of families who might use the center. Informal meetings have the advantage of establishing a basis of trust and open communication between the providers of the service and the families who will use it. Without the constraints of a specific questionnaire, parents are free to discuss their values and goals for their children, their unique needs and desires in terms of their family situation, and their feelings about different types of programs that might become available. However, this informal data collection process yields information that is often not as valid, is less reliable, and is more difficult to tabulate and analyze than questionnaire data. You may find it beneficial to work out a combination of the informal discussion and formal questionnaire procedures by holding a series of small group meetings in which parents fill out a brief questionnaire at the close of the meeting. Needs assessment data that are collected through both formal and informal channels can both provide the basis for the decision about whether or not to have a program and furnish information about family values and goals that will enter into formulating the program philosophy. Of course, the values and the educational interests of the program planners and the director also will have a significant impact on the philosophy.

## 2-2 PROGRAM MISSION AND VALUES STATEMENTS

The characteristics of an early child-  hood education program should emerge from the mission and values of the program. Developing the mission and values statements is part of the planners' strategic planning process. These carefully crafted statements guide directors' decisions about hiring new staff and designing appropriate professional development to ensure that all staff members are prepared to implement a program consistent with those statements.

### 2-2a Decisions about the Mission and Values Statements

Mission statements must reflect the principles of our profession and provide the indicators of quality that define good practice. Decisions about the mission of a program will also emerge from the data that are gathered in the initial planning process. If the data suggest that a full-day, 12-month program is needed for preschoolers of middle-class professional families who work from 8:00 a.m. to 5:00 p.m., then the mission of the center will reflect this need. A very different mission statement would likely be developed for

- children of military families who are frequently deployed overseas
- children of school teachers who need 9 or 10 months of care
- children whose families are in poverty and work split shifts

---

**REFLECTION**

Think about the three different groups of children and families described above. How might the mission of each group be crafted to reflect the needs of the children and families to be served?

---

The cultural, educational, and socioeconomic levels of the child and families are some of many factors that impact how the mission statement is developed. Understanding the construction and purpose of mission and values statements is important for planners engaged in the strategic planning process.

---

**REFLECTION**

Think about a program that you have taught in or observed. Identify the assumptions about how children learn in this program. Try to formulate an example from that classroom experience that supports the assumption about how children learn. Think about activities you may have planned or behaviors you encouraged, and try to determine the area of development you most value. What are your assumptions about how children learn?

---

### Mission Statements

A mission statement briefly defines the  focus or purpose of the organization. It appears on numerous program documents, including personnel policies, the parent handbook, brochures, newsletters, the program website, all promotional and fund-raising materials, as well as stationery and news releases. Having a well-developed mission statement is an indicator of program quality. Sections in both the NAEYC Accreditation Standards and the Program Administration Scale (PAS) require a mission statement. The Program Planning and Evaluation Section of the PAS indicates, under "Documents Needed," that programs must have a mission and/or vision statement. Vision and/or mission statements are mentioned in the NAEYC Accreditation Criteria for Leadership and Management Standard.

### Developing a Mission Statement

A mission statement should clearly and concisely state the purpose and business of the program in a manner that resonates with the current staff and stakeholders. Radtke (1998) recommends that mission statements be revisited every five years to "ensure relevance" and should also answer the following three questions:

1. What are the opportunities or needs that we exist to address? (the *purpose* of the organization)

2. What are we doing to address these needs? (the *business* of the organization)

3. What principles or beliefs guide our work? (the *values* of the organization) (Radtke, 1998. p. 2)

Figure 2-1 shows an example of how one university-affiliated center answered Radtke's three questions to develop a mission statement.

### 2-2b Decisions about Core Values and Value Statements

Establishing the core values that will serve as the foundation of the program is a critical step in establishing a meaningful and well-justified program. Core values come from a sound understanding of child development and core value. A classroom guided by this value statement would replace planned activities set up to teach letters or numbers with a print-rich environment that includes many books, charts, and a writing center, and children would enjoy the use of math games, measuring tools, and simple machines such as pulleys and pendulums. Consider Table 2-2 and note how core values are transformed into value statements.

It is important to have a director who fully understands and supports the core values because he or she will be the educational leader responsible for the implementation of a program that supports these values. When the planners have very specific ideas about either mission or values, or a new director is hired for an ongoing program, the new hire is expected to operate within the program's adopted framework. Frustrations over incompatible values or philosophies can create unworkable teaching

---

**FIGURE 2-1** Developing a Mission Statement.

**What is the purpose of the organization?** To provide high-quality early care and education for young children and professional development for early childhood college students and practicing professionals.

**What is the business of the organization?** To provide opportunities for a highly qualified staff to work together to learn about, critically reflect on, and collaboratively develop and deliver high-quality and research-supported programs to young children and seek opportunities to share their practice with students and practicing early childhood professionals.

**What are our values?** The staff and stakeholders value high-quality care and education for young children within a curriculum framework that is child-centered and supports intentional teaching, integration, and inquiry. We value curriculum that

- is created jointly by children and adults
- is assessment-supported versus assessment driven
- is emergent at times and negotiated at others so that children investigate important topics in authentic ways
- is intentional so that development and learning are supported throughout the daily routine and environment
- integrates early learning content, developmental domains, and family culture in personally meaningful and socially relevant ways

The mission of this program is to

- provide high-quality early care and education for young children while demonstrating an assessment-supported, child-centered, emergent, integrated, and science-focused curriculum
- work together as reflective decision makers who seek to improve the quality of care and education for young children by mentoring early childhood graduate and undergraduate students and sharing research-supported practice with the larger early childhood community

*Source: © 2013 Cengage Learning®*

---

the best practices in the field. The value statements are important in determining the curriculum and teaching strategies that reflect the program's core values. Suppose a group of program planners identify one of their core values as "children learn through inquiry," meaning that children come to understandings about things and people in their world through the process of inventing ideas and developing hypotheses. A value statement that reflects this core value might be developed that identifies children as autonomous investigators. In turn, decisions about how classrooms are set up would support this

**TABLE 2-2** Sample core values and value statements

| Core Values | Values Statement |
|---|---|
| Children are: | Therefore we provide: |
| Social beings | Opportunities for children to work and play with each other and with responsive adults. |
| Independent learners | Environments where children make choices about their learning with adult support when needed. |
| Problem solvers | Children with a variety of open-ended experiences and authentic materials that prompt a sense of wonder. |
| Communicators | Opportunities for children to communicate about their wants, needs, and wonderings within a respectful and responsive environment. |
| Literate learners | A print-rich environment where children see a purpose for letters, words, and numbers and have opportunities to use this emerging knowledge in meaningful ways. |

*Source: © 2013 Cengage Learning®*

situations for dedicated staff members who need the support of the new director (Kuykendall, 1990, p. 49). If the core values of a program are based on the philosophical assumption that the child is born a *tabula rasa* (meaning the mind at birth is a "blank tablet" to be written on by experience; the stated goal of education is to fill that tablet with experiences), it is helpful if the program director is committed to that same philosophy. A director with a cognitive developmental or constructivist point of view who does not accept the *tabula rasa* premise will find it difficult to develop or direct an educational program that reflects the stated program philosophy. For a discussion of constructivism and a comparison of programs sharing the cognitive developmental orientation, see DeVries and Kohlberg (1988).

Value statements typically emerge from a philosophical position. The need for a philosophical position as a base for program design seems clear (Decker et al., 2009). Whether it is based on developmental theory, social learning theory, the notion of multiple intelligences, or behaviorism, a well-grounded philosophical foundation gives substance and validity to the program. The program philosophy underlies most programmatic decisions. It should reflect the values, beliefs, and training of the director as well as the wishes and interests of the program planners and families who will participate in the program. When administrators attempt to implement programs for which they are unable to state a philosophy nor substantiate their curriculum and accompanying pedagogical strategies in terms of that philosophy, they risk internal confusion, lack of unity, loss of teamwork, and an inability to help parents understand their true purpose.

## What Is the Basis for Choosing a Philosophy?

When programs are planned and implemented, the curriculum content and teaching strategies either consciously or unconsciously reflect a philosophy that is based on

- assumptions about how children learn
- values of the program planners and the families involved
- views of the planners regarding basic issues in education

Although the three areas that influence the philosophy of the program can be discussed separately, they interact with one another and, in reality, are almost impossible to identify and delineate.

## Assumptions about How Children Learn

In the very broadest sense and most simplistic terms, assumptions about how children learn fall into three major categories: environmental, maturational, and interactional. The environmental position assumes that the child's learning is dependent on extrinsic motivators in the form of tokens, compliments, smiles, gold stars, and so forth. The adult decides what the child is to learn and then plans lessons designed to teach content and skills. One of the basic assumptions of this position is that anything worth teaching is also observable and measurable. Attempts to relate this particular assumption about learning to some theoretical base usually lead to the mention of people such as Thorndike, Watson, and Skinner.

Goals based on the environmental assumptions about how young children learn in preschool classrooms might include the following:

- Children learn to recite the alphabet through alphabet songs and stories.
- Children practice rote counting during group time and while at play.
- Staff help children with letter recognition by using flash cards and word games.
- Group-time activities include color recognition and color-naming exercises.

The maturational position assumes that there is an internal driving force that leads to the emergence of cognitive and affective systems, which, in turn, determine the child's readiness for mastery of developmental tasks. Mastery of the task is itself rewarding, so the reinforcement is based on intrinsic satisfactions derived from accomplishment and task mastery. Learning is controlled by an internal growth force, and the child selects from various offerings, thereby learning what she is ready to learn. The theorists associated with the extreme maturational position are Freud and Gesell.

Goals based on maturational assumptions about how young children learn might be that children in the program

- show interest and choose to work in various interest areas in the classroom
- choose activities based on their interests and their rhythms
- show evidence of satisfaction after having mastered a task (verbally, with actions, or with body language that communicates pleasure in the accomplishment)

The interactional position assumes that learning results from the dynamic interaction between the emerging cognitive and affective systems and the environment. The interaction with both the material and the human environment is not driven solely by an internal force but also is nurtured, facilitated, and intensified by the timely intervention of significant adults in the environment. The child is intrinsically motivated to select appropriately from the environment, but the adult is responsible for preparing the environment and for timely and appropriate questions and ideas to alert the child to the learning opportunities in each situation. The adult facilitates the development of intellectual competence. The impetus for the interactional approach came from Piaget's work. Additional insights into the interactive theoretical perspective come from Vygotsky's work in which he emphasized the important connection between a child's social and psychological worlds for cognitive development (Bodrova & Leong, 2006, p. viii).

Goals based on interactional assumptions about how young children learn might be that in all classrooms the following is true:

- Play is cherished, and play spaces are rich with learning opportunities.

- Children are encouraged to explore and create.

- Children enjoy successes that lead to greater self-confidence and independence.

- Staff members value and are responsive to each child's special abilities, learning style, and developmental pace.

---

**REFLECTION**

Think about the following mission statements. How well do they answer Radtke's three questions?

- MISSION—To develop and operate a model professional early child care program that meets the diverse needs of the children and families in the communities we serve.

- MISSION—To enhance the cognitive, social, and emotional well-being of the young children in our program and to serve the diverse needs of their families.

---

## Values of the Program Planners and the Families

The program philosophy is influenced by the priorities parents and planners set for the children. When questioned, most administrators state that they value the optimum development of the whole child: the social, emotional, physical, language, aesthetic, and cognitive development of the child. However, when the philosophy or the ongoing program is analyzed, it may become clear that priorities do, indeed, exist. Concern for the development of the whole child is the stated position, but careful analysis reveals that cognitive outcomes are given priority over social and emotional goals, or vice versa.

## Views on Basic Issues in Education

A number of basic issues in education are implied, if not directly addressed, in the philosophy and, in turn, the value statements. One of these issues is the content versus process issue, sometimes interpreted as school orientation

versus human orientation. Those who subscribe to the content orientation support the notion that the goal of education is to provide children with content that enables them to succeed in school as it exists. Their focus is on preparation for the next step in schooling; achievement is evaluated by relating each child's progress to norms or grade level. The goal of education for those who support human orientation, or what might be viewed as the developmental point of view, is the upward movement of the child as an independent learner to higher levels of intellectual competence. The process of learning and the development of problem-solving skills are more important than content mastery. Autonomy, collaboration, and cooperation are valued, and the years in school are considered an integral part of life itself. The major goal is for children to become autonomous problem solvers (Kamii, 1982). Schooling is not viewed as either preparation for later school or preparation for life. Achievement is not dependent on reaching a norm or the next grade level but on the ability to cope with the here and now.

Today, planners and program directors must find a way to be consistent with their philosophical orientation and also develop a program that is both content- and process focused. The reality of the school readiness movement, the need to overcome the achievement gap, and accountability pressures from federal, state, and local funders call upon leaders in early care and education to find a way to advocate for childhood as a unique and valuable stage in the human life cycle while providing all children access to rich and challenging experiences that support early learning content. These demands do not need to be mutually exclusive, and, with careful planning, it is possible to put a framework in place for curricular decision making that allows teachers to reflect both a grounded philosophy of how children learn and to develop with the realities of societal demands for school readiness, content knowledge, and accountability .

At first glance, discussions about program philosophy may seem unrelated to the problems of starting a center or to taking over as director of an ongoing program. However, making program decisions is impossible without a commitment to an agreed-upon philosophy. Identifying the elements of this philosophy will be addressed in more depth in Chapter 11.

## 2-3 TYPES OF PROGRAMS

After the need has been assessed and the mission and values statements are
written, another major item to be determined is the type of program to be offered. After deciding on the type of program in terms of sponsoring agency and funding, the decision about ages of children to be served must be made before making arrangements for site selection, licensing, budgeting, staffing and equipping the center, and enrolling the children.

Decisions about the type of program will depend on the assessed need, the development of the mission and values statements, the sources of available funds, and the source of the impetus for the program. Not-for-profit programs receive financial support through government funding or subsidies from sponsoring agencies, whereas proprietary programs are supported by capital investments of individuals or corporations. Many different terms such as *preschool, nursery school, child care center,* and *early education center* are used when referring to early care and education programs, but there is nothing inherent in these labels that identifies what type of program or philosophy is practiced in the center. A wide range of program philosophies, including Waldorf, Reggio Emilia, and those based on Jean Piaget's or Montessori's teachings, to name a few, can operate under any of the program types discussed in the following section.

## 2-3a Not-for-Profit Programs

Public and private not-for-profit programs (sometimes called nonprofit) range in size and scope from the small cooperative preschool to the large, complex, agency-sponsored child care center. Although not-for-profit and nonprofit may be differentiated for legal reasons in some states, in most places, the terms are used interchangeably.

## 2-3b Individual Cooperative Programs

Cooperative programs, often called parent co-ops, are owned and operated by a group. Parents are expected to help in the classroom, so the small co-op usually functions with one or two paid staff members, one of whom is usually a teacher/director. Costs are kept at a minimum, and tuition is lower than in other centers. Most co-ops are half-day programs because they require parent participation; however, there are co-ops organized as child care centers.

## 2-3c Agency-Sponsored Programs

Many not-for-profit early childhood education programs are sponsored by community agencies such as church groups, labor unions, service agencies, neighborhood houses, and United Way organizations. These programs may be set up as full-day care centers for working families or as half-day enrichment programs. Such programs are found in both rural and urban areas and can serve both low-income and middle-income families depending on how much support is provided by the sponsoring agency. Agency-sponsored programs sometimes receive partial support from a sponsor such as United Way and obtain the remaining support from tuition, government funds, and/or grants.

## 2-3d Government-Sponsored Programs

Head Start is perhaps the best known of the federal government-sponsored, early childhood education programs and is the nation's leading investment in early childhood care and education. Head Start provides a range of comprehensive education, health, nutrition, parent involvement, and family support services, and it has primarily served at-risk children and their families since 1965. Head Start actually consists of two programs: Head Start and Early Head Start. Head Start is a comprehensive early childhood development program primarily serving at-risk preschool-age children and their families (National Head Start Association, 2011).

Head Start is administered by the Administration for Children and Families in the U.S. Department of Health and Human Services. Head Start funds are sometimes distributed through and monitored by the local Community Action Agency. Funding for Head Start programs may go to public school systems, universities, and public or private not-for-profit agencies. Larger grantees such as public schools or universities often find creative ways to partner with other agencies to provide opportunities for more families to receive the benefits of this comprehensive government-sponsored child care program. For example, a public school may set up a partnership with a church child care program that serves a number of low-income families. The church, in collaboration with the public school, can offer Head Start income-eligible families various health and social service benefits with the help of a Head Start family advocate. The Head Start funding also helps the church cover program expenses for these families. Many unique collaborative arrangements are being worked out between and among various types of child care agencies across the country, all in an effort to better serve children and families.

Head Start programs may be center based or home based and may provide child care on a full-time or half-time basis. Formerly for only preschool children, Early Start, a part of Head Start, is now available to children under age 4. Those who receive funds from Head Start (grantees) are mandated to serve children with disabilities (10% of enrollment opportunities) who must be mainstreamed and receive a total care package through direct services from the grantee or from other resources in the community.

The Department of Defense and the Department of Veterans Affairs also sponsor child care programs in some regions of the country, as do some state governments. Of course, there are many military programs (see the "Military Programs" section).

## 2-3e Public School–Sponsored Programs

Most states are funding some prekindergarten programs, and many of these are in public schools (Neugebauer, 2003). Full-day or half-day public school programs are staffed by people hired through public school personnel offices, and the programs are housed in public school buildings. Local school boards, public school administrators, and teacher unions typically have a voice in making policy as well as in teacher and program evaluation. The building principal is the appointed instructional leader, and at the state level, these programs fall under the jurisdiction of the superintendent of public instruction or the commissioner of education.

Practices in public preschools still tend to focus on academic success, school readiness, and standardized testing, but advocates for developmentally appropriate practice in preschools are challenging this academic readiness position of some public school instructional leaders. With the current trend toward universal prekindergarten, additional government funds are flowing into public schools to support the interest in offering a prekindergarten experience for all children. The aim in some states is to increase the amount of state dollars that comes to those systems offering prekindergarten programs.

This could potentially lead to prekindergarten programs that focus on instruction and dilute the caring dimension of the daily interactions between teachers and children. Some states are making an effort to combine public and private funding, which may be a way to have a system that allows for a combination of education plus the caring and emotional support that young children require.

Before- and after-school programs for school-aged children often are housed in public schools. Some are also public school–sponsored, while others are run by community agencies or service groups such as the Salvation Army and YMCA. The public school–sponsored programs may be staffed by teachers in the building or by high school or college students who are free during early morning and late afternoon hours. Often, the person in the school system responsible for the preschool programs also oversees these before- and after-school programs and

*Many campus-based programs must meet the needs of a broader stakeholders group that includes not only children, families, and staff but also preservice and in-service teachers.*

other wraparound programs, and the building principal is the on-site administrator-in-charge.

### 2-3f Campus Child Care Programs

Laboratory (or demonstration) schools and child care programs for children of students, faculty, and staff are two types of programs found on college campuses. The programs may be sponsored and subsidized by the college or university or by government funds. These programs often provide facilities for research, observation, and teacher training. They may be full-day or half-day and may charge full, or in some cases, partial, tuition for those affiliated with the university. In some places where student groups as well as the university itself offer support for the care of students' children, the students pay minimum tuition for their children, and the program hours are flexible to accommodate the students' course schedules.

### 2-3g Privately Sponsored Not-for-Profit Programs

Many large industries, hospitals, and apartment complexes include child care centers in their facilities and offer services for the children of their employees and residents. These not-for-profit centers are set up for the comfort and convenience of the employees and residents. The hours are often flexible, and in some cases, fees are on a sliding scale to encourage full use of the available facilities. The fees for hospital- and industry-operated programs may be part of an employee benefit package implemented through the use of vouchers, direct payment to the caregivers, or a child care allowance to the employee.

Some employers offer a Dependent Care Assistance Program (DCAP) or Dependent Care Reimbursement Program (DCRP) that allows employees to set aside a certain amount of their yearly pretax salary for child care expenses, thereby providing a substantial tax savings to the employee.

Employers are realizing they cannot meet the challenge of fulfilling employees' child care needs on their own and are reaching out to the child care community for help in managing on-site centers. Some employers contract with centers for a reduced fee or funded slots for employees, whereas others prefer to contract for information and referral services in the area but are not involved in service delivery.

### 2-3h Profit-Making Programs (Proprietary)

Although much is written about not-for-profit programs such as Head Start, United Way centers, and public school programs, a large majority of the early childhood education programs in the United States are proprietary. These programs are set up to provide a service that will make a profit.

## 2-3i Independent Owner

Many full- and half-day child care programs are owned and operated by an individual or a small group (partnerships or small corporations). In the case of the proprietary center, tuition is usually the only source of income, and the operators frequently have budgeting and financial problems, although some proprietary and nonprofits can obtain supplementary funding from other sources, including state funds. The proprietary operators may be able to draw a salary from the tuition that is paid by families using the service, but the operators rarely make a profit over and above that because of the high cost of operating a quality program. Sometimes, proprietors open more than one center in a community or region and begin a small chain operation. Although it is difficult to make a profit from the small chain, quantity buying and shared service costs sometimes can reduce the cost per child and increase the possibility of making a profit over and above operating expenses.

## 2-3j Corporate Systems

Large, for-profit, child care organizations are operated by a parent company that develops a prototype and sets up a number of centers throughout a state or region, or across the nation and into Canada. Some of these corporations have gone public, and their stock is traded on the New York Stock Exchange. These national child care chains operate under a central administration that furnishes the financial backing and is usually very powerful in setting the policy and controlling the program. There often is a prototype building and program that are publicized by identifiable slogans, logos, brochures, and advertisements. Some corporate systems operate all centers carrying the chain name, while others work on a franchised basis. In the latter case, an individual purchases a franchise from the parent company for a basic purchase price, and then pays the company a percentage of gross intake for the ongoing use of the name and the program. In addition, the parent company supplies guidelines for fees, sample documents, brochures, advertising materials, and the like. Some of these sample documents must be changed by center operators to meet local regulations and/or be in line with local practice. The parent corporation often monitors the franchised centers to maintain the company standard of quality control. Because company policy often controls the program, directors are usually expected not only to adopt the program as outlined by the corporate body but also can adjust some practices based on their own philosophy.

## 2-3k Employer-Sponsored Programs

There is an increasing demand for employer-sponsored child care. Employers are analyzing the benefits of child care services and seeking creative ways to meet their employees' identified needs. During the early 2000s, the top players among the child care management organizations involved in employer-sponsored care were Bright Horizons Family Solutions and Knowledge Beginnings (now Knowledge Learning Corporation). They accounted for the lion's share of the phenomenal growth in employer-sponsored care in the late 1990s. Much of their growth resulted from contracts to take over centers that employers were previously managing on their own in addition to some acquisitions of other independent child care providers. The concept of employer-sponsored care is not new. In the 1940s, during World War II, the Kaiser shipbuilder corporation on the West Coast provided care for the children of women who were called into the workforce to support U.S. troops in the war effort. Companies such as Stride Rite and Levi Strauss also were pioneers in the on-site, employer-sponsored child care business. The availability of child care management corporations is relatively recent.

Demand by big industry for services provided by the leading employer child care management organizations leveled off in the first years after the turn of the century for some of the large for-profit child care providers. However, business held and improved slightly for Bright Horizons Family Solutions while it leveled off for others in this group. These companies continue to find that the families who use their centers demand some customized services. Some of these additional services include backup and sick child care; therapy services for children with special needs; crisis intervention; and a number of extracurricular programs, including karate, gymnastics, music, and dance. Other creative ways they serve families are to offer dry cleaning pickup, UPS pickup, gourmet meal pickup, and even haircuts for children. In most cases, parents contract with these special service providers, and the center is the appointed location for deliveries and pickups. Centers are not involved in billing or receiving payments for these special services.

When unemployment is low, growing numbers of employers begin to view child care as a recruitment and retention tool. For example, hospitals sponsor on-site centers to help with recruitment and retention of nurses and other technical personnel. Employers also look for child care solutions that will work for the employee who telecommutes from home as well as some who work at small satellite offices away from the main campus. Although many employer-sponsored centers are run by the large management organizations, there are employers who seek out public or private groups such as universities or the YMCA to run centers for them. In some cases, the employers provide generous subsidies by building new facilities that are rent-free or by offering low-cost leases for ground on which to build. Employers who not only strive to keep fees down for their employees—but also value quality care and want fully qualified staff as well as low teacher-to-child ratios—subsidize their centers to make up the deficits.

When universities or other nonprofits such as hospitals or YMCAs are called on to manage centers for large for-profit corporations, it is important for the center director to be prepared for many discussions with the corporate partners to clarify the mission and goals of the new program. Of course, families and children are always the focus of those who manage and staff the center. However, it is important to keep in mind that recruitment, retention, employee productivity, and morale are major goals of the corporation that subsidizes and sponsors the center. Directors know they have many customers, including families, children, and staff, but now directors must also realize that one of the most important customers is the sponsoring corporation. When issues and questions arise, the position of corporate customers must be taken into consideration. They may have questions about curriculum or hiring practices, but they are likely to accept the decisions of the early childhood professionals whom they hired to deal with those aspects of the program. For the director, this is no different from handling the usual inquiries and concerns from parents in any type of center. But a business sponsor may need to make decisions about hours of operation, changing schedules for children by the week (or even the day), backup care, sick child care, late day or night care, and weekend care in order to keep employees who work different schedules. Corporate sponsors respect the early childhood professional and value the beautiful classrooms and rich programming offered the children. However, to meet the expectations the corporation has for its employees, the center staff may have to reconsider what they view as best for the children and adjust to the interests and schedules of their sponsor without compromising the integrity of their own ethical and professional values.

Enigma/Alamy

*Programs that serve military families must be prepared to meet the sometimes intense needs related to having a loved one deployed for long periods of time. These programs need to have close connections with the social services offered on the base and also need to be tuned in to the sometimes exceptional emotional needs of the children and families served.*

## 2-3l Military Programs

The Department of Defense (DOD) operates child care programs at military installations across the country. Financed by a combination of government appropriations and sliding-scale parent tuition fees, the programs may be full-day, center-based care; part-day preschools; drop-in care; and, in some places, evening and weekend care. Some of this is center based and some is in family child care homes.

Each of the military services (Air Force, Army, Marines, Navy, and Coast Guard) operates its own child care service, but all must follow the mandates of the Military Child Care Act of 1989. The act addresses program funding, required training for staff, competitive pay rates for staff, and an internal inspection system. To meet the demand for child care services, the DOD has expanded preschool and school-aged child care options by increasing the number of programs on military installations. It accomplished this by using existing resource and referral programs to help families locate available child care and by contracting with off-installation centers to guarantee spaces for DOD children.

## 2-3m Family Child Care Homes

Family child care is reminiscent of an extended family, with a small group of children being cared for in the home of a child care provider (Gordon & Williams Browne, 2011). Although this type of child care service is most popular for infants and toddlers, these home providers also care for preschool children and offer before- and after-school care. The provider may be an employee of a system but most often operates independently, contracting directly with families who choose home care over center-based care. These providers run their own business. In some states, family child care homes must be licensed, whereas in other places, they are certified or registered by a community agency authorized to pay for children of low-income families who are in the home. Many providers join employer or community agency information and referral registries that take calls from parents seeking child care. Registered family child care homes may or may not be subject to inspection by a responsible community agency. In some places, inspections are made only after a complaint has been filed.

## 2-4 STANDARDS OF PRACTICE

All child care programs of every type **naeyc** listed in the previous section are expected to provide high-quality programs for young children. It is assumed that these programs meet local licensing requirements because without a proper license, programs are not permitted to remain open for business. However, to provide the very best for children and to meet the accepted standards of quality based on expectations of fellow professionals, directors are expected to go beyond meeting minimum standards established by the states and strive for higher standards of quality.

The best-known and most widely accepted standards for quality practice for any and all programs for children, birth through kindergarten, are those developed by the National Association for the Education of Young Children (NAEYC). School-age programs are accredited by the National After-School Association (NAA), while family child care programs are accredited by the National Association for Family Child Care (NAFCC). In some places, centers receive accreditation from the National Association of Child Care Professionals (NACCP). (For additional information on accreditation, see Chapter 3.) There is also a quality movement in many states that involves rating early care and education programs based on a series of quality indicators. These systems serve to increase awareness of the importance of quality.

## SUMMARY

Many decisions must be made concerning how needs should be assessed, what philosophy will be most representative of the thinking of the planners and the prospective director, what type of program is feasible in terms of financing, and so forth. To conduct an effective needs assessment, directors must do the following:

- Identify information that will help determine the types of child services needed now and in the future.

- Develop a mission statement that reflects the program's core values.

- Determine the various types of child care needed by families in the region.

- Identify where the standards of quality practice can be located and how they should be used when determining the program's core values.

## TRY IT OUT!

1. Review the sample needs assessment questionnaire in Director's Resource 2-1, and adjust it so you could use it for a 10-item online survey.

   a. How would you introduce the survey in an email that encourages potential program users to answer the questions?

   b. What incentive would you offer to encourage participation in the survey?

   c. What follow-up message would you send to those who participated in the survey?

2. Consider a program that you would most like to direct, and use Radtke's three questions to develop a mission statement. Be sure to describe the type of population that would be served by this program.

3. In groups of four, discuss and record the thinking of the group about the following items:

   a. What are your assumptions about growth and development?

   b. How does learning or the development of knowledge come about?

   c. During the early years of a child's life, what is the adult's role relative to

      - physical development?

      - social development?

      - emotional development?

      - cognitive development?

      - language development?

      - moral development?

   d. What goals do you have for the children in your care?

   e. What is your belief about how families impact development and how they should be served in your center?

4. Assume you have been hired as a director of a new center. Write a list of core values and corresponding value statements for your new center.

## Director's Resource 2-1

## SAMPLE NEEDS ASSESSMENT

1. How many adults are there in this household?

2. Do all adults in the household work? ☐ Yes ☐ No
   *If yes*, ☐ part time How many?_____ ☐ full time
   How many? _____

3. What is the total number of children under the age of 16? _____

4. What is the number of children under age 6?
   _____

   Check ages of children under 6:
   ☐ Under 1                How many? _____
   ☐ Between 1 and 2        How many? _____
   ☐ Between 2 and 3        How many? _____
   ☐ Between 3 and 4        How many? _____
   ☐ Between 4 and 5        How many? _____
   ☐ Between 5 and 6        How many? _____

5. Does any child in this family, younger than school age, regularly spend time away from home? ☐ Yes ☐ No
   *If yes*, how many? _____

6. Do any children in the family have special needs?
   ☐ Yes ☐ No
   *If yes*, how many? _____
   *If yes*, does the condition require attendance at a special school or program? ☐ Yes ☐ No
   *If yes*, describe program(s) needed:
   _____
   _____

7. Is/are your child(ren) regularly cared for every day in your home by someone who does not live with you?
   ☐ Yes ☐ No
   *If yes*, is the caregiver a relative? ☐ Yes ☐ No

8. How many children over 5 regularly spend time away from home before or after school? _____ What are their ages? _____
   Describe type of program: _____
   _____
   _____

9. For statistical purposes only, please give the total family income in this household:

   | | |
   |---|---|
   | $0–$15,000 | ☐ |
   | $15,001–$20,000 | ☐ |
   | $20,001–$35,000 | ☐ |
   | $35,001–$50,000 | ☐ |
   | $50,001–$75,000 | ☐ |
   | $75,001–$90,000 | ☐ |
   | over $90,000 | ☐ |

10. Approximately how much do you pay every week for the care of all your children? Give that figure in column A. In column B, mark how much you would be willing to pay for quality care for all of your children. Mark with X.

    | A | B | |
    |---|---|---|
    | _____ | $0–50 | ☐ |
    | _____ | $51–75 | ☐ |
    | _____ | $76–100 | ☐ |
    | _____ | $101–125 | ☐ |
    | _____ | $126–150 | ☐ |
    | _____ | $151–175 | ☐ |
    | _____ | Over $175 | ☐ |

11. Parents have a difficult time arranging for the care of their children. Indicate what has been your experience.
    ☐ Easy time
    ☐ Not very difficult
    ☐ Difficult time
    ☐ Extremely difficult
    ☐ No opinion

12. If you had a choice of arrangements for the care of your child, what would be your first choice?
    ☐ Care in child care center for four hours or less
    ☐ Care in child care center for more than four hours
    ☐ Care by another mother or someone in her own home
    ☐ Care by a sitter in your own home
    ☐ Care in a center before and after school

# DIRECTOR'S RESOURCE 2-1 *(continued)*

**13.** If you could have the type of arrangement you prefer, how many days per week would you want your children to spend there (insert number of days)?
_____ Infant _____ Toddler _____ Preschooler _____ After school (Age _____)

**14.** Where would you prefer to have your child(ren) cared for?

☐  Near where you work

☐  Near where you live

☐  Other location:

**15.** Generally speaking, in selecting an ideal child care arrangement, which is more important to you? (Assume that quality is equal.)

☐  Cost more important

☐  Closeness to home more important

☐  Closeness to work more important

☐  No opinion

**16.** If a child care center opens across the street from your office (insert home, church, factory, as appropriate), for which age child would you be likely to use it?

☐  Your infant

☐  Your toddler

☐  Your preschooler

☐  Your school-age child(ren)

**TeachSource Digital Download**

# REFERENCES

Bodrova, E., & Leong, D. J. (2006). *Tools of the mind: The Vygotskian approach to early childhood education* (2nd ed.). Upper Saddle River, NJ: Prentice Hall.

Children's Defense Fund. (2014). *The state of America's children: 2014 Report.* Washington, DC: Author.

Decker, C., Decker, J. R., Freeman, N., & Knopf, H. (2009). *Planning and administering early childhood programs* (9th ed.). Upper Saddle River, NJ: Prentice-Hall Merrill.

Denton Flanagan, K., & McPhee, C. (2009). *The children born in 2001 at kindergarten entry: First findings from the kindergarten data collections of the early childhood longitudinal study, birth cohort (ECLS-B)* (NCES 2010-005). Washington, DC: National Center for Education Statistics, Institute of Education Sciences, U.S. Department of Education.

DeVries, R., & Kohlberg, L. (1988). *Programs of early education: The constructivist view.* New York: Longman.

Gordon, A. M., & Williams Browne, K. (2011). *Beginnings and beyond* (8th ed.). Clifton Park, NY: Delmar Cengage Learning.

Kamii, C. (1982). *Number in preschool and kindergarten: Educational implications for Piaget's theory.* Washington, DC: NAEYC.

Kuykendall, J. (1990, July). Child development directors shouldn't leave home without it. *Young Children,* 49–51.

National Head Start Association. (2011). Basic Head Start facts. Alexandria, VA: Author. Retrieved from http://www.nhsa.org/files/static_page_files/48BADE30-1D09-3519-ADED347C39FA16A4/Basic_Head_Start_Facts_rev02212011.pdf.

Neugebauer, R. (2003). Update on child care in public schools. *Child Care Information Exchange: The Director's Magazine,* 150, 66–71.

Radtke, J. M. (1998). *Strategic communications for nonprofit organizations: Seven steps to creating a successful plan.* New York: John Wiley & Sons, Inc.

# LICENSING *and* CERTIFICATION

*The primary function of the licensing agent is to ascertain whether a program is in compliance with minimum requirements.*

## Learning Objectives

After reading this chapter, you should be able to:

**3-1** Explain the purpose of licensing.

**3-2** Describe various types of licensing regulations and their specific purposes.

**3-3** Identify the steps in the licensing process.

**3-4** Discuss the role of the licensing specialist.

**3-5** Compare and contrast licensing and accreditation of early childhood programs.

**3-6** Describe the function of state Quality Rating and Improvement Systems (QRIS) and how they differ from accreditation.

**3-7** Identify and explain the various levels of individual credentials available for staff in a child care and education center.

**3-8** Explain the relationship between director credentialing and career pathways.

## Standards Addressed in this Chapter

Accreditation Standard 1 – Relationships

Accreditation Standard 8 – Community Relationships

Accreditation Standard 9 – Physical Environment

Accreditation Standard 10 – Leadership and Management

Administrator Competencies – Management Knowledge and Skills 1, 3, 4, 5, 8, 9, 10

Administrator Competencies – Early Childhood Knowledge and Skills 2, 5, 10

Professional Preparation Standard 4 – Using Developmentally Effective Approaches

Professional Preparation Standard 6 – Becoming a Professional

Child care center directors are responsible for understanding licensing, certification, and other regulations pertaining to providing services for young children. Each type of regulation is developed by a governmental body and has specific purposes. Directors must understand which regulations apply to their programs and ensure that all requirements are fulfilled in a timely manner. They also must be prepared to pay the requisite fees. In the future, people who assume responsible roles in children's programs probably will have to deal with more and more regulatory functions. This increase in regulation is related to the expanded use of public funds and the broader acceptance of the fact that programs for young children must provide care and protection for children and be educationally sound. Also, educational accountability points to greater focus on the need for certifying or licensing the people responsible for children's programs, while protection of children's health and safety requires licensing of centers. The term *licensing* may cause confusion because it is used to signify that a governing body is giving permission to do something. In this case, what is being permitted is the operation of a child care program. Later in the chapter when we discuss licensing (also known as certifying or credentialing) teachers, what is being permitted is the opportunity to obtain a teaching position.

After programs comply with the minimum standards required for local or state licensing, they can move toward higher standards and gain some form of professional recognition. The National Association for the Education of Young Children (NAEYC) works with child care centers through its National Academy for Early Childhood Program Accreditation "to enhance children's well-being and early learning by improving the quality of early childhood programs serving children birth through kindergarten," which is how NAEYC describes the Academy's mission on its website (http://www.naeyc.org/academy/primary/academy). The Association for Early Learning Leaders (formerly The National Association of Child Care Professionals), the National Early Childhood Program Accreditation Commission (NECPA), the Council on Accreditation, and the American Montessori Association also provide opportunities for accreditation. On-site directors and boards are responsible for providing the necessary inspiration and leadership to improve the center. They work to move a program from compliance with minimum licensing requirements to meeting quality performance standards. Even beyond these standards lies the goal of dynamic development that continues to produce a quality educational program. Model program directors always are working to refine their programs as they move toward the goal of excellence. The knowledge base in child development and early childhood education is constantly growing, so no program can afford to be complacent about its quality.

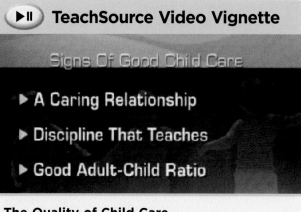

**TeachSource Video Vignette**

Signs Of Good Child Care

▶ A Caring Relationship

▶ Discipline That Teaches

▶ Good Adult-Child Ratio

**The Quality of Child Care**

This video provides an overview of the importance of quality programming for children's development. View the video vignette entitled *The Quality of Child Care*. Reflect on the following questions:

**1.** How do quality care and education support children's development?

**2.** As a director, what factors should you consider to ensure quality programming for the young children in your care?

## 3-1 THE PURPOSE OF LICENSING

Licensing of centers is required, but coverage varies from state to state. For example, in some states, only full-day child care programs are required to obtain a license, whereas in other states, all full-day, half-day, and home-based programs must be licensed. Depending on the type of program being planned and the geographical location of the center, both local and state requirements might need to be met. And when federal funding is involved, there will be additional requirements. In some states, program sponsorship determines program licensing. For example, programs affiliated with public schools may be licensed by the state department of education. Your licensing agent can provide updated licensing information. A directory of state child care licensing offices is available online through the U.S. Department of Education's Resource Organizations Directory. To view an individual state's child care licensure regulations, go to the National Resource Center for Health and Safety in Child Care. Both of these organizations provide numerous online documents and research results.

The licensing function is a result of legislation, and its thrust is accountability for the health and safety of children and staff. Licensing requirements are usually minimal, and enforcement practices in some localities are limited. As a result, program licensure does not guarantee quality of care or protection for children and rarely addresses the educational quality of the program. The licensing function is essential and valuable but is often misunderstood. A license gives *permission* to operate but does not indicate quality.

An estimated 312,254 licensed child care facilities are operational in the United States (National Association for Regulatory Administration and the National Center on Child Care Quality Improvement, 2014). Approximately 34 percent of these are centers while the remaining 66 percent are licensed family child care homes or other types of facilities.

Family child care homes are places in which people care for one or more children in their homes instead of in a center or the child's own home. Some states divide these into categories based on the number of children permitted. In larger child care homes, perhaps 12 children may be cared for. At least two adults are needed, and building regulations should be required. Many families prefer this type of care, particularly for infants and toddlers, because of the smaller setting. Although family child care (or family day care as it is sometimes called) has always been a frequently used source of child care, its regulation has been relatively recent.

*After programs are in compliance with minimum standards required for local or state licensing, they can work toward higher standards that may lead to accreditation.*

Although more and more states have established preservice qualifications for family home child care providers, the mandated qualifications related to early childhood training are limited. For example, much of the training may be in first aid, collecting fees, or completing forms for Child Care Food Program reimbursement. Because of the limited hours available for training, information about young children's development and learning is minimal.

Child care center staff preservice training shows a trend toward emphasizing early childhood education. Although not part of the regulatory system for child care centers, the American Association of Colleges of Teacher Education has called for all preschool teachers to have a bachelor's degree. This proposal far exceeds licensing requirements but

is consistent with requirements for kindergarten teachers. As a future early childhood teacher or director, you may want to discuss this proposal with your peers or instructors.

In addition to the licensing department, in most localities, the building department will review the plans, and the fire, building, and health or sanitation departments will send individual representatives to inspect the proposed space where the services for children will be offered. No matter what system is used in a particular state, an initial inspection and approval is required before the center can begin to operate. Even when the center is moving from one location to another, the inspection and approval must still be done. The regulating departments may be willing to send individual representatives to inspect the proposed space where the services for children will be offered. These inspections can alert the director to major and minor changes that need to be made. The decision about moving to a particular facility may hinge on the cost and time line for making these changes, as well as on the deadline for exiting the current premises.

The director must play an active role in the licensing process, which may include making frequent phone calls to agencies and walking papers from office to office if necessary. Communication breakdowns can occur, and directors must be proactive.

After initial inspection and approval, inspections and license renewals will be required on a regular basis. Directors are responsible for ensuring that their programs are in compliance with regulations and for being familiar with appeal and grievance procedures if conflicts arise regarding compliance with the regulations.

> ▶❚❚  **TeachSource Video Vignette**
>
>
>
> **Leadership Practices in Child Development Centers: The Regulatory System**
>
> This video provides an overview of the **naeyc** many responsibilities that directors of child care programs possess. As you view the *Leadership Practices in Child Development Centers* video, reflect on the following questions related to licensing:
>
> **1.**  What is the importance of regulatory compliance?
>
> **2.**  What steps can be taken to ensure that new employees are aware of licensing requirements?

## 3-2 LICENSING REGULATIONS

Local and state licensing regulations typically cover building safety and requirements for physical space and establish base teacher-to-child ratios. Although licensing regulations vary greatly from state to state, most licensing regulations include the following points.

### 3-2a Building Safety

Licensing regulations always include at least the minimum fire, sanitation, and building safety standards that apply to all private and public services. Fire regulations usually cover the type of building construction, ease of evacuation in the event of fire, alarm systems, smoke detectors, sprinkler systems, availability of fire extinguishers, and methods of storing combustible materials. Building codes usually cover wiring, plumbing, and building construction, including building materials. Health department regulations cover conditions in all areas of the building, with particular attention to the bathrooms and food service operations.

When infants and/or children who are nonambulatory are enrolled in the program, the director must be sure to meet licensing requirements for those groups. Typically, these requirements focus on egress in case of emergency. Usually housing these programs on the first (ground) floor is required.

### 3-2b Physical Space

Licensing regulations usually specify the amount of space necessary for programs for infants, toddlers, and preschool children. The requirement for 3- to 5-year-old children is typically a minimum of 35 square feet of indoor space per child and 50 to 75 square feet of outdoor space per child. Because programs for infants and toddlers require cribs, feeding tables, and diaper-changing areas, such programs require more space per child than do programs for 3- to 5-year-olds. Levels and sources of light, levels of heat, sources of fresh air, fencing of outdoor areas, protection from radiators and low windows, and numbers of toilets also are included in regulations covering physical space. These standards are minimal, and good programs usually exceed them. Providing more than minimal space, particularly for children who will be at the center all day, is likely to make both children and staff more comfortable. For additional state and national data regarding physical space requirements, see the collaborative report by the American Academy of Pediatrics, American Public Health Association, and National Resource Center for Health and Safety in Child Care and Early Education (2013).

### 3-2c Teacher-to-Child Ratios

Some licensing regulations include minimum teacher-to-child ratios. These state or local ratios vary, but they are in the range of 3 to 8 infants to 1 adult, 4 to 12 toddlers to 1 adult, and 6 to 20 preschoolers to 1 adult. The baseline licensing standards for child-to-staff ratios in child care centers in some states already meet the standards used by NAEYC, but most states are still below these significant ratios. Most regulations require that two responsible adults be on the premises at all times. The ratios are established to furnish a baseline standard for protecting the safety of children; however, group size is even more important and also is regulated by some states. A collaborative report from the American Academy of Pediatrics, American Public Health Association, and the National Resource Center for Health and Safety in Child Care and Early Education (2013, p. 2) recommends the group size and child-to-staff ratios shown in Table 3-1.

Licensing standards seem to be coming closer to these guidelines. Following are the most common child-to-staff ratios required by licensing in 2011 (National Center on Child Care Quality Improvement, 2011):

- Infants, 4:1
- Toddlers, 6:1 (18 months of age) and 8:1 (27 months of age)
- 4-year-olds, 10:1
- 5-year-olds, 15:1

NAEYC accreditation guidelines provide the rationale for establishing staffing criteria: "Across all the comprehensive research linking structural dimensions of child care to child care quality and to children's optimal outcomes, three dimensions emerge as most predictive: child care providers' compensation, providers' education and specialized training, and the teacher-child ratio" (2005b, p. 59).

### 3-2d Staff Qualifications

Teachers' training in child development and their interactions with the children are key factors in creating a quality program. NAEYC's standards continue to uphold the importance of well-prepared staff and appropriate group sizes. These standards also call for teachers

**TABLE 3-1** Recommended group size and ratio of children to staff

| Child Age | Maximum Group Size | Ratio of Children to Teacher |
|---|---|---|
| Infant | 6 | 3:1 |
| Toddler | 8 | 4:1 |
| 3-year-olds | 14 | 7:1 |
| 5-year-olds | 16 | 8:1 |

© 2013 Cengage Learning®

who have completed considerable formal education and specialized professional preparation in early childhood. Check the NAEYC website for current information related to qualification guidelines for teachers and directors.

Although licensing regulations sometimes address staff qualifications, requirements are often minimal. Some states require that caregivers be able to read and write, while others require at least a high school diploma for anyone who is hired as a teacher, teacher assistant, and/or aide. Most states require a director to have at least a high school diploma, while a few states require some college training, which may or may not be in child development or early childhood education. Others, however, require specific training in early childhood education or attainment of the Child Development Associate credential. Professional organizations are working to upgrade the criteria for early childhood staff as one component of the effort to improve staff salaries. As this process evolves, we can expect licensing standards to continue to improve. Psychologists, nurses, doctors on call, and other professionals must meet the appropriate credential requirements of their respective professions.

### 3-2e Transportation

In centers that provide transportation, the service usually must meet the state motor vehicle department standards for school bus service. These standards regulate numbers of children, type of vehicle, types of lights on vehicles, proper identification on the vehicle, use of car seats and seat belts, and appropriate licensing and insurance coverage for the vehicle and the driver. Even when it is not required, it is wise to provide drivers with training in child development and management so that time spent on the bus will be positive as well as safe for both children and drivers.

Having a second adult on the bus to assist in an emergency is also advisable. The driver, of course, should not leave even one child on the bus while seeking help or when walking a child to the door when that child's parent does not come out to meet the bus. Furthermore, some children have a difficult time leaving seat belts on. The driver, who must give full attention to the road, should not have to check constantly to ensure that all children are safely seated. The center also should establish a policy requiring the driver to check the interior of the vehicle thoroughly to be sure no child remains on board. This procedure should be in effect every time the driver leaves the vehicle. This procedure is required by law in some states.

### 3-2f Other Standards

In centers serving infants, licensing usually requires detailed plans for diapering, including the surface on which the baby is placed, a plan for disposing of soiled and wet diapers, and hand washing by staff after each diaper change. Additional requirements for storing food, feeding babies, and washing toys also are included.

As you review this section on licensing regulations, it should become clear that, depending on the size, location, and scope of the program for which you are responsible, you could find yourself working with local, state, and federal regulatory agencies. At times, the regulations from the various bodies are not totally compatible, and they even may be contradictory. As director you are tasked with handling all these regulatory agents so that your program is in compliance. If your program is not in compliance, you run the risk of having a fine imposed or of being unable to take full advantage of available funds and community resources. There also is the risk of having to delay the opening of a new program or having to close down an ongoing program because of failure to meet minimum licensing requirements. In some cases, noncompliance may jeopardize the well-being of children and staff.

## 3-3 THE LICENSING PROCESS

Directors who are seeking initial licensing **naeyc** should allow plenty of time for the lengthy process that includes on-site visits and conferences with inspectors from all the departments involved. It is wise to allow *at least* 90 days to complete the initial licensing process, although some states suggest that much more time may be required. For example, in Ohio, a minimum of 150 days is recommended to complete the steps in the process. All departments must provide clearance before the license is issued. On rare occasions, programs are permitted to continue operation when they are out of compliance because licensing specialists are trying to help provide sufficient child care in the community; but the regulatory agencies constantly monitor the work being done to bring the program into compliance with the minimum requirements. The burden is on the operator, who must present data to show that the program qualifies for a license or is working toward that goal within a well-defined, limited time line.

Total compliance with all regulations may be very expensive, so it is important to have a clear understanding of the changes that are essential before a program can operate and those that can be made as money becomes available. For example, the fire inspector may not allow children in the building until all required fire extinguishers are purchased, mounted appropriately, and made accessible. The health department might allow a child care program to begin before a separate sink for hand washing is available in the food-preparation area, provided that adequate hand-washing facilities are available elsewhere in the building and that there is a double sink in the kitchen. Monies must be budgeted to move toward compliance in areas that require further work. Therefore, the director and any board members who are involved in budget preparation should be well informed about any aspects of the program and the physical environment that might need modification to be in compliance with licensing standards. The time allowed for total compliance with all the licensing regulations will vary greatly and may be negotiable.

## Working Smart with Technology

*Familiarity with Licensing's
Use of Technology*

The U.S. Office of Child Care (OCC) works with state child care licensing programs to ensure that minimum health and safety requirements are being met. The OCC has recommended to states that technology be used to "enhance their licensing programs and create efficiencies that will lead to increased protection and improved quality of care for children" (National Center on Child Care Quality Improvement, 2012, p.1). Specific suggestions for integrating technology to improve service include using mobile technology during monitoring visits, providing resources and alerts for providers, and permitting providers to apply online for a license. Directors of programs must become familiar with these enhanced strategies as they are implemented within states

*Directors of programs must become familiar with the ways that technology is being used by the licensing specialist and agency.*

In general, the steps involved in the licensing process are as follows:

1. Request a copy of licensing requirements from the appropriate regulatory agency. Many agencies provide this information on governmental websites.

2. Complete any trainings specified by the regulatory agency that may be required of applicants for child care center licenses.

3. Ensure that the zoning authorities in the area have approved the land use; that is, does zoning allow child care at the site you have chosen? Because child care may be considered a business instead of an educational program or school, neighbors may be reluctant to allow a zone change. Some may be concerned

about setting a precedent that would allow additional businesses to locate in that immediate area. Others may be unhappy about increased traffic and noise, as well as about the compatibility of the building with others in the area. Whether or not a zone change is needed, one of the first jobs of the director is to reach out to neighbors and establish the center as a cooperative part of the neighborhood.

4. Obtain information from the licensing agent about contacting the sanitation inspector, the fire inspector, the building inspector, and the public health office.

5. Arrange for conferences with, and on-site visits from, representatives of all necessary departments.

6. When all inspections have been completed, and the inspectors have provided evidence of approval, complete the application for the license and send it, with the required fee, to the appropriate licensing agent. You may be required to submit a detailed plan for operating the center, including number of staff, daily schedule, equipment list, and center policies and procedures. (See Director's Resource 3-1 at the end of the chapter.) You also may have to show copies of forms you will use for gathering required information such as health and emergency data.

7. On receipt of the license, post it in a conspicuous place in the child care center so that it is visible to families and visitors.

8. Check the expiration date and establish a procedure to ensure that the renewal process will be set in motion in time to eliminate the possibility of having to interrupt the provision of services to the children or having to pay a fine.

Some states and localities provide a one-stop licensing process. The idea is that a director can contact one person to set the licensing process in motion. Such a plan eliminates most if not all of the frustration directors may feel they have experienced in the past when they tried to coordinate various departments and agencies. The goal of the various inspectors, as well as of the director, is to ensure that the standards are met.

The director or, in special cases, a designated member of the board, is responsible for obtaining a license for the child care center. Renewals, although less time-consuming for both the director and the licensing agents, must be taken care of on a regular basis. The cost of a state or local license is minimal when considered in light of a total budget, but it is an item that must be included in the budget. Although some states do not charge a fee, others charge varying amounts based on the number of children served. Some states have additional fees for special services such as review of a particular building prior to a decision to obtain that building.

*The licensing specialist should be viewed by directors as both a team member and valuable resource.*

## 3-4 THE LICENSING SPECIALIST

The primary function of the licensing specialist is to ascertain whether a program is in compliance with the licensing regulations and to issue, or recommend issuing, a license to those programs that meet the minimum requirements. When programs do not meet minimum requirements, the function of the licensing specialist is to provide support and suggest resources that will help bring the programs into compliance rather than close them. The specialist's goal is to improve services for children and families. Licensing specialists are being viewed more and more as people who provide services instead of as people who simply issue licenses or close centers.

Knowledge of the community, combined with a thorough knowledge of the licensing regulations, makes the licensing specialist a valuable resource for directors who are seeking training for staff; looking for educational program consultants; and exploring the best and least expensive ways to meet the fire, health, or building regulations. The licensing specialist also may be available as a consultant when a director is petitioning to have an unusual or unrealistic restriction varied or adjusted. In situations in which licensing regulations are inappropriate for children's programs, licensing specialists are available to support community efforts to have the regulations changed. Often, specialists are not in a position to initiate an action to change a very restrictive regulation. However, they may provide support and information to a group of laypeople or professional people who organize to bring about changes that will allow quality service for children, and at the same time, free the programs from unrealistic

restrictions. If you find yourself confronted with a local or state regulation that seems impractical or unworkable, enlist your licensing specialist's help in making contact with other directors who feel as you do about the regulation, and form a task force to investigate the process necessary to have the regulation changed.

In one locality where all staff people were required to hold first aid certificates, center operators and licensing specialists worked together to adjust the requirement and make it more realistic without jeopardizing the health or safety of the children. Having a first aid license is valuable for everyone, whether at the center or elsewhere. However, when a center experiences high rates of staff turnover, paying for training and providing paid time to complete the training can be a major burden. In some cases, centers require staff to meet this requirement during their own time and at their own expense. The key is ensuring that appropriate numbers of staff are prepared and properly certified to administer first aid at the center, while children are being transported, and on field trips.

An unreasonable or outdated requirement may be included in licensing and may need to be changed, but the regulation may remain until some very pragmatic, energetic director comes along who is willing to organize the forces necessary to create change. You may find yourself interested in doing just that with the help of other directors, related agencies, and your licensing specialist.

> ### DIRECTOR'S CORNER
>
> "I spend a lot of time keeping track of paperwork. I know that I have to have all the staff and child medical records as soon as a new child or staff member comes to the center. That's one of the first things I do. I also make a calendar each year that reminds me when to apply to renew our license, to get our fire inspection, and our kitchen inspection."
>
> —*Director, private not-for-profit center*

You also may find yourself in a situation in which the licensing requirements offer little effective protection of children. In this case, even though your center exceeds minimum standards, it is your responsibility to advocate for appropriate standards. The NAEYC Code of Ethical Conduct (2011) discusses, in Section IV, our ethical responsibilities to community and society and points out our obligation "to support policies and laws that promote the well-being of children and families" (p. 7). Often, licensing specialists support the need for more appropriate requirements, yet their authority allows them to enforce only the written rules.

The licensing specialist also can help you work through a grievance process if you encounter a unique problem with licensing. For example, one specialist explained a situation in which the fire inspector was holding to the letter of the law by requiring that an expensive, special type of glass be installed in the windows of a building that was not the required 30 feet from an adjacent building. The regulation requiring 30 feet is appropriate and necessary for adequate fire protection, but in this case, the center windows were 28 feet away from an all-brick, fire-resistant building separated from the center by a grassy area. There was no real hazard to the children in this particular center. The licensing specialist provided special help to the director to expedite the grievance process, and the requirement was waived for the center.

In another situation, a new, all-day program was to begin for a one-year period on an experimental basis. The kitchen facility was totally inappropriate for cooking lunches for children who were to stay all day. The director, with the help of the licensing specialist, was able to obtain a temporary permit to operate the experimental program for one year by having the children bring brown-bag lunches. Bag lunches are strictly forbidden in this particular locality under the center licensing regulations, so this particular experimental program could not have been implemented without the understanding support of the licensing specialists. It was agreed that the conditions in the center's food service area would have to meet minimum standards if the program were to be extended beyond the first experimental year and that the bag lunches would have to be appropriately stored each day during that period. The center provided information to parents about appropriate nutritional content of sack lunches.

Licensing specialists are well acquainted with many directors and teachers in the community, so they can serve as a communication bridge between centers by taking ideas and news from one center to another. For example, sharing the news about how a director in a neighboring community solved a budget or staffing problem (without breaking confidentiality) can be very helpful to the director who is dealing with seemingly unsolvable problems and is isolated from contact with colleagues facing similar problems. The specialist can assist directors who are trying to effect budget adjustments or staffing changes but who are meeting resistance from board members or influential community groups. Occasionally, for economic reasons, some board members will pressure the director to overenroll a group to increase revenue. Overenrolling is a risk because there are days when all the enrollees appear, and the classroom becomes overcrowded and understaffed. It may be difficult to convince some board members that overcrowding or understaffing for a few days a month can be demoralizing for staff members and disruptive for children. In some states, overenrolling is even illegal.

Although some prefer fewer government regulations, keep in mind that the quality of child care would almost certainly diminish rapidly if state regulations were reduced or eliminated. If child care center licensing were not in place, an individual could assume responsibility for large numbers of children. This is an unsafe condition that would jeopardize children's health, safety, and development.

---

### MAKING THE CASE FOR *PROGRAM ACCREDITATION*

While licensing of early childhood programs addresses the minimal regulations for operation, accreditation entails meeting standards that in many cases far exceed the requirements of licensing. Some administrators may feel that accreditation is not necessary or is too costly or time consuming. Reflect on the following questions:

1. What are the important similarities and differences between licensing requirements and accreditation? (Refer to Appendix D for an overview of NAEYC accreditation standards.)

2. How might the process of accreditation benefit an early childhood program, including the children, parents, staff, director, board members, and the community?

---

## 3-5 ACCREDITATION

While licensing implies meeting minimum standards, accreditation implies performing at a higher level and meeting additional standards. Directors volunteer to have their center reviewed by an accrediting agency, and those programs that are accredited are deemed worthy of the trust and confidence of both the private and professional communities. Approximately 11 percent of child care centers in the United States have achieved national accreditation (Child Care Aware® of America, 2013).

The accreditation process varies depending on the organization conducting the evaluation of the early childhood program. However, the process typically includes an extensive self-study of a center's facilities, staff, and programming, followed by validation, which may include a site visit by professional early childhood educators representing the accrediting body. Programs usually must seek renewal of their accreditation after a specified period to maintain their status as an accredited center.

Engaging in the accreditation process is productive for the director, staff, parents, and, ultimately, the children. The self-study process may be revealing to the director because it requires reviewing all facets of the center's operation. The process can also provide opportunities for the director and staff to work together in achieving the quality they desire. Groups such as the American Montessori Society, the Association Montessori Internationale, the Child Welfare League of America, the Association for Early Learning Leaders, the National Early Childhood Program Accreditation Commission (NECPA), and the YMCA have various programs to ensure that their centers provide quality child care. The Association for Early Learning Leaders and NECPA also accredit centers. The National Association for Family Child Care offers the only national accreditation system for family child care providers. The most far-reaching effort is that of the National Academy for Early Childhood Program Accreditation, a division of NAEYC. One facet of this professional organization's attempt to improve the quality of life for young children and their families is the accreditation system, based on research and criteria developed over several years with input from a wide range of early childhood educators. While many early childhood professionals and parents recognize the benefits of accreditation, individual states are beginning to recognize the value as well. For example, both Maine and Arkansas offer tax credits to families choosing to enroll their children in NAEYC-accredited programs (NAEYC, 2010). Additional information about NAEYC accreditation policies and procedures can be found on the organization's website. The NAEYC accreditation criteria can be found in Appendix D.

> **DIRECTOR'S CORNER**
>
> "We were a little bit leery of going for NAEYC accreditation. It was a lot of work, but the staff and parents really got interested. And when we got the letter saying we were accredited, I felt like we'd accomplished something as a team."
>
> —*Director, agency center*

# 3-6 QUALITY RATING AND IMPROVEMENT SYSTEMS (QRIS)

Within the past 15 years, many states have implemented another approach to increasing the quality of early care and education programming known as Quality Rating and Improvement Systems (QRIS). Quality improvement systems can be viewed as a "systemic approach to assess, improve, and communicate the level of quality" of early childhood programs (U.S. Department of Health and Human Services, Office of Child Care Technical Assistance Network, n.d.). These systems build on licensing systems within states and seek to improve the quality of care in early childhood

programs. Although not an accreditation system, the QRIS process provides a research-based framework of best practices that administrators and staff can use to evaluate and enhance programming. Additionally, quality rating systems provide parents with another indicator they can use to select programs for their children.

QRIS include multiple tiers where each level builds on the previous level. Each tier contains specific standards related to items such as staff-child ratios, administrator and staff education and experience, accreditation, benefits for employees, and implementation and assessment of research-based curriculum.

Most states have adopted a recognizable symbol that programs can use to advertise their center as having successfully completed the QRIS evaluation. For example, stars may be awarded to programs that have met criteria related to a specific tier. In Colorado, early childhood programs can earn up to four stars; in Ohio, those programs that reach the top tier are awarded five stars.

While completion of a QRIS should not be viewed as a substitute for accreditation, the two systems can work hand in hand to help directors and staff members provide the most appropriate program possible for young children. In fact, some states provide support to programs seeking and maintaining accreditation, and many have included accreditation as part of their QRIS as an indicator of quality. For example, some systems provide points for having accreditation while others require a program to be accredited in order to reach the top tier.

Additional information about QRIS can be found on the QRIS National Learning Network website.

# 3-7 CREDENTIALING

Individuals who work in a profession may be awarded a credential indicating that they have demonstrated the capabilities necessary for successful participation in that profession. While licensing is required for an agency to operate a program, credentials are related to the educational preparation of individual staff members. Credentials may or may not be required by licensing, but they are an indication that the individual has had appropriate preparation for the early childhood profession. There are several types of credentials in the field of early childhood education.

## 3-7a Staff Credentialing
### State Teacher's Licensure

Licensing or certification of early childhood personnel has been under discussion in many states for a number of years, and more and more states are creating prekindergarten or early childhood teaching licenses. Some people refer to the credential as a certificate, meaning a license to practice the profession of teaching, just as doctors, lawyers, real estate agents, or beauticians may obtain a state license to practice their professions. Although the term *certificate* was more widely used in the past, licensing is now considered to be the base. A certificate may be earned from the National Board for Professional Teaching Standards, which indicates that the individual exceeds minimal requirements for teaching. This system is parallel to center licensing and center accreditation.

The license usually is issued by the state department of education. In some cases, the state provides enabling legislation; that is, the license is available, but the state does not require that everyone who teaches preschool children be licensed. However, all 50 states and the District of Columbia require that public preschool teachers be licensed. Many different licensure configurations are available, including birth to 5 years, birth to 8 years, 3 to 5 years, and so forth.

Individual center policies may require that teachers be licensed, but often directors find that they are unable to find licensed teachers willing to work in child care centers at the salaries offered. Directors who require licensure as a qualification for their teachers must be aware of the many kinds of teaching certificates. Preparation for elementary or secondary teaching licenses, for example, does not include attention to most of the knowledge, skills, and attitudes necessary for those working with younger children. Therefore, these licenses may not be appropriate criteria for early childhood teaching positions.

## National Board Certification

Teachers who desire to demonstrate that they are accomplished in their field may apply to become National Board Certified Teachers through a voluntary program organized by the National Board for Professional Teaching Standards. This nonprofit organization is governed by a board primarily composed of classroom teachers.

Eligibility for the certificate requires the applicant to have the following:

- At least three years' experience working with children ages 3 through 8.

- A baccalaureate degree.

- A valid teacher license or certificate in the applicant's state. (In states where a license is not required, the candidate must have taught in programs/schools that are approved to operate by the state.)

Applicants are required to complete a comprehensive portfolio of teaching practice and an online assessment of early childhood content knowledge. Like any worthwhile effort, the process is time consuming and is itself a valuable learning experience for teachers. Nonetheless, more than 100,000 educators in the United States are National Board Certified Teachers in 25 certificate areas, including early childhood. In addition to the recognition the certification carries, a number of states have begun programs to provide compensation to board-certified teachers. For more information, check the National Board for Professional Teaching Standards website.

## Child Development Associate Credential

Another type of credential is the Child Development Associate (CDA) credential. The first CDA credentials were conferred in 1975 under the auspices of the CDA Consortium. Bank Street College administered the program until 1985 when the nonprofit Council for Early Childhood Professional Recognition was established. The Council was established by an agreement between the U.S. Department of Health and Human Services, Administration on Children, Youth and Families, and the NAEYC to administer the CDA program. To date, more than 300,000 credentials have been awarded to caregivers in four categories:

1. center-based infant

2. center-based preschool

3. home visitor

4. family child care

A bilingual endorsement for each of the four types of credentials is also available.

This national credential is included as one of the possible qualifications for directors and/or teachers throughout the United States. Candidates for the credential demonstrate their skill in six competency goal areas, including 13 functional areas such as advancing physical and intellectual competence (physical, cognitive, communication, creative). A combination of experience and training prepares candidates for assessment based on procedures established by the council. Now, almost 40 years since its inception, the credential is still tied closely to Head Start, the program that led to its creation. The CDA is widely recognized by the entire early childhood community as a valuable addition to professional development.

To be eligible to apply for assessment in the CDA process, candidates must

- hold a high school diploma/GED or be enrolled in a career/technical program in early childhood education at the junior or senior level

- be able to speak, read, and write well enough to perform CDA responsibilities

- have 480 hours of experience working with children within 3 years before application

- complete the Professional Portfolio within six months of application

- complete 120 clock hours of formal education prior to application in 8 subject areas

Candidates must be prepared to demonstrate their understanding of the following areas:

- safety
- health
- learning environment
- physical development
- cognitive development
- communication
- creative development
- self (emotional development)
- social development
- guidance
- families
- program management
- professionalism

Although fees are associated with participating in this credentialing process, scholarships are available, and some agencies pay all or part of the fees. Contact the Council for application materials and a list of fees (see Appendix F).

### Certified Childcare Professional Credential

The Certified Childcare Professional (CCP) credential is offered by the National Early Childhood Program Accreditation Commission (NECPA). The credential authenticates teaching skills and professionalism particularly for those who do not have a college degree or who

*Directors who are working toward a credential can review their understanding of child development by observing in the classroom.*

are entering the field from another discipline. Candidates must have a high school diploma or GED, be 18 years of age or older, and speak, read, and write English at a level that will allow the candidate to complete the duties of a CCP. Moreover, an opportunity exists for candidates to obtain college credit for their work. Additional details and application materials can be obtained from the NECPA website.

### U.S. Department of Labor Registered Apprenticeship for Careers in Child Development

The apprenticeship program for careers in child development is offered by many agencies and organizations throughout the United States. This certificate program, sponsored by the U.S. Department of Labor, targets practitioners and requires both on-the-job training with a mentor and classroom instruction. Increased compensation for participants must be provided as they progress successfully through their apprenticeships. Additional information about the program is available from the U.S. Department of Labor, Employment and Training Administration website or your state's apprenticeship agency.

## 3-7b Director Credentialing

During the past two decades, a movement toward director credentialing has grown significantly. The idea evolved through the work of advocates in the profession, such as Gwen Wheeler at Wheelock College and Paula Jorde Bloom at the McCormick Center for Early Childhood Leadership, who understood the importance of specific training, education, and recognition of center leaders (Bloom et al., 2011). Director credentials certify "that an individual has met a defined set of requirements set forth by the grantor of the credential, usually related to skills and knowledge, and may include demonstrations of competence" (National Child Care Information Center, n.d., p. 6-2). The body that awards the credential may or may not be the same organization that delivers the training. A credential may be awarded by a professional association, a state agency, a higher education consortium, or other organization, and it signifies a consensus by those groups of the validity of the standards set forth.

Many states have established director credentials or are in the process of developing credentialing systems. Because this movement is evolving quickly, check with your licensing specialist to determine the status of your state's progress toward the credential.

Several organizations offer national director credentials or certificates. For example, the National Administrator Credential (NAC), sponsored by the NECPA Commission, focuses its efforts on the licensed private child care community.

The McCormick Center for Early Childhood Leadership at National-Louis University offers the Aim4Excellence™ online director credential program that requires completion of nine self-paced modules. This credential was the first in the nation to be recognized by NAEYC as meeting the *relevant training and credentials* criterion for those directors seeking accreditation of their centers.

When seeking a credential or certificate, you must decide which program meets your needs and the requirements in your state. Typically, credentials are offered through states and reflect a more rigorous process of preparation than do certificates. Programs seeking accreditation from NAEYC must be able to demonstrate that teaching staff and administrators meet specific preparation and education guidelines. The organization does not offer a credential or certificate itself; however, it does provide credit for directors who have earned their NAEYC approved state administrator credential. Administrator credentials are important because they have the potential to increase the knowledge and skill level of administrators, particularly in the business and management roles they must assume. As a result, the quality of centers is likely to improve, and staff turnover under the leadership of a knowledgeable administrator may be reduced. The director makes the decisions that influence child outcomes while helping to create the culture of the center. Components such as creating suitable staff-to-child ratios, providing appropriate resources, creating partnerships with diverse families, and selecting well-qualified teachers lead to high quality. Being credentialed creates value for the role of director and encourages individuals to consider this position as a career. Moreover, credentialing can promote both public and private support as the directorship becomes recognized as a valid professional role. Because much of the early childhood education programming being offered today is of poor quality, the need for well-prepared directors is receiving greater attention.

## 3-8 CAREER PATHWAYS

Credentials are important indicators of one's developing skill and competency and, as a result, are now being included in many states' early childhood QRIS and career pathways, also known as *ladders* or *lattices*. Career pathways provide clearly defined routes by which professionals can enhance their qualifications, recognize professional possibilities that exist in the workforce, and be compensated appropriately (LeMoine, 2008). Pathways include a variety of experiences such as completion of in-service trainings or college coursework and attainment of degrees, credentials, or certificates.

One example of a state pathway is the Pennsylvania Keys to Quality Career Lattice. As part of the statewide professional development system, this lattice identifies eight educational levels that need to be achieved to fulfill a variety of roles in the field of early childhood education such as assistant teacher, lead teacher, or director. The lattice can be used by individuals to plan professional development experiences that will prepare them for the position they desire. Moreover, the pathway is directly linked to Pennsylvania's QRIS, known as Keystone Stars, and director credentialing. For example, at level three of the state's four-tier QRIS, 100 percent of teachers must have reached Level 5 on the career lattice (attainment of an associate's degree), and directors must have obtained the Pennsylvania Director Credential.

## SUMMARY

The director of a child care program is responsible for being familiar with licensing regulations, accreditation, and staff credentialing opportunities as these all work together to ensure quality care for young children. Specifically, the director should do the following:

- Understand that licensing of centers provides the minimum standards for early education programs and focuses on the health and safety of children and staff.

- Be familiar with licensing regulations and understand the purpose behind each requirement.

- Know the steps in the process that are required by the local or state agency responsible for issuing a program's license to operate.

- Recognize the important role of the licensing specialist as a resource and in ensuring that regulations are achieved and maintained.

- Understand the differences between the licensing and accreditation processes and the role that each plays in providing quality care and education for young children.

- Be familiar with the requirements of the QRIS in one's state, and recognize that while it is not a substitute for national program accreditation, the two can work together to provide high-quality programming for children.

- Differentiate among the various credentials for center staff and how they can contribute to professionalism and quality programming.

- Understand that credentials are not only an important indication of one's competency but also are important components of many states' career pathway systems, which provide defined routes to enhancing one's qualifications.

# TRY IT OUT!

1.  Invite the licensing specialist from your community to come to a class session to discuss all the services provided by the licensing agency. Prior to the licensing specialist's visit, review the local licensing regulations. After the visit, complete the following activities in class with a small group:

    a.  Review the licensing regulations and determine which sections of the code would help you do a more effective job as a center director.

    b.  Evaluate the regulations and determine which sections (if any) should be revised so that more effective service could be delivered to children.

    c.  Discuss what you consider to be the most challenging part of the licensing process.

2.  Many states require that a detailed plan of operation or business plan be developed as part of the licensing process. Review Director's Resource 3-1, which provides a sample of such a plan. In a small group, discuss the information that must be addressed when planning an early childhood center. Visit your own state's website to secure information regarding the requirements for business plans. Compare and contrast your state's document to Director's Resource 3-1.

3.  Divide the class into small groups to consider the pros and cons of licensure for prekindergarten teachers.

    a.  Can you think of any individuals or groups that provide services for young children who would be opposed to licensure? Discuss why.

    b.  Does licensure guarantee quality service to young children? Discuss the reasons for your conclusion.

    c.  What are the best ways to guarantee quality service to children? Report your conclusions and supporting rationale to the class.

4.  You are the director of an early childhood program who is considering working toward NAEYC accreditation for your center. Review and discuss the Four Steps of accreditation with a small group. Draw a time line of the process that you can present at your next board of directors and parent meetings. You may obtain information on program accreditation from the NAEYC website.

5.  With a small group, compare and contrast program accreditation, quality rating systems, teacher/director credentialing, and career pathways. How are they different? How are they related? How does each contribute to the quality of care and education of young children?

6.  Review the career pathway/lattice/ladder for your state or one provided by your instructor. Discuss the following questions with a classmate or small group:

    a.  How many levels are included in the pathway?

    b.  What requirements must be completed to reach each of the levels?

    c.  How are the individual levels related to specific positions in early childhood?

    d.  Given your current experience and educational background, in which level would you be placed in the pathway?

    e.  Consider your long-term professional goals. Identify those criteria you would need to meet or complete to achieve your goal.

7.  Working with a small group, review the three sets of standards that appear in Appendices B, C, and D. Identify those standards and competencies that relate to licensing, accreditation, and teacher and administrator qualifications. What are early childhood professionals expected to know and be able to do? Discuss you finding with the class.

## DIRECTOR'S RESOURCE 3-1

# OHIO DEPARTMENT OF JOB AND FAMILY SERVICES
# PLAN OF OPERATION FOR A CHILD CARE CENTER

Ohio Department of Job and Family Services
**PLAN OF OPERATION FOR A CHILD CARE CENTER**

| Dates of Attendance | | Do Not Write In This Space | |
|---|---|---|---|
| Opening a Child Care Program (Available through OCCRRA) | | Application Number | |
| Initial Plan of Operation Orientation (Provided by ODJFS) | | Assignment Number | |
| Plan of Operation Review (Conducted by staff from the local licensing field office) | | Date Plan Received | |

### SECTION 1: GENERAL INFORMATION/SPACE

| | | | |
|---|---|---|---|
| Name of Center | | County | |
| Address | | State | Address |
| Mailing Address (if different) | | State | Mailing Address (if different) |
| Name of Contact Person | | | |
| Center Telephone Number | | Contact Person's Telephone Number | |
| Proposed Date of Opening | | Owner/Corporation | |
| Directions to the Center | | | |
| Proposed Hours of Operation | Proposed Days of Operation | | Proposed Months of Operation |

#### PLANNED ENROLLMENT

| Age Categories | Number of Children Planned at Opening | Number of Groups Planned at Opening | Number of Children Planned at Capacity | Number of Staff needed at opening |
|---|---|---|---|---|
| Infants (0-18mo.) | | | | |
| Toddlers (18mo-3yr) | | | | |
| Preschoolers (3yr – school age) | | | | |
| School age Children (5 yr - 14yr) **Note:** School age children present more than 4 hrs per day are considered fulltime during school breaks, holidays, snow days, etc. | Before school / After School | Before School / After School | Before School / After School | |
| | Fulltime | Fulltime | Fulltime | |

**Total Number of Child Care Staff Members Needed at Opening**

---

## DIRECTOR'S RESOURCE 3-1 *(continued)*

### INDOOR SPACE
#### (Rule 5101:2-12-13)

Draw a diagram of the indoor space used by the child care operation. Indicate the following:
- Exits
- Walls, partitions or half walls
- Walls, partitions, or half walls that are moveable
- Sinks and water fountains
- Emergency exits and exits to the outdoor play space
- Room assignments (i.e., infant room, toddler room, preschool room etc.)
- Restrooms
- Diaper changing area with sink
- Food preparation areas

Is center building occupied by any other persons or groups other than those of the child care center during hours of operation? Explain:

*(Include what space is used by these persons as well as the children from the center.)*

Will the center care for children under the age of 2 ½ years? If yes, describe how the center will keep these children separated from other groups older than 2 ½ years.

### OUTDOOR SPACE
#### (Rule 5101: 2-12-14)

Diagram the space used for outdoor play.
- Include location of fence or barriers.
- Note gate locations, street locations, and parking lots.
- Sketch outdoor permanent play equipment which stays in space (i.e., slides, swings, sandboxes, etc.)
- Also include sidewalks, concrete, or blacktop areas.

If the play space is away from the center, diagram the outdoor space used.
If the center has no outdoor play space an indoor recreation area must be provided. Give dimensions of your indoor recreation area.

1) What type of protective fall surface will the center use on the playground? (Fall surface needed under slides, swings, climbers, bouncers, etc.)

2) How is the play area enclosed or otherwise protected from traffic or other hazards?

3) Describe how children will have access to <u>bathroom facilities</u> and <u>drinking water</u> during outdoor play time.

4) How will the center provide a shaded area when needed?

Note: When the playground does not meet the square footage requirement of 60 square feet per child, for all children at one time; then children will need to play in groups by staggered shifts.

---

## DIRECTOR'S RESOURCE 3-1 *(continued)*

### SECTION 2: SAFE/SANITARY REQUIREMENTS
#### SAFE/SANITARY EQUIPMENT
#### (Rules 5101:2-12-15, 5101:2-12-15.1, 5101:2-12-15.3 and 5101:2-12-15.4)

1) Describe the center's plan to maintain and clean indoor and outdoor play equipment, furniture and materials. (Be sure your answer includes all parts of this question.)

2) What supplies will be used for cleaning and sanitizing? (Refer to Appendix A for Rule 5101:2-12-15 for more information.)

3) How often is equipment cleaned?

4) How often is equipment sanitized?

5) Who is responsible for cleaning and maintenance?

6) Explain how you will keep track of when cleaning/sanitizing is completed. (Describe your tracking system.)

7) Describe how and where cleaning equipment and supplies will be stored.

8) Will the center care for pets? ☐ Yes ☐ No  If yes, explain and indicate how pet shot records will be maintained?

9) Will the center use fans? ☐ Yes ☐ No  If yes, what safety provisions will be taken?

10) Is the center's water publicly supplied?
☐ Yes ☐ No  If no, sampling by the local health department must be completed.

11) When are cots cleaned?

12) When are cots sanitized?

13) Describe the location of the hand washing facilities for children over 2 ½ years old and explain when children wash their hands.

14) If center staff is permitted to smoke, what will be your policy? (Refer to 5101:2-12-15.3 for restrictions.)

15) Will children be provided the opportunity to brush their teeth while at the center?
☐ Yes ☐ No  If yes, explain how you will keep brushes sanitary.

---

## DIRECTOR'S RESOURCE 3-1 *(continued)*

### SECTION 3: PROGRAMMING AND CENTER POLICIES
#### PROGRAMMING/EQUIPMENT AND COTS
#### (Rules 5101:2-12-16 and 5101:2-12-19)

1) Where will a copy of the daily program schedule for each age group be posted?

2) What provisions have been taken to provide enough equipment representative of all areas listed in Rule 5101:2-12-16? (Have you listed all categories? Have you listed all age groups?)

3) Who will monitor the equipment so sufficient quantities are maintained and replacements are ordered in a timely manner? (Describe your system.)

4) If you have school age children who rest/sleep at the center, what type of equipment will be provided?

5) How many cots are available at the center for daily use by toddlers and preschoolers?

6) How are cots assigned to the children?

7) What tracking system will be used to document when cots are cleaned and sanitized?

#### SWIMMING AND WATER SAFETY
#### (Rule 5101:2-12-17)

1) Will the center's program include swimming or water activities? ☐ Yes ☐ No  (If Yes, continue below, otherwise skip to Transportation and Field Trip Safety.)

2) Describe type of activity including the pool location if off the premises.

3) Describe the center's plan for supervision of children when they are out of the water and the system the center will use for supervising and tracking each child while in the water.

#### TRANSPORTATION/FIELD TRIP SAFETY
#### (Rule 5101: 2-12-18)

1) Does the center plan to offer: *(Check all that apply)*
☐ Field trips
☐ Routine trips

If the center will **not** take field/routine trips, skip to Supervision/Child Guidance and Management

2) Does the center provide transportation? ☐ Yes ☐ No

3) Describe the center vehicles or vehicles that are used (by a contracted agency, if applicable. i.e., mini-van, bus, car)

4) Explain the center's safety procedures in regards to transporting children.

5) What will be taken on trips?

## DIRECTOR'S RESOURCE 3-1 *(continued)*

6) How will identification for the children be provided?

7) How will permission be obtained?

8) Explain how the center will obtain verification of an appropriate valid driver's license for all drivers.

9) Who is responsible for obtaining an <u>annual</u> vehicle safety inspection? See prescribed form JFS 01230.

10) Who will be responsible for providing the transportation safety training each year to any employees who will be driving or riding?

11) Who will be responsible for completing the <u>weekly</u> vehicle inspection?

12) How will the administrator verify that any areas of concern, indicated on the weekly inspection sheet, will be addressed? (i.e., brake lights not working, low tire pressure, etc.)

### SUPERVISION/CHILD GUIDANCE AND MANAGEMENT
### (Rule 5101:2-12-20 and 5101:2-12-22)

1) Explain how all child care staff members will be made aware of the center policies.

2) Describe the center's procedure for taking attendance and maintaining attendance records.

3) Explain provisions made for compliance with staff/child ratios on occasions when staff is absent, late, or leave for breaks? (Describe your plan for each situation.)

4) Describe the center's plan for transitioning children into the next age group.

5) How will the transitioning child's whereabouts be tracked?

### EVENING AND OVERNIGHT CARE
### (Rule 5101:2-12-23)

1) Will the center be providing evening and/or overnight care? (Between 7:00 PM and 6:00 AM) ☐ Yes ☐ No
(If yes, complete the following questions otherwise skip to Center Administrative Policies and Procedures.)

2) Days and hours overnight and/or evening care will be provided?

3) Describe the center's security plan to ensure that access to the center is limited to parents and guardians of children in care and authorized persons.

4) Describe the center's sleeping arrangements, including how children will be grouped.

JFS 01250 (Rev. 9/2011)⊠      Page 5 of 15

---

## DIRECTOR'S RESOURCE 3-1 *(continued)*

### CENTER ADMINISTRATIVE POLICIES AND PROCEDURES
### (Rule 5101:2-12-30)

This refers to your Parent Handbook that you will attach.
(See Sample Form JFS 01268 for guidance)

### ADMINISTRATION OF MEDICATION AND
### FIRST AID SUPPLIES/PROCEDURES
### (Rules 5101:2-12-31 and 5101:2-12-36)

1) Describe the center's procedures for administering medication, and topical products or lotions. (Be sure to describe the plan for each type of product.)

2) Describe the center's procedures for administering food supplements and/or modified diets. (Describe the plan for each.)

3) Who is the designated individual(s) who will be assigned and responsible for the administration of medication?

4) How will the designee(s) document the administration of medication to assure accurate records?

5) Describe the procedure if medication is: not administered, delayed or incorrectly administered.

6) Describe the center's plan for safe storage of medication.

7) Describe the center's procedure for implementing standard precautions (5101:2-12-15.1)

8) Where will first aid supplies be stored?

### MEDICAL, DENTAL AND GENERAL EMERGENCY PLAN
### (Rule 5101:2-12-34)

1) Describe the center's plan for emergency transportation of children.

### INCIDENT/INJURY REPORT
### (Rule 5101:2-12-35)

1) Describe the center's procedure for completing incident/injury reports. (Use prescribed form JFS 01299)

2) Describe the center's procedure for notifying the appropriate licensing office when a serious incident, injury, illness, death of a child or unusual or unexpected event occurs.

---

## DIRECTOR'S RESOURCE 3-1 *(continued)*

### SECTION 4: STAFF REQUIREMENTS
### ADMINISTRATOR RESPONSIBILITIES AND QUALIFICATIONS
### (Rule 5101:2-12-24)

1) How will the center assure the administrator will be onsite for a minimum of one-half of the hours that the center is in operation?

### EMPLOYEE AND CHILD CARE STAFF MEMBER REQUIREMENTS AND STATEMENTS OF
### NONCONVICTION, CRIMINAL RECORDS CHECKS
### (Rules 5101:2-12-25 and 5101:2-12-26)

1) Explain the procedures used to maintain employee's group assignments, work schedule and the date of employment. (How will the Employee Record Chart be kept up to date?)

**Complete an Employee Records Chart, bold box only.**

2) Describe the center's plan for providing the orientation training for staff using the prescribed online curriculum. Include when it will occur and who will provide the training.

3) Describe plans for the administrator to review the licensing rules, and to provide a copy of the Medical and Dental General Emergency Plan, and the center policies and procedures to each employee.

4) Where will the ODJFS Licensing Rules be located for staff?

5) Has the administrator submitted requests for both BCII and FBI criminal records web checks?

**Be certain the results for <u>owners/administrators</u> are being sent directly to the appropriate <u>child care licensing field office</u> by the WebCheck agency.**

6) Describe procedures for submitting requests for BCII and FBI criminal records web checks, for each child care staff member prior to employment. (What is the system for tracking this?)

**Be certain the results for <u>employees</u> are being sent directly to the child care <u>administrator/center</u> by the WebCheck agency.**

7) Describe the center's procedure for assuring that child care staff members are not left alone with children until the results of their criminal records checks are returned, and reviewed and approved by the administrator.

8) Describe the center's system for tracking results for all child care staff members/employees when the results are not received in a timely manner.

9) Describe the center's procedure if the results of the records check indicate that an employee has been convicted of a crime that prohibits employment. (Note: Review background check requirements and considerations for rehabilitation contained in this rule.)

10) Will the center use a non-employee as a second adult as required in Rule 5101:2-12-20? ☐ Yes ☐ No
If yes, describe the center's plan for obtaining the required information and describe the means to summon the second adult.

---

## DIRECTOR'S RESOURCE 3-1 *(continued)*

### TRAINING IN FIRST AID, CPR, CHILDHOOD ILLNESSES,
### CHILD ABUSE PREVENTION AND INSERVICE TRAINING
### (Rules 5101:2-12-27 and 5101:2-12-28)

1) How will the center assure that child care staff members who are trained in First Aid, Common Childhood Illnesses, CPR (for all the needed age groups), and child abuse prevention, will be on the premises during all hours of operation, and in all buildings?

2) What tracking system will the center use to ensure child care staff members have maintained current certifications in the areas above?

3) Describe the center's requirements for staff and annual inservice trainings.

4) What tracking system will the center use to ensure child care staff members meet inservice training requirements?

### SECTION 5: CHILDREN'S RECORDS and FOOD REQUIREMENTS
### CHILDREN'S MEDICAL STATEMENTS AND RECORDS AND
### CARE OF CHILDREN WITH HEALTH CONDITIONS
### (Rules 5101:2-12-37 and 5101:2-12-38)

1) Describe the center's plans to ensure that all required children's medical statements will be secured within 30 days of each child's admission. (Be sure to note the difference in the medical requirements for school age children.)

2) What action will be taken if the child's medical examination records are not provided within the required time frame?

3) Describe the procedure the center will follow to assure medical examinations are updated as required.

4) Explain the center's system for obtaining and updating all required enrollment information for each child. (How often will information be reviewed?)

5) Describe how the center will obtain the medical/physical care plan, if needed. (How will these records be kept up to date?)

### MEALS AND SNACKS
### (Rule 5101:2-12-39)

1) List all meals and snacks that the center will be providing and the approximate serving times.

## DIRECTOR'S RESOURCE 3-1 *(continued)*

2) Will meals and snacks be prepared on site or brought in from another source?

3) Where will meals/snacks be eaten? Who will be responsible for getting the meals/snacks to the serving area? Who will serve the meals/snacks?

### SECTION 6: INFANT/TODDLER CARE

**INFANT DAILY PROGRAM/INFANT CAREGIVER**
**(Rule 5101:2-12-40)**

1) Describe the center's procedure for assigning staff to groups of infants. How will parents be informed of the primary caregivers assigned to their infant?

2) Describe the center's procedures for assuring that necessary information regarding infant's care is exchanged among staff and between staff members and parents.

3) Describe how the cribs will be separated from the play space. What type of barrier will be used?

**INFANT FORMULA AND FOOD**
**(Rule 5101:2-12-41)**

1) Describe the center's process for feeding infants.

2) How will the center adapt the menu to take into account the developmental levels of infants?

3) Describe the center's procedure for obtaining written instructions from the parent(s) about serving food to infants.

4) How often will this be updated?

5) If formula is prepared by the center, describe the technique used.

6) Explain where this preparation of formula takes place.

7) How is the infant food prepared?

8) Describe the center's plan for safe storage of baby food, formula and breast milk.

---

## DIRECTOR'S RESOURCE 3-1 *(continued)*

9) How will formula be heated?

10) How will the center assure that extra formula, for all enrolled infants, will be on hand and available for use?

**DIAPERING FACILITIES AND PROCESS**
**(Rule 5101:2-12-15.2)**

1) If the center's hand washing facilities are located in a space other than where the infants/toddlers receive care, describe the location of the hand washing facilities and the center's plan to maintain supervision while diapering.

2) What separation material will the center use during diaper changes?

3) What will the center use to disinfect the changing station?

4) Describe the storage of soiled diapers/clothing.

**CRIBS**
**(Rule 5101:2-12-42)**

| 1) How many cribs will the center have available? | Porta Cribs | Full Size Cribs |
|---|---|---|

2) When were the cribs purchased/obtained? (Do they meet the federal standards for cribs that were effective June 28, 2011?)

2) Describe the center's schedule for cleaning and sanitizing cribs. (If more than one infant will share a crib, how will the cribs be cleaned and sanitized in between children?)

3) Describe how staff will be trained on the safety requirements of this rule and who will provide the training.

4) What will the center's policy be on positioning infants when placing them in their cribs to sleep? (See prescribed form JFS 01235)

---

## DIRECTOR'S RESOURCE 3-1 *(continued)*

### STATEMENT OF UNDERSTANDING

**I understand that the department may revoke a license if:**

- A center fails to comply with the requirements of Chapter 5104 of the Revised Code or Chapter 5101:2-12 of the Administrative Code.

- The center is found to have furnished or made misleading or false statements or reports to the department.

- The center refuses or fails to submit reports requested by the department within required time frames.

- The owner or administrator has pleaded guilty to or been convicted of an offense described in Section 5104.09 of the Revised Code and has not met the standards of rehabilitation set out in Rule 5101:2-12-26.

- A center has refused to admit the director's representative onto its premises.

**I understand that the following must be obtained prior to an individual starting employment.**

- A medical that meets the requirements of Rule 5101:2-12-25.

- Educational verification showing completion of high school or equivalency per Rule 5101: 2-12-25.

- Signed non-conviction statement per Rule 5101: 2-12-26.

- Fingerprint impressions/web check, the administrator must assure that child care staff members and employees have submitted fingerprint impressions to BCII and FBI per Rule 5101:2-12-26 prior to the first day of employment.

- A signed statement that the administrator has reviewed the licensing rules and all center policies and procedures to the employee per Rule 5101-2-12-25.

**I have read and understand the requirements listed above.**

| Signature of Administrator | Date |
|---|---|

---

## DIRECTOR'S RESOURCE 3-1 *(continued)*

| SECTION 7 | REQUIRED ATTACHMENTS TO THE CHILD CARE CENTER PLAN OF OPERATION |
|---|---|
| **ATTACHMENT 1** | If the center is owned by a corporation, attach a copy of the **incorporation papers.** |
| **ATTACHMENT 2** | A copy of the **Certificate of Occupancy.** |
| **ATTACHMENT 3** | A copy of the completed **fire inspection report** (JFS 01303.) |
| **ATTACHMENT 4** | A copy of the center's **food service license**, exemption and/or caterer's food service license. |
| **ATTACHMENT 5** | **Diagrams** of indoor floor plan and outdoor play space. (See page 2 for instructions) |
| **ATTACHMENT 6** | The **laboratory test** of the water supply from the local health department per Rule 5101:2-12-15, if the center's water is **not** publicly supplied. |
| **ATTACHMENT 7** | A copy of the **center's inventory.** Divide the inventory by all age groups, infants, toddlers, preschool, school age, and by category. Be sure to include the number of each item listed. (See Rule 5101:2-12-16.) |
| **ATTACHMENT 8** | A copy of each parent **permission form** that applies: field trip, routine trip, swimming and water activities. |
| **ATTACHMENT 9** | A sample **attendance form** which the center will use to record daily attendance of all children at the center. |
| **ATTACHMENT 10** | A copy of the center's **evening program schedule**, if applicable. |
| **ATTACHMENT 11** | A copy of the **administrator's qualifications and job description.** |
| **ATTACHMENT 12** | A copy of the **Parent Handbook.** (See Rule 5101:2-12-30) |
| **ATTACHMENT 13** | A copy of the center's completed **medical, dental and general emergency plan.** |
| **ATTACHMENT 14** | One week **menu** for meals and snacks. |
| **ATTACHMENT 15** | If the center will not prepare food but only **serves food brought by the parents**, attach: (1) a list of foods kept on hand to supplement lunches which do not meet the one-third daily dietary allowance, (2) a copy of the nutritional information given to parents (3) a description of the center's food storage plan for lunches. |
| **ATTACHMENT 16** | A sample copy of the center's **infant daily record and basic information.** |
| **ATTACHMENT 17** | A copy of the **Employee Record Chart** (JFS 01306) with the bolded box information completed. |

## DIRECTOR'S RESOURCE 3-1 *(continued)*

### Portion Sizes for Meals Served at
### Child Care Centers and Type A Homes
(To be used when completing Attachment #14)

| Meal | Component | Minimum Serving | | |
|---|---|---|---|---|
| | Age of Child | 1 & 2 years | 3-5 years | 6-12 years |
| Breakfast | Fluid Milk | ½ cup | ¾ cup | 1 cup |
| | Juice/Fruit or Vegetable | ¼ cup | ½ cup | ½ cup |
| | Grains/Breads/Dry Cereal | ½ slice ¼ cup or 1/3 oz. | ½ slice 1/3 cup or 1/2 oz. | ½ slice ¾ cup or 1 oz. |
| Lunch or Supper | Meat or Meat Alternative | 1 oz. | 1 ½ oz. | 2 oz. |
| | 2 Fruits or Vegetables | ¼ cup | ½ cup | ¾ cup |
| | Grains/Breads/ Pasta/Noodles | ½ slice ¼ cup | ½ slice ¼ cup | 1 slice ½ cup |
| | Fluid Milk | ½ cup | ¾ cup | 1 cup |
| Snack | Meat or Meat Alternative | ½ oz. | ½ oz. | 1 oz. |
| | Fruit or Vegetable | ½ cup | ½ cup | ¾ cup |
| | Grains/Breads | ½ slice ¼ cup or 1/3 oz. | ½ slice ¼ cup or 1/3 oz. | ½ slice ¼ cup or 1/3 oz. |
| | Fluid Milk | ½ cup | ½ cup | 1 cup |

Additional information on meal preparation and nutrition may be found at:
http://www.fns.usda.gov/cnd/care/ProgramBasics/Meals/Meal_Patterns.htm

## DIRECTOR'S RESOURCE 3-1 *(continued)*

**Attachment 14**

| | | Component | Monday | Tuesday | Wednesday | Thursday | Friday |
|---|---|---|---|---|---|---|---|
| Breakfast | One serving of each | Fluid Milk | | | | | |
| | | Fruit or Vegetable | | | | | |
| | | Grain/Bread/Cereal | | | | | |
| Meal | One serving of each | Meat or Meat Alt. | | | | | |
| | | 2 Fruits or Vegetables (one of each is recommended) | | | | | |
| | | Grain/Bread/Cereal | | | | | |
| | | Fluid Milk | | | | | |
| Snack | Two serving of the four groups | Grain/Bread/Cereal | | | | | |
| | | Fruit or Vegetable | | | | | |
| | | Meat or Meat Alt. | | | | | |
| | | Milk | | | | | |

- Only 100%, undiluted fruit or vegetable juice shall meet the fruit or vegetable requirement for meals or snacks.
- Children under 12 months of age shall receive formula or breast milk unless otherwise directed in writing by a licensed physician.
- Children 12 months to 24 months of age shall receive whole homogenized Vitamin D fortified cow's milk, unless otherwise directed in writing by a licensed physician.
- Children over 24 months of age shall receive fluid milk that is Vitamin D fortified. Lowfat and skim milk shall be Vitamin A and Vitamin D fortified. Reconstituted dry powdered milk shall be used only for cooking and shall not be used as a beverage.

## DIRECTOR'S RESOURCE 3-1 *(continued)*

**Attachment 14**
**page 2 (if needed)**

| | | Component | Monday | Tuesday | Wednesday | Thursday | Friday |
|---|---|---|---|---|---|---|---|
| Evening Meal | One serving of each | Meat or Meat Alt. | | | | | |
| | | 2 Fruits or Vegetables (one of each is recommended) | | | | | |
| | | Grain/Bread/ Cereal | | | | | |
| | | Fluid Milk | | | | | |
| PM Snack | Two serving of the four groups | Grain/Bread/ Cereal | | | | | |
| | | Fruit or Vegetable | | | | | |
| | | Meat or Meat Alt. | | | | | |
| | | Milk | | | | | |

*Source: Ohio Department of Job and Family Services*

# REFERENCES

American Academy of Pediatrics, American Public Health Association, and National Resource Center for Health and Safety in Child Care and Early Education (2013). *Stepping stones to caring for our children* (3rd ed.). Elk Grove Village, IL: American Academy of Pediatrics, Washington, DC: American Public Health Association, and Aurora, CO: National Resource Center for Health and Safety in Child Care and Early Education. Retrieved from http://nrckids .org/index.cfm/products/stepping-stones-to-caring-for -our-children-3rd-edition-ss3/.

Child Care Aware® of America. (2013). *Child care in America: 2013 state fact sheets.* Retrieved from http://www.naccrra .org/sites/default/files/default_site_pages/2013/2013 _state_fact_sheets_082013.pdf.

*Directions in center director training: Insights of Paula Jorde Bloom, Yasmina Vinci, Donna Rafanello, and Chip Donohue.* (2011). *Exchange, 197,* 18–20.

LeMoine, S. (2008). *Workforce designs: A policy blueprint for state early childhood professional development systems.* Washington, DC: NAEYC.

National Association for Regulatory Administration and the National Center on Child Care Quality Improvement, Office of Child Care. (2014). *The 50-state child care licensing study: 2011–2013 edition.* Retrieved from http://www .acf.hhs.gov/programs/occ/news/nara-releases-the-2011 -2013-child-care-licensing-study.

National Association for the Education of Young Children. (2011). *Code of ethical conduct and statement of commitment.* Washington, DC: Author.

National Association for the Education of Young Children. (2005b). *Leadership & management: A guide to the early childhood program standard and related accreditation criteria.* Washington, DC: Author.

National Association for the Education of Young Children. (2010). State and local quality improvement support efforts. *Young Children, 65*(1), 54–56. Washington, DC: Author.

National Center on Child Care Quality Improvement. (2011). *Trends in child care center licensing regulations and policies for 2011.* Retrieved from http://www.qrisnetwork .org/resource/2011/trends-child-care-center-licensing -regulations-and-policies-2011.

National Center on Child Care Quality Improvement. (2012). *Use of technology to enhance licensing administration.* Retrieved from http://www.acf.hhs.gov/sites/default/files /occ/001_1209_technology_licensing_final_508c.pdf.

National Child Care Information Center. (n.d.). *Early childhood professional development system toolkit, qualifications, credentials and pathways.* Retrieved from https://childcare .gov/resource/early-childhood-professional-development -systems-toolkit-focus-school-age-professional.

U.S. Department of Health and Human Services, Office of Child Care Technical Assistance Network. (n.d.). *Quality improvement systems.* Retrieved from https://childcare .gov/topics/quality-improvement-systems.

*Board members can be extremely helpful to the director in carrying out the mission of the program.*

## Learning Objectives

After reading this chapter, you should be able to:

**4-1** Describe four types of business organization, and explain the advantages and disadvantages of each.

**4-2** Identify circumstances under which a business must have a board.

**4-3** Explain important considerations in the selection and orientation of board members.

**4-4** List the responsibilities of a center's board.

**4-5** Describe the various roles of board committees in conducting the work of the center.

**4-6** Explain the rationale for maintaining open communication with and among board members.

**4-7** Discuss the role that the board plays in the operation of the center.

## Standards Addressed in this Chapter

Accreditation Standard 8 – Community Relationships

Accreditation Standard 10 – Leadership and Management

Administrator Competencies – Management Knowledge and Skills 2, 3, 8, 9, 10

Administrator Competencies – Early Childhood Knowledge and Skills 6, 10

Professional Preparation Standard 6 – Becoming a Professional

# 4-1 ORGANIZATION OF THE CENTER

Anyone considering a position as director of an early childhood program must determine how the prospective center is organized and for what purpose before accepting the position. The roles of directors vary widely, based in large part on the organizational structure of the early childhood center or the requirements of the owner. In some cases, a director may also be an owner. "The legal structure . . . will determine how much paperwork you will have to do, how much personal liability you will incur, how you will be able to raise money, and how your business will be taxed" (Pinson & Jinnett, 2006, p. 59). Let's look at the four main organizational structures.

## 4-1a Sole Proprietorship

Individuals who create centers and maintain ownership are sole proprietors. They can make all the decisions, and they bear all the responsibility. They provide the financing, often through bank loans using their own property as collateral. Some individuals may obtain loans from friends or relatives. This type of operation usually is rather small but may later grow, perhaps then becoming a partnership or a corporation. These business owners, also called *entrepreneurs,* establish new companies to fill unmet needs (Greene, 2012).

Being the decision maker has benefits but also can be lonely, particularly when a crisis hits. When the center's furnace must be replaced on the coldest day of the year, or the lead teacher leaves, and a replacement can't be found, the proprietor may second-guess the organizational decision. When the waiting list is long, and a child gives the owner a hug, the decision seems just right. The owner is at risk, however, in the case of a lawsuit, for example, when a child is injured on the playground. All the owner's assets may be in jeopardy. Carrying liability insurance is essential, even for small proprietary programs.

Creating a sole proprietorship is relatively easy after the financial hurdles have been resolved. Papers must be filed with federal, state, and local governments. Usually a form indicating the name of the business is required. Even if Mary Smith decides to open Smith's Child Care Center, she should file the paperwork stating that she is doing business as (d/b/a) Smith's Child Care Center.

When the percentage of center income required for salaries is considered (see Chapter 5), it would seem almost impossible for an individual owner to make a profit. Nonetheless, over the years, many individual centers grow, with the owners gradually opening more and more centers. Soon regional chains are bought up by larger groups. Today, a corporation may oversee thousands of centers, some of which may have been started originally by individual owners.

One type of child care usually provided by a sole proprietor is home-based care. Many of these providers do not consider themselves to be in business, but in fact they are unless they care only for relatives. They are subject to business requirements such as keeping records of attendance, receipts, expenses, and so forth. They may be eligible for the government food program and, in some communities, may receive visitors who provide information about how children learn, activities and supplies, and answers to the provider's questions. In many communities, home care providers are not licensed, and there is no oversight. Serious problems have occurred too often. To protect children and those home providers who are providing appropriate care, every state should have home provider licensing in place, just as every state licenses child care centers.

## 4-1b Partnerships

Sharing responsibility and finances is another possibility. One option is to form a partnership, that is, "an association of two or more persons to carry on as co-owners of a business for profit" (Hatten, 2011, p. 38). For example, two people might be equal partners, or 60–40, or any other combination. This decision usually impacts the amount of decision making and responsibility each assumes and the amount of financial involvement of each. Being a silent partner—contributing financially but not being involved in decision making—is also a possibility. When profits are available, they usually are allocated according to the percentage of investment. In case of a lawsuit, each partner is liable on a percentage basis, and personal assets are at risk. The liability issue is based on the way in which the partnership is legally constituted. A formal contract between or among those entering the agreement is signed to delineate their obligations and responsibilities (Hatten, 2011).

Having one or more partners provides additional capital and a relatively stable business life. Partners can both (or all) contribute to decision making and share responsibilities so that each can have at least some free time (Cohen, 2006).

Because setting up a partnership is somewhat more complicated than setting up a sole proprietorship, employing a lawyer is essential. The paperwork must be prepared with care. Furthermore, even the best of friends or relatives may disagree and decide to end the partnership. Or one or more of the partners may decide that this is no longer the business investment desired. In addition, it must be made clear, in writing, what happens to the partnership in the event of a partner's death.

## 4-1c Franchise

One way to have your own business using a model that has already been standardized is to invest in a franchise. "A franchise is an agreement that binds a franchisor (a parent company of the product, service, or method) with a franchisee (a small business that pays fees and royalties for exclusive rights to local distribution of the product or service" (Hatten, 2011, p. 109). The owner of the franchise sells the rights to use the logo, program, and company reputation to a buyer and may provide free management training. Buying and using the company supplies and equipment is expected. Because the franchisor sells large amounts to franchisees, the cost may be lower to the individual program. In turn, the buyer probably will be required to follow specific policies and procedures and to complete company paperwork. If the center loses money, the company is unlikely to share in the loss (Hatten, 2011; Pinson & Jinnett, 2006).

Parents can expect that each franchise will be the same as others of the same name with which they may be familiar. The franchisor ensures that the franchisee follows company policies and standards. You may be familiar with this model based on some of the fast-food restaurants you patronize. If you like certain foods prepared a certain way, you expect to find the same product at all franchises of that restaurant. Getting a burger that's not the way you like it isn't a major problem; however, the same cannot be said for child care programs. If parents have had experience with a specific franchised center in the past, they will no doubt expect that all centers managed by this franchisor will offer equal quality. Getting involved with any major business opportunity requires careful checking in advance.

## 4-1d Corporation

To form a corporation, articles of incorporation must be filed, usually with the secretary of state (see Director's Resource 4-1). Bylaws, also referred to as regulations or a constitution, must be adopted, and a governing body, usually called a board of trustees, must be formed to set policy and assume overall responsibility for the operation of the corporation.

A corporation is a business owned by one or more shareholders. The shareholders elect directors to manage the affairs of the corporation, and the directors, in turn, elect officers to handle the day-to-day business of the corporation. Both federal and state laws regulate registration of stock issued to shareholders. Stock refers to shares or parts of ownership of a corporation. A stockholder provides an amount of money to a company, often through a broker, thereby becoming part owner of the company. In exchange, stockholders experience the possibility of profit or loss in their own accounts.

Large companies have thousands of shareholders, whereas a corporate child care center may be owned by a very small number of friends of the center. Some child care centers, however, become major corporations by creating or acquiring a large number of centers under one corporate name. Examples of large corporate child care programs are Knowledge Universe and Bright Horizons. These organizations serve thousands of children in hundreds of locations. When you go to their websites, you may see that they are encouraging early childhood program owners to consider selling their program to one of the large companies.

Like large corporate groups, federal, state, and local branches of government are taking on a larger share of the early childhood education role. In some cases, a governmental body will provide funding for child care and education programs. In other cases, a business will be chosen or created to run a tax-funded early childhood program. For example, a school board might hire a corporation that manages a number of children's programs. That corporation provides staff and equipment, usually at the school, and is paid to run child care for preschoolers and for older children before and after school. Increasingly, public schools are offering their own preschool programs, staffing them, and creating the curriculum. Many parents appreciate this, believing it is easier to have preschoolers in the same building as older siblings and feeling that the young child will not have to transition to a new place for kindergarten. The program may be partially or totally funded by tax dollars. One drawback may be that some programs operate on the typical school schedule, with no provisions for before- and after-school care or for holidays and vacations. In some cases, the program for young children and for after-school care may be primarily academic rather than focusing on the whole child. Infants and toddlers are rarely included in public school programs. An exception occurs when a school creates a program for the very young children of high school students, in large part to help the teens finish their education.

One aspect of the increased direct involvement in preschool education by public schools is the effect on child care businesses. Because the need for infant and toddler care will still be strong, centers may find that the high cost of care for the youngest children may no longer be balanced by the lower cost of care for 3- to 5-year-olds. As you read more about financing programs for young children in a later chapter, this idea will become clearer.

---

### REFLECTION

Do you think you would like to direct a center in a large chain, or would you rather operate a center independently? Have you thought about working in a child care program managed by an agency such as a hospital or faith-based group? What might be some of the pros and cons of each arrangement? Think about the centers with which you are familiar. How are they organized?

When a center is to be operated as a corporation, the board is responsible for initiating the incorporation process. Because laws vary from state to state, consulting an attorney is essential. The law does not require that child care centers incorporate, but it is desirable.

Although initially setting up a corporation is more complex and more costly than setting up a sole proprietorship or partnership, there are advantages. Corporations may attract funding more easily and may be more stable because they may be less dependent on the involvement of one or a few individuals. Nonetheless, a corporation can be very small and consist of only a few family members.

One advantage that accrues to corporations is the limitation on financial responsibility. Because the liability of the corporation is limited to the assets of the corporation, individuals holding positions in the corporation are generally protected from personal liability for acts or debts of the corporation. A corporation can be sued and lose all of its assets, in effect putting it out of business. However, the personal assets of the director or owners are not included. On the other hand, corporate assets of small child care centers often are obtained by using personal assets as collateral. In that case, individuals' assets are jeopardized.

## Profit or Not-for-Profit Corporations

When a center's management plan is to incorporate, the decision to be for-profit or not-for-profit must be made. In the case of a not-for-profit corporation, the corporate structure is different. For example, there are no shareholders in a nonprofit corporation. Instead, members elect trustees to manage the affairs of the corporation. The required number of trustees and officers varies from state to state. Once incorporated, the corporation must function in accordance with the state laws, the articles of incorporation, and the bylaws.

Although it is a common belief that nonprofit entities are organized to provide some sort of charitable, educational, or religious function, the law does not require such a purpose. An organization can provide "almost any kind of good or service on a not-for-profit basis. . . . Some nonprofits are supported by donations, others depend on income from sales of goods and services, and many receive most or all of their revenues from government" (Hall, 2010, p. 3). Although nonprofits can receive funds from donors and foundations, only a small percentage of early childhood program funding is from charitable contributions.

Not-for-profit corporation status does not automatically result in tax-exempt status. Based on Internal Revenue Code 501, a corporation must apply to the Internal Revenue Service (IRS) for tax-exempt status and to demonstrate that the organization's purpose is educational or falls under one of the other IRS-exempt categories. A specified Department of the Treasury form must be completed accurately. This form requires a statement of the

*No matter how the center is organized, individual attention to each child is essential.*

organization's sources of financial support, fund-raising program, purpose, activities (past, present, and future), relationship to other organizations, and policies (for example, nondiscrimination). This lengthy form also requires a statement of revenue and expenses and a list of governing board members. The process is time-consuming and expensive, often taking months to complete and costing thousands of dollars. However, centers that operate on a not-for-profit basis are subject to fewer taxes. For example, with the proper documentation, they usually are exempt from sales tax as well as some federal taxes. Exemption from state and local taxes, including sales tax, is often tied to exemption from federal income tax, but application for exemption must be made to each taxing body.

Because tax law is subject to change, the director and board must keep abreast of new requirements. New directors moving in to existing centers must check to see that the documents are in order and that proper procedures are being followed. Every director must be informed about current tax and reporting requirements of the federal, state, and local governments. Not knowing is not an acceptable excuse for improper filing and reporting.

When donors make contributions to a not-for-profit center, they may be allowed to deduct the amount on their federal income tax subject to applicable tax laws. It is common courtesy to send a written acknowledgement to each contributor, stating the amount of the contribution and the monetary benefit received, if any. Furthermore, your letter may enable the contributor to document a tax deduction. In the event that a not-for-profit program ceases operation, its assets must be donated to another not-for-profit organization. Although nonprofits can obtain grants, writing grant requests takes time, effort, and skill. Typically, grants do not cover the capital needed to start a program or cover operating costs.

The profit versus not-for-profit issue is complex. Organizations are advised to consult with attorneys and tax advisers before making this type of decision. When there is a corporate center's board, it will have an important role in this decision making.

---

## 4-2 THE EARLY CHILDHOOD CENTER BOARD

Board membership, board duties, committee structure, and board operations vary, depending on the size and type of center and on the relationship of the center to a sponsoring or funding agency. Despite the inevitable variation in the structure and function of center boards, you will be better equipped to assist in establishing a board or to work with an existing board if you have some basic information about governing boards and how they operate.

The center's director, who is responsible to the board, implements the center's program as mandated by the board. The board's major role is making policy. The director then creates procedures to carry out those policies. In practice, board involvement runs the gamut from heavy involvement with the center to deferment of all the work to the director. In the former situation, the board carries out all the functions described in this chapter and then charges the director with full responsibility to act on decisions that the board has reached. In the latter case, the board does not question the rationale or philosophical basis for the recommendations presented by the director for board review and gives carte blanche approval. Ideally, a board should function somewhere between these two extremes by carrying out some functions related to personnel, finance, facility, and program and by keeping in close contact with the director who also is working on fiscal and program matters. Although some proprietary centers operate without the guidance of a governing group, the organizational structure of most agency-sponsored and public-funded programs includes a board of directors.

When the center is an arm of another agency, such as a church-sponsored child care program, the agency board may serve as the governing board, sometimes with representation from the center. In other cases, an advisory committee for the center is formed. As the name implies, the role of the advisory committee is much less structured, and the committee has less authority than a board. When an early childhood program is part of a public school system, the principal often assumes many of the director's responsibilities, and a lead teacher assumes others. The actual board then is the elected board of education. Because of the great variation among organizations, the center's director may have several administrative levels above her. Generally, she reports to her immediate supervisor, one level above her position. Decisions may be made at a higher level in some cases.

## 4-3 BOARD MEMBERSHIP

Most well-planned boards consist of 10 to 20 members who are either elected or appointed to board positions. A board operates most efficiently when its size is small enough for members to know each other and feel comfortable about speaking out when issues are being discussed, yet large enough for members to cover all the committee assignments required to conduct business without overworking any board members. Tenure for board members is specified in the bylaws. Requirements for board membership are based on program philosophy and needs, state laws, and sponsoring agency mandates.

When for-profit corporations involve very large organizations, usually the parent organization manages all the centers by providing regional supervisors (a variety of titles may be used). In this case, because the corporation operates on a major business model and may be traded on a stock exchange, the board also operates commensurate with the rest of the organization. Board members are chosen from a national perspective and usually are paid. Shareholders vote for the board members, and their vote is weighted based on the number of shares they own. Shareholders are invited to the company's annual meeting, although rarely do small shareholders attend due to lack of knowledge, lack of influence, and inconvenience of travel distance. The boards described in the next sections refer to those affiliated with individual centers or small groups of centers. A center may also establish a local board when it is part of a very large agency. Such a board usually will not have fiduciary responsibility.

### 4-3a Selection of Board Members

At the outset, boards may be made up entirely of appointed members. After the bylaws are developed and incorporation is accomplished, ensuing boards usually are elected by a regulated process required by law and stated in the bylaws. When a director, a board, or a nominating committee chooses people to be appointed or elected to an early childhood education center's board, the background and personality of the candidates and the current board composition must be considered.

The nominating committee should create a process that will allow it to fill board positions effectively and efficiently. The committee may begin by deciding the types of people who are needed on the board. As the organization's circumstances change, the kinds of board members needed also may change. Although a variety of professionals can be valuable board assets, their expertise should not be exploited. Their perspectives will help guide the board, but when particular professional advice is needed, the board should allocate funds and employ someone not on the board. For example, although it may be advisable to have a physician on the board, that person's role should be one of commitment to the whole program rather than to the health needs only (Bess & Ratekin, 1999). When an organization and a board are small and in a start-up phase, some professionals may be willing to join the board and provide guidance that would not be needed for an established program. They may be serving out of friendship for the director or based on community spirit. Finally, consideration should be given to developing a board with diverse membership.

---

## MAKING THE CASE FOR *DIVERSE BOARD MEMBERSHIP*

Our society is becoming increasingly diverse, and board membership should reflect this diversity. Having a diverse board sends the message to staff, families, and the community that your program values unique perspectives and personalities. According to the National Council of Nonprofits, when diversity exists, "each person will bring to his or her own personal and professional contacts and life experiences to their service on a nonprofit board. With a diversity of experience, expertise, and perspectives, a nonprofit is in a stronger position to face opportunities and challenges" (National Council of Nonprofits, n.d.). The Council also notes specific benefits of diverse boards:

- Programs have greater opportunities to form relationships with potential donors or important policymakers in the community.

- Diversity of membership will increase the organization's ability to access resources in the community.

- When challenges or important decisions arise, the presence of diverse beliefs and perspectives will enable the board to identify potential risks and opportunities.

Diversity is more than politically correct, it is essential!

---

Professionals from the fields of health, education, finance, and law often are asked to serve on child care center boards. These professionals can provide support in decision making in their areas and often volunteer time and expertise to help solve problems. For example, the physician who is a board member may direct the board to accurate information about health practices in the center, or the accountant may help draw up the budget and prepare for an audit. A media specialist or a board member who can write effective proposals and has contacts with various funding sources can be a real asset. A person with knowledge of special education may support the board in its efforts to meet requirements of the Americans with Disabilities Act and may help the center's staff address issues related to inclusion of children with disabilities. A computer specialist also may be a valuable asset as a director ponders what types of hardware or software are best for the center. Some boards reserve a percentage of slots for parents, and a teacher also may be a member, although usually a nonvoting one.

After the nominating committee has decided on the types of members needed, it may solicit suggestions from existing board members. After creating a master list, the committee begins contacting potential candidates, explaining that it is considering board and committee nominees to determine interest. The committee may send interested persons an information sheet about the organization, including the purpose and philosophy, as well as job descriptions of board and committee members. Each potential candidate may be invited to tour the center. Then, the committee may interview several potential candidates and recommend putting them on the board slate or on a committee until a board opening occurs. No new board member should be surprised when asked to serve on a committee or when asked to contribute and solicit funds for the organization. Board members should be prepared to be active and committed to the organization.

Large agencies usually provide liability coverage for board members, but smaller organizations may be unable to afford this coverage. Nonetheless, board members usually are legally liable for the center's operation. Prospective board members should be informed that they will need to provide their own liability coverage if that is the case. Director liability is controlled by state law. Additional information on this important topic can be obtained from your insurance agent or attorney.

## ▶❚❚ TeachSource Video Vignette

`01:03:49:50`

### Leadership Practices in Child Development Centers: Orientation of Board Members

Effective boards are typically comprised of members from both inside and outside the field of early childhood. Although they bring their own professional experiences to the work, they do not necessarily have enough background in early childhood to be able to contribute fully. View the video Vignette entitled *Leadership Practices in Child Development Centers* as an example of what might be included in your board's orientation. Reflect on the following questions:

**1.** What segments from the video would be useful to helping board members obtain information about the complexities of managing a center?

**2.** What additional information would you provide board members at the orientation?

## 4-3b Orientating Board Members

New board members should be expected to participate in an orientation program led by the chair of the nominating committee. Board officers may be asked to participate, both to welcome the new members and to explain their components of the organization. Before this session, each should receive a board book, preferably a loose-leaf binder, containing the following:

- welcome
- board members' names, addresses, and pictures
- mission statement
- bylaws
- strategic plan
- board committees
- minutes from the past year
- fiscal statements from past year
- current year budget
- center's information, including philosophy, number of children and ages served, and calendar
- your state's guidelines for nonprofit board members

At the orientation, new members should learn about the role of the nonprofit agency board and should be alerted to the differences between the roles of board and staff. As a result, new members should be ready for their first meeting with a basic understanding of current and recent issues and decisions. They should enter the meeting knowing a few of the members and should be greeted individually by others. This approach helps new members recognize that they are valued and that the board functions in a businesslike manner with positive interpersonal interactions (Bess & Ratekin, 2000).

Those who have not served on a center board previously may have the misperception that as a volunteer, they are serving in an honorary or advisory capacity. As a result, the board orientation should include information about the specific leadership, fiduciary, and related legal responsibilities that accompany the position. Additional information about board membership can be obtained from the National Council of Nonprofits or your state attorney general's website.

## 4-3c Terms for Board Membership

Continuity in board membership is important. Therefore, many boards elect members for a three-year term, allowing for one-third of the members to be new each year. To achieve this ratio, the initial board members draw lots to determine who will hold three-, two-, and one-year terms. This time frame may not be workable for parent members who may not feel comfortable about joining the board until their child has been at the center for a while or who may no longer be interested after their child has left the center.

Although continuity is valuable, stagnation may occur when board members serve for too long. Consequently, bylaws should contain a provision for a limited number of terms of board service. Provision also should be made for replacing members whose attendance is poor. When a board member resigns, an exit interview may provide insight regarding possible changes in board operation. Members who feel overworked or undervalued may choose not to complete a full term.

## 4-4 BOARD DUTIES

Board members are responsible for the leadership and governance of the program and for "taking the care and exercising the judgment that any reasonable and prudent person would exhibit in the process of making informed decisions" (Renz, 2010, p. 128). This legal responsibility is known as the Duty of Care. The Duty of Loyalty requires members to "consider and act in good faith to advance the interests of the organization" (p. 128). The third fundamental responsibility is to demonstrate the Duty of Obedience, "which requires obedience to the organization's mission, bylaws, and policies, as well as honoring the terms and conditions of other standards of appropriate behavior such as laws, rules, and regulations" (p. 129).

Board members must be ready to thoughtfully, yet quickly, modify the organization's mission and practices to meet their communities' changing needs and values. They must also be prepared to find funding that is commensurate with the growing recognition of the importance of providing well-prepared staff. More specifically, the board is responsible for drawing up the bylaws for the center's operation. Subsequently, the board makes policy decisions and provisions for the operation of the center.

*Board members may be invited when a special activity is planned at the center, and they are always welcome to visit.*

## 4-4a Drawing Up Bylaws

Bylaws for operation of the center are written by the board and should contain the following points:

- name and purpose of the organization
- composition of the board of directors, including information about when and by whom its members are elected or appointed, their duties and terms of office
- description of the process by which officers are selected, including terms of office, duties, and election or appointment procedures
- policies related to the removal of directors or officers when necessary
- frequency of meetings or minimum number of meetings to be held annually
- standing committees and their composition and duties
- relationship of staff to board
- rules governing the conduct of meetings
- provisions for an annual meeting
- procedures for amending the bylaws
- procedures for dissolution of the corporation

Other items may be added to meet the needs of a particular board.

Bylaws should be extensive enough to meet legal requirements and to guide the board. However, when bylaws are too detailed, the board's operation is hampered. Furthermore, changes to bylaws appropriately involve rather detailed procedures that become burdensome if changes must be made frequently. For example, the bylaws should not list the specific month of the annual meeting or the exact number of board members.

Along with the establishment of bylaws, the board works on developing or revising (if needed) the organization's mission statement. The board may also create a vision statement, describing the future to be expected if the mission is carried out according to strategic planning.

## 4-4b Making Policy

After the mission and philosophy have been established, the board sets goals for the program based on the philosophy and purpose. If goals have already been established prior to the formation of the board, the board formally adopts them. The board then informs the director and staff about the philosophy and goals that form the basis for establishing the objectives for the daily program. In some cases, a knowledgeable director can take a leadership role in guiding the board's decision making about philosophy and goals that reflect sound theories. In any case, the board establishes policies, and the director uses these policies as the basis for formulation of procedures. A *policy* is a course of action that guides future decisions. A *procedure* is a series of steps to be followed, usually in a specific order, to implement policies.

---

**DIRECTOR'S CORNER**

"Our staff seemed rather mystified about the board—who they were and what they did. Many board members needed to know more about the center. One of our teachers volunteered to take pictures of the staff and board members and to make a montage of the photos. Afterward, we had an old-fashioned ice cream social, with board members serving the ice cream."

—*Director, early childhood center*

Creation of policies based on the center's philosophy should lead to a cohesive approach to the center's operation. This systemic approach facilitates staff commitment to the overall program because it has been made transparent. Ensuing decisions then will be consistent because they will be based on established policy.

Issues such as required orientation for all new staff should be in policy form, accompanied by procedures such as who will orient staff and what will be included. Regarding personnel, a policy might be, "Written personnel policies will be provided to all employees during their orientation." Procedures for signing in, getting a substitute, or holding parent conferences may be included. Policies regarding board membership and responsibilities should be in place in addition to the statements included in the bylaws. A policy regarding when the bylaws will be reviewed for possible revision should also be included. Because the policies should not be changed without serious consideration, the board should make them general and flexible enough so that the director is able to implement them without disregarding the goals of the center and without being required to request policy changes every time a new circumstance arises.

Procedures are more detailed than policies. Their purpose is to provide an implementation plan that is clear and uniform. Fire drill procedures or procedures for checking out material from the storeroom are good examples. Procedures also may be written for using the building after the children leave, for using equipment in the multipurpose room, or for filling a staff vacancy.

Policy decisions regarding personnel and program are ultimately subject to board approval; in practice, they are often made by the director with official board approval becoming a formality. Occasionally, an involved, knowledgeable board will scrutinize policies presented by a director, often asking for the rationale to support each policy. In some instances, staff and program policies are actually written by board members.

The type of program offered and the population served are both program policies subject to board approval. Decisions about the number and age span of children, the method of selection, and the population served are all board decisions. Examples include decisions about setting up the program schedule to include after-school care or care for children on a part-time basis. Although these policy decisions are usually based on the director's recommendations, the board makes the final determination.

Written policies and procedures are essential, but avoid creating so many that all creativity is eliminated. In fact, in a field such as early childhood education, it is impossible to predict exactly what will happen from day to day.

## 4-4c Operating the Center

The board is responsible for making provisions for the operation of the center. The major decisions in this category are as follows:

- selecting a director
- providing for appropriate staff members and for their suitable, in-service training opportunities
- providing facilities and equipment
- preparing or approving the budget and overseeing the finances of the center
- writing proposals and obtaining funding, including setting rates of tuition
- complying with local, state, and federal laws
- evaluating the operation of the program and the work of the director, and assisting the director in the evaluation of other staff
- arranging for an annual audit of financial records
- arbitrating problems between the staff and the director that cannot be resolved by the director
- replacing the director, as needed, and dismissing the director as the situation warrants

After provisions are made for operating the program, it becomes the director's responsibility to implement the program. At this point, the director becomes accountable to the board for the total program operation.

## 4-5 BOARD COMMITTEES

Board work is usually done by committees. **naeyc** Each standing committee has a charge that is spelled out in the bylaws. When all the standing committees are in place and working, the basic board functions are carried out. As special needs arise, ad hoc board committees are appointed by the board chairperson to perform specific, short-term tasks and report to the board. When the task has been completed, the committee is dissolved.

The board chairperson appoints members to each standing committee based on their interest and expertise and makes an attempt to balance the membership on committees by gender, race, age, point of view, and type of skill. Some boards have special requirements for committee membership. For example, the bylaws may state that each committee must have a parent member or a community representative.

Board committees convene at intervals that correspond to meeting the demands of their workload. When a center is being formed, most committees are extremely active; however, in an ongoing program, some committees have activity peaks. For example, the building committee deals with building maintenance, which is fairly routine. But if a decision is made to remodel, relocate, or build a new facility, the building committee becomes very active.

Decisions about the number and types of standing committees needed to carry out the board functions are made when the bylaws are written. Some of the typical standing committees include executive, personnel, finance, building, program, and nominating.

## 4-5a Executive Committee

The executive committee is composed of the board's officers with the center director often serving as an ex officio member. The executive committee advises the chairperson on actions to be taken, on changes to be made, and on committee assignments. This committee conducts board business between meetings and acts in place of the total board in emergency situations. However, it is critical that the executive committee plan far enough in advance to avoid as many "emergency" situations as possible, lest the way be opened for making important decisions without total board participation. Board members will become disgruntled and fail to contribute time or energy to board business if they find that crucial decisions are being made outside official board meetings. Whenever possible, board decisions should be made by the total board. In some situations, it may be illegal for the executive committee to make decisions.

---

### DIRECTOR'S CORNER

"My business partner and I decided to add a second site and to incorporate since our business was growing. At first, the board was just a few relatives. But gradually we realized that we needed people who could really help with the management and oversight of the corporation, particularly when we needed additional investors. Now we have a working board that helps keep us focused on the fact that an early childhood program that is good for children and families must be run as a business."

*—Director and president, incorporated for-profit center*

---

## 4-5b Personnel Committee

The personnel committee is responsible for hiring a director who will adhere to the philosophy of the center and implement the policies established by the board. To accomplish this task, the committee advertises the position, conducts the interviews, and prepares the director's contract. The personnel committee also is responsible for firing the director if that becomes necessary.

Personnel committee members usually assist the director in writing job descriptions, interviewing job candidates, and discussing the merits of each applicant. After these steps are completed, the hiring recommendations are made to the total board for final approval. Other boards set the basic criteria for staff members and set hiring and terminating employees as the director's responsibility.

In small centers where there is no evaluation committee, personnel committee members may be asked to conduct the evaluation process. In this capacity, the committee determines the method of evaluation, carries out the evaluation of the director, and monitors the director's evaluation of the staff and program.

## 4-5c Finance Committee

Because they prepare the budget and appropriate the funds, finance committee members must understand the program's overall operation and the way in which the operation relates to the program philosophy. In situations in which the director prepares the budget and secures the funds, the finance committee approves the budget, monitors the record keeping, and arranges for the annual audit. In some centers, the finance committee sets salary schedules and reviews bids for major purchases. This committee also should teach board members how to read financial statements and what they mean.

## 4-5d Building Committee

The responsibility for finding and maintaining a facility suitable for the type of program being offered rests with the building (or facility) committee. Prior to starting a center or establishing a new facility, the committee spends an extraordinary amount of time making decisions about purchasing, constructing, or leasing a building. The committee is responsible for locating the new facility or the construction site. Building committee members work closely with the architect when the construction or remodeling is in progress and must remember to involve the director who presumably has the most knowledge of what the center needs.

*The director and the board treasurer meet to review the financial report.*

The building committee is responsible for seeing that the building and grounds are clean, safe, and attractive. Preventive maintenance and emergency repairs also are authorized by this committee. Although directors usually manage the details of applying for a license and arranging for necessary changes at the center to keep the program and facility in compliance with licensing standards, the building committee may be the one designated by the board to monitor licensing.

Many boards also assign the building committee responsibility for the center's equipment. The director must obtain the approval of the committee on major equipment orders, and the committee sanctions orders after considering whether the suggested purchases are suitable, in both type and quantity, and are within the budget. The committee members may also ascertain whether the equipment is properly stored, maintained, and inventoried.

The building committee makes long-range plans by considering questions such as the center's future building needs. It projects the type and amount of space that will be needed and plans for ways to meet those needs. Equipment needs are considered in a similar way. Long-range planning prevents the board from suddenly finding that a major addition or repair is needed when no funds are available. Long-range planning also enables the center to stagger the purchase of equipment so that the quality and quantity are constantly maintained at a high level and so that the budget is not suddenly unbalanced by the need to replace large quantities of worn-out equipment.

## 4-5e Program Committee

The responsibility for all center programs ultimately rests with the program committee; however, in practice, any work on the program is handled completely by the director and the staff. The children's program, the parent program, and the in-service program for staff all may be under the auspices of the program committee. The committee recommends policies to the board focusing on the enrollment and grouping of children; the hours and days of operation; and the offering of ancillary services such as health, nutrition, and social services. Some boards set up separate committees for medical services and social services if these are major components of the center's program. These separate committees are responsible for working with the director to determine what services are needed, where, and at what cost they can be obtained. The committees also may help with transportation arrangements to the medical center, if required, and with recruitment of volunteers to assist children and families needing special social or educational services.

## 4-5f Nominating Committee

The nominating committee's function is twofold. Potential members of the board are screened by the committee, which also prepares the slate of board officers for election by the board. The process should be open, and the committee should check with prospective members for permission to nominate them.

A separate committee may be set up for the orientation of new board members, or the nominating committee may serve in this capacity. Continuing the process begun at nomination, the committee ensures that new board members understand their duties and the operating procedures of the board.

**Working Smart with Technology**

*Communicating with Board Members*

Regular and deliberate communication with board members and committees is an important responsibility of the director, and technology can simplify this process considerably. Email distribution lists or listservs can be used to share center news as well as information related to ongoing management issues, committee work, and developing concerns. Additionally, sending agendas and related background information prior to the meeting dates enhances the efficiency of meetings. Make sure that you check with board members to request the email address they want you to use for the purpose of sharing center mailings, and be cautious about flooding their inboxes with center mail.

*Directors can use technology to communicate with Board members on a regular basis to keep them informed of important management issues and decisions.*

## 4-6 BOARD COMMUNICATION

From the committee descriptions, it should be obvious that the functions of the committees are interrelated and that communication among committees is essential. For example, the building committee must know what kind of plans the program committee is making in order to provide an appropriate facility. However, the building committee cannot choose a facility without an understanding of how much the finance committee plans to allocate for physical space. To avoid duplication of efforts, each committee's task must be delineated clearly. Sometimes, a board member may be assigned to two closely related committees to facilitate communication between them. Care must be taken to divide the work of the board equitably among its members and to see that every board member is involved in and aware of the operations of the board and of the center.

The board shares responsibility with the director for maintaining open communication within the board itself and among the board, the sponsoring agency, the staff, and the families who use the center's services. The most successful boards are those whose members communicate effectively with the center's director and with each other. Both the board and the director have responsibilities here, and providing training in interpersonal communication for all concerned may be worthwhile. If staff and board members both attend the training sessions, communication skills are improved, staff and board members become better acquainted with each other's values, and the outcome is a greater sense of community among those people who are responsible for the center's operation. An obvious place to start is to make sure that new board members are introduced and that continuing board members also introduce themselves. Taking new board members on a tour of the facility and introducing them to the staff is another way to foster communication. When board members and staff members have developed effective communication skills, all will be expected to use the skills. Ideas will be expressed and considered openly; likewise, disagreements will be stated specifically and objectively. Board and staff members lacking these skills may be less willing to address problems directly, with the result that disagreements may not be resolved, and factions may develop within the organization.

As with all good communication, the communication between the board and the staff is two-way. The board informs the director of policies that have been formulated because the director is responsible for seeing that the policies are executed. The board also explains the reasons for its decisions and approaches any necessary changes in a positive way instead of in a dictatorial manner. The director, in turn, communicates to the board any difficulties the staff is having with the existing policies or suggests policy changes, providing reasons for these changes. For example, if the director finds a number of parents asking for a program for their 2-year-olds, the suggestion is presented to the board and is supported with arguments for and/or against the admission of 2-year-olds. Facts concerning the type of services that could be provided, the facilities available, the cost of such a program, and the advisability from an educational standpoint also should be presented to the board. Considering the data and the recommendation of the director, the board makes the final decision about the admission of 2-year-olds.

The board is responsible for using the director's recommendations and all other pertinent data in formulating policy. Policy decisions must be based on sound data so that they are fiscally responsible, developmentally and educationally sound, and legal. They must also follow good business practice and be realistic. For example, a policy requiring the director to be on duty whenever the center is open may seem sound but will be unrealistic in practice in a child care center that operates for 10 hours a day. Similarly, a board policy requiring the director to hire only well-qualified teachers with ECE bachelor's degrees would make the hiring task nearly impossible if available salaries are held at or near the minimum-wage level. Because the director is mandated to carry out board policy, the board ideally gives careful consideration to her recommendations to ensure that final policy is mutually agreeable and feasible.

The board serves as the communications liaison between the center's program and the sponsoring agency. The director keeps the board informed about the center's functioning by sending the board members copies of newsletters, special bulletins, and meeting notices; by reporting at board meetings; and by presenting a written report to the board at least annually. Board members may be invited when a special activity is planned at the center, and they are always welcome to visit. The board, in turn, communicates to the sponsoring agency by reporting regularly to the agency board. This type of communication is two-way in that the board also receives information from the sponsoring agency concerning the expectations of the sponsoring group.

### DIRECTOR'S CORNER

"I know that our board members are really interested in our program, but they aren't early childhood educators. So I have to make sure they understand the needs of the center and of our staff. I put a lot of effort into making sure key persons are well informed. Maybe I'll have lunch with the board chairperson or talk about an idea I have over coffee. You definitely don't want to surprise your chairperson with a new idea during a meeting."

—*Director, agency-sponsored child care and education center*

For example, a community group may provide partial funding for the center with the stipulation that it be used to provide training for a staff member or parent program, or a church sponsor may expect preferential admissions for members' families. As long as these stipulations and expectations are compatible with the center's philosophy and are legal, they should be fulfilled.

## 4-7 BOARD INVOLVEMENT IN CENTER OPERATION

When a new center is starting up, the board [naeyc] must meet frequently—even daily—during very busy planning periods. However, in ensuing years, boards may meet monthly, quarterly, or in some cases annually. When the board is working closely with the director and is intimately involved in policy making, monthly meetings are essential. On the other hand, the board that assigns most of the decision making to the director may meet only annually to receive the director's report; approve the budget for the ensuing year; and make any adjustments in goals, policies, or procedures that seem necessary. Notice how unrewarding service on such a board might be.

The board that meets frequently contributes to the operation of the center by working closely with the director and by using fully the skills of all board members. The board that meets less frequently provides the director with maximum freedom to operate on day-to-day matters, although within definite guidelines. Each board must decide which alternative seems to be more appropriate for the type of center being planned, and the director is chosen to fit into the selected method of operation.

Although each board has its own style, board meetings must be conducted according to recognized parliamentary procedures that may be covered in the by-laws. In large, formal organizations, a parliamentarian who is appointed or elected ensures that business meetings are conducted according to the procedures adopted. Although too much formality may be uncomfortable for some board members, total informality leads to loose practices, with disputes arising over decisions that are based on improper voting procedures or other points of order.

The board of an incorporated center is obligated by law to conduct its business in an organized manner and to keep accurate records of all transactions. In situations in which record keeping is not required by law, it is just sensible business practice to operate an agency in an orderly manner. Therefore, minutes of all board meetings, committee reports, and financial records must be kept. Copies of contracts and agreements, job descriptions, and correspondence also should be in the files.

---

### REFLECTION

Consider how you might work most effectively as a director. Would you prefer a board that left the decision making to you and expected an annual report about what you had done? Or would you prefer a situation in which you had to check back with people in authority on a regular basis to get the benefit of their thinking, after which you would follow their lead as you continued your work? You may be able to relate this idea to college classes in which you operated independently and received feedback from your instructor only on the final exam, compared with classes in which you regularly submitted written work throughout the course and subsequently received information from your instructor about your work. It would be wise to give careful consideration to your own needs and administrative style before accepting a directorship.

---

## SUMMARY

There are key questions to be decided when new centers are being planned:

- What business structure will be selected for the new center: sole proprietorship, partnership, franchise or corporation? Will this be a profit or not-for-profit center?

- Based on the type of program selected, will the program have a board of directors?

- What considerations exist when selecting and orienting board members?

- What responsibilities will board members be expected to carry out in supporting the work of the center?

- What board committees are required to assist with conducting the work of the center?

- How will open communication with board members be carried out by the director?

- What is the board's role in creating policy that results in a well-organized center?

# TRY IT OUT!

1. Visit your state government's website. Search for information about serving on nonprofit organization boards. (In many cases, this will be the attorney general's website.) Discuss with classmates the following questions:

   a. What type of information is provided related to board member responsibilities?

   b. Based on the requirements and responsibilities, what types of people would be important for you to include as board members?

2. Interview (or invite to class) a director of an early childhood center that has a board of directors. Ask the following questions, and then compare responses with members of your class:

   a. How are members chosen?

   b. What type of orientation is provided for new board members?

   c. How long is a member's term?

   d. What are the duties of board members?

   e. How often does the board meet?

   f. Are minutes of each meeting kept?

   g. What is the relationship between the director and the board?

   h. Is the director a voting member of the board?

   i. What challenges have you experienced working with a board?

   j. If the center does not have a board, who carries out the responsibilities that would have been met by the board?

3. Obtain a copy of the bylaws of an early childhood organization with which you are associated or of any type of community agency. (Consider your YMCA, your church group, PTA, and so forth.) In class, compare and contrast the bylaws of the group you select with the bylaws provided by other students.

   a. How are they similar in structure?

   b. What are the substantive differences?

   c. How do the differences in the documents reflect the differences in the purposes of the organizations?

4. Investigate the process that must be followed in your state to start a for-profit or nonprofit center for young children. Review the forms that must be filed to incorporate your center. (See Director's Resource 4-1 for a sample.) You may find the information you need on your state's secretary of state website or by using library resources.

## DIRECTOR'S RESOURCE 4-1

## INITIAL ARTICLES OF INCOPORATION – NONPROFIT

**JON HUSTED**
OHIO SECRETARY OF STATE

180 East Broad Street, Suite 103 (ground floor) • Columbus, Ohio 43215
Toll Free: (877) SOS-FILE (767-3453)  Central Ohio: (614) 466-3910
www.OhioSecretaryofState.gov • busserv@OhioSecretaryofState.gov

**Please return the approval certificate to:**

Name: _____
(Individual or Business Name)

To the attention of: _____
(If necessary)

Address: _____

City: _____

State: _____  ZIP Code: _____

Phone Number: _____  E-mail Address: _____

☐ Check here if you would like to receive important notices via e-mail from the Ohio Secretary of State's office regarding Business Services.

☐ Check here if you would like to be signed up for our Filing Notification System for the business entity being created or updated by filing this form. This is a free service provided to notify you via e-mail when any document is filed on your business record.

Type of Service Being Requested:  (PLEASE CHECK **ONE** BOX BELOW)

○ **Regular Service:** Only the filing fee listed on page one of the form is required and the filing will be processed in approximately 3-7 business days.  The processing time may vary based on the volume of filings received by our office.

○ **Expedite Service 1:** By including an Expedite fee of $100.00, **in addition** to the regular filing fee on page one of the form, the filing will be processed within 2 business days after it is received by our office.

○ **Expedite Service 2:** By including an Expedite fee of $200.00, **in addition** to the regular filing fee on page one of the form, the filing will be processed within 1 business day after it is received by our office. **This service is only available to walk-in customers who hand deliver the document to the Client Service Center.**

○ **Expedite Service 3:** By including an Expedite fee of $300.00, **in addition** to the regular filing fee on page one of the form, the filing will be processed within 4 hours after it is received by our office, if received by 1:00 p.m.  **This service is only available to walk-in customers who hand deliver the document to the Client Service Center.**

○ **Preclearance Filing:** A filing form, to be submitted at a later date for processing, may be submitted to be examined for the purpose of advising as to the acceptability of the proposed filing for a fee of $50.00. The Preclearance will be complete within 1-2 business days.

---

## DIRECTOR'S RESOURCE 4-1 (continued)

Form 532B Prescribed by:
**JON HUSTED**
**Ohio Secretary of State**

Central Ohio: (614) 466-3910
Toll Free: (877) SOS-FILE (767-3453)
www.OhioSecretaryofState.gov
Busserv@OhioSecretaryofState.gov

Mail this form to one of the following:
Regular Filing (non expedite)
P.O. Box 670
Columbus, OH 43216
Expedite Filing (Two-business day processing time requires an additional $100.00).
P.O. Box 1390
Columbus, OH 43216

### Initial Articles of Incorporation
(Nonprofit, Domestic Corporation)
Filing Fee: $125
(114-ARN)

**First:** Name of Corporation _____

**Second:** Location of Principal office in Ohio
_____
City _____ State _____
_____
County

**Effective Date (Optional)** _____ mm/dd/yyyy  (The legal existence of the corporation begins upon the filing of the articles or on a later date specified that is not more than ninety days after filing)

**Third:** Purpose for which corporation is formed
_____

\**Note for Nonprofit Corporations:** The Secretary of State does not grant tax exempt status. Filing with our office is not sufficient to obtain state or federal tax exemptions. Contact the Ohio Department of Taxation and the Internal Revenue Service to ensure that the nonprofit corporation secures the proper state and federal tax exemptions. These agencies may require that a purpose clause be provided.

\**Note:** ORC Chapter 1702 allows for additional provisions to be included in the Articles of Incorporation that are filed with this office. If including any of these additional provisions, please do so by including them in an attachment to this form.

---

## DIRECTOR'S RESOURCE 4-1 (continued)

**ORIGINAL APPOINTMENT OF STATUTORY AGENT**

The undersigned, being at least a majority of the incorporators of _____ hereby appoint the following to be statutory agent upon whom any process, notice or demand required or permitted by statute to be served upon the corporation may be served.  The complete address of the agent is

_____
Name

_____
Mailing Address

_____
City _____ State _____ Zip Code

Must be signed by the Incorporators or a majority of the incorporators

_____
Signature

_____
Signature

_____
Signature

**ACCEPTANCE OF APPOINTMENT**

The Undersigned, _____ , named herein as the
Statutory Agent Name

Statutory agent for _____
Corporation Name

hereby acknowledges and accepts the appointment of statutory agent for said corporation.

Statutory Agent Signature _____
Individual Agent's Signature / Signature on behalf of Corporate Agent

☐ If the agent is an individual and using a P.O. Box, check this box to confirm the agent is an Ohio resident.

---

## DIRECTOR'S RESOURCE 4-1 (continued)

By signing and submitting this form to the Ohio Secretary of State, the undersigned hereby certifies that he or she has the requisite authority to execute this document.

**Required**
Articles and original appointment of agent must be signed by the incorporator(s).

_____
Signature

If the incorporator is an individual, then they must sign in the "signature" box and print his/her name in the "Print Name" box.

_____
By

_____
Print Name

If the incorporator is a business entity, not an individual, then please print the entitiy name in the "signature" box, an authorized representative of the entity must sign in the "By" box and print his/her name and title/authority in the "Print Name" box.

_____
Signature

_____
By

_____
Print Name

_____
Signature

_____
By

_____
Print Name

_____
Signature

_____
By

_____
Print Name

Form 532B     Page 3 of 3

### Instructions for Initial Articles of Incorporation
### (For Domestic Nonprofit Corporation)

This form should be used if you wish to file articles of incorporation for a domestic nonprofit corporation.

**Name of Corporation**
As set forth in Ohio Revised Code §1702.05, the name must be distinguishable on the records in the office of the secretary of state.

**Ohio Principal Office Location**
Please provide the address in Ohio where the principal office of the corporation is to be located.

**Effective Date**
An effective date may be provided but is not required. Pursuant to Ohio Revised Code §1702.04(D), the legal existence of the corporation begins upon the filing of the articles or on a later date specified in the articles. The effective date cannot (1) precede the date of filing with our office or (2) be more than ninety (90) days after the date of filing. If an effective date is given that precedes the date of filing, the effective date of the corporation will be the date of filing. If an effective date is given that exceeds the date of filing by more than ninety (90) days, our office will return the filing to you and request that a proper effective date be provided.

**Purpose**
Pursuant to Ohio Revised Code §1702.03, a nonprofit corporation must provide a purpose in the articles. A nonprofit corporation may be formed for any purpose or purposes for which natural persons lawfully may associate themselves. **Note:** The Secretary of State does not grant tax exempt status. Filing with our office is not sufficient to obtain state or federal tax exemptions. Contact the Ohio Department of Taxation and the Internal Revenue Service to ensure that the nonprofit corporation secures the proper state and federal tax exemptions. These agencies may require that a purpose clause be provided.

**Additional Provisions**
If the information you wish to provide for the record does not fit on the form, please attach additional provisions on a single-sided, 8 ½ x 11 sheet(s) of paper.

**Original Appointment of Statutory Agent and Acceptance of Appointment**
Pursuant to Ohio Revised Code §1702.06, an Ohio Corporation must appoint and maintain a statutory agent to accept service of process on behalf of the corporation. We cannot accept articles of incorporation unless the statutory agent information is provided. The statutory agent must be one of the following: (1) an Ohio resident; (2) an Ohio corporation; or (3) a foreign corporation that is licensed to do business in Ohio and is authorized by its articles of incorporation to act as a statutory agent and that has a business address in Ohio.

If the statutory agent is an individual using P.O. Box address, they must also check the box below the address to state they are a resident of the state of Ohio. The statutory agent must also sign the Acceptance of Appointment at the bottom of page 2.

**Signature(s)**
After completing all information on the filing form, please make sure that page 3 is signed by the incorporator(s).

**\*\*Note: Our office cannot file or record a document which contains a social security number or tax identification number. Please do not enter a social security number or tax identification number, in any format, on this form.**

*Source: Ohio Secretary of State*

# REFERENCES

Bess, G., & Ratekin, C. (1999, May). Recruiting effective board members. *Child Care Information Exchange, 127*, 14–20.

Bess, G., & Ratekin, C. (2000, November). Orienting and evaluating your board of directors. *Child Care Information Exchange, 136*, 82–87.

Cohen, W. A. (2006). *The entrepreneur & small business problem solver* (3rd ed.). Hoboken, NJ: Wiley.

Greene, C. L. (2012). *Entrepreneurship: Ideas in action* (5th ed.). Stamford, CT: Cengage Learning.

Hall, P. D. (2010). Historical perspectives of nonprofit organizations in the United States. In D.O. Renz (Ed.), *The Jossey-Bass handbook of nonprofit leadership & management* (3rd ed., pp. 3–31). San Francisco: Jossey-Bass.

Hatten, T. S. (2011). *Small business management: Entrepreneurship and beyond* (5th ed.). Stamford, CT: Cengage Learning.

National Council of Nonprofits. (n.d.). *Diversity on boards*. Retrieved from http://www.councilofnonprofits.org/resources/resources-topic/boards-and-governance/diversity-boards.

Pinson, L., & Jinnett, J. (2006). *Steps to small business start-up: Everything you need to know to turn your idea into a successful business* (6th ed.). Chicago: Kaplan Publishing.

Renz, D. O. (2010). Leadership, governance, and the work of the board. In D.O. Renz & Associates (Eds.), *The Jossey-Bass handbook of nonprofit leadership & management* (3rd ed., pp. 125–156). San Francisco: Jossey-Bass.

*The director must be aware of the needs of all the stakeholders in the center. Ongoing communication with teachers can provide insight into how well needs are being met.*

## Learning Objectives

After reading this chapter, you should be able to:

**5-1**  Describe the process for creating a financial plan for a child care center.

**5-2**  Explain how to prepare and operate a budget.

**5-3**  Identify the financial responsibilities of a well-managed center.

## Standards Addressed in this Chapter

Accreditation Standard 10 – Leadership and Management

Administrator Competencies – Management Knowledge and Skills 2, 5, 10

Administrator Competencies Early – Childhood Knowledge and Skills 10 Professionalism
Preparation Standard 6 – Becoming a Professional

---

The director's role as one who sets the tone for the center has already been established, but the director also must be a pragmatist capable of dealing with all the financial obligations of running a center. To meet the needs of children, families, and staff within a balanced budget, a financial plan must be in place. A well-constructed financial plan is comprised of two major components: a system for managing financial resources and a means of obtaining adequate funding. This chapter focuses on financial planning while methods of funding the center are discussed in Chapter 6.

To effectively manage financial resources, the director must create policies and procedures that

- develop and follow a plan for using funds
- keep records, including those mandated by law
- provide required documentation

Every center needs both a long-range financial plan and a plan for the upcoming year. Poor financial planning and fiscal management can lead to a lack of funds, which will likely hinder personnel as they work to achieve program goals. High-quality care for young children is expensive, and funds must be allocated properly to provide a developmentally sound program on which children and parents can depend. No matter how well intentioned the staff, a program cannot continue to operate for long without a balanced budget and a reserve fund. Therefore, before publicity is in place, before staff are hired, and before detailed plans are made, the board must be sure that sufficient funds for start-up are available, keeping in mind that it may be many months before the revenue stream can offset the expense of a new child care center (see Chapter 6).

## 5-1    CREATING A FINANCIAL PLAN

In a new center or one that is reorganizing, **naeyc** a decision must be made regarding who will be responsible for the center's financial management. In a sole proprietorship or partnership, the owner/director may assume these duties. When the owner has hired a director, he may turn the responsibilities over to the director, while requiring regular reporting. In a corporation, the board is responsible. A corporate system may have a regional or national financial officer for all of the system's centers. Franchisees manage their own budgets within company constraints; for example, fees may be set by the parent company. No matter what the center's organizational structure is, someone must ultimately be responsible for fiscal management. Throughout this chapter, therefore, we will use *director* to include others who may bear responsibility. We will also assume the center could have a financial officer. When that is not the case, the director may have to assume all fiscal duties.

Usually, the director has some responsibility for creating and managing an annual budget. If a board is involved, the members bear ultimate responsibility. When a center has multiple sites, a financial officer may be part of the staff. This person would be expected to keep day-to-day records, produce financial reports, and consult regularly with the director.

### 5-1a Policies and Procedures

The policies and procedures manual must include a section on fiscal management. Although not all policies and procedures are reviewed annually, reviewing those related to finances helps everyone involved check to ensure that these requisites are being met. Following are some of the policies that must be in place:

- All financial transactions must be checked for accuracy.
- Standard accounting practices will be followed.
- The director will prepare a long-range fiscal plan.

- The annual operating budget will be prepared prior to the start of the fiscal year.
- The budget will be used as a guide throughout the year.
- Every financial transaction must be recorded in a specific location.
- Transactions must be recorded at least weekly, preferably daily.
- A business checking account must be used for all transactions.
- Personal funds and business funds must never be mingled, even if the owner is the director.
- All receipts must be deposited rather than used to pay bills.
- All payroll checks must be available to each employee on the expected date.
- All taxes must be paid by the required date.
- A budget variance report will be prepared at least quarterly.
- Money will be handled by two people, one to receive and record the funds and the second to deposit the funds and record the deposits.
- Amounts, due dates, and payment methods for tuition, as well as consequences of delinquent tuition, must be provided to parents.
- An income and expense statement and a balance sheet must be prepared annually.
- Reports to funders and requests for release of funds will be made on the required schedule.

This list is more detailed than most policy lists. Specific procedures for each of these policies must be written and placed in the policies and procedures manual, available for review by all staff. Spelling out financial requirements in detail can help avoid problems in the future. When staff knows what to expect, they are better able to implement policy and adjust their practice when needed.

> **REFLECTION**
>
> You have just read a long list of items that must be carried out by the business manager or director. Make a list of the items that are unfamiliar to you. Check the item off as soon as you learn about it. If you cannot find an explanation, ask your professor to provide more information on the topic. Directors must understand the center's finances. Imagine how much easier it will be to learn now rather than when you are a director in the midst of setting up or reorganizing a center.

The director works with staff to prepare policies that are clear and workable. He may spend part of a staff meeting discussing this topic, ask staff to submit suggestions, or prepare the policies and procedures with the financial officer and make them available for staff information.

Having the entire staff spend time writing financial policies is a poor use of their time. Encouraging the staff to provide input lets them know that their perspectives are valued and will be taken seriously by both director and staff.

---

## MAKING THE CASE FOR *STAFF INPUT INTO BUDGET PRIORITIES*

Highly effective directors are well informed **naeyc** about the needs of the center and consider staff input when constructing a budget. Obviously, the director is ultimately responsible for establishing the budget. However, staff feel more empowered when they are able to provide input to define the priorities. When budgets are tight, staff need to have enough information to understand why financial decisions are being made. Problems with morale can be minimized if staff members feel that they are part of the solution.

1. Provide staff with an opportunity to state their needs as part of the budget-building process.

2. Keep staff informed of the general financial condition of the center. Directors will need to find a balance between maintaining confidentiality and providing enough information to keep staff informed.

---

## 5-1b Establishing a Fiscal Calendar

Because there are so many important financial tasks, the director and the financial officer, when appropriate, must work together to create a calendar of due dates. Working backward, they schedule dates for reviews of drafts of the proposed budget. A review of the budget will be of interest to most staff, so time should be allowed for their input. Preparation of items, such as submission of withheld taxes to government offices, can be done by the financial officer as a routine matter but should appear on the calendar.

*Despite the need to attend to business matters, highly effective directors recognize that the center exists to support children's development.*

If your fiscal year begins January 1, the budget for the coming year should be under way in October. The board will be able to review preliminary numbers based on those from the current year, yet modified based on plans for the coming year. For example, a proposed staff raise might be included. By November, with recommendations for changes made, the budget should be resubmitted to the board with hopes of final approval. Because the financial records should be closed as of December 31, it is important that the new budget is ready for January 1.

## 5-1c Managing Payroll

A number of dates must be scheduled for payroll items. It is essential that staff receive paychecks on time. Preparing them is complex, however, even with advanced computer software. Each staff member's name, ID number, address, wage or salary (hourly, weekly, biweekly, or monthly), and local taxing district must be entered into the computer. The financial officer must contact federal, state, and local agencies to determine withholding rates, current minimum wage, overtime laws, Family and Medical Leave Act (FMLA) requirements, and any other laws that may affect payroll.

The employer must obtain a federal taxpayer ID number from the IRS because, before an employee is paid, the employer must make appropriate deductions from the amount earned. When submitting these deductions and the company's equal contribution, the company ID and the employee's ID are listed.

The financial officer is responsible for withholding from each person's pay the appropriate amount of money for various taxes as well as Social Security and other federal, state, and local payments that are required. The employer pays an amount equal to the percentage withheld from the employee's pay for Social Security and Medicare. The employer must also pay unemployment compensation and workers' compensation. These programs cover payments to the employee for job-related injuries, diseases, and disabilities that occur as a result of working conditions. These amounts must be put aside so they are available for submission to the respective governments on specified dates each quarter. The center may be charged interest and penalties if these payments are not timely or are for incorrect amounts. Your accountant can help you determine the taxes for which you are liable.

## 5-1d Health Care Costs

Quality and affordable health insurance is an important employee benefit that contributes to maintaining a quality staff and also impacts the budget. The role of the employer in providing health care has been the focus of media attention since the roll out of the Affordable Care Act in 2013. While expectations for employers have increased, the options for quality and affordable health insurance have also increased. It is important for directors to understand the new law and its implications for the budget.

The employer mandate of the Affordable Care Act states that starting January 1, 2015, employers with 50 or more full time equivalent (FTE) employees are required to provide health coverage to full-time employees or pay a tax penalty. "To avoid a payment for failing to offer health coverage, employers need to offer coverage to 70 percent of their full-time employees in 2015 and 95 percent in 2016 and beyond, helping employers that, for example, may offer coverage to employees with 35 or more hours, but not yet to that fraction of their employees who work 30 to 34 hours" (U.S. Treasury Department, 2014, p.1).

Supporting your employees in obtaining health care insurance can be an incentive for joining your organization, whereas not offering health care or keeping employees at a part-time status to avoid the cost of health care is likely to be a detractor for highly qualified teachers as they consider their employment options.

## 5-1e Tax Forms and Pay Roll

Whenever new employees are hired, the financial officer must obtain IRS form W-4 indicating the number of dependents they are claiming. Calculations for the amount of tax to be withheld are made on this basis. Each year, all employees may submit new forms if changes need to be made to the number of dependents. By January 31 annually, a statement of earnings and deductions must be provided to each employee who worked at the center during the year, even if they are no longer employed there.

When all the categories affecting pay are entered into payroll software, the deductions can be readily made. Nonetheless, because preparing the payroll accurately is challenging and time-consuming, quite a few centers hire a payroll company to take care of this aspect of their business. Still, the information must be collected and entered by the financial officer or by the contracting payroll company. The director is responsible for seeing that these requirements are fulfilled.

---

### REFLECTION

Think about the tuition paid by parents, particularly in regard to its relationship to the salaries paid by a center. Consider a situation in which a teacher's annual salary is $27,000, and the assistant teacher's annual salary is $18,000. With a total of $45,000 a year for salaries, 15 families would each pay $3,000 a year to cover these salaries alone. Unless the center has other sources of income, tuition costs also must cover costs of equipment, supplies, food, facilities, utilities, benefits, taxes, administration, and so forth. The last child will leave the center from 10 to 12 hours after the first child has arrived, so staff members will have to be present on a staggered schedule, and additional help will be needed, all of which will increase salary costs. What would tuition have to be to produce a profit for the program sponsors? Think about how much you will probably earn as a teacher in a child care center. If you were to earn minimum wage as a child care center teacher, working eight hours a day, five days a week for a year, what would your total salary be? If you were a parent earning minimum wage, how much could you afford to pay for child care?

---

Center directors must ensure that they comply with the Fair Labor Standards Act (FLSA). A number of complex issues and conflicting results of court cases make it difficult to determine who is considered a teacher for the purposes of FLSA. This determination can make a difference in whether an employer is required to provide overtime pay and pay for hours spent at in-service training and parent meetings "after hours."

The U.S. Department of Labor regulations of 2004, still in effect today, consider exempt from FLSA those staff members who are paid a regular salary of at least $23,660 annually, no matter how many hours they work. Their work must relate directly to the management or general business operations of the organization to be exempt. Keep in mind that professional advice is still important, especially when addressing complex legal matters.

Another major personnel policy relates to hours worked. Will staff be paid for break time, planning time, and required meeting time? Be sure to check labor laws before making this and other policies. Because many child care centers are open for 10 or more hours, no teacher is in a classroom for the entire program day. Therefore, many part-time staff members are employed. Will they have paid time to meet with the lead teacher? Will the center provide for an overlap in the schedules of the departing teacher and the arriving teacher so that the children's day is not disrupted?

## Planning Reports

Throughout the year, the director and others will need to know how close the center is to meeting budgetary projections. Is your enrollment on target? Is tuition being paid in a timely manner? Do you have enough cash on hand to meet payroll? Then, when the year is over, how did you fare? Was it a good year financially?

Reports that will help you determine the answers to these questions include a cash flow report, which can be prepared monthly; a variance report (monthly, quarterly, or annually); and an end-of-the-year balance sheet. Any of these reports that a center uses can be prescheduled on the annual calendar. We discuss their contents later in this chapter.

▶❙❙ **TeachSource Video Vignette**

### Financial Planning for Early Childhood Programs: Establishing a Budget

View the video vignette entitled *Financial Planning for Early Childhood Programs: Establishing a Budget.* Critical to the management of every well-run child care center is the development of the center's budget. The budget is a statement of the center's goals for one year stated in financial terms. Responsible fiscal management, in fact, starts with this important document. Watch this video to see Chief Financial Officer Clement James provide concrete and specific information about the development of a budget.

**1.** What is the difference between a variable expense and a fixed expense?

**2.** Which of these two types of expenses can be considered when a center needs to trim costs?

# 5-2 PREPARING AND OPERATING A BUDGET

A major task of the director or finance committee is the preparation of a budget. A budget is a plan or financial forecast usually set up for a period of one year. One section of the budget contains a list of income categories and dollar amounts; the other section shows a list of categories and dollar amounts for expenditures. The director's goal is to balance income and expenses and, in most cases, show a profit. Recall that in a for-profit center, the profit may be distributed to shareholders or used for the center. In a nonprofit or not-for-profit center, the profit stays with the center and can be saved to build financial reserves, can be used to reduce tuition, or can be spent on the center in some other way.

## 5-2a Types of Budgets

Budgets are classified in several ways. They may be based on the stage of development of the center, or they may be categorized according to the stage to which the budget itself has been carried. The creation of a new center demands one kind of budget while the ongoing operation of a center requires a budget of a different type.

The director prepares a budget by

- estimating the cost of the program (based in part on the center's goals)

- determining how much income will be available (see Chapter 6)

- seeking more income to equal expenditures, adjusting expenditures to equal income, or doing both

### Start-Up Budgets

The creation of a new center presents a crucial opportunity for the financial aplomb of the director. When a center is being created, the director prepares *two* budgets: the start-up budget and the operating budget. As discussed in Chapter 6, the *start-up budget* consists of all the expenses incurred in starting the center. These expenses include initial building expenses (down payment on the purchase of the building, the cost of building renovations, or rent deposit), the purchase of major equipment, the cost of publicizing the center, the director's salary for several months prior to the children's arrival, the deposit on telephone service, and the utility charges during the start-up period. Salaries for any additional personnel needed to assist the director of a large center also must be provided. Total start-up costs vary widely. When these costs are incurred, the usual sources of revenue ordinarily have not become available. In these cases, a special grant may be needed, or the organizers of the center may arrange for a loan or invest their own funds. When a loan is obtained, the cost of the interest must be recognized as a very real budgetary item.

Occasionally, suppliers will permit purchasers to defer payment for 90 days, and the center can schedule purchases so that the first tuition is received before the 90-day period ends. However, the first receipts certainly will not cover all the expenses. If receipts are due from agency or government funds, those first payments usually are made after the services have been provided. In the meantime, suppliers may charge interest on unpaid bills.

Therefore, it is important to obtain as much assurance as possible that funds for start-up will be available when needed. Searching for "GSA Child Care Center Startup" on the Web will provide you with a wealth of information, although specific costs are not provided.

Geographic area, projected size of the center, ages of children to be served, in-kind support (such as free or reduced-price space offered by a church), and amount of money to be borrowed all factor into start-up costs for new centers. Therefore, it is difficult to project the cost of a specific center. The Small Business Administration (SBA) recommends that those interested in starting a center create a business plan. Using this approach, prospective owners can determine whether their plan is realistic in terms of potential resources (loans and so forth) and potential success. More information about start-up is available in Chapter 6 and online at www.sba.gov.

## Operating Budget

The *operating budget* consists of an income and expense plan for one year and is used when centers enroll children and begin the program, and annually thereafter. The center may operate on a calendar year (from January 1 to December 31) or on a fiscal year, a 12-month period chosen for ease of relating financial matters to other operations of the center. Centers funded by agencies that operate on a fiscal year running from July 1 to June 30 find it easier to work on the same schedule as the funding agency, but many early childhood education centers choose September 1 to August 31 for their fiscal year because those dates relate closely to the start of their school year. After a center has selected its fiscal year, no change should be made without serious reason. Planning one year's budget from January 1 to December 31 and then changing to a September to August fiscal year in the following year causes confusion and may need to be justified for tax purposes.

## 5-2b Estimating Costs

The financial director's first task is to figure program cost. The task requires an overall understanding of the early childhood education program and its goals and objectives. It also requires reviews of the child care industry spending patterns nationally and locally.

At the local level, the director determines what is needed for children in the particular community and program, and then analyzes the cost of meeting these needs. These data are essential in preparing a realistic budget. If other people are preparing the budget, the director works with them in interpreting program needs. Priorities should be established on the basis of the program goals, while the cost and the availability of funds determine the scope of the program. For example, a center may select improving salaries as a primary goal. If new playground equipment is also desirable, the decision about

*In planning a budget, directors must be aware of the day-to-day needs of everyone in the center.*

providing equipment in addition to improving salaries will be made based on the availability of funds, as well as on which is the greater need. If the planned primary goal is related to salaries, the center staff may work together to create workable playground enhancements until the desired equipment can be purchased. Nonetheless, in many cases, additional funding will be needed. The director must take a leadership role in implementing a plan for obtaining funding.

Another question that has an impact on both program and finances is the following: What is the population to be served? For example, does the program serve children from infancy through preschool age, and does it provide after-school care? If so, the director will have to recognize that costs for infant programs are considerably higher than costs for preschoolers, based largely on the staff-to-child ratio that infants require.

School-age children need fewer adults, and they are usually at the center fewer hours. Consequently, their care is less expensive.

Other questions include these: How many teachers will be needed and for what hours? Will it be necessary to have aides? A cook? A janitor? A secretary? A bus driver?

---

### REFLECTION

It may be easier to think about the financial aspects of an educational program by looking at your own educational finances. Think about the following questions: How is your college course work being financed? If you are paying tuition, what percentage of the actual cost of your education do you pay? Who finances the balance? Taxpayers? Endowments? How are other school expenses (high school and elementary school) financed?

Answers to these and dozens of additional questions should be available from the people who are responsible for designing the program and will come primarily from the director. By using this method, the director keeps the goals and philosophy of the center paramount.

Some directors have difficulty with the initial phase of budgeting. Instead of starting with the goals and objectives, they start with the dollars available and attempt to determine what can be done with them. Such a center is truly ruled by the budget (or by the finance director), and maintaining an educationally and financially sound program under these conditions is extremely difficult.

Although program and financial decisions in a corporate system may be made at the national or regional level, the director of each center is responsible for implementing these decisions. The national or regional financial officer provides information about how much money is budgeted for each category; each local director then orders equipment and supplies through the main or regional office and is responsible for generating the required tuition. Some franchisees create their own budget, including fees paid for the right to use the franchised name and logo in the community.

Determining the dollar amount of a budget is a major part of the overall financial plan. This figure is arrived at by listing the items needed to operate the program for a year in categories such as salaries, rent, and equipment. Next, the budget director determines how much each of these categories will cost with as much accuracy as possible. The sum of the costs for each category is the amount of income needed for a year. A sample budget in Director's Resource 5-1 provides an idea of the costs of each category and of the costs of the total program for a hypothetical center. This sample budget is not meant to be used in the form presented here but may be used as a guide to budget preparation. In your area, costs may be much higher or lower. More important, the philosophy and goals on which you base your planning may differ widely from those used in this sample. Center directors and other professional groups and organizations in each community may provide helpful local information. Companies, such as gas and electric companies, kitchen equipment suppliers, toy suppliers, and business associations, can furnish more specific and relevant cost information for individual centers.

Following are factors that influence the total amount spent by a center and the ways in which that amount is allocated:

- number, ages, and special needs of children enrolled
- teacher-to-child ratio
- staff training
- type and location of building
- amount of equipment already owned or available
- type of program and services provided
- section of the country in which the center is located
- general economic conditions
- amount and type of in-kind contributions
- special considerations, such as free rent

The sum of the costs for each category is the cost of running the center for one year. Dividing this figure by the number of children to be served establishes the cost per child, a figure that can be further examined on a monthly, weekly, daily, or hourly basis. The cost of various program components, such as infant or school-age programs, can be figured this way also. (See the description of the break-even point in Chapter 6.)

It is important to consider whether the center is a nonprofit organization or whether one of the goals is to make a profit. This question is sometimes hotly debated among early childhood educators, many of whom feel that early childhood education centers should not be operated for profit because someone then makes money at the expense of the children. Admittedly, early childhood education costs are high, and it is difficult to make a profit. Nonetheless, if a person or group can provide a good program, meeting the needs of both children and staff while showing a profit, there is no reason to discourage such a financial plan. The director is responsible for ensuring that children are not shortchanged in the interest of making a profit. Nor should teachers receive inadequate pay and benefits. This ethical issue may become even more challenging if the director's salary is tied to the amount of profit.

## 5-2c Adjusting Budget Figures

While it is relatively easy to change the budget figures on paper, the budget must remain balanced. Expenses must not exceed income. Chronic budgetary problems will drain staff energy from the daily operation and will remain unless the center can actually pare costs to the level of income earned. When one budget category amount is increased, obviously another budget category must be decreased.

Each expense must be analyzed with an eye toward its relative importance to the overall program. Can the equipment budget be lowered by substituting some free or inexpensive materials? Can food costs be lowered by cooperative buying? Can the consumable supply budget be reduced without a major effect on program quality? What effect will a particular cut have on the quality of the children's program? How will the cut affect the staff?

At the same time, both new and current funding sources can be approached with clear documentation of the need in relation to goals because expenses must not exceed income. If professional early childhood educators take the approach that it is better to have a poor program than none at all, the problem of adequately funding child care will never be solved. When a center's financial management is poor, the director may continue operating past this point without becoming aware that the inevitable outcome will be a poor-quality program or bankruptcy. If the year begins with a deficit budget (that is, expected expenses exceed expected income), it is highly unlikely that the year will end with a balanced budget. For that reason, deficit budgets should not be approved.

*The director understands that all children need a wide variety of books from which to choose and provides adequate funds to maintain the center's collection.*

> ### DIRECTOR'S CORNER
>
> "Our needs assessment indicated that more than 100 children would use our center. Two major corporations in the neighborhood worked with us, and many of their employees expressed interest in enrolling their children. We were shocked when we spent the whole first year with only nine children enrolled. Luckily, we had strong financial backing, and we have now reached capacity enrollment."
>
> —*Director, private not-for-profit center*

## 5-2d Analyzing Budget Categories

Even when a financial officer assumes major responsibility for preparing the budget, the director is still responsible for understanding and articulating what is needed to operate the program successfully. Many board members have limited knowledge of the actual cost of child care. The director must help them develop this understanding.

Some centers budget by function rather than simply by category; that is, administrative costs and the costs of each aspect of the program are budgeted separately. For example, if 20 percent of the director's time is spent working directly with the children, and 80 percent is spent on administration, then 20 percent of the director's salary would be allocated to the children's program salaries category and 80 percent would fall under administration. A complex center may provide and budget several separate functions such as infant program, preschool program, and after-school program. This budgeting method clearly delineates the actual cost of the children's program. When coupled with a description of the services offered, it provides a mechanism for comparing costs with other programs and for including the value of the services provided in relation to the costs incurred. This method also provides information used in determining tuition However, ever-changing tax laws make it essential for even small centers to have the services of an accountant to guide the director in setting up financial systems and to provide information about new governmental requirements. An attorney also may be needed to help ensure that the center is operating within legal limits. The cost of these services must be included in the budget.

Although requirements at each center vary widely, new directors may be given a general idea of costs if they consider the following rough estimates:

- 70 percent personnel
- 10 percent facility, utilities
- 5 percent equipment
- 3 percent supplies
- 3 percent food
- 9 percent other categories

Attempting to design a budget to fit these percentages, however, would be inappropriate because these figures are provided as general guides.

The following budget categories will provide a rough idea of the costs of early childhood education and the formats used for presenting a budget.

### Salaries

In any early childhood education budget, the major component is salaries. A center can expect to spend 70 percent and even up to 80 percent of its operating costs for personnel. This figure includes salaries and wages for full- and part-time staff members (such as director, teachers, cooks, janitor) and for substitutes. It also includes fringe benefits for the full-time staff. In determining the budget for salaries, the personnel policies should be consulted in regard to pay rates and fringe benefits. The salary policies may address issues such as staff members' education level, previous experience, or meritorious service. The director also must comply with the minimum wage laws, tax laws, and laws regarding employer responsibility.

Salaries are considered in budgeting as a cost of doing business. Of course, to the employee, salaries represent livelihood. Employees expect and are entitled to fair pay for the amount and type of work they do. Their job category is usually determined by the preparation and experience they bring to the role. By now, you are well aware that salaries in the demanding field of early childhood education are relatively low. Parents are paying higher and higher tuition. Why, then, aren't staff salaries higher?

Child Care Aware of America (2012) corroborates the salary conundrum and recognizes, along with many others, how low the salaries or pay scales are in relation to the important type of work being done in early childhood centers. This report offers data on the relationships among salary, quality of staff, and quality of program for young children nationally and by state.

The Bureau of Labor Statistics of the U.S. Department of Labor regularly reports wages by occupation. Salaries of preschool teachers and child care workers are separated for analysis and reported by mean (average) and annual dollar amounts. See Table 5-1.

While not all preschool teachers have degrees, the wage assumption is that preschool teachers are more qualified than child care workers. The Bureau of Labor Statistics lists teachers, beginning with kindergarten teachers, by annual salary rather than by hourly wage. Kindergarten teachers were listed as earning a mean salary of $52,840. Mean annual salary for preschool teachers was listed as $31,420. The preschool figures appear to be based on a work schedule of 40 hours per week at 52 weeks per year. Because hourly rates are not provided for kindergarten teachers, one can assume that the annual salary is for the school year rather than for 52 weeks at 40 hours each. If preschool teachers, based on this report, worked from September to June, their annual mean salary would be $23,565 (Bureau of Labor Statistics, May 2013).

You probably quickly noticed the large disparity between public school teachers, preschool, and child care staff. Consider that in a public school, one teacher is responsible for 25 children for 6 or 7 hours a day. (Most public school teachers also work before or after school and on weekends, planning and preparing for their work.) In child care programs, many more staff are needed for each class of fewer children. When staff work 8 hours a day for 5 days a week, the director still has many "staff hours" to fill. Because many centers are open 10 or more hours a day, many staff are employed on a part-time basis. In the following section, you will learn how directors determine how many staff members they need.

Keep in mind that these figures group all teachers in a given category. For example, you may know a beginning public school teacher who is making much less than $52,660. In that same district, a teacher who has taught for 30 years would be earning much more than $52,660 per year. Also, all the figures mentioned in this section were based on national averages. However, salaries vary widely from state to state and from program to program.

## 5-2e Staffing and Full-Time Equivalents

As discussed previously, approximately 70 percent of your operating budget will be spent on staff salaries and benefits. But how does an administrator determine the number of teachers that will be needed and the salaries that can be provided? One strategy you might employ involves computing the full-time equivalents (FTEs) or number of full-time employees that will be needed to meet teacher-child ratios. The following is an example of how you could approach this aspect of the budgeting process.

Assume you are the director of a child care center that serves 140 children, 12 hours a day, 5 days a week. Your program has an annual operating budget of $1 million. Based on the 70 percent figure, we can presume you will budget approximately $700,000 for salaries and benefits ($1 million × 70%). Let's also assume that your state's teacher-child ratio and group size licensing requirements are less stringent than those found in the NAEYC standards. As a center that will be applying for accreditation, let's assume you have decided to try to meet and, in some cases, exceed the more rigorous guidelines provided by NAEYC.

**TABLE 5-1** Comparison of wages by job title, May 2013

| Job Title | Hourly Wage | Annual Wage |
|---|---|---|
| Preschool Teacher* | $15.11 | $29,200 |
| Child Day Care Services | $10.33 | $21,490 |
| Elementary School Teacher | | $56,420 |

*It should be noted that preschool teachers employed by public schools typically earn the same salary and work the same calendar as elementary school teachers.

*Source: Bureau of Labor Statistics, May 2013*

You may love working with numbers and immediately want to explain Table 5-2 to everyone else—or you may give up as soon as you see so many numbers in one place. In either case, proceed slowly so that you will gradually be able to plan staffing for one classroom, and eventually move to a much more complex setting. Every director must understand this, even if he or she hires someone else to handle it. Showing it to parents, funders, and elected officials should help them appreciate that early childhood centers have complex financial needs.

Table 5-2 presents an overview of your center's staffing needs. You have planned for three groups of infants, four groups of toddlers, and five groups of preschoolers. Based on the caregiver-child ratios you have adopted, *each classroom* will require 24 "caregiver hours" each day (2 teachers × 12-hour day, which equals 24 hours per day). Each classroom will need 120 hours each week (24 teacher-hours per day × 5 days per week). Note that this does *not* mean that teachers work a 12-hour day. This number reflects the number of hours that must be covered by a staff person.

We know that there are 12 classrooms.

Each room needs the equivalent of two teachers for 12 hours a day or 120 hours a week.

12 hours × 5 days × 2 teachers = 120 hours

120 hours a week × 52 weeks a year = 6,240 teacher-hours per room

6,240 teacher-hours per room × 12 classrooms = 74,880 teacher-hours per year

We can see that the total number of caregiver hours required in your center each year is 74,880. If all teachers are full-time employees, then we can assume that they will work a total of 2,080 hours per year.

40 hours per week × 52 weeks = 2,080 hours per year

Therefore, your center would require a total of 36 FTEs.

74,880 caregiver hours ÷ 2,080 hours per year = 36 FTEs (FTE = full-time equivalents)

That is, to maintain your caregiver-child ratios, you would need to hire the *equivalent* of 36 full-time teachers.

Let's assume you are hiring child care workers at a mean hourly wage of $9.46. Therefore, a full-time teacher would have an annual salary of $19,677 (2,080 hours × $9.46 per hour), and your annual budget for teaching staff would need to be $708,372 ($19,677 × 36 FTEs). Based on your original figure of $700,000 for salaries, it appears that you will not be able to cover your

**TABLE 5-2** Overview of center staffing needs

| | No. of Children in Each Classroom | Caregiver-Child Ratios | No. of Caregivers Required to Meet Ratio | No. of Caregiver Hours Required Each Day (12-hour day) | No. of Caregiver Hours Required Each Week (5 days per week) | No. of Caregiver Hours Each Year (52 weeks per year) |
|---|---|---|---|---|---|---|
| Infants | 6 | 1:3 | 2 | 24 | 120 | 6,240 |
| Infants | 6 | 1:3 | 2 | 24 | 120 | 6,240 |
| Infants | 6 | 1:3 | 2 | 24 | 120 | 6,240 |
| Toddlers | 8 | 1:4 | 2 | 24 | 120 | 6,240 |
| Toddlers | 8 | 1:4 | 2 | 24 | 120 | 6,240 |
| Toddlers | 8 | 1:4 | 2 | 24 | 120 | 6,240 |
| Toddlers | 8 | 1:4 | 2 | 24 | 120 | 6,240 |
| Preschoolers | 18 | 1:9 | 2 | 24 | 120 | 6,240 |
| Preschoolers | 18 | 1:9 | 2 | 24 | 120 | 6,240 |
| Preschoolers | 18 | 1:9 | 2 | 24 | 120 | 6,240 |
| Preschoolers | 18 | 1:9 | 2 | 24 | 120 | 6,240 |
| Preschoolers | 18 | 1:9 | 2 | 24 | 120 | 6,240 |
| **TOTAL** | 140 | | 24 | 288 | 1,440 | 74,880 |

*Source: Thanks to Dr. Ellen Lynch for contributing this activity and chart.*

staffing needs. However, you must also consider that fringe benefits, which may add approximately 25 percent onto the salaries, were not budgeted. Moreover, you must consider that this example does not account for administrator and support staff salaries or variations in wages based on the staff member's position (e.g., lead teacher, classroom assistant, aide) or teacher experience.

If, instead of thinking about child care workers' salaries, you wanted to provide *at least* the national average preschool teacher pay of $12.47 per hour, what would your classroom staff cost be? As the program's director, it becomes your responsibility to balance the budget while addressing the needs of your staff and the children and families you serve.

Table 5-2 can be modified to meet your needs and can be used when you have some full-time and some part-time children. You may not need two teachers in each classroom for the first and the last hour of each day, depending on how many children arrive and leave during those hours, but you must always have a minimum of two staff available at all times.

With this guideline, you can get a starting point in deliberations about the salary requirements for your center. However, you will still need to make your own chart showing each teacher by name, assuming that each teacher's salary is based on qualifications, years of experience at your center, merit, and other potential salary criteria included in your policies and procedures manual. You will also need to make a chart for each room showing what time each staff member arrives and leaves and when they are on break or have planning time. These charts will ensure that you have the desired number of staff in each classroom at all times. Your focus should be on maintaining consistency for the children and avoiding having too many different caregivers in one room over a one-week period.

### Consultants

A second component of a center budget that is closely related to salaries is contract services or consultant fees. This category covers payments to people who agree to perform specified services for the center or its clients. Most centers have an accountant and an attorney available for consultation on a retainer or an hourly rate. Other possible consultants might be doctors, dentists, social workers, real estate agents, psychologists, nutritionists, and educational consultants. These types of professionals could be employees of a large center or system. However, they usually serve as consultants by agreeing, for example, to give dental examinations to all children enrolled in the center or to provide workshops for teachers one day a month. When the center's staff is not well trained, or when a broad range of services is provided for children,

many consultants are needed. Although some centers do not hire consultants, and most will hire only a limited number, the overall quality of the program may be increased by the services they provide.

When consultants come from out of town, their transportation, meals, and lodging may be additional costs. Sometimes, consultants are paid a per diem rate to cover meals and lodging. The current per diem rate of the federal government might be used in budgeting. Both the center and the consultant should agree in writing on all financial arrangements and performance expectations in advance of any services rendered. Under no circumstances should the director attempt to classify a staff position as a consultancy to avoid paying taxes and benefits. Serious legal ramifications may be the result.

## 5-2f Plant and Equipment

The largest cost in the physical plant category is rental, lease, or mortgage payments on the facility. The costs for the maintenance of, and the repairs to, the building and grounds also are part of this budget component. When maintenance work is done on a regular basis, the costs usually will be lower in the long run. However, because it is impossible to predict all maintenance and repair needs in advance, a lump sum for this purpose should be allocated each year. A preliminary assessment of the main components of a building (foundation, roof, plumbing, wiring, heating and cooling system, termite damage, and so forth) will provide a rough idea of when major repairs may be expected. Periodic assessments must also be scheduled.

Also included in the physical plant category in the operating budget are utilities (heat, electricity, and water). In some cases, one or more of the utility charges may be covered in the lease, a point that should be fully understood and in writing before an agreement to lease is made. Some centers also may have to pay for garbage removal. When utilities are not included in the lease, an approximate budget figure can be obtained by checking with previous tenants or with the utility companies.

In budgeting for a new center, equipment for the children, the office, and the kitchen is a major part of the start-up budget. For a continuing center, the operating budget includes supplementary pieces, as well as repair and replacement where needed. Leasing and rental charges for equipment are included here. For example, a center may rent a carpet cleaner for a day or two or lease a copy machine for a year. The continuing equipment budget will be about 10 percent of the start-up equipment budget, so if the start-up equipment budget is $1,000 per child, the continuing equipment budget would be $100 per child per year.

## Depreciation

One of the costs of doing business that may be overlooked is depreciation of major equipment. When a center purchases major playground equipment or furniture such as tables, chairs, and shelves, it would appear that the center had added that amount of dollar value to its assets. However, after an item is purchased and put into use, its value begins to drop or depreciate. Let us assume that the children's furniture will last 15 years, whereas the computer and copy machine will have to be replaced in 5 years. Dividing the initial cost of the item by the anticipated length of its useful life yields the annual depreciation amount. A $2,000 computer divided by 5 years results in depreciation of $400 per year. That is, the computer is worth $400 less each year. Table 5-3 depicts the annual value of the computer. Although the computer may still be functioning adequately, it now has little or no value. When you consider the assets of your child care business, this computer is no longer an asset even though you may continue to use it.

In listing assets, the annual amount of depreciation is deducted so that the value of the equipment is more realistic than if the full cost were listed. At the same time, wise directors build an equipment replacement fund so that when eight infant cribs must be replaced, the center is prepared for that expense.

## Supplies

Three types of supplies must be purchased: office and general supplies, classroom supplies, and food supplies. The first category—office and general supplies—includes items such as pencils, stationery, toilet paper, paper towels, cleansers, and brooms. Construction paper, paint, crayons, pet food, and doll clothes are included in classroom supplies. Food supplies encompass all items available for human consumption. Usually, two meals and two snacks per child per day are served in full-day centers, with one snack offered in a half-day program. In any case, sufficient food should be provided so that teachers can eat with the children. Food costs vary depending on the availability of federal food subsidies and on factors in the economy. A nutritionist engaged as a consultant can aid the director in setting up a nutritionally and financially sound food plan. (See Chapter 12 for a discussion of nutrition and the U.S. Department of Agriculture)

## Transportation

This category may include the purchase or lease of several buses for transporting children to and from school and on field trips. In such cases, insurance, gas, maintenance, and license fees must be budgeted. Some centers contract with a company to provide transportation for children, and others may rent a bus for special occasions. Vehicles must be equipped with child safety seats or seat belts, depending on the size and age of the child, and other governmental regulations regarding vehicles must be followed. Based on a ruling by the National Highway Traffic Safety Administration, buses rather than vans are to be used. They must comply with both federal and state laws. Your state may require that you transport children in vehicles meeting special school bus regulations and that drivers have special licenses. The many financial, safety, and liability issues involved frequently lead centers to require parents to provide the child's transportation to and from school.

Costs for staff members to travel to professional meetings, other centers for observation, and homes for home visits are included in the transportation category. The mileage rate for automobile travel reimbursement is usually based on the current federal government mileage rate.

## Communication

Telephone costs can be determined by checking with the telephone company. In deciding on the number of telephones to order, consider the center's staffing pattern. For example, if a classroom staffed

**TABLE 5-3** Five-year depreciation of a $2,000 computer

| Year | Worth = | New Value |
|---|---|---|
| 1 | $2,000–$400* | $1,600 |
| 2 | $1,600–$400* | $1,200 |
| 3 | $1,200–$400* | $800 |
| 4 | $800–$400* | $400 |
| 5 | $400–$400* | $0 |

*$2,000/5 years = $400 depreciation per year.

© 2013 Cengage Learning®

*Supplying art materials to allow children's creativity to develop requires careful budgeting.*

families, colleagues, vendors, home offices, and others. The director and other staff also will use various websites for gathering information, contacting legislators in their roles as advocates, and marketing the center. The monthly charge for this access is included under the communication category.

Having a presence on sites such as Facebook and Twitter is a great PR tool for some centers, while others have a policy of not participating and requiring staff to agree that they will not discuss the center online. Such policies must be carefully written.

## Staff Training and Development

Even when a center is fortunate enough to have a staff of well-prepared teachers and assistants whose education was in the early childhood field, continuous in-service programs will be needed. Recognizing that learning is lifelong and that research continues to provide new information about children's development, both directors and staff members need opportunities to participate in conferences, classes, and visits to other programs. When the staff is underprepared, the director must begin their in-service program immediately. State licensing regulations may require a particular number of hours of training annually, usually a minimal level. The director is responsible for determining what is needed and facilitating the acquisition of that training or education. Some centers provide partial scholarships for classes and may reimburse the staff member on successful completion of a course. Providing current professional journals and books in the staff lounge or supply room will support teachers' growth and development as well.

## Insurance

In addition to health insurance, it is important for directors to have other types of insurance. Insurance agents can quote rates and provide information about appropriate kinds of insurance. A center usually needs at least fire, theft, and liability insurance. If the center provides transportation or owns vehicles, various types of insurance are required. A child accident policy is valuable and relatively inexpensive. If the center has a board of directors, directors and officers insurance is important. Be sure to read each policy carefully and ask questions about any items you do not understand. Find out whether your legal expenses would be covered if, for example, you were sued by a family who claimed you were negligent. What are realistic deductibles for your situation? What exclusions, if any, are written in your policy ("Does Your Insurance Coverage Fit," 2002)?

## Postage

Postage covers the cost of mailings to parents, prospective client families, and past and prospective donors. The

by one adult is located on another floor away from other classrooms, an extension or cell phone is needed to allow that teacher to get help when necessary. When a teacher is outside or on a field trip, even though at least one other adult is present, it is a good idea to provide a cell phone. In an emergency, the teacher can get help. Licensing requirements in some states specify where a telephone is required. In any case, enough lines should be provided to enable parents and other callers to reach the center without undue delays. Call waiting, often less costly than a second line, improves accessibility for outside callers but can be annoying to some. Although many people now use cell phones, some centers require that they be turned off in the center.

Getting emergency messages through immediately is a priority. Providing staffers with access to a telephone for personal calls during breaks is a benefit that recognizes their needs and helps them feel they are respected members of the organization. In fact, it is a requirement in at least one state.

Many centers rely heavily on email for much of their within-agency communication, as well as contact with cost of shipping and other business mailing is included. In some cases, fax or email may be appropriate and less costly, but in all cases, a record of important communication should be maintained.

Billings, especially notices of overdue accounts, usually are mailed. Many families prefer to receive and pay bills on-line. Some centers establish the policy that payment is due on a particular date each month, and no bills are sent. Postage costs can be held down to some extent if information is distributed by sending notes home with the children, but keep in mind that these items may not always reach the parent. If you have a flexible software package, you should be able to accommodate each family's preferences.

## Marketing

Marketing includes newspaper and telephone book advertisements, brochures and fliers, and radio or television announcements. Some agencies design a logo and use it on products such as T-shirts, stationery, business cards, and mugs. Also included are promotional items such as open house events, announcements of staff activities (e.g., names of teachers who recently attended a national conference), and information about a speaker coming for staff development. In fact, any opportunity to highlight the center without, of course, compromising the privacy of children, families, and staff can be considered *marketing* (see Chapter 16).

## Licensing

Information about licensing costs can be obtained from the licensing agent; these costs will vary according to the center's location. Other professional fees, such as those for NAEYC accreditation, also belong in this category (see Chapter 3).

## Audit

Yearly audits are essential. They assure the board and funders that the center's financial matters are being handled properly. You should ask your accountant for a cost estimate and build that into the budget.

## Miscellaneous/Other

This category includes funds for small items that do not fall under any of those previously mentioned. However, attributing expenditures to a particular category provides a more accurate picture of the center's financial status and eliminates slippage in expenditures. For example, if postage and advertising were both included under miscellaneous, postage expenditures could skyrocket and not be recognized as a budgetary problem.

## In-Kind Contributions

Some budget items are not received in cash and not paid for in cash. These are called *in-kind contributions* and should be shown in the budget so that the true cost of operating the center is known. For example, a center may rent two 600-square-foot rooms in a church building for $200 per month per room. The church may charge the center $4,000 for a 10-month program. If the fair rental cost is at the rate of $10 per square foot (a total of $12,000), then the church is, in effect, contributing $8,000 to the center program. Note that the reverse is also true. Some church schools provide income for their church.

Consultants may volunteer their services, and such services also should be shown as in-kind contributions. For example, assume that a child development specialist conducts a half-day workshop without charging the center. If the specialist's regular fee is $300, her contribution is valued at $300.

Sometimes, directors expect staff to volunteer to work additional hours without pay. This practice is usually inappropriate and may be illegal. Many teachers already spend time at home planning and preparing materials. Furthermore, staff salaries usually are alarmingly low. If staff members are expected to attend meetings and programs outside regular work hours, these conditions should be spelled out in the job descriptions. Some centers include policies relating to staff caring for

### Working Smart with Technology

*Technology Supported Budgeting Tools*

The financial decisions facing the director of the twenty-first century require accuracy in accounting and the ability to complete "what if" financial modeling projections. A director who is faced with trimming the budget needs to know how closing a classroom might impact the bottom line. Another who is seeking a high rating on the state's Quality Rating and Improvement System (QRIS), needs to know if the monetary award offsets the additional expense of hiring a more qualified staff. In the past, calculating these impacts would be onerous. Today, technology-based budgeting tools allow directors to respond to "what if" scenarios with just a few clicks.

Photograph by Nicholas Dworsack

*Technology allows directors to utilize "what if" financial projections.*

children who are center clients outside of work hours. At the very least, staff members who are required to work more than 40 hours in a week must be paid overtime rates for the additional hours, unless they are exempt under U.S. Department of Labor regulations.

## 5-2g Using Budget Systems

After the sources and amounts of income have been determined, these facts must be written down along with the plan for spending discussed earlier in this chapter. This written plan must be prepared in such a way that the people who need to read it will be able to understand it.

Small centers can use a very simple format. Centers that are publicly funded may be required to use whatever system is designated by the funding agency. Many centers use budget codes or account numbers, assigning a code number to each budget category and using separate numbers for each item within that category. For example, if the budget item *equipment* is coded as 110, then the subcategories might be

111 office equipment
112 classroom equipment
113 kitchen equipment

Similarly, personnel might be coded as 510, with

511 salaries
512 Social Security
513 workers' compensation

Such a system enables the financial director to record transactions according to appropriate budget categories and to ascertain quickly how much has been spent and how much remains in a given category.

Centers with a large number of classrooms, a range of age groups, or more than one site will certainly use a computer program to manage budgets. These may be modified to meet the center's needs.

An additional consideration in keeping accurate records is the responsibility to maintain ethical and legal practices. Having access to large sums of money is tempting to some people. If safeguards are not in place, the director or an employee who has access to financial records may manipulate them in unethical and illegal ways. A system of checks and balances can deter this behavior. For this reason, board members should be tenacious in insisting on current and thorough financial reports and should not hesitate to question any items they do not understand.

## 5-2h Approving the Budget

Before spending can begin, the budget must be approved by the board and the funding sources. The budget must balance; that is, income and expenses must be equal. When there is a surplus in the income side of the budget, it is categorized as profit or may be put in a reserve fund for large expenses that may occur in a future year. Because

not-for-profit businesses obviously do not show a profit, such funds would be added to appropriate budget categories or would be put in a reserve fund. However, if the budget projects a loss, serious attention must be paid to immediate financial trimming. Believing that "something will turn up" is a poor way to conduct business and should not be accepted by a board or funders. At this point, conflict may arise among the board, the funding agency, and the director as each group may have varying interpretations of the center's goals and the means for reaching these goals. After a consensus has been reached and the budget approved, the budget becomes the working financial plan, and the director must see that it is followed.

## 5-2i Budgeting for Subsequent Years

Several months prior to the end of the year, the director and members of the finance committee meet to review the budget prepared for the ensuing year. For the second and subsequent budgets, the previous year's figures can serve as a guide, but the new budget figures, based on experience and on program changes, will usually differ from those of the previous year. Still, income and expenses must balance.

# 5-3 FINANCIAL RESPONSIBILITIES

The budget is the major tool used by the financial director for management of center finances, but balancing income and expenses is only one aspect of an overall, ongoing financial system. The director has a number of continuing financial responsibilities, all of which relate ultimately to the budget.

## 5-3a Managing Cash Flow

To be sure you will have enough cash on hand to pay staff and order budgeted equipment, you must keep track of cash flow. Often, budgets are divided into monthly components with the assumption that each month you will spend approximately one-twelfth of the annual amount. You can assume that income will be received in a similar pattern: one-twelfth of the annual income is expected each month. Realistically, some items are paid for annually, semiannually, or quarterly. Similarly, total tuition expected in summer may be lower because some children stay home with older siblings or with parents who work as teachers and are home during the summer. The reverse may occur if you have a school-age program. Children who from September to June come before and after school may spend all day at the center during the summer, thus increasing center income. But suppose your budget includes $1,200 for classroom supplies. Does that mean you can spend $100 a month or can you place a $500 order in March? You need to know whether the cash will be available.

## REFLECTION

You have $120 in your checking account. An item of clothing that you have desired for a month has just gone on sale for $100. What factors will you take into account in determining whether to buy it?

Now assume you direct a center. In examining your records for this month, you note the following:

- Income for March 2006 = $20,359.
- Expenses for March 2006 = $15,250.

Can you, as the director, purchase $5,000 of needed equipment for the center? Why or why not? If you have recorded that you had placed an order for $2,000 worth of equipment (even though the bill has not been paid yet), and if you also realize that several other major required expenses are coming up in the next three months, you would know that you had already encumbered (or planned for) $5,000 for equipment that hadn't arrived yet.

## DIRECTOR'S CORNER

"I thought we were in good financial shape. We were showing a solid bank balance, and we had full enrollment. What our cash accounting system didn't show was that we had several thousand dollars in bills that the bookkeeper hadn't paid yet. I learned that checking the cash on hand and even looking at how much we had budgeted for a category weren't necessarily appropriate ways to make decisions about what I could spend."

—*Director, for-profit proprietary center*

To accomplish this, you make a cash flow chart, showing each income and each expense item on a monthly basis. Often, these amounts are shown on a one-twelfth per month basis. At the end of January, you record the amount actually received and disbursed in each category. In another column, you show the difference between what you expected to receive or spend in that category, and what actually happened. Your accountant may refer to these as *accounts receivable* (money that people owe you) and *accounts payable* (money you owe others).

You also may record year-to-date expenses and receipts, as well as year-to-date expectations. Let us assume you listed $100 each month for classroom supplies for an annual total of $1,200. If you spent $0 in January, $50 in February, and $0 in March, you would have a $250 favorable balance in the supplies line. It is not necessary to spend money only as it is available in that line. However, you must be sure you can meet all expenses and not exceed the annual amount allocated without either receiving unexpected, unbudgeted income or decreasing the amount to be spent for the year on another item. Recognize, too, that if you purchase items or services monthly before cash is available to pay for them, you may be faced with high finance charges. Using a good software package to help you keep these records will simplify your task. Director's Resources 5-4 and 5-5 provide examples.

## 5-3b Handling Salaries

After the budget is approved, the financial director informs the personnel committee of the allocation for salaries. In a new center, the committee then may begin the employment process in accordance with the personnel policies. In continuing centers, pay raises should be considered.

The director keeps additional records relating to the budget category *salaries*. Professional staff may be paid monthly, biweekly, or weekly, but their salaries are a fixed expense regardless of the number of hours worked as long as those individuals remain on the payroll. Other staff members receive wages based on the number of hours worked during the pay period. Employees who are paid hourly must have some way to record the amount of time spent on the job if that is the basis on which they are paid. Some centers have employees record their working time on weekly time cards or by signing in and out on the computer. These records are referred to when paychecks are prepared or may be recorded in one step by the software when the employee checks in and out. The director keeps a record of the sick days and the professional days used for all employees, including those who are salaried.

Payments are made to each individual employee on the basis agreed on in the employment contract. In small centers in which staff have the same schedule daily, time sheets may not be kept. In any event, the director is responsible for keeping track of hours worked, sick leave, and vacation time. Here again, entering this information into a computer database enables the financial officer to prepare up-to-date reports and facilitates preparation of the payroll.

Staff members also may be on unpaid leave. Current laws require that certain leaves be available to staff for circumstances such as childrearing. The returning staff member is not guaranteed the exact job but is guaranteed employment when the legal leave concludes. Centers also may create additional opportunities for leave. In any case, accurate records must be kept of leaves requested, granted, and used, and the director or designee is responsible for knowing and following related laws.

## 5-3c Ordering Goods and Services

With an approved budget in hand, the director or purchasing agent (or someone else assigned to this role) can begin to order supplies, equipment, and services. The first step is to consult the person or people who will use the item or services. The janitor may be consulted about a waxing machine, while the teachers should be involved in decisions about tables and chairs for the children. Both janitor and teachers could participate in selecting carpeting for the classrooms. However, when it comes to the actual ordering of the goods and services, as few people as possible—one is preferable—should be involved.

Several methods of ordering goods and services are used, depending on the nature of the purchase. Major purchases usually are approved by the director, the board, or a committee. If outside funding has been received, the center's contract may require that bids be submitted for large items or for large quantities of items such as food or paper goods. The purchaser writes out required specifications to suppliers or advertises for bids in the case of a large order. Then, the purchaser examines the bids and contracts that each supplier offers. The lowest bid must be accepted unless the bidder does not meet the specifications. Specifications can refer to a description of the item in question (e.g., a commercial dishwasher), to the performance of the item (with water temperature of 180 degrees), or to its delivery date (to be delivered by September 1).

Smaller purchases or those that are routine, such as art supplies, may be ordered from a wholesaler. However, some centers require that price information on such items be obtained and that the item of appropriate quality having the lowest price be purchased. Sometimes, purchases are made with particular outlets because they allow credit, but this choice will be false economy if the quality is not satisfactory.

In some large cities, several centers may band together to purchase large quantities of items at reduced prices in a plan called *cooperative buying*. Each center may contribute to the salary of the person who manages the co-op and must transport items from a central location to its own center.

## 5-3d Making Payments

The director (or someone so designated) is responsible for making all payments. When shipments arrive, they are checked and paid for as soon as possible within the terms of agreement. For example, if the vendor gives 30 days to pay, the center should use the money until the payment is due but should monitor bill payment carefully so that unnecessary interest is not incurred. In cases in which a discount is offered for prompt payment, that may be a wise course to follow. Before paying for any item, it is important to verify that the items received are proper in quantity and quality and that the price on the invoice is correct.

A center should establish a checking account immediately so that payment for goods and services can be made promptly and safely. If the center is small, there may be the temptation to pay expenses directly from cash income. This practice is a major mistake because under such a plan, money can easily be lost or stolen, and errors or misunderstandings are more likely. Furthermore, no audit trail of these items is available. Most centers use checking accounts, and some centers require two signatures on each check, perhaps the signatures of the board treasurer and the director. In small centers or proprietary centers, the director signs all checks. Of even greater importance is the appointment of a person other than the bookkeeper to reconcile the bank balance. When procedures for money management are in place and followed, fewer errors are likely to occur.

There must be a specific place to store bills and a specific time set aside to pay them. In small co-ops, a parent may work at home recording transactions. In large, complex organizations, all finances may be handled through a central administrative office that may be in another city or state.

## 5-3e Recording Transactions

Whenever a financial transaction occurs, it should be recorded promptly in a specific form and in a specific place. Access to a personal computer and appropriate software makes this task relatively easy and provides clear, readily available reports that show the financial position of the center on a monthly, weekly, or even daily basis.

In fact, many directors who now use computers for record keeping wonder how they ever managed without these tools. At first, using this technology can be time-consuming, particularly if you are completely unfamiliar with the way these machines can work for you. However, after the system is set up, it takes no more time (and probably less time) to enter figures by means of the keyboard as opposed to pencil and paper. The result usually is easier to read, may be converted readily to chart form on the computer, and can be cross-referenced. For example, you can enter in each child's record the tuition received that month from that family, and without rewriting all the amounts, query the computer for the total amount of tuition received that year to date.

Billing is easy. After you have enrolled a child, and entered the parent(s) names and addresses, you can direct your computer to print bills to each family, customized with the specific amount owed. You also may want to add a message to each bill such as a reminder about registration for the following autumn or an advance notice of the date of the school picnic. If a family must make tuition payments in cash, provide a numbered and signed receipt and keep a copy. Both checks and cash must be deposited quickly, generally within the week.

Although not directly related to the center's fiscal operation, you may want lists of center children or families by the child's birth date, health checkup due date, ZIP code, or class at the center. You can print out attendance reports (often required by funders), which is a task that is made even easier if the parent signs the child in and out using a computer. Clip art or your own creative graphics add zest to notices. Just remember that you are directing a professional program and not a "Kutesy Korner."

Getting your payroll out on time can be much simpler with a computer. Once programmed with the hourly or monthly rates, the percentages to be withheld or deducted for various purposes, and other data to be recorded such as sick days used and available, your computer will do the calculations and print the checks. You'll have a record of the transactions, but, as with any other document, you'll make a backup disc or use an external drive and keep it in a secure place.

As you work on budgets, reports to funders, cash flow statements, and any other data, you can use a password that will prevent those who do not need or should not have access to the data from viewing or modifying it. For example, a parent may not want the child's address published on the class list.

Every year, hardware and software manufacturers develop new capabilities for this technology. If you are relatively new to computer usage, finding a knowledgeable board member, volunteer, or consultant to assist you is essential. Choosing computer components requires understanding how you will use your computer. Most centers can't afford to buy a more powerful computer than they will need in the next few years, yet buying strictly on price will probably prove to be false economy. If your computer cannot run the software you need, you may wind up with nothing more than an expensive typewriter.

Purchasing software also can be challenging, though not as costly as the hardware. Just as you can add hardware components as you acquire the need and the funds, so, too, can you add software packages. For example, you may add an accounts receivable package. You may also modify or customize existing programs, or you might purchase a basic program and create your own system.

When purchasing software, some of the items you'll want to consider include the following:

- What kind of hardware is needed to run this software?
- Can you try out the software?
- Does it do what you need?
- What kind of support is available and at what cost?
- Are seminars available? Where and when are they held?
- Is there a telephone help line? What are the hours in your time zone?
- Are upgrades provided?
- How long has the company been in business?

Because both computer hardware and software are changing so rapidly, it's a good idea to check with colleagues about what has worked effectively and what they would like to add. Professional journals such as *Child Care Information Exchange* provide regular reviews. Most reputable software companies will permit you to try out the software instead of watching someone else work with it and telling you about it as they go. Pro-Care Software and Softerware (maker of EZ-CARE2) are two of the most active players in this market. However, you also may find an excellent package developed by individuals who have been or are directors and have worked with computer programmers to design software that meets specific needs. Of course, whether a center uses computerized records or handwritten reports, these will be timely and accurate only when timely, accurate information is recorded.

## 5-3f Summarizing Data

Shortly after a fiscal year ends, the financial director should prepare an income statement for that year. This statement shows all revenue and expenses for the past year and points out the net income or loss. Director's Resource 5-2 provides an example of an income statement.

To monitor the center's financial position, the financial director lists all assets and all liabilities as well as the equity the owner or owners have in the center. Directors need this total picture to enable them to understand their total financial position.

For example, if the assets are much less than the liabilities, the center is obviously in financial trouble. Notice how important accrued accounting is in creating the statement of financial position. Director's Resource 5-3 provides a sample statement of financial position.

*Sometimes children enjoy and learn by using materials that do not appear in the budget. Nonetheless, the director must carefully plan and monitor the center's financial functions.*

### 5-3g Auditing

In most businesses, including early childhood education centers, an auditor reviews the books annually. The director makes the financial records, including the checkbook, canceled checks, receipts, and invoices, available to the auditor, whether on computer or in a ledger,. The director or bookkeeper must keep these documents in an organized manner, and they must be regularly updated. Shoe boxes or laundry baskets full of invoices are totally unacceptable and certainly unprofessional. At the very least, such lack of organization leaves the impression that the financial transactions of the center are not accurately maintained.

Auditors can perform several levels of audit or verification that the financial operation of the center is based on generally accepted procedures. The board will determine which level is needed, but in any event, the auditor will not verify each individual transaction. An annual audit protects the financial personnel of the center by making sure their job is being done according to procedures and protects the entire operation by ensuring that the use of funds is being recorded as planned and that procedures are being followed.

### 5-3h Handling Petty Cash

There are several ways to operate the petty cash fund. Each teacher may receive a specified sum of money to spend for the classroom, or the director may allocate a certain sum per staff member, paying cash when the staff member presents an appropriate receipt. Some centers use petty cash for all unexpected small needs. The director keeps a sum of cash on hand and gives it to staff members who present legitimate requests. For example, if the cook has run out of bread, petty cash may be used to purchase a loaf or two. Petty cash should be used as little as possible to avoid obscuring substantial program expenditures under its heading. If $20 worth of food is purchased weekly with petty cash, then the item *food* in the budget is underrepresented. All expenditures should be recorded (or allocated) to the correct account. This can be accomplished by the bookkeeper when the user presents receipt documentation. Some directors prefer to eliminate petty cash altogether.

### 5-3i ... And Finally

If you are not already knowledgeable about financial planning and record keeping, gaining this knowledge is essential, at least at a basic level. Even when a director has no direct responsibility for financial records, inability to understand them is unacceptable. Many books and articles are available to guide you. If you are a real financial beginner, Gail Jack's book, *The Business of Child Care: Management and Financial Strategies,* will start you off with the basics (Jack, 2005). It contains several sample forms to give you an idea of how they look and what they include. The numbers included are not meant to be used by a center. Rather, you will need to create your own budget and, therefore, your own financial reports.

## SUMMARY

Handling financial matters is a challenging but essential function of the director. Directors must develop a financial plan based on the priorities for meeting children's needs and on the available funds. The major tool used by the financial director is the budget, a plan for balancing income and expenses. The director is responsible for all other financial matters, including designing budget systems, ordering goods and services, making payments, recording transactions, and preparing the new budget.

To plan for and maintain a fiscally healthy center, the director must do the following:

- Describe the process for creating a financial plan for a child care center.

- Explain how to prepare and operate a budget.

- Identify the financial responsibilities of a well-managed center.

## TRY IT OUT!

1. Work with a partner. Create a plan for staffing two classrooms for one week. Show what time each staff person will arrive, leave, and be on break. Assume the center is open for 10 hours a day. Compare your plan with others created by your classmates. How many full-time staff did you include? How many part-time? How many FTEs did you need?

2. Examine Director's Resource 5-2: Income Statement, and Director's Resource 5-3: Statement of Financial Position. What information can you obtain from each of these statements?

# DIRECTOR'S RESOURCE 5-1

## SAMPLE CHILD CARE CENTER BUDGET

**INCOME**

Tuition

| | | |
|---|---|---|
| Infants (8 × $160 × 51) | $65,280 | |
| Toddlers (12 × $150 × 51) | 91,800 | |
| Preschoolers (51 × $135 × 51) | 351,135 | |
| **Total Gross Tuition:** | | 508,215 |

Discounts

| | | |
|---|---|---|
| Vacancy (3%) | | |
| **Total Discounts:** | | <15,246> |

Other Income

| | | |
|---|---|---|
| Application Fees (30 × $20) | 600 | |
| Interest on Account | 600 | |
| Fund-Raisers | 1,000 | |
| Grant Award (Literacy Program) | 2,500 | |
| **Total Other Income:** | | 4,700 |
| **Total Income:** | | $497,669 |

**EXPENSES**

Personnel

| | | |
|---|---|---|
| Director | 30,000 | |
| Head Teachers (5) | 135,000 | |
| Teachers (5) | 100,000 | |
| Assistants (10 part-time) | 46,800 | |
| Substitutes | 2,000 | |
| Secretary | 8,000 | |
| Custodian | 7,000 | |
| Cook | 8,000 | |
| FICA, Workers' Comp., Unemploy., and Insurance | 62,500 | |
| **Total Personnel:** | | $399,300 |
| Rent | 31,000 | |
| Utilities and Telephone | 17,465 | |
| Advertising | 1,000 | |
| Food | 35,000 | |
| Office Supplies | 1,000 | |
| Custodial Supplies | 700 | |
| Classroom Equipment and Supplies | 5,200 | |
| C.P.A. Fees | 1,000 | |
| Insurance | 3,500 | |
| Licenses | 500 | |
| Staff Development/Training | 1,500 | |
| Teachers' Petty Cash | 504 | |
| **Total Nonpersonnel:** | | 98,369 |
| **Total:** | | $497,669 |

# DIRECTOR'S RESOURCE 5-2

## SAMPLE INCOME STATEMENT
## FOR THE YEAR ENDED DECEMBER 31, 20XX

**(For use with Try It Out! 5-2)**

### Revenues

| | | |
|---|---:|---:|
| Infant Program Income | $70,500 | |
| Toddler Program Income | 64,500 | |
| Preschool Program Income | 247,120 | |
| Federal Child Care Food Program | 41,500 | |
| Donations/Contributions | 500 | |
| Parent Fund-Raising | 1,100 | |
| Other Income | 50 | |
| **Total Income:** | | $425,270 |

### Expenses

| | | |
|---|---:|---:|
| Salaries/Wages | 267,100 | |
| Health Benefits | 19,650 | |
| Employment Taxes and Insurance | 21,840 | |
| Management Services Fee | 15,000 | |
| Training/Consultant Fees | 7,200 | |
| Food/Beverage Supplies | 21,300 | |
| Educational Supplies | 4,100 | |
| Office and Paper Supplies | 3,300 | |
| Rent | 16,000 | |
| Payroll Service Fees | 1,420 | |
| Cleaning Service Fees | 8,920 | |
| Custodial Supplies | 950 | |
| Equipment Expense | 2,800 | |
| Utilities/Telephone Expense | 11,300 | |
| Garbage Removal | 650 | |
| Advertising | 850 | |
| Travel/Field Trips | 1,600 | |
| Bookkeeping/Audit Service Fees | 11,500 | |
| Licenses | 625 | |
| Maintenance and Repair Expense | 5,920 | |
| Insurance Expense | 3,200 | |
| **Total Expense:** | | 425,225 |
| **Net Income (Net Loss)** | | $45 |

# DIRECTOR'S RESOURCE 5-3

## SAMPLE STATEMENT OF FINANCIAL POSITION AS OF APRIL 30, 20XX

**(For use with Try It Out! 5-2)**

### Assets

| | |
|---|---:|
| Cash–Operating | $7,000 |
| Cash–Payroll | 8,000 |
| Accounts Receivable | 11,200 |
| Educational Supplies | 900 |
| Office Supplies | 400 |
| Property, Plant, and Equipment | 42,000 |
| **Total Assets:** | $69,500 |

### Liabilities

| | | |
|---|---:|---:|
| Accounts Payable | $11,000 | |
| Wages Payable | 5,000 | |
| Mortgage Payable | 32,000 | |
| Long-Term Liabilities | 11,000 | |
| Depreciation | 4,000 | |
| Total Liabilities: | | 63,000 |

### Equity

| | |
|---|---:|
| Capital | 6,500 |
| **Total Liabilities and Equity:** | $69,500 |

TeachSource Digital Download

# DIRECTOR'S RESOURCE 5-4

## HYPOTHETICAL BUDGET BY MONTH CREATED ON SPREADSHEET

### Felton Family Preschool
#### Monthly Budget

| | "Reasonable" Budget A3 | September | October | November | December | January | February | March | April | May | June | July | August |
|---|---|---|---|---|---|---|---|---|---|---|---|---|---|
| **INCOME** | | | | | | | | | | | | | |
| Tuition | 344,235 | 25,000 | 28,000 | 30,000 | 30,000 | 30,000 | 30,000 | 30,000 | 30,000 | 30,000 | 27,078 | 27,078 | 27,078 |
| Fund-Raising | 3,500 | 292 | 292 | 292 | 292 | 292 | 292 | 292 | 292 | 292 | 292 | 292 | 292 |
| County Grant | 27,000 | 2,250 | 2,250 | 2,250 | 2,250 | 2,250 | 2,250 | 2,250 | 2,250 | 2,250 | 2,250 | 2,250 | 2,250 |
| Other | 2,000 | 167 | 167 | 167 | 167 | 167 | 167 | 167 | 167 | 167 | 167 | 167 | 167 |
| TOTAL INCOME | 376,735 | 27,708 | 30,708 | 32,708 | 32,708 | 32,708 | 32,708 | 32,708 | 32,708 | 32,708 | 29,787 | 29,787 | 29,787 |
| **EXPENSE** | | | | | | | | | | | | | |
| Payroll Expense | | | | | | | | | | | | | |
| Salaries-Staff | 270,000 | 22,759 | 23,793 | 20,690 | 23,793 | 23,793 | 20,690 | 21,724 | 22,759 | 22,759 | 21,724 | 23,793 | 21,724 |
| Payroll Taxes | 24,300 | 2,048 | 2,141 | 1,862 | 2,141 | 2,141 | 1,862 | 1,955 | 2,048 | 2,048 | 1,955 | 2,141 | 1,955 |
| Worker's Comp | 13,500 | 1,138 | 1,190 | 1,034 | 1,190 | 1,190 | 1,034 | 1,086 | 1,138 | 1,138 | 1,086 | 1,190 | 1,086 |
| Staff Benefits | | | | | | | | | | | | | |
| Health Ins. | 27,250 | 2,271 | 2,271 | 2,271 | 2,271 | 2,271 | 2,271 | 2,271 | 2,271 | 2,271 | 2,271 | 2,271 | 2,271 |
| Dental Ins. | 4,000 | 333 | 333 | 333 | 333 | 333 | 333 | 333 | 333 | 333 | 333 | 333 | 333 |
| Education Allow. | 875 | 73 | 73 | 73 | 73 | 73 | 73 | 73 | 73 | 73 | 73 | 73 | 73 |
| Rent | 4,800 | 400 | 400 | 400 | 400 | 400 | 400 | 400 | 400 | 400 | 400 | 400 | 400 |
| Janitor | 6,000 | 500 | 500 | 500 | 500 | 500 | 500 | 500 | 500 | 500 | 500 | 500 | 500 |
| Insurance | | | | | | | | | | | | | |
| Liability | 2,914 | 243 | 243 | 243 | 243 | 243 | 243 | 243 | 243 | 243 | 243 | 243 | 243 |
| Accident | 1,575 | 131 | 131 | 131 | 131 | 131 | 131 | 131 | 131 | 131 | 131 | 131 | 131 |
| Directors Ins. | 944 | 79 | 79 | 79 | 79 | 79 | 79 | 79 | 79 | 79 | 79 | 79 | 79 |
| Supplies | 15,000 | 1,250 | 1,250 | 1,250 | 1,250 | 1,250 | 1,250 | 1,250 | 1,250 | 1,250 | 1,250 | 1,250 | 1,250 |
| Utilities | 2,835 | 236 | 236 | 236 | 236 | 236 | 236 | 236 | 236 | 236 | 236 | 236 | 236 |
| Capital Improvement | 2,000 | 0 | 0 | 1,000 | 0 | 0 | 0 | 1,000 | 0 | 0 | 0 | 0 | 0 |
| TOTAL EXPENSES | 375,993 | 31,461 | 32,640 | 30,102 | 32,640 | 32,640 | 29,102 | 31,282 | 31,461 | 31,461 | 30,282 | 32,640 | 30,282 |
| SURPLUS (DEFICIT) | 742 | (3,753) | (1,932) | 2,606 | 68 | 68 | 3,606 | 1,427 | 1,247 | 1,247 | (495) | (2,854) | (495) |

*Source: From JACK, The Business of Child Care, 1E. © Cengage Learning.*

# REFERENCES

Bureau of Labor Statistics. (May 2013). *National occupational employment and wage data estimates*. Washington DC: author. Retrieved April 10, 2014, from http://www.bls.gov/news.release/pdf/ocwage.pdf.

Child Care Aware of America. (2012). *Child care in America: 2012 state fact sheets*. Arlington, VA: author. Retrieved April 10, 2014, from http://www.naccrra.org/sites/default/files/default_site_pages/2012/full2012cca_state_factsheetbook.pdf.

Does Your Insurance Coverage Fit Your Needs? (Nov-Dec 2002). *Child Care Information Exchange, 148*, p. 80–83.

U.S. Treasury Department. (2014). *Fact sheet: Final regulations implementing employer shared responsibility under the Affordable Care Act (ACT) for 2015*. Washington DC: Author. Retrieved April 10, 2014, from http://www.treasury.gov/press-center/press-releases/Documents/Fact%20Sheet%20021014.pdf.

*When the director is seeking funds, she must be prepared to explain her request to bankers or representatives of a foundation.*

## Learning Objectives

After reading this chapter, you should be able to:

**6-1** Explain how multiple programs can work together to secure funding.

**6-2** Describe the director's role in obtaining funding for a center.

**6-3** Identify several resources potentially available for child care financing.

**6-4** Explain the purpose of a break-even analysis and how it can be useful in determining funding needs.

**6-5** Differentiate between start-up and operating funds and how tuition rates may be determined.

**6-6** Explain the steps that must be taken in preparing for a fund-raising campaign.

**6-7** Describe several types of financial reports that funders may require.

**6-8** Identify potential challenges to your program's reserve of available funds.

## Standards Addressed in this Chapter

Accreditation Standard 8 – Community Relationships

Accreditation Standard 10 – Leadership and Management

Administrator Competencies – Management Knowledge and Skills 2, 3, 7, 8, 9, 10

Administrator Competencies – Early Childhood Knowledge and Skills 1, 6, 10

Professional Preparation Standard 6 – Becoming a Professional

All directors, whether previously experienced in business or not, must understand the finances of operating a center. Even the director who does not have day-to-day responsibilities for the financial component of the center's structure must have financial knowledge and understanding. Directors who have moved up from teaching must remember that as teachers they were authoritative, rather than authoritarian. They knew what was appropriate for children and classrooms. Now they must also become authoritative about business.

A major component of the director's responsibility is ensuring sufficient funds to establish and operate the program. Although this assignment is ongoing, responsibilities mount when a new program is created, a new facility is needed, or components are to be added to an existing program. Of course, every director annually addresses the upcoming year's funding, and experienced directors recognize the need for long-range fiscal planning. Certainly, seeking additional funding is important, but shepherding carefully the funds one has is essential. In child care, there are no dollars to waste or lose through carelessness.

## 6-1 GETTING STARTED IN RAISING FUNDS

Typically, in early childhood centers, the director's role is demanding in terms of time, energy, and talent. Throughout this text, you have read about the wide range of expectations placed on the director. When it comes to funding, it often is wise to obtain needed assistance in one of several ways. To begin with, the director must understand that "few organizations are successful in raising funds from their communities without significant and sustained involvement by the board" (Bergman, 2010, p. 19). That is one of the reasons for creating a board with a broad community and business base rather than a collection of outstanding early childhood educators.

Everyone involved with the center should play a fund-raising role, directly or indirectly. For example, the director may assign other staff or enlist the aid of one or more volunteers to assume some additional responsibilities, such as organizing equipment orders or conducting inventory, thereby providing time for the director to engage in fund-raising. A well-trained volunteer may conduct center tours for prospective clients; an enthusiastic parent may do an excellent job of pointing out things parents are especially interested in knowing. A volunteer may answer the telephone one afternoon a week to provide the director with uninterrupted proposal-writing time. Finally, volunteers may participate in the fund-raising process in myriad ways that will be discussed throughout the chapter.

Centers with several sites may be able to afford a full- or part-time funding specialist. Directors of several centers may support each other by creating a joint fund-raising plan. They even may be able to hire a fund-raising consultant to guide their efforts, particularly if they have limited knowledge of the process. In the long run, such an expense may be quite productive.

An example of such cooperative planning and funding occurred when several center directors, together with their local Child Care Resource and Referral Association (CCRRA), were involved in monthly discussions. They were interested in supporting children with social and emotional needs beyond those expected in typical development. As a result, they formed a consortium specifically to work together on funding and implementing the program they all needed. They wrote proposals and received grants. A team of specialists was employed, and a volunteer teacher coaching program was implemented. Many children, families, teachers, and directors are benefiting from this collaborative approach, yet each center maintains its identity. No matter which approaches to funding you, as director, decide to take, it is essential to recognize that the director alone cannot manage the entire fund-raising process. Every staff member and every family member of the center's children should be involved. "Spreading the word" is one way. Keep everyone aware

**▶‖ TeachSource Video Vignette**

**Financial Planning for Early Childhood Programs: Establishing a Budget**

This video provides an overview of the issues that must be considered when planning a budget for your program. You are planning to show the video to members of your center fund-raising committee. Reflect on the following questions:

1.  What information is provided that would enable your fund-raising team to better understand the expenses associated with operating a child care program?

2.  Mr. James comments that "there may be instances where cutting too much could jeopardize the very core of your program." What does he mean by this statement? What examples could you provide to members of the committee to help them understand this idea?

that you have a high-quality program for young children and that a high-quality program requires a strong financial position.

## 6-2 FUNDING A NEW CENTER

Obviously, starting a new center or expanding an existing center requires a significant  amount of planning and money. Before seeking a loan or investing personal assets, remember that you are starting a business. The U.S. Small Business Administration (SBA) and the Service Corps of Retired Executives (SCORE) are good resources. Some business textbooks provide easy to understand and detailed descriptions of start-up funding (see Greene, 2012, and Hatten, 2011).

A prospective center developer who does not have a strong business background should seek assistance. The SBA recommends that before starting a business, you answer the following questions:

- What niche or void will my business fill?
- What services or products will I sell?
- Is my idea practical, and will it fill a need?
- Who is my competition?
- What is my business's advantage over existing firms?
- Can I deliver a better-quality service?
- What skills and experience do I bring to the business?
- What will be my legal structure?
- How will my company's business records be maintained?
- What insurance coverage will I need?
- What equipment or supplies will I need?
- How will I compensate myself?
- What are my resources?
- What financing will I need?
- Where will my business be located?
- What will I name my business?

Another possibility is purchasing an existing business. Such a purchase involves real estate, possibly equipment, the name of the center, and the goodwill the center has established (if that is the case). (See Greene, 2012, to find out what to look for.) Linsmeier (2003) explains how a child care business is valued. As a buyer, you will need to research the value that the seller uses and how that amount was calculated. At the same time, maintaining confidentiality is essential so that the current enrollment is not diminished based on parents' anxiety about changes in ownership. You would not want to buy a center whose status was being compromised by rumors.

In any case, check with your state department of labor about specific policies that will govern your business. (You'll read about other business requirements in other chapters.) You may need to register your business name and get a business license and sales tax number, and you must definitely open a separate business bank account. You will need to know the federal and state laws governing employees and stay current with business publications in your area. Gather data on whether the market for child care is growing or declining in the area in which you are planning your business. Your local chamber of commerce or child care resource and referral agency may be able to help with information and may provide valuable contacts. Even when your business is going well, stay current with your community and its needs.

### Working Smart with Technology

*Using Technology to Find Funding Sources*

Finding funding sources is one of the most important challenges faced by early childhood center owners. Your computer can be a tremendous help in surveying many of the grant opportunities available to you. Federal program information can be accessed at the Grants.Gov and Small Business Administration websites as well as on the Resources for Child Care Providers section of the Office of Child Care website. Information about the Child and Adult Care Food Program that provides reimbursement for meals can be found on the USDA Food and Nutrition Services website. One of the largest databases of grant sources can be found on the Foundation Center's website. And do not overlook your local library system. Search the library's website to see if it offers services related to locating and writing grants, including free workshops. Also note that many libraries are partners with the Foundation Center. This means that you may be able to access the Foundation's resources through your local library.

*Directors of programs should become familiar with the many funding sources available to them online.*

To obtain money, you must know exactly how much you need, why you need it, when you will need it, and how you will pay it back. You must also commit sufficient capital such as a second mortgage on your home. If you are working as an incorporated company, the corporation will need to demonstrate its sources of funding in addition to the loan being sought. The lender will obtain your credit report; therefore, it is wise to check your own credit report, or that of the corporation, before applying for a loan.

Can you convince key people in your community of the importance of a new child care and education center? Are you and your board confident that your new program is what your community needs so that preschoolers can have the experiences and support they need to learn and develop?

## 6-3 START-UP FUNDS

Start-up capital is the money that must be available before the center is opened and for some time thereafter to support the initial program operation until the flow of tuition and other funds is sufficient to support the ongoing program. After a director is hired, it takes a *minimum* of two to three months (and much more in some cases) to complete the necessary preliminary planning before the program begins. Money for space, equipment, office supplies, and some staff salaries must be available during these early months before the center opens. Programs often are underenrolled during the first few months of operation. Checks from funding sources are sometimes delayed until the program operation is well under way. Therefore, it also is wise to have sufficient capital on hand at the outset to operate the program for at least six months. These operating monies that need to cover costs for both the planning period and the initial operation of the center are in addition to the capital needed to finance the purchasing or remodeling of a site and to purchase equipment and supplies for the children's program. In other words, it takes a considerable amount of money to start a program, and it is important to make careful calculations to ensure that the start-up money is adequate to cover the costs until regular operating funds become available.

A director who has been a teacher and is now planning to open a center will notice that lenders, suppliers, inspectors, and insurers will not ask about what kind of relationships she plans to establish with children and families, what the curricular objectives are, or what kinds of special activities will be provided. They are interested in *business*. The director will have to have or develop this new focus while continuing to focus on the needs and interests of staff, children, and families. Although the director may have a close relationship with families because both she and they care about their children, she is still the administrator. She must be careful to avoid crossing an invisible line. At some point, the director may have to follow up on a slow tuition payment. A family may decide to dispute the way an injury was handled or to complain about the food being served. The director must maintain an objective and ethical stance. (See NAEYC Administrators' Code of Ethics Supplement in Appendix A.)

At the same time, the board and the director must seek out the leaders in their community who can be shown the need to go beyond a bare-bones program. Help them see that young children aren't "just" playing and that the learning that is occurring will be a foundation for continued learning and development. The process of cultivating individuals and businesses that can help is ongoing. Keeping the program and its importance in the forefront is a major job. The results can be quite rewarding for the center, children, and families.

Most agency-sponsored centers are nonprofit, and many are eligible to receive funding from other community or governmental agencies after there is an established, ongoing program to fund. To get started, however, the agency may need to apply to foundations or other sources for funding. A sample grant application is shown in Director's Resource 6-1.

### DIRECTOR'S CORNER

"The bank wouldn't lend me the money to start a center. They said it would take too long to show a profit. Finally, we put our house up as collateral and we got the loan. But I didn't get any salary for three whole years. We're in good shape now after five years and we're expanding."

—*Director, private for-profit center*

You may be preparing grants for much larger amounts of money for bigger projects, but this example provides an idea of how a proposal looks. Often, agencies conduct campaigns, soliciting first from their own board members, who are expected to contribute. Next, businesses and others who have expressed interest in the work of the agency are approached. Some corporations that operate many centers, or very large centers, obtain funds from investors. Operators of small proprietary centers that are established for profit or that have no sponsoring agency must invest personal capital or arrange for a loan to get started. Foundation money is rarely offered to proprietary centers; it is reserved for serving particular populations chosen by the foundation that meet specific foundation-determined goals.

## 6-3a Community and Governmental Support

When the community expresses great interest in getting a program started, it may be possible to promote a successful fund-raising program. However, only relatively small amounts of money can be obtained through raffles or bake sales. Established philanthropic groups such as Kiwanis, Lions, various community groups, and fraternal organizations sometimes are willing to donate money to cover start-up costs such as equipment or to support a capital improvements fund-raising campaign. They may fund specific activities such as field trips. But like other funders, they seldom provide operating expenses.

A company may provide start-up funding for a center for its employees' children with the understanding that the director will need to secure adequate funding for operating costs from other sources, including tuition. If the company makes something the center could use, such as diapers or packaged food products, it may offer a continuing supply to the center. Other companies may offer a flex plan, a benefit that allows employees to set aside before-tax income to pay for child care. This benefit makes child care more affordable for families. In turn, it provides relatively reliable tuition payments for centers because employees must show a paid receipt from the center or caregiver to collect their own before-tax dollars. If, by the end of the year, the employee has not used all of his child care benefit fund, the money reverts to the employer.

Centers in public schools are usually funded through special government grants, and the central administration may manage the budget. In some cases, public schools offer government-supported programs for children, sometimes specifically for children with special needs. However, families within the community are encouraged to enroll and are expected to pay for children who are typically developing, thus creating a diversified class. In the case of large chains of centers, the corporate office secures investors and then funds the start-up of new centers based on its market research. It may also arrange for franchises, finding individuals who are interested in contracting with the corporation to be a franchisee. (You may be familiar with family restaurants, ice cream stores, or dry cleaners that operate as part of a franchise system. You may also find franchised early childhood programs in your area.)

Centers not connected with other institutions or programs usually need a major source of income beyond tuition. When a center is operated day to day on tuition and small funding campaigns such as raffles or cookie sales, the board and the director will come to realize that a major pool of funds is needed to make any real changes, handle an emergency such as water damage from a broken pipe, or cover a sudden drop in enrollment, such as if parents lose jobs and can no longer afford their children's programs. That is one reason for choosing members of the board of directors carefully. When the board has members who have "connections" to people and companies with major resources, they may be able to organize and implement a campaign for a children's

program. Such plans must be made well in advance, using a rationale that will appeal to a wide range of contributors. Simply saying, "Our family center needs financial help," won't sell well. But creating a slogan that ignites interest can be quite effective. Programs that start without a sufficient funding base are in fiscal trouble from the outset. Maintaining a balanced budget for an early childhood education program is very difficult. Therefore, it is paramount to keep a balanced budget at the outset by finding enough capital to cover start-up costs as well as to plan for unexpected needs and to enhance the program in a major way when needed.

## 6-4 BREAK-EVEN ANALYSIS

In determining the amount of funds needed, a break-even chart is useful. You want to know how many children you need to enroll to break even financially as well as to make a profit or provide some funds for future initiatives. You and your accountant can prepare such a chart by first determining the fixed costs of operating the center, such as rent, utilities, and director's salary. These are costs that will remain at the same level, regardless of enrollment.

Variable costs are calculated. These are the costs for operating the program that change as enrollment increases or decreases. For example, when four or five children are added, the cook probably orders more food, more art materials are needed, and so forth. If you have several years of budget experience available for this program, you can figure the cost of food per child from the previous year by dividing the cost of food by the number of children. In the same manner, you can determine the cost of equipment per child and the cost of teaching staff per child. As prices rise, you will need to increase amounts accordingly.

Although you don't change the line every time an additional child is admitted, it is clear that the more children you enroll, the more expenses you will have. Some figures can be computed per child such as the amount of food or of disposable materials (crayons, paper, soap, etc.). However, when you have a sufficient number of children, you will need additional teachers, furniture, and even an additional classroom, depending on the number of children added.

Let's finish the break-even chart so you can see what the financial effect might be.

At this point, the analysis becomes more challenging. Based on licensing requirements and center policies, when a certain enrollment is reached, an additional teacher must be employed. For example, think of a center with 30 children in which a 1:10 ratio is required. When the 31st child is added, the center must provide an additional teacher, even though the additional tuition generated by a single child surely will not pay a teacher's salary.

However, if six new children are added, it *may* be feasible financially to have four groups of nine children. Of course, if tuition from 10 children is required to pay a teacher's salary expenses, then the director should not add children until she can ensure a class of 10 or realize that money will be lost on that class and must be made up by charging higher overall tuition.

The director or accountant can figure a break-even analysis, that is, how many children and what tuition rate will be needed to offset costs. To get an idea of how this works, use the following steps (Hatten, 2011):

1. Calculate fixed costs (see Figure 6-1). These must be paid no matter how many children are enrolled (see Figure 6-2). These include rent; phone; utilities; insurance; equipment; and salaries and benefits for director, cook, maintenance staff, secretary, and any other nonclassroom staff.

2. Determine the number of children you will serve.

3. Based on the number of children per teacher, calculate the number of teachers and the cost of teacher and assistant salaries and benefits.

4. Based on the number of children, estimate the cost of food and supplies.

5. Add the costs to be incurred (items 1, 3, and 4).

6. Divide the total (from line 5) by the number of children.

The dollar figure in line 6 represents the amount you will have to receive in tuition to break even (see Figure 6-3). If, at any time, you do not have full enrollment, you will lose money. Therefore, you will want to build into your budget a cushion that will allow for underenrollment.

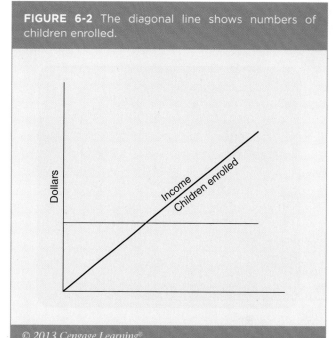

**FIGURE 6-2** The diagonal line shows numbers of children enrolled.

© 2013 Cengage Learning®

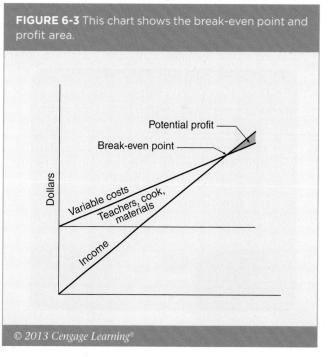

**FIGURE 6-3** This chart shows the break-even point and profit area.

© 2013 Cengage Learning®

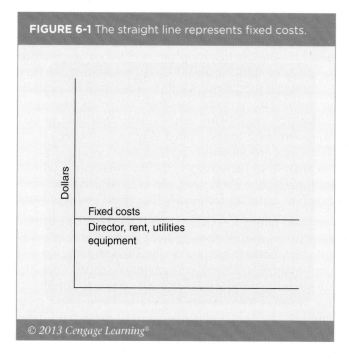

**FIGURE 6-1** The straight line represents fixed costs.

© 2013 Cengage Learning®

One way to accomplish this is to charge higher tuition than required to break even. However, if any of your tuition comes from government vouchers, you may be limited to the current voucher rate, which will almost certainly be below your tuition costs.

Costs for infants and toddlers are higher than for preschoolers, while costs for school-age care are lower, based primarily on the teacher-to-child ratio. Because infants require a lot more individual care and attention than older children, a teacher can care for only three or four

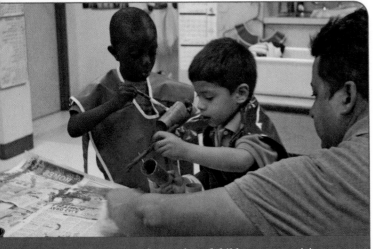

*Teachers manage the number of children at an activity. Directors must manage the number of children enrolled to break even.*

infants at the most. To determine break-even costs when you serve a variety of age groups, do the following:

1. Divide the fixed costs by the total number of children in all age groups (as described previously). The fixed cost for every child, regardless of age, is the same.

2. Calculate the variable costs for each age group separately (teaching staff, food, supplies).

3. Divide each age group's variable costs by the number of children in that age group to find the variable cost per child.

4. Add the variable cost per child and the fixed cost per child. This amount is the tuition that must be collected from that child to break even.

To carry this further, you may want to investigate how you would figure costs for a center serving 8 infants

*Individuals who have visited the center may be more likely to contribute to your fiscal campaign.*

and 36 preschoolers. Notice that although the variable costs for infants will be considerably higher than those for preschoolers, the fixed cost for each child remains the same. Therefore, preschool tuition, although spread over more children in this example, must, in effect, cover part of the cost of caring for infants. (A sample budget in Chapter 5 demonstrates that a center may lose money on infant care but cover that loss with tuition from preschoolers.) Nonetheless, infant care is important for at least two reasons: (1) there is a major need for infant care in many communities, and (2) when children start in a center during infancy, the center hopes to retain them throughout their preschool years. If the number of preschool children in a center decreases, the cost of infant care may have to increase, or the fees for all children must increase.

By the same premise, school-age care can potentially balance the cost of care for younger children. Centers must carefully plan school-age tuition to be reasonable for families. However, because fewer staff are needed, before- and after-school care is less costly than preschool and may be financially helpful to centers serving preschoolers. The key factor remains retention of high-quality care for all age groups.

Using a break-even chart, the director projects the income based on the enrollment. She then looks for the points at which the total costs meet the income and checks to see at what enrollment levels that occurs (Cohen, 2006; Hatten, 2011).

# 6-5 OPERATING FUNDS FOR NEW AND CONTINUING CENTERS

*Operating funds* refers to the amount needed **naeyc** to run the center after it is open for business. Operating funds must include all the regular budget items needed in the day-to-day operation of the center. After the facility is established, and the basic equipment has been purchased using start-up funds, income must be adequate to ensure daily program operation as well as provide an emergency fund. Many centers have depended heavily on government funds, United Way, and other charitable monies to provide most or all of their operating funds. An analysis of these sources for the twenty-first century indicates that in many cases, it is unlikely they will be sufficient to maintain the quality that centers must provide.

Fund-raising for operating costs must be planned carefully in terms of the benefit to be derived from the contributor's dollars. Imagine a contribution being used to pay for rather mundane, yet certainly essential, categories such as utilities and insurance. Such usage may not encourage the giver. The creative fund-raiser frames requests in terms of projected program accomplishments. One director in an annual fund-raising letter labeled contributions as "your opportunity to nourish the minds and bodies of 62 of our young children." During the preceding weeks, she had sent the local newspapers (with parental permission) pictures of several children engaged in interesting projects such as visiting several local small businesses and discussing with the proprietors how they now use what they had learned in school. Based on this project, the director of their before- and after-school program submitted a proposal for a homework coach. She included quotes from the children who had discussed and written about their community visits. Besides helping with school-assigned homework, the coach was to engage children in games and activities involving logic, problem solving, and creativity. The local businesspeople were invited to join them in these activities. As a result, this successful grant paid for a well-qualified staff member and a wide variety of materials.

### 6-5a Tuition

When the center is largely dependent on tuition for operating funds, it will be necessary to balance the number of children to be enrolled, the amount of tuition their families can reasonably be expected to pay, and the amount of money needed to operate the program. The program will not always be fully enrolled; therefore, the budget should have at least a 3 percent to 8 percent vacancy rate built in. Programs just beginning may have only a few children enrolled for many months, necessitating close management of the initial budget and reduction of variable costs to the lowest possible level. Even some fixed costs can be reduced. For example, a director may employ one or two salaried teachers until the tuition receipts warrant the addition of more staff.

Because the salaries of most preschool teachers are unreasonably low, and salaries comprise the biggest expenditure by far in an education budget, it is sensible to charge an amount that will provide the fairest possible salary to the staff. Therefore, the tuition rate should be based on a number of facts, including the following:

- the amount needed to meet professional commitments to staff

- the amount that is reasonable in terms of the type of program offered to families

- the amount charged by comparable centers in the area

### Adjusting Tuition

For many centers, payments by parents are the major source of income. There may be an application fee, which will be applied to the child's tuition when she enrolls. If the child is not enrolled, the center retains the application fee. To assist parents or to attract clients, centers may decide to offer one or more weeks' tuition free for vacation or illness for each child. If you decide to do this,

*When the center director can convince a funder of the importance of physical and motor development opportunities for children, he may be able to secure funding for outdoor equipment.*

remember to multiply the weekly tuition by 51 instead of 52 weeks or to divide the annual tuition by 51 weeks. Keep in mind that if parents pay 51 times a year, there may be a week when you receive no tuition income. However, if you are following your budget, you will recognize that you should not be spending more than the total amount initially approved. You may specify in your enrollment agreement that the 52nd week of the child's attendance is the week during which no tuition will be due. You may also decide to require two weeks' tuition in advance. If the child will be leaving the center, the parents are expected to give two weeks' notice to the director. They will then not pay for the last two weeks, but the director may have time to find a child to fill the spot.

You may also offer a discount to the second child enrolled from the same family at the same time. But remember, if Jamala's tuition is $5 less per week than that of the other children in her class just because her older brother is also attending the center, you still need to get that $5 per week from some source. If you have 10 children who have a sibling at the center, keep in mind, this means that each week you are receiving tuition minus $50.

$5 × 10 children = $50 less per week
$50 × 52 weeks = $2,600 less income per year

You then need to reduce the budgeted amount of tuition by $2,600 and reduce (by $2,600) the amount allocated to the expense side of your budget, or find a way to acquire the $2,600 from some other source.

Similar situations arise when parents request that you hold a space for their child. For example, holding a space for a newborn who will be coming to the center in two months can mean that you lose two months of infant tuition. Working parents face the dilemma of finding infant care, while center directors face the dilemma of keeping full enrollment.

The director must balance this loss of income against the potential loss of enrollment and still make the initial tuition rate high enough to cover such factors. However, because these costs are quite variable depending on how many two-child families are enrolled in the center at a given time or how many infant spaces become available, they may add to budget instability.

Some centers charge tuition on a sliding scale based on the parents' ability to pay. Often, these centers receive government or agency funds to supplement tuition income. A sliding fee scale formula is prepared that takes into account the amount of income, the number of dependents, and other circumstances such as extraordinary medical bills. However, whenever a family pays less than the actual cost of care, the difference must be covered by making the top of the scale higher than the cost so that some families pay more than the cost of care, or by securing outside funds. A sample sliding fee scale appears in Director's Resource 6-2.

## Scholarships

Many center directors encounter situations in which parents want to enroll their children but are unable to afford the tuition. You may want to plan for some sort of aid for either partial or full tuition. This can be accomplished by establishing a scholarship fund created by charging more tuition than the cost per child and using the excess for scholarships, or by contacting individuals, agencies, and foundations to ask them to support full or partial scholarships.

Think about the purpose of a scholarship. Do you want to assist families that are temporarily unable to afford tuition, families whose income falls between eligibility for government support and the ability to pay tuition, children from other cultures, or children with disabilities? In any event, the purpose must be clear. To create a scholarship program, you will need an application process, a review process, and a thorough system for keeping records of funds that have been contributed and those that have been disbursed. If the tuition-assistance program is large, particularly in a multiple-site organization, additional staff time may be needed to maintain thorough oversight of the scholarship initiative.

Assume you need 100 children paying $160 a week ($16,000 tuition per week) to balance your budget. Think about having 10 children on partial scholarship. Of the $160 weekly preschool tuition, each of the 10 families is able to pay $70 per child. The $90 per week that those families do not pay ($160 − $70 = $90) has to come from somewhere:

$90 per week not charged × 10 children = $900
(weekly amount needed to
compensate for scholarships)

If no special scholarship funds are available, the $900 weekly would, in effect, have been divided among the remaining 90 children. (Of course, this would be done before the tuition was announced to the parents.)

100 children total − 10 children at reduced rate =
90 children paying full price

*Calculating the Potential Effect of Scholarships on Tuition*

> $900 per week (scholarship money) ÷ 90 children =
> $10 per fee-paying child per week
>
> $160 per full-paying child + $10 per full paying child
> = $170 per full paying child
>
> Tuition for the year: $170 per week ×
> 90 children = $15,300
>
> $70 per week × 10 children = $700
>
> $15,300 + $700 = $16,000 per week tuition
> for the 100 children at the center

Parents might not be aware that their $170 per week tuition is contributing to scholarships, or you may choose to tell them. Such a plan is effective unless the tuition rate becomes higher than non-scholarship families can or will pay.

## Tuition Rates

Tuition charges are set by estimating what families are willing and able to pay for services and by considering what rates are charged by competing agencies in the community. Local professional organizations or the local or state universities may have information about the amount of tuition that reasonably can be charged in a particular community. Unless a program offers something very different from that offered by nearby centers (such as NAEYC accreditation or top ranking in state QRIS programs), it may be difficult to convince parents to pay significantly higher tuition for one program over another; therefore, tuition rates must be reasonably competitive. On the other hand, if tuition is lowered to attract clients, it may be difficult to cover costs and compete with other centers in offering teachers appropriate salaries and in hiring competent staff. Directors of quality centers often have to educate members of the community about the differences in program quality and, in particular, about the value of well-prepared and more costly staff.

Although most programs charge tuition, sometimes that charge is even higher than tuition at a college. A typical range for early care and education in a community might be $115 to $215 per child per week. Infant tuition is higher than tuition for preschoolers because of the higher teacher-to-child ratio in infant rooms. Usually, parents of children needing child care have had limited opportunities to save for tuition because they are just beginning a career or because they are working in low-paying jobs. College tuition is often supplemented by governmental support, endowments, and grants. Completing college is important for many people, but more and more attention is now being given to the importance of the early childhood years as the foundation for future learning. One factor influencing child care costs is the general cost of living in an area (see Table 6-1).

Employer-supported child care has become much more prevalent during the past two decades. According to a Families and Work Institute study, employers are most likely to provide less costly support options such as dependent care assistance plans enabling workers to pay child care costs with pretax dollars as well as share information with employees about child care services near the worksite (Matos & Galinsky, 2012). Additionally, the study showed that larger employers, when compared to smaller businesses, are more likely to provide access to child care at the worksite or offer vouchers to assist with child care costs.

**TABLE 6-1** Lowest and highest child care charges for 2012

| | | |
|---|---|---|
| Lowest price for infant care | Mississippi | $4,863 |
| Highest price for infant care | District of Columbia | $21,948 |
| Lowest price for preschool care | Mississippi | $4,312 |
| Highest price for preschool care | District of Columbia | $16,908 |

*Source:* From Parents and the High Price of Child Care: 2013 Update. *Appendix 1. 2012 Average Annual Cost of Full-Time Care by State. Child Care Aware: http://usa.childcareaware.org/sites /default/files/cost_of_care_2013_103113_0.pdf.*

---

**DIRECTOR'S CORNER**

"We really couldn't charge more tuition. Parents just couldn't afford it. It means that the board can't pay me for planning time. My contract calls for a 3 percent raise annually, but this summer, the board president said to me, 'Jeanine, we're going to have to use your raise to cover the unexpected moving expenses. There's no other way.' I know they tried hard to get other funds."

—*Teacher/director, incorporated not-for-profit center*

## 6-5b Community Resources

Many early childhood education programs are subsidized by local charities and church groups. These groups typically do not provide cash to help meet the operating budget. Instead, they provide in-kind contributions such as free rent, janitorial service, coverage of utility bills, volunteer help, and so forth. If the director and the board find themselves with an unbalanced budget at the end of the year because of unforeseen problems with enrollments or unexpected expenditures, some sponsoring agencies will cover the losses. This practice is particularly prevalent when one of the sponsoring agency's goals is to provide child care services to low-income members of the community. However, the director who is not managing her budget well is not likely to be bailed out more than once.

Boards and directors may want to respond to newly identified needs and to creative ideas. To meet these needs, seeking funding is almost inevitable. Occasionally, whoever funds operating costs also may fund special projects. More often, special funding must be sought. Consider the program that served several children—Mindy, Dashawn, and Ronnie—who had developmental delays. The teacher observed that they seemed very interested in caring for classroom plants. She asked the director for gardening supplies and a section of playground so that her whole class could create a garden. Mindy, Dashawn, and Ronnie were to be assigned special responsibilities. Recognizing a creative idea, the director went to a local nursery for help. The owner not only contributed tools and seeds but also volunteered to help the class create the garden and joined them at circle time to discuss her job. Later, the class visited the nursery. Having been so delighted with the children's interest and the positive response from parents, several of whom later made purchases from her, the owner made a follow-up call to the director. She offered to provide a small greenhouse for the school so that the children could start plants earlier the following year. Imagine how much everyone benefited from one idea and one director's efforts to provide funding.

United Way funds, raised through a United Appeal campaign, are available for child care services in some communities. Usually, this is a grant for a specific purpose. Eligibility for these community funds varies depending on the locale, the amount of money available, and the demands placed on that source of funding.

As a director of a program that may need community support money, you should familiarize yourself with eligibility requirements in your community so that you can plan accordingly. Often, a number of preliminary steps must be taken before a program can be presented for funding consideration. Also, some United Way agencies will not give start-up money or operating funds to new programs. Eligibility requirements for funds typically include the following points:

1. The agency must be an incorporated, voluntary, nonprofit, charitable organization possessing tax-exempt status under Section 501(c)(3) from the Internal Revenue Service. The agency must be licensed by the appropriate authority; must provide a needed health-, welfare-, or social service; and must have a qualified and representative governing body that serves without compensation.

2. The agency must have and must implement a written policy of nondiscrimination and nonsegregation on the basis of race, ethnic origin, disabling condition, sex, or religion regarding its governing body, its employees, and the people it serves.

3. The agency must have been established and must have continued to function for a minimum of three years (number of years varies) before applying for funds.

4. The agency must be willing to cooperate in the United Way fund-raising campaign and to abide by all the policies of the United Way agency.

After the minimum eligibility requirements have been met, the necessary steps for funding consideration must be taken by the director of the center or by a designated board member. The director usually is the only person who has all the necessary information for completing application forms and, therefore, is the one ultimately responsible for filing the numerous ongoing attendance and financial records most agencies require. If a board member assumes this responsibility, the director still must provide the necessary data. Therefore, it is important that the director be familiar with the application procedures and clearly understand the ongoing requirements, including reporting requirements for funded programs *before* entering into any agreements with any funder.

The application for funding may seem intimidating to some directors and hinder them from applying for available funds. The process does become easier as the director gains more experience in applying and finds that many applications require similar information. After the information has been gathered, some of it can be reused in subsequent proposals. Nonetheless, directors must be prepared to spend a great deal of time and energy on routine reporting if they expect to use outside funds. Keep in mind, too, that some funders are targeting certain areas. The area may be a well-baby initiative or ensuring that all school-agers have a safe place to go after school. With national attention currently focused on early childhood education, you may find that an organization in your area will also support that initiative.

## 6-5c Foundations

A *foundation* is a fund administered by trustees and operated under state or federal charter. Foundation funds sometimes are made available to child care centers for major equipment purchases or for a special project. Occasionally, a foundation will provide funds for building or remodeling a facility or for training staff. Foundation support for a program depends on whether the trustees of the foundation have declared education, or more specifically, early childhood education, as an area of interest.

Large philanthropic foundations such as the Ford, Carnegie, and Rockefeller Foundations have broad-ranging programs with specific interest areas that change periodically. For example, there may be a general interest in funding innovative educational programs, but monies may be going into literacy or single-parent programs during one funding period, only to shift to programs for preschool children with developmental delays or to innovative child care models during the next funding period. Smaller foundations may limit support to programs in a certain geographic area or to a given problem area that may change every few years, while other special-interest foundations limit support efforts to very specific interest areas that do not change.

The Foundation Center is an organization with branches in several major cities. Free classes on various aspects of funding are frequently offered at its sites. In addition, individuals may register to receive regular emails from the center The Center publishes research reports, which you can view at its locations, view at its partners' locations, or purchase online. The reports include helpful information for those interested in applying for grants, including national trends and priorities of foundation giving. The website also includes a large section labeled "Foundations Supporting Early Childhood Care and Education." Consider this source when you are looking for funds.

Money from corporate foundations is available in many communities. In smaller cities, it is wise to solicit funds from small, local corporations that often have some funds set aside for use by local agencies.

Frequently, the small corporate funds are controlled by corporate managers who are very sensitive to the public relations value of making a gift to local agencies that, in turn, will give due credit and recognition to the funder. The company name may be attached to the contribution, which is a reasonable expectation. For example, when the XYZ local branch of a department store funds new block areas in all your classrooms, you may install a small plaque that reads "Donated by the XYZ Company." You may submit pictures of a store official handing you a check, building with the children (with parental permission for the photo), or in some other way promoting the company and your center. You, your staff, and the center families may support the store with your business in return.

In an earlier example, a small-business owner recognized a creative and worthwhile idea. She was interested in helping children learn about plants and, therefore, responded to the center's request. Foundations, too, are looking for innovative ideas and approaches to solving problems. You can approach foundations with your opportunity for them to support a good cause (Mitchell, 1996). Mitchell's article, although written a while ago, still offers excellent advice. Your well-prepared and enthusiastic presentation, as well as your strong interpersonal and communication skills, will improve your chances of obtaining funding. Keep in mind, however, that foundations provide only a small portion of the large amounts of money required to provide good child care.

When directors plan to approach a foundation for money, they must know precisely what they expect to do with the money and how they expect to do it. Their appeal for money must be tailor-made to the foundation's interest areas, and all funding requests must move through the proper channels. However, personal contacts with foundation trustees or other people connected with the foundation are considered very helpful. Perhaps a member of the center's parent group or a board member has personal contacts with a foundation or can help find the best channels to use for personal contacts.

### DIRECTOR'S CORNER

"When I write a proposal, I always try to think of something that will appeal to the proposal reader—a catchy title or an intriguing goal such as introducing preschoolers to good nutrition through 15 microwave cooking projects. In the long run, we not only meet the goal, but we still have the microwave to use for daily food preparation."

—*Director, agency-sponsored not-for-profit center*

Funds tend to flow toward challenging and interesting programs in well-run organizations rather than to needy institutions that are faltering. A few letters of reference from respected sources may increase your chances of receiving funds.

## Government Funding

Federal, state, and local governments all have some commitment to the care of the children of working mothers, with the federal government being the forerunner of that movement as far back as the early 1940s. Although state and local government agencies have been involved in licensing and monitoring early childhood care and education programs for some time, the availability of state and local money for child care for working mothers is relatively recent when compared with federal monies available on a somewhat sporadic basis for more than 50 years. Government monies typically are available for programs that serve low-income families or those that serve children with special needs. Currently, the Head Start program and the proliferation of programs for young children with disabilities serve as evidence of the federal government's focus on these children's education. California was the first state to establish an extensive network of state-supported child care centers. However, many other states are moving to expand their state-supported systems. In 2011–2012, 40 states provided state-funded preschool at a cost of $5.1 billion. With more than a million children attending these programs, states became the largest source of public preschool (Barnett et al., 2012). Then in 2010 and 2011, with prices rising and unemployment high, many states reduced funding for education at all levels. In 2012, state spending per child dropped below the $4000 mark for the first time since the National Institute for Early Education Research began collecting data in 2002.

Nonetheless, many children, particularly in certain areas, are underserved or receive no services. Others receive no services because their parents do not enroll them for a variety of reasons.

A number of major sources of federal funding were established during the 1960s and continue to provide some basic support for child care and for children with disabilities. Although some of these programs have ended, advocates for high-quality early education continue to work to find ways to provide qualified teachers for every child and support for early childhood education and care programs. Additionally, the current focus on providing universal early care and education in the United States may result in increased funding in the future from the government.

## Head Start

One of the most well-known federal early childhood initiatives has been Head Start. This large, well-funded

*Some funders may send representatives to observe in classrooms, view center records, and confer with the director.*

their families. Both programs are comprehensive early childhood development programs. Since Head Start's inception, more than 25 million children have been enrolled. Fiscal year 2012 program statistics show the enrollment as 959,280 children ages 3 to 5 years (U.S. Department of Health & Human Services, 2012). For the 2012 fiscal year (the latest year for which data were available), Congress appropriated $7,968,544,000 for Head Start projects and activities.

## Child Care and Development Block Grants

Another source of federal funding is the Child Care and Development Grant Fund (CCDF). In 1996, to provide eligible low-income families with subsidies to help them afford child care, the welfare reform law consolidated several sources of federal funding to create the Child Care and Development Block Grant (CCDBG). In fiscal year 2012, this fund provided approximately $5.2 billion in federal block grants to improve the affordability, supply, and quality of child care in the United States and to enable low-income families to work, attend training, or enroll in education programs. States and territories use some CCDF funds to support child care start-up or expansion grants and loans to providers. Additionally, many states have used block grant funding to help early childhood programs improve their star or quality rating level in the state's Quality Rating and Improvement System (QRIS).

program was created in 1965 as part of the "War on Poverty." Designed to serve low-income children and their families, Head Start now focuses on two age groups. The original Head Start program serves low-income preschool children and their families. Early Head Start serves low-income children prenatal to age 3, pregnant women, and

## MAKING THE CASE FOR *ADEQUATE FUNDING OF AN INTEGRATED SYSTEM OF CARE*

As support for universal early childhood education increases, we find ourselves at a crossroads. The current system of prekindergarten education has developed in a somewhat piecemeal fashion, resulting in a wide variety of programming: public and private preschools, center-based and family home child care, and Head Start programs. Some educators and policy makers believe that as we move forward, public schools should serve as the foundation for all early childhood programming as they have the demonstrated capacity to provide affordability

and quality (McCartney, Burchinal, & Grindal, 2011). Others contend that a mixed-delivery system of educating young children, making use of existing programs in modified configurations with adequate funding, will provide the greatest potential for quality education (Barnett & Ackerman, 2011; Gilliam, 2011). As the director of a program, you have the opportunity, and perhaps the responsibility, to become involved in this critical debate over the future of early education in our country. For additional information, see Zigler, Gilliam, & Barnett (2011).

## Advocacy

Despite the best efforts of early childhood educators nationwide, the issue of funding child care centers presents several dilemmas. First, many parents simply cannot afford to pay the cost of care. Although the government already provides large sums of tax revenue, those amounts have never been enough to provide even basic quality for

all the children who need care. Nor has it provided for all the children whose parents want them to participate in preschool education. At the same time, by far the largest part of the child care budget goes to staff salaries. Yet most staff salaries are deplorably low. A plan for financing universal early care and compensation has been proposed by many early childhood educators. Major ideas include delineating a career lattice that would allow entry-level child care staff to begin work with limited previous training and then participate in professional development at no cost. Staff members with bachelor's degrees would be paid salaries in line with those of public school teachers. All staff would be expected to continue to participate in professional development activities. Directors need to be aware of such initiatives, to contribute ideas, and above all, to work for improved quality in child care and education.

Often, legislation involving child care is controversial. As more women work outside the home and more children grow up in single-parent families, child care has taken on new political importance. (See the U.S. Department of Education website for updated information regarding federal policies and initiatives related to early care and education.) Center directors need to keep informed of current and pending legislation and make their views known to state and federal legislators who can provide up-to-date information. Local and national organizations such as Child Care Aware of America (formerly the National Association of Child Care Resource and Referral Agencies) and NAEYC are good sources of information on legislation related to young children. You can easily find the names and contact information for your state and federal legislators online. The Children's Defense Fund provides a newsletter available through email. Regular updates and bulletins on pending legislation are provided. Governmental bodies, individual government officials, and myriad organizations related to funding, education, and similar issues are easy to locate on the Internet. Two publications addressing the overall issues of early childhood care and education are *The Pre-K Debates: Current Controversies and Issues Vision for Universal Preschool Education* (Zigler, Gilliam, & Barnett, 2011) and *Ready or Not: Leadership Choices in Early Care and Education* (Goffin & Washington, 2007).

Center directors are responsible for maintaining current knowledge of how federal, state, and local dollars are being allocated. They should make their opinions known to their legislators and determine whether their programs or the children they serve might be eligible for various types of funding. If so, they certainly should give serious consideration to applying for those dollars.

Some programs are funded almost entirely by state or federal government tax dollars. Although one might argue that 3-year-olds are just as entitled to government funds as are 7-year-olds who attend public schools, relying on tax monies to support a program totally can be risky. Funding for some programs or individuals has been eliminated rather abruptly, and there is no guarantee that funds will continue from year to year. Many public elementary and secondary schools engage in additional fund-raising for aspects of the program that are usually considered integral parts of schooling such as music, athletics, field trips, and transportation to school. You must be prepared to participate in the universal preschools

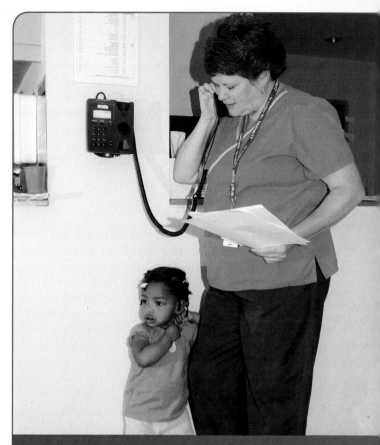

*On some days, directors are expected to take care of the needs of homesick children, answer the phone, and, in addition, work on obtaining funds for the program's needs.*

debate with information rather than relying solely on your personal opinions.

## 6-6 SOLICITING FUNDS FROM CORPORATIONS AND INDIVIDUALS

The fund-raising we have addressed so far  relates to major government grants and to relatively small amounts raised for a specific immediate purpose such as additional books for classrooms or cooking activities. Most centers require funding that far exceeds tuition paid by parents. Not all centers are eligible for government funding, and the owners of home centers prefer to solicit funds from nongovernmental programs.

Because most directors will need to be involved in annual and special fund-raising from corporations and individuals, they must establish policies and procedures regarding this responsibility. These policies and procedures then can be used to create individual funding campaigns.

Step one of a funding campaign is to find the people who will be the fund-raisers. If board members have been selected with this activity in mind, at least some of them will be able to contribute significantly, monetarily or in service, to the fund-raising program. All board members should understand their responsibility to make a contribution to the center, no matter how small. Some board members may have connections with community members or corporations that are prospects for center support. All should be willing to ask for contributions.

## 6-6a Preparing for Fund-Raising

Before beginning any fund-raising program, the board and director must make sure that the center has been formally chartered by the state and has IRS exemption. Forms for the latter can be obtained from the IRS. This status permits individual donors to deduct the amount contributed to the center as a charitable contribution. Specific procedures must be followed depending on the size of the contribution and the value (if any) that the contributor receives in return such as a dinner, book, or ticket to an event. Written reports are required in these cases, and it is the director's responsibility to know and follow the law or to see that the person assigned to this task has complied. Many agencies disseminate this type of information in a special brochure. When the contributor does not receive the proper documentation from the agency, future contributions may be jeopardized.

Whether the center retains an attorney, relies on the volunteer services of an attorney who also is a board member, or keeps abreast of legal requirements in some other manner, the board is responsible for knowing and following the law. Professional organizations and journals are helpful in alerting directors to potential changes and to those that have been adopted. But not knowing the law is not accepted as an excuse for not following it.

After the agency is in a position to seek contributions, the board approves the plan to conduct a fund drive. Next, the director oversees preparation of attractive and informative materials that make the case for the program's current and future operation. The information must be free of jargon and accurate, not overblown or overly dramatic. Important points must stand out with clarity to aid the busy reader who initially may be totally unfamiliar with the center and its mission. Be sure to include the purpose of the request, the total amount being sought, and information on current funding. If the document is based on a request for proposals (RFP) created by a funder, the proposal must state clearly how the funds will be used and relate that information to the funder's goals. RFP guidelines must be followed closely, and meeting the funder's deadline is essential.

A number of reference sources are available to help you plan your fund-raising strategies and to help you target foundations, corporations, and government agencies that are likely contributors to your type of request. *Not Just Small Change* (Bergman, 2010) provides detailed information about working with your organization's board to create and implement a fund-raising program. Your public library is a good resource, as are websites related to foundations. Your board members are usually good sources of contacts, and you may want to engage a professional trainer to help you develop your solicitation plan.

### Requesting Contributions

The director is responsible for ensuring that board members are prepared to speak knowledgeably and enthusiastically about the agency and the fund purpose and that they know how to ask comfortably and specifically for funds. Board members (or whoever will request contributions) should determine who will be approached, by whom, and in what time frame. Then the designated person either telephones or writes for an appointment. The latter is usually more successful and may be followed with a brief letter of confirmation. Targeting a specific amount or range for an individual or organization gift is necessary. You may receive a "no" followed by "but I can contribute a lower amount." A request for a vague amount or for a contribution may net you $100 when a specific request for $1,000 may have produced that amount. Many people are uncomfortable discussing money, and even more cringe at the thought of asking someone else for funds. Good fund-raisers focus on the value of the contribution to the agency's clients and on providing the prospective funder an opportunity to engage in important work. In most cases, the enthusiasm and sincere approach of the requesters go a long way toward eliciting a positive response.

Let us assume that you called on someone for funds. Whether or not the response was favorable, writing a brief thank-you letter will win friends for the agency and is common courtesy. If a contribution is made, your appreciation is certainly warranted, and if the prospective funder chose not to contribute, appreciation for the time spent with you is in order.

---

**REFLECTION**

Think about a time when you needed a loan from a bank, your parents, or a friend. Did you plan ahead what you would say and how you would explain your need? Did you mention the amount you needed and the purpose of the loan? How did you decide whom to approach for a loan? A director who writes a proposal must answer similar questions. A fund-raiser seeking contributions must be equally well prepared.

## 6-7 REPORTING TO THE BOARD AND FUNDERS

Whether the funders are organizations provid- **naeyc** ing support to assist needy families, stockholders investing for profit, members of a parent co-op, school board members, or individuals who own and direct the center, every funder needs to know how the business is doing. Accurate, timely, and understandable reports are essential. The director uses the daily transaction records to prepare monthly financial reports available to funders as well as for internal use in making budgetary decisions. (These reports also should be available to those staff members who choose to read them.) The director may present this information at a board meeting or may mail it to board members and other concerned people. Either way, the information should be presented in a clear, neat, and concise format. Computer-generated reports can be revised readily so that the most current information is available. The director must be prepared to answer questions regarding the month's operating budget and to justify the figures in the report.

Because the purpose of the report is to inform the reader, it is meaningless to present a highly technical report to a group with no background in reading such reports. On the other hand, large organizations may require that each center follow a particular reporting format. In any event, the information must be presented in such a way that the reader can grasp it easily. Brief comments may clarify various aspects of the report.

The director prepares or oversees the preparation of several types of reports.

### 6-7a Center Enrollment Report

How many children are enrolled, and how many are on the waiting list? If the center serves various age groups, the report should be subdivided into the various subgroups such as infants, toddlers, preschoolers, and after-school care. The director also may project the number of children expected to move up to the next age group on a month-by-month basis. For example, if six children will no longer be eligible for the toddler group in March, will there be room for them, based on licensing rules, in the preschool classrooms?

### 6-7b Accounts Receivable

The director should receive a report at least weekly of accounts receivable. In a child care center, this figure will consist primarily of tuition owed. Repeated billing on a specific schedule (usually weekly) is essential.

### 6-7c Budget Comparison Report

This report may also be called the budget variance report. Each month, the director prepares or receives a report from the bookkeeper showing what was spent the preceding month in each category. The report also shows budgeted spending for that month, as well as actual and budgeted spending for the year to date. The director or board then can spot cash flow problems, analyze expenditures, project remaining expenses, and revise the budget if necessary. If a funder requires monthly reports, the budget comparison report may be used.

### 6-7d Statement of Financial Position

On an annual basis, a statement of financial position should be prepared, showing assets (what you own) and liabilities (what you owe). This statement may be helpful as you seek additional funding.

### 6-7e Income Statement

The director or accountant must create an income statement at the end of each year. This statement reflects the total of all revenue earned and all expenses incurred during the fiscal year. The difference between revenue and expense is net income if revenues are greater than expenses, and the difference is net loss if expenses are greater than revenues. The income statement is widely considered the most important financial statement because it is a measure of how well a business is doing at the end of the year. The statement shows whether the company has generated a profit or is incurring losses. The income statement represents the actual figures for each of your previously budgeted categories. It can be used as a tool to evaluate monies allocated to specific categories on your budget. For example, if maintenance and repair expense was actually $7,000 for the year according to the income statement but was budgeted at $2,500 on your operating budget, you would want to reevaluate your budgeted figure, provided that the dollars spent for maintenance and repair were not one-time, unusual expenditures. In addition to this latter example, the income statement can be helpful for other kinds of statistical analyses.

### 6-7f Annual Report

At the end of the fiscal year, the director presents a final report showing the amount budgeted in each category and the amount actually spent. Up-to-date cash flow statements make it relatively easy to prepare the annual report, and the income statement may be used in this capacity. In some cases, the report will consist of income and expenses for a particular grant only. The annual report from the center or organization may be distributed to everyone who contributed, to families, to prospective donors, and to local press. The report should be designed to capture the recipients' attention. Information should be succinct, while at the same time conveying the accomplishments of the program. If your organization is large enough, you may want to employ a professional firm to prepare and mail the report.

Purchasing the software you'll need for processing your financial reports is essential. Invest in programs that will make fund-raising presentations more interesting and informative.

# 6-8 SHEPHERDING EXISTING FUNDS

Although obtaining additional funds often requires a significant portion of a director's time and effort, putting into place policies and procedures to manage available resources also is essential. Of course, the director presents these tools in a positive light while making it clear to staff and families that these policies and procedures will be followed. A knowledgeable, skilled director does this without rancor and without antagonizing anyone. The director helps all concerned recognize that lax procedures can lead to reduced resources. From the staff point of view, this can mean reduction in salary, staff, or supplies and equipment. For families, it can mean a lowering of program quality. And for everyone, it can mean eventual closure of the center.

Following are three areas that can lead to unexpected diminishing of funds:

- collections
- fraud
- lawsuits against the center

## 6-8a Collections

It is not uncommon for a family to have difficulty paying bills. Recognizing this, center policies and procedures, such as the following, must be explained clearly and agreed to during the enrollment procedures.

- State verbally and in writing when payment is due and how it can be made (check, credit card, cash, or voucher).
- Establish procedures regarding the timing, method, and number of overdue reminders and whether a penalty will be charged for late payment.
- Consider a plan for accepting partial payment when a family is hit with a crisis, but keep in mind that the money is needed to meet your budget and that some families will fail to pay when their children leave the center.

Your policy may be to inform the parents that the child may not attend the center program until all past due payments have been made and that the child will be readmitted only if the space has not been filled. Because positive relationships have presumably been established with every child and family, this is one of the most difficult tasks a director faces. It should never be turned over to the classroom teacher. In fact, neither the teacher nor any of the other staff need to have this confidential information.

If your policy is to require a week or two of tuition in advance, when a problem occurs, you will have payment for that period of time while you try to replace the child who must leave. This policy also will help when a family decides to move out of the area or finds another child care arrangement.

## 6-8b Fraud

Clear policies and procedures must be in place to protect against fraud. Huge amounts of money are embezzled each year, and a large percentage of that occurs in small businesses. Fraud refers to "a false representation of a matter of fact—whether by words or by conduct, by false or misleading allegations, or by concealment of what should have been disclosed—that deceives and is intended to deceive another so that the individual will act upon it to her or his legal injury" (Batten, 2011, p. 532).

Some examples of fraud include theft of cash and charging for more hours than actually worked. An employee who has access to the financial records can commit fraud by keeping an employee on the payroll for a period after they leave, writing extra checks to themselves, or charging personal expenses to the business.

Fraud occurs when a person of low integrity is unwittingly given the opportunity to steal. For example, when one person is in charge of receiving, recording, and depositing funds, it may be easy to keep some of that money for personal use. Not accepting cash will limit this opportunity to an extent.

To prevent fraud, the director must be aware of what is happening with the financial records and periodically must cross-check records such as time cards and payroll. The board must review all financial statements carefully. Members must know how to read and understand these reports and must not be afraid to question items that seem out of line to them. However, the most important deterrent is clear, enforceable (and enforced) policies and procedures.

## 6-8c Lawsuits

Directors also should establish and enforce policies that will reduce the likelihood of being sued. For example, training staff and documenting that the training occurred, coupled with adequate ongoing staff supervision, will help prevent accidents. Regularly scheduled checking of equipment, buildings, and grounds, as well as maintenance, is another preventive component. You should document who checked what and on which date. Policies regarding who has access to the premises and who may take children from the center are essential and must be followed strictly. Hand-washing, food storage, and serving procedures should be reviewed regularly, as should all other health and safety policies and procedures. The licensing process may dictate some requirements, such as background checks of center staff. Even if licensing does not require such information, it should be included in your personnel policies.

Maintaining positive relations with all families and keeping them informed on a regular basis and whenever anything out of the ordinary occurs also may lessen the probability of a lawsuit. Certainly, centers should carry insurance that will cover families' expenses in the event of an accident at the center.

The well-prepared director takes a proactive stance in seeking funds for the center and using existing resources wisely. The director also assumes responsibility for coaching the staff to follow the policies and procedures essential to the maintenance of a financially stable organization that provides high-quality care and education. For more information related to preventing lawsuits in early childhood programs, see Bruno and Copeland (2012). Additionally, the center's attorney can provide guidance.

# SUMMARY

Operating a good quality center requires a significant amount of planning. All directors must understand their fiduciary responsibilities related to operating an early care and education program. Specifically, directors should do the following:

- Understand the value of joint fund-raising initiatives to meet specific needs of the program.

- Investigate the roles that she plays in obtaining funding for a center.

- Be familiar with the numerous local, state, and national sources, both private and governmental, that are available for providing funding, and develop some skill in writing applications and proposals.

- Be able to complete a break-even analysis that can be used to ascertain how much funding will be needed to operate a center.

- Understand the differences between start-up and operating funds and the manner in which tuition rates may be determined.

- Be aware of the steps involved in fund-raising campaigns and the director's role in these efforts.

- Develop skill in preparing the multiple reports that must be submitted to board members and potential funders.

- Be aware of potential circumstances that may arise unexpectedly and that may threaten the program's reserve of available funds.

# TRY IT OUT!

1. Investigate who provides funding for early childhood education in your community. Are any programs funded by the federal, state, or local governments; United Way; private individuals; chain or franchised centers; universities or colleges; businesses; or proprietors? Is anyone else funding early childhood education in your community? Your instructor may assign one student or a group to explore each of these potential resources and provide a written or oral report for the class. Identify the purpose of the funding, conditions for receiving funding (e.g., start-up, operating, or special project funds), potential amount available, and the procedures that must be followed to apply for the funds.

2. Contact or invite to class a rural or inner-city child care center director (not a Head Start center). Inquire about the funding base.

   a. How much tuition do parents pay?

   b. How much of the total budget is covered by tuition?

   c. What outside funding sources are available to support the program, and how much money is available through those sources?

   d. How were outside funds obtained?

Discuss your findings in class. Do the resources seem adequate? What else might the center director do to secure funding for the program?

3. With one or two classmates, examine the sample grant application in Director's Resource 6-1. Identify the individual sections of the proposal, and discuss the following:

   a. What is the purpose of this particular grant application?

   b. How much funding has been requested?

   c. What information has been provided to justify the request for funding?

   d. What is the importance of the Statement of Agency Commitment?

   e. Identify the type of information included in the Statement of Need.

4. Use the figures in Director's Resource 6-3 to determine how many children will be in each group for the next six months. If licensing requires one adult for every four infants, one for every eight toddlers, and one for every 12 preschoolers, what effect will the changing enrollment have on your budget?

## DIRECTOR'S RESOURCE 6-1

### SAMPLE GRANT APPLICATION*

### (for use with Try It Out! 6-3)

Doe Learning Center Inc. is a nonprofit corporation that operates four child care centers in the greater metropolitan area. The centers provide quality child care for children ages 3 months through 5 years and also offer school-age care at two of the sites. As a United Way agency, the centers' common goal is to work toward alleviating the current crisis of child care, as outlined in the Long Range Plan for Child Care of the United Way in 2000. This study shows that there is an urgent need for quality programming for children identified as having special needs. Doe Learning Center Inc. has responded to this need by operating four centers whose common goal is the inclusion of all children.

### Statement of Agency Commitment

Metropolitan Learning Center (MLC) is located in the central area of the city. The program serves 67 children ages 3 months through 5 years. In the summer, we enroll an additional 20 children in our school-age program. Established in 1984, MLC was the first full-day program in this city to be accredited by the National Association for the Education of Young Children.

Largely based on the theories of Piaget and Erikson, the center's philosophy reflects a focus on the development of the whole child and the formation of strong, trusting relationships.

*Names of people and places are fictitious.

## DIRECTOR'S RESOURCE 6-1 *(continued)*

The developmental constructivist approach holds the belief that children develop sequentially from one stage of development to another. Because of this, we believe that children must be provided with opportunity that will challenge them and aid in their progression from one stage to the next. It is a necessity that learning be based on actual experience and participation. Talking without doing is largely meaningless to young children.

We believe that for children to grow, they must be placed in a setting that meets their basic needs. Therefore, it is our utmost concern that our program provides a nurturing, comfortable environment that is specifically structured to meet the physical, emotional, and cognitive needs of each individual child.

This philosophy was the foundation for the development of the agency. Due to this commitment, the question of inclusion was never discussed, only how to do it well.

In this time of severe staff shortages in the ECE field, MLC feels fortunate to have an outstanding quality and quantity of professionals.

- Four preschool head teachers—M.Ed.
- One toddler head teacher—Associate in Early Education
- Two infant teachers—Bachelor Education and two infant teachers—Associate Education
- Dr. John Jones, professor emeritus at the Metropolitan University, has been consulting with our agency for three years. This past year, Dr. Jones has been working strictly at MLC, coordinating our educational services.

MLC has worked extensively with the Early Childhood Education Department, Metropolitan University. The program has

## DIRECTOR'S RESOURCE 6-1 *(continued)*

been a training site for the past five years and works with an average of three to four students per quarter.

According to Washington County Child Day Care: The State of Today and Plans for 2010: "Special needs children are still at a great disadvantage. Most child care providers feel ill equipped to serve children with developmental problems and physical disabilities." MLC has successfully integrated approximately 25 children identified as having special needs. One family called more than 60 child care centers before finding a placement at MLC for their child with cerebral palsy. The center has served many children with a wide variety of special needs, including, but not limited to, pervasive development disorder, fragile X syndrome, autism, mild mental retardation, receptive language disorder, and visual impairments, to name a few.

One of the primary goals of the organization is to meet the needs of the family, parent, and child. MLC has identified its ability to meet these needs as follows:

### Needs of the Child

- Placement in a program meeting the standards of developmentally appropriate practice
- Master-level staff capable of identifying and working with high-risk children

### Needs of the Family

- Providing high-quality care for their children
- Providing quarterly parent education/training programs
- Providing assistance in identifying (or working with existing) available services (i.e., early intervention) for their children

## DIRECTOR'S RESOURCE 6-1 *(continued)*

MLC has been identified in the community as a program that will not only serve children with special needs but also give them access to the services they need or support the work of other service providers as part of the daily program. Metropolitan University acknowledged the endeavors of the center by placing students from the Special Education department under the guidance of our experienced staff. We have worked with many agencies to provide more comprehensive services to these children. These agencies include the following:

- Washington County Department of Human Services
- Special Education Regional Resource Center (SERRC)
- Cerebral Palsy Services Center
- Center for Developmental Disorders
- Speech and Hearing
- Speech Pathology
- Child Advocacy Center
- Association for the Blind
- Metropolitan University—Early Childhood/Special Education Department
- Foster Grandparent Program
- The Council on Aging
- The Single Parent Center

### Statement of Need

There are currently eight children enrolled in the program who have been identified as having special needs. There are several children who are integrated into the environment and are receiving services from support agencies. MLC feels

DIRECTOR'S RESOURCE 6-1 *(continued)*

confident that we can meet their needs without additional services. There are two children that pose challenges to our existing program. One child is currently enrolled in our infant program; he is 20 months old and has cerebral palsy. When we enrolled Ed, we assessed that we could meet his needs in the infant program. Although Ed is nonmobile and nonverbal, he uses smiles, cries, and coos to communicate with his caregiver. To continue serving Ed:

- We need to be able to meet the challenge of facilitating his growth through experiences with the toddlers.
- We need to acquire the equipment to encourage his further development.
- We need release time for his caregiver to meet with his therapist to learn how to use specialized equipment and participate in his IEP meeting.

Our second child has been identified with pervasive developmental disorder and mild characteristics of autism. Communication has been the primary barrier in the progression of Ryan's development. This aspect of his disorder carries over into other areas of his growth, including the development of self-control. Ryan has been enrolled in our program for one year and within that period has gone from single-word utterances to communicating in four- to five-word sentences. Because of this increased ability to communicate, the agency believes that a transition to the oldest preschool classroom is the next step. The goal of this move is to place Ryan in an environment of his same-age peers where he might benefit from the modeling of age-appropriate behaviors and participation in activities. Any changes in daily schedule and transition times are extremely difficult for Ryan, and separation

DIRECTOR'S RESOURCE 6-1 *(continued)*

from his current classroom teacher will be a tremendous undertaking.

Our belief is that to best aid in this transition, MLC will need the assistance of an additional staff person for the following reasons:

- To meet the needs of Ryan during the period of transition so that classroom staff may continue to meet the needs of his peers
- To act as a facilitator, giving Ryan assistance with social interactions so that he might form relationships with his peers and staff
- To give the classroom staff opportunity to focus on forming trusting relationships with Ryan, without concern that the experiences of his peers are being limited

### Purpose of Funding/Budget

The purpose of our funding breaks into three categories: equipment, consulting/training, and additional staff to decrease ratios.

DIRECTOR'S RESOURCE 6-1 *(continued)*

### Equipment

| Type | Purpose | | Cost |
|---|---|---|---|
| Outdoor swing | | | $126.95 |
| Floor sitter | Seat for severely challenged student allows a nonmobile child to interact with peers but have necessary support | | $150.00 |
| Button switch toy | | | $ 42.00 |
| Jelly bean switch toy | | | $ 42.00 |
| Circus truck | | | $ 27.00 |
| Bumper car | | | $ 25.00 |
| Brontosaurus | | | $ 29.50 |
| Oversized ball | Easier to manipulate than typical ball | 18" | $24.35 |
| | | 34" | $ 69.50 |

### Consulting/Training

Topic (we would like to open these to the public)

| | |
|---|---|
| How to adapt "typical" equipment to meet the needs of physically challenged children | $100.00 |
| How to use switch toys | $ 80.00 |
| How to write an appropriate IEP and how to make the IEP meeting work for the child | $100.00 |

### Consulting

| | |
|---|---|
| How to arrange the toddler environment to meet the needs of a physically challenged child | $100.00 |
| How to encourage positive peer relationships with typical and atypical children | $ 50.00 |

### Support Staff

Enrolling a physically challenged child into the infant program was within the abilities of our staff. Allowing time for this child to interact with peers of his own age and slowly transitioning him into the toddler room will be a challenge for us. We need time for his caregiver to visit the toddler room with him, and then time for the toddler teacher to have one-on-one time for him. This cannot be done without additional staff. Any choice we make with the current staff situation will either shortchange Ed or the other children enrolled. We are requesting a part-time assistant for six months.

| | |
|---|---|
| Cost | $ 6,656.00 |

Having children that model age-appropriate behaviors has been the most vital ingredient to Ryan's development. To continue his progress, it is imperative that he be surrounded by children exhibiting the behaviors that Ryan is striving for. As mentioned earlier, any transition is very difficult for Ryan. To continue servicing Ryan and meet his needs by transitioning him to be with children of his own age, we will need additional staff.

We are requesting a part-time assistant for six months.

| | |
|---|---|
| Cost | $ 6,656.00 |
| **TOTAL REQUESTED** | $14,278.30 |

### Expected Outcome

This grant will enable us to purchase equipment that will

- allow physically challenged children to become more accessible to the other children by being positioned near them on the floor.
- provide stimulation and encourage peer interaction.
- lessen isolation so that relationships with peers will increase.

## Director's Resource 6-1 *(continued)*

This grant will enable us to provide sufficient staff to

- allow challenged children to be surrounded with children of their own age providing appropriate models.
- allow staff to meet the requirements of our children with special needs without denying other children the attention they need.
- facilitate smooth transitions that encourage success with meaningful relationships with other children.
- make inclusion a successful experience that will encourage staff to include additional children.

This grant will provide technical assistance that will

- give the staff and management the knowledge to include these children and additional children in the future.
- encourage other early childhood programs to attend these training sessions and build support through networking with other teachers participating in inclusion.

We will be asking staff who are working with Ed and Ryan to fill out a short questionnaire before we provide additional services and then again after. We would like to see if these support services change any possible insecurities or feelings of being overwhelmed that had previously occurred.

## Director's Resource 6-2

### SAMPLE SLIDING FEE SCHEDULE

| Parent pays: | 20% | 30% | 40% | 50% | 60% | 70% | 80% | 90% |
|---|---|---|---|---|---|---|---|---|
| Infant | $30/wk | $45 | $60 | $75 | $90 | $105 | $120 | $135 |
| Toddler | $25 | $37.50 | $50 | $62.50 | $75 | $87.50 | $100 | $112.50 |
| Preschooler | $20 | $30 | $40 | $50 | $60 | $70 | $80 | $90 |

## Director's Resource 6-3

**(for use with Try It Out! 6-4)**

### CENTER ENROLLMENTS IN FEBRUARY

*Currently Enrolled*

| Infants | 10 | **Infants Transferring to Toddlers in:** | |
|---|---|---|---|
| Toddlers | 16 | March | 1 |
| Preschool | 24 | April | 0 |
| | | May | 2 |
| *Waiting List* | | June | 1 |
| Infants | 12 | July | 1 |
| Toddlers | 3 | August | 0 |
| Preschool | 0 | | |

**Toddlers Transferring to Preschool in:**

| March | 0 |
|---|---|
| April | 1 |
| May | 0 |
| June | 2 |
| July | 0 |
| August | 0 |

# REFERENCES

Barnett, W. S., & Ackerman, D. J. (2011). Public schools as the hub of a mixed-delivery system of early care and education. In E. Zigler, W. S. Gilliam, & W. S. Barnett (Eds.), *The pre-k debates: Current controversies and issues* (pp. 126-129). Baltimore, MD: Brookes Publishing.

Barnett, W. S., Carolan, M. E., Fitzgerald, J., & Squires, J. H. (2012). *The state of preschool 2012: State preschool yearbook.* New Brunswick, NJ: National Institute for Early Education Research.

Batten, G. (2011). *Gale encyclopedia of American law* (3rd ed.). Farmington Hills, MI: Gale/Cengage Learning.

Bergman, R. L. (2010). *Not just small change: Fund development for early childhood programs.* Redmond, WA: Exchange Press.

Bruno, H. E., & Copeland, T. (2012). *Managing legal risks in early childhood programs: How to prevent flare-ups from becoming lawsuits.* New York: Teachers College Press.

Child Care Aware (2013). *Parents and the high cost of child care: 2013 report.* Retrieved from http://usa.childcareaware.org /sites/default/files/cost_of_care_2013_103113_0.pdf.

Cohen, W. A. (2006). *The entrepreneur & small business problem solver* (3rd ed.). Hoboken, NJ: John Wiley.

Gilliam, W. (2011). Preschool programs should be coordinated in the public schools with supports from head start and child care. In E. Zigler, W. S. Gilliam, & W. S. Barnett (Eds.), *The pre-k debates: Current controversies and issues* (pp. 120–126). Baltimore, MD: Brookes Publishing.

Goffin, S., & Washington, V. (2007). *Ready or not: Leadership choices in early care and education.* New York: Teachers College Press.

Greene, C. L. (2012). *Entrepreneurship: Ideas in action* (5th ed.). Mason, OH: South-Western, Cengage Learning.

Hatten, T. S. (2011). *Small business management: Entrepreneurship and beyond* (5th ed.). Stamford, CT: Cengage Learning.

Linsmeier, D. (2003, May). Valuing your child care business. *Child Care Information Exchange, 151,* 56–59.

Matos, K., & Galinsky, E. (2012). *The 2012 national study of employers.* New York: Families and Work Institute.

McCartney, K., Burchinal, M., & Grindal, T. (2011). The case for public preschool. In E. Zigler, W.W. Gilliam, & W.S. Barnett (Eds.), The pre-k debates: Current *controversies and issues* (pp. 116-120). Baltimore, MD: Brookes Publishing.

Mitchell, A. (1996). Fishing for dollars in philanthropic waters. *Child Care Information Exchange, 111,* 7–10.

U.S. Department of Health & Human Services, Administration for Children & Families. (2012). *Head Start program fact sheet.* Retrieved from http://eclkc.ohs.acf.hhs.gov/hslc /mr/factsheets/2012-hs-program-factsheet.html.

Zigler, E., Gilliam, W., & Barnett, S. (2011). *The pre-k debates: Current controversies and issues.* Baltimore, MD: Brookes Publishing.

# DEVELOPING *a* CENTER FACILITY

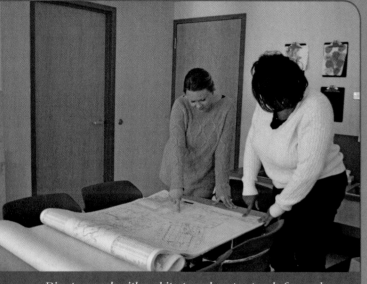

*Directors work with architects and contractors before and during the building or renovation process.*

## Learning Objectives

After reading this chapter, you should be able to:

**7-1**   Identify and describe the many factors that must be considered when planning a facility that meets the needs of children, staff members, and families.

**7-2**   Explain the director's role in creating a new center.

**7-3**   Identify the individual consultants involved in planning an early childhood facility.

## Standards Addressed in this Chapter

Accreditation Standard 5 – Health

Accreditation Standard 7 – Families

Accreditation Standard 8 – Community Relationships

Accreditation Standard 9 – Physical Environment

Accreditation Standard 10 – Leadership and Management

Administrator Competencies – Management Knowledge and Skills 2, 5, 10

Administrator Competencies – Early Childhood Knowledge and Skills 2, 4, 5, 7, 8, 9, 10

Professional Preparation Standard 1 – Promoting Child Development and Learning

Professional Preparation Standard 6 – Becoming a Professional

An early childhood education program should be housed in a spacious, attractive facility that has been created or redesigned for children and that also meets the needs of staff members and parents. The director is responsible for ensuring that appropriate space is available; therefore, space needs are analyzed carefully for both ongoing and new programs. The director may assume full responsibility for analysis of space needs, or this job may be done in cooperation with the board building committee or with staff members. Corporate systems often have a prototypical design for all centers in the system, and they usually designate an employee to provide and manage the physical facilities for the system's centers. Similarly, preschool facilities in public schools may be planned by central administration, although the principal may have a major decision-making role. In any case, the facilities must be well maintained. The director is responsible for the development of a maintenance system and for seeing that it is implemented.

As we work to meet all the standards and requirements imposed for good reason, let us also reflect on the words of beloved early childhood educator and author, Jim Greenman: "An environment is a living, changing system. More than the physical space, it includes the way time is structured and the roles we are expected to play. It conditions how we feel, think, and behave; and it dramatically affects the quality of our lives" (Greenman, 2007, p. 1).

# 7-1 ANALYZING SPACE REQUIREMENTS

In providing a suitable facility, the first task is **naeyc** to analyze the space needs. When a program is already in operation, this analysis is made periodically to ensure the availability of proper facilities for both present and future needs. If the center's program or enrollment changes, it may be necessary to modify, add, or eliminate space in the existing center. In some cases, a different location may be needed. Under any of these circumstances, the director may have to assume major responsibility for ensuring that appropriate facilities are provided. A thorough space analysis should be made before any renovation, relocation, or initial facilities choices are made.

---

**REFLECTION**

Think about a place you often go. Maybe it's a library, a store, or a college building. What kind of experience do you have as you approach the building? Is it easy to find the entrance? Is it accessible? Do you feel comfortable entering, or are you a little bit intimidated? After you enter, can you find the area you need? If not, is help available (receptionist, signs, computer information kiosk)? How do you feel when everything seems quite unfamiliar and no one seems to care that you have arrived?

How might a 3-year-old feel on his first day in preschool?

---

Users of an early childhood education facility fall into three groups: children, staff, and families. An analysis of space requirements must be based on the needs of each of these users. Space needs are based on consideration for the users, program requirements, and governmental regulations. Therefore, the director must have up-to-date information in all these areas. One option for creating a

space analysis is to chart the hours that the center is used by one or more persons. How many people will use each space, at what times, and for what types of activities? Of course, the desired number of children to be enrolled will be of major importance. Very small centers may be more costly (per child) to operate while those that serve hundreds of children may overwhelm the child. Large centers must be very carefully designed so that children have private spaces. What the child encounters on a daily basis, in terms of both facilities and people, must be manageable for each child.

---

**DIRECTOR'S CORNER**

"When we received funds to move out of a church basement, we designed our new center in two pods. Each pod has rooms for infants, toddlers, and preschoolers. Each pod has playground spaces, one for infants and toddlers and one for preschoolers. The large motor activity area, office, staff space, and area for visitors serve both pods. A few years later, when our enrollment continued to grow, we added a third pod. We find that the children, families, and staff identify the pod as 'their' school, while the teachers and families feel part of a school community as well as of a specific pod.

—*Director of an employer-sponsored child care center*

---

## 7-1a Basic Requirements

NAEYC describes the standard for physical **naeyc** environment as "a safe and healthful environment that provides appropriate and well-maintained indoor and outdoor physical environments" (NAEYC, 2007, p. 63). Lella Gandini, official liaison in the United States for the Administration of Early Childhood Education of the Municipality of Reggio Emilia, Italy, emphasizes the importance of recognizing the "special qualities of local life." She also points out, "One of the greatest challenges in designing institutions is to transform a physical plant into a human environment. One part of the transformation has to do with discovering ways to allow impersonal rooms and hallways to reflect the lives of the children and adults who spend so many active hours in that space" (Gandini, 1994).

Both children and adults are bombarded with stimulation. Using decorations judiciously can minimize environmental "noise." For example, limit what is on walls and windows. Children's art and photographs, documentation of projects, and information for parents and staff are all legitimate items to be posted. When space surrounds each posting, it is more likely that someone will notice the item. When displays are changed frequently, the newness draws children and adults alike to inspect them.

Because a child care center is planned primarily to meet the needs of children, all child care facilities should be comfortable and convenient in terms of children's sizes, their developmental levels and needs, and their interests. Preschool children need space for active and quiet play; for having breakfast, lunch, and snacks; and for taking naps. Very young infants need a play area that is safe from crawlers. And crawlers need plenty of space to move around and explore their environment without being stepped on by children who have just begun to walk.

> ### REFLECTION
>
> When you visit a friend's home or apartment, how does the space reflect who they are? Does your home convey to others your own culture? What was the place in which you grew up like? Was there a community feeling? Think about schools you attended. Recall whether or not they were influenced by the surrounding community. Did you feel welcome there?

Each child needs an individual space to keep outdoor clothing and for a change of clothes. Infants and toddlers need separate storage areas for diapers and other personal items that are provided by parents. Preschoolers need a place to store special items they bring to show others but not to share with them.

Programs for school-age child care before and after school require space for older children and must take into account the need for active play as well as relaxing, studying, and preparing and eating snacks. Children who spend six or seven hours in a school classroom need a change of pace and should not feel they are in a schoolroom before and after school.

The building also must be comfortable and convenient for adult users. To work effectively with the children, staff members need a place designed for breaks and planning time. To feel comfortable in the center, families need a welcoming entry experience and a place to meet with other families and with staff.

The primary needs that planners must consider for each of these users are

- health and safety
- accessibility of facilities
- controlled traffic flow
- personal space
- opportunities for independence and growth
- aesthetic character of all spaces

Meeting the needs of each group of users has a cumulative and reciprocal effect because when the needs of one group are met, a step is taken toward meeting the needs of the other two groups. The dynamics of a human environment involve the impact of each group on the others. In a well-run center, the three groups interact effectively because each is involved in the joint, sensitive process of child development.

## 7-1b Health and Safety

Center planners must be aware of the safety aspects above and beyond those stipulated in licensing regulations. A hazard-free building meets the needs of staff and parents, as well as children. Directors must stay abreast of environmental issues. For example, asbestos and lead paint, once considered appropriate building materials, now are not used in child care centers. Some sealed buildings in which air is recirculated may be simply redistributing poor-quality air. Recently, several schools have extensively renovated sections of buildings in which mold had developed, usually from a leaking pipe. Although not ordinarily visible on the surface, mold may cause children and teachers to become ill. The solution is to close off the area while qualified personnel remove contamination. In some cases, the director may be required to close the center while the work is done.

Governmental regulations usually will determine the type of building and decorative materials (such as carpeting) to be used; the number and type of exits (including panic hardware and lighted exit signs); the number and location of fire extinguishers, smoke detectors, and fire alarm systems; and the location of furnaces and water heaters relative to the children's play area. All these regulations protect children and staff from dangers associated with fire. Choosing environmentally friendly materials whenever possible will ultimately enhance the environment and the health of everyone.

Children also must be protected from such hazards as tap water that is too hot, slippery floor surfaces, unsafe or unprotected electrical outlets and wiring, and poorly

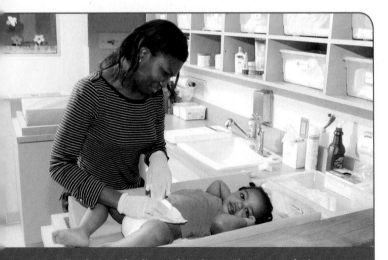

*The design of a diaper-changing station must take into account the child's needs as well as staff convenience and back health. Maintaining safe and sanitary procedures is essential.*

lighted spaces. Because of the hazards to both children and adults, smoking must not be permitted in the building or on the grounds. Covered convenience outlets or specially designed safety outlets are needed throughout the classroom for audiovisual equipment, computers, aquaria, and so forth. The director must ensure that the flooring is even; that there are no protrusions to cause falls; that stairs are provided with sturdy, low rails; and that protective screening is installed on all windows. Although the director is primarily responsible for establishing and maintaining a basic safety plan for the center, every staff member must remain alert to potential hazards and must teach children simple safety procedures such as reshelving toys and mopping up spilled water.

In public schools where older children use the hallways, plans for entering and exiting the building and moving about must be made so that young children experience minimal encounters with large groups of grade-schoolers. Although older children can move about the building independently, additional staff may be required so that young children will have escorts when they go to the library, the office, or the restroom. Ideally, each classroom for young children will have its own adjoining bathroom.

In any building, many safety practices revolve around the enforcement of center safety rules, such as prohibiting children from climbing on window sills, but it is preferable to adapt the building itself so that it is a safe place for children. Placing locks on the furnace room door is less disturbing to everyone and far safer for children than telling them they must not enter the furnace area. Be sure, however, that security devices such as locks or gates do not block an emergency exit. Guidelines for fire safety can be obtained by consulting the fire inspector. All staff must understand and follow written procedure for everyone's safety. Situations that may require calm and immediate use of these procedures include fire, tornadoes, hurricanes, presence of an intruder, a building lock-down because of a situation in the area, and so forth.

For safety reasons, programs for children usually are housed on the ground-floor level of the building, even when licensing regulations do not require this. Stairways are dangerous obstacles to quick and safe building evacuation. In the event of a fire or other emergency that requires building evacuation, preschool children may become confused or frightened and will need individual guidance to reach safety. In such situations, staff members caring for infants, toddlers, and nonambulatory preschoolers will be able to remove only the one or two children they can carry. Some centers place several babies in a crib and roll the crib to safety. If children are on an upper floor, remember that it is unsafe to use elevators in an emergency.

Over and above promoting the ease of evacuation, other safety considerations make ground-level facilities immediately adjacent to fenced outdoor space very advantageous. When children can go directly from their classrooms to a fenced outdoor area, the teaching staff can supervise both those children who choose outdoor play and those who remain indoors. One teacher would be outside with children there, and another teacher would be inside with those children. An adult must be able to see every child at all times and to reach each of them quickly and easily. The outdoor space is viewed as an extension of the indoor space. Fenced-in play areas prevent children from leaving the play space and prevent others from entering and damaging equipment, interfering with children's play, or leaving dangerous materials such as broken glass around the area. A covered outdoor space provides an additional advantage because it can be used on rainy days or on very hot, sunny days. You may find it helpful to review the national standards for physical activity in group care presented in the *Stepping Stones for Caring for Our Children* report from the American Academy of Pediatrics, American Public Health Association, and the National Resource Center for Health and Safety in Child Care and Early Education (2013).

All exits from the building and the outdoor playground should be in locations where supervision of who comes and goes can be maintained readily. While the center may welcome community visitors, strangers should not be permitted to wander through the building. Similarly, children should not be able to leave unnoticed, either alone or accompanied by anyone other than authorized personnel. Panic hardware must be provided on all exit doors, but they should be locked so that visitors cannot enter without being admitted. Parents and staff probably will have to be reminded that holding the door open for an arriving visitor is unwise because that person's presence in the center may go unnoticed.

## 7-1c Accessibility of the Facility

All users must have easy access to the building. Many parents do not want to subject their children to long daily trips to and from the center, and they prefer a center close to home. Others will look for a center close to the workplace so that they can visit the child during the day. Location near public transportation also is desirable for staff and parents.

Access to the center is increased when people feel comfortable about entering the building; therefore, the scale of the building is another consideration. As children approach the center, they should feel that it fits them. Even a large building should have some features that indicate to each child that the building is theirs. Entranceways and the areas surrounding them can be scaled to the children's requirements so that the children are not overwhelmed by a huge, heavy door or a stairway wide enough for a regiment.

Because parents and visitors often form opinions about a program on the basis of external appearances, the grounds must be well maintained, and the building itself

*A pleasant greeting from a receptionist makes everyone feel welcome.*

must be inviting. A building welcomes people through its scale, color, texture, and design. When the building is compatible with other buildings in the neighborhood, the center can begin to establish itself as a positive force in the community and be considered as an integral part of the total community. Understandably, an ultra-contemporary building might not be welcome in a traditional residential neighborhood.

The parking area should be located near the center's entrance and should be large enough to accommodate the cars of staff, parents, and visitors. A safe walkway from parking to entry is essential because many parents will arrive with several children, diaper bags, and favorite toys.

*Often, staff and visitors are required to wear identification badges. Another important identifier of you and your staff is the warm greeting you give one another each day.*

Some children are so excited about arriving at their center that they may run quickly, but not safely, to the door.

## Building Entry

When a child care center is housed in a building shared by other users, the center should have a separate entrance that is clearly marked so that families and visitors can find it. Entrances used by older students, agency clients, or other tenants may mean heavy traffic that can intimidate children and may make supervision of their arrival and departure more difficult. Many centers now have entry systems requiring visitors to ring a bell, while designated family members enter a code that unlocks the door. The code may be changed periodically for security.

Inside the building, there should be clear indications of where to proceed. Signs, supergraphics, or pathways incorporated in the flooring (such as tile arrows) can lead visitors to the proper place, even if no receptionist or secretary is available. A pleasant greeting from a receptionist is ideal, especially when the child and parent are called by name, but many centers are unable to afford a staff member to fill that role.

When the receptionist's or secretary's office has a large glass window overlooking the entry, visual contact can be made with people as they arrive, and parents or visitors will feel more comfortable about asking for assistance. In the office adjacent to the entry, the center staff can greet people and receive forms and payments from families. If parents or visitors find no one with whom to communicate when they enter the building, they may become disgruntled and leave, feeling that no one cares about their needs. Or a visitor may search out the classrooms and begin a conversation with a busy teacher, disturbing activities there and probably inviting a cursory response that is detrimental to good public relations. The entry also should be accessible to the director's office so that he is highly visible and readily available. Furthermore, it is imperative that all visitors be screened to ensure that everyone who enters has a legitimate purpose.

### DIRECTOR'S CORNER

"This morning, Mrs. Adams stopped in to see me. She just wanted to let me know how much she and Ralinda missed Marion, our receptionist, who has been home with the flu for a week. She said, 'Marion always calls everyone by name. She greets us with a smile and, especially on days when I'm rushing, I really enjoy the welcome.'"

—*Director, urban center*

Many centers require an access code to open the door of the center. As technological development continues, an even wider variety of options, such as voice and fingerprint recognition, may be readily available to programs. Although some centers have already installed surveillance cameras at exterior doors and in hallways, these may become more commonly used by centers. Some programs have these cameras in classrooms so that parents can access views of their children's activities from their places of employment. A simple safety feature, such as well-lighted exterior doors, makes it easier and safer for staff and parents arriving and leaving the center during early morning and evening hours.

In many centers, staff wear identification badges. Visitors are given a temporary visitor badge. In other centers, parents sign their children in and out via computer, connected to the center's software package. More elaborate screening devices are used in very large centers, requiring visitors to insert their driver's license into a machine that records the data with the exact date and time of arrival. To exit, the process is repeated.

In any case, the entry itself should say "welcome." The colors used in the entry should indicate that this is a place for growth and vitality; grayness and drabness do not belong here. Lighting is as important here as it is in the classrooms. The area should be bright but not harsh. Avoid glare, perhaps by using sheer window covers, awnings, or shades. Sunshine is ideal, but when that is not available, an artificially, brightly illuminated area with softer lighting in cozy areas sets the tone for the real warmth that children and families can expect to experience throughout the center. Entry surfaces also are important and must be designed to withstand muddy shoes or boots and dripping umbrellas. Although the entry should be large enough to accommodate several people without being crowded, it should not be too large because such space has minimum use but still costs about as much per square foot as areas that are heavily used. Furthermore, large entranceways may overwhelm a child or intimidate an unsure parent. Some children will interpret large open spaces as an invitation to run.

The required minimum number of entrances and exits is determined by fire laws, but to determine the best locations for these doors, the planners should take into consideration the traffic patterns of people who come to the building. Teachers like to greet parents as they arrive with their children; therefore, locating the arrival point close to the classrooms helps parents and children as well as teachers. Similarly, when the children leave, teachers can see the parents briefly.

Just as children should be able to reach their classrooms without walking through long, uninteresting, and perhaps frightening hallways, adults should be able to get to their areas conveniently and without disturbing children's play. For example, deliveries to the kitchen or other service areas should be easy to make without having to negotiate stairs or move through the children's space.

## Working Smart with Technology

### *Applying Principles of Universal Design*

All too often when we hear the word "technology," we may think of cell phones, laptops, and interactive whiteboards. However, technology has a much broader definition and can refer to the knowledge that is used to create items as well as the use of scientific principles to solve problems (National Institutes of Health, n.d.). Nearly 25 years ago, Ronald Mace and his colleagues began applying their scientific knowledge to the design and construction of buildings. Mace, an architect who used a wheelchair, coined the term *universal design* (UD) to refer to "designing all products, buildings and exterior spaces to be usable by all people to the greatest extent possible" (Mace, Hardie, and Place, n.d., p. 2). The goal of UD as it relates to buildings is to ensure that structures are planned *from the beginning* to be accessible to all potential users without the need for retrofitting at a later date.

One of the foundational principles of the field of early childhood education is embracing diversity and celebrating difference. This important value can be seen in the facility we provide for young children. If we use our knowledge of the science of child growth and development as we plan with consultants from other disciplines, we can provide a welcoming facility that meets the needs of the diverse children, families, and communities we serve.

*A facility with automated doors makes entering the center easier for everyone—children with and without disabilities, parents carrying children, and visitors making deliveries to the front desk.*

Accessibility carries an additional importance for those who have special needs. The Americans with Disabilities Act (ADA) requires that facilities be designed so that all services can be used by all clients and employees. Entrances and exits, traffic flow patterns, and facilities throughout the building and grounds should be designed for ease of use by people who have disabilities. People (children included) in wheelchairs or on crutches should be able to move about comfortably; to use bathrooms, drinking fountains, and telephones; and to participate in all aspects of the center's program. Seemingly small items such as the type of faucet on sinks or the handles on cabinets can be designed to facilitate use by people who otherwise would have to ask for assistance. The ADA requires these accommodations for most centers that meet certain conditions, but even in situations where the accommodations are optional, concern for the comfort of all individuals necessitates that efforts be made to modify buildings. Additional information on accessibility and UD in early childhood can be found on the University of Maine's Center for Community Inclusion and Disability Studies website.

## Control of Traffic Flow

Planners should consider the children's daily traffic patterns between indoor and outdoor spaces, as well as within those spaces. For example, children will move from classroom to multipurpose room and back, and from classroom to outdoor area and back. They may leave from the outdoor area if they are playing there when their parents arrive. A good floor plan takes into account the fact that young children should be able to go directly outdoors, preferably from their own classroom, or at least with minimal walking in hallways or in areas used for other purposes.

Coat storage should be near the door where the children enter. When coats are stored in the classroom, shelving may be used to create a coat area separate from the play space.

Well-planned children's areas are designed so that teachers can supervise all areas from almost any vantage point without excessive walking and certainly without screaming at children. A teacher in a room with an alcove may have to walk over to that area repeatedly to know what is happening there. An L-shaped outside area may be spacious, but such an area becomes very difficult to supervise without extra staff because as soon as children turn the corner, they are out of sight and beyond the reach of their teacher.

## Food Service

Serving meals to children further complicates the traffic flow in the center. Because preschool children usually eat in their classrooms, there is no need for a separate cafeteria. In fact, in a public school, the noise and confusion of a cafeteria is inappropriate for preschoolers, and the furniture is too large to accommodate them comfortably. Preschool classrooms, therefore, must be large enough to contain tables and chairs for all the children and teachers without crowding the play space. The kitchen should be nearby. Steps or doorways between the kitchen and the classrooms make moving food carts or carrying trays difficult, and long distances between the kitchen and classrooms may

mean long walks for teachers and long waits for children when something extra is needed during mealtime.

When teachers sit at the table with children and eat the food that is served to the children, they model good eating habits and appropriate manners without lecturing children on how to behave and what foods are good for them. The center budget should include enough food for teachers because this is part of their job. Some teachers will prefer to provide their own lunch to be eaten during their break time. Nonetheless, those teachers should still have lunch with the children and eat at least small amounts of the food served.

The kitchen must function primarily in relation to the classrooms and secondarily in relation to adult areas. The amount of kitchen space required varies according to the activities to be conducted. The center that uses a catering service for lunches may need very little space, while the center in which hot lunches are prepared will require additional equipment and space. In very large centers, a kitchenette may be provided for staff use and for preparation of refreshments for various meetings.

---

### REFLECTION

Think about how the traffic pattern of a building you use frequently affects you. When you arrive at this building, which room do you go to first? Where is that room in relation to the door you use to enter the building? Think about the directions in which you move through the building during the day. Are there any places that could be rearranged to save you steps?

Classrooms can be arranged for variety and ease of traffic flow if areas within the room are clearly demarcated and exits are located so that traffic does not cross through a number of areas. Shelves for blocks are excellent room dividers that can be used to separate the block area from the housekeeping area and from the heavy traffic area, thereby providing a special space for undisturbed block building. Reading and writing areas can be separated from noisy carpentry or music areas by shelves or dividers; then children can find quiet, secluded spaces for solitude and concentration. Children can work comfortably without being disturbed when traffic patterns in the classroom are taken into consideration. One of your roles as director will be to help teachers recognize the value of planned traffic flow.

---

## Bathroom Locations

Licensing laws regulate the number of toilets and sinks required, but the location of the bathroom is equally important. Children need bathrooms immediately adjacent to their classrooms, multipurpose room, and outdoor play areas so that they can get to them quickly. Each of these areas may not need a separate bathroom, but planning can include location of one bathroom to serve two areas. Prekindergarten boys and girls are comfortable sharing the same bathroom. However, the philosophy of some programs and the requirements of some governmental bodies now necessitate separate toilet facilities for boys and girls. Certainly these are needed for school-age children. As with all other areas, restrooms require adequate adult supervision.

Location of adult bathroom facilities is often determined by designing a plumbing core around which the bathrooms and kitchen are built. Although a plumbing core design is economical, it may not be practical in terms of the traffic pattern and the program needs because adult bathrooms must be placed appropriately to serve the people in classrooms, offices, meeting rooms, and the kitchen.

## Arrival Area

Figure 7-1 shows an example of a plan for a child care center, but because each center should be designed to meet the needs of its clients and staff, it is not meant as a model. Several of this plan's characteristics are worth imitating, however. Note that as families arrive, the receptionist (or director) can greet them, and then they can go directly to the classrooms. (The arrow to the right on Figure 7-1 indicates the entrance.) An observation booth is shown overlooking one classroom. When space is available, this feature may be desired for all of the children's spaces. Parents and visitors can

observe without being seen by the children. Observation booths enable future teachers to learn about children's development and related good teaching practices. Note, too, that each classroom has an adjoining restroom for children and that a multipurpose room is available for large-muscle activities.

## Staff Area

In planning for traffic flow, the staff's daily traffic patterns also must be considered with attention focused on which areas they use in what sequence on a typical day. Figure 7-1 shows the relationship of staff members' spaces to children's spaces in one center. Teachers need a conveniently located general storage room to enable them to set up the day's activities efficiently. They must be able to move comfortably and quickly from the storage areas to the classroom, the outdoor area, or the multipurpose room, depending on where the equipment or the supplies are needed. Teachers each need a locked cabinet or drawer in which to store personal belongings of value. In or near the classroom, they need a place to hang coats, gloves, and so on, which are needed when they go outside with the children.

Bathroom facilities for teachers should be separate from those used by the children, and there should be a lounge area in which to have refreshments during break times. Work space includes places in which they work with children, places in which they prepare materials for classrooms, and places in which they do paperwork or hold conferences. Work space that meets the staff

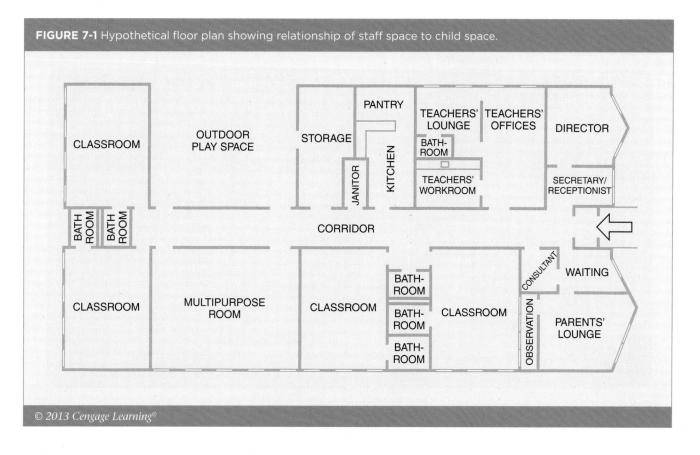

**FIGURE 7-1** Hypothetical floor plan showing relationship of staff space to child space.

© 2013 Cengage Learning®

members' needs assists them in performing their duties well. Some personnel have specialized work spaces (maintenance staff; the cook; and specialists such as a nurse, speech and language therapist, psychologist, or other consultants). Each workplace must be of a size suitable for the activity in question. For example, full-time office staff each need approximately 100 square feet of office space. This space should be arranged to provide for some privacy and sound control so that work can be accomplished with minimal interruption.

Sometimes, with proper written documentation from parents and the child's physician, a teacher will be asked to administer medication at school. Therefore, a locked cabinet is necessary in each classroom. In or next to the cabinet, one should find a clipboard or notebook on which to document the administration of the medication. This responsibility is very important; making a mistake could be quite damaging to the child. Paying attention to licensing guidelines as well as center policies and procedures related to these issues is essential.

Office space sometimes is placed close to the classrooms so that immediate additional supervision can be provided in an emergency situation; however, planners may decide to place the offices farther away from the classrooms to eliminate distractions for the director, off-duty teachers, or other staff members. An intercom system can be installed to facilitate communication in emergency situations and to eliminate disturbances. The intercom or a telephone may be a necessity if a classroom or any other area used by children is isolated from direct contact with the rest of the center. For example, all classrooms may be located on the ground floor while the multipurpose room is a level above them. A teacher using the multipurpose room needs a telephone to reach additional help if a crisis occurs. In any case, policies regarding the use of the intercom and telephone should be in place, largely to eliminate unnecessary noise and disturbance in the classrooms.

Figure 7-2 shows additional ideas for arranging center facilities. If you have ever browsed through

**FIGURE 7-2** Hypothetical floor plan.

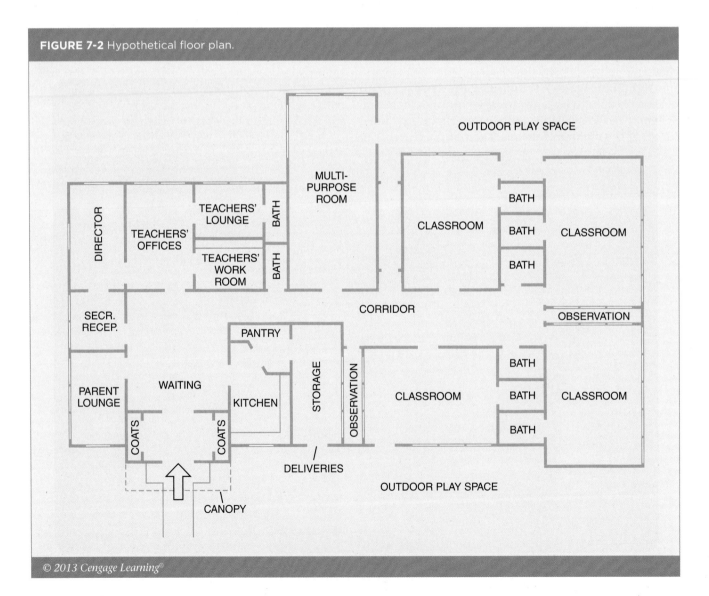

magazines showing floor plans of various homes, you may have found yourself saying, "There's a feature I like" or "I'd never want to have a room like that." Consider these floor plans in the same way. Examine them to see what you would like and why. Keep in mind that the ages and numbers of children to be served will have a major effect on the plan for the building and grounds. Geography and topography also will play important roles. For example, on a sloping lot, both the front and the back of a building may be at least partially at ground level, which is an important planning issue.

### ▶❚❚  TeachSource Video Vignette

### Space Planning, Equipment, and Facility Maintenance

This video provides an overview of the issues that must be considered when planning children's spaces for a facility. Reflect on the following questions:

**1.** How does the director meet the needs of differing age groups of children?

**2.** How might you use this video with members of your board and fund-raising committee to justify your request for maximum square footage, beyond that required by licensing, for your new facility?

### Spaces for Children

A comfortable and convenient classroom for young children includes enough space for each child to work and play without being disturbed by other activities. Thirty-five square feet per child is considered minimum, so a classroom for ten 3-year-olds must have at least 350 square feet, measuring about 18 feet by 20 feet. Fifty square feet per child is more realistic, and more space should be provided whenever possible. However, extremely large classrooms are difficult to supervise and may feel overwhelming to children. When determining classroom square footage, do not include permanent fixtures such as a sink in the classroom or immovable cabinets. Also keep in mind that when children's storage cubbies are in the classroom, the space immediately in front of the cubbies is rarely usable for classroom activities (except

getting outdoor clothing on and off). Space in front of doors is also not usable for activities (entrance door, bathroom door, and door to outside play area).

Rooms for infants require more space because of their cribs. Infants need a quiet area so that they can sleep on their own schedules. Infants able to play on the floor need space to practice moving from place to place by scooting, creeping, and crawling, while others are trying to roll from side to side, to work on sitting up, and to reach a toy that is just slightly out of reach. Meanwhile, one of the caregivers may be rocking and soothing an uncomfortable child, feeding a hungry baby, or changing a diaper. Therefore, groups of infants are kept quite small with a 1:3 or 1:4 adult-child ratio and two adults at all times.

Toddlers are becoming a little more independent, more mobile, and more interested in exploring *everything* in the environment. They still need the support of and access to an adult frequently during their waking hours. Toddler rooms should also be a little larger per child than are rooms for preschoolers.

In all classrooms where diapers are changed, a special area is needed with a changing table; access to supplies needed such as gloves for the adult, cleansing supplies, and clean diapers; and a place to deposit used diapers—all within the reach of the adult who is at the side of the child being changed to prevent falls. A sink immediately adjacent to the changing table is needed for adult hand washing. Keep in mind that while diaper changing is occupying one adult, the other adult must be alert to the needs of the remaining five to seven babies. One can see why infants and toddlers are placed in small groups!

All children need cozy places where they can relax while they look at books, examine interesting objects, or just daydream. These spaces should be small enough to promote a sense of privacy and intimacy, yet large enough to be shared with a friend or two. For preschoolers, a loft can meet this need. It must be quite sturdy and have some kind of siding to prevent objects from falling to the floor and hitting anyone below. The space under the loft can be used for storage or small group activities. The teacher must be able to supervise the area. Furthermore, a loft and all other spaces designed for children's use should be accessible to each child.

The classroom also must include a meeting area that is large enough for a number of children to gather for a story or special activity. Furniture can be moved for these occasions: movable shelving and furniture facilitate such rearranging. These movable pieces also will be valued when teachers are placing cots for children's naps. Too much furniture moving detracts from the teacher's real role, but most centers do not have a separate nap room and must consider how to place cots so that children will not be too close to one another (a requirement of many licensing rules). When cots are too close together, children may find it difficult to rest. Space also must be available for cot storage.

Some centers also offer care to children from kindergarten through third or fourth grade or older. These children come to the center for before- and after-school care and may even be transported between sites by a center bus. School-age children will treasure some personal space. Imagine spending 10 hours a day in a relatively small space with 30 people, primarily following someone else's directions. Although many adults do spend 8 hours in a work environment crowded with equipment and people, they have the opportunity to go out for lunch or take a short break. Children in schools usually are required to stay with their class for the entire day. After school, having some private space provides a welcome respite.

Before and after school, elementary-grade children also need spaces for organizing clubs and playing games, for informal sports, and for creating and carrying out their own wonderful ideas. They need adult supervision, but at the same time, they need much more independence in organizing and reorganizing the space, perhaps decorating it so it is theirs. Because these needs are quite different from those of younger children, they need separate spaces.

## Family Space

Parents and visitors need a comfortable lounge area in which to wait for their children or to talk with each other. Parents also need a space that is large enough for group meetings and space that is small enough for individual conferences with a teacher or the director. Even if a whole room is not available, centers can at least provide some seating in another area. Fire laws may preclude having furniture in hallways. Facilities for observing the classrooms, while going unnoticed by the children, represent both a convenience and a learning experience for parents and visitors.

*In after-school care, many children enjoy working on projects.*

Often, employer-sponsored child care is provided near the worksite. Parents will appreciate an area in the classroom where they can spend quiet time with their own children, sharing a book or puzzle. In infant centers, a private space for nursing offers a relaxing time for mother and baby.

## 7-1d Opportunities for Independence and Growth

The facility should be planned to promote the independence of both children and staff. An environment for children fosters independence and growth when it is arranged so they can make decisions and solve many of their own problems. Such a setting has child-size appointments, including sinks, toilets, and drinking fountains; doorknobs that children can reach and operate (where that is desirable); and wall decorations that are placed at the children's eye level. Planners must keep in mind that independence is equally important for children with special needs.

A setting that encourages independence also has classroom storage that is directly accessible to children, enabling them to find and reach all the materials and equipment they use. When such shelving is adequate, each piece of equipment is displayed so that the children can see it easily, remove it from the shelf without moving other items stacked on top of it, and return it to its proper place. Clearly marked storage space for children's personal belongings, located so that children can get to it, also will promote independence. In addition, however, storage space that is out of children's reach also is needed in each classroom so that teachers can store materials and supplies they do not want the children to obtain, such as gallon jugs of glue.

Single-purpose buildings allow programming to be based on users' needs (especially those of children) rather than requiring that the program be planned based on the needs of a range of occupants. A center allows teachers to feel independent when the design of the facility enables them to plan programs for their children without constantly checking with other teachers. For example, teacher independence is curtailed when a preschool class is housed in a public elementary school where the young children must use the bathroom, lunchroom, or outdoor play space for specific time blocks because older children use these facilities at other times. Even if the children's needs suggest a deviation from this schedule, the teacher may be required to follow it. Some teachers in centers that move children from room to room for various activities find that they are not able to plan as independently if they have to direct children from the art room to the music room and then to the playroom on a daily basis at a predetermined, scheduled time rather than having the children move at their own pace. Children may feel frustrated at having to move to another area just as they are getting interested in writing a message or serving dinner in their "restaurant." Obviously, balance is needed. Children and teachers usually have to stop at a particular time for lunch. And when it's time to go home, a parent may be able to spend a few minutes while her child finishes an art project, but then it's really time to leave.

The environment that fosters independence and growth is one in which variety is apparent, offering children an *appropriate* number of choices. They are not overwhelmed with choices or bored with repetitive sameness in the design of space. Variety in color, texture, floor level, and building materials, if not overdone, can give children a sense of vitality that can be stimulating. Noise level is another area in which variety can be appropriate. Some spaces may be set aside for noisy play while others are retained for quieter activities. Although acoustical ceilings, carpeted floors, and curtains all absorb sound and contribute to the auditory comfort of everyone in the center, children still can learn to use appropriate sound levels in each space and to choose their activities accordingly. The environment leads to cooperation as well as to independence. When staff members find themselves working in a well-designed, appropriate space, they are happier, which leads to a better program for parents and children.

## Aesthetic Character

An environment for children should be aesthetically pleasing to them. The factors relating to other users' needs and to program requirements can be designed so that they appeal to the children's sense of beauty. For example, it is just as easy to have an interesting painting in the classroom as it is to put up a fake window with curtains over the play sink. Both are intended to make the room more attractive. Children can enjoy a wide range of art, but the value of a fake window is limited, at best.

Provide as much natural light as possible while avoiding glare. Artificial lighting should be bright enough for children's activities but also adjustable. Lamps that cannot be tipped over, ceiling lighting that can be controlled with dimmer switches, and area lighting all contribute to a feeling of physical and emotional well-being and help foster productivity, relaxation, and comfort. Incandescent lighting and full-spectrum lighting seem more appropriate than fluorescent. Consider purchasing energy-efficient lightbulbs, which, though initially more expensive, are longer lasting and environmentally friendly.

Wall surfaces can provide texture and color that contribute to the room's vitality. Garish decorations or "cute" wall coverings, emblems, or cutouts contribute little to children's appreciation of beauty. Carpets replete with numbers and letters add "busyness" to the environment and provide neither aesthetic nor intellectual stimulation. Children and staff probably will be more inclined

*Children develop independence and friendships when they enjoy meals together. Teachers always sit with the children and share the meal.*

to take care of an attractive environment. It is easy to develop messy habits when the surroundings are poorly designed with inadequate facilities and unappealing spaces. It is equally easy and more satisfying for everyone to develop good habits and an appreciation of beauty when the facilities are well designed. Note that the touches a teacher adds may be inexpensive or free: a single flower from her garden, attractively mounted pictures of the children at play, or a crystal hanging in the window to catch the light and project interesting colors and patterns throughout the room.

Having analyzed the facility requirements for a high-quality early childhood education program, and the information provided by a specific needs assessment, the director can determine the center's current facility needs and project the building and ground needs of the center for several years. This long-range planning is useful in enabling a center to coordinate program, facility, and financial decision making. Whether the director is analyzing need in terms of possibly rearranging or remodeling the existing center's facilities, or of leasing or constructing a new center, the users' needs are kept in the forefront when working toward a decision.

**MAKING THE CASE FOR *SUPPORTING PHYSICAL ACTIVITY***

We are in the midst of an obesity epidemic among children today. Child care programs have been found to be effective environments for encouraging healthy eating and physical activity to combat this epidemic (Lyn et al., 2013). When planning a facility, consideration should be given to providing children with physical activity on a daily basis. Reflect on the following questions:

**1.** What is the climate where you want to create a center? What do these conditions mean for you as you plan your facility that supports regular physical activity?

**2.** What do you know about the physical development of young children that should be considered when planning indoor and outdoor spaces for large motor activity?

## 7-1e Programmatic Requirements

The director and building committee members must be thoroughly familiar with the early childhood education program before they attempt to evaluate an existing or proposed facility. They must understand the types of activities planned, the program goals, and the enrollment projections. For example, in contrast to a half-day program, a full-day program must provide a place for resting and for eating meals. Many children who spend the entire day at a center also need room in which to seclude themselves from the group for short periods of time, that is, a quiet place supervised by the teacher but free from the intrusion of other children.

The center's philosophy influences the type and arrangement of space. If the philosophy places heavy emphasis on parent involvement, space will be needed for meeting rooms and a lounge, and additional parking will have to be provided. The prevailing climate also affects the type of building. If children are able to be outdoors most days on a year-round basis, they will need more outdoor space and slightly less indoor space. On the other hand, a center located in a region with temperature extremes will put emphasis on indoor areas and will give major consideration to effective heating, ventilating, and air-conditioning systems. Floor-level temperature in the children's areas is critical because children frequently play on the floor.

Planning for carpeting and tiling sections of the classroom floor should be done with activities in mind. Cleaning is facilitated when art and food activities take place on hard surfaces, and teachers will be able to focus on the children's needs instead of protecting the carpeting. A sink in the classroom is a much-used and much-desired convenience and also should be on the tiled area.

Keep in mind the importance of the outdoor environment. Just as children need to test ideas in the classroom, they also need to test ideas outdoors. They need opportunities to test what they can do physically as they explore an environment created to challenge and stimulate them. Similarly, children need time to try new ways of doing things—new ways of interacting with water, mud, plants, and people. As more and more information becomes available on the problems caused by childhood obesity, directors must plan for spaces and opportunities for children to engage in significant periods of large motor activity.

Children need extensive opportunities to interact with the green environment. Digging in the soil, planting, caring for, and enjoying what they helped produce provide important science learning. Walking and running on paths surrounding green spaces provides much more interest than running on a concrete surface surrounded by more concrete, metal, and wood equipment. When the outdoor environment is aesthetically pleasing for children and adults, well maintained, and designed with lots of movement in mind, it beckons them to come out and be involved.

*Flowers (nonpoisonous) and grassy areas can enhance the children's playground.*

## 7-1f Governmental Regulations

In communities that have zoning laws, an early childhood education center that is operated for profit may be limited to locating in a business or less restrictive zone, while a nonprofit educational facility generally may be located in any zone. Local rulings may also limit non-profit use of certain areas. Prior to signing a lease or contract to purchase property, the director must check with the local zoning board to see if usage of the particular piece of property is in compliance with the zoning code. In some cases, a zoning variance may be allowed; that is, the director may petition to use the location for a center if it can be shown that the presence of the center will not have a negative effect on neighboring sites. Zoning ordinances also may include parking requirements, and off-street parking provisions may have to be made for center staff and visitors, including those who have special needs.

When a new facility is built or an existing building renovated or put to a new use, current codes usually apply. For example, a building being used as a public school would be inspected based on the codes in existence when that building was put into use. However, if a child development center leases the space, the owner will be required to meet the *current* regulations. When a building is renovated or a new facility is constructed, the ADA must be followed. Some requirements include access by means of ramps instead of, or in addition to, stairs; accessible restroom facilities; doors that can be opened by a person in a wheelchair; and low drinking fountains.

Other governmental regulations pertain to licensing. These are discussed in Chapter 3 and include number of square feet of space for children's use both indoors and outdoors, fencing, exits, building materials, and toilet and hand-washing facilities. Before you purchase, lease, or renovate a building, ask your licensing agent to ensure that the facility is in compliance with governmental regulations or can be renovated appropriately and at an affordable price. There may be a charge for this consultation. Also make sure that your lease and all conditions make it worthwhile for you to pay for the required changes to the building.

Sometimes, a church, community service organization, or school will permit or invite an early childhood education center to use its facilities at little or no charge. Available rooms also may be found in school buildings. This contribution is a major cost benefit to the program. Before agreeing to this use of the building, however, both the contributor and the center's board should have a clear, written understanding of the rights and responsibilities of each party. For example, both will need to know how liability and property insurance will be handled and exactly what is covered.

Get written answers to your questions, such as the following:

- Will the center be able to operate if the agency or school is closed for vacation or for a holiday, such as Presidents' Day, when many parents must still go to work?

- What maintenance responsibilities will the early childhood center have?

- How will the rest of the property be maintained?

- Will the agency or school be responsible for all grass cutting, snow removal, utilities, garbage collection, and recycling?

- Will the center area be wired for phones, computers, and other technology?

- How many parking spaces will be reserved for staff and parents?

- With whom can the director communicate if a problem occurs, such as a leaking roof?

Check details carefully. You don't want to be in a situation in which the agency's behavior leads to serious problems for the center. For example, suppose the agency neglected to pay the utility bills as agreed, leaving the center without heat or water.

## 7-1g Cost and Quality

Cost is a factor in every aspect of facility development and maintenance. Using low-quality materials to save money often proves to be expensive in the long run. For example, inexpensive carpeting may be difficult to keep clean and may have to be replaced frequently. Many "cute" or unusual details put in place to attract parents may do that in some cases but may add nothing to the quality of the children's experience. Examples include elaborate entryways, themes related to TV or film characters as part of the permanent decor, and so forth. Center directors have many opportunities to choose environmentally conscious materials, such as electrical appliances that use reduced amounts of energy. Ensuring that a building is well insulated can save many dollars on heating and cooling bills.

## 7-2 PLANNING A NEW CENTER

In planning for a new center, the sole proprietor, the partners, or the corporate board will be the final decision maker(s). As discussed in an earlier chapter, the director may also be an owner. In any case, it is the owners who must decide or agree that a new center is needed. They must also raise the necessary funds and employ appropriate contributors (realtor, architect, attorney, banker, and contractor). If the director is an employee, the owner may charge him with the tasks of performing a preliminary property search, providing a list of criteria for the building, and, in some cases, taking on the major responsibility of planning and implementing the entire construction process. To avoid conflict, wasted energy, and probable cost overruns, roles and responsibilities must be clearly delineated early in the planning stage. The decision may be to construct a building; to buy, rent, or lease an existing building; to renovate an existing facility extensively;

or to locate space that would be donated by the owner on a temporary or permanent basis.

Planning for a new center involves the same analysis of space requirements that is done when an ongoing program facility is assessed. The one item that usually stands out as being important in decisions about planning a new center is cost. Although cost is a major factor, the key concept is the value of the setting to children, staff, and families.

Let us assume that a new center is being created. The owners already have several centers in other cities. They are not early childhood educators, and they do not want to spend time on the details. Therefore, they have hired a director and given him the major responsibility of planning the center. He is to report to the designated owner on a weekly basis. The owners will make the final decision on all major issues.

The director starts facilities planning with a needs assessment in the community (recall that needs assessment was discussed in Chapter 2). The director must also obtain applicable information about zoning and licensing. These data, combined with the availability of a particular amount of money, are applied as criteria in the search for appropriate facilities. Some centers assess needs, locate facilities, and then mount a fund drive, anticipating that sufficient money will be obtained. The director or building committee must assess realistically the amount of money that will be *available* for establishing and maintaining the center facility and the amount of money that will be *required* to meet the assessed need.

The building committee works closely with the budget committee to determine the amount of money needed and available for constructing, purchasing, renovating, or leasing a building. Costs of real estate and construction vary widely depending on geographical location, and within a given city, they vary from the inner city to the suburbs. Costs must be checked for each locale. Careful planning is essential because after construction starts, changes are costly.

## 7-2a Considering New Construction

Both land and building costs must be considered. The lot must be large enough for a building of the required size; for a playground of at least 75 square feet per child (groups of children may use this area at different times); and for parking for staff, parents, and visitors. The cost of the building will depend on the size of the building, on the quality and elaborateness of the materials used, and on the intricacy of the design. A major advantage of new construction is that the building can be created to meet the specific needs of children. Furthermore, it can be designed to look like a place for children. And if well designed, it will be a place in which the program can

be delivered efficiently, effectively, and with a high level of comfort for all users. Talk with your architect about "going green," that is, using environmentally friendly materials and design, as well as taking advantage of the natural setting. Often a company that owns many centers will have a standard building plan that will be used no matter where the building is located.

## 7-2b Using Existing Buildings

Costs involved with the use of an existing building are purchase price, lease or rent, and renovation. A center may incur none, one, or two of these costs, depending on the owner and on the condition of the building.

If funds are available, a down payment on the purchase of a lot or a building, or plans for extensive remodeling, may be made. The board must be certain that funds for monthly payments, including interest as well as principal, will be available. A bank or savings and loan company can provide information on interest rates, length of mortgage, and payment procedures, as well as explanations of penalties, foreclosures, and insurance requirements.

## 7-2c Renting or Leasing

Because purchasing a building involves high initial costs, many centers rent or lease all or part of a building. Both renting and leasing involve periodic payments. Under a lease, the lessor and the lessee agree that the space will be available and paid for during a specified length of time, usually at least a year. A longer lease is preferable because moving can be expensive, and clients may be lost if the center changes locations. Relocation costs include staff time spent in the following activities:

- fund-raising
- attending additional board committee meetings
- locating a new site
- negotiating the lease
- arranging a loan for additional costs
- communicating with staff and families about the move
- arranging for required and desired renovations
- planning logistics of the move
- working with a licensing specialist
- arranging for reaccreditation as needed
- managing the unexpected

Following are direct costs of relocation:

- attorney fees
- architect and contractor fees
- materials needed for renovation
- cleaning prior to the move

- movers
- changing address or other information on stationery, brochures, website
- reaccreditation fee
- paying staff overtime to prepare the new site just before the center opens

One of the most challenging aspects of moving a center is making the move so that service to children and families will be interrupted as little as possible. Another challenge is the possible loss of families if the new location is not as convenient for them. The director is then faced with recruiting new families quickly while managing the settling-in period in the new center. When a space is rented, the renter may have to pay only for the period during which the space is actually used. For a nine-month preschool program, this savings could be important and significant. Such a situation occurs primarily when renting from a church. The school's equipment may have to be moved out during the summer months or may be used by other groups as part of the rental agreement. If you are renting space, try to negotiate limitations on rent increases.

A lease should spell out these conditions and include answers to questions such as the following:

- What are the beginning and ending dates of the lease?
- Is the lease renewable?
- If renewable, what limits, if any, will be set on a fee increase?
- Can the lease be terminated early?
- If terminated, what penalties apply?
- Can we sublet?
- Who is responsible for maintenance and repairs? What is included in maintenance and repairs? Who pays for it? Who provides materials, supplies, and tools? When will maintenance and repairs be done?
- Who is responsible for compliance with the building code?
- Who pays for utilities?

For example, if the board of health requires the addition of a hand-washing sink (a permanent fixture), will the center or the landlord pay for the sink and its installation? The center cannot operate a program without the sink because a license will not be granted; but if the center should move, the landlord will still have the sink.

If the landlord is responsible for maintenance, can an agreement be reached that the grass is not cut during children's regular playground hours? Think about securing a written agreement about spraying for insects and rodent control. Insist that it be done when children are not present and that no residue harmful to children will remain.

If the facility is shared because the landlord uses part of it or rents part of it to someone else or because the center owns a building and rents or leases part of it to someone else, all the preceding items must be considered. In addition, the building committee or director will settle the matter of who has access to the building and when they may have access. For example, if a teenage group uses the building in the evenings, will they be allowed to use the playground during the late afternoon before all the children have left? Other points to be considered include the following:

- Who may have master keys?
- Who may use what equipment and supplies?
- Who is responsible for ordering and paying for shared equipment and supplies?
- Who pays the telephone bill? Internet service?

Other questions involve use of the center's space by other organizations or individuals when the children are not present, such as during the evenings or on weekends. The use of the facilities (their own and that of others) by center staff members and the parent group during evening, weekend, and holiday hours also must be considered.

It is easier to reach agreement on these issues before the building committee signs a lease and takes occupancy. If a lease has been signed, the center usually cannot be moved without financial penalty, which could mean that an uncomfortable situation exists for a number of months. When the lease clearly details the rights and responsibilities of each party, most questions can be settled amicably.

---

### DIRECTOR'S CORNER

"When the renovation was initially being planned and the architects were working up the drawings, the chairperson of the committee and I went in and talked about what we would like to see happen. It seemed to break down after the initial meetings, and there were some outcomes that we were not that pleased with. Everything was ordered and halfway done before I realized what was happening. There wasn't any way that we could go back and ask for changes."

*—Director, preschool in a church facility*

---

## 7-2d Renovating

Renovation costs also vary widely depending on the location of the building and the type of work to be done. Complex changes such as relocating plumbing; rewiring electrical circuits; or installing exits, stairways, and fire-resistant surfaces are costly. The type and amount of renovation to be done will be based on the particular licensing requirements, including fire and building codes, and on the requirements of the planned program. If the center owns the building, renovation usually is a worthwhile investment.

# 7-3 WORKING WITH OTHER PROFESSIONALS

A variety of professionals outside the field of early childhood education can be helpful in planning a space for young children. Usually, the cost of their services is relatively high on an hourly rate, but in the long run, the expertise they contribute to the center's development is worth far more than the actual expenditure. However, checking references and credentials before you sign an agreement with the individual or company is critical. Written agreements with each service provider also are essential.

## 7-3a Licensing Agent

Because most programs must be licensed, the building committee contacts the licensing agent first. This specialist often provides free services and is funded through state or local taxes. Through this agent, the committee works with other professionals in the building, sanitation, and fire departments. Community planners also may be involved, either at the governmental level or through community councils. Even though these professionals are not paid by the center, the licensing and inspection fees must be paid as required.

## 7-3b Realtor

Whether you are looking for an existing building or land for a new building, a realtor may be able to save you a lot of time. Many realtors specialize in certain areas and may know of property that will be available but has not been advertised. They can also look for the type of property you need, keeping your price range in mind. The realtor can assist you in determining the zoning requirements in the area you select and may be able to help you determine whether a zone change or exception can be obtained. After you are settled into your new center, your realtor will be well aware of your program when home buyers ask about programs for young children in the area.

## 7-3c Architect

During the very early planning stage, retaining an architect can produce positive results. An architect can evaluate a site in terms of a center's needs or can examine an existing building and make recommendations about the renovations that are necessary for safety, efficiency, and aesthetics. And, of course, an architect can design a new building to fit your needs.

Ongoing architectural services can be contracted at an hourly rate, flat fee, or on a percentage (of building

or renovation cost) basis. The contract should include the fee for services and the payment due dates. In addition, the architect should spell out clearly in the contract the services that are to be provided—such as survey, site selection, design, working drawings from which a building can be built or remodeled, building permit clearance, contractor selection, construction supervision, and/or final inspection.

Your architect also will assist you in selecting materials if that is part of your contract. For instance, gypsum wallboard (which is inexpensive) is readily dented, gouged, and subject to corner damage. It is usually not the best choice in areas used by children. If you are not familiar with building materials, the architect's recommendation of an alternative material could save you money and repeated repairs in the long run.

When selecting an architect, choose someone with whom you feel comfortable. Some architects are unfamiliar with child care center needs, and you will want to choose one who is willing to listen to your concept and incorporate your ideas. Keep in mind, however, that architects have knowledge about design and construction that can help you attain a more attractive, more functional building within your budget. A few architects will want to put a great deal of emphasis on the exterior of the building, using such a large portion of the budget there that little money remains for finishing and furnishing. Listen to your architect with an open mind, but be willing to insist on components essential to your program.

Also be sure to let your architect know what kind of budget you are working with. You may have dreams of an elaborate center with all kinds of wonderful enhancements, but your budget may dictate that you have a much more straightforward approach. A good architect can help you get the most for your money. Figure 7-1, earlier in this chapter, shows a very simple, relatively inexpensive design. Only the essential spaces are included for this hypothetical half-day program. A rectangular building is often the least expensive to build.

When the plans are complete, asking a colleague to review them with you may help uncover details you hadn't considered. Changes made at this stage are relatively easy; changes made after construction begins may be impossible. At the very least, they usually are quite expensive.

Generally, the architect will oversee the job, but the general contractor is responsible for scheduling subcontractors, ordering materials, and so forth. Some architects also serve as construction managers, and some contractors offer building design services.

## 7-3d Contractor

A contractor may plan the construction or remodeling of the center's building and carry the work through to completion. Parts of the job, such as the electrical or plumbing work, may be subcontracted, but the contractor retains responsibility for the satisfactory and timely completion of that work. Nonetheless, the director must pay attention to the job as it moves along. Balancing frequent site visits with allowing the contractors to do their work is necessary, but asking questions is essential when you aren't sure about an aspect of the construction or when the work is not completed as promised. Sometimes, directors feel intimidated because they don't understand the drawings and specifications for the work. Part of the contractor's job is to ensure that the work is done to the client's specifications as determined by the written contract.

### 7-3e Accountant

The building committee works with an accountant to determine the amount of money that can be invested responsibly in construction, purchase, or rental. The ac-

countant also may help locate a lending agent and may help the building committee find the best interest rate. Information about depreciation and taxes also may be provided. An accountant may charge an hourly rate or a flat fee for a particular piece of work. Some centers pay an accountant a monthly retainer in exchange for whatever services are needed, including preparation for the annual audit.

### 7-3f Attorney

When the building committee decides to enter into a contract or sign a lease, its attorney reviews the document to ensure that the center's needs are being met and that all legal aspects have been covered. The attorney also participates in settling disputes in relation to payment, failure to perform work satisfactorily, and so forth. In a few cases, these disputes may be taken to court. In those special situations, the attorney would represent the center in court. The attorney may be on retainer or paid an hourly fee.

## SUMMARY

Whether it is a brand-new building or one that was constructed years ago for another purpose, directors or center owners must do the following:

- Become familiar with the numerous factors to be addressed in meeting the needs of children, staff members, and families while at the same time satisfying all licensing requirements.

- Understand the complex role played by the director in planning and building a new center.

- Be able to collaborate with a variety of professionals such as architects, contractors, and realtors to create a center that is best suited for carrying out the program for which it has been designed.

## TRY IT OUT!

1. Work with a classmate to design a floor plan for a child care center for 44 children (six infants, eight toddlers, 14 three-year-olds, and 16 four-year-olds). Also show the spaces that are used by adults. Be prepared to explain your design to the class.

2. Work with a classmate to design a building plan for a half-day preschool for 14 three-year-olds and 16 four-year-olds. Make your drawing approximately to scale.

3. Compare the drawings in Try it Out! 7-1 and 7-2. Are any of the differences attributable to full-day versus half-day child care? Explain.

4. Assume that you and your classmates are board members of a child care and education center for 60 preschool children located in a community center

building. They had asked you to set up the program four years ago. Now the community center director feels he needs your space for additional adult activities during the day. You need to move out of the building in 30 days. What will you do? Consider all the options, and then make a plan.

   a. Consider children, families, and staff as you make your decision.

   b. If you decide to move, consider what you will do to avoid this type of occurrence in the future.

5. Examine Director's Resource 7-1. Discuss with members of your class the ways in which development of this program's facility might be affected by its philosophy and belief statement.

# Director's Resource 7-1

## PHILOSOPHY STATEMENT

**(for use with Try It Out! 7-5)**

We are dedicated to care for and educate all the children at the Bombeck Family Learning Center. We believe that positive experiences for infants, toddlers, and young children are critical to healthy development and that these experiences serve as the foundation for future development and learning. Our philosophy is based on the work of such classic early childhood theorists as Ainsworth, Bandura, Bowlby, Bronfenbrenner, Erikson, Gerber, Honig, Montessori, Partens, Piaget, and Vygotsky. We have learned from prominent early childhood approaches such as the Project Approach (Katz and Chard) and the programs of Reggio Emilia, Italy. We believe that children benefit from practices that are well grounded in research. We also strive to maintain a program where diverse children and families are welcome and engaged. We believe in the following developmental principles:

1.  Each child's uniqueness is the result of interplay between genetic and environmental factors. Child development involves interrelated physical, cognitive, emotional, and social changes. Rates of development vary from one child to another, but the sequential progression of growth does not.

*Source: Bombeck Family Learning Center*

2.  With these principles in mind, we believe that infants, toddlers, and young children are individuals in their own right and must receive the same respect and consideration afforded older children and adults.

3.  We believe that it is our responsibility to provide responsive care and responsible guidance where strong social and emotional development is promoted and modeled. Furthermore, we are committed to providing a developmentally appropriate environment in order to nurture growth in all areas of development, while treating each child as a whole person.

4.  We believe that it is the job of adults to provide children with enticing and accurate learning experiences that are based on sound content knowledge and developmentally appropriate practices. Our science-focused curriculum is intentional, integrated, inclusive, inquiry-based, and innovative.

# REFERENCES

American Academy of Pediatrics, American Public Health Association, and National Resource Center for Health and Safety in Child Care and Early Education. (2013). *Stepping stones to caring for our children* (3rd ed.). Retrieved from http://nrckids.org/index.cfm/products/stepping-stones -to-caring-for-our-children-3rd-edition-ss3/.

Gandini, L. (1994, March). Not just anywhere: Making child care centers into particular places. *Child Care Information Exchange*, 48–50.

Greenman, J. (2007). *Caring spaces, learning places: Children's environments that work*. Redmond, WA: Exchange Press.

Lyn, R., Maalouf, J., Evers, S., Davis, J., & Griffin, M. (2013). Nutrition and physical activity in child care centers: The impact of a wellness policy initiative on environment and policy assessment and observation outcomes, 2011. Retrieved from http://www.cdc.gov/pcd/issues /2013/12_0232.htm.

Mace, R., Hardie, G. J., & Place, J. P. (n.d.). Accessible environments: *Toward universal design*. Retrieved from http://www.ncsu.edu/ncsu/design/cud/pubs_p/docs /ACC%20Environments.pdf.

National Association for the Education of Young Children. (2007). NAEYC early childhood program standards and accreditation criteria. Washington, DC: Author.

National Institutes of Health, National Center for Research Resources. (n.d.). Retrieved from http://www.science .education.nih.gov/supplements/nih4/technology/guide /implementing.htm.

# EQUIPPING *the* CENTER

*Supplying appropriate equipment contributes significantly to the success of early childhood programs.*

## Learning Objectives

After reading this chapter, you should be able to:

**8-1** Identify the necessary equipment that will meet child, adult, and service area needs.

**8-2** Identify and explain criteria for choosing equipment and vendors.

**8-3** Describe the issues to be addressed when working within an equipment budget.

**8-4** Describe a system for ordering equipment that meets program needs.

**8-5** Describe a system for managing equipment over time.

## Standards Addressed in this Chapter

Accreditation Standard 2 – Curriculum

Accreditation Standard 3 – Teaching

Accreditation Standard 5 – Health

Accreditation Standard 9 – Physical Environment

Accreditation Standard 10 – Leadership and Management

Administrator Competencies – Management Knowledge and Skills 4, 5, 9, 10

Administrator Competencies – Early Childhood Knowledge and Skills 2, 4, 5, 7, 8, 9, 10

Professional Preparation Standard 1 – Promoting Child Development and Learning

Professional Preparation Standard 4 – Using Developmentally Effective Approaches

Professional Preparation Standard 6 – Becoming a Professional

It is both challenging and rewarding to equip a child development center. Your personality will be reflected in the physical environment you create as you strive to meet the needs of the children and their families and as you select components that enable the entire staff to maintain congruence with your program philosophy. Although many programs are being implemented with inadequate, unsuitable materials, supplying equipment that is appropriate contributes significantly to successful program implementation. Creating rich learning environments that are replete with abundant opportunities for children to be actively involved with age-appropriate and individually appropriate materials requires thoughtful, careful selection of classroom equipment and supplies. Furthermore, staff members are able to do their assigned jobs more efficiently and comfortably when they work in adequately equipped environments.

One component of your organization's systems approach (described in Chapter 1) will center on equipment. Establishing a center-wide value to the role of equipment and supplies in carrying out your mission will support staff decision making as they develop curriculum, arrange their classroom environments, and support children's learning on a day-to-day basis. Whole staff discussions on the role of equipment in support of children's learning and development helps teachers create a more cohesive, meaningful philosophy. As new teachers enter the staff, they can observe the similarities across classrooms as well as the individual differences in equipment selection, arrangement, and use.

Establishing clear and pared-down policies and procedures for selecting, ordering, storing, and maintaining equipment and supplies will streamline this element of your system. Within the system and the philosophy it supports, staff members will be free to create classrooms they and their children find to be joyful and productive.

## 8-1 ESTABLISHING NEEDS

There are three major areas to equip in a child **naeyc** care center. The director, with input from the staff, must determine the type and amount of equipment needed for each one. When the center is already operating, teachers will join in this decision making. Following are the three areas to be equipped:

- children's spaces, both indoors and outdoors

- adults spaces, including offices, waiting rooms, conference rooms, and lounge areas

- service areas

Equipment refers not only to furniture but also to appliances, computers, and other durable goods. Included in this budget are supplies, which are items that have a relatively short useful life or that are disposable. Examples are paper for the printer, finger paint, food, and paper towels. The equipment and supplies budgets should provide for initial purchases as well as for long- and short-term replacement of both basic furnishings and consumable supplies.

Directors entering an ongoing program begin by taking inventory of what is on hand, setting up a priority system for securing new equipment, replacing worn-out items, and replenishing supplies of consumable materials. Directors of new centers are confronted with the somewhat overwhelming task of equipping an entire center. Some companies will provide lists of equipment you will need and suggest room arrangement.

One detailed equipment list, *Selecting Educational Equipment and Materials for School and Home* (Moyer, 1995) addresses both methods and materials for classrooms for infants through elementary school. Each section has been authored by a well-known early childhood specialist. Another valuable source is *Community Playthings*, which produces sturdy blocks, wood trucks, and other accessories and furniture for children. This company can provide you with drawings of sample room arrangements and a description of materials needed for your classroom. The company also offers free floor plans and room arrangement information for students who are preparing to be teachers or for individuals needing information for grant proposals. Visit their website to explore their products and resources.

### ▶❚❚ TeachSource Video Vignette

### Space Planning, Equipment, and Facility Maintenance

This video provides an overview of the issues that must be considered when planning children's spaces in an early education program. As you view the video, reflect on the following questions:

1. What domains of development should be considered when planning spaces for young children?

2. What factors should be considered when purchasing equipment for children's classrooms?

## 8-1a Children's Spaces

Program philosophy and the needs of children dictate what will be ordered for the children's spaces in the center. Let's assume that every child comes with a parent or "comfortable-to-him" adult to visit the classroom before school starts or at a time when no other children are present. Think about what the room says to a child opening the door. Some children may be overwhelmed with delight as they quickly visually take in a world of interesting walls, shelves, areas, and a new-to-him adult. Other children may be frightened by the magnitude of the space, the overwhelming variety of objects to see, and the sounds that they can't yet decode. Some children may take days, even weeks, to feel comfortable. Others can't wait to move right in.

Too much in a room can overwhelm a child, as well as his parents, even after they have been enrolled for months. Having everything in bold, bright colors can make a room seem "loud." Well-designed classrooms with uncluttered shelves, walls, floors, and tables help children find their way. Organizing space so that areas are somewhat separate helps children decide on a place to start. Everything needed for a particular type of activity should be available in that area.

When a building has a common storage area for classroom materials, teachers can share toys, tools, or objects to be used by children. When children's interests change or teachers want to present new materials to support children's learning, they can choose what they need from the shared storage area. Later, some of the same objects may be returned to the classroom as children are ready to use them in different ways. The director's role is to see how this system is working and to encourage teachers to establish policies and procedures for using shared equipment and supplies.

Most early childhood programs provide basic interest areas in each classroom. These usually include areas for art, music, blocks, books, science, manipulative activities, and pretend play as well as spaces for math games and writing materials. All of these curricular areas require special furnishings and materials. Provisions also must be made for water and sand play, carpentry, cooking, building, and large-muscle activities. Note that an interest area often addresses more than one content area. For example, puzzles in the manipulative area may depict characters from a book that the teacher has read to the children. In the science center, children may be recording observations of an animal; in the block area, you may find a child working on developing symmetry; and in the music area, a child may be listening to a song sung in Chinese or Spanish. You'll read more about the director's role in curriculum in Chapter 11.

Furniture for working, resting, and eating is needed, including such accessories as clocks, planters, wastebaskets, and curtains. Most preschool groups gather together daily and need a space large enough so that everyone is comfortable. Children need spaces to work alone or in small groups. Low dividers can define spaces, but shelving is often used for the same purpose. Often a few rolling shelves are moved back to make the gathering space available. When quickly and easily locked by the teacher, the shelves won't roll.

Children of all ages need outdoor play time. Almost every activity that can be done indoors can be moved outdoors as well. Infants can enjoy the swaying and rustling of leaves. Toddlers can feel powerful climbing a low grass-covered hill and running or rolling down it. Outdoor play also offers essential opportunities for gross motor activities and skill development such as climbing, swinging from rung to rung, running, jumping, and so forth. Some large equipment may be provided to encourage some of these motor activities, but plenty of space, along with cushioning material, must surround each piece of large equipment. Such equipment must be installed with firm, deep anchors that are below ground level and should be checked regularly for protrusions, splinters, or any other potential hazard.

Although this type of equipment is found on many playgrounds, explorations of nature also appeal to children and help them begin to understand its importance in our lives. Running around curving paths and "hiding" in bushy alcoves easily supervised by a teacher are exciting

**▶‖ TeachSource Video Vignette**

**Appropriate Learning Environments and Room Arrangements**

This video provides an overview of the impact of appropriate equipment and room arrangement on play. View the video vignette entitled, *Appropriate Learning Environments and Room Arrangements*. Reflect on the following questions:

1. What environmental factors contribute to supporting meaningful play and appropriate behaviors in the classroom?

2. As a director, how might these factors affect the items you select for purchase?

and fun for children. Planting and caring for their own gardens also interest and teach children. Even digging in soil and finding "treasures" such as a stone, a root, or an insect can fascinate children, especially those who live in areas where there are no yards. Walking in a summer rain, making and throwing snowballs, and crunching fallen leaves all go beyond going up and down a slide (although that is fun too).

If the director is not familiar with early childhood curriculum and the associated equipment, room arrangement, and scheduling, the center definitely will need an education coordinator who has this knowledge and who is an experienced early childhood teacher. She must also be familiar with programs for infants, toddlers, and school-age children if those groups are to be served. Taking courses in early childhood education curriculum and child development will also enable the director to develop a better understanding of why some materials are important and why others are not supportive of program goals and children's needs. Curriculum courses also provide information on how and why to integrate curriculum. Suggested books on curriculum and child development are included in the Director's Library in Appendix H.

## 8-1b Adult Spaces

Adults, working together to meet the common goal of providing rich, fulfilling experiences for children, need space to meet together, to think and plan together, and, at least briefly, to relax together. They need space to write reports and to converse with parents in private. Teachers need access to a telephone for parent contacts and for personal calls when they are on break. The location of the telephone should allow for quiet talks and for privacy. Staff members also need a few comfortable chairs for lounging during breaks, a refrigerator and microwave for snacks, and any other amenities that the center can provide. A bowl of grapes, cherries, or even, once in a while, mini chocolate bars would be welcomed by most teachers, especially after a week of staying inside due to very bad weather.

Even a very small center requires some office space with a locked file cabinet for records at the very minimum. Because adult desks are not used in classrooms for young children, some desk space for teachers is essential. A resource library and a work table with a paper cutter, laminator, and storage for supplies such as poster board, scissors, and markers support teachers in their work.

Almost every professional child care center director now relies on a computer for record keeping, billing, correspondence, writing reports, information gathering, and emailing. Many teachers also use computers to maintain professional currency via the Internet. Therefore, purchasing appropriate hardware

*Experiences with nature allow children to enjoy and learn about their world.*

and software becomes a significant contribution to the smooth running of a center. If your knowledge of computers is limited, recognize that everyone has experienced this beginning stage, and avoid saying you understand if that is not the case. Other staff members can assist you, or you may find free courses at your library or online. Purveyors of software want you to like and use their material. Although it is not uncommon to find glitches in computer software, you still should expect the vendor to provide needed support in rectifying the problem. Protecting against computer viruses with special software is essential.

Directors of large centers find that a copy machine is a worthwhile investment in terms of the time and money saved in duplicating such items as newsletters, menus, forms, and interesting articles to share. Although these machines are initially expensive, they pay for themselves over time by saving staff time and enabling the center to produce materials of professional quality. At the same time, consider ways to avoid overcopying by using other ways to communicate whenever possible.

When the families who are affiliated with your center have access to the Internet, you may want to send information via email. This process may be used for communicating with the entire center's population, with families from a particular classroom, or with an individual parent. Setting up a listserv with the email addresses of those families who choose to be included makes communication easy and quick. However, other ways of reaching those who are not using this technology must be provided. Remember, too, that personal, face-to-face communication is still highly desirable whenever possible. Look for ways to communicate in the language most familiar to the recipient. Parent or community volunteers may be available to facilitate translation, including through the use of sign language. You may also want to communicate with members of the broader community by creating and maintaining a website. In some areas, this approach can be developed into a successful marketing tool.

---

### DIRECTOR'S CORNER

"Our director has created a separate group email list for the families of each class. If we are working on something in my class, I can easily send a brief email to all the families telling them that the children have become quite interested in ants. Some parents will use this to start a dinnertime conversation with their child. Others will go outside and see if they can find ants together, watch them, and suggest that it would be a good thing to tell the other children the next day. It's a way for me to communicate quickly and positively with all my families."

*—Teacher in a franchised child care program*

---

In addition to communications tools, the staff needs a place for meetings. When staff meetings are held after children leave, the classrooms can be used. However, it certainly is more comfortable for the adults attending meetings to have a space furnished with adult-size chairs and tables. Comfortable furniture should be provided for use by parents who come to the center for conferences and by consultants who come to meet with staff members. Bulletin boards and coat racks are convenient accessories for adult spaces. Consider the seating and other furnishings and equipment in terms of adults who may have special needs.

*Some centers provide a lounge area for parents and visitors.*

Some centers provide a separate lounge for parents and visitors. This area should have comfortable seating, lamps, tables, a bookshelf for pertinent reading materials, and perhaps facilities for coffee or other refreshments. Wall hangings or pictures, plants, a rug or carpet, and curtains all enhance the appearance of the space. A shelf of toys and books for visiting children indicates that the center is sensitive to children's needs. The goal is to let families know that they are valued and welcomed.

## 8-1c Service Areas

Basic equipment in the bathrooms, kitchen, laundry room, and janitor's closet is usually built in and, therefore, is not purchased from the equipment and supplies budget. In a new facility, some appliances may be included in the equipment line. Consumables for service areas must be furnished, and, of course, appliances must be replaced over time. Dishes, cutlery, cooking utensils, and serving carts must be provided in centers where lunch is served. In large centers, special appliances such as commercial dishwashers, rug shampooers, heavy-duty automatic washers and dryers, and large refrigerators and freezers are needed. The local board of health may have very specific requirements about the type of kitchen equipment that must be provided. The fire department will usually require alarm systems and may also require a fire suppression system. A battery-operated radio with weather channel is an important tool to help the center prepare for weather emergencies. Flashlights in every classroom are also helpful. However, these items are useful only if you replace batteries regularly.

First aid supplies must be available in all classrooms, in the office, and in vehicles used to transport children. You may want to install an alarm system that would notify the police in the event of an emergency or a break-in when the center is closed.

If you have decided to provide child transportation, you will find many companies offering small buses equipped with seat belts and outfitted to accommodate car seats. Because the driver needs to focus on safe driving, a second adult should ride with the children to see that they remain in their car seats and that they are delivered directly to the previously agreed-upon adult.

When ordering cleaning supplies for your center, keep child friendly and environmentally friendly items in mind. Keep in mind also that some children or staff members may have allergies or asthma. Some states now require schools to use environmentally sensitive cleaning products. This requirement reduces exposure of children and staff to dangerous chemicals. Early attempts to regulate emission of formaldehyde used in producing some furniture may become law in some states. Find out from vendors of furniture, toys, and other equipment what kind of glue and paint are used (White Hutchinson Leisure & Learning Group, 2007). Also check periodically with the U.S. Consumer Product Safety Commission to determine whether various products have been recalled.

Choose recycled paper and encourage everyone in the center, including children, to recycle. In addition to paper, glass, and plastic, ink cartridges can be recycled. Everyone in the center can learn to conserve water, and the director can ensure that leaky faucets are repaired quickly (Stoecklin, 2005).

---

### MAKING THE CASE FOR *DIGITAL LITERACY*

The inclusion of digital technologies in early childhood facilities is no longer considered optional. However, to make responsible choices about what should be purchased for new programs, administrators must first understand the technology being considered. NAEYC and the Fred Rogers for Early Learning and Children's Media (2012) contend that educators "need training, professional development opportunities, and examples of successful practice to develop the technology and media knowledge, skills and experience needed" to meet the needs of children. It is also true that those making decisions about costly purchases must educate themselves about the technologies under consideration.

---

## 8-2 USING SELECTION CRITERIA

Selection of all equipment should be based on a set of pre-established criteria that you have created as part of your system. The primary consideration is usefulness; that is, will a specific piece of equipment meet the needs of this center? Other criteria are versatility, safety, suitability, durability, ease of maintenance, attractiveness, and user preference. Some equipment for children should encourage and even necessitate cooperative play. All equipment should work the way it is supposed to and should be durable and economical. Although these criteria apply to all equipment purchases, this chapter primarily covers information about equipment that children will use.

The goals and objectives of a particular center will dictate purchases. That means that the director and all staff members must focus on the goals and objectives that have evolved from the center's mission. The recent emphasis in the media on preparing children for kindergarten has led some centers to focus heavily on academic content and may lead some directors to order materials suitable for older children as an approach to preschool learning. As director, you must assume responsibility for keeping current on developments within the early childhood field as well as within the broader population. Helping staff maintain familiarity with these issues enables them to speak knowledgeably with parents and community members and to offer a curriculum that meets the needs of children. For example, many elementary schools are reducing or eliminating recess so that children will have more time to develop literacy skills. You can help staff understand how to explain the value of play, particularly outdoor play. One would hope that most staff could respond comfortably and professionally.

*Equipment and supplies for maintaining cleanliness must be child- and environment friendly. Keep in mind also that some children or staff members may have allergies or asthma.*

## Working Smart with Technology

*Identifying Technology Needs before Making Purchases*

Equipping a center today must include reflecting on how technology and interactive media will be used in the program for children, families, and staff. As you contemplate your purchases of equipment, you may wish to consider the following:

1.  What types of computer hardware will be needed for children and staff members? Desktops, laptops, tablets with touch screens?

2.  What software should be purchased to manage finances, the food program, children's records, licensing data, and so on? What software should be purchased for use in classrooms?

3.  What devices will be used in the classrooms to provide opportunities for listening to recorded books and music or for taking photos?

4.  What telephone, security, and alert systems (e.g., carbon monoxide, smoke, and fire) should be considered for your program?

5.  Is closed-circuit television appropriate or financially possible?

6.  Will you provide smartphones or other wireless devices to enable emergency communication among staff and families?

7.  If you are including a separate space for parents in your facility, will you provide a computer for those who may not have access at home?

*Managing today's early childhood program requires that directors and teachers understand how to use technology to facilitate their work.*

As director, you may feel pressure from parents and from observing how some early childhood centers operate, and you may begin to question your system's goals. Would it be better to use funds for prekindergarten workbooks? To find the answer, you must return to your understanding of how children learn. Is your program providing opportunities for children's development in all areas, including literacy? Consider the children's small motor development, understanding of recording a correct answer rather than choosing an interesting picture to circle, and ability to work in silence in a group, all of which are often necessary for completing required worksheets. Many people would agree that children entering kindergarten should be prepared and that the kindergarten system should be prepared for the children. When you are a director, your role is to determine how best to prepare children for kindergarten as well as for their lives in the here and now. You must base this on knowledge on how children develop, how learning occurs, and the needs and interests of each child in your class rather than on more narrowly focused goals such as readiness for kindergarten in a particular content area. Most kindergarten teachers value children's age-appropriate social and emotional development as more important to them at the beginning of kindergarten than whether children are well versed in letter-sound relationships.

### REFLECTION

As a student, you are required to spend a certain number of hours observing and assisting in a preschool classroom before student teaching. The teacher starts the day with a drill on the sounds that letters make. (You wonder when was the last time she ever heard a letter make a sound. Oh well, it's her classroom.) Then they practice counting from 1 to 30. You are surprised because yesterday, you asked two children who were playing a game, "Which is more—7 or 9?" Neither of them had any idea. You begin to wonder whether you will teach this way or you will do something different.

After you finish reading this, ask yourself what you plan to do in your own classroom. Why?

Today's standards-driven educational approaches require that administrators and staff become familiar with standards set forth by state departments of education and national professional organizations. In some cases, working to ensure that all children meet these standards will be mandated. For example, in some states, preschool centers that receive state funds are expected to be guided by the standards and to demonstrate how standards are met in each "lesson" or activity. More and more, children entering kindergarten are being tested to determine what they know, particularly related to specific literacy skills. Directors who have a good grasp of developmentally appropriate curriculum will be able to help teachers work toward the standards within the context of routines, schedules, and plans that meet each child's needs while supporting children's progress toward meeting the content standards. Eliminating play and the related materials and equipment is not an option.

How will such knowledge relate to purchasing equipment and supplies? You must think about how equipment will be used and how it will support children's interest in learning in all areas. For example, early childhood educators understand that providing blocks and offering long periods of time and space to explore ways to use them can help children learn in all the content areas (math, science, social studies, literacy) and in the arts (Chalufour & Worth, 2004; Dodge, Colker, & Heroman, 2010).

Knowledgeable directors realize that during block play, children also develop skills in planning, balance, organizing, cooperating, and persistence toward a goal. The other interest centers in an early childhood classroom lead to similar development with the guidance of a well-prepared teacher.

Elsewhere in this book, you can read about the important role of the director in selecting and orienting teachers who will support children's development. You'll also consider how the director supports teachers as they develop more competent ways of enhancing children's growth and change in all areas. It is the director's responsibility to use a systematic approach, blending facility, equipment, staff, families, and finances to accomplish the mission related to children's care, growth, and development. Equipping a center is costly, and when mistakes are made, replacements are doubly costly. Therefore, plan your purchases carefully by first assessing your needs, then developing criteria for equipment selection, and finally relating needed and desired items to your budget.

Many equipment suppliers will be happy to provide sample equipment and supplies lists. Additionally, some states now provide online equipment lists that can assist owners and directors in planning purchases. For example, the Utah Department of Workforce Services, Office of Child Care (2012), provides a guide entitled *Opening a Quality Child Care Center*. This document includes separate lists of equipment and materials needs for infants, toddlers, preschool-kindergarten, and school age. You may find local resource and referral agencies can provide information as well. For example, the *Child Care Facility Development Guide* by Child Care Aware of North Dakota (2013) includes excellent suggestions for planning equipment needs for young children.

These comprehensive lists are not intended as mandatory purchases but as guides to be adjusted and supplemented based on the needs of particular children, staff, and families. As new materials become available, they can be considered based on their appropriateness for the children who will use them. For example, although vinyl records and audiotapes were widely available in preschools some years ago, today centers are more likely to purchase CDs, DVDs, or digital music files.

Suitability of specific curricular materials is not discussed here because a number of texts include this information in the context of program development. Please see Appendix G for related books.

> ### REFLECTION
>
> Think of yourself as a director who is responsible for equipment purchases. Did you realize that you would pore over websites and catalogs for classroom equipment and materials and would find yourself searching through office equipment and restaurant supply catalogs, websites, and ads? Your duties now have expanded from educator and administrator to purchasing agent. This responsibility probably seems overwhelming at the moment because many of you have been responsible for purchasing only personal items and, in some cases, basic household equipment. You are, no doubt, beginning to realize that the role of the director has many facets and requires a wide variety of special skills.

## 8-2a Developmental Needs

The developmental levels, capabilities, and age range of the children enrolled influence what will be purchased. A center serving 2-year-olds will need some pull toys and small climbers that would not be needed if the youngest child were 3. Infants require special furnishings such as cribs and changing tables. Although younger infants are always held during feeding, infants who are able to sit independently are also ready to help feed themselves and should be encouraged to do so. High chairs had been standard equipment for this purpose, but because of the danger of children falling from the chairs, they are usually replaced by low feeding tables, similar to high chairs but with shorter legs. A teacher sits in a low chair opposite the children and helps when help is needed. Infants also require washable and chewable toys, bibs, sheets, blankets, and disposable diapers. Parents may be asked to furnish some of those necessary items and to take responsibility for their infant's laundry.

When center bathrooms have adult-size toilets and sinks, children will need step stools to be able to use the equipment independently. Preferably, the center will have installed child-size toilets and sinks at the appropriate height. Toddlers also need toys that provide opportunities for filling and dumping, big toys that can be carried during early walking stages, and lots of duplicates so that sharing will not be necessary. Toddler rooms are arranged in interest centers, but because many toddlers like to practice walking and carrying items in each hand, materials are often found in a variety of places. Preschoolers can understand that everything in their classroom has its own place, and they usually learn quickly to return things to their specified location. Many creative preschoolers find new uses for classroom items. For example, a child may take yarn from the art area to use as spaghetti in the house play area. Whether or not this creative use is encouraged depends on the philosophy of the program.

*Duplicate materials should be provided for toddlers to minimize potential conflict.*

*The director who understands child development and ways of learning is prepared to equip classrooms appropriately.*

Preschool children need equipment and materials in all of the interest areas. Some of these materials will be specifically designed for children, while many others will be of interest to both children and teachers, such as items from nature; maps; and books and posters depicting and identifying birds, flowers, cars, or dinosaurs. Adult musical instruments often appeal to children, especially if the children are permitted to both listen and try their hand at bowing or strumming. Opportunities to prepare and eat most kinds of food provide chances to learn about nutrition, food from other cultures, heat and cold, textures, comparisons, contrasts, the safe use of tools and appliances, math, literacy, social studies, science, arts, turn taking, preferences, and sharing good times with friends.

School-age children in after-school care programs need games and crafts that are far too complex and frustrating for younger children. They also need well-lighted working areas for homework; larger furniture in which they can sit and work comfortably; and equipment for active, semi-organized sports and games. A place to store and eat snacks and an area to relax away from the group provide some feeling of being independent.

Programs for school-age children should enable them to participate as fully as possible in activities that other children their age enjoy. When the center is well equipped to meet these needs, it will provide not only activities that the children could have been doing at home after school but also enriching group activities that encourage children to develop new interests and hobbies.

Children with special needs may require modified equipment or equipment designed to meet a particular need. A director with contacts at agencies serving people with disabilities can seek their assistance in providing modifications or special equipment. The equipment should allow the child to function as independently as possible. If the director is new in the area and does not have the necessary contacts, one of her priorities should be to become familiar with the community and its resources.

## 8-2b Usefulness

The usefulness of a piece of children's equipment is measured first by how well it meets the developmental needs of the children in the program and second by whether the equipment can be put to multiple uses by those children. When a piece of equipment meets both these criteria, a director may be able to convince a potential funder to support a request for funding. For example, a set of large, sturdy, wooden boxes can serve as cozy places to hide, as houses for pretend play, and as places to climb on and jump from; a wooden board added to the area can function as a stage, slide, or tent. Of course, all the wood needs to be well sanded and protected from weathering.

## 8-2c Versatility

A piece of equipment that can be used in several ways is a bonus, both financially and in terms of enriching the learning environment for children. Such a piece saves space and money and gives children the opportunity to use their imaginations in creating different functions for one object. For example, the large, hollow blocks that can be used to make a puppet stage or a grocery store can serve as individual work spaces for children's small projects. A bookshelf can be a room divider and a storage facility. Two-year-olds may find the water table to be a relaxing place for splashing, while 4-year-olds may be more interested in using this equipment for constructing a water maze. Many pieces of equipment may be shared by two or more classes for the same or different purposes, eliminating the purchase of duplicate materials and freeing up money for other purchases.

Some equipment can be used both indoors and outdoors, a practice that is economical and provides a wider variety of learning experiences for children. Easels, water tables, and a workbench are a few items that may be moved outside if the building and play area have been planned to facilitate such indoor–outdoor movement. When that planning has not occurred, teachers will not be able to leave the children in order to make several trips to carry equipment, and the children will not have access to those items. Perhaps a janitor, or older children in elementary settings, may be able to help set up outdoor equipment. In some situations, equipment must be put away and locked up when children are not in the outdoor area.

## 8-2d Safety

No matter how versatile, attractive, durable, economical, and suitable a piece of equipment may be, it must be rejected if it is not safe. A climber with protruding bolts, blocks of soft wood that splinter, and tricycles that tip over easily must not be used in the center. A kitchen appliance that requires a long extension cord is a hazard to the cook and should be avoided. All equipment used by the children must be made of nontoxic material and must not have sharp or pointed edges. Safety is maintained by staff members who make a point of being constantly alert to the condition and the arrangement of the equipment that is placed in the learning environment (Aronson, 2012).

No one but a curious toddler seems able to spot a small button that has fallen from another child's clothing. Nonetheless, every classroom should be checked for safety hazards daily and throughout the day. Items used in infant/toddler rooms must not have small pieces that

*Providing safe equipment is an important first step to planning for playground safety. Positioning it with safety in mind is the next step, followed by regular evaluation of the condition of the equipment and vigilant supervision by the staff.*

could be dislodged, such as the eyes of stuffed animals or small beads on a wire in a board counting book. Even some 3-year-olds are still mouthing small items.

However, a safety issue may be inadvertently overlooked. Three areas to which staff must give special attention are fall zones, entrapment, and protrusions (Wardle, 1999). Fall areas occur under climbers and swings. Entrapment refers to the possibility of a child getting a body part trapped in a piece of equipment (e.g., when fence slats are close together, but not close enough, a child may get an arm or a leg caught). Look carefully at elaborate climbing towers with tunnels. It is possible for a child to become frightened while in the tunnel, yet the tunnel may be too long or narrow for the adult to reach the child. Protrusions also may pose safety issues. Sharp corners on furniture or screw heads extended from a flat surface may injure a child.

The U.S. Consumer Product Safety Commission (CPSC) provides voluntary standards for children's playgrounds as well as up-to-date safety alerts on its website. Additionally, you can request email alerts or download their cell phone app. The 2009 CPSC update reported that the majority of injuries requiring hospital treatment during 2001–2008 resulted from swings, climbers, slides, and monkey bars. This does not mean that this equipment should be banned. Rather, they should be surrounded by appropriate and adequate cushioning material and should be located away from other activities to avoid having children run or ride through the climbing area. Other playground injuries result from hot surfaces, entanglement of clothing in the equipment, head entrapment in openings, and entanglement in ropes. Selection of appropriate equipment and close supervision on the playground are major factors in preventing injuries. Nonetheless, the active play, motor skill development, confidence building, and enjoyment that children experience on the playground should not be denied. An excellent resource for directors is the U.S. Consumer Products Safety Commission's *Public Playground Safety Handbook* (2010).

Some furniture may tip over and is particularly dangerous if a heavy object such as a computer monitor or aquarium has been placed on top. A child may try to pull or climb on the furniture, causing it to tip over.

It is not unusual for child care programs to have at least one potential safety hazard. This can include the use of clothing with drawstrings at the neck, lack of safe playground surfacing, and cribs with soft bedding. If you visit the U.S. CPSC website, you will find a very lengthy list of toys that have been recalled due to lead paint use, swallowing hazard, and so on. As center director, you may be diligent to purchase safe toys and equipment; however, a child may bring his own favorite toy to school. Some centers have policies encouraging children to show their toys at group time but to put them in their cubby immediately afterward.

Most directors know that lead paint has been banned for consumer use for many years, but they may not be aware of the lead hazard lurking in playground equipment. Older equipment that has been painted several times may still contain lead. Products from other countries, especially toys, should be checked for lead paint. Children need consume only small quantities on a regular basis to create a harmful lead level. In 2007, news media reported that millions of toys in homes and schools contained lead, small magnets, and other components harmful to children, leading to a massive recall. Be aware that even the surface under playground equipment may contain lead. Having a trained inspector check a playground periodically for lead and other hazards is a wise investment (Aronson, 2012). Paying attention to recalls is essential.

Purchasing equipment for infants and toddlers requires particular consideration regarding safety. The U.S. Consumer Product Safety Commission (2013) reports that in 2012, there were approximately 77,900 injuries treated in emergency rooms in children under 5 years of age that were associated with nursery products such as cribs and mattresses, high chairs, infant carriers, and strollers. Falls caused the greatest percentage of injuries. It should be noted that in some instances, these injuries were not caused by the product itself and could have been prevented with greater supervision or other interventions. Additional information regarding the purchase of safe equipment can be found in the *Stepping Stones for Caring for Our Children* report from the American Academy of Pediatrics, American Public Health Association, and the National Resource Center for Health and Safety in Child Care and Early Education (2013).

## 8-2e Suitability

Some equipment must be provided in several sizes to meet the needs of each user. For example, the secretary must have a standard, adult-size chair, preferably ergonomically designed. Chairs for children are usually 10-, 12-, and 14 inches high, depending on the child's age and height. Chairs that are so tall that seated children cannot put their feet on the floor are not suitable for them. Children's chairs also should have a wide base so they will not tip.

For meals, school cafeteria tables and chairs are not at all suitable for toddlers and preschoolers. If these children are to use a school cafeteria, they must have low tables and chairs. Eating in their own classroom is often a better option. When older children are also present, the noise and activity levels may be distracting for preschoolers and toddlers. Children in before- and after-school programs should never be expected to use preschool-size chairs and tables. They need furniture, space, and equipment designed to fit their needs.

### Stereotypes

Equipment must be chosen with the understanding that it may be used equally by all children. Staff members who plan curricula in a stereotyped way will need special guidance on this point so that boys are not relegated to playing with blocks and trucks, and girls are not always expected to dress dolls and play quiet table games. People with special needs should be depicted in books, puzzles, and classroom displays, and they should be shown participating in a variety of activities. Classroom materials should reflect many cultures and depict a variety of roles being chosen by members of various cultures and of both genders. For example, dolls of many races should be available. The play figures that are used as block accessories might include a female postal worker and a black doctor rather than depicting all white males. Books, music, food, and posters should be carefully selected to avoid any stereotyping and to depict the culturally pluralistic society in which the children live. This principle applies even when the center serves children from only one racial or ethnic group, a situation that may occur when students all come from a segregated neighborhood.

### Children with Disabilities

Educators today focus on planning a curriculum and environment that allows all children to participate. As discussed previously, the principles of universal design (UD) are important to providing an inclusive program and should be considered when planning equipment purchases. This idea does not mean that everyone does the same thing the same way at the same time, but that each child can participate in a meaningful way in understanding the activity, in implementing it, and in demonstrating what he is learning. Often, consulting a special educator or intervention specialist facilitates this type of planning.

In determining the suitability of equipment, you must consider children with special needs. A child who cannot walk, for example, may need easels and water tables that can be used while the child sits in a chair or a wheelchair. Sometimes, such equipment is very low to enable children who are sitting on the floor to use it. In selecting the equipment, you should consider the height of the chair or wheelchair that is used and the length of the child's arms. In this way, you can determine the optimum height of the working space for a particular child. Consider purchasing tables with adjustable heights. If children are crawling in body casts or leg braces, they need comfortable floor surfaces. Wheeled equipment such as a sturdy wagon or a special buggy with seat belts will make it possible for *all* children to enjoy tours around the center's neighborhood.

---

**REFLECTION**

Think about your previous experiences with individuals with disabilities. Have you had enough experience to be aware of their special needs? If you have a friend or relative with a lifelong disability, imagine what his or her special needs might have been during the preschool years. Now consider yourself responsible for equipping an environment that is suitable for that child along with a group of typically developing children. What special provisions would have to be made for your friend or relative with special needs to provide a suitable learning environment?

---

Some children may require the use of assistive technologies to be successful in the classroom. For example, children may need an augmentative communication system so they can interact with staff and other children. A child with cerebral palsy who has reduced fine motor control may benefit from an adapted computer keyboard or mouse. Others may find that a touch screen enables them to be more successful. Children with hearing loss may need ample visual cues such as pictures attached to storage areas so they can tell where equipment belongs, even though they cannot hear the teacher's directions. Children with visual impairments may need some toys that vary in terms of weight, texture, and sound. Balls with a bell inside and storage containers covered with different materials (e.g., velvet on a container of beads or corduroy on a box holding small blocks) are especially appropriate for these children. When children who do not have disabilities use these same materials, they may develop greater insights into the experience of children with disabilities.

In purchasing equipment for a center, the director will need to know, in general, what the lifestyles of the families are and what the learning styles and interests of individual children are. Children must be provided with enough ordinary, simple equipment so that they need not be bombarded nine hours a day with novelty. This is particularly true for children who have sensory issues such as those with attention deficit hyperactivity disorder, autism, visual impairments or hearing loss. A balance of the familiar with the novel creates a learning environment that is neither overstimulating nor boring; the proper balance may be different in full-day child care centers than in half-day programs.

Watson and McCathren (2009) provide an excellent *Preschool and Kindergarten Inclusion Readiness Checklist*, based on UD principles, for program administrators and teachers to use as they plan for children with disabilities. Numerous companies now sell adaptive equipment that can meet the differing needs of most children as well. For example, Rifton Equipment, an offshoot of Community Playthings, provides high-quality equipment for children and adults with disabilities. Some directors purchase packaged kits or curricula for their centers, particularly when the staff members have had little early childhood educational background. In such cases, it is essential that the materials are appropriate as they may be used with the belief that they must be good just because they were included in a curriculum package. The director has a major responsibility for ensuring that the components meet the needs of children and teachers. (Often, similar materials can be purchased separately at lower cost.) The director must also provide training to ensure that teachers are using a curriculum plan to meet the needs of children rather than following a page-by-page or random plan. Not every component must be implemented. Such a preplanned curriculum can be viewed as a framework rather than a mandate. It is the director's responsibility to determine who prepared the curriculum and what premises about teaching and learning are supported through its use. Keep in mind that it is unlikely that someone who does not know the children in your center could develop a day-to-day curriculum that would meet the needs and interests of your children. You will read more about providing appropriate curriculum in Chapter 11.

## 8-2f Ease of Maintenance

Ease of maintenance also should be a consideration in choosing equipment. Sinks, toilets, and drinking fountains that must be cleaned daily and tabletops that must be washed several times each day should be extremely simple to clean. The surfaces should be smooth, and all areas must be easy to reach. Small pieces that are hard to clean around may cause problems and harbor dirt and germs. Equipment parts that are cleaned separately, such as feeding table trays, should be easy to remove and replace. Some plastic chairs have surfaces that are slightly roughened or ridged. And although the surface feels relatively smooth to the hand, there are actually shallow indentations that attract and hold dirt. It is almost impossible to wipe or even scrub these chairs so that they look clean. This type of furniture may be slightly less expensive than other furniture, but maintenance problems outweigh the possible savings. A clean, well-maintained environment is important for all children and staff, but it may be critical for children and staff who have allergies or asthma. In those cases, it may be helpful to have curtains, drapes, and carpeting cleaned frequently, or they may have to be eliminated.

Outdoor equipment that must be repainted frequently should be designed so that it can be sanded and painted easily. Places that are difficult to reach are a nuisance, and surfaces that catch and hold rain increase the need for maintenance. Equipment that will rust or rot easily should not be purchased for outdoor use.

## 8-2g Aesthetics

Child care center equipment should be well designed and aesthetically attractive. Most parents and teachers would like their children to appreciate beauty, and one of the best ways to help children acquire this appreciation is to surround them with beauty. An attractive environment also carries the subtle message that children, families, and staff who enter the setting are much appreciated and that great care is taken to make their environment beautiful. A material that is aesthetically appealing need not be expensive. In fact, it often is the ability of the director or teacher to find beauty in nature that provides the most attractive places for children. For example, a colorful tablecloth on the housekeeping area table with a small vase of wildflowers in the center makes that classroom area attractive and inviting. A large square of interesting gift-wrapping paper, neatly trimmed, or a square yard of fabric serves as an attractive and inexpensive wall hanging and can be changed or cleaned often.

Be aware of the wide variety of art forms and styles developed by each culture. Displaying these introduces children and families to beauty they may not have had the opportunity to experience and provides an interesting and appropriate way to begin discussions and explorations of other cultures.

When equipment is made for the classroom, it should be prepared with special attention to its visual appeal. A math game, for example, can be made using well-designed stickers or beautiful pictures cut from duplicate copies of magazines instead of cartoonlike gimmicky stickers or drawings. The cardboard should be cut evenly and laminated or covered with a plastic coating instead of being presented to children with rough, crooked edges. Preparing beautiful materials takes a little longer and may require initial costs that are somewhat higher, but the product is worth the investment. One of the director's roles is to help staff and children value quality rather than quantity and to appreciate and care for the beauty in the objects around them.

## 8-2h User Preference

The classroom is a place in which the teacher can express her personality. By including some items that represent her interests, she communicates to children and families that she has preferences just as they do. It's reasonable to expect that sometimes teacher preference determines the type of equipment ordered. One teacher may choose to buy many books while another depends heavily on the library, or one sees an autoharp as a necessity while another finds this instrument encumbering. One teacher may choose a guinea pig as the ideal classroom pet, another prefers fish, and still another considers all pets to require an inordinate amount of the teacher's time. As long as these teacher preferences are not contrary to appropriate classroom practice, they are legitimate and should be honored if at all possible. When budgeting constraints or other equipment needs make it impossible to fill all teachers' requests, the director must notify teachers that their preferences are under consideration and that plans are being made to fill all requests as soon as possible. The teacher who wants an autoharp may have to wait until next year's budget provides it, but meanwhile, the director can support that teacher by informing the staff of planned equipment purchases. Each teacher's preference deserves careful consideration because each teacher will ultimately set the stage for learning through the use of the center's equipment. Of course, the director will have to intervene if a teacher chooses to order inappropriate items such as toys and games with very small pieces for toddlers or flash cards for preschoolers.

# 8-3 WORKING WITHIN A BUDGET

As you bring together information about purchases to be made, notice how various components of your program's systems come into play. You are addressing finances, staff, and equipment simultaneously, and you will follow the policies and procedures established around the center's equipment. With that perspective in mind, you will be ready to relate the choices that you and the staff have made, the needs of the children, and a component of the budget.

*Children enjoy working with found materials collected on the playground.*

Major considerations when working with an equipment budget are durability and economy, which often go hand in hand. The climbing apparatus that costs three times as much as a competitor's product is worth the original investment if it lasts three times as long or is safer and sturdier. When more durable items are purchased, the center is not faced with the problem of replacement so often, and considerable shipping costs are saved, particularly with large pieces of equipment. Price and durability are not always perfectly correlated, but it is safe to say that inexpensive tricycles, which may be appropriate for home use, are inappropriate for group use. When used at a center, the standard equipment that is used at home will be in the repair shop far sooner and more frequently than will the sturdier, more expensive equipment that is designed for school use. Keep this fact in mind when well-meaning board members want to donate items their children have outgrown instead of including sufficient dollars in the equipment budget.

In child care center kitchens, many adults (and occasionally children) use the equipment. This heavy usage (and perhaps misuse), coupled with lack of care, may lead to the need for earlier replacement. Refrigerator and freezer doors are opened frequently and often are left standing open while children, accompanied by a teacher, of course, take out ice cubes or put in trays of sloshing Jell-O™.

Dishwashers may be improperly loaded or overloaded, and sinks are sometimes scoured with rough scouring

*Order furniture based on the children's age, size, and ability.*

pads or abrasive powders. It is important to provide heavy-duty kitchen equipment because equipment made for home use will require costly service calls when it is subjected to the hard use it inevitably will get in a center. A prepaid maintenance agreement may be a cost-effective way to manage equipment repairs. Checking the total cost of the maintenance agreement against the record of repairs typically needed over time for a particular type of equipment is a smart practice. Two possible sources of such information are consumer guides, usually available at libraries, and discussion with other directors. Furthermore, instructions on how to use equipment may be posted on each item, and a short in-service session may be helpful.

In setting up a new center, the director can expect to spend $10,000 to $30,000 per classroom on equipment. The variance is due to the number of children in each classroom and the quality of the items purchased. A typical budget for manipulatives (puzzles, table toys, and small blocks) for a center of about 75 children is about $4,000, assuming that the items are centrally stored so that teachers can share them. Morgan and Emanuel (2010) suggest allocating $60 per child for classroom supplies and $60 per child for kitchen and office supplies as part of the start-up budget. They also suggest you will need $700 to $1,000 per child for all equipment, including kitchen and office, with $50,000 to $98,000 for playground equipment. They offer many examples to help you with all aspects of managing your center's money. Directors often search for free materials and supplies to reduce these costs. However, the director then may have to pick up the items or enlist a volunteer for this service. Recognize that free items are not necessarily worthwhile, and expensive items are not always better.

*Preschoolers and their teachers lunch together using child-sized tables and chairs.*

## 8-4 ORDERING EQUIPMENT

Decisions about what, when, and where to buy equipment are usually left to the director. In any case, directors are consulted, and they have considerable control over what is bought with the money that is budgeted for equipment and supplies.

### 8-4a Equipment Requisition

Directors usually develop an equipment request procedure. Staff members notify the director, in writing, of the type of equipment needed or desired, providing additional information such as the rationale to support the need, a possible vendor, and an estimated purchase price. All of these data are helpful when final purchase decisions are made. Some centers use purchase order or requisition forms, which are nothing more than request forms that can be sent to vendors with a duplicate retained for center records (see Director's Resource 8-1). Even though this request procedure is formal and perhaps cumbersome, it puts the purchase of equipment on a businesslike basis and gives each staff member an equal opportunity to bid for the equipment dollars in the budget.

In corporate systems, requisitions are processed through a central purchasing agent, and shipments are made directly to the center from the manufacturer. The central office handles all the orders and saves money through collective, quantity buying and careful selection of suppliers. This approach cuts costs but limits the options for those staff members selecting equipment. Public school programs usually have specific purchasing procedures to follow, with supplies requisitioned through the principal or through a supervisor responsible for the preschool or after-school programs. However, if a nonschool organization is implementing the program within a school building, that group may have wisely negotiated an agreement that will allow them to provide and own their own equipment. The program director will then be able to maintain the

---

**DIRECTOR'S CORNER**

"When I think about ordering equipment for our center, I recall a five-generation Community Playthings block family. About 40 years ago, a great-grandmother and her daughter ordered blocks for a little boy on several occasions, providing him with quite a collection that he used daily. This year, the boy's mother ordered more blocks to be added to his collection and given to his two sons. The boys are still too young to understand that this tradition of block giving was started years ago by their great-great grandmother, but they (and their father) are maintaining the tradition of playing with their blocks daily."

*—Director of a nonprofit child care program*

philosophy that the center espouses. If the school system no longer has room for the center or prefers to run its own program, the organization maintains its equipment.

In centers where directors are fully responsible for receiving staff requests and placing orders, they check requests against the established selection criteria and the budget allowance before completing order forms. All order forms should include quantity, price, catalog order number (if available), and name or description of each item. When making final decisions on purchases, make certain that careful consideration is given to possible savings through bulk buying. For example, newsprint for painting can be bought from some vendors for much less per ream when bought in 48-ream packages. Economies realized through bulk buying are practical only if adequate storage space is available for the unused materials.

Equipment costs also can be reduced in nonprofit centers by applying for tax-exempt status. When orders are sent to suppliers, the center will not be charged sales tax if the order includes the center's tax-exempt number. Some centers have provisions for teachers to purchase specified dollar amounts without permission and within a given time period. For example, a teacher may receive $200 to spend for the classroom each year (in addition to the center-wide purchases that the director makes). In most cases, the purchase is made, and the teacher is reimbursed on presentation of the receipts to the director or fiscal manager. Giving teachers some freedom to provide for special program needs helps them meet children's interests without having to wait for more formal procedures.

---

### REFLECTION

Assume that your classroom, which is stocked with basic equipment for your 15 four-year-old children, has been allocated $200 from petty cash. Think about how you might spend it.

---

## 8-4b Purchase Time Line

Equipment purchasing occurs in three different time frames:

- start-up
- supplementary
- replacement

First, there must be a major start-up equipment purchase when a center is opened so that all the basic aspects of the program can function with appropriate equipment. This phase obviously is the most expensive of the three, but extensive purchases at this point are absolutely essential because it is unfair to children and staff to operate a program without basic equipment. To save money, some secondhand, borrowed, or homemade equipment can be used, keeping in mind the criteria described earlier. There

is no formula that can tell a director exactly what must be provided, but the staff will need equipment of the type, quantity, and quality that will allow them to focus on the children and their needs instead of on the equipment or the lack thereof. Children in a classroom with inappropriate or inadequate equipment will be quite likely to engage in inappropriate behavior as they seek to create something interesting to do.

Providing enough appropriate storage is also essential. In the classroom, teachers need storage for supplies that they will use later in the day or week. Major classroom storage space should be available to the children so they can independently choose and put away materials. Crowded shelves and cluttered spaces make it difficult for children to find the materials they want to use. Children are also more likely to leave materials strewn about the classroom when it is not clear where they belong.

The second phase of equipment purchasing is the supplementary phase that provides for additional equipment purchases throughout each year. When supplementary equipment purchases are spaced throughout a program year, both children and staff members enjoy greater variety and a change of pace. Furthermore, teachers can adjust equipment requests to meet the needs of particular children such as a child with special needs who enrolls midyear and requires a chair with particular supports, a prone board, or a walker. Although outside funding may be available for some of these larger items for an individual child's use, teachers still need to consider books with large print, puzzles with large knobs, or writing tools that have been adapted for easier handling.

Lastly, the replacement phase helps maintain a constant supply of equipment that is in good repair and allows for adjustments in available equipment and

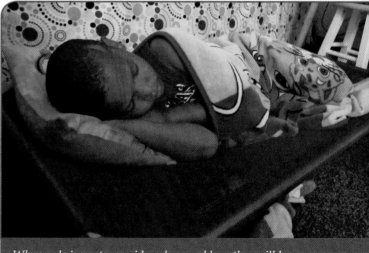

*When ordering cots, consider where and how they will be stored, as well as ease of setting them up daily and keeping them clean.*

materials as program needs change or as new items come on the market. For example, a few years ago, all African American dolls had Caucasian hairstyles and facial features, but newer dolls have features that more closely match the ethnic group being represented. Nontoxic, washable markers have replaced the old odorous markers. Similarly, film-strips have been replaced by videos and DVDs. At the same time, much-loved children's books such as *Goodnight Moon* (Brown, 1947) remind us that new is not always better.

The budget also should include enough money for emergency replacements. Although careful usage, combined with a fund for maintenance, minimizes the need for emergency replacements, unexpected breakage or loss is sure to occur. When a copier repair is too costly, it is sometimes more economical to buy or lease a new model than to repair the old one. As for buying a maintenance plan, consider what the warranty covers and for how long before paying for a plan.

## 8-4c Sources of Equipment

Much of the equipment for early childhood education centers is purchased from catalogs. If the dealers are reliable, this arrangement is satisfactory. It is wise to check with other directors, professional organizations, or the Better Business Bureau to determine the suitability of making purchases from a particular company. Among the advantages of purchasing by catalog are the wide variety of merchandise that is available and lowering of costs with bypassing the retailer. On the other hand, shipping costs may be charged, and returning

*All children need access to a wide range of books, some of which may come from the public library.*

unsatisfactory merchandise may be cumbersome. It is helpful to have a supply of catalogs offering good quality merchandise available to the staff. Catalogs from companies that sell easily breakable toys, items that are always in only very bright colors, cars and trucks with faces, and so on should be discarded. Most companies will be pleased to put your center on their mailing list. Refer to the list in Appendix E.

When you are placing a large order, request a discount. Another opportunity for price reduction is prompt payment. Vendors who establish a relationship with your center are more likely to inform you of upcoming special prices. Then it is up to you to purchase items because the center needs them instead of because they are on sale. Many companies charge about 30 percent of the cost of items that have been returned, unless, of course, they arrived damaged. In addition, the center pays the return shipping. Impulse buying is irresponsible when you are in charge of purchasing equipment.

Equipment purchased from local retail outlets can be seen and tried out, which has obvious advantages. But most retail outlets cater to home users and carry a limited stock of classroom equipment. If a local outlet has access to a manufacturer of school equipment, it may be possible to order from a catalog through a local retailer. A buying co-op is another equipment source worth investigating because group buying can be very economical. In this system, the co-op group buys in quantity at a wholesale price and sells items to co-op members at just enough above cost to pay the co-op's operating expenses.

Exhibit areas at state or national early childhood conferences provide great opportunities to view a huge range of products for early childhood classrooms and to talk with the vendors. Keep in mind that their goal is to sell their products, but a careful shopper can garner a wealth of information and sometimes a special price. Particularly at the end of the exhibit hours, vendors would just as soon give you a discount as ship materials back to their home base. Remember also that conference sponsors rarely endorse products being displayed. Conferees are responsible for using their own good judgment because what is available is not always appropriate for early childhood education.

Toy libraries are popular equipment sources in some areas. A center director or teacher may borrow anything from a puzzle to a complete set of house-keeping equipment, just as one borrows library books. Sometimes, a group of center directors finds it worthwhile to help establish a toy library for their mutual benefit, and it is especially helpful to have toy-lending programs that furnish materials for special-needs children. Occasionally, toy-lending or toy-sharing systems are set up by community organizations to make equipment available to centers and parents.

Secondhand shops, discount stores, antique shops, and garage or yard sales frequently are excellent sources of equipment or raw materials for pieces needed by the center. The buyer may discover a garlic press that can provide an interesting physical knowledge experience for children when they are working with Play-Doh. Using imagination and effort, directors can turn large ice cream cans into storage places for musical instruments or some other equipment that demands a number of relatively small, easily accessible spaces. Perhaps a used desk or file cabinet for the center office can be located. When such discoveries need to be put into finished, usable, and attractive form, it sometimes is possible to enlist the help of the parent group, a high school vocational class, or a senior citizens' organization whose members enjoy repairing and painting. In some regions, high school woodworking or metalworking classes make new equipment and sell it to centers at reasonable prices.

Another way to obtain equipment is to solicit the help of parents, teachers, board members, or residents of the community in equipment-making parties. This activity enhances the feeling of community in the center's program. Child care center staff members often take advantage of the children's nap time to make classroom materials. Encouraging staff members to make some materials is important because few centers have unlimited resources, and commercial equipment cannot always be suitably adapted to meet individual children's needs.

Gifts of equipment are usually welcome, but their suitability must be measured against the same criteria employed for equipment purchases. A gift such as a toy gun in a center where pretend gunplay is discouraged or the gift of an animal that induces allergic reactions in some children must be refused graciously.

Most center directors keep a record of at least the major items purchased, and some directors keep a running account of all small items and consumables as well. An inventory of purchases can be recorded as items are unpacked by listing each item on the computer or a file card, noting the description, supplier, price, date of purchase, and location in which the item is to be used. Some directors mark equipment with the name of the center, with an inventory number, or with an identifying number so that if a center owns four identical computers, each is individually identifiable. In public schools, the usual practice is to put the room number on each piece of equipment. The labeling practice is helpful when pieces are sent out for repair, when school buildings are cleaned during vacation periods, or when items are stolen. Of course, valuable equipment should be insured. When equipment is added or removed from the center, the inventory must be updated.

An accurate record of equipment will always be available when the inventory is updated regularly. Director's Resource 8-2 shows a suggested inventory form. A backup disc of the inventory should be kept in a safe place—a fire-resistant file cabinet or other storage unit if possible—so that losses can be reported accurately in the event of fire or theft. Furthermore, an ongoing, updated inventory minimizes the work of taking an annual inventory (usually necessary for insurance purposes) for annual reporting to the board or the sponsoring or funding agency or for reporting to a corporate central office that must have an accurate annual inventory to determine the assets of the corporation. Updated inventories also give directors a clear picture of what is available in the center and help pinpoint areas or types of equipment that are incurring

## 8-5  MANAGING EQUIPMENT

Even before equipment is delivered to the **naeyc** center, the director must consider how it will be managed. All equipment must be checked and inventoried on delivery, and before it is stored or put into use, a maintenance plan should be set up to minimize repair and replacement needs.

### 8-5a Checking and Inventorying Equipment

When equipment is received, it must be checked against the order to ascertain that it corresponds with the order in terms of quantity, size, color, and so forth. It also is important to make certain that only the items actually received are listed on both the order and the packing slip and that prices are correct. If discrepancies are found, the vendor must be notified immediately. Keep original packing materials in case any equipment needs to be returned.

*Most center directors keep a record of at least the major items purchased, and some directors keep a running account of all small items and consumables as well.*

heavy damage. This information is useful in determining how much and when to reorder and in making decisions about changing vendors or brands of equipment ordered. Information about persistent damage in certain areas should lead to a careful examination of the storage and maintenance system.

After the equipment is checked in and inventoried, the director must notify the staff that the new equipment is available for use. No doubt, everyone will know when a new climbing tower arrives or when a new microwave oven is available, but if a dozen new puzzles are placed on the shelves or a fresh supply of felt markers is stored, it could be weeks before all teachers in a large center discover the new materials.

## 8-5b Maintaining and Storing Equipment

As soon as equipment is placed in the center, the job of maintenance begins. In the very act of placing equipment, maintenance decisions are made. For example, an untreated wooden climber that is placed outdoors in a rainy area is doomed to rot. It will need immediate treatment, followed by periodic coatings of a penetrating, nontoxic stain if it is to withstand weathering. Large tempera paint containers that are left open will dry out quickly, as will clay that is not properly stored.

Equipment used by the children must be checked daily and removed if in need of repair, even if immediate replacement is impossible. Children need attractive, usable equipment and should not be subjected to the frustration of trying to make sense out of broken or incomplete classroom materials. Puzzles with missing pieces, tricycles with broken pedals, or books with torn or defaced pages should not be left in the classroom.

Storage of equipment also is directly related to its maintenance. It is easy to return equipment after it has been used when each piece has a specific, clearly delineated storage space. The space, whether in a storage room or on a classroom shelf, must be large enough so that the object does not have to be jammed into place and perhaps damaged. The space must be accessible to staff members (and in many cases, to children) to ensure that it will be used for storage purposes. When storage is far from a classroom or the teachers have to go through another area such as the director's office to get to the storage room, it is more likely that the equipment and materials will be shoved out of the way in the classroom rather than returned to the storage room. Each center must work out a method for storing certain equipment and supplies that are used daily and must remain in the classroom. Other supplies should be designated for return to a central area. Storage also must be provided for items such as tricycles that are used daily but must be protected from weather and theft. Additional storage is needed for items that are purchased in quantity for long-range use such as paper towels and paint.

When a large number of people have access to the central supply storage areas, there is some tendency for each person to assume that someone else will maintain order and cleanliness in the area. Therefore, many of the users feel little or no responsibility for maintaining the area. When this happens, some users return materials in a haphazard way, fail to place them on the correct shelves, or return them in poor condition. Other staff members become irritated when they try to find what they need and have to cope with a messy storage area. These frustrations lead to conflict and a breakdown in positive staff relationships. Sometimes, this problem can be avoided by assigning each teacher the responsibility for maintaining a specific storage area, such as the area for art materials, outdoor equipment, or books and records, for a given length of time. In other centers, periodic work sessions are scheduled to involve the entire staff in cleaning and straightening central storage areas. Some centers institute a system for checking equipment in and out of the storage room that is similar to how libraries operate; an example is shown in Figure 8-1. In a large center, putting the checkout list on a computer may be helpful, but in most centers, posting a clipboard with a checkout sheet is more likely to be convenient for teachers. A few centers keep all the equipment in classrooms on shelves available to the children or in closed cabinets available to the teacher, but this practice is expensive because it requires so much duplication.

In whatever way equipment is stored, its placement should be neat and easy to find so that children and teachers alike will be encouraged to maintain some degree of order in their attractive environment. The director's job is to establish and follow routines that lead to the easy accessibility of all equipment to everyone. These routines make putting things away far less burdensome for both teachers and children. Orderliness does not have to be an obsession; rather, it is an appropriate way to manage a large variety of equipment that is used in a number of ways by a wide range of people.

**FIGURE 8-1** Sample checkout sheet for equipment and materials.

| Date | Item | Teacher | Date Returned |
|------|------|---------|---------------|
| 10/7/16 | Large Legos | Denice | 10/28/16 |
| 10/7/16 | Magnetic Letters | Sam | |
| 10/10/16 | CD: Ella Jenkins | Maria | 10/31/16 |
| | CD: Elgar violin | | |

© 2013 Cengage Learning®

## SUMMARY

Appropriate equipment allows the staff to focus on the essentials of their work as they provide an excellent early childhood program. Directors must be able to do the following:

- Select appropriate equipment that meets the needs of children, staff members, and families.

- Understand criteria that should be used to select equipment and reliable vendors.

- Work within a budget to purchase the most useful, durable, economic, easily maintained, attractive, and safe equipment possible.

- Revise a plan for the use and regular care of equipment.

## TRY IT OUT!

1. Obtain the prekindergarten learning standards for your state. In a small group, review the standards and discuss the implications of what children should know and be able to do on the equipment purchases you would need to make for a new center.

2. Work with fellow students on the following role-play situations. Have several students role-play using different approaches to each problem. Discuss the strengths and weaknesses of each group's approach.

   a. You are a preschool director. Mrs. Jane Jones has just given you 24 coloring books with an advertising message for her husband's business on the cover. You never use coloring books at the center because you believe they are not developmentally appropriate and would not meet NAEYC guidelines. How might you handle this situation?

   b. Suppose that the same situation in problem (a) occurred but that the donor is Mrs. Thomas Vanderbilt. Last year, she gave your center $10,000 for equipment. What might you say to Mrs. Vanderbilt? How might you try to prevent this situation from occurring in the future?

3. Your public preschool class is in the planning stages and will be held in a public school building. Discuss with your principal your 4-year-olds' needs and ways in which their equipment will be different from that of older children. Use a role-play format, working in pairs, or perhaps volunteering to role-play for the class.

## DIRECTOR'S RESOURCE 8-1

**PURCHASE ORDER FORM**

REQUISITION/PURCHASE ORDER

THE CHILDREN'S CENTER

To: _____

_____

_____

| Catalog No. | Description | Quantity | Price | Total |
|---|---|---|---|---|
| | | | | |
| | | | | |
| | | | | |
| | | | | |
| | | | | |
| | | | | |

Ship to: The Children's Center 1099 Main Street Centerville, CA 00000–0000

Account charged: _____

Approved by: _____

Date ordered: _____

Date received: _____

© 2013 Cengage Learning®

**TeachSource Digital Download**

## DIRECTOR'S RESOURCE 8-2

**SAMPLE INVENTORY FORM**

| INVENTORY FORM | | | | | |
|---|---|---|---|---|---|
| Date Purchased | Description | Identifying Number | Source | Price | Location in Center |
| | | | | | |
| | | | | | |
| | | | | | |
| | | | | | |
| | | | | | |
| | | | | | |
| | | | | | |
| | | | | | |
| | | | | | |
| | | | | | |
| | | | | | |
| | | | | | |

© 2013 Cengage Learning®

**TeachSource Digital Download**

# REFERENCES

American Academy of Pediatrics, American Public Health Association, and National Resource Center for Health and Safety in Child Care and Early Education (2013). *Stepping stones to caring for our children* (3rd ed.). Elk Grove Village, IL: American Academy of Pediatrics, Washington, DC: American Public Health Association, and Aurora, CO: National Resource Center for Health and Safety in Child Care and Early Education. Retrieved from http://nrckids.org/index.cfm/products/stepping-stones-to-caring-for-our-children-3rd-edition-ss3/

Aronson, S. (2012). *Healthy young children: A manual for programs* (5th ed.). Washington, DC: National Association for the Education of Young Children.

Brown, M. W. (1947). *Goodnight moon*. New York: Harper.

Chalufour, I., & Worth, K. (2004). *Building structures with young children*. St. Paul, MN: Redleaf Press.

Child Care Aware of North Dakota. (2013). *Child care facility development guide*. Retrieved from http://www.ndchildcare.org/providers/build-business/center-startup.html.

Dodge, D. T., Colker, L. J., & Heroman, C. (2010). *The creative curriculum for pre-school* (5th ed.). Washington, DC: Teaching Strategies.

Morgan, G., & Emanuel, B. (2010). The bottom line for children's programs: What you need to know to manage the money (5th ed.). Watertown, MA: Steam Press.

Moyer, J. (1995). *Selecting educational equipment and materials for school and home*. Washington, DC: Association for Childhood Education International.

NAEYC and the Fred Rogers Center for Early Learning and Children's Media. (2012). *Technology and interactive media as tools in early childhood programs serving children from birth through age 8: A joint position statement issued by the National Association for the Education of Young Children and the Fred Rogers Center for Early Learning and Children's Media at Saint Vincent College*. Retrieved from http://www.naeyc.org/positionstatements.

Stoecklin, V. (2005, July). Creating environments that sustain children, staff, and our planet. *Child Care Information Exchange, 164*, 39–48.

U.S. Consumer Product Safety Commission. (2009). *Injuries and investigated deaths associated with playground equipment, 2001–2008*. Retrieved from http://www.cpsc.gov/PageFiles/108596/playground.pdf.

U.S. Consumer Product Safety Commission. (2010). *Public playground safety handbook*. Retrieved from http://www.cpsc.gov/PageFiles/107329/325.pdf.

U.S. Consumer Product Safety Commission. (2013). *Injuries and deaths associated with nursery products among children younger than five*. Retrieved from http://www.cpsc.gov//Global/Research-and-Statistics/Injury-Statistics/Toys/nurseryproductsinjuries121313FINAL.pdf.

Utah Department of Workforce Services, Office of Child Care. (2012). *Opening a quality child care center*. Retrieved from https://careaboutchildcare.utah.gov/pub/qualityCenter.pdf.

Wardle, F. (1999). The story of a playground. *Child Care Information Exchange, 128*, 28–30.

Watson, A., & McCathren, R. (2009). Including children with special needs: Are you and your early childhood program ready? *Beyond the Journal: Young Children on the Web*. Retrieved from http://www.naeyc.org/files/yc/file/200903/BTJWatson.pdf.

White Hutchinson Leisure & Learning Group. (2007, May–August). Illinois becomes second state to require green cleaning, reducing chemical exposure for children. *Children's Learning Environments eNewsletter, VI*(2), 1.

*The center director sets the emotional tone for the program.*

## Learning Objectives

After reading this chapter, you should be able to:

**9-1** Discuss ways to create a positive climate and motivate staff.

**9-2** Describe the major sections of an employment policy.

**9-3** Explain the steps in the hiring process

**9-4** Identify strategies that facilitate staff retention.

## Standards Addressed in this Chapter

**naeyc**

Accreditation Standard 10 – Leadership and Management

Administrator Competencies – Management Knowledge and Skills 1, 2, 3, 9, 10

Administrators Competencies – Early Childhood Knowledge and Skills

This chapter focuses on the importance of developing good leadership skills, and then using these skills—with good communication skills—to be an effective administrator of a child care program. Obviously, the person in charge must have knowledge of how to develop and oversee a budget, write policy and job descriptions, and determine the program's facility and equipment needs. However, writing policy, hiring staff, developing budgets, and ordering equipment all will be wasted efforts unless the manager has the interpersonal and communication skills necessary to hire and motivate the staff. After the policies have been established, the staff are hired, and the children enrolled, the function of the director is to develop structures that motivate staff and create a climate that inspires adults and children alike.

## 9-1 CREATING A POSITIVE CLIMATE AND MOTIVATING STAFF

Clearly, the interpersonal issues and the time  it takes to resolve them are at the very core of being an effective administrator. Much of what is discussed in this text deals with budgets, boards, licensing, and record keeping, but the real task of the director as a manager is to work effectively with, and provide support to, those who will implement the program. The terms *manager, director, administrator,* and *leader* used throughout this book, all refer to the person in charge of, and responsible for, the program. The manager must relate to the staff and motivate them to do the tasks delegated to them. Members of the staff implement the program, but the director, acting in the capacity of leader and motivator, orchestrates so that all the components work together.

## 9-1a Creating a Positive Climate

As a leader, the director has the major responsibility for creating a climate of care, trust, and respect. This climate can be achieved best by demonstrating caring behavior, by taking steps to build a feeling of community or partnership, and by creating a climate for good communication among and between all members of the center community. The goal is to optimize the developmental potential of children, families, and staff in an environment that respects diversity. The director not only sets the emotional tone of a center but also works with staff to develop structures that empower, organize, and build a sense of community.

---

### DIRECTOR'S CORNER

"In most cases, to be successful as a director of a child care center, you have to be a people person. You have to realize that this job goes far beyond administrative policy and doing paperwork—that being the boss here is not really being a boss in the traditional sense. Being the boss here has to do with forming trusting relationships with your staff, respecting their individuality, being firm when you need to be firm and being gentle when they need a gentle hand. It's important to remember that you won't get respect if you don't show respect. Also, remember that others can do the paperwork, but you are the one who must build the relationships with your staff. Of course, you are also responsible for building and maintaining relationships with parents and the community."

*—Director of a community nonprofit child care center*

---

### Modeling

The director creates a climate of warmth, caring, and acceptance by relating to staff members, parents, and children with honesty and openness. Mutual trust will grow in an environment in which respect is earned, and the best way to earn respect is to show respect for others. When respect for difference is modeled, the tone is set for the entire center.

Maturity and self-awareness are the basic characteristics of a leader who can maintain professional interaction in even the most intense situation. Self-awareness is being able to identify one's own emotions and the ability to link those emotions to one's actions. Leaders who are self-aware and attuned to their emotions and actions are better equipped to understand the emotions of others (Bloom, 2007). These leadership attributes create a climate that, in turn, motivates others to be understanding, accepting, and warm. Most of you have read about and observed "modeling" in young children. One child who is perceived as the leader displays a pattern of behavior, and others imitate it. One child might say, "Yuck! Spinach!" and soon everyone at the table is saying "Yuck, spinach!" However, if the child were to say, "Yummm, spinach!" then other children are more likely to respond positively to the vegetable being served. Although this example is clearly an oversimplification of what typically happens in a group, behavior *is* contagious, and there is evidence that a leader who serves as the model does, indeed, drive the behavioral climate of the setting.

Modeling begins with the very first encounter the director has with new staff members as they come into the center for interviews or when a newly hired director is introduced to the staff for the first time. The trust and mutual respect that are communicated during these initial meetings are the building blocks for the relationships that will develop over time. During the first meeting of a new year, at a new center, or with a new director, there is a unique opportunity to establish procedures and practices that will set the stage for future respectful interactions. Additionally, the director who shows intellectual curiosity and is always seeking more information to do a better job can inspire others to do the same. A leader who does not serve as a model of professional commitment and enthusiasm for learning more about children, families, human relationships, and trends and issues in early childhood cannot expect staff members to invest energy in these areas. The leader's responsibility is to show interest and enthusiasm for what is going on in the program and in the profession and to serve as a resource for staff members and parents.

## 9-1b Community Building

The director is responsible for developing and maintaining a sense of community among staff, parents, and children. Morale will be higher and the environment more conducive to growth for all involved if there is a "we" feeling of belonging. As the feeling of belonging increases, feelings of anxiety, self-doubt, hostility, and rejection decrease.

Staff members who feel a sense of ownership about the program will be more self-assured and enthusiastic about assuming responsibility. They will not only perform the tasks they were hired to perform but will be more likely to invest energy into learning more so they can extend their area of responsibility. The total task of serving children and families becomes *our* task, and *we* provide the richest and best service we can.

The "we" feeling radiates beyond staff to families and children. It becomes "our" center or "our" program, and children begin to talk about "my" school. The feeling of community permeates the entire environment; all who participate in the many aspects of the center program feel they play an important part in the total program. All participants feel that they *own* a piece of the program and contribute to its success or failure. Parents and children alike recognize that they, and their cultures and languages, are valued; that diversity is at the very core of the program; and that their contribution to the program is important. They come to understand that they are the very reason for the center's existence. There would be no reason for the center to continue if there were no families and children to serve.

---

### DIRECTOR'S CORNER

"I often think back on my own experiences in the classroom when I was there eight hours a day. I remember that I was expected to be nurturing and giving of myself *all* day long—it helps me remember how much I, in turn, needed to be nurtured. That's why I have an 'open door' policy for my staff—I take time to actively listen, to problem-solve with them, to encourage them. I often have to put my paperwork aside because I know that a staff person sometimes needs to talk *right now*! This job goes beyond, 'I'm the boss, and you're the staff person' relationship. The other side of this is knowing when and where to set the boundaries. When and how do I set limits on my availability to staff members or family members so that I can focus on what will be best for others and for me, as well as what is best for the program?"

*—Director, for-profit corporate center*

---

### REFLECTION

Take a moment to reflect on your own experiences. Think about whether there was a sense of community in the center in which you gained experience. Consider whether you were made to feel that you were an important member of the community. If you recall feeling positive about the experience, who was most instrumental in creating that accepting environment for you? Did you sense the children also felt this was *their* place? Who was responsible for creating the "we" feeling in the classroom?

---

## Communication

Every director will engage in written communication. When there is a need to communicate in writing, the first question to ask is, "Who needs to know?" Interpersonal relationships are often damaged inadvertently because some members of the group do not receive information that they feel should have been relayed to them. For example, although a change in next week's menu may, on the surface, affect only the cook in a child care center, a teacher who has planned a special science activity around one of the foods to be served on a given day may be very annoyed to learn about the change in menu on the day of the lesson. The message itself, including the exact wording, can be more easily drafted when the audience for the message has been determined. Therefore, the audience receiving the message will determine both the content and the wording.

Although some communication will be in writing, much of it will be face-to-face verbal or nonverbal. To be an effective leader, the director must be a competent communicator and must take responsibility for helping the entire staff develop communication skills.

Verbal communication skills can be learned. The director can learn to send effective messages, to become a good listener, and to engage in effective problem solving. It is possible to define specific behaviors, both verbal and nonverbal, that block communication. It is possible to improve communication skills and, as a result, enhance interpersonal relationships. Note that we have said this is *possible*, but it is not easy. Unless directors believe wholeheartedly in the importance of open communication for good interpersonal relationships, they are unlikely to invest the energy necessary to develop the skills and to practice them until they become totally integrated into a personal communication style. However, after this integration has come about, the director's communication style inevitably will serve as a model for others. The model will set the pattern for all the other people in the center and will create an atmosphere more conducive to open communication.

Verbal and nonverbal messages must be congruent. Sensitive leaders will take care to convey the *real* message with both their words and body postures. Words that convey approval or acceptance but are accompanied by a frown and a closed body posture conveying rejection and hostility send a mixed message that is confusing to the receiver. Supportive, positive words and actions will help build trusting relationships among the people in the center. In a trusting relationship, criticism or negative reactions can be handled without destroying the relationship, provided they are given discreetly and are carefully timed. For the director to criticize a teacher in front of the receptionist when the teacher is on the way to the classroom to help a crying child is the epitome of poor communication skills and will have a negative impact on future attempts at open communication. Other, more subtle blocks to communication that will set the stage for a defensive response, hostility, or feelings of inadequacy include the following:

- demanding and controlling messages
- put-downs
- use of sarcasm or threats
- flip, humorous responses to serious concerns

It is important to consider what needs to be said, how to say it, and when to say it, while always being aware of the cultural nuances of language.

A sensitive leader is well advised to consider carefully whether a situation calls for *telling* or *listening*. Telling often comes more easily than listening but must always be done with full awareness of the cultural nuance of language. However, in many situations, listening is a better vehicle for maintaining open communication and strengthening a relationship. Dealing with the personal problems of families or professional issues of staff members often requires listening instead of telling. The benefit of listening is not only to gain information but also to validate the message of the sender. Such communication can be energy draining and time-consuming but when done well, it has a powerful and positive influence on the network of interpersonal relationships. Listening is time and energy well spent.

Despite all the care and planning that go into creating a supportive atmosphere, conflict will arise. This is human nature and does not necessarily mean poor management, nor does it imply weakness in the network. It does, however, require attention. The director and the staff can learn specific communication skills to facilitate conflict resolution. Recognizing that conflict will exist is the first step in developing a system for dealing with it. Because many find conflict to be uncomfortable, people commonly try to avoid it. Effective leaders overcome the natural tendency to overreact or to avoid, blame, or punish those who are involved in the conflict. They maintain a calm, rational style of interaction. Being proactive is an effective tool to deal with conflict as it arises. It includes developing a conflict resolution policy and communicating it to both teachers and families as part of the orientation process. Addressing expectations for dealing with conflict before the emotions of an actual tense situation arise is an important strategy to implement. Consider the conflict resolution policy shown in Figure 9-1.

## 9-1c Motivating the Staff

The director does the orchestrating, but programs are implemented through the efforts of staff. The staff of a center must be motivated to plan and implement the total program. Just as communication skills can be learned, the skills for guiding mental and physical energies toward defined goals can also be learned. Without training in how to guide and to motivate human energy toward shared goals, the director will follow some rules of thumb that may leave the role of director-as-motivator to chance. This practice may be compared to designing a program for young children based on knowledge gained from having been a child, having parented a child, or having been through a public school system. Although these experiences may be useful, they cannot substitute for theoretical knowledge and a sound educational background in the field.

---

**DIRECTOR'S CORNER**

"As a director, I want my staff to know that it is good to have different opinions about any number of things, and when I hear about these differences, I want to provide an opportunity for discussion rather than have concerns turn into bad feelings, unproductive activity, and gossip."

—*Director, church-based not-for-profit program*

---

As directors begin to think about ways to motivate employees, they usually think about salary increases, a better building, new equipment, more help in the center, and a number of other items that are related to money and budget. Certainly, low salaries and poor working conditions can lead to dissatisfaction, but the promise of more money—or the threat of less—probably will not have far-reaching or long-lasting effects on individual or group performance levels. However, if a leader is using dollars to control and motivate performance, it becomes increasingly more difficult to find the necessary supply to meet the demand. In addition, extrinsic incentives motivate employees to get the rewards but rarely alter the emotional or intellectual commitments that underlie behaviors.

What, then, is a director to do? A number of useful strategies are available for motivating people to commit themselves to a task and to actualize their potential. Two of the strategies that seem particularly applicable to the early childhood setting are use of encouragement and provision of job enrichment.

### Use of Encouragement

Rewards or reinforcements may motivate the staff, but as with teaching, they tend to increase dependency on the one who controls the source of the rewards. They also heighten competition, thereby defeating the overarching goal of developing a sense of a cooperative community. Encouragement, on the other hand, tends

**FIGURE 9-1** Sample conflict resolution policy.

### Conflict Resolution Policy

We provide a safe, secure environment where children learn to respectfully resolve conflicts that naturally occur in a child care setting:

- Adults help children develop vocabulary that expresses not only their wants and needs but also other's feelings as well as their own.
- Adults model respectful interactions with others, using their own words and actions to develop an understanding of how to deal with conflict.
- Adults affirm everyone's right to be safe emotionally as well as physically by setting standards for behavior and implementing caring, consistent consequences aligned with developmentally appropriate expectations according to the children's age levels.
- Adults facilitate resolution between preschool children by asking guided questions but resist solving the children's problems for them, thus providing children the opportunity to make decisions and practice self-regulation of socially responsible behavior.

### Conflict between Adults

While every effort is made to meet the needs of children, parents, and staff, we realize that from time to time a conflict may occur between parents, staff, and administrators. The following process is followed should a conflict occur:

- Step One – A respectful discussion is held between the persons directly involved at a time and place that assures privacy and sufficient time for a thorough resolution to take place.

- Step Two – If resolution is not found at the first meeting, a second meeting is held with the director for the purpose of creating a plan for resolution and a timeline for expected success.
- Step Three – If the conflict is not resolved according to the timeline, adjustments may be made to the plan, and an additional timeline be established, or:
- Step Four – If at any time the director determines that resolution is not possible s/he will consider one of the following for immediate action:
  - Removal of the child from the classroom
  - Withdrawal of services from the center
  - Suspension of the staff member until disciplinary steps can be taken
  - Involvement of the Assistant Dean of the School of Education and Allied Professions

Grounds for determining that a resolution is not possible include but are not exclusive of the following:

1. any person involved displays inappropriate behavior such as shouting, accusing, name-calling, swearing, or physical assault
2. any person involved refuses to follow the prescribed process
3. any person involved jeopardizes the process by spreading information concerning the conflict to those outside the immediate conflict or those involved in the resolution of the process.

*Source: Reprinted with permission from the Bombeck Family Learning Center of the University of Dayton.*

*The director needs to recognize when teachers design quality experiences and communicate that recognition regularly.*

to build self-confidence and a sense of intrinsic job satisfaction.

Just as the classroom teacher makes sure that encouragement is specific, focused on process, usually given in private, and neither judgmental nor evaluative, the director also keeps these same principles in mind when working with staff. To encourage a teacher who has just helped a screaming toddler, you might say, "I noticed how calm you managed to be with Tommy while he was having such a hard time in the bathroom. It worked out well." These words of encouragement are more specific and process oriented than, "I like the way you work with toddlers." Telling the teacher of 4-year-olds, "You must have done some detailed planning for the science experience you did today to make it go so smoothly. It's surely fun for you to watch how engaged the children were in inflating their model lungs" is more specific and less evaluative than, "That was a nice science activity."

## Job Enrichment

Carter and Curtis (2010) encourage leaders to view teachers as competent thinkers and learners:

> How you (the director) see teachers and the scope of their work is critical to your success in helping them develop. If you view your staff as people with problems, only noticing their lack of skills and knowledge to manage behavior or plan lessons for learning, you will most likely approach your coaching with quick fixes, one-size-fits-all techniques, and impatience rather than engage them in the dynamics of the teaching and learning process. In contrast, if you acknowledge the complexities of working with children and regard your teachers as competent human beings with rich life experiences, important perspectives, and the potential to rise to their best selves, you will invest the time, resources, and enthusiasm to engage with them in their work. (p. 131)

Job enrichment is a management strategy that enhances job satisfaction and honors the strengths of staff by presenting more challenges and increasing responsibility, which, in turn, produce a sense of personal achievement and on-the-job satisfaction. It is possible to design a job enrichment program for a child care center so that staff members are motivated to higher levels of commitment. As a result, they will experience greater intrinsic rewards. The job enrichment principles particularly applicable to child care centers are listed here:

1. Give new and added responsibilities to staff members so they are constantly challenged and empowered to control aspects of their work setting.

2. Provide opportunities for ongoing training and college-based education that will contribute to quality of performance and to personal and professional growth.

3. Give staff members special assignments by occasionally delegating coworkers' or supervisors' jobs to broaden each person's understanding of the total operation of the organization. This is recognition but has no monetary reward. This procedure can bring more recognition from other staff members and open up greater opportunities for advancement.

Obviously, there is some overlap among the three stated principles, both in terms of the method used and the outcome expected. There also are other ways to enrich staff members' jobs that will broaden their experience and bring them both intrinsic and extrinsic rewards. The many possibilities are limited solely by the creativity and imagination of the person in charge.

At first glance, it may seem that added responsibility will lead to dissatisfaction and demands for more money or other material rewards. However, there is evidence to suggest that, more often than not, the person who is challenged and who "stretches" to assume more responsibility will feel a sense of pride and achievement. For example, the classroom aide who, at midyear, is given the added responsibility of meeting and greeting parents and children at arrival time probably will find that job intrinsically satisfying. The aide will develop better skills for helping children make that first daily break from a trusted caregiver and acquire new skills for accomplishing the added responsibility. Assigning added duties can be accomplished best in an atmosphere of mutual trust, and it must be done through the use of positive communication skills.

The training needed to develop the skills necessary for managing a new task effectively often can be offered informally by other members of the staff and by exposure to resources such as books, pamphlets, videos, PowerPoint presentations, or opportunities to observe. Ongoing training can be expanded to include more formalized in-service sessions on curriculum, child abuse, communication skills, working with children with special needs and their families, or other topics selected to serve a specific need within the center program. Use of release time or financial support for workshops and seminars, online resources, and additional course work are still other ways to provide job enrichment opportunities for the personal and professional growth of staff members.

Delegating special assignments to staff members usually evokes a sense of achievement and recognition, even though it means extra work. A cook who is consulted about menu planning and buying, and who is later asked to help evaluate the total food service program when the center is undergoing a self-study for accreditation, not only gains an understanding of what is involved in the total food planning and preparation program but also develops a greater potential for advancement, whether in the current job or in another work setting.

## 9-2 DESIGNING EMPLOYMENT POLICIES

Directors of new centers are faced with the daunting task of developing new  employment policies while directors of existing centers must deal with the recurring task of reviewing and revising these policies. Employment Policies are required documents for NAEYC accreditation in the Leadership and Management Standard. The Program Administration Scale (PAS) has Employment Policies as part of the Human Resources Development System. When writing or revising employment policies, it is important to consider the purpose served by the policies, the best interests of all parties covered and affected by the policies, and what is to be included in the policies.

## 9-2a Purpose

Personnel needs for security and confidence in job performance should be balanced with the center's need to function effectively in the establishment of carefully conceived employment policies. When staff members are unsure of their rights and responsibilities, some may tend to probe and test to determine where the limits lie. The dissension among staff members that ensues drains energy from child care. Staff members who know what is expected can recognize how their assigned roles fit into the overall organization and can function more comfortably in those roles. Administrators also can function more effectively when there is little doubt about policies.

Inclusive employment policies tailored to a specific child care operation, whether staffed by a few or by many, serve two purposes.

1.  They reduce procedural errors and free administrators from unnecessary involvement in resolution.

2.  They reduce anxiety by helping each staff member to understand expectations and move, independently and as part of the team, toward efficient operation of the program.

A written statement of the employment policies and procedures should be given to each employee at the beginning of the term of employment. These policies set the parameters within which the staff will function. Of course, the administrator should periodically check with employees to ascertain whether the policies are understood. Although these policies must be tailored to the needs of each program, the samples in Director's Resource 9-1 can serve as a guideline for their preparation.

## 9-2b Source

The task of writing employment policies is complex, and the sphere of their influence is extensive. They must not only be precise, well written, and inclusive but also take into consideration the best interests of staff, children, and families. The interest of the sponsoring group, whether it be to make a profit or not, deserves consideration as well. Those who are responsible for writing the policies must have both an understanding of the scope of the program and insight into the vested interests of all involved.

Employment policies might be prepared by such persons as the hired director of a community-sponsored center, an owner of a proprietary center, a human resources department for a center sponsored by a corporation or institution, or the human resources director of a national child care chain. Existing public school employment policies for teachers or, in some cases, for civil service employees often will be applicable in programs sponsored by public schools or on military bases. When the center staff is part of a labor union, the union contract will likely impact how policies and procedures are written to reflect agreements that were made during the contract negotiations.

> ### DIRECTOR'S CORNER
>
> "During my new staff orientation program, I sit down with each new employee and read through the employment policies, leaving time for questions and discussion. I give special attention to the section on holidays, sick days, personal days, and vacation time. It helps me feel comfortable that this new staff person has at least looked at the employment policies once and not just put the document in a file or on her night table to read later when she has more time."
>
> —*Director, private not-for-profit center*

*Good employment policies need to be revisited with staff in order to be fair and current.*

It is somewhat common practice for child care settings to have policies drawn up by a subcommittee or a standing human resources committee of the policy-making board. The bylaws, as drawn up by the policy board, should contain the mechanism for creating a human resources committee and should detail the manner in which the membership of that committee will be selected. The center director serves on the committee and represents the staff's interest. Other members of the committee might be parents, people from the community, and representatives of licensing and/or certifying groups who would, in each case, represent the interests and diversity of special-interest groups.

## 9-2c Inclusions

Employment policies cover all matters relating to employment and include job responsibilities, organizational charts, schedules of reimbursement for services, evaluation and grievance procedures, and description of the steps necessary to change the policies themselves. They must conform to union requirements, where applicable, and to all regulations that apply to employment practices. For example, as of July 1994, employers with 15 employees or more must comply with the Americans with Disabilities Act (ADA), which covers nondiscrimination practices related to recruitment, advertising, tenure, layoffs, leave, fringe benefits, and all other employment-related activities (Americans with Disabilities Act, 1991). Because many of these elements are included in the employment policies, it is important to understand the implications of the ADA for you and your staff to ensure compliance with these regulations, as well as to protect your program. Employment policies specifically spell out the rights of employees and what they may expect from the employer, and they should include the items described in the following sections.

### Job Descriptions

The job description is a detailed outline of what is expected from the person who fills a specific position.

### Career Lattice

Developing a career lattice or opportunity for progression is a challenge to the director and/or the board. Each center must develop a career lattice after reviewing the roles and responsibilities of each staff position, budget limitations, and the professional goals of the center. The career lattice clearly defines education, experience, and corresponding salaries and benefits for every step in the hierarchy (Bloom, Sheerer, & Britz, 2005).

### Contract

The contract usually is a bilateral agreement signed by both parties that mutually binds the employee and the employer to agree upon certain rights from each other. In this case, the employee agrees to provide a service (as defined by the appropriate job description), and the employer agrees to reimburse the employee for the service at a given rate for a specific length of time. Of course, those employers who have an at-will policy do not use employment contracts.

### Salary Ranges

Salary ranges for each position on the career lattice should be indicated clearly. Salary ranges should be based on the training, experience, and years of service required for each position. If salary increases are performance based, the plan for those increases is stated in the employment policies.

Each state may have its own laws regulating minimum wage and overtime pay, but all state regulations must be compatible with the federal Fair Labor Standards Act (FLSA). In that act, employees classified as "exempt" from FLSA are professional, salaried staff, while those who earn an hourly wage and are entitled to overtime pay are considered "nonexempt" and are covered by the FLSA. (The federal government has instituted new rules that clarify employee rights and employer obligations relative to overtime pay.) Because these definitions and rules are scrutinized and revised regularly, it is important to consult an attorney with expertise in labor law when making decisions concerning questions related to compliance with government regulations. The Child Care Law Center can provide information on the current status of the issues involving how the FLSA affects child care employees in different states.

### Staff and Fringe Benefits

Fringe benefits available to employees must be stated clearly in the employment policies. Retirement plans, health insurance, educational opportunities, and other policies that impact the lives of employees should be reviewed in detail during orientation and should also be available for reference when questions arise. Changes in benefits must be communicated with staff in writing, and updates must be maintained in benefits documents.

### Employment at Will

"Employment at will" is common in most states and refers to an employment status in which the employee does not have an annual or ongoing contract and can be terminated without reason. "Even in states which allow for 'at will' employment (as opposed to states which require 'good cause' for termination), an employer may still be found liable if the employer violates its own employment policies" (Cohen, 1998, p. 86). The sample employment policies in Director's Resource 9-1 provide exact wording for those who choose to use the employment at will provision. But that being the case, it is important to use caution when wording the staff handbook to avoid wording that can be viewed by the court as a contract. Employment law is changing all over the country, and regulations vary state by state; therefore, it is wise to consult an attorney on employment-related questions or issues.

### Health and Safety Measures

A health examination for all staff members is required upon hire in most states. In many localities, the law requires the health examination of center administrators who are viewed as being ultimately responsible for the health and safety of the children in the center. Those who work with children should be free of any infectious disease, whether or not there is a local certifying or licensing group responsible for monitoring health regulations. In addition, all staff are required in most states to have universal precautions (blood-borne pathogens) and hazardous materials training. It also is recommended that child care staff be advised to update their immunizations because close contact with children puts them at risk for contracting a variety of infectious diseases. Furthermore, because the work is often physically demanding, the examination protects members of the staff by exploring their health limitations and by reminding them to follow basic practices such as getting adequate rest and proper nutrition.

Child abuse and other child safety issues are a major concern among child care professionals. Therefore, there is an increasing trend to seek ways to certify that employees do not use drugs and have no criminal records. Some states and government-funded programs require that prospective staff be screened for one or more of these. Employers with more than 15 employees must comply with the ADA when dealing with employment issues. The problem of AIDS is causing concern as well. Congress intended that the ADA protect people infected with AIDS and HIV. Therefore, employers may not ask candidates for their AIDS and HIV status on applications or during the prehiring process.

Most states require that applicants for positions working with children complete a form declaring that they have not been convicted of a crime involving children. It is also common to require background checks. Many states have required forms for this important information, which can be used to glean information that is not permitted to be asked directly in an interview. The sample form in Figure 9-2 that covers the criminal record issue will serve as a guide for a way of obtaining information from staff members as well as job candidates about some sensitive areas of inquiry. If there are questions about the legality of making inquiries of this nature, contact the Equal Employment Opportunity Commission (EEOC) or seek legal counsel.

Employment policies should state clearly that professional staff must submit certified copies of credentials and that personal and professional references furnished by all new employees will be contacted before job offers are made.

## Daily Hours and Employment Period

Careful scheduling of personnel is critical for effective and efficient operation of all centers. This schedule should be stated in the employment policies and should be reiterated in each contract or letter of employment if these are used. Daily hours will not be the same for each staff member. Some staff members must arrive before children to prepare the learning environment. A large child care center will need extra staff to cover peak hours. For example, if school-age children come to the center before and after school, or for lunch, the staffing needs will be increased during those hours. A key staff member must be present late in the day to chat with people who pick up the children near closing time. When all children have gone, the center must be in order for the early arrivals the following day; therefore, some of the staff must stay beyond the time that all children leave.

The complexity of the staffing schedule and the format used to lay out the schedule in an understandable way will vary. It should be set up to provide sufficient coverage to meet the licensing requirements, where applicable, and to guarantee safety of children and adequate staff to maintain high standards of quality throughout each day. In planning the staffing patterns, directors should keep in mind the concerns about child abuse in child care centers and take preventive measures. Schedule at least two caregivers to be present at all times, particularly early and late in the day and during nap and toileting routines. This will help protect children and staff if one is unjustly accused of abuse (Cohen, 1998). Director's Resources 9-2 and 9-3 will serve as guidelines for setting up staffing schedules and staffing plans. Use of graphing, listing by staff member, listing by room, or listing by program are a few of the ways to record a staffing schedule so it is clear to those who are interested in it, including staff, board members, licensing agents, and especially parents.

## Relief Periods

A planned system of daily relief periods or breaks should be stated. The policy on rest periods may be very flexible or carefully scheduled. In either case, the policy should clearly state and include the designated space where staff may take breaks. In half-day programs, it is rare to find a set policy on rest periods due to the short time span of concentrated effort required by staff members. On the other hand, in child care programs in which a teacher may work an eight- or nine-hour day that includes having lunch with children, it is essential to provide time to rest and be away from the children. Some centers prefer to have some staff members work a split shift to provide time for rest, shopping, or study at midday. This serves to reduce costs at a time of low need.

## Vacations, Holidays, and Sick Leave

A statement on vacations and holidays should appear in the employment policies. Specific details about lead time for vacation applications and the length and timing of vacations is advisable for larger, year-round centers, but smaller centers in session only during the typical school year may not require the same specificity in their policy. However, both large and small centers observe certain holidays. These holidays will vary depending on the religious and ethnic orientation of the staff and/or the children served, the agency with which the school is affiliated (church or public school), and the community standards. All employees should know exactly which holidays will be observed by the center.

Ohio Department of Job and Family Services
## STATEMENT OF NONCONVICTION
## FOR CHILD CARE CENTERS AND TYPE A HOMES

This statement must be signed by every individual owner, administrator and employee of a child care center, Type A Home and all persons eighteen years of age and older who reside in a Type A Home. This statement must be kept on file at the center or Type A Home. Please note that owners and administrators must also attach the JFS 01314 which is a supplement to this form.

**Employee Name** (please print or type)

☐  I hereby attest that I have never been convicted of or pleaded guilty to child abuse or other crimes of violence set forth in section 5104.09 of the Revised Code and that no child has been removed from my home as described in section 2151.353 of the Revised Code.

| Employee Signature | Date |
|---|---|

**Street Address**

| City | State | Zip Code | Telephone Number |
|---|---|---|---|

☐  I am unable to sign the statement above because I have been convicted of a crime included in section 5104.09 of the Revised Code. However, after reviewing the rehabilitation requirements of rule 5101:2-13-26 or 5101:2-12-26 of the Administrative Code with the administrator, it has been determined I meet the rehabilitation requirements. Please see attached verifications that the requirements for rehabilitation have been met.

**Note:** Anyone who withholds information from, or falsifies information on this statement is guilty of falsification, a misdemeanor of the first degree. If the offender is an owner of a center or a licensee of a Type A Home, the conviction constitutes grounds for denial, revocation, or refusal to renew a child day care license application. If the offender is an employee of a center or Type A Home, or is a person eighteen years of age or older who reside in a Type A Home, and if the owner or licensee had knowledge of, and acquiesced in the commission of the offense, the conviction constitutes grounds for denial, revocation, or refusal to renew a child day care license application.

Please note: effective June 1, 2006 all civilian background checks must be submitted electronically through use of WebCheck or other approved methods. More information can be accessed at: www.webcheck.ag.state.oh.us.

**The administrator is required to sign and date below verifying that fingerprints have been electronically submitted to the Ohio Bureau of Criminal Identification and Investigation (BCII), or mailed if electronic processing exemption criteria are met.**

A criminal records check for the above named individual was requested on (date) _____

☐ Ohio records check        ☐ FBI records check  (please check)

| Signature of Administrator | Date |
|---|---|

### TYPE A HOMES ONLY

In addition to the above, the licensee of a Type A Home must sign the following statement.
I hereby attest that no one who resides in my home and who is under eighteen years of age has been adjudicated a delinquent child for committing a violation of any offense listed in section 5104.09 of the Ohio Revised Code.

| Signature | Date |
|---|---|

This is a prescribed form which must be used to meet the requirements of section 5104.09 of the Revised Code. Failure to complete the form shall preclude issuance of the child care license or certificate.
JFS 01313 (Rev. 9/2006)

Page 1 of 2

**FIGURE 9-2** (*Continued*)

## Section 5104.09 Prohibitions Against Employment

**Homicide**
1. R.C. 2903.01 – Aggravated murder
2. R.C. 2903.02 – Murder
3. R.C. 2903.03 – Voluntary manslaughter
4. R.C. 2903.04 – Involuntary manslaughter

**Assault**
5. R.C. 2903.11 – Felonious assault
6. R.C. 2903.12 – Aggravated assault
7. R.C. 2903.13 – Assault
8. R.C. 2903.16 – Failing to provide for a functionally impaired person

**Menacing**
9. R.C. 2903.21 – Aggravated menacing
10. R.C. 2903.22 - Menacing

**Patient abuse and neglect**
11. R.C. 2903.34 – Patient abuse, neglect

**Kidnapping and related issues**
12. R.C. 2905.01 – Kidnapping
13. R.C. 2905.02 – Abduction
14. R.C. 2905.04 – Child stealing (as this law existed prior to July 1, 1996)
15. R.C. 2905.05 – Criminal child enticement

**Sex offenses**
16. R.C. 2907.02 - Rape
17. R.C. 2907.03 – Sexual battery
18. R.C. 2907.04 – Corruption of a minor
19. R.C. 2907.05 – Gross sexual imposition
20. R.C. 2907.06 – Sexual imposition
21. R.C. 2907.07 – Importuning
22. R.C. 2907.08 – Voyeurism
23. R.C. 2907.09 – Public indecency
24. R.C. 2907.12 – Felonious sexual penetration (as this former section of law existed)
25. R.C. 2907.21 – Compelling prostitution
26. R.C. 2907.22 – Promoting prostitution
27. R.C. 2907.23 – Procuring
28. R.C. 2907.25 – Prostitution
29. R.C. 2907.31 – Disseminating matter harmful to juveniles
30. R.C. 2907.32 – Pandering obscenity
31. R.C. 2907.321 – Pandering obscenity involving a minor
32. R.C. 2907.322 – Pandering sexually oriented matter involving a minor
33. R.C. 2907.323 – Illegal use of a minor in nudity-oriented material or performance

**Arson**

34. R.C. 2909.02 - Aggravated arson
35. R.C. 2909.03 - Arson

**Robbery and Burglary**
36. R.C. 2911.01 – Aggravated robbery
37. R.C. 2911.02 – Robbery
38. R.C. 2911.11 – Aggravated burglary
39. R.C. 2911.12 – Burglary

**Offenses against the family**
40. R.C. 2919.12 – Unlawful abortion
41. R.C. 2919.22 – Endangering children
42. R.C. 2919.24 – Contributing to unruliness or delinquency of a child
43. R.C. 2919.25 – Domestic violence

**Weapons control**
44. R.C. 2923.12 – Carrying a concealed weapon
45. R.C. 2923.13 – Having a weapon while under disability
46. R.C. 2923.161 – Improperly discharging a firearm at or into a habitation or school

**Drug offenses**
47. R.C. 2925.02 – Corrupting another with drugs
48. R.C. 2925.03 – Trafficking in drugs
49. R.C. 2925.04 – Illegal manufacture of drugs or cultivation of marijuana
50. R.C. 2925.05 – Funding of drug or marijuana trafficking
51. R.C. 2925.06 – Illegal administration or distribution of anabolic steroids
52. R.C. 2925.11 – Possession of drugs or marijuana that is not a minor drug possession offense in section R.C. 2925.01

**Other**
53. R.C. 2905.11 - Extortion
54. R.C. 3716.11 – Placing harmful objects in food or confection
55. R.C. 2909.04 - Disrupting public services
56. R.C. 2909.05 - Vandalism
57. R.C. 2917.01 - Inciting to violence
58. R.C. 2917.02 - Aggravated riot
59. R.C. 2917.03 - Riot
60. R.C. 2917.31 - Inducing panic
61. R.C. 2921.03 - Intimidation
62. R.C. 2921.34 - Escape
63. R.C. 2921.35 - Aiding escape or resistance to authority
64. Or an existing or former offense of any municipal corporation, this state, any other state, or the United States that is substantially equivalent to any of these offenses.

JFS 01313 (Rev. 9/2006)

Sick days, personal days, maternity leave, newborn parental leave for either parent, and special leave days for jury duty should be included in the employment policies. Directors can check the Family and Medical Leave Act (FMLA) regulations when dealing with these requests. It also is wise to cover details such as the use of unused leave days, the necessity for documenting illness, and policies about closings due to bad weather. The center's plan for hiring substitutes for each staff position during vacation periods, for special holidays, and for sick days must be spelled out clearly. The policy should state that all health, safety, and training qualifications for staff also apply to substitutes. Maintaining a substitute file that includes the necessary employment information and payroll paperwork on available people will make it easier to find substitutes on short notice. A plan for hiring substitutes prevents confusion when emergencies occur and also facilitates budget planning for these special needs.

## Probationary Periods

Many programs include probationary periods after initial employment to allow an adjustment period for both adults and children in the program. A director may be appointed on an "acting" basis for as long as a year. The time period must be long enough for the new employee to demonstrate competency in a given position but not so long that valuable aspects of the program can be undermined by an incompetent individual.

Teacher competency can be validated in a three- to six-month probationary period by an experienced director who operates under a clearly defined philosophy of education and evaluates with an experienced eye. Because the teacher works directly with the children and any incompetence could have direct detrimental effects on them, the probationary period for teachers should be delineated carefully and understood clearly at the time of employment. This practice not only protects the welfare of the children but also is more equitable for the teachers in the long run because they come into a new role with a clear understanding of the time allowed for initial review and evaluation. Precise and thorough evaluation and documentation throughout the probationary period is essential because this trial period could lead to termination of the employee.

## Staff Evaluation and Grievance Procedures

Performance evaluations should be scheduled on a regular basis. Evaluation and grievance procedures are included in the employment policies (Figure 9-3). These procedures should be made available to all center personnel. Ideally, they will include details about the following:

- who evaluates whom
- when the periodic evaluation will take place
- what techniques or instruments will be used in the evaluation

- who makes the decision on whether or not the criteria are met
- what the consequences are of not meeting the stated criteria

Not meeting stated criteria could mean no recommendation for a raise, no opportunity for advancing to a higher-level position, or termination. When there are other actions that could cause dismissal, such as use of corporal punishment, these should be in writing. In some situations, there may be no recourse after a decision to deny a raise or to terminate an employee has been made. Although that may seem unfair, it is better to state it at the outset than to deal with all the negative feelings generated by the decision when an employee is unaware that there is no way to appeal it.

## Performance Evaluations

Staff members are entitled to know evaluation procedures as well as evaluation criteria. Therefore, performance evaluations for all staff positions should be part of employment policies and/or the orientation materials and discussed during staff orientation. Teaching staff are usually evaluated by the director who, in turn, may be evaluated by the human resources committee of the board or by the human resources director in cases where centers are part of a larger organization. Other support staff may be reviewed and evaluated by the director or by other designated staff. The sample Performance Appraisal (Director's Resource 9-4) might be used as a prototype for performance evaluation tools. Although there may be some overlap in areas covered by the evaluation forms, such as physical and mental health, ability to work well with other adults, and personal attributes such as enthusiasm or sense of humor, some are unique to a given position. For example, the cook must be able to manage time well in order to have meals ready for serving at a given hour, whereas a teacher must adjust the daily schedule based on the changing needs of children. Performance evaluation forms usually are based on job descriptions. Knowledge of evaluation criteria helps build a sense of trust and partnership between the staff to be evaluated and the evaluator, who is either the director or another staff member.

## Organizational Chart

An organizational chart that is sometimes part of the employment policies and is made available to all members of the staff can clarify lines of communication and responsibility for everyone in the center. For a newcomer, even a very simple organizational pattern may be difficult to see unless it is presented in a diagram or flowchart (Figure 9-4). An organizational chart enables an employee to determine how each position meshes with other positions in the center. This information, coupled with complete job descriptions, performance evaluation procedures and

**FIGURE 9-3** Townville child development center (a United Way agency) evaluation and grievance procedures.

**Evaluation and Grievance Procedures**

1. Frequency of Evaluation

Performance evaluations will be made twice during the probationary period for every new staff member—at the midpoint and the end of the probationary period—and annually thereafter. It is the responsibility of the Personnel Committee to evaluate the work of the director and the responsibility of the director to evaluate all members of the staff. All evaluations will be shared with the employee and then become part of the employee's file.

2. Purpose of Evaluation

The primary purpose of the annual evaluation is to create a mutual understanding between the director and each member of the staff of what is expected and how they both view the best way to move toward fulfilling those expectations.

Annual evaluations will be used as a basis for continued employment, horizontal or vertical movement on the career lattice, salary increments in cases where the job description allows for merit raises, and demotion or dismissal.

3. Basis for the Evaluation

Staff members will be evaluated on knowledge of the job as described in the job description, quality of skill demonstrated in fulfilling the job, interest and initiative, dependability, personal and professional growth, attendance and punctuality, and ability to work effectively in cooperation with other staff members.

Evaluation forms for each staff position in the center are included in these personnel policies.

4. Evaluation Procedure

Each staff member will be notified as to when his/her evaluation will take place. The evaluation will be discussed with the staff member, at which time the staff member will be given the opportunity to express his/her agreement or disagreement with the evaluation. The outcome of this discussion will become part of the staff member's record.

5. Review of Grievances

The staff member who wishes to present a grievance must present it first to the director. Failing to reach settlement with the director, the staff member may submit to the chairperson of the Personnel Committee a written statement of the situation, requesting that the grievance be reviewed by the Personnel Committee. The Personnel Committee will review the grievance and report with recommendations to the Board of directors for action.

*Source: © Cengage Learning, 2013.*

*Staff are entitled to know evaluation procedures and criteria.*

forms, and open staff communication, leaves little doubt about expectations, areas of responsibility, and who will be the evaluator for each position. It, in a sense, defines reporting relationships as well as limits of authority.

## Amending and Changing the Policies

The employment policies should contain a section that details the procedure for amending the policies. The amending procedure presumably parallels the one that was used initially for developing the policies and that is stated in the bylaws, but the policy-making body now may be expanded to include staff members or parents who were not available during the initial stages of development. As the center undergoes its regular evaluation period, the employment policies also should be checked to determine whether changes are needed. Then the board or the policy-making staff can follow the amendment procedures when it becomes necessary to make changes. After a change has been adopted, it is important to inform all personnel of the changes, and the director is charged with implementing the new policy.

**FIGURE 9-4** Sample organizational charts.

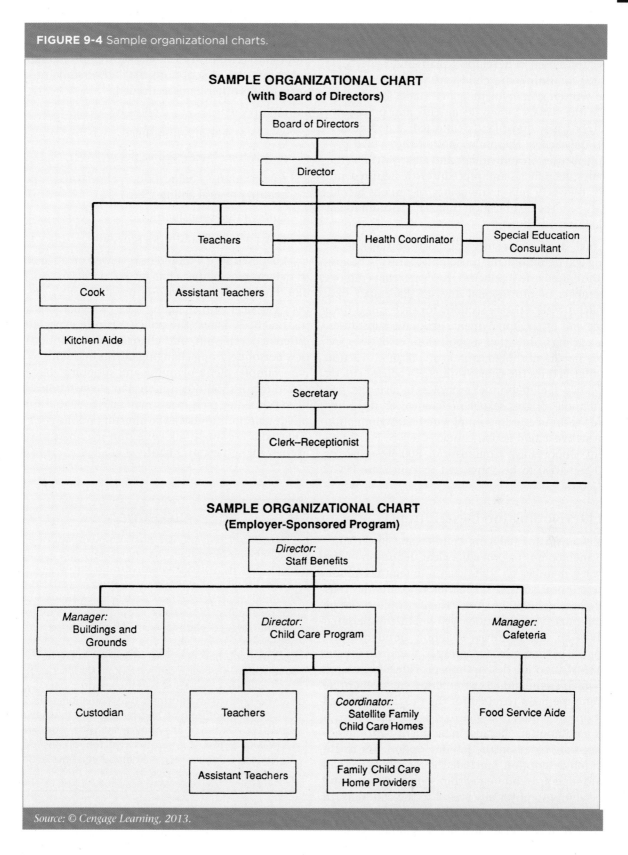

**SAMPLE ORGANIZATIONAL CHART**
**(with Board of Directors)**

**SAMPLE ORGANIZATIONAL CHART**
**(Employer-Sponsored Program)**

Clearly, small, private centers will not use all the preceding items in their employment policies. However, large, complex organizations undoubtedly will include all of these and more. Policies are drawn and shaped to the unique needs of each center and are constantly evaluated and modified to meet the ever-changing and growing needs of the program for which they are written.

# 9-3  THE HIRING PROCESS

The basic tools used in developing plans and procedures for hiring the child care center staff are written employment policies and job descriptions. On the surface, these documents and procedures appear to be easily drawn and delineated; at a more subtle level, they reflect the philosophy of the overall program as it focuses on individuals and their worth as human beings. As policies and procedures are adjusted and changed, they will reflect the ability of responsible administrators in the organization to make optimum use of available human resources.

An analysis of each center's purposes and manner of operating will determine the broad policy areas to be covered in the employment policies. The center that employs large numbers of professional and ancillary staff may have policies with separate sections for each category of employee and other employment, including substitutes, resource teachers, and other support staff. In all cases, every policy statement should contain an affirmative action section that verifies the center's intent to adhere strictly to acceptance of all personnel regardless of race, age, sex, creed, national origin, sexual preference, or disability. (For information regarding employment discrimination and affirmative action issues, contact the U.S. Equal Employment Opportunity Commission, 800-669-3362, or call 800-669-4000 to be connected to your state EEOC office.)

## 9-3a  Developing Job Descriptions

One mechanism for reducing conflict and uncertainty for staff members is to provide a clear definition of the role of each member on staff. Each role requires a thorough description so that no matter who fills the role, the same basic job will be done. The description can be written to clarify expectations yet retain the personal freedom of all staff members to follow through in the performance of their roles according to their own unique style. Well-written job descriptions provide a framework within which an individual can function creatively while performing the tasks required for the program. Detailed descriptions of required knowledge, skills, and physical abilities are important because subsequent performance evaluations are based on the job description. For teaching staff job descriptions, include the idea that staff will be able to supervise children within sight and sound and have the ability to physically attend to the children. For infant and toddler teachers, also add that the staff person will have the ability to lift at least 40 pounds regularly during an eight-hour period. The applicants then are asked if they can perform the duties as described in the job description.

A sample job description (Director's Resource 9-5) provides a prototype for writing descriptions for various staff positions, including full-time and part-time professional and support staff for both agency-sponsored and proprietary child care centers, as well as public school preschools. Job descriptions may cover some of the following, plus other items as needed:

- job title
- person to whom responsible
- people for whom responsible
- qualifications (education, experience, personal health, physical abilities, etc.)
- duties and responsibilities
- salary schedule and work schedule

Job descriptions should be reviewed on a regular basis to determine whether changes are necessary. Such periodic review is useful because the director or governing body can deal with changing rules or regulations governing practices, adjust the policies as role expectations at different levels shift, and change job descriptions when new personnel bring changing talents and skills to a staff. For example, menu planning and shopping may be part of a director's job description, but a new cook who has been trained to plan meals may take over that function. Job descriptions for both the director and the cook can be adjusted accordingly, allowing staff members to perform at their highest creative level.

---

**REFLECTION**

Think about yourself as a practicum student or a new teacher, and remember the uncertainty and accompanying anxiety you felt when you did not have a clear understanding of what was expected of you. How did you feel when you were unsure about who was to set up the snack or who was to straighten up the storage room? How did you manage when you were not sure about who to call when you knew you would be late because you had missed the bus? How did you react to criticism when you did not put all the blocks on the shelf while another adult had the children outside, and you had not been informed that you should do that? Can you remember how energy draining these experiences were and how they interfered with your creative work with children? A carefully written job description for your position might have helped you have a clearer understanding of your role.

---

Initial writing of job descriptions is only the first step in an ongoing process. This process requires expertise in using information from the program evaluation and an ability to adjust to changing and growing strengths of personnel to make efficient use of available talent for a more effective program.

## Recruiting

After the job descriptions have been written, the major hiring procedure begins. In fact, in many large centers or in programs with a board, the first task assigned to a new director is to initiate staff-recruitment procedures. Each center establishes and follows some general procedures regarding advertising, interviewing, and selecting employees to use during initial hiring in a new center and in filling vacant staff positions for an ongoing program.

Advertising for new staff is usually the director's responsibility. However, in some public schools and in corporate settings, the human resources office may set up school district or company advertisements that cover available positions throughout the organization. If the center program is ongoing, the director first should notify current staff members, board members, and parents about job openings as they become available. People in the

organization may choose to apply for the new job, or they may know qualified individuals who would like to apply. For employees to learn of openings in their own center from an outside source is disconcerting, and it exemplifies poor communication within the center.

Affirmative action statements must be included when advertising for center personnel.  These statements are always included in advertising for staff, not only because that has been the usual practice, but, more important, because it is essential that centers strive to maintain and enhance staff diversity. It is helpful to have advertising appear in a range of publications to make the information available to diverse segments of the population. Figure 9-5 shows examples of some advertisements. Local professional organizations that publish classified ads in their newsletters are good places to advertise for classroom staff, as are high schools, colleges, or universities that have child care training programs. Ads also may be placed in national professional journals or put on their websites if there is sufficient time to meet publication deadlines. Some colleges and vocational high schools maintain placement services, and some hold placement conferences so that employers can interview applicants. Notices of job openings also can be posted on community bulletin boards and in community papers that reach special segments of the population, such as the African American or Native American community and non-English-speaking groups, and on various appropriate websites.

The classified section of newspapers is frequently used for advertising, but the result may be large numbers of unqualified applicants who then must be screened before interviewing can begin. Nonetheless, when a position must be filled quickly, advertising in both small community weekly newspapers and large city daily newspapers is helpful because information is quickly disseminated to large numbers of people.

Personnel ads should include enough information to minimize the number of applications from completely unqualified people but should not be so narrowly written that qualified people fail to apply. If you are expected to write the advertising copy, you must be completely familiar with all the qualifications that are essential for performance of the job. Careful review of the job description is a good way to become familiar with the desired qualifications for potential candidates. Each advertisement should include the following:

- job title

- brief job description

- essential qualifications

- method of applying (telephone, letter, application form)

- name of the person to contact with a telephone number, street address, or email address

### Working Smart with Technology

*LinkedIn and Web-Based Applications*

With online professional networking and recruiting websites such as LinkedIn and Monster.com, the task of recruiting has shifted from one of pencil-and-paper applications and classified ads in the Sunday paper, to an online system where job seekers and job openings connect. Today's director needs to be aware of strategies that lead to the best possible candidate pool. Many new hires have grown up using technology and are very comfortable with electronic forms, portfolios, and home pages. Efforts to become part of the digital age can promote the program and also make it easier for qualified candidates to become aware of openings when they are posted. Another benefit of posting positions online is that the length of the position description is not limited by a cost per word. Postings can include detailed information about the program and the position that would be cost prohibitive in a newspaper posting.

*LinkedIn and other professional networking and recruiting websites have rewritten the rules for recruiting.*

**FIGURE 9-5** Sample advertisements.

### Sample LinkedIn Job Posting

Are you a creative and caring person with a desire to make a difference in the lives of children? Do you have a strong understanding of child development and teaching and want to join an organization that values your skills? Are you interested in a career with opportunities for advancement? Our NAEYC accredited program is seeking dedicated teachers who wish to become part of our preschool team.

Position Summary

Works as part of an educational team to plan and implement a high-quality preschool program. Maintains strong communication with families and administration. Works with the team to maintain a clean, safe, and effective learning environment.

Essential Functions

Provides care and education to children

Works as part of an education team to develop and implement curriculum

Engages with current and prospective parents and family members and is responsive to their needs

Is aware of and complies with all licensing standards

Completes timely and accurate assessment and documentation of children's learning and development

Attends and participates in all staff meetings, center events, and parent/customer meetings as requested

Requirements: Skills, Education/Knowledge, Experience

Education

Bachelor's Degree in Early Childhood Education

Experience

2+ years of early childhood education experience desirable

1+ years of experience working with assigned age group desirable

You are applying to an Equal Opportunity employer. All qualified applicants will receive consideration for employment without regard to race, national origin, age, sex, religion, disability, sexual orientation, marital status, military or veteran status, gender identity or expression, or any other basis protected by local, state, or federal law.

Click to submit application.

### Sample notice on the local Early Childhood Leadership online group

Director wanted for the Community Head Start Center. Responsibilities include hiring and supervision of entire staff for a program serving 75 children, record keeping, proposal writing, and working with Center staff, Community Action agency, parents, and other community agencies. Applicant must have a master's degree in Early Childhood Education with some training in at least one of the following: social work, special education, administration. Three years' administration experience required—Head Start teaching experience preferred. Send resume to Community Head Start Center, 352 Ninth St., Sioux City, Iowa. Deadline for applications, July 1. We are an Equal Opportunity Employer.

### Sample Classified Advertisement for *the New York Times*

Preschool teacher wanted for suburban church-affiliated preschool. Responsibilities include planning and implementing an age-appropriate developmental type early education program for a group of fifteen 3- and 4-year-old children. Bachelor's degree required—early childhood education teacher experience preferred. Write for application to Ms. D. L. Jones, Director, Upper Plains Christian Church, 130 Meadows Place, Upper Plains, New York 11112, or call (713) 431-6037 Monday through Thursday from 1:00 to 3:00 p.m., or e-mail upperplains@hotmail.com. We are an Equal Opportunity Employer.

### Sample Classified Advertisement for the *Parkville Times*

Cook wanted for child care center at outskirts of town. Responsibilities include preparing snacks and lunch for 65 preschool children, cleaning kitchen appliances and cupboards, and making weekly shopping list. Experience preferred. Please send resume to P.O. Box 932, Parkville, VA 23221. Equal Opportunity Employer.

Starting date, working hours, starting pay, fringe benefits, and goals of the organization also may be included.

Advertisements that clearly state all nonnegotiable items will eliminate practically all unqualified applicants. On the other hand, negotiable items stated equivocally tend to attract a more diverse pool of candidates from which to choose. For example, "experience necessary" is much more restrictive than "experience preferred." If experience is a nonnegotiable qualification, then say, "experience necessary." However, if the position could be filled by a person with good training and a variety of life experiences that may or may not have been with children, then say "experience preferred." The latter phrase appeals to a broader population and will not only increase the number of applicants but will also have appeal to a more diverse group.

The director should be cautious about luring people into the field by presenting a glowing picture of life in a child care center. Hiring staff members under false pretenses can lead to job dissatisfaction quickly. Rapid staff turnover disrupts program continuity and is very hard on the families and children who must constantly establish new relationships. During the past decade, the staffing crisis in the early childhood field has increased the challenge for directors who prefer to wait until they find qualified candidates to fill vacancies but are unable to meet required teacher-to-child ratios because of staff shortages. Many well-qualified early childhood teachers are choosing to move into public school or Head Start programs where pay and benefits often are better than those in other child care settings. The availability of qualified staff is limited, and the competition for their services is keen. But dealing with the consequences of hiring staff members who are unable or unwilling to do a good job inevitably leads to more turnover that is hard on other staff, families, and children. Therefore, a job opening notice that lists the required job qualifications in specific and realistic terms and careful hiring increase the probability of getting the best match between applicants and available positions and reduces turnover.

Careful consideration must be given to the best method for receiving applications. If the need is urgent and immediate, it may be necessary to accept applications by telephone. This option means that a new employee can be found quickly because an interview can be scheduled moments after a notice is seen. But it also means that current staff members may have to spend hours on the telephone, which detracts from their work with the children and puts them in the position of answering questions from people who are not seriously interested in the job.

Listing a post office box number in an ad places fewer demands on the director and the staff because potential candidates do not know the identity of the center and are unable to call. On the other hand, qualified people may decide not to apply if they are unsure of the source of the ad. Others may feel that they could be applying to the center in which they work, another reason for notifying all employees of every opening. In fact, occasionally ads read, "Our employees know about this advertisement."

Allowing applicants to apply in person can be very inconvenient and is inappropriate for some positions. Unless the center has its own human resources director or is affiliated with a sponsoring agency such as a public school, having applicants appear at the door during the hours in which children are present is awkward. However, this problem can be handled by setting specific hours during which interviews may be scheduled. In neighborhoods where many people do not have telephones and where writing letters is difficult for some adults, it may be appropriate to have people apply in person. If the job

does not entail making written reports, such as in the case of a cook or a housekeeper, then the ability to communicate effectively in writing may not be a criterion for selection, and there is no need to see a resume or written application. On the other hand, in the case of a teacher, teacher assistant, or special education resource teacher, writing skills are important. For these positions, a written response offers helpful data for initial screening of applicants and should be mandatory before an interview is scheduled.

The advertiser also will have to decide whether to have the candidates request an application form or send a resume. If a secretary is available to answer requests for application blanks, the process can be speeded up. If the director will be distracted from work by recording the name and address of applicants and mailing out applications, it is wiser to have candidates mail in resumes and fill in a formal application when they are interviewed. Sample application forms (Figures 9-6 and 9-7) show how applications are adjusted depending on availability of a resume from the applicant.

When all the applications have been collected, they must be screened to eliminate obviously unsuitable candidates. If no suitable candidates have applied, and attempts to recruit staff from other centers have failed, the advertising and application process is reopened. The director or the chairperson of the human resources committee usually screens the applications for those that meet the job requirements, particularly in the areas of education, health, or experience. Then interviews can be arranged. Interviewers should not be burdened with candidates who have no qualifications for the job. Therefore, the careful writing of the job opening notices to interested qualified candidates and the initial screening process to eliminate totally unqualified candidates are both important steps in the recruiting process.

Applications that are received from people who are not subsequently called for an interview should be retained so that affirmative action procedures can be completed where that is a requirement. A record must be kept listing the reasons why any applicant was not interviewed, and they should receive written notification that they will *not* be interviewed. Applicants who are called for an interview should be advised to bring identification to prove citizenship. A candidate who is not a U.S. citizen will be required to prove eligibility to work in this country. To be in compliance with the Immigration Reform and Control Act of 1986, every person hired must complete Form I-9, available from the Immigration and Naturalization Service (INS).

## Interviewing

Interviewing is essential and should not be eliminated no matter how urgent the need for obtaining a staff member

**FIGURE 9-6** Sample application form (no resume).

Sample Application Form
(Suggested for use when no resume is on file)

**Application for Employment**

Jewish Community Child Care Center—Fairmount, Pennsylvania

Name of Applicant _____
                           Last             First          Middle or Maiden

Address _____

State _____ ZIP _____

Telephone _____ Social Security No. _____

Citizenship:   USA _____ Other _____

**Record of Education**

| School | Name and Address of School | Check Last Year Completed | List Diploma or Degree |
|---|---|---|---|
| High | | 1 2 3 4 | |
| College | | 1 2 3 4 | |
| Other (Specify) | | 1 2 3 4 | |

© 2013 Cengage Learning®

TeachSource Digital Download

may seem. Even though a candidate can make an excellent impression during an interview and then turn out to be an ineffective staff member, interviewing will provide insights that cannot be gleaned from written applications or resumes and will facilitate judicious hiring decisions in the majority of cases. The relative amount of time spent interviewing can be extremely profitable when compared with the amount of time that might otherwise be spent solving personnel problems and higher staff turnover because a poor candidate was hastily selected. "Although not a magic solution to cure all turnover woes, effective interviewing is a step in the right direction" (Hamrick, 2000). The person or group responsible for staffing the center must decide who will review applications and interview the candidates and must develop the plan for the interview.

## Reviewing Applications

Reviewing applications is the first step in the total interviewing process. The director or group in charge of staffing the center first must make sure that the job de-

**FIGURE 9-6** (Continued)

**List below all present and past employment, beginning with your most recent**

| Name and Address of Employer | From Mo./ Yr. | To Mo./ Yr. | Describe in detail the work you did | Weekly Starting Salary | Weekly Last Salary | Reason for Leaving | Name of Supervisor |
|---|---|---|---|---|---|---|---|
| | | | | | | | |
| | | | | | | | |
| | | | | | | | |
| | | | | | | | |
| | | | | | | | |
| | | | | | | | |

List all professional and community organizations with which you are affiliated. *(Indicate if you hold office in the organization.)*

Write your educational philosophy.

What do you feel most qualifies you for this position?

What are your professional goals?

List names and addresses of three references.

_____

_____

_____

I give permission to contact references _____

*(signature)*

*Source: © Cengage Learning, 2013.*

TeachSource Digital Download

scription for the position being filled is up to date. It also is helpful to think about what type of person will best fit the position. Consider not only what the job description defines as required for the position but also the center's culture, the match with other staff, and the comfort level for working with the center's families. These considerations will keep the focus on finding a good match with the existing center "family" as well as enhance and support the center's interest in diversity. Using a systematic approach for application screening makes the job easier and will cover you later if anyone questions your hiring decision.

Begin the application review process by developing a form that covers the required qualifications for the job, including education, experience, and specialized training. Add qualifications that may not be required for the position but are preferred and could contribute to the candidate's ability to do the job. For example, experience working with diverse populations may be a requirement, but special experience on a Native American reservation or student teaching in Latin America could be a plus, depending on the location of your program and the population served. Include items on the form that would cover those special experiences by

**FIGURE 9-7** Sample application form (resume on file).

## Sample Application Form
(Suggested for use when a resume is on file)

**Application for Position**

University Day Care Center—Ogden University, Ogden City, Michigan

Name of Applicant _____
                      Last             First            Middle or Maiden

Address _____

State _____ ZIP _____

Telephone _____

Title of position for which you are applying. _____

What do you feel best qualifies you for this position? _____

_____

_____

Would you be willing to continue your education by taking college courses or in-service training if recommended to do that? _____

_____

_____

What satisfaction do you expect to receive from this position? _____

_____

_____

List three references (preferably one former employer, one former teacher, and one community person).

    1. _____

    2. _____

    3. _____

I give permission to contact references _____
                                               *(signature)*

*Source: © Cengage Learning, 2013.*

TeachSource Digital Download

having a place to check whether or not the candidate has had experience with diverse groups and a place to note which ethnic, cultural, and socioeconomic groups were part of that experience. The changing demographic profile in our society calls attention to the im-portance of adjusting staff hiring practices so they will be responsive to the diversity among families, children, and program staff. The screening form should include all the items that are on the application and also cover the job description.

Develop a rating scale for the items on the screening form so each reviewer can arrive at a total score for each applicant (Hamrick, 2000). A three-point scale can be used for this purpose. It is helpful to provide reviewers with some definitions for the three levels on the scale. If the candidate does not meet the requirement at all, the score on that item would be 0. Ratings might be defined as follows:

1 = barely meets requirement

2 = meets requirement

3 = exceeds requirement

Definitions of ratings will vary, depending on exactly how the requirements or criteria for the job are stated. In any case, a rating scale gives those who screen the applications a way to evaluate the qualifications of the candidates and provides a score for each one. There should be places on the screening form for comments and recommendations of reviewers and a place where they can note that the candidate does not have the qualifications to fill the position that is open. All applications are kept on file should there be any question about the hiring procedures.

When the reviewers meet to discuss the next step in this process, they can eliminate those candidates who do not have the qualifications for the job as described in the job description and use their scores on the screening forms to rank the remaining candidates. The next steps are to decide who will be interviewed and who will do the interviewing.

## Interviewers

While applications are being collected and screened, decisions are made about who will interview the viable candidates. In a very small program, the director may take full responsibility for all interviewing or may do it with the help of one or more of the following:

- staff person
- member of the board
- community person
- other professional (social worker, special educator, physician, school principal)
- person responsible to the new employee
- parent representative

In some programs, the interviews are conducted by committees, often by the human resources committee.

The composition of the interview committee may be established by the board beforehand, as in the case of the human resources committee; the committee can also be set up by the director to pertain specifically to the job being filled. For example, when there is an opening for a teacher, the committee might include the director, a teacher, and a parent. The expertise of a teacher on the interviewing team is very valuable. Including teachers also makes them feel valued and appreciated. Community people could be included as well as people from other professions, such as community health or special education. There might be more than one person from a given category, but if the committee is too large, its effectiveness will diminish. It can be difficult for large numbers of people to interview a given candidate at one time, and the procedure can be very threatening for the candidate. Nonetheless, it is best if the committee is diverse and is representative of the center staff with whom the person will work, of the families who use the center, and of the people who represent the sponsoring agency.

Although the committee makeup may vary depending on the type of center and on the position to be filled, both the committee members and the candidates must be aware that the organizational structure of the center takes precedence in making hiring decisions. For example, if a janitor is being hired, it may be appropriate to have the teachers express a preference for the candidate who would be most able to meet their needs for classroom maintenance. However, if the person who becomes janitor is going to be responsible to the center director, then the director's opinion must weigh heavily in the final hiring decision.

A major exception to this hiring and interviewing procedure is in programs sponsored by public schools in which hiring is based on established school district policies. Public school union contracts often dictate hiring policies and procedures. Sometimes, the human resources office will handle advertising, interviewing, and hiring. Involving teachers or parents in the process is unlikely. This could result in a team that will have to spend time building a partnership and working through possible philosophical differences.

## Preparation for the Interview

Just as candidates should come to the interview prepared to express their strengths, weaknesses, goals, expectations, and past experiences, so the interviewers should be prepared for each interview. Their questions should reflect a thorough knowledge of the center, its program, its staff, and the clients served by the program. Interviewers should be familiar with the information in the candidate's resume, application form, and reference letters, and they should look for evidence of warmth, good-natured calmness, and ease of relating to others. As Greenberg notes, it is important to select caregivers who have "the right stuff" to start with (1993, p. 5). An interview is conducted most productively when all parties are well prepared and when the environment has been set up for a meaningful dialogue between interviewers and interviewee.

## Interviewer Information

Each interviewer should be totally familiar with the job description for the vacant position and should have copies of the candidate's application and references. When contacting references, it is important to have a consistent process so that references will provide comparable data for all candidates. It has become more common for responses to be collected using electronic questionnaires that are sent via email. The most popular method of collecting feedback from references is by phone. Figure 9-8 shows a sample questionnaire that is administered by phone.

## Interview Plan

Interviewers plan the type of interview they will conduct. Sometimes, a predetermined list of questions is developed so that all candidates will respond to the same questions. This procedure provides uniform data but is somewhat inflexible and may not elicit the most useful data from each candidate. Sometimes, questions are developed as the interview progresses. This spontaneous procedure is more likely to give rise to potentially constructive data but requires more skill on the part of the interviewers.

The person who develops the questions should keep in mind the parameters of the job description and should understand the requirements of Title VII of the 1964 Civil Rights Act, the EEOC, and the ADA. There must be a "business necessity" for all questions asked during the interview. Consider the list shown in Figure 9-9 when determining what questions to ask and avoid during an interview.

The first question of the interview should be open ended and require more than a simple yes or no answer. Furthermore, it should focus on previous jobs, education, hobbies, or any other subject matter with which the candidate is very familiar. This technique puts the candidate at ease and creates an environment for more focused probing later in the interview. For example, the interviewer might say, "I see in your resume that you have worked for Head Start in California and that the committee was made up of Mexican and Asian parents. What were the aspects of that job that you liked best?" or "I see you studied at Wheelock in Boston. Tell us about that program." From these questions, it is possible to cull out material that can be examined at greater depth. "You said you enjoyed working with the Parent Policy Committee in California. What did you do with that group that you think is applicable to this job?"

Interviewers can learn a great deal about the ways in which a teacher candidate would fit into their center's program by posing hypothetical situations and asking questions such as, "What would you do if a child kicked you?" or "How would you work with a toddler who is not yet talking?" This type of question can produce ideas

**FIGURE 9-8** Telephone reference check list.

### University of Dayton Telephone Reference Check List

This list includes suggested questions for telephone reference checks. Please select questions you wish to uniformly and consistently use for each candidate. If you wish to ask other questions, please contact the Office of Human Resources Staffing Department at 229-2722 for guidance on whether questions are legally permissible.

My name is (___), and I work at the (name of center/program). We are filling a position within our department and would like to verify employment information on (applicant's name), who was employed by you from (beginning date) until (ending date).

1. What was the nature of his/her job?
2. What did you think of his/her work?
3. What are his/her strong points?
4. What are his/her weak points?
5. How did he/she get along with other coworkers?
6. Would you comment on his/her:

   - Attendance:
   - Dependability:
   - Ability to take on responsibility:
   - Ability to follow instructions:
   - Degree of supervision needed:
   - Overall attitude:
   - Quality of work:

7. Why did he/she leave the position? Would you rehire the person? Yes or No? If No, why not?
8. Is there anything else you would like to comment on regarding (applicant's name) employment or job performance?

*Source: From the University of Dayton, Office of Human Resources.*

about curriculum, classroom management, parent involvement, staff relations, and understanding of the development of young children. Of course, the questions should relate to the job for which the person is applying. For example, a prospective cook might be asked, "What would you do if sandwiches were on today's menu, and the bread delivery had not been made by 10:00 a.m.?" A list of sample questions in Director's Resource 9-6 can give you some ideas for questioning both degreed and nondegreed job candidates.

## Interview Setting

Before the interview, give careful thought to the setting:

- Will the candidate be as comfortable as possible?
- Will everyone be able to see and hear everyone else?

## ▶❚❚ TeachSource Video Vignette

### Infants and Toddlers: Creating an Optimal Learning Environment

In this video, a center director has moved the interview process from her office to a classroom. Watch as the candidate for a position in the center reveals her philosophy of children and knowledge of developmentally appropriate practice.

**1.** By extending the interview to the classroom, what is the director able to learn about the candidate that might not be evident in an interview confined to an office or conference room?

**2.** As the center director, now that you have heard the candidate's responses, what have you learned that can inform your decision as whether or not to hire this person? What do you still want to know?

- Is the seating arrangement comfortable and planned so that desks or large tables do not separate the candidate from the interviewers?

- Is the interviewing room free from distractions?

- Has the time of the interview been chosen appropriately so that everyone can focus on the interview instead of on the next appointment, and are all cell phones turned off?

- Is adequate time available for developing rapport and exploring details of the answers to the questions?

- Has provision been made to offer water or some refreshments to the candidate?

When the goal is to make applicants feel welcome and at ease, the interview setting becomes a matter of central concern. The interviewers are revealing to the candidate a major part of the center's culture and philosophy as they create an accepting environment for an interview and are more likely to obtain an accurate picture when the candidate is at ease.

### REFLECTION

Can you recall your first job interview? If so, you may be able to remember some of your reactions during that interview. Were you put at ease when you entered the room? Were you introduced to everyone before the questioning began? Did you feel the interviewers had prepared for the session by reviewing your resume and credentials? Were you given time to ask questions? How did they close the interview? As you think about being interviewed and recall the stress you experienced, you will increase your sensitivity to an applicant's feelings.

The director sets the nonverbal tone for the interview by being relaxed and friendly. It is important to sit back, smile, and maintain an open posture with arms down in the lap and body facing the candidate.

### The Interview

At the beginning, candidates should be given some idea about the length of the interview and informed that there will be a time at the end of the interview to ask questions. Interviewers should be prepared to present information about the program's philosophy, the job, and the center, and they should clearly and honestly answer the applicant's questions. The interviewers should maintain eye contact and let the applicant do most of the talking. They can refer to the employment policies and clarify thoroughly the expectations regarding performance standards for the position.

The interviewers will look for an applicant who plans to stay with the center for a number of years because staff stability provides continuity for children and nurtures a sense of community at the center. Nonetheless, caution should be used about requesting any information in sensitive areas mentioned earlier. It is recommended that employment records be limited to that information relevant to employment decisions, and disclosures of that information to third parties should be strictly limited when not authorized by the candidate or employee. It is advisable that child care centers develop written policies and procedures concerning this issue. Also, because federal law provides only a portion of the employment discrimination picture, and many states have their own discrimination laws, it is wise to consult an attorney regarding applicable state laws for your center and to clear up uncertainties about the content of interview questions.

Interviewers should obtain as much information as possible during the interview, but note taking or discussing the candidate's qualifications should be done after the interview. Some discussion about the candidate

**FIGURE 9-9** What not to ask when interviewing candidates.

| Subject | Questions Permissible to Ask in an Interview | Question to Avoid in an Interview |
|---|---|---|
| Name | Inquiry whether an applicant's work records are under another name, for purposes of access to these records: "Have you worked for the University under a different name?" | A. Inquiry into any title which indicates race, color, religion, sex, national origin, handicap, age, or ancestry.<br><br>B. To ask if a woman is a Miss, Mrs., or Ms. |
| National Origin/Citizenship | A. To indicate that the institution is an equal opportunity employer<br><br>B. "What languages do you read, speak, or write fluently?" (This question is fine, as long as this ability is relevant to performance of the job) | A. If native-born or naturalized.<br><br>B. Proof of citizenship before hiring.<br><br>C. Whether parents or spouse are native-born or naturalized. |
| Age | Any inquiry limited to establishing that applicant meets any minimum age requirement that may be established by law. | A. Requiring birth certificate or baptismal record before hiring.<br><br>B. Any inquiry which may reveal the date of high school graduation.<br><br>C. Any other inquiry which may reveal whether applicant is at least 40 years of age. |
| Sex/Gender/Sexual Orientation | None. | A. Any inquiry which would indicate sex.<br><br>B. Any inquiry made of members of one sex, but not the other. |
| Marital/Parental/Family Status | A. Whether an applicant can meet specified work schedules or has activities, commitments and responsibilities that may hinder the meeting or work attendance requirements. "This job requires overtime occasionally; would you be able and willing to work overtime as necessary?" (This question is fine as long as *all* applicants for the job are asked consistently).<br><br>B. "Would you be willing to relocate as necessary?" | A. Before hiring: to ask marital status: "What's your marital status (married, single, divorced, engaged)?"<br><br>B. To ask the number and/or age of children, who cares for them, and of applicant's plans to have more children?<br><br>C. "Whom do you live with?"<br><br>D. "Do you plan to have a family? When?"<br><br>E. "How many kids do you have?"<br><br>F. "What are your child care arrangements?" |
| Education | A. Inquiry into nature and extent of academic, professional or vocational training.<br><br>B. Inquiry into language skills, such as reading and writing of foreign languages, if job related. | A. To ask the racial or religious affiliation of schools attended.<br><br>B. Inquiry as to what mother tongue is or how foreign language ability was acquired. |

| Subject | Acceptable | Unacceptable |
|---|---|---|
| **Work Schedule** | Inquiry into willingness or ability to work required work schedule | Any inquiry into willingness or ability to work any religious holidays. |
| **Religion/Creed** | Questions pertaining to the applicant's familiarity and/or their interest in coming to work for a Catholic/Marianist Institution. | A. Any inquiry which would indicate or identify religious denomination or custom of the applicant. B. Request pastor's recommendation or reference. |
| **Organizations/Affiliations** | Inquiry into membership in professional organizations and offices held, excluding any organization, the name or character of which indicates the race, color, religion, sex, national origin, handicap, age, or ancestry of its members. | Inquiry into every club and organization where membership is held. |
| **Personal/Physical** | Inquiries as to ability to perform actual job requirements. | Being a certain height or weight will not be considered to be a job requirement unless the employer can show that no employee with the ineligible height or weight could do the work. |
| **Disabilities** | To ask whether the applicant is capable of performing the essential functions of the job with reasonable accommodation. Note: This question may be asked after the interviewer thoroughly described the job and if all applicants are going to be asked in a consistent manner whether they are able to carry out all the necessary job assignments and perform them in a safe way. | A. Before hiring: to initiate questions regarding the specific accommodation needed. B. Inquire if job applicant is handicapped or ask about nature and severity of handicap: "Do you have any disability." C. "Have you had any operation or recent/past illnesses?" |
| **Criminal Record** | Inquiries into conviction of specific crimes related to qualifications for the job applied for. | Any inquiry relating to arrests if not substantially related to functions and responsibilities of the particular job in question. "Have you ever been arrested?" |
| **Military Service** | A. Inquiry into service in U.S. Armed Forces when such service is a qualification for the job. B. Require military discharge certificate after being hired. | A. Inquiry about the type of discharge. B. To request military service records. C. To ask about military service in armed service of another country. |
| **References** | To request general and work references not relating to race, color, religion, sex, or national or ethnic origin, age, disability, or marital status. | To request references specifically from clergy or any other person who might reflect race, color, religion, sex, or national origin, age, disability, or marital status. |

*Source: Reprinted with permission from the University of Dayton, Office of Human Resources.*

is useful, and reaching a group consensus serves a worthwhile purpose. Discussion provides the opportunity for interviewers to share their impression of the candidate as they draw on each other's perceptions. Confidentiality is a critical issue, and all committee members must understand that information on candidates and any committee discussion must be kept confidential.

## Teaching Interview

Observing a teacher or assistant teacher candidate in a classroom setting provides the committee with additional data on classroom presence and skills with children. Some candidates are able to give interviewers all they want to hear in an interview, but when observed in a classroom, it becomes obvious they are not comfortable with children. It is unfair to have the regular classroom teacher leave a new person alone in the classroom because of the anxiety that would be produced in both the candidate and the children, but a great deal can be learned by observing a prospective teacher read a story to a few children or join a small group for snacks. Asking to see sample lesson plans, resource files, or picture files also provides useful information to the interview committee. Some centers select candidates from the substitute list or from among a pool of student teachers whom they know. In this case, the center staff will have worked with the candidate before the interview.

*Observing the candidate in a classroom setting provides the committee with data on rapport with children and classroom presence.*

## Second Interview

A second interview for prospective candidates after the teaching interview can be helpful when there are several candidates with comparable training and credentials or when more information is needed prior to making the final hiring decision. Having a second interview also offers opportunities to discuss the teaching interview and to answer questions the candidate may have at this point in the interview–hiring procedure. Additional questions that focus on the candidate's opinions and personal style also can be discussed at a second interview. Director's Resource 9-6 gives sample interview questions for first and second interviews.

## Selecting the Employee

When interviewing is completed, the person or committee responsible for selecting the employee uses material such as the employment policies and the job description, combined with all the information from the interview and the observation, to reach a final decision. All data are weighed and balanced until the best match among job description, current staff composition, and candidate qualifications is obtained. It also is important to review the nondiscrimination prohibitions in this decision-making process, especially if you have an applicant who is disabled. An employer is not required to give preference to a qualified applicant with a disability over other applicants; however, the employer may not consider the candidate with disabilities unqualified if that person can perform the essential functions of the job. It may be helpful to have a second interview with selected candidates from the pool who seem best qualified for the position to further narrow down the choice. The procedure for making a decision should be clear to all interviewers. Will the director ultimately choose the employee? Will the director present two or three names to the board, and have the board make the decision? If there is a board, will that group make the decision, or will the committee rule by majority vote? Generally, the director will make the decision, taking into account the recommendations of the interviewing committee. Final approval from the board sometimes is part of the hiring policy.

The selected candidate should be notified of the job offer by the director or the chairperson of the committee. On acceptance, the new employee may be asked to sign a contract stating the salary and the length of time covered by the contract, provided the employment policies do not state that all employees are employees at will. Immediately after the new employee has been informed of the job and has accepted it, all other interviewees are informed of the selection, thanked for their interest, and told that their resumes will be kept on file in case another vacancy occurs.

# 9-4 RETAINING STAFF

Hiring the staff is only part of the work to be done. Directors can put substantial effort into hiring a qualified staff, and efforts must be made to support new employees and maintain a positive work environment in order to retain an effective staff.

## 9-4a Employee Orientation

The director is responsible for introducing the new employee to the work environment. The new person will need to know where to find work space, what storage facilities and materials are available, and what schedule is to be followed. A tour of the building and introductions to all other staff members, either during the tour or at a staff meeting shortly thereafter, are essential to the orientation procedure. The person who conducts the tour and makes the introductions sets the tone for the employee's future interpersonal relationships with the other staff members. Each staff member has an obligation to become involved with making the new employee's transition to the staff position as smooth and satisfying as possible. For an in-depth discussion of staff orientation, see Sciarra and Dorsey (2002).

The new employee also should be introduced to parents at the earliest possible time. Some directors notify parents of staff additions or changes by mail; others use their bulletin boards, email, website, or newsletters; and still others introduce the new member informally as the occasion arises or at a regularly scheduled meeting.

During the initial weeks of employment, it is important for the director to check with the new staff member to answer any questions and make a conscious effort to build a positive relationship. At the same time, the director can continue to reiterate expectations and expand on ways to follow and implement the program philosophy. A carefully planned staff orientation program can promote better staff relationships and reduce staff turnover. A written Staff Orientation Plan document is required as part of the Human Resource Development system for the Program Administration Scale (PAS).

Sometimes, it is difficult for the director to be available to the new teacher often enough. It can be helpful to establish a mentor program or assign a staff member to watch over the new staff person. Mentors can help new staff with basic orientation questions, like where to find and file various forms, and introduce them to all staff and support people such as the van driver and custodian. Mentors also can provide new staff with information about special talents of other teachers, such as planning effective group times, planning and carrying out smooth transitions, or making challenging math games. A mentoring system assists the director with orientation of new

staff and enriches and enhances the self-esteem of the mentor (Carter, 1998).

It also helps for the director to leave a note in the teacher's box asking questions such as, "What went well today?" or "What did I miss today in your room that you would like to share with me?" The director also might leave a message about being available the next day at nap time or a plan to stop in before lunch to see how things are going. These steps help make the new teacher feel that the director really is available to give support and help.

Some centers have handbooks for each employee. In corporate centers, the parent firm may prepare a handbook for use in all centers, whether franchised or run by the corporation. Guidelines in this handbook may detail how many children should be permitted in blocks or dramatic play at any given time, or exactly how the daily cleaning is to be done by the classroom teachers. However, handbooks are rarely that detailed and usually do not include expectations for teachers to clean

*A mentoring system assists the director with orientation of new staff.*

the premises. More often, they include items such as the following:

- philosophy of the center
- bylaws of the board (if applicable)
- employment policies
- policies and procedures for the children's program
- copies of forms used by the center
- information about the community the center serves
- information about the staff (job titles, home addresses, telephone numbers, etc.)
- NAEYC Code of Ethical Conduct (see Appendix A)

A handbook is useful because it gives everyone a common reference point and provides new employees with materials that familiarize them with the center.

---

### REFLECTION

Perhaps you can recall your first day as a new student or employee in a child care center. How did you feel on that first day? What else do you wish you had known about the center or the program? Do you recall what it was like not to know where the extra paper towels were kept or how awkward it was when you could not find the easel paper? As you recall those feelings, consider what you would tell a new teacher in your center if you were responsible for orienting the new employees.

---

## 9-4b Handling Turnover

Each year, approximately 30 percent of the early childhood workforce changes jobs or leaves the field altogether. Such instability in the child care workforce has a negative impact on quality (Gable, Rothrauff, Thornburg, & Mauzy, 2007). It is estimated that staff turnover can cost, at a minimum, $3,000 for each lost employee. Centers cannot afford the high cost of staff turnover, especially when turnover results not only in financial costs but also damage to employee morale, customer satisfaction, and center image (Hamrick, 2000). Although some would say low wages and poor benefits are the major causes, it is important to recognize that there are many different ways to think about turnover. As Hamrick (2000) points out, poor hiring decisions are a major factor, along with compensation concerns.

In making hiring decisions, take time to reflect on what type of person would best fit the position. What are you looking for in this person in terms of the fit with

- the center culture?
- the parent group?

- the support staff?
- the teaching staff?
- the administrative staff?

The first step in reducing turnover is to hire the right people. Collins (2005) emphasizes how important it is to "get the right people on the bus." He goes on to point out that it is often difficult to "get the wrong people *off* the bus," thus making it doubly important to get the right ones on in the first place.

Although compensation and careful hiring have an impact on turnover, they are not the only factors affecting staff stability. There is evidence that highly trained teachers are more likely to remain at their jobs. It follows that these teachers are usually compensated at a higher level and work with other highly trained staff who are also inclined to stay with a job. These qualified staff people are also more often in accredited centers, and there is evidence that accredited centers have a more stable workforce and less turnover.

Finding dollars to offer the kind of wages and benefits to keep qualified staff is difficult. Although some staff turnover is inevitable, and some may even allow for positive changes, clearly, much of the time, loss of a staff member is disappointing and traumatic for the families, children, and staff who remain.

The director's task is to try to reduce staff turnover by attending to variables that can be adjusted and changed. There are a few inexpensive perks that may compensate staff and help them feel good about their job. Consider the following:

- flex time
- treats in the staff lounge for break times
- occasional personal use of the office copier (limits are necessary here)
- token gifts for birthdays and other special days
- opportunities to attend conferences as well as take additional education courses

This last item does involve some cost to the center, but there may be tax breaks for this benefit (check with your tax adviser or attorney).

Striving to give staff higher wages and more benefits is worthy, but stabilizing the workforce by refining hiring practices, improving the work environment, and making sure a thorough orientation plan is in place for all new hires can all be done without great cost. Because there are no magic solutions to solving the problem of staff retention, directors are almost always involved, at some level, in looking for and hiring new staff.

### Work Environment

*Work environment* is an inclusive term covering the physical space and, more important for our purposes, the interpersonal climate—that is, relationships with coworkers. An involved director constantly evaluates the quality of the work environment and makes adjustments when possible. (See Chapter 15 for more discussion on evaluating work environment.) Sometimes, alterations in the physical environment are costly and can happen only if the budget allows. However, adjustments can be made to alter other aspects of the work environment with little or no added expense. For example, it is very important for every staff member to feel respected and valued. Offering staff opportunities to write for the newsletter, help with the design and equipment choices for the new playground, join an advocacy group, or serve on the committee to plan the center's tenth anniversary celebration is but a few ways staff can feel a sense of ownership in the center's total program. Pride, commitment, and collegiality abound among those who share ownership in a successful enterprise.

"In child care we tend to spend very little time on adult development. We are often more democratic and participatory in spirit with children than we are among ourselves" (Whitebrook & Bellm, 1999). Although classroom teachers are encouraged to help children solve problems, resolve conflicts, and make decisions, in some programs, major decisions are made by administrators with minimal input from staff who are very much affected by those decisions. Adults who are accustomed to top-down management may initially need a lot of support and encouragement from the director who really wants active participation in writing articles, planning center events, leading staff meetings, or joining focus groups. When staff are invited to help plan meeting agendas and submit their questions and concerns for group meetings, they feel they are valued and important to the organization. When directors seek staff participation in decision making and help teachers feel valued, they are nurturing loyalty and commitment in the work environment.

Issues of race, class, and culture are aspects of the work environment that impact interpersonal relationships and can affect staff turnover. Directors like to describe their programs as color blind, but on careful analysis of the reasons for turnover, they may find that issues of class, color, or culture contributed to friction that led to resignations. Constant attention to open communication with a focus on understanding and acceptance of diversity is essential because diversity can never be taken for granted.

## MAKING THE CASE FOR *GROWING YOUR OWN LEADERS*

Many leaders in the field of early childhood started out as teachers. Characteristics that allow teachers to guide the behavior of young children and manage a classroom often do not translate to the supervision of adults and management of an early childhood program. Likewise, bringing in administrators who have developed their management skills outside of the field of early childhood can result in leadership that does not grasp the nuances of a developmentally appropriate practice in a child care setting. Many have found that understanding the distinctive complexities of early care and education is critical to being a successful director, and developing leadership skills within existing staff is the most effective approach. This notion of being intentional and growing your own leaders can lead to job satisfaction in the staff as new skills are developed, and opportunities for career advancement are made available.

## 9-4c Exit Interview Questionnaire

It is important for the director to try to understand the cause of turnover. One approach to collect this information is the exit survey or interview. Some turnover situations result in strained relationships in which the exiting staff member is unlikely to participate in an open and sincere exit interview or complete and return a survey. However, many exiting staff members leave the center on good terms and are willing to provide feedback about the factors that led to their decision. It is important to try to get information from both disgruntled former employees and those who left the center on good terms. Whether using an exit interview or survey, careful thought needs to be given to the types of questions to be asked. Director's Resource 9-9 shows a sample Exit Interview Questionnaire. This sample is extensive but provides a variety of questions to select from and add to in order to develop a questionnaire that meets the needs of the center. After results are collected, they should be analyzed and strategies developed to minimize future turnover when possible.

### REFLECTION

Think about the best job and the worst job you ever had. What made you stay with the best one? What made it appealing? What was bad about the worst job? How much were your feelings about the best and worst jobs affected by the relationships you had with other adults in the setting?

# SUMMARY

The importance of good interpersonal relationships and trust within a center cannot be overstated. Only through a feeling of community and a spirit of cooperation can a director create a supportive environment in which both adults and children can grow to their fullest potential. There must be a strong element of acceptance and positive regard in the surrounding climate to establish a mutually helping relationship for staff, families, and children. It is the responsibility of the director as a leader to serve as a model of caring and respect for others in order to build a strong sense of community among all the diverse people involved in the center program. Effective interpersonal communication among the staff members, children, and families also is an important basic element in creating a supportive, comfortable environment at a center, and it is up to the director to be the model of good communication to create an atmosphere of openness, warmth, and acceptance. To successfully staff an early childhood center, directors must do the following:

■ Discuss ways to create a positive climate and motivate staff.

■ Describe the major sections of an employment policy.

■ Explain the steps in the hiring process.

■ Identify and implement strategies that facilitate staff retention.

# TRY IT OUT!

1. In small groups with other class members, discuss the motivating factors that you as a director can control or change.

   a. List five effective motivating factors directors can control.

   b. Compare the lists produced by the small groups, and develop a final list of strategies (that do not cost money) to encourage staff and enrich jobs.

2. Think about yourself as the director of a center where you have observed or taught. Based on your understanding of the use of encouragement as a motivator, write an appropriately phrased positive acknowledgment for

   the secretary

   the cook

   the custodian

   a volunteer

3. Describe a way you could use the job enrichment strategy with

   the assistant infant teacher

   the van/bus driver

   a student teacher

   a lead teacher

4. Review the job description for the cook in Director's Resource 9-5, and develop a list of questions that would be appropriate to ask candidates applying for the job.

   a. Select three class members to serve as interviewers of applicants for the cook. Select one class member as a candidate for the position.

   b. After the three interviewers review the candidate's application for the position, have them role-play an interview with the candidate using the questions that the team developed.

   c. After the interview, have all class members participate in summarizing the candidate's qualifications for the job.

## DIRECTOR'S RESOURCE 9-1

### BOMBECK FAMILY LEARNING CENTER HANDBOOK

UNIVERSITY *of* DAYTON

## DIRECTOR'S RESOURCE 9-1 *(continued)*

## DIRECTOR'S RESOURCE 9-1 *(continued)*

### What We Believe

The Characteristics of a Marianist University
Marianist Universities Educate for Service, Justice, and Peace
The Marianist approach to higher education is deeply committed to the common good. The intellectual life itself is undertaken as a form of service in the interest of justice and peace, and the university curriculum is designed to connect the classroom with the wider world. In addition, Marianist universities extend a special concern for the poor and marginalized and promote the dignity, rights and responsibilities of all peoples (2006, p. 27)

As part of a Catholic Marianist university, we readily adapt and change with the times. We build communities of faith and educate in what we call a "family spirit." We provide an integral, high-quality education on a campus that's known for its hospitality and inclusiveness.

### The Bombeck Center Commitment to Community

*Three foundational elements represent who we are and define how we interact.*

Respect — **We are a community of learners in an environment of respect for children, families, staff, early childhood faculty, and students.**

Reflective Practice — **Quality care and education requires intentional reflection of the people, policies, and practice that takes place.**

Research — **We base our practice on a sound understanding of the literature of the field.**

## DIRECTOR'S RESOURCE 9-1 *(continued)*

### Mission Statement

Provide high quality early care and education for young children while demonstrating assessment-supported, child-centered, emergent, science-focused, and integrated curriculum.

### Vision Statement

Work together as reflective decision makers who seek to improve the quality of care and education for young children by mentoring early childhood graduate and undergraduate students and sharing research-supported practice with the larger early childhood community.

*Goal 1* – Promote the optimum social, emotional, physical motor and health, cognitive development, and approaches to learning of the children at the center.

*Goal 2* – Promote the professional development of early childhood students in the University of Dayton's School of Education and Health Sciences.

*Goal 3* – Provide professional development opportunities for the Bombeck Family Learning Center staff and the greater early care and education community.

*Goal 4* – Advocate for children, their families, and the profession in community and society.

*Goal 5* – Model the Catholic Marianist tradition of faith formation, service, adaptation, and change by providing, in the family spirit, a quality education for children, teacher candidates, and staff.

### Philosophy Statement

We are dedicated to care for and educate all the children at the Bombeck Family Learning Center. We believe that positive experiences for infants, toddlers, and young children are critical to healthy development and that these experiences serve

*Source: Reprinted with permission from the author S. M. Adams, Family Engagement Collaborative of the Miami Valley, 2014.*

as the foundation for future development and learning. Our philosophy is based on the work of such classic early childhood theorists as Ainsworth, Bandura, Bowlby, Bronfenbrenner, Erikson, Gerber, Honig, Montessori, Partens, Piaget, and Vygotski. We have learned from prominent early childhood approaches such as the Project Approach (Katz and Chard) and the programs of Reggio Emilia, Italy. We believe that children benefit from practices that are well grounded in research. We also strive to maintain a program where diverse children and families are welcome and engaged. We believe in the following developmental principles:

1. Each child's uniqueness is the result of interplay between genetic and environmental factors. Child development involves interrelated physical, cognitive, emotional, and social changes. Rates of development vary from one child to another, but the sequential progression of growth does not.

2. With these principles in mind, we believe that infants, toddlers, and young children are individuals in their own right and must receive the same respect and consideration afforded to older children and adults.

3. We believe that it is our responsibility to provide responsive care and responsible guidance where strong social and emotional development is promoted and modeled. Furthermore; we are committed to providing a developmentally appropriate environment in order to nurture growth in all areas of development, while treating each child as a whole person.

4. We believe that it is the job of adults to provide children with enticing and accurate learning experiences that are based on sound content knowledge and developmentally appropriate practices. Our science-focused curriculum is intentional, integrated, inclusive, inquiry-based, and innovative.

This complete Handbook is available as a TeachSource Digital Download

## DIRECTOR'S RESOURCE 9-2

### STAFFING SCHEDULES

Staffing Schedule

| Classroom | Full-Time Staff Arrive | | | Lunch and Nap | | | | | | | |
|---|---|---|---|---|---|---|---|---|---|---|---|
| | | | | Children Eat 11:45 – 12:30 | | Children Nap 12:30 – 3:00 | | Staff | | | |
| | | | | Staff Lunch | | Plan | | Depart | | | |
| | 7:30 | 8:30 | 10:00 | 11:00 | 12:00 | 1:00 | 2:00 | 3:30 | 4:30 | 5:00 | 6:00 |
| Young Infants | A | B | C | A | B | C | ABC | A | B | | C |
| | | | | Part-time teacher D arrives at 11:00 and departs at 5:00 | | | | | | | |
| Older Infants | A | B | C | A | B | C | ABC | A | B | | C |
| | | | | Part-time teacher D arrives at 11:00 and departs at 5:00 | | | | | | | |
| Toddlers | A | B | C | A | B | C | ABC | A | B | | C |
| | | | | Part-time teacher D arrives at 11:00 and departs at 5:00 | | | | | | | |
| Preschool 1 | A | B | C | A | B | C | ABC | A | B | | C |
| | | | | Part-time teacher D arrives at 11:00 and departs at 5:00 | | | | | | | |
| Preschool 2 | A | B | C | A | B | C | ABC | A | B | | C |
| | | | | Part-time teacher D arrives at 11:00 and departs at 5:00 | | | | | | | |

A = Teacher A
B = Teacher B
C = Teacher C
D = Part-time Teacher arrives at 11:00 to help with lunch and cover nap time so that teacher can plan and attend meetings. He or she departs around 5:00 when ratios allow.

## DIRECTOR'S RESOURCE 9-3

### SAMPLE STAFFING PLAN—MULTIPLE PROGRAM B

Staff Plan by Staff Member

| Title | How Many | Schedule | Recommended Salary | Total Yearly |
|---|---|---|---|---|
| Director/ Administrator | 1 | MWF 7:30 a.m.– TTH 12:00 p.m. | $ 11.00/hr $22,880/yr | $ 22,880 |
| Head Teachers | 5 | 7:30–3:00 p.m. 30-min. break between 12:00–1:30 p.m. | $ 8.50/hr $17,680/yr | $ 88,400 |
| Teachers | 5 | 11:00–7:00 p.m. 30-min. break between 1:00–2:30 p.m. | $ 7.00/hr $14,560/yr | $ 72,800 |
| Morning Assistants | 5 | 7:30–12:30 p.m. 15-min. break between 11:00–12:00 p.m. | $ 5.00/hr $ 6,500/yr | $ 32,500 |
| Afternoon Assistants | 5 | 12:30–7:00 p.m. 15-min. break between 2:30–3:00 p.m. | $ 5.00/hr $ 8,450/yr | $ 42,250 |
| Secretary/ Bookkeeper | 1 | 9:00–5:30 p.m. 1-hr. lunch | $ 6.00/hr $10,400/yr | $ 12,480 |
| Custodian | 1 | 5:00–10:00 p.m. Mon.–Thur. 5 hrs. on Sat. 15-min. break | $ 5.00/hr $ 6,500/yr | $ 6,500 |
| Cook | 1 | 7:30–3:00 p.m. 30-min. lunch | $ 5.00/hr $10,400/yr | $ 10,400 |
| **Total Yearly Salaries:** | | | | **$288,210** |

## Director's Resource 9-3 *(continued)*

### STAFF PLAN BY CLASSROOM

| Classroom | No. of Children | Staff/Child Ratio |
|---|---|---|
| Infants Rm: 101 | 8 | required: 5:1 maximum: 8:3 minimum: 8:2 |
| Toddlers Rm: 201 | 11 | required: 7:1 maximum: 11:3 minimum: 11:2 |
| 3-year-olds Rm: 202 | 17 | required: 12:1 maximum: 17:3 minimum: 17:2 |
| 3- and 4-year-olds Rm: 203 | 17 | required: 12:1 maximum: 17:3 minimum: 17:2 |
| 4-year-olds Rm: 204 | 17 | required: 14:1 maximum: 14:3 minimum: 14:2 |

| 1 Head Teacher | 7:30 a.m.–3:00 p.m. |
|---|---|
| 1 Teacher | 11:00 a.m.–7:00 p.m. |
| 1 Assistant | 7:30 a.m.–12:30 p.m. |
| 1 Assistant | 12:30–7:00 p.m. |

This flexible schedule allows ample time for classroom planning in the morning and evening when the ratios will be low because most children arrive at the center between 8:00 and

## DIRECTOR'S RESOURCE 9-3 *(continued)*

9:00 a.m. and leave between 5:00 and 6:00 p.m. Nap time is when team planning and communication takes place.

### ADDITIONAL COMMENTS ABOUT STAFFING

- Breaks must maintain staff-to-child ratio at all times.
- Flexibility in scheduling breaks is necessary to meet the immediate needs of the classrooms.
- Short restroom breaks or emergency phone calls could be arranged as needed, as long as the ratio is maintained.
- Staff schedules are designed for enhancing staff communications and for meeting the needs of the children.
- Swing scheduling for directors is designed to encourage and maintain communication with all staff members, family members, board, and community contacts.
- It is the teacher's responsibility to take care of housekeeping emergencies during the day.
- The cook is solely responsible for cleaning the kitchen, other than the cleanup after the afternoon snack, which is the teacher's responsibility.
- One morning snack, one afternoon snack, and one full meal will be provided each day.
- Encourage male applicants for all positions to balance male-female models.
- Parent(s)/surrogate(s) provide transportation.
- Tuition is $95/week for infants and $85/week for all others.
- Eighty percent of tuition income goes for salaries.

*Source:* © Cengage Learning, 2013.

## DIRECTOR'S RESOURCE 9-4

### UNIVERSITY OF DAYTON

### Performance Management Assessment

Employee: _____ Evaluation Period:_____

Position Title:_____

### Planning

I. Please attach current position description. Has the position description been reviewed for accuracy? Yes [WOL]_____ No _____

II. Result-Based "Smart" Objectives:

1.
2.
3.
4.

III. Professional Competencies for focus this year:

1.
2.
3.

## DIRECTOR'S RESOURCE 9-4 (continued)

IV Plans for Professional Development:

Employee Signature _____

Date_____

Supervisor Signature_____

Date_____

### Assessing

I. Employee Self-Assessment: Please comment on your performance in achieving each result-based objective that was included in your performance plan.

1.
2.
3.
4.

Please comment on your demonstration of the professional competencies that were listed for focus in your performance plan.

1.
2.
3.

## DIRECTOR'S RESOURCE 9-4 (continued)

Please comment on your progress in Professional Development and achieving the associated goals that were established in your performance plan.

II. Supervisor Feedback: Please comment on employee's performance in achieving each result-based objective that was included in the performance plan.

1.
2.
3.
4.

Please comment on the employee's demonstration of the professional competencies listed for focus in the performance plan.

1.
2.
3.

Please comment on the employee's progress in Professional Development and in achieving the associated goals that were established in the performance plan.

## DIRECTOR'S RESOURCE 9-4 (continued)

### Supervisor's Overall Assessment:

**Performance Summary:** Consider overall performance in realizing objectives and competencies, and in accomplishing responsibilities as defined in the position description. Select the appropriate descriptor from the following list.

| | |
|---|---|
| Exceptional Performance. Always exceeds expectations for this position. | |
| Above average performance. Frequently exceeds expectations for this position. | |
| Expected level of performance. Consistently performs acceptably in this position. | |
| Improvement is expected. Sometimes does not meet expectations for this position. | |
| Major improvement required. Usually does not meet expectations for this position. | |

Employee Signature _____

Date_____

Supervisor Signature_____

Date_____

Source: Reprinted by permission of the University of Dayton Office of Human Resources.

# DIRECTOR'S RESOURCE 9-5

## JOB DESCRIPTION

**(For use with Try It Out! 9-4)**

Cook

Schedule: Monday through Friday—7:30 a.m. to 3:30 p.m.

Reports to the Head Start director.

Responsible for the following:

1. safely preparing all food (breakfast, lunch, and snacks)
2. requisitioning appropriate amounts of foodstuffs based on designated menus
3. checking food deliveries against orders
4. storing foods appropriately, before preparation, in refrigerator, freezer, bins, cupboards, and the like
5. preparing all foods using methods that maintain food value and freshness
6. following menus, recipes, or other directives furnished by Head Start nutrition consultant
7. recording amounts of food used daily and maintaining an inventory of staples on hand
8. washing and sterilizing dishes and all utensils according to sanitarian's directions
9. cleaning appliances and storage areas according to a designated schedule
10. supervising assistant cook

Summarize the qualifications for each applicant:

**TeachSource Digital Download**

# Director's Resource 9-6

## INTERVIEW QUESTIONS

Be intentional in choosing interview questions. Identify the attributes that you are seeking. Remember that a candidate's priorities and beliefs are typically part of who they are and will be difficult to change after hiring. Consider starting with a "Grand Tour" statement that can give insight into what is most important to the applicant. It can also put the applicant at ease and give the interviewer ideas for good follow-up questions.

What applicants believe about early care and education will likely drive their actions. Consider asking questions that uncover what the applicants believe about themselves, about children, about families, about their role in a team, and about the field of early care and education.

It is common to ask applicants about their education and experience. Also try to access their level of commitment to the profession. One way to find out more about this is to see how well prepared they were for the interview. Commitment can often be predicted by how well applicants can answer questions about their future in the field of early care and education.

Below you will see examples of questions or statement prompts that are designed to gain different types of information.

**Sample "Grand Tour" prompts:**

Tell me about yourself.

Describe your experience with children.

**Belief questions:**

What do you wish the public knew about early care and education?

How do you think children learn best?

What do you believe is important for a teaching team to be effective?

Describe the ideal relationship between families and teachers in an early care and education setting.

How do you think children at the various age groups should be disciplined?

What would you see as your role in staging and maintaining a classroom environment?

How important do you believe play is in the daily curriculum?

**To learn about the applicant's experience:**

What is your experience in working with young children?

What are your greatest strengths?

What are your greatest challenges and how have you worked to address them?

Describe yourself as a member of a teaching team.

Describe strategies that you have used to establish relationships with families and maintain open communication.

**To learn about how the applicant might contribute:**

What can you bring to our center that would be an asset?

Why do you want to work here?

What can we (the center's administration) do to help you be successful?

**To learn about what the applicant knows:**

What types of activities would you do with the children as infants, toddlers, preschoolers, and schoolagers?

What do you think is most important in taking care of infants?

If two children were disagreeing over something and became physical, what would you do and how would you deal with the situation?

How would you address a situation in which non-nappers are preventing nappers from sleeping?

How would you address early learning and development standards in the classroom?

Describe a high-quality curriculum.

How would you help new parents of infants feel that you are providing the best care to their baby?

How do you feel that you communicate with parents?

Describe how you would handle a behavior-challenged child.

**Commitment Questions**

What do you know about our center, and what attracted you enough to apply for this position?

What are your long-term career goals?

**TeachSource Digital Download**

# REFERENCES

Americans with Disabilities Act: Questions and answers. (1991, July). Washington, DC: U.S. Equal Opportunity Commission.

Bloom, P. J. (2007). *From the inside out: The power of reflection and self-awareness.* Lake Forest, IL: New Horizons.

Bloom, P. J., Sheerer, M., & Britz, J. (2005). *Blueprint for action: Achieving center-based change through staff development.* Lake Forest, IL: New Horizon.

Carter, M. (1998). Principles and strategies for coaching and mentoring. In R. Neugebauer & B. Neugebauer (Eds.), *The art of leadership: Managing early childhood organizations.* Redmond, WA: CCIE.

Carter, M., & Curtis, D. (2010). *The visionary director* (2nd ed.). St. Paul, MN: Redleaf Press.

Cohen, A. J. (1998). Bettering your odds of not getting sued. In R. Neugebauer & B. Neugebauer (Eds.), *The art of leadership: Managing early childhood organizations.* Redmond, WA: CCIE.

Collins, J. (2005). *Good to great and the social sectors.* New York: Harper Collins.

Gable, S., Rothrauff, T. C., Thornburg, K. R., & Mauzy, D. (2007). Cash incentives and turnover in center-based child care staff. *Early Childhood Research Quarterly, 22,* 363–378.

Greenberg, P. (1993). *Character development: Encouraging self-esteem and self-discipline in infants, toddlers, and two-year olds.* Washington, DC: NAEYC.

Hamrick, J. (2000). Reduce staff turnover through effective interviewing. *Child Care Information Exchange, 134,* 26–28.

Sciarra, D. J., & Dorsey, A. G. (2002). *Leaders and supervisors in child care programs.* Clifton Park, NY: Thomson Delmar Learning.

Whitebrook, M., & Bellm, D. (1999). *Taking on turnover: An action plan for child care teachers and directors.* Washington, DC: Center for Child Care Workforce.

*Families are more likely to choose a program where they feel they belong.*

## Learning Objectives

After reading this chapter, you should be able to:

**10-1** Identify how early care and education meets the needs of all children, including those with special learning and developmental needs.

**10-2** Demonstrate how to make informed decisions about grouping children in centers.

**10-3** Identify effective practices for enrolling children.

## Standards Addressed in this Chapter

naeyc

Accreditation Standard 4 – Assessment

Accreditation Standard 6 – Teachers

Administrator Competencies – Management Knowledge and Skills 2, 4, 6, 10

Administrator Competencies – Early Childhood Knowledge and Skills 1, 5, 10

Professional Preparation Standard 2 – Building Family and Community Relationships

Professional Preparation Standard 6 – Becoming a Professional

Effective directors are informed decision makers who consider multiple and sometimes competing factors before coming to conclusions. Decisions related to enrolling and grouping children are complex as many factors related to the needs of children and families as well as the quality of the program must be considered. Of course, there are pressures to admit all applicants when enrollment is not full. However, it is important for the director to exercise good professional judgment and base admission decisions on what is in the best interests of children and families.

Ultimately, the director is responsible for the decisions about how children will be admitted to the program and how they will be grouped. The teachers may be called on to assist in these decisions, and sometimes a standing committee authorized by the board is asked to make policy or give advice. An admissions and recruitment committee might be charged with policy-making decisions about the population the program is designed to serve as well as the procedures to be followed when enrolling children. Decisions must also be made about how children will be grouped and how the program can support children with disabilities.

## 10-1 MEETING THE NEEDS OF ALL CHILDREN AND FAMILIES

Quality programs are inclusive and strive to meet the needs of all the children and families admitted to the program. This means that directors must have a realistic understanding of the strengths and limitations of the program and the unique needs of the children and families to be served. Developing this understanding requires that the director and staff engage in ongoing program evaluation to understand what the center can do, where improvement or support is needed, and what the realistic limits are to the types of services a program can offer.

For example, a program may want to increase enrollment by serving a larger number of subsidized children, but an economic downturn at the state level has led to severe cuts in the reimbursement rates. The center must now look elsewhere to increase enrollment or end up with a budget shortfall. Additionally, many of the families that are eligible for a county subsidy are also eligible for Head Start, where children have access to additional program options such as dental and medical evaluations and, in some instances, mental health services. Directors need to make an honest assessment of what their program can provide for children and families and if services can be enhanced by partnering with other agencies.

A center director may understand the need to include children with special learning or developmental needs. Noting an increase in the number of children with autism spectrum disorders, a director might recognize a limitation in the expertise of his or her staff and determine that special training is needed so that teachers understand and can implement strategies that support children with autism. The director might also note that many children with autism require early intervention services to best meet their needs. Directors need to maintain an ethical balance of striving to be inclusive, working with families to find services to best meet the needs of children, and recognizing the strengths and limitations of their program.

Professionals at the center must decide if the available staff and the particular program offerings at the center can provide the most enriching experience for a particular child. In other words, can *this* program provide what *this* child needs to develop to his or her fullest potential? If there is any doubt in the minds of either the members of the family or the director, careful consideration should be given to a number of questions.

- Can the program be adjusted to accommodate this child?

- Is there another program with a different focus that would provide a better match for this child and family?

- Are there programs to partner with that would enhance what can be offered in order to meet the needs of children and families?

Partnering with the local school district or the county early intervention program can provide access to itinerant special educators who will work with children with special needs in child care and home settings. Likewise, many Head Start grantees have developed partnerships with child care programs, allowing children and families to reap the benefits of Head Start services in a child care setting.

---

### MAKING THE CASE FOR *INCLUSION*

The inclusion of children with special learning and developmental needs can be challenging and also very rewarding for the child, his or her peers, and for the teaching staff. The fear of the unknown and a lack of understanding of special education law can prevent centers from accepting children with special needs. For those centers that have been inclusive, the benefits for the center children and staff frequently outweigh the disadvantages.

In an inclusive center, typically developing children learn about diversity and compassion while also learning that children with disabilities are more like them than not. Staff members learn to differentiate and support learning throughout the day. Including children with special needs often helps teachers to be more intentional in their planning and assessment. They become better collaborators and are often more ready to view families as partners. Children with special needs are often eligible for itinerate services that bring new expertise to the classroom, broadening the teachers' skill base, which benefits all children. To support inclusion, directors need to do the following:

- Be aware of the services that are available to children with special needs in child care settings. Visit the special education resource center in your region to learn how to access support services.

- Become familiar with the special education intake team in the schools where the children in the program tend to go to kindergarten. Inquire about the processes they use to handle referrals from child care centers. When you have a question about the development of one of the children in your care, work with the family to connect with the school district. If the referral pertains to an infant or toddler, learn about the early intervention services that are available for very young children in your county.

Inclusive directors see that their program can be one option on a continuum of program options for children and families. Progressive directors need to be realistic while also understanding the need to grow and change to meet the needs of children and families facing the demands of the twenty-first century. One particular challenge is to understand the myriad of federal laws, mandates, and procedures that govern how children with special needs are to be served in inclusive settings.

## 10-1a Admission of Children with Disabilities

A federal law that directors must be familiar with is the Americans with Disabilities Act (ADA), which was enacted in 1990 and amended in 2008. Knowledge of the ADA is important as directors review requests for admission of children with disabilities. Centers are prohibited from denying admission to a child simply because of a disability *unless* such admission would "fundamentally alter the nature of the program" (ADA Amendments Act, 2008). Likewise, children who pose a *direct threat* or "a substantial risk of serious harm to the health and safety of others" do not have to be admitted into a program. The determination that "a child poses a direct threat may not be based on generalizations or stereotypes about the effects of a particular disability; it must be based on an *individualized assessment* that considers the particular activity and the actual abilities and disabilities of the individual" (U.S. Department of Justice, n.d.).

Directors in early childhood education programs must be prepared to address the challenge of providing quality inclusive environments for increasing numbers of young children with disabilities. They are obligated

Roger Bamber/Alamy

*Effective directors support teachers as they make intentional decisions about how to include children when special learning and developmental needs in their classroom.*

to understand that a child may not be excluded simply because he or she has a disability. It is important for them to know how the law applies to infants, toddlers, and preschoolers and to understand how early childhood programs are likely to fit into the scheme of services for children with disabilities. They also should know what role they and their staff can play as part of the interdisciplinary, interagency team effort to give these children the benefit of quality early childhood education experiences. The well-being of the child is best served when families are a part of the team.

Another important law that was enacted by Congress is Public Law 99-457, which amended the Education of Handicapped Act (EHA, PL 94-142). This 1986 amendment mandated services for children 3 to 5 years of age. The reauthorization of both PL 94-142 and PL 99-457 came in 1990 with the passage of PL 101-476, Individuals with Disabilities Education Act (IDEA). It was further amended in 1997 as PL 105-17. The law requires that states provide a free, *appropriate* public education to everyone with a disability between the ages of 3 and 21. In the past, IDEA was specific to public school–based programs for preschoolers and older children with special needs. However, states are now applying the early childhood itinerant model, which brings early intervention services to community-based early childhood programs (Dinnebeil and McInerney, 2011). This means that children with disabilities can now receive inclusive intervention services in child care and other community-based programs, opening a wide variety of options for families.

### Provisions of the IDEA

IDEA, as amended by PL 105-17, the Individuals with Disabilities Act Amendments of 1997, extends all rights and due process protection to children with disabilities ages 3 to 5. Therefore, preschool children with disabilities are ensured free public education in a least-restrictive environment based on an individualized education plan (IEP) developed by a team that includes the child's parents. The programs are to be administered through state or local education agencies (LEAs), which may contract with other service providers to offer a range of service models. The designated state agency ultimately is responsible for monitoring overall services and use of the federal funds. Other sources of funding such as Medicaid or Maternal and Child Health also must be used when the children are eligible, and the new funds are to supplement, not supplant, these existing sources. Therefore, the new funds may be used *in addition to* but not *instead of* existing sources of funding.

According to Allen and Cowdery (2011), IDEA also establishes a state grant program to provide financial assistance to states to maintain and implement a comprehensive, multidisciplinary system of services for infants and toddlers with disabilities. Part C of IDEA, known as *discretionary legislation,* says that states may serve this age group but are not required to do so. The exception is for those states that serve nondisabled infants and toddlers: they must serve those children who are disabled in that age group. The governor of each state designates a lead agency in the state to administer the program. That agency develops eligibility criteria, and the law allows but does not require extension of services to those babies viewed as "at risk" for developmental delay based on medical or environmental factors, in addition to identified infants with disabilities. A case manager, sometimes called a service coordinator, must be designated for each child. That person, who is the liaison between agencies and services needed, also is responsible for the development of the individualized family service plan (IFSP), which must have evidence of multidisciplinary input and include information about the child's level of development, the family's strengths and needs as these relate to the child, the specific intervention services planned, and the projected outcomes for the child and the family. Therefore, the IFSP is somewhat comparable to the IEP required for children ages 3 to 5 and brings the focus to the importance of the family in each young child's life.

## Role of Child Care Centers

IDEA allows for variation in length of day, as well as range and variety of  programs. This means that services to be used may be part-time or full-time, home-based or center-based. This is likely to lead to more inclusion models as state and local agencies contract with half-day and full-day child care programs to expand the continuum of services to include more center-based care in integrated settings. Now that the values of early childhood education programs are sufficiently high and demand public notice, state education agencies that have discretion to choose program models see that these programs offer viable alternatives to the current typical public school categorical model. In addition to integrated child care options that are now available through itinerant services, Head Start is an option for many low-income families, as 10 percent of Head Start's classroom slots must be reserved for children with disabilities.

The vast majority of unserved children with disabilities who come into programs under the new law are identified as needing mild to moderate intervention. Most children who require intensive intervention already receive services and may or may not be included in preschools or child care centers, depending on how well their needs can be met in an inclusive environment. However, based on ADA, each applicant must be considered on a case-by-case basis and may not be excluded merely due to a disabling condition. If the program can include the child by making reasonable accommodations in the

Jim West/Alamy

*The needs of applicants with disabilities must be carefully assessed to determine how best to serve them.*

environment, then it is expected to do so (U.S. Department of Justice, n.d.).

IDEA requires that children with disabilities have access to the "least-restrictive environment" (LRE). Legally, this means that every effort must be made to integrate children with their peers in a regular educational setting. In practice, the LRE facilitates opportunities to function and grow optimally in all areas of development. Directors of centers are responsible for providing such an environment for children with disabilities, who must share the pedagogical and social environment; teachers are expected to be specifically trained to facilitate interaction among and between typically developing children and those who have special needs. They should also have an understanding of the implications of developmental differences and be able to adapt the learning environment to enhance the development of children with diverse abilities.

Although there is evidence that significant benefits accrue to children with special needs who participate in groups with typical peers, these benefits are not the result of merely being in the same classroom. The factors that determine how well children with special needs do in an inclusive environment depends on the quality of the program and the presence of a teacher who has developed specific intervention plans to support interaction between and among the children with disabilities and their typically developing peers (Allen & Cowdery, 2011).

When available staff struggle to find sufficient time or lack the background to provide the special support for children with special needs in the classroom, it may be possible to reach out into the community for additional help. In addition to reaching out to school districts and early intervention providers, volunteers from parent groups, senior citizens, service organizations, or students from university early childhood or special education programs can help in the classroom. Special training for the volunteers and the staff can be arranged through special educators at the local school or university, or from other community agencies (Allen & Cowdery, 2011).

Including children who have been identified with special needs can be both inspiring and challenging for the teaching staff and the director. However, because so many resources are available to children with special needs and their families, inclusive can work out to benefit everyone involved. The more vexing challenges are those faced when a new child enters the program and, soon after admission, begins to manifest social and/or emotional problems through disruptive emotional outbursts in the classroom. In these cases, neither the director nor the teaching staff has had a chance to prepare themselves or the children for this new student. It becomes stressful and time-consuming to work with this new family and to provide the necessary support for the troubled child and the classroom teacher. In these situations, directors are pulled in many directions, sometimes struggling with a screaming, angry child; sometimes talking with hostile, defensive, or bewildered parents; sometimes taking time after hours to give support to an exhausted teacher. These are the times when directors must call on all their professional skills to help the child, the family, and the teacher cope and eventually move forward toward resolution.

In the past decade, the challenge of working with troubled, angry children has created a great deal of interest among early childhood educators as they consider preventive measures as well as explanations for the phenomena and any remedies that might help children, their families, and their teachers. One sample of such a remedy focuses on refining and adjusting classroom practice to promote the emotional well-being and resilience of all children in the classroom, not just of those who are seen as "troublesome." This type of refined and modified approach to children and families requires training and coaching for all staff, including administrators, with a director who participates and serves as a model for other staff. It is essential that everyone who sees, greets, or talks with children and families reflects the same focus of respect and caring. Everyone must engage in what the center views as *best practice*. The adjusted attitude and practice focuses on strengths of children and families and provides very predictable, safe, and supportive experiences throughout the center. The classroom is a place where children come to know and trust that they are respected, protected, and heard by trusted adults. When this modified approach is implemented throughout a program, it seems to minimize the need for the more traditional identification/referral/intervention procedure for troubled children. That traditional routine is reserved for those children and families who require specialized support in addition to the support provided by the uniquely trained and qualified staff that understands the importance of the emotional well-being of children, families, and colleagues.

### ▶❚❚ TeachSource Video Vignette

**Response to Intervention: The Three-Tier Model in a Preschool Environment**

This video provides an overview of how the "Response to Intervention" (RTI) process might be used to meet the needs of young children with special needs in a preschool setting. View the video vignette entitled, *Response to Intervention: The Three-Tier Model in a Preschool Environment*. Reflect on the following questions:

1. How do you think the RTI process might impact the child-centered and play-based practice that is valued in many early childhood settings?

2. As a director, how might you support teachers who are exploring how to use RTI in their classrooms?

### Role of the Director in an Interdisciplinary/Interagency Effort

Cooperation among education agencies, social service agencies, medical groups, and early **naeyc** childhood education providers is essential if young children with special needs and their families are to be well served. Directors conversant in the law and its implications for child care programs will be able to respond more knowledgeably to professionals from related agencies who make inquiries about placements for children with special needs. These directors may be called on to make decisions about whether their programs can meet the needs of the selected special needs children; to serve on interdisciplinary teams where IEPs are developed and referral decisions are made; and to support their teachers who will be working with special educators, therapists, and the children's families. If the children are to benefit from what early childhood educators have to offer, "turf guarding" must be set aside; yet directors must assertively advocate developmentally appropriate practice, which is the area of expertise they bring to the interdisciplinary and interagency team.

To facilitate communication between and among members of interdisciplinary teams and to support their work, directors must understand how and why inclusive works and what prevents it from working. That often means directors must learn more about children with special needs through additional training and reading to prepare themselves for coaching classroom staff and for working with an interdisciplinary team. When members of the interdisciplinary team view each other as colleagues, all of whom bring special skills and training to the situation, and when they keep in mind that their common goal is to provide the best environment for the children and their families, they can work together to that end.

## 10-2 GROUPING THE CHILDREN

As part of the process of meeting the diverse **naeyc** needs of children and families, directors need to make informed decisions about how the structures of the center impact a variety of stakeholders, including children, families, and staff. Decisions about how children are grouped create structures that affect how staff are called upon to work together, how children and families interact at the center, and how much such care costs. Decisions about grouping also reflect a program's philosophy of education and the approach that the program has adopted. These decisions need to be carefully considered as they are more than logistical but will have a long-term impact on the children, families, staff, and budget of the program.

Decisions about grouping the children—group size, ages of children, and composition of the groups—must be reached before making the group assignments and pursuing all the subsequent steps in the enrollment procedure. After assignments have been made, teachers can contact families and initiate the enrollment process. Although the degree of flexibility around grouping in ongoing early childhood education programs is sometimes more limited than in half-day programs, even there the cyclical nature of demand usually follows the public school year, thereby giving rise to numerous grouping decisions for newcomers in the fall.

A number of factors are considered in dealing with the complex question of how children should be grouped appropriately. The size of groups is determined by a variety of factors, including the physical space available, the licensing requirements, the number of staff members, and the program philosophy. Appropriate group size has a positive influence on both children and teachers (Freeman, Decker, & Decker, 2012). Other factors that relate to the grouping of children are the needs and skills of the staff, the needs of the children, the question of chronological age grouping versus vertical grouping (sometimes called family or multiage grouping), the number of children with special needs to be enrolled, and the nature of their disabilities.

### 10-2a Total Number of Children

To a large extent, the number of children **naeyc** available and the size of the physical space determine the total number of children in a center. If it is a new program, after the needs assessment in the community has been completed (Chapter 2) and the facility has been selected (Chapter 7), the final decision about the total number of children in the center must be made. Often, this decision is simply to take all available children. However, when the requests for service are overwhelming or when the available space cannot accommodate large numbers of children, the director and/or the board may want to limit the enrollment. Accreditation standards and many state licensing regulations limit total group size as well as adult-to-child ratios, both of which affect program quality. (See Chapter 3 for further details.)

Centers for young children must radiate a feeling of intimacy and warmth. Little children often feel frightened and uncomfortable about entering a large, forbidding building. The noise, the inevitable confusion, and the motion created by many people concentrated in one area can provoke anxiety in young children. It is difficult to maintain an inviting, comfortable atmosphere for small children when buildings are very large and when children are moved through crowded play yards, hallways, or receiving areas before they reach *their* room and *their* teacher.

Because the atmosphere in large public school buildings can be overwhelming for very young children, it is important for early childhood professionals and public school educators to give special attention to the selection of the classroom and play yard space for the preschool children. Partnerships between early childhood educators and public school personnel can result in site selection for public school–sponsored programs that may be in a separate wing of the building or in a facility completely separate from the school building. Some of the advantages of funneling preschool and full-day child care services into public school sponsorship include greater stability, insulation from political attack, and protection from sudden economic shifts.

## 10-2b Space and Group Size

Group size varies according to the licensing regulations and how the available space is organized. Licensing regulations often limit the number of children in a room and usually dictate the adult-to-child ratio for children of different ages. Because space requirements and adult-to-child ratio standards in the licensing regulations are not always based on the knowledge of experienced professionals, it is wise to follow a standard of small groups with low teacher-to-child ratios, meeting NAEYC standards or achieving even lower ratios under special circumstances (National Association for the Education of Young Children, 2013).

---

### DIRECTOR'S CORNER

"Children had to go down the hall and upstairs when the teachers wanted to take them to the gym for large-muscle activities. I always asked my teachers to try to avoid having the preschoolers in the halls of the school building when the older children were moving in and out of the auditorium or the lunchroom. It was very confusing for the younger children to be taken through the long lines of older children—especially if remarks were made like 'make room for the baby group' by the children or the elementary teachers."

—*Director, Head Start program in a public school building*

---

The organization or plan of the available space affects the size of the groups that can be accommodated. When bathrooms are two floors down or outside areas are not directly adjacent to the classroom, groups must be smaller to be manageable during the transition periods when children move from one place to another. If fenced-in play areas outside can be reached directly from the classroom, the total space can be supervised more easily, and a larger group could be assigned to the space.

When space is adequate to accommodate large numbers of young children, some directors and teachers find

---

### REFLECTION

Can you recall how you felt as a first-year high school student when you initially entered your big high school building? Were you afraid and anxious? How did it feel to be the youngest or the smallest in the whole school? Did you feel that you might not be able to find your room or your locker? Did you ever have nightmares about forgetting your schedule or losing your most important notebook? If you can recall any of those feelings, perhaps you can begin to relate to the young child who leaves a familiar home environment and enters a large, strange, crowded building.

---

creative ways to use dividers, draperies, or movable partitions to break the space into smaller units. Even where available space would accommodate larger groups, smaller groups are viewed as optimal.

## 10-2c Skills of Staff and Group Size

In deciding on the size of groups, the director considers the skill level of the staff and factors that into the decision about how many children should be assigned to each classroom. The staff for each group must be available to provide frequent personal contact; promote age-appropriate, meaningful learning experiences; create a nurturing environment using effective classroom management strategies; and respond immediately to all emergencies.

## 10-2d Needs of Children and Group Size

Discussing the policy of making group size or placement decisions on the basis of differing individual family and child needs or ages of children is beyond the scope of this book, even though every director must consider such needs carefully. However, some basic considerations apply to all children, whether infant, toddler, preschool, or school age.

The needs of children will vary depending on their experiences, their level of development in all areas, and their ages. However, it is generally agreed that very young children in their first group experience find it most satisfying to relate to a constant adult. After the initial shift in attachment from the primary caregiver (usually the mother) to a constant adult at the center, the child begins to branch out and relate to other adults and other children in the group. This developmental progression suggests that the child's first experience should be in a small, intimate group with a consistent adult. The children in this group may be the same chronological age, or they may range over a year or two in age. Volunteers, student teachers, or parent helpers may rotate through the classroom, but the one primary constant caregiver becomes the trusted adult figure to whom children can turn when they need caring and attention. Continuity of care is especially important for infants and toddlers, who should have an assigned primary caregiver who works closely with the parents. When change is carefully planned and minimized, infants and toddlers begin to be able to predict what will happen, thus feeling less powerless or uneasy and more secure (Gonzalez-Mena & Widmeyer Eyer, 2011).

For young children spending the full day in a center, it is wise to consider small, intimate grouping patterns. Because children in full-day programs spend practically all of their waking hours in the center, it becomes a surrogate home for them. Young children who are dealing with all the stimulation and interpersonal relationships of a large group for an extended period of time may be exhausted by the end of their long day. Small groups in a carefully planned space provide both time and space for the child to be alone, to establish close relationships with just one or two children, or to spend time alone with just one adult. Quiet and intimacy in a comfortable setting with a few people more closely resembles the home environment and can soften the institutional atmosphere that prevails in many large centers.

Careful planning and adequate staffing enable directors to maintain consistency in caregivers and to avoid having to regroup children to maintain required staff-to-child ratios throughout each day. In fact, some programs take significant steps to maintain continuity of care by grouping children in broader age ranges such as 3 months to 3 years or by implementing a practice called "looping," in which teachers follow a group of children from infancy through preschool. Both of these grouping practices offer the children the benefits of consistency throughout these formative years. Moving children to different spaces for the critical and sometimes fragile times of separation and reunion creates tension for everyone involved. If at all possible, directors should plan staffing so that children stay in the same familiar space with their caregivers from the time they see that special parent disappear behind that closed door in the morning to the time they see that familiar face reappear for pickup at day's end. It is recommended that children of all ages have an assigned primary caregiver.

## Chronological versus Vertical Age Grouping

There is no consensus on the best grouping practice. Although there has been some movement toward greater homogeneity in classrooms for young children, which usually results from chronological age grouping, there is a resurgence of interest in multiage or vertical grouping (Freeman, Decker, & Decker, 2012). Program philosophy may dictate the preferred approach to grouping the children. However, unless licensing regulates how children should be grouped, the way classrooms are organized within the program is left to the discretion of the director and the professional staff.

Stan Adams

*The younger the child, the more important it is that experiences should be in a small, intimate group with a consistent and responsive adult.*

---

> ### REFLECTION
>
> Think about your first practicum experience in a classroom. Think about how many children you were able to manage at one time. Could you comfortably work with 5 children? If you were asked to work with 10 children without a second person to help, did you still feel that you could practice effective management skills? What adult-to-child ratio and total group size is most comfortable for you, keeping in mind your philosophy of early childhood education?

Directors are faced with the challenge of maintaining full enrollment while keeping groups balanced and exercising caution when decisions are made about moving children among established center groupings.

When infant-toddler groups are at capacity, but there are openings in the preschool, it is tempting to move some of the older toddlers to the preschool to make space for families on the waiting list. It is important to balance the need for full enrollment to meet budget requirements against the social-emotional readiness of these very young children and their ability to manage a more complex environment with older children and new adults.

Too often, children are moved based solely on their chronological age or in response to pressure to make room for new children, rather than on a careful analysis of the readiness of the children involved in the move. The first step is to give careful consideration to a child's readiness to thrive and grow with the older children. Then take note of the challenges to the family and teachers involved in supporting the child through this critical adjustment to many unknowns, such as different spaces with new adults and few familiar faces. The transition process for any child to a new group in the center can be eased by setting up a transition plan that parallels the phasing-in process described in the "Intake Procedures" section of this chapter (page 221). The family and the teachers from both rooms will be involved in the transition process, just as a parent and the teacher are involved when a new child enters the program.

Parents may need a special conference with the director to clarify the importance of the parent role in the transition process, not only when the child enters the program but also for all subsequent transitions from one group to another and the final one when the child leaves the center. Meeting with the child's parents as these transition times approach offers the director the opportunity to help them understand how their presence in the new room can help reduce stress for their child as both are adjusting to the families and staff. It is helpful to parents if they understand that taking time for their child during potentially stressful changes will contribute to the emotional well-being of their child.

## Chronological Grouping

Grouping by age traditionally has been a more common practice in early childhood programs than vertical grouping. It involves grouping based solely on the basis of age: 3- and 4-year-olds are in different groups, and toddlers are separated from infants. When children are grouped chronologically, there is little discussion about which group a given child will join. The director's task is simplified because in accepting the center program, parents understand that their 3-year-old will be in Group 1 and their 4-year-old will be in Group 2. Of course, there will be ranges of ability and behavior within an age group due to individual differences, but the child's exposure to differences is inevitably lessened when chronological grouping is used. Therefore, the child's opportunity to develop a broad appreciation for diversity is diminished. On the other hand, there are advantages to age grouping, such as simplifying the planning of the learning environment and making classroom management less troublesome. The less experienced teacher may find this type of grouping more comfortable.

**▶❙❙ TeachSource Video Vignette**

### Preschool: IEP and Transition Planning for a Young Child with Special Needs

View the video vignette entitled, *Preschool: IEP and Transition Planning for a Young Child with Special Needs.*

Transitions meetings are common when children move from public school preschool programs to kindergartens that are part of the same school system. Child care providers who work with children and families but who are not part of the school system are often not included in the transition planning meeting. As director, how might you facilitate avenues to support children and families to be more involved in this transition process?

Chronological age grouping is based on the assumption that children of the same age are within the same range in ability and level of development. Because children of the same age are not homogeneous, many programs go to multiage grouping where children advance at their own rate through individualized or differentiated programming. Multiage grouping allows for children's uneven development and provides an environment in which younger children engage in more interactive and complex types of play with older children, who are easily accessible. There is also compelling evidence that children will do well when they are in a mixed-age group where children not only differ in age but also in ethnic and socioeconomic backgrounds. With the guidance of a well-trained teacher, children will engage in projects that match their interests and move toward more cooperative play (Katz & Chard, 2000).

## More on Multiage Grouping

Multiage grouping, or vertical grouping as it is sometimes called, involves placing children of different ages in the same group; the children in any one group may range in age as much as 2 to 3 years. This multiage grouping more closely resembles one that would occur in a family and is sometimes referred to as *family grouping*. Depending on licensing requirements, infants and sometimes even toddlers must be kept in separate groups. When vertical grouping is the pattern, decisions about the size and the composition of each group, as well as the number of adults needed for each one, become more complex. The broad age range also complicates managing the children and planning their learning environment.

Sometimes, parents object to having their 2-year-old with older children who may be viewed by the toddler's parents as being loud and rough. These parents often are concerned about the safety of their toddler and sometimes fear that their young child will be unable to cope in a group covering a wide age range. However, many of these parents can be helped to see that a young child in a multiage group has more opportunity to learn from older children in the group and that every child has a chance to teach the other group members. Peer teaching and learning have intrinsic value because they not only enhance a child's sense of mastery and worth but also facilitate cooperation and appreciation of others. For example, 2-year-olds may not be as efficient as 5-year-olds about putting equipment back on the shelf, but the total concentration they give to an activity such as water play and the curiosity they show in exploring this material may help their more controlled 3- or 5-year-old counterparts to try splashing in the water.

Parents who are familiar with programs that have chronological age grouping are usually aware of differences in tuition as children move up from infant to toddler to preschool in these programs. Costs are lower because of more generous ratios in classrooms for older children, which is a financial benefit for families as children move up from one level to the next. This cost differential and its inevitable result are a reality that program sponsors and directors must deal with when they choose to do vertical age grouping. Fees per child in vertical grouping are usually the same, regardless of the child's age.

The director must cope with the skeptical parents and with the teachers who are reaching out for support as they work with a broad age range. However, sometimes the advantages of multiage grouping, such as peer modeling and peer tutoring, are outweighed by the challenges of planning for the age span and equipping and managing the classroom. Helping families understand that it is typical for the development of 3- to 5-year-olds to vary across developmental domains comes from teachers who also understand this concept and can communicate it in clear and consistent ways. Consider using graphics that show how the profiles of individual children might intersect with the skill levels of older and/or younger children.

As children mature into the primary grades, this variation in developmental rate tends to even out. However, typical 3- to 5-year-olds are very sporadic in their rate of development, and many children have peaks and valleys that make the opportunities to connect with older and younger children in a multiage group configuration very appropriate (see Figure 10-1).

### REFLECTION

How might you, as a director, use Figure 10-1 to equip your staff so they can convey a clear explanation of multiage grouping to families?

Directors become coaches and sources of support for staff as they try to meet challenges. Teachers who are able to individualize planning for a multiage group also will be better qualified to create culturally responsive programs for children from diverse backgrounds and inclusive programs

**FIGURE 10-1** The development of young children varies in rate so that typical children of different ages are often working on the same developmental skills.

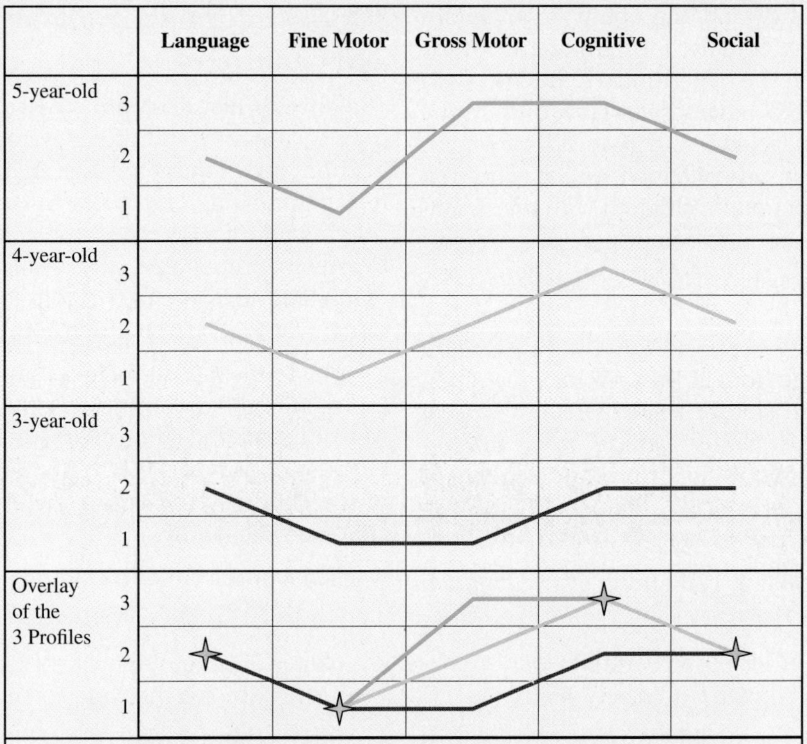

✧ See where these three typical children of different ages connect developmentally. Because the developmental rates of typical young children vary greatly, there are many natural opportunities for children of different ages to connect. There are also opportunities for children to scaffold the development of their peers and for emerging skills to be learned by working with slightly advanced peers. Note that profile scores shown here are intended to represent lower, mid-level and higher scores commonly used in screening devices.

for children with special needs. These teachers develop a keen awareness of the fact that "one size does not fit all." Directors can help teachers both develop these skills and also become proficient in communicating what they do and why to families.

## 10-2e Impact of Children with Exceptionalities on Group Size

When children with exceptionalities are included in the group, the size and composition of the group may need to be adjusted accordingly to ensure that enough adults will be available to respond to the children's needs. Consider which group can best meet the needs of the child with the disability, as well as how that child can offer something to the group. Unless the child is truly integrated into the group, which will likely require scaffolding from the teachers, there is a risk that the child with the disability will be ignored and will not reap the benefits of being included with typical peers. The least-restrictive ruling is not necessarily a mandate to enroll all children with a disability into regular programs; however, the advantages of inclusive for both nondisabled children and children with developmental disabilities are numerous and well documented (Allen & Cowdery, 2011). Social competence and the ability to maintain higher levels of play are enhanced for children with exceptionalities who have the opportunity to interact with typically developing peers in inclusive classrooms. At the same time, their language and cognitive gains are comparable to their peers in self-contained special education classrooms. On the other hand, children without disabilities in inclusive classrooms become more accepting of others who are different and become more comfortable with those differences.

There is no ideal exceptional-to-typical ratio, and recommendations range from at least two or more to an even balance (50–50), to more disabled than nondisabled, sometimes called "reverse mainstreaming" where nondisabled make up one-quarter to one-half of the enrollment (Allen & Cowdery, 2011). Variables that must be considered include the following:

- severity of the disabling conditions of the children with special needs
- characteristics of the nondisabled children
- how to explain and understand peers' disabilities
- expertise of the available adults who are to work with the inclusive group (Taylor, 2002)

Multiage groups are advantageous for children with special needs because they provide peer models who have a broad range of skills and abilities. The atypical child is exposed to the peer model who has higher-level skills or abilities and also will have a chance to develop friendships with younger children who may be more compatible developmentally.

Decisions about group size or group patterns will affect program planning, child and teacher behaviors, group atmosphere, and ultimately the experiences of both teacher and child in the learning environment. An inclusive program must consider the uniqueness of every child and family in the classroom and how each child's strengths and needs will be addressed (Allen & Cowdery, 2011). Therefore, grouping the children is a complex issue that has far-reaching results.

## 10-3 ENROLLING THE CHILDREN

Filling out forms, interviewing parents, and visiting back and forth between home and school are the major components of the enrollment procedure. The director is responsible for developing forms that will provide the center staff members with the information they need about the families and the children. The director also manages the planning and timing of this procedure; however, these plans must be discussed with staff members and parents who will be required to carry them out.

## 10-3a Information about Families and Children

The director first determines what information is needed from each family and then develops a plan for obtaining it. Both forms and interviews can be used for this purpose. It is up to the director to design the forms and to develop the plan for interviews or conferences. The ultimate goal is to assemble the necessary information for each child and family and to make it available to selected adults at the center who will be responsible for the child and the family.

The following list includes the type of preenrollment information that is typically obtained from the family. Note that all the information is important to efficient business operation of the center, to the health and safety of the children, and to the better understanding of the child and the family.

- name of the child (including nickname)
- names of family members and ages of siblings
- names of other members of the household and their relationship to the child
- home address and telephone number
- name, address, telephone number (home, work, cell), and email addresses of employer(s) of parent(s)
- arrangement for payment of fees
- transportation plans for the child (including how the child will be transported and by whom)
- medical history and record of a recent physical examination of the child by a physician

- social-emotional history of the child

- name, address, and telephone number of the child's physician or clinic

- emergency medical treatment authorization

- name, address, and telephone number of a person (outside the family) to contact in an emergency if a member of the family cannot be reached

- permission to participate in the total school program (field trips, photos, videotaping, research, etc.)

To ensure that you have all the information and signed releases required to satisfy licensing and to cover liability questions, contact your local licensing agent and consult an attorney.

## 10-3b Forms

A number of sample forms included in the Director's Resources demonstrate various ways in which the information just listed can be recorded. These are only sample forms and cannot be used in the exact format presented, but they can provide a basis for developing appropriate forms to meet the specific needs of each center. For example, the director of a small cooperative preschool does not need all the data on family income that is required by Head Start or publicly funded programs but does need details on family schedules to plan for parent participation.

Programs sponsored by public schools may or may not require family income information but will require a Medicaid number for those children entitled to the benefits of that program and also may need a birth certificate to validate the age of the child.

Because programs vary so much concerning the information required on children and families, directors must develop forms that meet the specific needs of the program.

In the case of early childhood education centers and preschools, applications for admission are often included on the center's website, which allows families to print out the forms that are relevant to them. In some instances, the forms are automated so they can be submitted to the center electronically. If selection and grouping of the children require more subjective data than can be gleaned from the application form or any other written information that has been collected prior to admission, the director can arrange to talk with the parent(s).

After most of the children have been admitted and assigned to groups, those who have not yet been placed are held for deferred enrollment, or in the case of ongoing programs, put on a waiting list. If a child is rejected for reasons other than full enrollment, the reasons should be discussed with the family to avoid any misunderstandings that quickly could undermine the public relations efforts of the center staff and impair communication between the staff and potential clients from the community.

### Working Smart with Technology

*Developing an Effective Website*

Developing an effective website can facilitate communication with parents and also provide access to the forms needed for a wide variety of center needs. It is important that the development of the website reflect collaboration with staff and families to determine how the website will be used as well as the kinds of materials that will be included on the site. Some centers choose to use a password-protected section of the site that includes the handbook and forms for families and staff as well as pictures of children and their work. Having a password-protected section of the website is especially important if your program serves children with special needs as special education laws are very clear about maintaining confidentiality. It is also important to have an open-access section of the program website, which is designed to market the program and include application and enrollment information. The website developer must understand the intended use and audience for the website as well as the need to protect children and their identity from public view. After the website is developed, it must be maintained, which can involve ongoing costs. Consider using a free or inexpensive user-friendly website development tool such as Weebly.com to create a website. Not only is it possible to develop a free or inexpensive website using drag-and-drop technology, but it is also very easy to keep the website up-to-date without incurring additional costs.

Photograph by Stan Adams

*A well-developed website is essential for today's child care program. Website development should be a collaborative effort between center staff and families in order to design a website that meets the needs of all involved.*

## 10-3c Confidentiality

Information on families and children that is recorded on forms or obtained by staff members during interviews or home visits is confidential and *must not be released* to unauthorized people without parental consent. Furthermore, the Family Educational Rights and Privacy Act of 1974 (FERPA) provides that any public or private educational institution that is the recipient of federal funds made available under any federal program administered by the U.S. Department of Education must give parents access to their children's educational records. Because all information in the files must remain available to parents, it is important that staff members use discretion when recording information to be placed in a child's permanent record. Parents should be informed of what information will be kept confidential and what will be available to teaching staff, office staff, and other support staff. Parents decide how much detail they are willing to release. They realize that emergency telephone numbers and names of people authorized to pick up the child will be needed by all teaching and office staff. However, they may choose to have medical histories and income information available only to the director and the lead teacher (Taylor, 2002).

Records and other confidential information should not be disclosed to anyone other than center personnel without written consent of the parent or guardian, unless its disclosure is necessary to protect the health or safety of the child. Written parental consent is required to pass information on to the public school by any preschool or Head Start program. As a general rule, parental consent should be obtained except in emergency cases or when it appears that the parent is a threat to the child (Family Educational Rights and Privacy Act, 1974). Centers that receive funds from government sources should be familiar with any regulations or guidelines on confidentiality and privacy that are tied to the funding source.

Center directors in collaboration with staff, parents, and board members can develop written policies for the protection of confidentiality and the disclosure of children's records. These policies should be made available to all program personnel and families (Feeney & Freeman, n.d.). The trust that develops between staff and families will be damaged if there is a breach of confidentiality. Setting aside one staff meeting each year to review the confidentiality policies is one way to encourage the staff to reaffirm their pledge to maintain confidentiality.

## 10-3d Intake Procedures

The director decides which staff members will be involved in each step of the intake proce-dure, but it is imperative that the child's teacher actively be involved throughout. The adult who will work directly with the child must interact with the child and family to begin to establish feelings of mutual trust among the child, the family, and the teacher.

Parents often feel apprehensive about placing children in an early childhood program. A carefully planned intake process that provides frequent opportunities to talk with the teacher, the director, and the social services staff (if available) can help parents cope with their feelings. At the same time, young children are often upset when they first are separated from their parents and family. Children worry about who will take care of them or how they will get home. Some children display regressive behaviors. Both teachers and parents need help to understand that children are uneasy about this new experience and must have special attention and care during this initial transition. Because children feel frightened and lonely, their transition to a new physical and social environment is done gradually and must be accompanied by continuous support from family members. For the mental health of both the parents and children, the sequences followed in the intake process should be arranged so that everyone involved will be able to cope successfully with the separation experience. Four steps are commonly employed in introducing the family and the child to the center program and to the teacher. They are discussed here because it is the director's responsibility to ensure that this careful intake procedure is implemented.

## 10-3e Initial Interview with Parents

The purpose of an initial interview is to get acquainted with the parent(s), answer their questions about the center program, communicate what will be expected of them, take them on a tour of the center, and familiarize them with the forms that must be filled out before their child can be admitted. It may be useful to go over the family information, the child's social history, the medical history, the emergency information record, and the various release and permission forms during the interview to answer questions about any confusing items. The sample forms in the Director's Resources give some idea of the way these forms may look. The informality and friendliness of this first personal contact will set the tone for all future contacts. This is precisely the time to establish the foundation for mutual trust among director, teacher, parent, and child, so it is important that these interviews be conducted in a nonthreatening manner.

Scheduling the interview is usually done at the convenience of the family. Even though the teacher or the office staff may do the interview scheduling, it is essential that the director monitor it to ensure that families are not unduly inconvenienced. Careful consideration of family needs indicates that the center staff is sensitive to individual lifestyles and family preferences. When parents work, evenings or weekends may be best for interviews. Center staff members also must consider the transportation problems for some families, the availability of baby-sitters, and the schedules of other children in the family.

## 10-3f Home Visit with the Family

A home visit may be the next step in the intake procedure. The director first de-scribes the purpose of home visits to the staff and goes over a home visit report with them before family appointments are made (see Director's Resource 10-4). The purpose is not

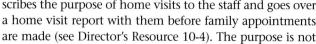

to evaluate the home, but rather to gather information that will enable the staff to have a better understanding of the child. Trust between the parent(s) and the staff will be destroyed and communication impaired if the family interprets the purpose of these home visits as evaluative. Observing a family at home will help the teacher understand the family lifestyle, culture, and attitudes about childrearing.

---

### DIRECTOR'S CORNER

"We make it clear at the outset and are fairly firm with parents about spending some time here with their child because we know, from experience, that even a child who comes in with apparent ease may have a problem two months hence, which harks back to skipping the gradual transition into the group. Even if a parent can spend only 15 minutes in the morning with a child for a week or two, we accept that and make it clear we expect it. My staff is sold on the importance of gradual separation and will even come in 15 or 30 minutes early—before we open—to give a new child time in the classroom with both the parent and the teacher present."

*—Director, corporate-sponsored center*

---

### Initial Visit to the Center

The scheduling of the initial visits to the center is arranged by the director and the staff before home visits begin so that information about visiting the center can be given to parents during the home visit.

This initial visit to the classroom is planned to help the child make that first big step from home and the trusted caregiver to the center and a new caring adult. For preschool children, the visit can last from 30 to 45 minutes and should terminate before the child is tired or bored. This entire orientation process is longer and more complex for infants and toddlers. Although the teacher is clearly responsible for working with the child and the accompanying adult during preliminary visits, it is important for the director to be available to greet the newcomers and answer any questions that might arise. It provides a perfect opportunity for the director and the parent(s) to get to know each other better and is a good time to give them a copy of the parent handbook. (A sample parent handbook is available as a TeachSource Digital Download.)

`TeachSource Digital Download`

### 10-3g Phasing in the Children

The first three intake steps for preschool children described here can be implemented in **naeyc** all types of center-based programs. The scheduling of each step should be adjusted to individual family needs and obviously is much more difficult for working parents. In fact, the scheduling of these steps may seem to be somewhat unrealistic for full-day child care programs but can be done through very creative planning. Implementing the intake

procedures for all ages of children in child care programs could involve evenings, early mornings, or weekends. The director, therefore, must work out the scheduling with the staff and may give comp time to professional staff or overtime for hourly employees.

The phasing in (or "staggered entrance"), which is the fourth and last step in the intake procedure, will, of necessity, be very different in ongoing child care programs than in programs that are just starting or in those based on the typical school calendar. Arranging for the staggered entrance of a group of 12 to 15 preschool children at the beginning of the year poses a complex scheduling problem, but it is an essential step in the orientation process. Because scheduling is very involved, it is important for the director and staff to consult with parents about convenient times for them to come and stay with their child. Successful implementation of the plan depends on staff and family commitment to it. Extended intake procedures for younger children can require special planning.

In public school–sponsored programs, which usually have no precedent for gradual intake of new children, early childhood staff will have to meet with administrators and building principals to explain the importance of this procedure for the well-being of children and families. Because some early childhood programs in public schools are considered part of the elementary school and are accredited with the elementary school in the local school district, they usually are expected to provide a given number of instructional days to maximize the amount of state funds they receive. Often, the developmentally appropriate practice of phasing in children is one of the first issues that creates conflict between developmental early childhood educators and the more academic-school, readiness-focused elementary educators.

In full-day child care programs, the major problem is to find a trusted adult to stay with the child until all people involved feel comfortable about the child being at the center every day for the full day. When a family needs full-day care for a child, both parents usually are working, or the child may be a member of a one-parent family or in foster care. In these special cases, a grandparent or other member of the extended family may be the best person to provide the emotional support necessary for the child during the phasing-in period.

If there is any question among staff members about the importance of the gradual orientation program for the child, the family, and the success of the total program, it is up to the director to help everyone understand that this process represents the next logical step in developing mutual trust within the teacher-child-family unit. Orienting children is usually exciting and productive for the teacher, but it is also time-consuming and energy draining. The process can be successful only if the entire staff understands its relevance to the total program and recognizes it as being consistent with developmentally appropriate practice.

## SUMMARY

Most of the decisions about grouping children appropriately are made by the director, who must consider the unique needs of the children, available space, and licensing regulations about ratios and group size. Policy decisions about chronological or multiage grouping must be made before children are assigned to groups. Skills and experience of staff, ages of children, and the numbers and types of children with special needs selected for admission are all factors that will affect where children will be assigned.

Enrolling children involves filling out forms, interviewing parents, making home visits, and gradually phasing in the children. Although the staggered enrollment procedure is complex and time-consuming, it is a critical step in the process of building trust among the school, the child, and the family. To effectively recruit and enroll children, directors must do the following:

- Identify how early care and education meets the needs of all children, including those with special learning needs, and their families.

- Demonstrate how to make informed decisions about grouping children in centers.

- Identify effective practices for enrolling children.

## TRY IT OUT!

1. Using Director's Resource 10-1, work out a staggered enrollment schedule for 12 children, then reflect on your personal reactions to the information in this chapter under the heading "Intake Procedures" (page 221).

   a. Did you think about how parents might feel about the procedures described in the various steps of the intake procedures?

   b. Were you having any particular negative (or positive) feelings about the intake procedures?

   c. Did you identify with this material as a
      - student?
      - classroom teacher?
      - prospective parent?
      - director?
      - other?

2. Working with another student, role-play an initial interview with a young mother who is sending an only child who is 3 years old to your program. The Sample Personal History (Director's Resource 10-2) and the Policy Summary Form (Director's Resource 10-3) are to be explained during this interview. At the close of the interview, discuss reactions to this role-play with the entire group.

3. In groups of four, role-play a home visit with a mother, father, and their 3-year-old daughter. When you arrive, you see no evidence of toys in the home, and you find the child dressed and sitting in a chair with her hands folded, apparently having been told to "be good and sit quietly while we talk to your teacher." The purpose of the visit is to explain the initial visit to the center and the staggered enrollment plan for the child.

4. After the role-play, stay in groups of four and evaluate your reaction to the child and to the family. Evaluate your reactions as you played teacher, mother, father, or child. Consider how successful the teacher was at developing a relationship with the child. Fill in the Home Visit Report (Director's Resource 10-4) in sufficient detail so the director will have a clear picture of what transpired during the visit.

# Director's Resource 10-1

## DEVELOP A STAGGERED ENROLLMENT PLAN

**(For use with Try It Out! 10-1)**

Enroll 12 children over a period of eight days.

The plan is for a half-day preschool that meets from 9:00 a.m. to 11:30 a.m. daily.

Remember to have children come for shorter hours, in small groups, and gradually move toward having all children together for the full 2 1/2 hours on the ninth day of school.

Fill in the time slots with the child's number—1, 2, 3, ..., 12.

Time slots can be adjusted to suit your plan.

| Week 1 | Monday—1 | Tuesday—2 | Wednesday—3 | Thursday—4 | | Friday—5 | |
|---|---|---|---|---|---|---|---|
| 9:00 | | | | | | | |
| 9:30 | | | | | | | |
| 10:00 | | | | | | | |
| 10:30 | | | | | | | |
| 11:00 | | | | | | | |
| 11:30 | | | | | | | |
| **Week 2** | **Monday—6** | **Tuesday—7** | **Wednesday—8** | **Thursday—9** | | **Friday—10** | |
| 9:00 | | | | Children 1–12 | | Children 1–12 | |
| 9:30 | | | | | | | |
| 10:00 | | | | | | | |
| 10:30 | | | | | | | |
| 11:00 | | | | | | | |
| 11:30 | | | | | | | |

## DIRECTOR'S RESOURCE 10-2

### SAMPLE PERSONAL HISTORY—YOUR CHILD'S DEVELOPMENT

**(For use with Try It Out! 10-2)**

Date _____

Child's Name _____ Nickname _____
Address _____ ZIP _____ Phone _____
Date of Birth _____ Placeofbirth _____
Sex _____

I. The Child's Family
   Parents or Guardians
A. Name _____ Birth Date _____
   Education (include highest grade completed or degrees)
   _____
   _____
   Occupation _____ Usual working hours _____
                     Work phone _____
B. Name _____ Birth Date _____
   Education (include highest grade completed or degrees)
   _____
   Occupation _____ Usual working hours _____
                     Work phone _____
   Status of Parents (Check)      Living together
   _____            Living apart _____
   Child lives with _____
   If parents work or are students, who keeps the child in their absence?
   Circle one    Grandparent    Other Relative    Friend    Paid Sitte    Other

## DIRECTOR'S RESOURCE 10-2 *(continued)*

Other children in the family (list in order of birth)

| Name | Sex | Birth Date | What grade if in school |
|------|-----|-----------|------------------------|
|      |     |           |                        |
|      |     |           |                        |
|      |     |           |                        |
|      |     |           |                        |
|      |     |           |                        |
|      |     |           |                        |

Additional members of household (give number)
Friends _____          Others _____
Boarders _____         Relatives _____

(Indicate relationships)

What part do these other persons have in the care of your child? _____

Has your child been separated from his/her parents for long periods of time, and if so, why?
_____

Have you moved frequently? _____
What language is usually spoken at home? _____
(If more than one, what other language(s) are spoken?)
_____

## DIRECTOR'S RESOURCE 10-2 *(continued)*

C. Income _____ (per month) _____
   (per year) _____
D. Medical card number _____ (parent)
   Child's number _____

II. Development in Early Childhood
    Comment on the health of the mother during pregnancy
    _____

    Comment on the health of your child during delivery and infancy _____
    _____

    When did your child walk? _____
    When did your child talk? _____
    Is your child adopted? _____
    Does he/she know it? _____
    Does your child have bladder control? _____
    Child's terminology _____
    Does your child have bowel control? _____
    Child's terminology _____
    Does your child need help when going to the bathroom?
    _____
    Does your child need reminding about going to the bathroom? _____
    Does your child usually take a nap? _____
    At what time? _____
    Describe any special needs, handicaps, or health problems.
    _____
    _____

## DIRECTOR'S RESOURCE 10-2 *(continued)*

Does your child have any difficulty saying what he/she wants or do you have any trouble understanding his/her speech? _____

III. Eating Habits
     What is your child's general attitude toward eating?
     _____
     What foods does your child especially like? _____
     For which meal is your child most hungry? _____
     Does the child feed himself/herself entirely? _____
     Does your child dislike any food in particular? _____
     Is your child on a special diet? _____
     Does your child take a bottle? _____
     Does your child eat or chew things that are not food? Explain. _____
     Do you have any concerns about your child's eating habits? Explain. _____
     Is there any food your child should not eat for medical, religious, or personal reasons? _____

IV. Play and Social Experiences
    Has your child participated in any group experiences?
    _____
    Where? _____
    Did your child enjoy it? _____
    Do other playmates visit the child? _____
    Does your child visit other playmates in their homes?
    _____
    How does your child relate to other children? _____
    Does your child prefer to play alone? _____ With other children? _____

## DIRECTOR'S RESOURCE 10-2 (continued)

Does your child worry a lot or is he/she very afraid of anything? _____

What causes worry or fear? _____

Does your child have any imaginary playmates? _____

Explain _____

Does your child have any pets? _____

What are your child's favorite toys and/or activities? _____

What is your child's favorite TV program? _____

How long does your child watch TV each day? _____

What are your child's favorite books? _____

How many times a week is your child read to? _____

Is there anything else about your child's play or playmates that the school should know? _____

V. Discipline

In most circumstances, do you consider your child easily managed, fairly easy to manage, or difficult to manage? _____

What concerns do you presently have about your child? _____

How are these concerns dealt with? _____

TeachSource Digital Download

## DIRECTOR'S RESOURCE 10-2 (continued)

VI. Parent's Impression and Attitudes

From your point of view, what were the events which seemed to have had the greatest impact on your child (moving, births, deaths, severe illness of family members, divorce)? _____

How would you describe your child at the present time? What changes have you seen in your child during the past year? _____

Does your child have any behavior characteristics which you hope will change? Please describe. _____

In what ways would you like to see your child develop during the school year?

_____
_____
_____
_____
_____
_____

_____
Signature(s) of person(s) filling out this questionnaire

## DIRECTOR'S RESOURCE 10-3

### SAMPLE POLICY SUMMARY FORM

**(For use with Try It Out! 10-2)**

**BOMBECK FAMILY LEARNING CENTER SUMMARY**

**OF POLICIES**

PLEASE SIGN AND RETURN THAT YOU HAVE RECEIVED AND READ THIS NOTICE. THANK YOU!!!!

_____

I have received and read the summary of Bombeck Family Learning Center polices.

Child(ren)'s name: _____

Parent Signature: _____

Date: _____

The following is a summary of some of the policies that impact daily life at the center. Complete information can be found in the Parent Handbook which we encourage you to read and keep on hand for reference. Please address questions or concerned to the director.

#### Attendance

A parent should notify the Center by 9:00 a.m. when a child will not be attending on a scheduled day. This procedure also applies to those children who attend half-day kindergarten.

## DIRECTOR'S RESOURCE 10-3 (continued)

#### Drop Off–Pick Up

Children must be brought to and picked up inside the child's classroom. A Child Release Form must be on file in the office for anyone other than a parent or guardian to pick up a child. Picture ID is required. Children may be dropped off at any time during the day except lunch and naptime.

#### Illness/Sick Policy

As a Center licensed by the State of Ohio, we are required to strictly follow procedures concerning communicable diseases to protect the children and staff at the Center. *The parent will be expected to pick up the child immediately if a child exhibits the following symptoms:*

Temperature of at least 100 degrees Fahrenheit – or less if accompanied by another symptom of illness

Two or more bouts of diarrhea

Severe coughing

Difficult or rapid breathing

Yellowish skin or eyes

Redness, discharge, burning, itching of the eye

Infected skin patches, spots or rashes

Dark urine or gray or white stool

Stiff neck with elevated temperature

Lice, scabies or other parasitic infestation

Vomiting one or more times, or if accompanied by another symptom of illness

## DIRECTOR'S RESOURCE 10-3 *(continued)*

The child or staff member will not be readmitted to the center until s/he is symptom free for a period of 24 hours, or until a physician's written permission verifies that there is no risk of contagion.

### Medications

"Administration of Medication by the Center Personnel" form must accompany any medication, prescription or over-the-counter drugs to be administered to a child. The child's name and specific times and dosage must be written on the form provided in the classroom each day. "As needed" is insufficient information.

Administration of medication by a person other than a center staff member and other than the parent, requires written permission signed by the parent. Name of the person, date, time and dosage should be included.

### Payment of Tuition

Tuition payments are to be paid one full week in advance. If payment is not received on time a *$25.00 late charge will be added to the balance.*

*Tuition payments and late charges not paid by the following week are cause for withdrawal of service by the center.*

### Late Pick Up Fees

A late fee will be charged for children left at the Center after 6:00 p.m. Late fees are charged as follows: (center clock used as basis). Calls ahead do not negate late charges.

## DIRECTOR'S RESOURCE 10-3 *(continued)*

6:01–6:30 – one dollar per minute 6:31 – on is five dollars per minute

### Back Up Plan

Please have a back-up plan in place for medical exclusions or emergency closings.

### Parent Participation, Visitors and Custody

Any custodial parent, custodian, or guardian of a child enrolled at the Center is welcome to visit at any time.

Visitors to the center are required to sign in and out of the building at the front desk.

When custody rights or visitation of a child has been determined by a court or other legal entity, a copy of the order must be provided to the Center.

### Medical Emergencies

The center's staff is trained in First Aid procedures. If a serious medical emergency should arise, a call to the University Public Safety Department would summon an emergency vehicle staffed with EMTs who would evaluate the situation and transport to an area hospital if necessary. Parents will be notified immediately and a staff member will stay with the child until parents arrive. The child's emergency transport, health and medical records will accompany them. A child safety seat is available if needed.

## DIRECTOR'S RESOURCE 10-3 *(continued)*

### Accidents

In case of accidents, a staff member will complete an incident report that is given to the parent on the day of the occurrence, which must be signed and returned to the teacher.

### Child Abuse

If any abuse or neglect is seen or suspected involving a child enrolled at the Bombeck Center, the situation must be reported to the Children's Services Board in the county in which the child resides.

### Discipline

Discipline is not punishment. If conflicts occur, staff members strive to help children find alternative modes of behavior and explain why inappropriate behavior is not acceptable. The Center strictly adheres to the discipline guidelines set forth by the Ohio child care Licensing Code.

### Emergency Closings

The Bombeck Center will make every effort to remain open in the event of inclement weather. However, if weather conditions warrant closing, the center will follow the University's directions for the closure. Please check your local television broadcast of school closing. Closing will also be posted on the Bombeck Center Facebook page.

## DIRECTOR'S RESOURCE 10-3 *(continued)*

### Vacations

Families are entitled to five vacation days annually. One week advance notice is requested. Vacation request forms may be picked up at the front desk

### Grievance Procedures

**In the event that a problem or complain should arise, the following are suggested procedures for resolution:**

It is strongly encouraged that the issue be resolved with the staff member involved. If the issue is not resolved at that level, the issue should be brought to the attention of the director, who will counsel with all individuals involved in order to resolve the issue in a positive way.

### Use of Videotapes and Photographs

The parent of every child enrolled at the Center must sign a "Permission to Videotape and Photograph Form." University students may be required to periodically videotape or photograph the children as they participate in classroom activities. The university photographer also takes photographs at the Bombeck Center.

*Source: Reprinted by permission of the Bombeck Family Learning Center of the University of Dayton.*

## DIRECTOR'S RESOURCE 10-4

### SAMPLE HOME VISIT/PARENT CONTACT REPORT

**(For use with Try It Out! 10-4)**

**Center** _____
**Type of Program** _____

1. Name of visitor _____ Title _____
2. Child's name _____
3. Parent or guardian _____
4. Address _____
5. Date and time of visit or meeting _____
6. Purpose of visit or meeting _____
   _____
   _____
7. Specific action taken as result of visit or meeting _____
   _____
   _____
   _____
   _____
   _____
   _____

## DIRECTOR'S RESOURCE 10-4 *(continued)*

8. Observations and comments _____
   _____
   _____
   _____
   _____
   _____

## DIRECTOR'S RESOURCE 10-5

### SAMPLE PERMISSION FORM

While your child is enrolled in this program, he/she will be involved in a number of special activities for which we need your permission. Please read the following information carefully. You are encouraged to ask questions about anything that is unclear to you. You, of course, have the option of withdrawing permission at any time.

_____
(Child's Name)
(Please circle your choice)

A. I DO   DO NOT give my permission for my child to go on walks with the classroom teacher and class in the nearby neighborhood.
B. I DO   DO NOT give my permission for my child to be screened for speech and language.
C. I DO   DO NOT give my permission for my child to be screened for hearing.
D. I DO   DO NOT give my permission for my child to be screened for specific educational needs.
E. From time to time photographs of our preschool program will be made for educational and publicity purposes. These pictures will be representative of the enriching experiences offered your child during the year.

I DO   DO NOT give my permission for my child to be photographed for use in educational, nonprofit publications/presentations intended to further the cause of public education. This permission is applicable for current as well as future project use.

## DIRECTOR'S RESOURCE 10-5 *(continued)*

As part of this program, your child's records may be included in research that evaluates the value of the program. In all cases, the confidentiality of individual children's records is maintained.

_____
Parent's Signature

_____
Date

## DIRECTOR'S RESOURCE 10-6

### SAMPLE CHILD CARE APPLICATION (REQUESTING INCOME INFORMATION)

For office use only

District Status: _____

Income Status: _____

Priority Status: _____

Date Application Received: _____

Date Eligible for Entrance: _____

Enrollment Age: _____

Child's Name: _____ Date of Birth: _____

Sex: _____

Race, Nationality, or Ethnic Group: _____

Address: _____ Phone: _____

Mother's Name: _____ Date of Birth: _____

SS # _____

Father's Name: _____ Date of Birth: _____

SS # _____

Child lives with _____

Children attend the center-based program four (4) half days per week; they eat lunch and snack at the center. Transportation is provided for handicapped or special needs children.

Do you wish to apply for the center-based program? Yes _____ No

Session preferred A.M. _____ 8:45–11:45

P.M. _____ 12:45–3:45

Children and families in the home-based program are visited once per week in the home and are transported to the center on

## DIRECTOR'S RESOURCE 10-6 (continued)

Friday for a group experience. The home-based teacher will assist parents in creating a home environment to promote children's growth and development. This program is in the morning only.

Do you wish to apply for the home-based program? Yes _____ No _____

\* \* \* \* \* \* \* \* \* \* \* \* \* \* \* \* \* \* \* \* \* \* \* \* \* \* \* \* \* \* \* \* \* \* \* \* \* \* \* \* \* \* \* \* \* \* \* \* \* \* \* \* \* \* \*

Family Size: _____

Family Income:

$ _____ per week $ _____ per month $ _____ per year

Source of Reimbursement or Services (Circle "Yes" or "No" for each source)

| | | | |
|---|---|---|---|
| YES | NO | EPSDT/Medicaid (Latest certification #): | ___ |
| YES | NO | Federal, State, or Local Agency: | ___ |
| YES | NO | In-Kind Provider: | ___ |
| YES | NO | Insurance: | ___ |
| | | I.D. #: | ___ |
| YES | NO | WIC | |
| YES | NO | Food Stamps | |

Does this child or any of your family members have a disability or special need?

Describe: _____

How well does your child speak and understand English? _____

How did you obtain information about this program? _____

## DIRECTOR'S RESOURCE 10-7

### SAMPLE APPLICATION (NO INCOME INFORMATION REQUESTED)

Walnut Corner Children's Center Preregistration Form

**CHILD'S FAMILY INFORMATION**

Child's Name _____ Name Used _____

Date of Birth, or Expected Date of Birth _____

Child's Address _____

Father/Guardian Name _____ Mother/Guardian Name _____

Home Address _____ Home Address _____

Employer _____ Employer _____

Address _____ Address _____

Business Phone _____ Business Phone _____

**REQUESTED DAYS OF ATTENDANCE**

Days: M  T  W  TH  F  Hours: _____ AM _____ PM

Requested Start Date: _____

**HOW DID YOU LEARN ABOUT WALNUT CORNER CHILDREN'S CENTER?**

Personal Referral/If so, who? _____

Newspaper _____  Radio _____  Website _____  Other _____

Thank you for this information

## DIRECTOR'S RESOURCE 10-7 (continued)

PLEASE INCLUDE THE NONREFUNDABLE $25 REGISTRATION FEE WITH THIS FORM.

THIS FEE WILL SECURE YOUR CHILD'S NAME ON OUR WAITING LIST.

## DIRECTOR'S RESOURCE 10-8

### SAMPLE STUDENT ENROLLMENT FORM

(*Public School–Sponsored Program*) STUDENT ENROLLMENT FORM
(MUST BE RETAINED IN STUDENT'S CUMULATIVE RECORD)

Assigned to: Gr _____ Hr _____
SDF sent to Census _____
Type a new CR _____
CR in office file _____
CR requested _____
Health Record Yes _____
No _____
Rec'd. 4-part SDF _____

Name of school student is entering_____ Grade Enter
_____ Special Ed _____
Name _____

Student's Legal Name (as listed on birth certificate)

Circle                    Circle
Sex:   Male   Female        Race:   Black   White   Other

Address _____ Apt. No. _____ ZIP Code _____ Phone No. _____

Place of birth _____ Date of birth _____
        City   State   Country            Mo   Day   Yr

## DIRECTOR'S RESOURCE 10-8 (continued)

Check one of the birth verifications listed below:
☐ Birth Certificate No. _____    ☐ Baptismal Certificate
_____
☐ Physician's Record                 ☐ Passport

| | DPT | Polio | Measles | Rubella | Mumps |
|---|---|---|---|---|---|
| IMMUNIZATION DATA | | | | | |

SOCIAL RECORD

| | Place of birth | | Deceased (Date) |
|---|---|---|---|
| **Name** | State | Country | |
| Father:_____ | | | |
| Mother: _____ | | | |
| Step-Parent:_ | | | |
| Guardian: _ | | | |

If family is supported by another source indicate: _____

| | Occupation | Place of Employment | Business Phone No. |
|---|---|---|---|
| Father's occupation ___ | | | |
| Mother's occupation ___ | | | |

## Director's Resource 10-8 (continued)

| Name of Brothers and Sisters: | Still in School: | |
|---|---|---|
| School Attendance | School or Preschool | |

Circle one:
FamilyStatus:   Married   Single   Divorced   Separated
                Remarried

Of parent:   Student is living with _____ Relationship_____

LANGUAGE OTHER THAN ENGLISH SPOKEN IN HOME: _____
Did student attend this school last year?

☐ Yes

☐ No  Name of school _____ Address _____

☐ Yes – Privacy Requested: If this box is checked, no information pertaining to this student will be released to any person or institution (including colleges or universities) without your written approval.

☐ No – Privacy is not requested

Parent/Guardian's Signature _____ Date: _____

In case of emergency, call _____
        Name          Relationship          Phone No

## DIRECTOR'S RESOURCE 10-9A

### PREENROLLMENT FORM OF CHILD DEVELOPMENT LEVELS

Demonstration School for
the School of Education
and Allied Professions
941 Alberta St.
Dayton, Ohio 45409
(937) 229-2158
http://www.udayton.edu/education/Bombeckcenter

**Child's Name:** _____**Today's Date:**_____
**Child's Date of Birth:**_____**Current Age:**_____**yrs.**
_____**mos.**
**Parent/Guardian filling out form:**_____
**Birth to 9 months: Security Stage**

Sensory Preferences: My child enjoys learning about his/her world **most** by: _____seeing _____hearing _____tasting _____smelling _____touching

Relationships:
    My child responds to others by:
_____gazing _____ making faces _____smiling _____making sounds _____other: _____

My child gets my attention by: _____

*Source: Developed by Diana Smith, Director of Program Development, University of Dayton, Bombeck Family Learning Center,   November 4, 2011.*

**DIRECTOR'S RESOURCE 10-9A** *(continued)*

_____crying _____gesturing _____holding on tight _____squealing _____other:

<u>Language:</u> My child's language development is shown by:
_____ smiling/gurgling when spoken to
_____ using different cries/sounds for different needs
_____ imitating sounds, rhythms, tones of adult talk
_____ playing games like peekaboo, pat-a-cake, etc.

<u>Movement:</u> My child's physical development is evidenced by:
_____ moving his/her arms, legs, and other body parts
_____ enjoying touching and being touched
_____ rolling over _____holding up his/her head _____ scooting/crawling _____ other: _____

<u>Emotions:</u> My child is generally:
_____ calm _____agitated _____fussy
_____ sensitive _____alert _____happy
_____ demanding

<u>Health:</u> My child has _____ no health issues _____ colds _____ allergies _____ fevers _____ other: _____

---

**DIRECTOR'S RESOURCE 10-9B**

**PREENROLLMENT FORM OF CHILD DEVELOPMENT LEVELS**

Demonstration School for
the School of Education
and Allied Professions
941 Alberta St.
Dayton, Ohio 45409
(937) 229-2158
http://www.udayton.edu/education/Bombeckcenter

**Child's Name:** _____ **Today's Date:** _____
**Child's Date of Birth:** _____ **Current Age:** _____ yrs. _____mos.
**Parent/Guardian filling out form:** _____
**8-18 months: Exploration Stage**

<u>Sensory Preferences:</u> My child enjoys learning about his/her world most by:
_____ seeing _____ hearing _____ tasting _____smelling _____touching

<u>Relationships:</u> My child responds to others by:
_____making sounds _____physically approaching /touching _____watching _____ imitating _____ other: _____
My child gets attention by:
_____squealing/crying _____touching /hitting _____ pinching/biting _____ watching/waiting _____other: _____

---

**DIRECTOR'S RESOURCE 10-9B** *(continued)*

<u>Language:</u> My child's language development is demonstrated by:
_____responding to his/her name, to directions, or to questions
_____expressing emotions through verbalizing
_____demonstrating an awareness of concepts of cause/effect, more/less
_____adding words to his/her vocabulary, imitating the tone and rhythm of adult speech
_____recognizing people and objects by name
_____demonstrating an interest in books and pictures

<u>Movement:</u> My child's physical development is evidenced by:
becoming mobile by _____ scooting _____ bouncing _____ crawling _____ cruising _____ walking _____ other: _____
_____standing or sitting _____going up or down ramps/steps _____bending over without falling
_____holding objects _____ pushing toys
_____ opening/closing items _____ using tools
_____ gesturing

<u>Emotions:</u> My child displays his/her emotion by:
_____ smiling/laughing _____ cuddling
_____ crying _____ tensing/screaming when angry _____ other: _____

<u>Health:</u> My child generally has:
_____ no health issues _____ colds _____ earaches _____ allergies _____ breathing problems _____ fevers _____ other: _____

---

**DIRECTOR'S RESOURCE 10-9C**

**PREENROLLMENT FORM OF CHILD DEVELOPMENT LEVELS**

Demonstration School for
the School of Education
and Allied Professions
941 Alberta St.
Dayton, Ohio 45409
(937) 229-2158
http://www.udayton.edu/education/Bombeckcenter

**Child's Name:** _____ **Today's Date:** _____
**Child's Date of Birth:** _____ **Current Age:** _____yrs. _____ mos.
**Parent/Guardian filling out form:** _____
**16 to 36 months: Toddlers – Independent Stage**

<u>Sensory Preferences:</u> My child enjoys learning about his/her world most by:
_____seeing _____hearing _____tasting _____smelling _____touching

<u>Relationships:</u> My child responds to others by:
_____communicating wants/needs _____asserting himself/herself _____ displaying empathy _____other: _____

My child gets attention by:

## DIRECTOR'S RESOURCE 10-9C *(continued)*

_____ asking    questions    _____ demanding
_____ cooperating    _____ physical    interaction
_____ other: _____

Language: My child's language development is demonstrated by:

_____ initiating conversations, back and forth discourse, conflict over "mine" or "no"

_____ repeating after others or reenacting series of events or daily adult tasks

_____ saying    single    words    _____    phrases
_____ sentences _____

_____ following directions, asking questions, naming objects, people, places

_____ demonstrating understanding of concepts of shape, size, color, type, other cognitive skills

_____ "telling" stories through play—with or without words

Movement: My child's physical development is evidenced by:

_____ walking _____ running _____ climbing
_____ jumping _____ stepping "over" _____ up and down stairs

_____ using small objects _____ using writing and art materials _____ pouring/serving food _____ other: _____

Emotions: My child displays emotional responses such as:

_____ empathy    _____ pride    in    accomplishment    _____ generosity    _____ comforting
_____ demanding _____ other: _____

## DIRECTOR'S RESOURCE 10-9C *(continued)*

Health: My child generally has:

_____ no health issues _____ cold/flu _____
earaches _____ allergies _____ asthma _____
fevers _____ other: _____

## DIRECTOR'S RESOURCE 10-9D

### PREENROLLMENT FORM OF CHILD DEVELOPMENT LEVELS

Demonstration School for
the School of Education
and Allied Professions
941 Alberta St.
Dayton, Ohio 45409
(937) 229-2158
http://www.udayton.edu/education/Bombeckcenter

Child's Name: _____ Today's Date: _____
Child's Date of Birth: _____ Current Age: _____ yrs.
_____ mos.
Parent/Guardian filling out form: _____
**3-5 years – Preschooler**

Physical Development: My child's physical activity includes:

_____ running _____ jumping _____ climbing _____ skipping _____ galloping _____ creative movement such as dancing

_____ coordinated movements _____ small muscle control _____ large muscle control _____ other: _____

Social/Emotional Development: My child displays the following behaviors:

_____ enjoys    learning    _____ develops    friends
_____ follows directions/rules _____ relates well to adults/peers

## DIRECTOR'S RESOURCE 10-9D *(continued)*

_____ emotional    awareness    _____ shares    easily
_____ takes turns _____ resolve conflicts without aggression

_____ develops conscience _____ copes with stress
_____ shows resilience to adversity _____ exhibits self-control

Cognitive Development: My child has the ability to:

_____ think about past/present/future

_____ reenact storylines accurately following sequence of events

_____ coordinate and assume roles during dramatic play

_____ organize thoughts into explanations, questions, and other categories

_____ use symbols to represent reality—i.e., pictures, words, numbers

_____ understand "pretend" and the difference between imaginary and real in most instances

_____ predict what will happen next with some accuracy

_____ solve problems through thoughtful reasoning with guidance

_____ express thoughts and feeling several ways (verbalizes, draws, sings, moves creatively)

Health: My child generally has:

_____ no health issues _____ cold/flu _____
earaches _____ allergies _____ asthma/breathing difficulty _____ fever

_____ within normal range of physical growth
_____ has regular check-ups _____ has received immunizations

*Developed by Diana Smith, Director of Program Development, University of Dayton, Bombeck Family Learning Center,  November 4, 2011.*
*Source: Reprinted by permission of the Bombeck Family Learning Center of the University of Dayton.*

## DIRECTOR'S RESOURCE 10-10

### SAMPLE CHILD'S MEDICAL STATEMENT

Enrollment Date _____

Day Care Center/Preschool Certificate of Medical Examination to Be Completed by Family Physician or Clinic

This is to certify that _____

Child's Name _____ Birth Date _____

Mother _____ Address _____ Phone _____

Father _____ Address _____ Phone _____

was examined by me on _____, and based on his/her medical history Date of Examination _____ and physical condition at the time of this examination, is free from apparent communicable disease, and is in suitable condition for enrollment in a child day care facility; and has had the immunizations required by Section 3313.671 of the Revised Code for admission to school, or has had the immunizations required by the State Department of Health for infants and toddlers, or is to be exempted from these requirements for medical reasons.

Tuberculin Test (within last year for new enrollee) Date _____

Type of test _____ Results _____

DPT Series and booster dates 1st _____ 2nd _____ 3rd _____ 4th _____ 5th _____

Oral Polio

Series dates 1st _____ 2nd _____ 3rd _____ 4th _____

The 5th DPT and 4th polio are normally administered just prior to kindergarten.

---

## DIRECTOR'S RESOURCE 10-10 (continued)

| Measles (Rubella, 10-day) | Date _____ | |
|---|---|---|
| Rubella (3-day) | Date _____ | |
| Mumps | Date _____ | |
| Haemophilus b Polysaccharide (HIB) | Date _____ | (HIB vaccine is required for children ages 2 years through 4 years) |

Is able to participate in all regular activities except _____

Remarks _____

Physician's Signature _____ Date _____

Clinic Name _____ Phone _____

Office Location _____

City, State, ZIP _____

Parent should retain this sheet when child withdraws from center.

---

## DIRECTOR'S RESOURCE 10-11

### SAMPLE EMERGENCY INFORMATION RECORD

Child's Name _____

Home Address _____

_____

Father's name/Husband _____ Place of Employment _____ Bus. Phone _____

(or guardian) _____

Mother's name/Wife Place of Employment _____ Bus. Phone _____

(or guardian) _____

Please fill in information below so that the school may act more effectively in event of illness or injury to the child.

EMERGENCY: Person to be called if parent (husband or wife) cannot be reached:

Name _____ Address _____ Phone _____

Date _____ Parent's Signature (or guardian) _____

---

## DIRECTOR'S RESOURCE 10-12

### CHILD RELEASE FORM

To maintain the safety and protection of your child, please provide us with a complete list of persons who may pick up your child or children from the center. Anyone other than the parent should sign in at the front desk. The staff will ask for picture identification before releasing the child(ren).

Child's name: _____ Classroom: _____

Child's name: _____ Classroom: _____

Child's name: _____ Classroom: _____

Child's name: _____ Classroom: _____

The following individuals have my permission to pick up the child(ren) listed above from the Bombeck Family Learning Center:

Name: _____ Relationship: _____

Name: _____ Relationship: _____

Name: _____ Relationship: _____

Name: _____ Relationship: _____

I have instructed these individuals to sign in at the front desk and be prepared to present picture identification when requesting release of the child(ren). Questions or concerns should be directed to me at the following phone numbers:

Work: _____ Home: _____ Cell: _____

If efforts to reach me should fail, please call the following person to verify permission to pick up my child(ren):

Name: _____ Relationship: _____

Parent Signature: _____ Date: _____

*Source: Reprinted by permission of the Bombeck Family Learning Center of the University of Dayton.*

© Cengage Learning®

# REFERENCES

Allen, K. E., & Cowdery, G. E. (2011). *The exceptional child: Inclusion in early childhood education* (6th ed.). Clifton Park, NY: Thomson Delmar Learning.

ADA Amendments Act of 2008, Public Law 110–325, 122 Stat. 3553 (2008).

Freeman, N. K., Decker, C. A., & Decker, J. R. (2012). *Planning and administering early childhood programs* (10th ed.). Upper Saddle River, NJ: Prentice Hall.

Dinnebeil, L. A., & McInerney, W. F. (2011). *A guide to itinerant early childhood special education services*. Baltimore, MD: Brookes.

Family Educational Rights and Privacy Act (Buckley Amendment). (1974). The 1974 Education Amendments, 20 U.S.C.A., Sec 1232g. (Supp. 1975).

Feeney, S., & Freeman, N. (n.d.). *Ethics and the early childhood educator: Using the NAEYC Code of Ethics, Section ll.* Washington, DC: NAEYC.

Gonzalez-Mena, J., & Widmeyer Eyer, D. (2011). *Infants, toddlers and caregivers: A curriculum of respectful, responsive, relationship-based care and education* (9th ed.). New York: McGraw-Hill.

Katz, L. G., & Chard, S. C. (2000). *Engaging children's minds: The project approach* (2nd ed.). Stamford, CN: Ablex.

National Association for the Education of Young Children. (2013). *NAEYC Early Childhood Program Standards and Accreditation Criteria & Guidance for Assessment.* Washington, DC: Author.

Taylor, B. (2002). *Early childhood program management: People and procedures.* Columbus, OH: Merrill.

U.S. Department of Justice (n.d). Commonly asked questions about child care centers and the Americans with Disabilities Act. Retrieved from http://www.ada.gov/childq%26a .htm.

# 11 SUPPORTING QUALITY CURRICULUM

*Program administrators support curriculum so that enriching experiences are woven throughout every child's day.*

## Learning Objectives

After reading this chapter, you should be able to:

**11-1** Describe quality early childhood curriculum.

**11-2** Explain the importance of teacher feedback, support, and intervention.

**11-3** Describe how to support intentional teaching.

**11-4** Identify strategies that support a seamless birth to age 8 early childhood system.

## Standards Addressed in this Chapter

Accreditation Standards 2 – Curriculum

Accreditation Standards – 3 Teaching

Accreditation Standards – 4 Assessment

Accreditation Standards – 9 Physical Environment

Administrator Competencies – Management Knowledge and Skills 4, 8

Administrator Competencies – Early Childhood Knowledge and Skills 2, 3, 4, 9

Professional Preparation Standard 1 – Promoting Child Development and Learning

Professional Preparation Standard 3 – Observing, Documenting, and Assessing to Support Young Children and Families

Professional Preparation Standard 4 – Using Developmentally Effective Approaches

Professional Preparation Standard 5 – Using Content Knowledge to Build Meaningful Curriculum

Professional Preparation Standard 6 – Becoming a Professional

For the director and educational leader of an early childhood program, decisions about curriculum are among the most difficult to make. The increasing national focus on the importance of the early years for brain development, school readiness, and sound emotional development provides both opportunities for the field and pressure to make informed decisions for the director and staff (Denton, Flanagan, & McPhee, 2009; Dickinson & Porche, 2011; Education Commission of the States, 2009; Kagan & Kauerz, 2007; Klein & Knitzer, 2006; Yoshikawa et al., 2013). Public awareness of the importance of quality early care and education is growing. Understanding the many factors that constitute quality and impact today's curriculum decisions is a monumental task for the director, who must understand developmentally appropriate practices, early learning content standards, accountability, appropriate assessment, school readiness, achievement gaps, and teaching children in poverty, children with disabilities, and children who are English-language learners. Not only do young children require an experience-rich environment, but it is now apparent that children who lack key experiences are more likely to start kindergarten without the fundamental knowledge and skills necessary for school success (Preschool Curriculum Evaluation Research Consortium, 2008). With this in mind, the director must be the "curriculum mentor" who embraces the challenge of leading a program that meets the needs of the whole child while also sorting through societal pressures that challenge the traditional notions of early childhood curriculum. (In some larger programs, the director may share the role of curriculum mentor with a curriculum specialist.)

As the educational leader of an early childhood program, the director needs to be aware of curriculum requirements that constitute a quality program and that support the center's mission. The director must monitor the richness and appropriateness of the curriculum and serve as a curriculum mentor for teachers who need a forum for critical reflection and feedback as well as support and resources. The director is responsible for ensuring that all teachers in the center know that everyone is accountable for offering a high-quality program each and every day. The curriculum should be part of the center's culture, which means that it reflects the culture of the children and families who use the center and its programs and is also informed by the culture of the professionals who design and implement it. By being part of the center's culture, high-quality curriculum should be apparent to all who enter the center and see children's work samples and documentation on the walls. Evidence of the importance placed on curriculum should be apparent when teachers talk in the break room, during staff meetings, and most definitely during dedicated planning time. Parents should see evidence of curriculum in the parent handbook and should hear about it informally during drop-off and pick-up transition times and more formally during the centers' open house events and parent conferences. The importance placed on curriculum should also be evident on the center's website and Facebook page, where parents and other stakeholders can get daily updates, including the curriculum in action.

By meeting regularly with teaching teams to discuss the curriculum that is evolving in each classroom, the director and the curriculum specialist, if applicable, clearly articulate the importance placed on curriculum quality.

These meetings help to establish a climate in which staff reflect critically on their practice, and center leaders come to understand the decisions that teachers make and the resources and support that they need. As a curriculum mentor, the director works with staff to establish curricular expectations and to ensure that teachers feel valued for their quality curriculum contributions. The director also needs to be aware of areas of weakness or lack of follow-through so that teaching teams in need of curriculum intervention are given the support and oversight needed to improve.

## DIRECTOR'S CORNER

"We are an NAEYC Accredited center and have earned the highest level on our state's quality rating system. Of all of the indicators of quality that parents and visitors see when they enter our building, our curriculum which reflects our mission is what they comment on most. Part of our mission is to demonstrate high-quality science and inquiry experiences with young children. This emphasis on science transforms our environment and is obvious to all who enter the building."

—*Director of a university-affiliated demonstration school*

## ▶❙❙ TeachSource Video Vignette

Signs Of Good Child Care

▶ A Caring Relationship

▶ Discipline That Teaches

▶ Good Adult-Child Ratio

### The Quality of Child Care

In this video, Ellen Galinsky, from the Families and Work Institute, describes the findings of three research studies related to early care and education. She discusses the characteristics of high-quality child care and the warning signs parents should look out for.

View the video vignette entitled, *The Quality of Child Care*. Reflect on the following questions:

1. As a director, what factors should you consider to ensure quality programming for the young children in your care?

2. How might you use this information to communicate the benefits of a quality program for the children?

## 11-1 QUALITY EARLY CHILDHOOD CURRICULUM

The focus on "quality" early childhood programs includes a curriculum that reflects a strong understanding of the philosophical underpinnings of the field, a comprehensive definition of curriculum, and a well-grounded understanding of developmentally appropriate practices.

### 11-1a Philosophical Underpinnings

Although some may see selecting a curriculum as the purchase of commercially prepared activities and assessment, quality programs see curriculum as an extension of the theory base that represents beliefs about children and families. Time needs to be taken to discuss how teacher beliefs represent the theory base for the field and also align with the mission, vision, and purpose of the center. Taking the time to establish a shared understanding of the program's educational philosophy means that practice will be consistent and intentional. This common understanding should not be left to chance, and the failure to take the time to have these conversations will likely result in a curriculum that reflects the beliefs and practices of individual teachers and not a cohesive reflection of the program's mission and vision.

### 11-1b Defining Curriculum

To establish a culture that embraces high-quality curriculum, communicates curriculum to others, and participates in curriculum reflection and mentoring, there must be a common understanding of what is meant by *curriculum*. Kostelnik, Soderman, and Whiren (2010) define curriculum as "all the organized educational experiences provided for children by the early childhood program [that] take place inside the classroom or beyond, involving educators, family members, and other people in the community" (p. 226). Others go beyond experiences for children and include program content as well as training and supervision of staff so that they can implement high-quality programs, and also include evaluations that assess program effectiveness (Epstein, Schweinhart, & McAdoo, 1996). While the field uses a variety of definitions of curriculum, a literature review conducted by Grisham-Brown, Hemmeter, and Pretti-Frontczak (2005) revealed that "many consider a curriculum to be a comprehensive guide for instruction that is composed of several elements, including assessment, content, and teaching methods" (p. 19). For the context of this book, a comprehensive definition of curriculum will be used and will include the following:

- well-informed understanding of what to teach as defined by children's interests, developmental skill

expectations, and early learning content standards/guidelines

- the incorporation of developmentally appropriate methods that support learning and development

- the use of effective assessment strategies that inform instruction, document child progress, and provide data for continuous program improvement

- careful staging of the environment (in the classroom, in the building, and on the grounds), which, when carefully planned, inspires children to learn and provides opportunities for development

- thoughtful selection of authentic materials that make learning meaningful and that facilitate development

- the implementation of professional development that enhances the teachers' ability to work with children and families to construct high-quality curriculum

- opportunities for curriculum mentoring that support critical reflection, quality curriculum, and intentional teaching

The importance of a quality and developmentally appropriate curriculum is evident; however, the reality is that for many, the term *curriculum* refers to a commercially produced book that is adopted by the program to satisfy a regulation or mandate. Moving the curriculum from a book on the shelf to an integral and visible component of the program's culture requires staff buy-in and strong educational leadership.

### 11-1c Developmentally Appropriate Curriculum

For a program to maintain a developmentally appropriate curriculum, the director needs to be aware of, understand, and be able to articulate the positions established by early childhood professional organizations. Keeping up-to-date with position statements and standards provides evidence of a commitment to the profession. One important document related to early childhood curriculum is the joint position statement on *Early Childhood Curriculum, Assessment, and Program Evaluation* developed by NAEYC and the National Association of Early Childhood Specialists in State Departments of Education (NAECS/SDE) (2003). The guidelines presented in this statement are considered to be necessary components of an early childhood program that provides developmentally appropriate and long-lasting benefits to the children attending the program (see Figure 11-1). NAEYC and NAECS/SDE present developmentally appropriate and effective curriculum as a *shared responsibility* between policy makers, early childhood professionals, and others who share in the care and enrichment of the lives of young children. Key components of this position statement include a comprehensive system of curriculum,

**Figure 11-1** Essential Findings in Child Development Research

In its Summary of Essential Findings, the Center for the Developing Child at Harvard University found the following:

- Early experiences determine whether a child's developing brain architecture provides a strong or weak foundation for all future learning, behavior, and health.

- Young children who grow up in homes with high incomes and high parent education levels have more than twice the expressive vocabulary at age 3 compared to children raised in homes characterized by low socioeconomic status.

- The basic principles of neuroscience tell us that providing the right conditions for healthy development in early childhood is likely to be more effective than treating problems at a later age.

- It is possible to improve a wide range of outcomes for vulnerable children well into the adult years, as well as generate benefits to society far in excess of program costs.

*Source: National Forum on Early Childhood Program Evaluation & National Scientific Council on the Developing Child, 2007.*

**Figure 11-2** Evidence of an Effective Curriculum

NAEYC Program Standards and Accreditation Criteria Standard 2: Curriculum

**Program Standard:** The program implements a curriculum that is consistent with its goals for children and promotes learning and development in each of the following areas: social, emotional, physical, language, and cognitive.

**Rationale:** A curriculum that draws on research assists teachers in identifying important concepts and skills as well as effective methods for fostering children's learning and development. When informed by teachers' knowledge of individual children, a well-articulated curriculum guides teachers so they can provide children with experiences that foster growth across a broad range of developmental and content areas. A curriculum also helps ensure that the teacher is intentional in planning a daily schedule that (a) maximizes children's learning through effective use of time, materials used for play, self-initiated learning, and creative expression, as well as (b) offers opportunities for children to learn individually and in groups according to their developmental needs and interests. (NAEYC, 2008, p. 1)

*Source: From NAEYC, NAEYC Early Childhood Program Standard and Accreditation Criteria: The Mark of Quality in Early Childhood Education, (Washington, DC: NAEYC, 2008), 9.*

assessment, and program evaluation based on sound early childhood practices, effective early learning standards, and a core belief in values, ethical behavior, and support for children and families (see Figure 11-2). Curriculum is to be "thoughtfully planned, challenging, engaging, developmentally appropriate, culturally and linguistically responsive, comprehensive, and likely to promote positive outcomes for all young children" (2003, p. 1). Indicators of an effective curriculum include evidence of the following:

- Curriculum is comprehensive.

- Children are active and engaged.

- Goals are clear and shared by all.

- Curriculum is evidence-based.

- Valued content is learned through investigation, play, and focused, intentional teaching.

- Curriculum builds on prior learning and experience.

- Professional standards validate the curriculum's subject-matter content.

- Curriculum is likely to benefit children. (NAEYC, 2003, p. 2)

Another important document that the informed early childhood director should be well versed in is the NAEYC Program Standards and Accreditation Criteria (2008).

This set of standards demonstrates the evolving priority that the field places on curriculum and is the standard that directors should strive to achieve.

This standard is effective in negating the "either/or" perspectives on curriculum that many in the field have practiced as the call for more accountability has become more prominent. The standard moves the conversation from, "Should curriculum for young children be child-centered and play-based *or* should it focus on content standards?" to "How can children be exposed to early learning content standards within the context of a child-centered and play-based curriculum?" This standard encourages a "both/and" dialog such as, "It is possible to be intentional in our planning and also rely on an emergent curriculum that follows the child's lead." The role of the director is to facilitate ongoing "both/and" conversation about how this standard can be implemented in each and every classroom. Each classroom will demonstrate this standard in its own unique way as the curriculum must reflect the individual children in the room, the culture of their families, and the personalities and teaching styles of the teaching staff. This means that the director must provide opportunities for discussion of and reflection on classroom curriculum.

# 11-2 ESTABLISHING OPPORTUNITIES FOR FEEDBACK, SUPPORT, AND INTERVENTION

As the educational leader of an early childhood program, the director must be able to provide valuable and informed feedback that reflects an understanding of what developmentally appropriate and quality practice for young children looks like. Some directors rely on formal tools such as the Early Child Environment Rating Scale-Revised (ECERS-R) and the Infant/Toddler Environment Rating Scale, Revised Updated Edition (ITERS-R), which can evaluate the quality of such aspects of the classroom as space and furnishings, personal care routines, support for language and reasoning, as well as the quality of activities, interactions, and more (Harms, Clifford, & Cryer, 2006). Another tool that is well regarded for assessing high-quality teacher-child interaction is the Classroom Assessment Scoring System (CLASS) (Pianta, La Paro, & Hamre, 2008). The CLASS assesses emotional support, classroom organization, and instructional support, and it offers insight into important but sometimes difficult-to-measure qualities of teaching such as active and engaged learning and concept development. Results from both the ECERS-R/ITERS-R and the CLASS can serve as impartial data that can inform teaching goals. In addition to relying on formal tools, directors also need to consider the following as clues to quality as they are observing their staff and providing feedback.

*This child-centered classroom is investigating how bridges are built. While all of the children are investigating the topic, they are encouraged to explore an aspect of the topic that most interests them. This child is interested in how much load different types of supports can hold and is stacking blocks on a variety of columns. The children in the background have chosen to work together to explore different types of bridge-building materials.*

## 11-2a Is the Classroom Curriculum Child-Centered?

"Child-centered practice" has been synonymous with quality for many early childhood professionals. However, the meaning of the phrase is not conclusive, as more than 40 definitions have appeared in the literature, starting with Froebel in 1778 (Chung and Walsh, 2000; Tzuo, 2007). The term, in one of its simplest interpretations, encourages a curriculum that focuses on the child's interests. It is often contrasted with teacher-directed approaches that give the control for content and selection of materials and activities to the teacher. In reality, the notion of child-centeredness is complex but should "attempt to balance the requirements of building a secure, socially responsive environment in which all individual and group interests are respected, and attention to progress in the acquisition of academic skills" (Tzuo, 2007, p. 34.).

In a child-centered classroom, the director should note the classroom's emotional climate, as children whose needs are not being met often become disengaged, emotionally distraught, and/or disruptive. A child-centered classroom can include some large group and even teacher-directed activities, but it also needs to include opportunities for children to make choices, play and learn in small groups or individually, and be active in experiences that support developmental skills across all domains (motor, social, emotional, cognitive, language, and aesthetic) and academic content. When mentoring a teacher, it is important for the director to look for evidence that all of the developmental domains are being addressed. The children must be given opportunities for large-motor activity every day, preferably outdoors whenever weather permits, and for artistic expression as part of a comprehensive program that supports all developmental domains and academic content areas.

## 11-2b What Is the Role of the Adult in the Classroom?

If a child-centered approach is favored in your curriculum, the director's approach may be to encourage teachers to let children solve their own problems and be responsible for their own achievements. However, Honig (2010) suggests there are times when a bit of teacher intervention may be just the right thing to do:

> Children can accomplish some tasks on their own after trying hard. Others are too easy or too difficult. Children get restless and bored when toys or tasks are too easy. They feel frustrated when tasks are too challenging. The Russian child-development theorist Vygotsky taught that teachers are priceless in supporting child learning and accomplishment when a task is just a bit too difficult at the child's present level of development. Then a teaching adult provides just that bit of help that will result in further child learning and satisfaction. Vygotsky used the term "zone of proximal development" for the

### Young Children's Stages of Play: An Illustrated Guide

This video provides a description of play as the medium through which young children learn. An overview of the stages of play is presented with examples of real children engaging in play at each stage.

View the video vignette entitled, *Young Children's Stages of Play: An Illustrated Guide.* Reflect on the following questions:

**1.** As director, what will you look for in a toddler classroom that suggests play is being adequately supported? What kinds of materials and equipment should be available? How should the adults in the room be supporting play?

**2.** Now consider an observation of a preschool classroom. What will you look for in a toddler classroom that suggests play is being adequately supported? What kinds of materials and equipment should be available? How should the adults in the room be supporting play?

difference between what a child can do on his or her own compared with what the child can do with adult help. With the assistance of an adult, a child will be able to succeed at a cognitive or social learning task beyond what he or she could have accomplished alone (p. 47).

## 11-2c How Does the Teacher Communicate the Use of Play to Support Learning and Development?

Early childhood educators typically understand the importance of play as a vehicle for learning in young children. People outside the field, including many parents, often miss the connection between play and learning and, unless its importance is explained proactively and consistently, may question its value. One role of the director can be to help teachers be proactive and explain and

*Taking the time to listen to children is the basis for high-quality teacher-child interaction. Children can read the listener's face to see if they are being heard.*

document what children are learning. Directors should find ways to help teachers articulate their practice so that the information flow becomes an automatic part of what teachers do, allowing others to understand the learning that is occurring in their classroom.

One reason that some teachers have difficulty explaining what children learn during play is that many use free play as a time to do other things; many are not involved in children's play. While play is an ideal time for children

*The children in this picture are engaged in dramatic play around a bike-washing service on the center's playground. They are developing oral communication skills while also learning the purpose of money when providing their service to other children who brought their bikes to school for the day. The teacher is enhancing their play by asking them how they might attract more customers. She will chart each child's response in order to document their ability to answer questions and solve problems.*

to practice evolving skills that can be enhanced with the support of an adult, many teachers use free choice or play time to attend to housekeeping, paperwork, or other classroom organization duties. Additionally, some teachers are not accomplished in supporting play and do not understand how to augment play without dominating it. Directors can help teachers understand how to become participant observers who support language, concept development, and social development through play. They can also learn to use play as a vehicle for assessing and documenting learning and development.

### 11-2d Is the Curriculum Emergent?

Emergent curriculum has been considered a hallmark of quality in early childhood programs. It is, for many teachers, a difficult concept to understand, and it frequently challenges the teacher who is inclined to plan well in advance to meet his or her need for control. To facilitate instruction that follows the children's lead and incorporates their interests, the director can ask teachers how the children and their interests were included in instructional decisions. Some teachers cite the need to focus on content standards as a reason not to use an emergent curriculum framework. The director

*This teacher is taking advantage of a teachable moment in which children showed an interest in the difference between a stick, a branch, and a tree. Because this teacher has collected data on what the children know and are able to do related to content standards, she knows that she can easily incorporate the standards into an extended investigation of trees.*

needs to facilitate a "both/and" paradigm shift and point out that it is possible to create a child-directed and emergent curriculum that addresses content standards. Specifics about how this can be done are explained in more detail in the following section.

### 11-2e How Does the Teacher Plan and Integrate Curriculum?

While the NAEYC identifies an integrated curriculum as a preferred practice, many early childhood professionals struggle with how to plan connected and meaningful experiences for young children. The new NAEYC Position Statement (2009) identifies as good practice that "[t]eachers make meaningful connections a priority in the learning experiences they provide children, to reflect that all learners, and certainly young children, learn best when the concepts, language, and skills they encounter are related to something they know and care about, and when the new learnings are themselves interconnected in meaningful, coherent ways." This standard includes the following element: "Teachers plan curriculum experiences that integrate children's learning *within* and *across* the domains (physical, social, emotional, cognitive) and the disciplines (including language, literacy, mathematics, social studies, science, art, music, physical education, and health)" (NAEYC, 2009, p. 21). It is clear that an integrated curriculum is identified as good practice, but how can the director support teachers who are uncomfortable with this process?

The director can be instrumental in supporting teachers in the planning process by establishing expectations for connected curriculum and by working with teachers to develop a planning system that supports integration. One easy strategy that can have a huge impact on the types of curriculum created is the lesson planning form that is adopted by a program. Consider the form that is currently used: Does it support the notion of interconnected and meaningful curriculum? Or does it represent a perceived need to keep children busy? Consider the lesson planning format shown in Figure 11-3.

This form represents the type of planning that is very common in many early childhood classrooms. Directors will very often collect such lesson plans weekly and review them. For some teachers, the lesson-planning process is perfunctory, with the goal being to fill the boxes communicating that the children in their classroom will be busy and, perhaps, even engaged. The director often tends to review these plans at a cursory level, looking to see that all of the boxes are filled. Now take a closer look at the types of experiences that a child might encounter in a given day by examining Figure 11-4. Note that the items with an asterisk are strategies or programs listed on the USDE *What Works Clearinghouse* list of programs that have been shown to improve reading or math skills in young children (IES What Works Clearinghouse, n.d.). Imagine that

**Figure 11-3** Fill the Week Lesson Planning Format—Blank

| | | Monday | Tuesday | Wednesday | Thursday | Friday |
|---|---|---|---|---|---|---|
| **Morning Meeting/ Circle Time** | | | | | | |
| **Free Play/Center Time** | Art | | | | | |
| | Blocks | | | | | |
| | Housekeeping/ Dramatic Play | | | | | |
| | Science | | | | | |
| | Math/ Manipulatives | | | | | |
| | Writing | | | | | |
| | Computer | | | | | |
| **Snack** | | | | | | |
| **Gross Motor/ Play Ground** | | | | | | |
| **Closing** | | | | | | |

*Source: © Cengage Learning, 2013.*

TeachSource Digital Download

you are a child in this program, and consider your experience for each of the days as planned. Even though you, as the child, are able to experience these research-based strategies, what are your thoughts on the continuity of the day? Do you see any connection between one activity and the next? Do you understand why you are engaged in the activity? Are you asked to engage in inquiry or study a topic in depth?

As director, it is imperative that you understand the complexity of planning curriculum for young children. Your role is to push planning beyond the surface level—a mere clerical activity. Effective directors guide teachers into reflective and intentional planning that connects learning

in deep and meaningful ways. As our society continues to be invested in research-based, research-supported, and evidence-based practice, it is important to understand the curriculum as a whole and maintain your vision for the complete program.

**REFLECTION**

Think about yourself as a director and curriculum mentor to the teacher who created the plans in Figure 11-4. How would you support this teacher to create more connected and inquiry-based experiences for young children?

**Figure 11-4** Fill the Week Lesson Planning Format—Completed

| | | Monday | Tuesday | Wednesday | Thursday | Friday |
|---|---|---|---|---|---|---|
| **Morning Meeting/ Circle Time** | | Dialogic picture book reading* | Dialogic picture book reading* | Dialogic picture book reading* | Dialogic picture book reading* | Dialogic picture book reading* |
| **Free Play/Center Time** | Art | Finger painting | Found object collage | Watercolor markers | Pudding painting | Tempera at the easel |
| | Blocks | Add farm animals to the blocks this week | | | | |
| | Housekeeping/ Dramatic Play | Kitchen with pretend food this week | | | | |
| | Science | Aquarium observations | Sensory table | Plant seeds | Water the seeds | Water the seeds |
| | Math/ Manipulatives | SRA real math activity* | Geoshapes | SRA real math activity* | Puzzles | SRA real math activity* |
| | Writing | Phonemic awareness* the letter g | Phonemic awareness* the letter h | Phonemic awareness* the letter i | Phonemic awareness* the letter j | Phonemic awareness* the letter k |
| | Computer | Headsprout early reading* | SRA real math* | Headsprout early reading* | SRA real math* | Headsprout early reading* |
| **Snack** | | Goldfish and juice or milk | Apple chunks and juice or milk | Pretzel sticks and juice or milk | Mini muffins and juice or milk | Cheese chunks and juice or milk |
| **Gross Motor/ Play Ground** | | Outside play or obstacle course in the gym | Outside play or trikes in the gym | Outside play or balls in the gym | Outside play or parachute in the gym | Outside play or trikes in the gym |
| **Closing** | | Sing goodbye song | Sing goodbye song | Sing goodbye song | Sing goodbye song | Sing goodbye song |

*Included in the USDE *What Works Clearinghouse* list of programs that have been shown to improve reading or math skills.

*Source: © Cengage Learning, 2013.*

Planning webs are a way to assist teachers in integrated planning. It has become common for teachers to identify a curriculum goal as the basis for integration. In Figure 11-5, note how the curriculum goal "To become familiar with shapes" has been used to connect the experiences throughout the day. This planning strategy places great value on having children learn a discrete skill. The children experiencing this plan are likely to have a more cohesive and meaningful day and, depending on the quality of the experiences, are likely to learn the skill.

Another planning process shifts away from "skill-centered" planning and toward planning focused around "in-depth investigations of various topics—ideally, topics worthy of the children's time and energy" (Katz & Chard, 1998, p. 1). Eliason and Jenkins (2008) describe a variety of planning webs that focus on themes, units, concepts, projects, or extended investigations, and they identify the following as helpful steps for web-based planning:

1. Identify a theme and related subtopics.

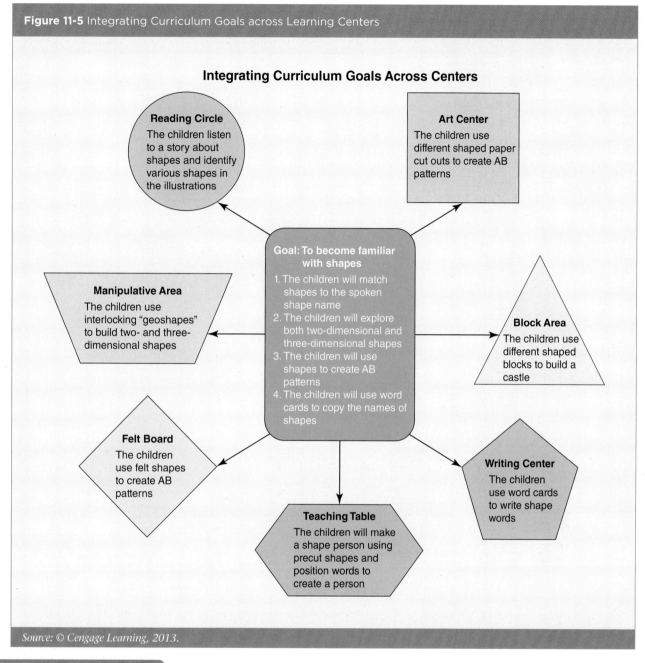

Integrating Curriculum Goals Across Centers

**Reading Circle**
The children listen to a story about shapes and identify various shapes in the illustrations

**Art Center**
The children use different shaped paper cut outs to create AB patterns

**Manipulative Area**
The children use interlocking "geoshapes" to build two- and three-dimensional shapes

**Goal: To become familiar with shapes**
1. The children will match shapes to the spoken shape name
2. The children will explore both two-dimensional and three-dimensional shapes
3. The children will use shapes to create AB patterns
4. The children will use word cards to copy the names of shapes

**Block Area**
The children use different shaped blocks to build a castle

**Felt Board**
The children use felt shapes to create AB patterns

**Teaching Table**
The children will make a shape person using precut shapes and position words to create a person

**Writing Center**
The children use word cards to write shape words

Source: © Cengage Learning, 2013.

TeachSource Digital Download

2. Brainstorm.

3. Identify desired learning outcomes.

4. Prepare for teaching. (Eliason & Jenkins, 2008, p. 82)

Extended investigations are the basis of such early childhood approaches as the Reggio Emilia Approach developed by Loris Malaguzzi and the Project Approach created by Lilian Katz and Sylvia Chard. Inspired by the work of Malaguzzi, Katz, and Chard, the *ACCESS to Science Concept Planner* (Figure 11-6) was developed to facilitate in-depth concept development through the investigations of science topics (Adams, Baldwin, Comingore, & Kelly, 2013; Baldwin, Adams, & Kelly, 2009).

In contrast to many web-based planning strategies that focus on a theme, unit, or topic and culminate in a topic-related literacy lesson, a math lesson, an art activity, or another discipline specific lesson, the *ACCESS to Science Concept Planner* generates experiences that lead to deep understanding of concepts related to the science topic. Content-area skills are incorporated into the experiences in authentic ways that give the skills a purposeful context. When children see how discrete skills can help them understand or document an investigation, they tend to be more motivated to learn new skills.

To complete the planning process using the *ACCESS to Science Concept Planner*, teachers identify a science topic

**Figure 11-6** *ACCESS to Science Concept Planner*

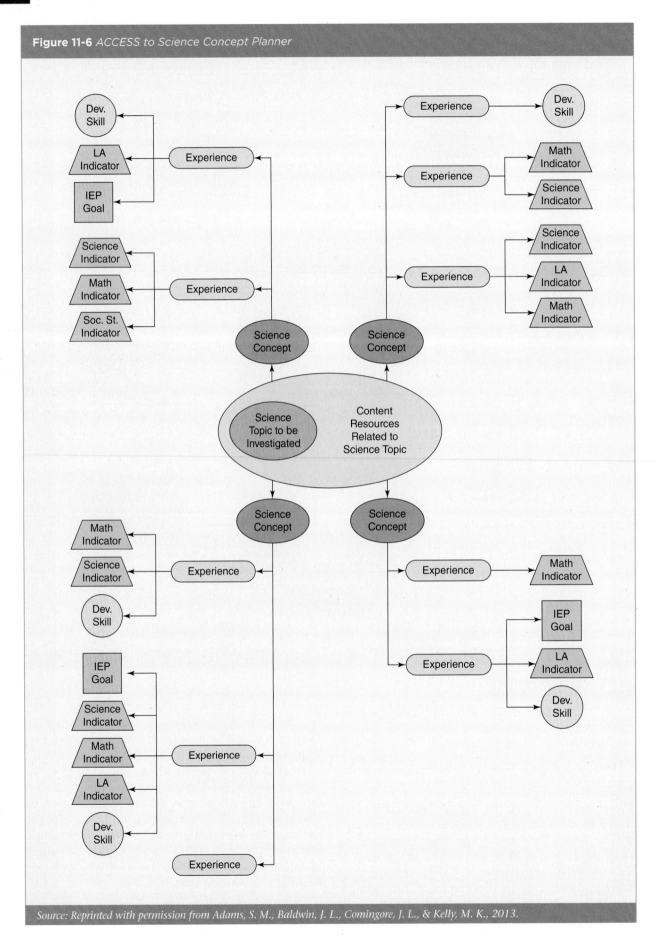

*Source: Reprinted with permission from Adams, S. M., Baldwin, J. L., Comingore, J. L., & Kelly, M. K., 2013.*

that is worthy of study and that reflects the children's interests. The quality of the investigation is dependent, in part, on the teacher's content knowledge related to the investigation. This is not to say that teachers should only teach what they know; rather, teachers need to be lifelong learners who seek out new information about the topics to be investigated. One goal of the *ACCESS to Science Concept Planner* is for teachers to develop in-depth understanding of science content related to the topic of study so they can plan experiences that lead to a deeper understanding by the children. In contrast to the planning web in Figure 11-5, in which the activities are focused on a discrete skill, the *ACCESS to Science Concept Planner* provides opportunities for inquiry, depth of understanding, and a context for the discrete skills that children are learning. Connected and meaningful learning is also a goal of the planning method,

*Integration that is centered on an important topic can bring meaning to content areas while supporting developmental domains. This investigation of ants grew out of the children's fascination with an anthill on the playground. The investigation inspired children to count, problem-solve, and re-create the ants' habitat. This group of children asked the teacher to include ant-related words in the habitat so that they could write them when they recorded their observations in their science journals.*

### ▶❚❚ TeachSource Video Vignette

### Exploring Math Concepts through Creative Activities: Integrated Curriculum in Early Childhood

This video shows how a series of lessons were integrated around the curriculum goal, "The children will become familiar with shapes." The lessons included whole group direct instruction and center-based, small-group experiences designed to teach discrete skills related to shapes. View the video vignette entitled, *Exploring Math Concepts through Creative Activities: Integrated Curriculum in Early Childhood.* Reflect on the following questions:

1. The teacher tells us there is a language of spatial relations that children learn best "if there is a visual attached to the word." This teacher is very intentional in her planning and can articulate her purpose well. As a curriculum mentor, what processes can you put into place so that other teachers can be intentional planners who can explain why they do what they do?

2. How well did the lessons that this teacher planned teach the curriculum goal and lesson objectives? Explain why.

3. How well did the lessons make the material connected and meaningful? Explain your answer.

4. How well did the lessons support inquiry?

which illustrates for teachers how it is possible to accomplish the following:

- Focus on interesting topics.

- Identify the important concepts needed to understand the science topic.

- Design experiences that allow children to explore, investigate, and understand the concepts deeply.

- Identify how those experiences support developmental skills, and address early learning content standards (indicators) and individualized education plan (IEP) goals in meaningful and connected ways.

Examine the planning progression in Figure 11-6 from the central science topic outward to the concepts, and then the experiences. Notice how the experiences are designed to support the science concepts but also support meaningful and connected integration, as math and science indicators might be emphasized in one experience while art, science, and language arts might be included in another. Now consider Figure 11-7, in which the central unifying science topic is obscured; with the *Fill the Week* planning method, it is possible to address academic content standards, developmental skills, and IEP goals without a unifying topic of study. The result is a series of unrelated or disconnected experiences in which children are left to determine the relevance of what they are learning. Directors may find these figures to be useful training tools as they guide their staff toward deeper and more meaningful curriculum development.

**Figure 11-7** *ACCESS to Science Concept Planner* with Topic Covered

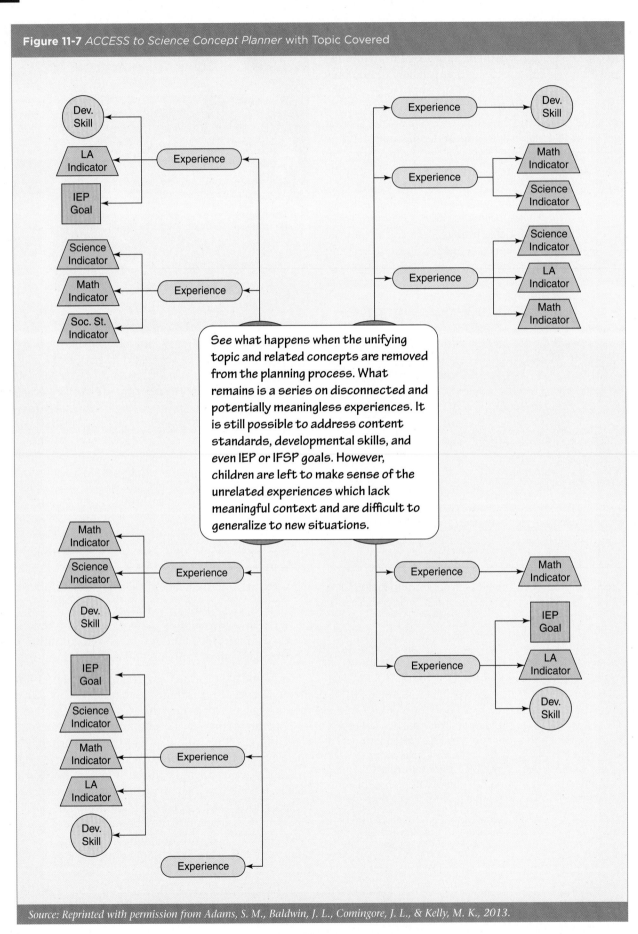

See what happens when the unifying topic and related concepts are removed from the planning process. What remains is a series on disconnected and potentially meaningless experiences. It is still possible to address content standards, developmental skills, and even IEP or IFSP goals. However, children are left to make sense of the unrelated experiences which lack meaningful context and are difficult to generalize to new situations.

*Source: Reprinted with permission from Adams, S. M., Baldwin, J. L., Comingore, J. L., & Kelly, M. K., 2013.*

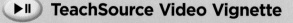

**The Reggio Emilia Approach**

This video describes the Italian approach to early childhood education known as Reggio Emilia, which focuses on the organization of the physical environment, child-directed activities, opportunities for creative thinking, and collaborative problem solving. View the video vignette entitled, *The Reggio Emilia Approach*, and reflect on the following questions:

**1.** How does the Reggio Emilia Approach facilitate integrated curriculum and inquiry?

**2.** What is the role of the physical environment in the Reggio Emilia Approach?

**3.** How well does this approach translate to programs outside of Italy?

## 11-2f How Are Early Learning and Development Standards Implemented?

As of 2010, all states have developed or are in the process of developing early learning content standards (also known as early learning guidelines) for preschool children, and 30 have adopted guidelines for infants and toddlers (National Child Care Information and Technical Assistance Center, 2011). Early learning content standards are new to some early childhood educators and may appear to contradict the child-centered practice and emergent curriculum model that has been preferred practice in the field. Many early childhood teachers struggle with the notion of how to blend systematic instruction of content with NAEYC's 12 Principles of Learning and Teaching (NAEYC, 2009).

One common concern about content standards for young children is the potential for academic content to be taught inappropriately. Working together to address this concern and clarify the purpose of content standards for young children, the NAEYC and the NAECE/SDE developed a joint position statement stating that early learning content standards must align with K-12 standards in a very "careful" manner. This means that early learning standards are to be developed in an age-appropriate manner, giving emphasis to all domains of early development and learning. Likewise, content standards are to be "mean-

ingful and important to children's current well-being and later learning" (NAEYC & NAECS/SDE, 2002, p. 2).

The role of the director in addressing content standards in the curriculum is to work with teachers to establish a planning process that includes standards but does not allow standards to be taught as a series of disconnected activities. Content standards should not drive the curriculum, but they must be addressed in connected, accurate, and meaningful ways. It is also important for teachers to have an understanding of the content represented in content standards. Directors need to provide opportunities for the staff to gain current professional knowledge in literacy, mathematics, science, and social studies in addition to development and appropriate teaching strategies. It is no longer acceptable for children to learn inaccurate content because teachers only know the myths associated with Thanksgiving, or they still think Pluto is a planet because they haven't had any exposure to science content since high school.

Directors need to have a big-picture view of curriculum and understand that developmentally appropriate content standards can be taught within the context of a wide variety of projects, units, or themes. This reality allows for emergent curriculum. It is also important to note that within an emergent curriculum model, it is common for teachers to gravitate to projects, units, or themes that interest them. Because of this, some project topics, units, or themes are often overused. For example, many teachers include the study of butterflies, dinosaurs, apples, leaves, and pumpkins in their curriculum. It is quite possible for young children to study these topics every year from the age of 2 through the primary grades. Teachers are less likely to focus on topics related to earth or physical science, in part, because they are unfamiliar with or intimidated by the content. The director needs to encourage a more comprehensive curriculum that pushes teachers to learn new content so that they can provide enriching experiences for children (see Figure 11-8).

**Figure 11-8**

Several children were engaged in an investigation of race cars and the physics that makes them go faster or farther down an inclined plane. The teacher provided the children with ramp-making materials, small toy race cars, and a variety of measuring tools. Up until this point, the children had shown little interest in learning about measurement using blocks, cubes, and other nonstandard units of measurement considered to be appropriate for preschoolers. After racing their cars down the ramps for a while, the children decided that they wanted to keep track of the distance that the cars traveled. They constructed a long measuring tool and sought out a pencil and paper so that they could record the distances after each race. This experience provided a context and purpose for measurement and a reason to learn to write numbers.

© Cengage Learning®

## 11-2g How Does the Program Facilitate the Development of Language and Emergent Literacy Skills?

The role of the early childhood program as a vehicle to reform education in the United States has altered the way that language development and emergent literacy is viewed for children from birth through age 5. Research-based literacy instruction has been identified as a means of reducing the achievement gap between children from the middle and upper socioeconomic classes and those who are raised in poverty. After the National Early Literacy Panel (NELP) reported that "conventional reading and writing skills that are developed in the years from birth to age 5 have a clear and consistently strong relationship with later conventional literacy skills" (2008, p. vii), national reform dialogue focused in on literacy instruction for young children. What does this mean for the director who must advocate for appropriate practice for young children, address the concerns of worried parents, and deal with the forces from outside the field that are pushing for more accountability related to systematic literacy instruction? Today's director must address the needs of multiple stakeholders while still keeping the needs of the children front and center. The research review conducted by NELP has impacted what is considered to be best practice for young children, and teachers must be aware of the panel's findings. Directors should ensure that teachers are aware of the research on emergent literacy and also provide their staff with a forum to discuss how best to infuse research-supported practice into a developmentally appropriate curriculum.

The National Early Literacy Panel has identified several core competencies as having a consistently strong relationship with later conventional literacy skills: Many early childhood professionals who are well grounded in developmentally appropriate, child-centered, and play-based curriculum may review these competencies with intense reservation (see Figure 11-9). There is a very real possibility that inappropriate and potentially harmful practice could be developed to address these skills. Children face long-term harm when they lack experiences that support the development of these skills. The role of the director is to make sure the staff is well grounded in both the early literacy research and developmentally appropriate practice so that curriculum can be developed that infuses these skills in age-appropriate, meaningful, and connected ways. Directors should also be watchful for teachers who see these skills as typical for older children and who might thus be inclined to use instructional strategies that are common in the primary grades. Set the expectation that curriculum in the program will honor the age of the child and support a system that encourages critical reflection and problem solving so that the skills identified in Figure 11-9 are included in the curriculum in developmentally appropriate ways.

The NELP's list of competencies that have a moderate relationship to long-term literacy acquisition includes skills

**Figure 11-9** Early Literacy Skills with a Strong Relationship to Later Literacy Skills

- alphabet knowledge (AK): knowledge of the names and sounds associated with printed letters

- phonological awareness (PA): the ability to detect, manipulate, or analyze the auditory aspects of spoken language (including the ability to distinguish or segment words, syllables, or phonemes), independent of meaning

- rapid automatic naming (RAN) of letters or digits: the ability to rapidly name a sequence of random letters or digits

- RAN of objects or colors: the ability to rapidly name a sequence of repeating random sets of pictures of objects (e.g., "car," "tree," "house," "man") or colors

- writing or writing name: the ability to write letters in isolation on request or to write one's own name

- phonological memory: the ability to remember spoken information for a short period of time

*Source: National Early Literacy Panel, 2008, p. vii.*

**Figure 11-10** Early Literacy Skills with a Moderately Strong Relationship to Later Literacy

- concepts about print: knowledge of print conventions (e.g., left–right, front–back) and concepts (book cover, author, text)

- print knowledge: a combination of elements of AK, concepts about print, and early decoding

- reading readiness: usually a combination of AK, concepts of print, vocabulary, memory, and PA

- oral language: the ability to produce or comprehend spoken language, including vocabulary and grammar

- visual processing: the ability to match or discriminate visually presented symbols

*Source: National Early Literacy Panel, 2008, p. viii.*

that may be more comfortable for teachers of young children (see Figure 11-10). These broader skills are common in print-rich early childhood environments, which tend to emphasize oral language, including vocabulary development, matching, and book handling skills. A comprehensive language and emergent literacy component of a complete early childhood curriculum establishes a purpose for literacy. When observing in a classroom, the director can note how print is used. For example, is there a purpose for print where the teacher has decided to label and name everything in the room? Children begin to understand that there is a purpose for print when they use a picture label on a shelf to decide where to put a toy. When everything in the room is labeled (i.e., door, table, chair), however, it communicates that the purpose of print is to label. Are the environment and experiences set up so that children understand how writing can help them to record, remember, track, and communicate? The teaching staff needs to be aware of the literacy research but also needs feedback and support so that they have a purposeful print-rich environment in which literacy has context and meaning.

### 11-2h How Do Teachers Support Math, Science, and Inquiry in the Classroom?

Science, Technology, Engineering, and Math (STEM) has emerged as an important concept and acronym in the educational reform movement. While STEM may be relatively new, theorists such as Jean Piaget and Constance Kamii have a long history of exploring mathematical concepts with young children. The importance and appropriateness of mathematics for young children was further validated in the National Mathematics Advisory Panel (NMP) report, which found that "most children acquire considerable knowledge of numbers and other aspects of mathematics before they enter kindergarten. This is important because the mathematical knowledge that kindergartners bring to school is related to their mathematics learning for years thereafter—in elementary school, middle school, and even high school. Unfortunately, most children from low-income backgrounds enter school with far less knowledge than peers from middle-income backgrounds, and the achievement gap in mathematical knowledge progressively widens throughout their PreK–12 years" (2008, p. 18). Like the NELP report, the NMP report highlights the importance of experience with academic competencies as an important factor in later learning and in reducing the achievement gap.

The release of national reports such as the NMP report has impacted policy recommendations for both math and science. The National Institute for Early Education Research (NIEER) Preschool Policy Brief on Math and Science made the following policy recommendations:

- Mathematics and science should be treated as essential components of a comprehensive, high-quality preschool program, not as extras.

- Policy makers must be certain that curricula, learning standards, and teaching expectations for early mathematics and science are research based and must outline expectations that are attainable and appropriate for preschool learners.

- Early education policies should define mathematics as more than counting and numbers, and science should be treated as more than learning lists of facts.

- Preservice and in-service educators need improved preparation to understand math and science content

*Children are more likely to choose to write when the purpose is clear. This child is fascinated by the investigation of seeds in which his class is engaged. Using attractive nonfiction books has inspired him to keep track of his own seed collection by locating the seed and "writing" its name in his science journal.*

and to provide experiences integrating this content into their teaching practice.

- Appropriate accountability systems that focus on the classroom, the teacher, and the child must be built to support high-quality early mathematics and science education.

- Mathematics and science learning should be integrated with each other and with other content domains. (Brenneman, Stevenson-Boyd, & Frede, 2009, p. 1)

This policy statement emphasizes the need for the director to oversee the quality of science and math experiences but also encourages the meaningful integration of science and math. It is important for teachers to be aware of these policy recommendations, which should be considered as part of the program's professional development plan.

### 11-2i What Is the Role of Technology in This Classroom?

"The push to integrate technology into **naeyc** early childhood settings can lead to inappropriate use of technology" (Cruikshank, 2010). While there are appropriate ways to include the use of technology in developmentally appropriate programs for young children, there has been a reluctance on the part of many who fear that the passive use of technology will replace active play and high-quality, play-based interactions between children and/or adults. Educators who are grounded in child development theory and developmentally appropriate practices, and are technologically and media literate have the knowledge, skills, and experience to select and use technology and digital media that are appropriate for the ages and developmental levels of the children in their care, and they know when and how to integrate technology into the program effectively. Educators who lack technological and media literacy are at risk of making inappropriate choices and using technology with young children in inappropriate ways that can negatively impact children's learning and development (National Association for the Education of Young Children & Fred Rogers Center for Early Learning and Children's

Media at Saint Vincent College, 2012). Because of the impact of what is being called the "digital divide" on children in poverty, it is no longer an option for early childhood professionals to be uninformed about the use of developmentally appropriate technology with young children (see Figure 11-11). Children who have access to technology tools and the Internet at home are more likely to have highly developed technology skills at an early age. Children who lack these experiences, commonly because of limited financial resources, start school behind their peers (Becker, 2000; Burdette & Whitaker, 2005; Calvert et al., 2005). Directors should remind teachers about the important role they play in ensuring equity by providing access to developmentally appropriate technology for all children (Judge, Puckett, & Cabok, 2004). The director also needs to find opportunities for teachers to develop technology skills and reflect on how technology might be incorporated in meaningful ways.

---

**Figure 11-11** Technology Recommendations for Classroom Practice

### Infants and Toddlers

During the earliest years, infants and toddlers need interactions primarily with human beings. They need to freely explore, manipulate, and test everything in the environment. Increasingly in today's world, this includes the exploration of digital technology and interactive media. Children of this age are drawn to button sand cause-effect toys. Technology tools that infants and toddlers might use must be safe, sturdy, and not easily damaged. Just as toddlers tend to chew on their books, children under 2 are very likely to chew on technology tools.

- Allow children to explore digital materials in the context of human interactions, with an adult as mediator and coplayer. As with shared book reading, use shared technology time as an opportunity to talk with children, use new vocabulary, and model appropriate use.

- Avoid passive screen time. Although many parents claim that baby videos calm an otherwise fussy child, there is little research to suggest that infants and toddlers learn from watching videos. If they are distressed, they need the comfort of a caring adult, not an electronic toy.

- Provide children with toy representations of digital objects to encourage toddlers to begin pretending about the ways in which others use technology: cell phones, cameras, laptops, CD players, and so on.

### Preschool and Kindergarten

During the preschool years, young children are developing a sense of initiative and creativity. They are curious about the world around them and curious about learning. They are exploring their ability to create and communicate using a variety of media (crayons, felt-tipped markers, paints and other art materials, blocks, dramatic play materials, miniature life figures) and through creative movement, singing, dancing, and using their bodies to represent ideas and experiences. Digital technologies provide one more outlet for demonstrating their creativity and learning.

- Freely explore touch screens loaded with a wide variety of developmentally appropriate interactive media experiences that are well designed and enhance feelings of success.

- Begin to explore and feel comfortable using "traditional" mouse and keyboard computers for using Flash-based websites or looking up answers with a search engine.

- Capture photos of block buildings or artwork that children have created; videotape dramatic play and replay for children to view.

- Celebrate children's accomplishments with digital media displayed on a digital projector or on a classroom website.

- Record children's stories about their drawings or their play; make digital audio files for documentation of progress.

*Source: From NAEYC, "Technology and Interactive Media as Tools in Early Childhood Programs Serving Children from Birth through Age 8." Position Statement. Washington, DC: NAEYC.*

# 11-3 SUPPORTING INTENTIONAL TEACHING

The director can be informed by the policies, position statements, and research reports that  have been highlighted thus far in this chapter, but creating an environment where teachers use this information to inform their practice requires structures that support intentional teaching. "Intentional teaching means teachers act with specific outcomes or goals in mind for children's development and learning. Teachers must know when to use a given strategy to accommodate the different ways that individual children learn and the specific content they are learning" (Epstein, 2007, p. 1). Intentional teaching requires that teaching teams have time for reflection and planning and that assessment is an integral part of instructional decision making. Directors can establish ground rules that support a climate where it is safe to express opinions in respectful ways. They will need to be creative in how they develop a center schedule so time exists for teachers to plan as a team. The program should have an established assessment system with the expectation that documentation will be collected, recorded, and used to make instructional decisions, track the progress of individual children, and inform program evaluation.

## 11-3a Time for Planning and Critical Reflection

### ▶❙❙ TeachSource Video Vignette

**Curriculum Planning: Implementing Developmentally Appropriate Practice in an Early Childhood Setting**

The video case reveals how excellent curriculum planning must be based on developmentally appropriate practice; be inclusive and integrated; highlight play; and take cues from the children. You'll see all these principles implemented in an early childhood center, as Ke Nguyen and her colleagues plan activities and interact with the children. You'll also see the children engage in teacher-initiated and child-initiated activities, and learn together in small and large groups.

View the video vignette entitled, *Curriculum Planning: Implementing Developmentally Appropriate Practice in an Early Childhood Setting*, and reflect on the following questions:

1. How does the center director define developmentally appropriate practice?

2. Ke, the lead teacher, tells us that her teaching team meets regularly to discuss developmentally appropriate practices and related curriculum development. Describe the dialogue that takes place during Ke's team meeting that suggests the team is responding to the developmental needs of at least one child.

---

## Working Smart with Technology

### Working Smart with Technology

*Effective Use of Technology with Young Children*

When supporting teachers to consider how best to use technology, encourage them to rely on the same decision-making process used when identifying developmentally appropriate practices. They should use knowledge of children's interests, what engages them, and also what they need to know and be able to do. The learning and development standards need to be considered along with family culture. Using the developmentally appropriate practice decision-making framework helps teachers use technology to enhance existing curriculum.

Although not every experience can be enhanced with technology, teachers should think critically about the goals they have for the students or the experiences to decide what will work best and whether technology can enrich the experience and deepen the children's understanding.

Help teachers understand that when they are planning to include technology devices in the classroom, they should be intentional in their planning. Ask them about their purpose for technology use. Too often, teachers provide access to technology without an intended purpose. The computer station becomes a way to fill the children's time but may not be used intentionally to enhance the curriculum. The director's role as educational leader and curriculum mentor can help teachers use technology effectively.

*While the time at a computer should be limited and the software carefully selected, the computer can support focused collaboration and inquiry.*

*Peer observation is a valuable practice for both the teacher being observed and the peers who are observing. Ideas can be shared between classrooms, and teachers have an opportunity to articulate their practice.*

## 11-3b Intentional Teaching in the Daily Routine

Planning is an important component of intentional teaching. Teachers are often much more enthusiastic about planning big projects and special celebrations than they are with establishing daily routines that constitute a significant portion of the program. Daily routines can serve as excellent vehicles for teaching with a purpose. Consider something as ordinary and mundane as the daily sign-in procedure. One teaching team noted that persistent upheaval occurred each morning when parents were trying to sign in with children clinging to their legs. Several children expressed an interest in being able to "sign-in" on the same chart as the parents. The teachers met to reflect on this situation. They referred to the early learning content standards and related assessment data and determined that, while the children were at various stages on the emergent writing continuum, most, if not all, of the children could benefit from a station where they could "sign in" while their parents signed in. Not only did this practice ease transition time strife, but it also provided a purposeful opportunity for children to write their name at least once every day. Periodically, teachers collected and documented work samples, which showed the progression of skills that started with mark-making and advanced over time until all children were able to print their name using uppercase and lowercase letters. As director, be on the lookout for examples such as the one just described and find a place to showcase examples that demonstrate intentional teaching.

## 11-3c Time for Planning, Sharing, and Critical Reflection

Consider a profession in which teams of adults are expected to work together to implement a complex and coordinated program with a very unpredictable client group whose education, health, and safety is dependent on the team's ability to know what each other is thinking from across the room. Now consider that the team has little or no time to plan together in order to develop a common understanding of the goals of a lesson or educational philosophy for the classroom. This scenario is all too common in early childhood classrooms, where the budget is so tight that paying two or three teachers to plan is incredibly difficult to manage. An early childhood teaching team without planning time is like an orchestra without practice time.

### MAKING THE CASE FOR *CURRICULUM MENTORS*

With all that a director has to do to manage the operations of the center, it may be tempting to view the curriculum as the responsibility of the teaching staff. The importance of a rich and engaging curriculum cannot be overstated, and quality experiences require teachers to be intentional in their planning. The curriculum mentor can serve as a support to teaching teams who benefit from reflecting on their practice. This role can be served by the director or by another person whose leadership is acknowledged by the staff. Each teaching team should meet with the curriculum mentor at least monthly to share their planning process, reflect on how the curriculum is being implemented, and identify where they are going next. Teaching teams work better when they have a shared understanding of what is happening in the classroom. By establishing the routine of meeting with a curriculum mentor regularly, teaching teams come to understand that intentional decision making about curriculum is valued (Frede & Ackerman, 2007). Additionally, the curriculum mentor can come to understand the strengths and needs of the teaching teams so that support, resources, and professional development can be provided as needed.

It does not matter how talented the musicians are: Notes will be missed, the timing will be off, and the audience will be left unimpressed. Teams who plan together are able to brainstorm and plan in a way that allows the talents of the individuals to emerge. Classroom tasks can be chosen by team members who have the skill and enjoy the task in contrast to being assigned based on some institutional hierarchy. Directors must find and support team planning time and, in order to encourage the best use of this time, must help teams establish models for respectful interaction and critical reflection as well as a team decision-making process that encourages open communication.

## 11-3d Assessment Supported versus Assessment Driven

Assessment data is an important tool for teachers who are engaged in intentional teaching and is considered to be an essential component of a quality curriculum. While the NAEYC and NAECS/SDE recommendations state that quality curriculum is dependent on appropriate assessment to support instructional decisions, assessment of content and development in early childhood settings is an emerging practice for the field (Meisels, 2004; Meisels et al., 2002). Assessment techniques that are used with older students are not valid or reliable for preschoolers. Additionally, many experienced early childhood educators are unfamiliar with assessment strategies that are appropriate for young children. An important role of the director is to help teachers make sense of assessment and how it can be used and managed in their classroom. It is not enough to require that teachers collect assessment data and documentation for their children; a system must be in place that helps teachers collect meaningful data and organize it in way that is useful and that informs instruction. Many teachers are committed to data collection and have found ways to observe children and note their progress. The challenge becomes what to do with all of the work samples, anecdotal records, post-it notes, and portfolios that accumulate in piles around the classroom. Many teachers struggle with how to pull data together in a way that allows them to make instructional decisions for a class or track the progress of an individual child.

Methods for collecting data often represent a combination of program requirements and teacher preference. If teachers are given the freedom to design a method of collecting data that works for them, then they are more likely to follow through and make the system work. The director needs to make teachers aware of the required components of the program's assessment system while also communicating where teachers have freedom to design their own strategies. The director also needs to make sure that intentional planning informed by ongoing assessment is part of the curriculum culture of the center. The expectation for data collection needs to be clear, and teachers need to know that their assessment efforts will be discussed during curriculum mentoring sessions.

*Meals and snacks can be planned with intentionality. This teacher knows that toddlers need opportunities to develop independence. The teacher has provided a small pitcher partially filled with milk and a much larger cup in order to increase the child's ability to pour his own milk with success. Staging the environment in this manner involves reflective, insightful, and intentional planning as well as a sound understanding of what the child is able to do.*

*This preschool teacher worked with her team to plan naturally occurring and meaningful ways for children to recognize their name and the names of the other children in the class. After a while, the placemats will be moved, motivating children to identify who they get to sit next to at the next meal.*

*Team planning time is essential for teachers to brainstorm ideas, develop a planning web, share resources, and establish a common understanding of the children and the curriculum.*

Figure 11-12 represents the assessment system developed by the Bombeck Family Learning Center of the University of Dayton. The teachers and leadership at this center worked with early childhood faculty to develop a tracking system that allows teachers to record the data collected through a variety of teacher-determined assessment strategies. The curriculum mentor works with teachers to ensure that they have an understanding of appropriate and unbiased ways of documenting what children know and are able to do. After the teachers understand sound assessment practices and are aware of a wide array of tools and strategies that they can use to collect data, they are allowed to develop an assessment plan that works for their teaching team. The teachers determine who will collect data, when the data will be collected, and what tools will be used, realizing that a variety of tools will be necessary. Each teaching team shares its assessment plan and is held accountable for follow-through. It is important for the director to understand how teachers have chosen to assess children so that he or she can ensure that assessment is completed in an ongoing and sufficient fashion. By expecting teachers to compile their assessment data onto the ACCESS Classroom Tracking Sheet (ACTS) and to bring an up-to-date ACTS to all curriculum planning sessions, teachers are held accountable for implementing their assessment system and for using data to make instructional decisions. While there is a program-wide assessment system in place, teachers determine the data collection methods that work best for them.

**Figure 11-12** ACCESS Assessment Funnel

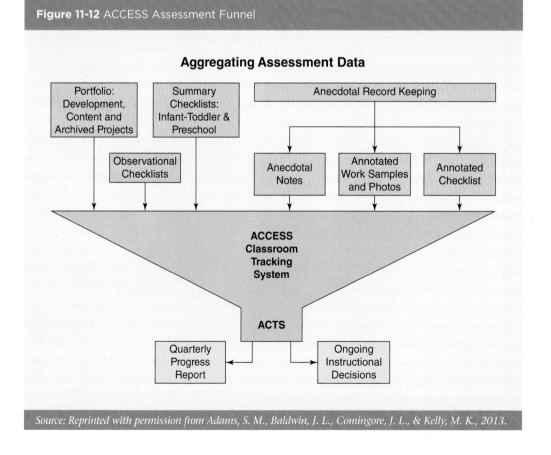

*Source: Reprinted with permission from Adams, S. M., Baldwin, J. L., Coningore, J. L., & Kelly, M. K., 2013.*

## Developing an Assessment System

One of the director's responsibilities is to work with staff to develop and oversee an assessment system that provides strategies to support teachers as they make decisions about children's learning in order to meet their current developmental needs and, in turn, to lay the foundation for their success in K-12 schools while maintaining developmentally appropriate classrooms that rely on play and other child-directed instructional techniques (Meisels et al., 2001). Additionally, assessment is to be an integral component of the curriculum, with results used to guide teaching, identify concerns for individual children, and provide information to improve and guide interventions if needed. Assessment methods to be used are those that are "developmentally appropriate, culturally and linguistically responsive, tied to children's daily activities, supported by professional development, and inclusive of families" (NAEYC, 2003, p. 2). Indicators of effectiveness for assessment systems include the following:

- Ethical principles guide assessment practices.

- Assessment instruments are used for their intended purposes.

- Assessments are appropriate for ages and other characteristics of children being assessed.

- Assessment instruments are in compliance with professional criteria for quality.

- What is assessed is developmentally and educationally significant.

- Assessments use multiple sources of evidence gathered over time.

- Use of individually administered, norm-referenced tests is limited.

- Assessment evidence is used to understand and improve learning.

- Assessment evidence is gathered from realistic settings and situations that reflect children's actual performance.

- Screening is always linked to follow-up.

- Staff and families are knowledgeable about assessment.

## 11-4 SUPPORTING A SEAMLESS BIRTH THROUGH AGE 8 SYSTEM

Early childhood educators agree that an emergent, play-based, child-directed, and constructivist approach is preferred practice (Copple & Bredecamp, 2009; National Association for the Education of Young Children & National Association for Early Childhood Specialists at State Departments of Education, 2002). However, the recent results of a multistate study of prekindergarten classrooms make it clear that 48 percent of children experience

### ▶❚❚ TeachSource Video Vignette

**Progress Monitoring: Using Transitional Time in an Early Childhood Classroom**

The teacher in this video demonstrates how, through intentional planning, she can collect data to document the progress of the children in her class. View the video vignette entitled, *Progress Monitoring: Using Transitional Time in an Early Childhood Classroom.* Watch how the teacher engages the children as they prepare to transition to the next experience in the day, and reflect on the following questions:

1. Click on the "artifacts" button and examine the "Progress Monitoring Form." List the three curriculum goals on which the teacher is gathering data. How many children met their goals and how many did not? How might the data that she has collected inform her instructional decisions?

2. Note that this teacher is using the form a little differently than it was intended. How was the form supposed to be used, and how did the teacher adapt it? Was this appropriate? Why or why not?

moderate to serious problems in making a successful transition into kindergarten (National Center for Early Development & Learning, 2005; Clifford et al., 2005; Pianta et al., 2008). There is often a poor fit between the skills of incoming kindergarteners and the expectations of their teachers. Additionally, there has been no common definition of kindergarten readiness, meaning that preschool teachers are often preparing children to meet standards that vary greatly from school district to school district, from school to school, and, in some instances, from teacher to teacher. In the past, it was common for early care and education to exist in a separate silo from K-12 schooling. This separation leads to misperceptions and a lack of understanding of what programs for younger children accomplish and what kindergarten and primary grades programs expect.

Pianta and Kraft-Sayre (2003) note the importance of effective kindergarten transition practices that are enhanced by a seamless system of early childhood for children ages birth through third grade. Directors of programs for young children need to understand their role in this system and act accordingly. Looking for opportunities to reach out to the kindergarten teachers and principals of the schools that receive your children is important. One effort that can provide for this process is the 2009 *Linking Ready Kids to Ready Schools* policy brief that represents the commitment of the governors of five states. Funded by the W. K. Kellogg Foundation and the Education Commission of the States, this effort calls for a mind shift toward a seamless birth to third grade system and also provides supports for center directors and K-12 principals and teachers who want to establish these connections.

---

### DIRECTOR'S CORNER

"Like many other communities, our county's children and families are subject to a void of communication between preschool and kindergarten. There is no common definition of kindergarten readiness, and the methods used to screen readiness are varied and inconsistent. My teachers dreaded the time of year when local school districts start screening children for kindergarten entry because parents want answers to the ongoing question, 'Is my child ready for kindergarten?' We believe that the readiness process starts before birth and is enhanced through rich and engaging experiences that grow the brain. We also hold firm to the idea that all children are ready to start school when they are chronologically eligible and that it is the responsibility of the kindergarten teacher and receiving school to meet the needs of all of the children who come to them. What we believe, however, can be irrelevant when a family has their child screened by three different schools only to have one school report that the child is ready, a second identify the child as advanced, and a third say that the child should be held out for a year because he has a summer birthday and cannot write his name. No wonder parents are confused and doubt our stance on readiness even though it is supported by NAEYC."

—*Director of a university-affiliated child care center*

## SUMMARY

In this chapter, the importance of the role of the director as the educational leader and curriculum mentor in the program was described. One important component of this role includes a sound knowledge of the research that informs quality curriculum. The chapter was organized around a series of considerations that directors may find helpful when preparing staff feedback. It also described how directors can support intentional teaching and enhance a seamless system for children ages birth through grade three. To be able to support quality curriculum, a director must do the following:

- Identify quality curriculum.

- Establish opportunities for teacher feedback, support, and intervention.

- Support intentional teaching.

- Support a seamless birth through age 8 system.

## TRY IT OUT!

Work in a team to integrate curriculum using the *ACCESS to Science Concept Planner* shown in Director's Resource 11-1. Assign one member of the team to be the curriculum mentor and the others to be members of the teaching team.

> *Background Information: The teachers determined that ants would be a worthy topic of investigation after the preschoolers found an anthill on the playground. The children became fascinated in watching the ants enter and exit the nest and were amazed at the strength of three ants that were able to carry a potato chip across the sidewalk. The teachers followed the children's interest but were also aware that there was a need to address an area of life science sometime during the year.*

1. The curriculum mentor should begin by facilitating a brainstorming session to generate the concepts about ants that children can learn more about. Avoid introducing activities at this stage, and redirect team members who start with activities, materials, or experiences. Focus on the science concepts that support an understanding of ants. Use Director's Resource 11-1 to record your concepts. Note that several concepts have been done for you. If the Internet is available, look up ants to add to the team's content knowledge; if not, take time after class to do some research. What new information did you learn that would have made your concept planner more complete?

2. Now that you know what is possible for children to know about an interesting topic, consider the experiences that you facilitate so that children can investigate the topic. How will the teachers find out about what questions the children have about ants? What authentic materials would support their inquiry?

3. After the team has completed the concepts and experiences, consider language/literacy, math, science, social studies, art, music, social/emotional, and/or movement goals that children can learn through the experience. Try to identify two main goals from two different content areas and developmental domains that can also be supported through the experience.

4. How did this planning process support inquiry and connected learning? What were the pros and cons with planning in this manner?

# DIRECTOR'S RESOURCE 11-1

## ACCESS TO SCIENCE CONCEPT PLANNER: A STUDY OF ANTS

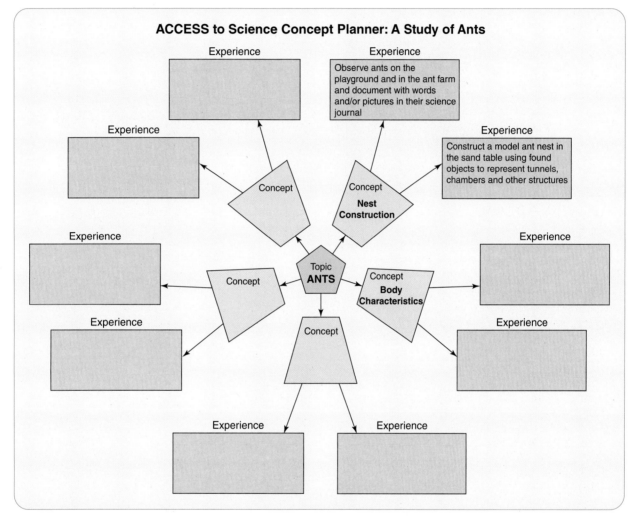

**ACCESS to Science Concept Planner: A Study of Ants**

Experience

Experience — Observe ants on the playground and in the ant farm and document with words and/or pictures in their science journal

Experience

Experience — Construct a model ant nest in the sand table using found objects to represent tunnels, chambers and other structures

Experience

Experience

Experience

Experience

Experience

Experience

Experience

Concept

Concept — **Nest Construction**

Concept

Concept — **Body Characteristics**

Concept

Topic **ANTS**

*Source: Reprinted with permission from Adams, S. M., Baldwin, J. L., Comingore, J. L., & Kelly, M. K., 2011.*

# REFERENCES

Adams, S. M., Baldwin, J. B., Comingore, J. L., & Kelly, M. K. (2013). *The ACCESS Curriculum: Intentional, integrated and inquiry-based for infants through grade 5.* Bloomington, IN: Xlibris.

Baldwin, J. L., Adams, S. M., & Kelly, M. K. (2009). Science at the center: An emergent, standards-based, child-centered framework for early learners. *Early Childhood Education Journal, 37,* 71–77. DOI 10.1007/s10643-009-0318-z

Becker, H. J. (2000). Who's wired and who's not: Children's access to and use of computer technology. *The Future of Children (Children and Computer Technology),* 10 (2).

Brenneman, K., Stevenson-Boyd, J. S., & Frede, E. (2009). Math and science in preschool: Policies and practice. Preschool Policy Matters, Issue 19. New Brunswick, NJ: National Institute for Early Education Research. Retrieved from http://nieer.org/resources/policybriefs/20.pdf.

Burdette, H. L., & Whitaker, R. C. (2005). A national study of neighborhood safety, outdoor play, television viewing, and obesity in preschool children. *Pediatrics,* 116 (3): 657–662.

Calvert, S. L., Rideout, V. J., Woolard, J. L., Barr, R. F., & Strouse, G. A. (2005). Age, ethnicity and socioeconomic patterns in early computer use: A national survey. *American Behavioral Scientist,* 48 (5): 590–607.

Chung, S., & Walsh, D. J. (2000). Unpacking child-centeredness: A history of meanings. *Curriculum Studies, 32*(2), 215–234.

Clifford, R. M., Barbarin, O., Chang, F., Early, D., Bryant, D., Howes, C., et al. (2005). What is prekindergarten? Characteristics of public prekindergarten programs. *Applied Developmental Science, 9*(3), 126–143.

Copple, E., & Bredekamp, S. (2009). *Developmentally appropriate practices in early childhood programs.* Washington DC: NAEYC.

Cruickshank, A. (2010). Empowering images: Using photography as a medium to develop visual literacy. *Exchange for Early Childhood Leaders,* (Sept./Oct.). Retrieved from https://secure.ccie.com/resources/view_article. php?article_id=5019553&action=view.

Denton Flanagan, K., & McPhee, C. (2009). The children born in 2001 at kindergarten entry: First findings from the kindergarten data collections of the early childhood longitudinal study, birth cohort (ECLS-B) (NCES 2010–005). National Center for Education Statistics, Institute of Education Sciences, U.S. Department of Education. Washington, DC.

Dickinson, D. K., & Porche, M. V. (2011). Relation between language experiences in preschool classrooms and children's kindergarten and fourth-grade language and reading abilities. *Child Development, 82*(3), 870–886.

Education Commission of the States. (2009). *Linking ready kids to ready schools: A report on policy insights from the governors' forum series.* Denver, CO: author, and Battle Creek, MI: W. K. Kellogg Foundation. Retrieved from http://www.ecs.org/docs/4208_COMC_report_forweb.pdf.

Eliason, C., & Jenkins, L. (2008). *A practical guide to early childhood curriculum* (8th ed.). Columbus, OH: Merrill/ Prentice Hall.

Epstein, A. S. (2007). *The intentional teacher: Choosing the best strategies for young children's learning.* Washington, DC: National Association for the Education of Young Children.

Epstein, A. S., Schweinhart, L. J., & McAdoo, L. (1996). *Models of early childhood education.* Ypsilanti, MI: High/Scope Press.

Frede, E., & Ackerman, D. (2007, March). Preschool curriculum decision-making: Dimensions to consider. *NIEER policy brief* (Issue 12). New Brunswick, NJ: National Institute for Early Education Research. Retrieved from http://nieer.org/resources/policybriefs/12.pdf.

Grisham-Brown, J., Hemmeter, M. L., & Pretti-Frontczak, K. (2005). *Blended practices for teaching young children in inclusive settings.* Baltimore: Brookes.

Harms, T., Clifford, R. M., & Cryer, D. (2006). Early Childhood Environment Rating Scale-Revised. New York: Teachers College Press.

Honig, A. S. (2010). *Little kids, big worries: Stress-busting tips for early childhood classrooms.* Baltimore: Brookes.

IES What Works Clearinghouse. (n.d.). *Early childhood education abstract.* Retrieved from http://ies.ed.gov/ncee/wwc/reports/early_ed/abstract.asp.

Judge, S., Puckett, K., & Cabuk, B. (2004). Digital equity: New findings from the early childhood longitudinal study. *Journal of Research on Technology in Education, 36* (4), 383–396.

Kagan, S. L., & Kauerz, K. (2007). Reaching for the whole: Integration and alignment in early education policy. In R. C. Pianta, M. J. Cox, & K. L. Snow (eds.), *School readiness and the transition to kindergarten in the era of accountability,* 11–30. Baltimore: Paul H. Brookes.

Katz, L., & Chard, S. (1998). Issues in selecting topics for projects. *ERIC Digest, 8,* 1–2.

Klein, L., & Knitzer, J. (2006). Effective preschool curricula and teaching strategies. *Pathways to early school success* (Issue Brief 2). New York: National Center for Children in Poverty. Retrieved from http://www.nccp.org/publications/pdf/download_100.pdf.

Kostelnik, M. J., Soderman, A. K., & Whiren, A. P. (2010). Developmentally appropriate curriculum: Best Practices in early childhood education (5th ed.). Upper Saddle River, NJ, and Columbus, OH: Pearson Prentice Hall Merrill.

Meisels, S. J. (2004). Should we test 4-year-olds? *Pediatrics, 113,* 1401–1402.

Meisels, S. J., Harrington, H. L., McMahon, P., Dichtelmiller, M. D., & Jablon, J. R. (2002). *Thinking like a teacher: Using observational assessment to improve teaching and learning.* Boston: Allyn & Bacon.

Meisels, S. J., Bickel, D. D., Nicholson, J., Xue, Y., & Atkins-Burnett, S. (2001). Trusting teachers' judgments: A validity study of a curriculum-embedded performance assessment in Kindergarten–Grade 3. *American Educational Research Journal, 38* (1), 73–95.

National Association for the Education of Young Children. (2009). Developmentally appropriate practice in early childhood programs serving children from birth through age 8. Washington, DC: Author.

National Association for the Education of Young Children. (2008). Overview of the NAEYC early childhood program standards. Washington DC: Author.

National Association for the Education of Young Children. (2008). NAEYC early childhood program standards and accreditation criteria: The mark of quality in early childhood education. Washington, DC: Author.

National Association for the Education of Young Children. (2003). Position statement with expanded resources: Early childhood curriculum, assessment, and program evaluation: Building an effective, accountable system in programs for children birth through age eight. Washington, D.C.: Author.

National Association for the Education of Young Children & Fred Rogers Center for Early Learning and Children's Media at Saint Vincent College. (2012). *Technology and interactive media as tools in early childhood programs serving children from birth through age 8.* Washington DC: author.

National Association for the Education of Young Children & National Association of Early Childhood Specialists in State Departments of Education. (2003). *Early childhood curriculum, assessment, and program evaluation: Building an effective, accountable system in programs for children birth through age 8.* Joint position statement. Retrieved from http://www.naeyc.org/dap.

National Association for the Education of Young Children & National Association of Early Childhood Specialists in State Departments of Education. (2002). *Early learning content standards: Creating conditions for success* [Joint position statement]. Washington, DC: National Association for the Education of Young Children.

National Center for Early Development & Learning. (2005). *Multi-state study of prekindergarten.* Chapel Hill: University of North Carolina.

National Child Care Information and Technical Assistance Center. (2011). State early learning guidelines. Washington DC: U.S. Department of Health and Human Services.

National Early Literacy Panel. (2008). *Developing early literacy: Report of the national early literacy panel.* Jessup, MD: National Institute for Literacy at ED Pubs. Retrieved from http://lincs.ed.gov/publications/pdf/NELPReport09.pdf.

National Forum on Early Childhood Program Evaluation & National Scientific Council on the Developing Child. (2007). A science-based framework for early childhood Policy: Using evidence to improve outcomes in learning, behavior and health for vulnerable children. Cambridge, MA: Center on the Developing Child at Harvard University.

National Mathematics Advisory Panel. (2008) *Foundations for Success: The Final Report of the National Mathematics Advisory Panel.* Washington, DC: U.S. Department of Education.

Pianta, R., Howes, C., Burchinal, M., Bryant, D., Clifford, R. M., Early, D., et al. (2005). Features of prekindergarten programs, classrooms, and teachers: Do they predict observed classroom quality and child–teacher interactions? *Applied Developmental Science, 9* (3), 144–159.

Pianta, R., La Paro, K. & Hamre, B. (2008). Classroom assessment scoring system. Baltimore: Brookes.

Pianta, R., & Kraft-Sayre, M. (2003). *Successful kindergarten transition: Your guide to connecting children, families, & schools.* Baltimore: Paul H. Brookes.

Preschool Curriculum Evaluation Research Consortium. (2008). *Effects of preschool curriculum programs on school readiness* (NCER 2008-2009). Washington, DC: National Center for Education Research, Institute of Education Sciences, U.S. Department of Education. Washington, DC: U.S. Government Printing Office. Retrieved from http://ies.ed.gov/ncer/pubs/20082009/index.asp.

Tzuo. P. W. (2007). The tension between teacher control and children's freedom in a child-centered classroom: Resolving the practical dilemma through a closer look at the related theories. *Early Childhood Education Journal, 35* (1), 33–39.

Yoshikawa, H., Weiland, C., Brooks-Gunn, J., Burchinal, M. R., Espinosa, L. M., Gormley, W. T. … Zaslow, M. J. (2013). Investing in our future: The evidence base on preschool education. Ann Arbor, MI: Society for Research in Child Development.

# 12

# MANAGING *the* FOOD *and* *the* HEALTH AND SAFETY PROGRAMS

*Health and safety information should be posted where both parents and teachers can see it.*

## Learning Objectives

After reading this chapter, you should be able to:

**12-1** Describe the components of a complete food service program.

**12-2** Explain staff responsibilities related to maintaining health and safety regulations, liability concerns, preventing and managing communicable disease, and providing sick child care.

**12-3** Describe factors that must be considered when planning and implementing disaster and emergency policies, and explain the importance of staff training on the content of the plans.

**12-4** Explain the need for staff training and reporting in the area of child abuse and neglect.

**12-5** Discuss strategies that directors can use to address legal issues related to health and safety and strategies that may help avert potential lawsuits.

## Standards Addressed in this Chapter

naeyc

Accreditation Standard 1 – Relationships
Accreditation Standard 5 – Health
Accreditation Standard 7 – Families
Accreditation Standard 8 – Community Relationships
Accreditation Standard 9 – Physical Environment
Accreditation Standard 10 – Leadership and Management
Administrator Competencies – Management Knowledge and Skills 2, 5, 10
Administrator Competencies – Early Childhood Knowledge and Skills 5, 7, 10
Professional Preparation Standard 1 – Promoting Child Development and Learning
Professional Preparation Standard 3 – Observing, Documenting, and Assessing to Support Young Children and Families
Professional Preparation Standard 6 – Becoming a Professional

## 12-1 FOOD SERVICE PROGRAMS

The total food service program, whether it is **naeyc** limited to a midmorning snack or consists of a two- or even a three-meal-a-day program, is important, not only because nutrition affects the mental functioning and the physical well-being of the child but also because nutritional habits and attitudes toward eating are established during the early years. Establishing an appropriate emotional atmosphere and providing variety in food choices and the style of serving the food are foremost considerations, whether the children's meals and snacks are catered, served from frozen prepackaged microwave dinners, come from public school or company cafeterias, or are prepared completely from start to finish in the center's kitchen.

In some programs, children bring brown-bag lunches, a practice that can be a boon to your budget and provide an opportunity to help parents learn more about good nutrition. All brown-bag lunches must be dated and properly labeled. They must be refrigerated, and all leftover foods must be discarded and not sent home in the child's lunch box. It is also important to make certain that children do not trade food with their friends. Nutritious foods should be offered daily, using variations in serving styles such as self-help and group snacks, family-style and cafeteria-style meals, picnics, bag lunches, and more casual food service for special occasions.

It should be understood that the adults in the classroom sit down with the children when food is served, that the adults eat the same food that is served to the children, and that the adults take charge of creating pleasant conversation among the entire group during snack time or mealtime. Conversation can focus on food, on what children have been doing or expect to do later in the day, or on any topic that is of interest to most children. An accepting adult who avoids having children wait to be served, who encourages but doesn't demand tasting new foods, who uses utensils appropriately and suggests that children try to manipulate their own small forks or spoons, and who avoids associating unpleasantness or punishment with food is demonstrating healthy habits and attitudes toward eating.

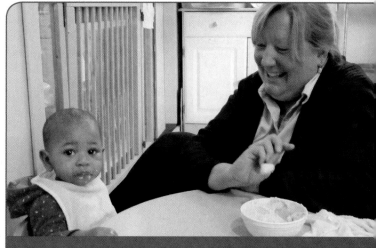

*Adults should sit with children during meals and encourage pleasant interaction.*

For the young infant, a caring, familiar adult who is unrushed is important during feeding time. Infants should be held while taking a bottle but encouraged to begin to hold it for self-feeding as voluntary control progresses. Staff must be reminded *not* to prop bottles for infants because of dangers of choking and of falling asleep with milk or juice in the mouth, which is detrimental to healthy gums and teeth and could lead to a possible increase in ear infections. In addition, for their emotional and social well-being, it is critical that babies be held and cuddled while being fed.

Older infants benefit from sitting in adapted chairs near the table with older toddlers and preschoolers, whenever that is possible. They often can enjoy finger foods with the toddlers and participate in the pleasant atmosphere of eating time. Choking may be a problem for babies who are beginning to feed themselves, so a caregiver must be close by at all times. Foods should be cut in bite-size pieces, be of proper consistency, and at the very beginning, be offered one piece at a time. Make sure the cook and the caregivers in the program know that there are high-risk foods that are likely to cause choking in young children. Ninety percent of all fatal chokings occur in children

### MAKING THE CASE FOR *USING FOOD THOUGHTFULLY*

As a director, you understand that making conscientious decisions regarding your food program is critical. Your menu can provide children with clear messages about what constitutes healthy eating. But have you considered that other uses of food in the center may send messages you did not intend? One area of debate concerns the use of food as a learning material. For example, does "playing with food" send the message to younger children that play items can be eaten? Or, does the use of food as an art or sensory table material

demonstrate a lack of respect for a vital resource that is valued by some cultures? How might adults who have come from impoverished areas perceive the "wasting" of food? There is no clear-cut solution to this debate. Nonetheless, as a director, you must make decisions regarding your stance and that of your program on this important issue. For an expanded discussion of this topic, see Swim and Freeman (2004) and NAEYC (2011b).

under age 4. Additionally, the Committee on Injury, Violence and Poison Prevention of the American Academy of Pediatrics (2010) reports that approximately one child dies every five days in the United States due to choking on food.

Foods that may cause choking include the following (American Academy of Pediatrics et al., 2011):

- hot dogs
- nuts and seeds
- popcorn
- raw carrots
- chunks of meat
- marshmallows
- chips
- peanut butter (spoonfuls)
- pretzels
- whole grapes
- hard candy
- raw peas
- rice cakes

Candy is the leading cause of nonfatal choking incidents (Chapin et al., 2013). Nonetheless, it is essential for children to sit down and to be supervised while eating or drinking any food item to avoid the dangers of choking.

Directors are responsible for all aspects of the food service program, so they must monitor and supervise the atmosphere, health, and safety features of mealtimes. They also must oversee the planning, buying, and preparation of food and provide opportunities for in-service training to the food service staff members and other adults who work with the children during snack time and mealtime.

## 12-1a Menu Planning

The proportion of the total daily food requirement provided by the center depends on the total number of hours the child spends in the center. Licensing regulations vary, but general guidelines state the following:

- Children in care eight hours or less should be offered at least one meal and two snacks, or two meals and one snack.

- Children in care for more than eight hours should be offered at least two meals and two snacks, or one meal and three snacks.

- A nutritious midmorning and midafternoon snack should be offered to all children.

- Children should be offered food at intervals of not less than two hours and not more than three hours apart unless the child is asleep (AAP et al., 2011).

Of course, infants in group care have very different needs and require individualized eating schedules with carefully prepared formulas and special diets.

The MyPlate food guidance system (Figure 12-1) has been developed by the USDA to provide guidelines for daily food intake. Portion sizes and food selections for young children are presented in the *Dietary Guidelines for Americans, 2010* publication available from the USDA website.

Nutritious meals and snacks can be selected from among the following food groups:

- bread, rice, cereal, and pasta
- vegetable
- fruit
- milk, yogurt, and cheese
- meat, poultry, fish, dry beans, eggs, and nuts
- fats, oils, and sweets

### REFLECTION

Think about your earliest recollections of eating with the family or with a teacher. Do you recall being pressured about table manners, finishing your main course before dessert, and tasting new foods that you disliked? Can you recall how you felt at those times? What emotions did you feel? How did you feel about the adults who made demands on you? How did you feel about eating and mealtime when you were put under pressure to eat too much or eat foods you disliked? What are your current attitudes about eating and about unfamiliar foods? Can you relate these current attitudes to your earlier experiences with eating and sampling new foods?

**FIGURE 12-1** The USDA's MyPlate logo is designed to remind individuals to eat healthfully.

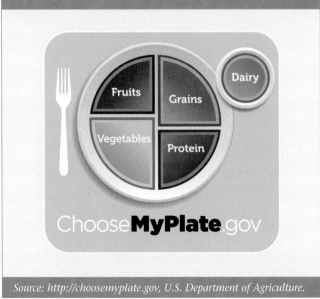

*Source: http://choosemyplate.gov, U.S. Department of Agriculture.*

Careful planning involves including ample choices of fruits and vegetables along with dairy products; some meat, fish, and poultry; and some selected items from the bread and pasta group. It is important to check local licensing standards for additional details on nutrition requirements. For centers involved in the USDA Child and Adult Care Food Program (CACFP), nutritional standards for meal and snack serving sizes for children birth through age 12 can be found on the USDA website.

Every precaution must be taken to ensure that children with food allergies or other conditions requiring a special diet, such as cultural or religious customs or family food practices (e.g., vegetarianism), are served only those foods on their prescribed diet. Both the cook and all classroom staff must be alerted to these special dietary requirements, and both the director and the staff must know the emergency procedures to follow in the event a particular child has an allergic reaction. According to the U.S. Food and Drug Administration (n.d.), the most common foods that cause allergies are milk, eggs, fish, shellfish, tree nuts (e.g., almonds, walnuts, pecans), peanuts, wheat, and soybeans. With the increasing incidences of peanut allergies among young children, some programs choose to eliminate all peanut products, including peanut butter, from their menus. For some special diet cases, parents may choose to send food for the child. These packed lunches must be properly refrigerated until served and must *not* be shared with other children. Any food from home also must be labeled, showing the child's name and date.

▶❚❚ **TeachSource Video Vignette**

### Children and Food Allergies

Food allergies in children have risen dramatically in the past 20 years, and these allergies can result in mild to potentially deadly reactions. View the video vignette entitled, *Children and Food Allergies*. Reflect on the following questions:

**1.** Why has the number of food allergies risen so dramatically?

**2.** As a director, what strategies would you use to make sure that your program is addressing the needs of children with food allergies?

Nutritional considerations in meal planning for young children are necessary but not sufficient to guarantee that children will be adequately nourished. Children's appetites and food preferences also must be taken into consideration when meals are planned. Three- and four-year-old children tend to have small, unpredictable appetites, and they are prone to food sprees. Their foods must not be too hot nor too cold, not too spicy or gluey, and cut into bite-size and manageable portions. Variation in texture, color, and flavor also are important considerations in planning children's meals. Every effort should be made to limit use of salt and sugar as well as foods high in fat. Serving certain ethnic foods will provide wider variation for all the children and make available familiar foods to the children from specific ethnic groups represented in the classroom. It is always a good idea to introduce a new food along with old familiar favorites.

Further considerations that affect menu planning are the availability of equipment and utensils and the preparation time for each menu item when all foods are prepared in the center kitchen. It is virtually impossible to prepare hot breads, an oven-cooked main dish, and a baked dessert for one meal if only one oven is available. Also, the number and sizes of pots and pans must be checked when menus are planned to ensure an adequate supply of equipment of an appropriate size to prepare the foods for a particular meal. Preparation time is another factor that influences meal planning. Meals that require too much last-minute preparation create problems for the cook, which, in turn, could delay the serving time. Hungry children who are forced to wait for their food become impatient and restless, and teachers then must find ways to help them cope with these unnecessary delays.

Meal and menu planning can be systematized and simplified by using meal planning guides, standardized recipes, and sample menus. A number of government booklets and other menu planning guides are useful in planning four to six weeks of basic menus. Menu changes based on the availability of seasonal or plentiful foods can be made on a weekly basis. But beyond those minor changes, basic menu patterns can be repeated every four to six weeks.

Teachers and parents often have helpful suggestions about changes in the basic menu patterns, so a process for collecting feedback should be established. Some lunches include too many items that are difficult for children to manage or too time-consuming to serve. For example, a menu of soup, banana sections that have to be peeled, and packaged crackers that have to be opened is both difficult to serve and a problem for children to manage.

To demonstrate respect and support for diversity, programs will want to consider families' cultural and religious needs during menu planning. Additionally, some parents may be interested in organically or locally grown foods. Inviting the cook to lunch with the children provides an opportunity for the cook to hear comments from the children about the food and to observe how well they manage the foods served. A "cook's mailbox" not only invites children to write requests for favorite foods and send thank-you notes to the cook, but also serves as an excellent meaningful literacy experience as well. The mailbox and the lunch with the children also give the cook a chance to feel more a part of the total center program, rather than one who spends all day in the kitchen and away from the children.

Parents often are interested in what children have been served for snacks and/or for breakfast and lunch, so it is helpful to post weekly menus or publish them regularly in the parent newsletter. Posting menus not only helps the parents plan for a child's meals at home but also serves as a model for parents who may be inexperienced with planning balanced family meals.

An interesting feature to add to the menu-posting area is a pictorial menu for the children. The cook, another staff member, or an interested parent may be willing to collect food pictures and post each day's snack and lunch on an eye-level bulletin board for children to "read." It creates interest among the children, who can look forward to a dish they especially enjoy, and it becomes part of the center's nutrition program.

### ▶❚❚ TeachSource Video Vignette

### Early Childhood Nutrition

Nutritious meals and snacks are an important component of early childhood programming. Additionally, young children can learn about making healthy food choices—behaviors that can guide them throughout their lives. View the video vignette entitled, *Promoting Children's Health: A Focus on Nutrition in an Early Childhood Program.* Reflect on the following questions:

**1.** What strategies does the teacher use to teach children about healthy snacking?

**2.** As a director, how could you support teachers' integration of appropriate nutrition information into the curriculum?

## 12-1b Food Buying

Careful menu planning reduces cost and waste and provides a clear-cut basis for setting up shopping lists for daily, weekly, and monthly food buying. Whether meals are catered, partially prepared from prepackaged meals especially designed for children, or fully prepared in the center kitchen, the food budget will affect both meal planning and food purchasing. Quantity buying and cooperative buying arrangements among a group of centers sometimes results in lower prices but also might limit choices, increase the pressure to purchase foods of lesser quality, and create storage problems when quantity purchases exceed the available storage space. Therefore, although price is an important consideration, quality, available storage space, and, of course, food preferences of the children, must be taken into consideration when food-purchasing decisions are made.

Catered meal services require practically no shopping time, no storage space, and very little time selecting foods and developing the shopping lists. They also eliminate the need for a complete meal preparation space and a full-time cook, but the services may be more expensive than meals prepared at the center. In addition, the food could turn out to be less satisfying to the children, and the number of food choices available may be limited.

The prepackaged frozen meals that are prepared in convection or microwave ovens are a very expensive convenience. This type of food service requires large freezers and special ovens, yet requires neither a full-time cook nor complete meal-preparation space. The director must select carefully so the choices are appropriate for young children and there is variety in the menu. Fresh foods and beverages must be bought daily or weekly as needed to supplement prepackaged meals.

An important movement that has developed over the past 15 years is the Farm to School (F2S) program. The F2S Network (F2SN) "envisions a nation in which Farm to School programs are an essential component of strong and just local and regional food systems, ensuring the health of all school children, farms, the environment, economy and communities" (Farm to School Network, n.d.). F2SN links food service programs in schools across the country with local farms that are able to provide locally grown food for meals and snacks. Additionally, some state programs include other activities such as school gardens and classroom education related to nutrition and agriculture (The Ohio State University Extension, 2013).

You can find additional information about F2SN and its programs in all 50 states on its website. Additionally, information related to the USDA's efforts in supporting food to school programming, managed by the Food and Nutrition Service, can be found on its website (U.S. Department of Agriculture Food and Nutrition Service, n.d.a).

Using company or public school cafeterias requires planning with the cafeteria manager and staff. Foods brought from cafeterias serving adults or older children are sometimes served in containers or in portions difficult for young children to manage. A whole hamburger, a large strip of dill pickle, catsup in a sealed foil container, and milk in a sealed carton are all difficult for young children to handle. But because that is standard public school cafeteria fare, you may find no other choices for your children. Also, cafeteria service customarily means self-help and carrying trays. That is out of the question for young children. It is important to develop clear-cut guidelines for portion sizes, family-style service, and alternative menus so you can work with the cafeteria food service staff to find ways to make appropriate adjustments for young children.

Meals prepared at the center mean that the center must have a complete meal-preparation space that meets all licensing requirements and must employ a full-time cook if it is a full-day child care program. Preferably, the cook will have planning and buying skills. If not, a staff person (sometimes the director) plans and purchases the foods in consultation with the cook. Planning purchases, doing the shopping, and checking deliveries are all time-consuming; however, total meal preparation at the center allows for greater variation in foods served and more involvement of the children in shopping, preparation, and serving. It also guarantees that items on the menu will be prepared and served with young children in mind.

## USDA Child and Adult Care Food Program

Some centers serve children who are eligible for free or reduced-price meals from the USDA Child and Adult Care Food Program (CACFP). While CACFP is federally funded, individual states are responsible for management of the program. Determination of a family's eligibility is based on income, and child care centers (not-for-profit or for profit), home-based programs, and after-school care programs may participate. For-profit centers may participate when 25 percent of the center's enrollment or licensed capacity receives either Title XX assistance or is eligible for free or reduced meals. For those providers who may not qualify under the Title XX criteria, they may meet other qualification expectations. The National Child Care Association (NCCA) is a helpful resource for for-profit programs. Although some programs may have a designated staff person or cook do some of the paperwork to receive the USDA reimbursement, in most cases, the director does the necessary paperwork or at least is responsible for making sure it is done correctly.

Eligibility of children for free or reduced-price meals is based on family income. Income levels for family eligibility and reimbursement rates for providers are adjusted

### Working Smart with Technology

*Data Management Systems for Child Care*

Today's directors have many resources at their fingertips thanks to the continuing growth of technology. One advancement that provides numerous benefits has been the development of data management systems for child care centers. One key advantage of these software programs is the reduction in time that must be spent developing weekly menus. For example, directors might be able to plan one or two months of menus at one time using a management system and then be able to reuse them over time. If changes are desired to the menu, adjustments can be made quite easily. Additionally, many programs enable you to print out food shopping lists based on the number of meals to be served. Another significant benefit is that data management systems can assist directors in purchasing and preparing only what is needed. In this way, food is not wasted, which saves money. For more information on the use of child care data management systems, see Ho, Schoenberg, Richards, and Morath (2009) and Simon (2012).

*Many data management systems are now available for directors to facilitate their work.*

### DIRECTOR'S CORNER

"One of the things I learned quickly when I started to work with this program in the public school was to become friendly with the cafeteria manager. Now she cuts the hamburgers in quarters, sends pickle slices instead of those huge strips of dill pickles, and includes a sharp knife for my use when there are apples to be cored and sliced or oranges to be quartered."

*—Director, public school Head Start program*

annually effective July 1 of each year. To obtain the most recent information regarding eligibility and management of the food program, view the *Income Eligibility Guidelines* on the USDA's Food and Nutrition Services (n.d.b) website. Other helpful sources of information include your state licensing agent or your state agency that administers the CACFP. A Meal Benefit Form must be on file for every child who receives meals under the USDA food program. These forms must be kept on file for at least three years to ensure they will be available at the time your agency undergoes monitoring reviews. It is essential that the information on the forms is complete and accurate to avoid the possibility of penalties if errors are discovered at the time of periodic reviews. USDA forms vary from state to state, so the federal form may not match those required by your state. Also, new forms are issued yearly with updated income guidelines.

To obtain forms from your state, contact your state agency that administers the CACFP. In most cases, this will be the state Department of Education. The state agency will provide updated application forms, worksheets that can be used to determine eligibility of your clients, and worksheets for record keeping and for applying for reimbursement. Most states require centers to submit the final information and request for reimbursement online.

Providers who fit into one of the following categories may receive USDA reimbursement for eligible children enrolled:

- nonresidential public or private not-for-profit child care and ADC centers (some forms or documents replace ADC with Temporary Assistance for Needy Families [TANF])

- profit-making child care centers that receive Title XX compensation for at least 25 percent of the children attending

- Head Start programs

- settlement houses and recreation programs

- family child care homes (only if they participate in the CACFP under a sponsoring organization that has tax-exempt status)

All participating agencies must serve foods that follow the USDA CACFP meal patterns that are updated regularly and published on the USDA Food and Nutrition website. You may also find updated meal pattern information on the website of your state agency that oversees CACFP.

The patterns provide information about the types and portions of foods that must be served to each child for meals and snacks in order for programs to receive reimbursement. Following USDA guidelines ensures well-balanced meals; however, some recommended serving sizes may be overwhelming for young children if put on the plate all at one time.

Directors of centers enrolled in the USDA food program must complete extensive paperwork on a regular basis. Reimbursement claims and financial reports must be filed monthly, reporting data on the following:

- attendance

- number of meals served

- cost of food, which is calculated on the basis of information obtained from a monthly food inventory

- labor and purchased service costs

- income from reduced lunch fees and other sources

To complete these claim forms, you must have accurate attendance records, invoices or cash tapes and receipts for all food and some nonfood purchases, canceled checks, and financial records on all cash received from those families who pay full or reduced lunch costs. The reimbursement form helps with record keeping. Some states provide worksheets to assist with record keeping. Directors may also develop their own worksheets.

Even when there is an extra person on staff to do the USDA paperwork, data collection for the reports and preparation for reviews involve the director, the cook, and the teaching staff. Some states require regular training for all staff involved in the food program. Items such as point-of-service meal counts, safe and sanitary food handling, record keeping procedures, and size of servings are appropriate topics for these mandatory staff training sessions. Although the sessions are time-consuming and costly, it is important that all staff understand details of the requirements to qualify for reimbursement from the CACFP because it is the center's primary source of revenue to finance the food program for eligible families. Federal regulations require that programs taking part in CACFP must be reviewed periodically. The purpose of these reviews is to ensure that all CACFP regulations are being addressed. Documents that will be examined during reviews include the following:

- income eligibility forms

- attendance records

- enrollment forms (to confirm that children listed as eligible for reimbursement are enrolled)

In addition to reviewing records on children, the food program official will examine the following administrative records:

- record of meal counts

- menus

- monthly food inventories

- documentation of food and supply costs

- documentation of labor costs

- documentation of Title XX enrollments if it is a proprietary center

As a director, it is essential that you understand the USDA program so you can do the paperwork if it is part of your job description, or delegate the responsibility and then coach those who are doing the detailed record keeping and reporting.

### 12-1c Food Storage

Food storage requires careful planning so that sufficient quantities of food items are conveniently accessible to the preparation area and so that storage areas and containers are sanitary and chilled. The available shelf space and containers must be appropriate to accommodate the packaged size of the food items as they are delivered from the supplier. All food items should be stored separately from nonfood items, and food storage rooms should be dry, relatively cool (60°F to 70°F), and free from insect or rodent infestation. Commodities should be stored in tightly covered, labeled metal or heavy plastic containers that are at least six inches above the floor level to permit air circulation and to protect them from dirt. Dating containers ensures food supplies will be used in the order received.

Perishable foods must be stored at temperatures that prevent spoilage. Refrigerator temperatures must be 41°F or lower; freezer temperatures should be 0°F or lower (AAP et al., 2011). Shelf space must allow for air circulation around the refrigerated foods, and thermometers in the warmest sections of refrigerators and freezers should be checked daily.

### 12-1d Food Preparation

Cooks must be instructed to follow recipes in meal preparation and are expected to adhere to directions about cooking times and temperatures, proper techniques, temperatures for holding prepared foods, and proper methods for storing and using leftovers. Sanitation in the food preparation area is of utmost importance. The food service staff must follow sanitary food-handling practices and maintain good personal hygiene while handling foods and cleaning food preparation equipment and utensils. Even though a nutritionist or other staff member may be responsible for the total food service program in the center, it is advisable for you, as director, to make periodic checks on the food preparation techniques and the sanitation practices of the cook as food is prepared and served to the children. It often becomes the director's responsibility to coach the cook when correct preparation procedures are not being followed.

Sanitation guidelines are available from your local health department or your state or local licensing agent. The licensing regulations at all levels include clearly stated sanitation requirements related to food preparation in child care centers. A local health department staff member or your center licensing agent is an excellent resource for helping interpret and implement the sanitation regulations applicable in your area.

*It is advisable for you, as the director, to make periodic checks on food preparation and service.*

### 12-1e Resources

Every state has a child nutrition agency. These agencies can supply copies of laws, regulations, and guidelines in response to questions about nutrition and health. The following list includes additional places to go for printed material and for consultation on the center's nutrition component:

- public health nutritionists in your state or local health department, or the county extension agency
- nutritionists in local dairy councils or comprehensive health centers
- USDA extension home economists
- dietitians in nearby high schools or universities
- dietitians in local hospitals

## 12-2 HEALTH AND SAFETY PROGRAM

The center's staff members are responsible for the health and safety of the children while they are at the center; therefore, directors must be knowledgeable about health and safety regulations as stipulated in the licensing regulations, about staff liability in cases of accidents at school, and about procedures for protection from and reporting of communicable disease and child abuse and neglect. Although some large centers may have a health consultant on staff, in most places, the director is the designated individual responsible for the health program.

The health services provided through the child care center may range from no service at all to comprehensive service, including regular physicals, dental checkups and treatment, vision screening, hearing screening, and mental health services. The scope of the health services program depends on the program's health policies set by the funding agent, the socioeconomic status of the families, the family expectations, and the licensing regulations. All centers should maintain up-to-date health and immunization records on the children, whether or not direct health services are provided.

## 12-2a Health Records for Children and Staff

Children's health records cover information up to the time of registration and any new health or medical information received while the child is in the program. Formats for these records vary and may be set by local health departments. The information provided (in addition to the basic demographics such as name, birth date, parents' names, and the like) should include medical and developmental information and must be completed and signed by the child's health care provider. The medical report on the child should include the following:

- results from the child's most recent well-care visit with physician's signature

- health history, including records of the child's immunizations

- description of any disability or special need and a care plan for how these needs will be accommodated

- assessment of the child's growth based on height, weight, and head circumference (percentile for these if the child is younger than 24 months)

- results of developmental screenings as well as those for vision, hearing, dental health, nutrition, tuberculosis, hemoglobin, urine, lead, and so on

- dates of significant communicable diseases

- prescribed medications, including information on recognizing and reporting potential side effects

- description of current acute or chronic health problems under care or needing treatment

- description of serious injuries sustained by the child in the past

- special instructions for the caregiver

- emergency medical/dental care authorization form (AAP et al., 2011).

It is preferable to have the child's medical report on file prior to or on admission, but it is imperative that it be completed within six weeks after admission or as required by licensing laws. These records should be updated every six months for children under 2 years and every year for children ages 2 to 6.

### ▶❚❚ TeachSource Video Vignette

**Communicating with Parents about Health Issues**

Informing parents about the health-related policies and procedures of an early childhood program is an important responsibility of administrators and teachers. View the video vignette entitled, *Communicating with Parents about Health in Early Childhood: A Parent-Teacher Meeting*. Reflect on the following questions:

**1.** What types of information should be shared with parents related to health-related issues?

**2.** What are the benefits of meeting face-to-face with the parent to discuss health policies and procedures?

**3.** What advice is given to parents regarding a child's return to the classroom following an illness?

A dental screening should be included in the medical report. An authorized health care provider often does the dental screening on children under age 3, at which time the child should visit a dentist. If the earlier dental screenings reveal special oral or dental problems, the child should see a dentist immediately.

Staff medical records that follow the licensing requirements must be on file at the center. Even when not required by licensing, there should be a medical record on every adult who has regular contact with the children, including substitutes, volunteers, practicum students, cooks, and van drivers. The staff records should include not only a physical assessment but also an evaluation of the emotional fitness of those who are to care for the children. The staff health appraisal should include the following:

- health history

- physical and dental exams

- vision and hearing screening

- tuberculosis (TB) screening with the Tuberculin Skin Test (TST) or the interferon gamma release assay (IGSA)

- review of immunizations (measles, mumps, rubella, diphtheria, tetanus, polio)

- review of occupational health concerns

- assessment of need for immunizations against influenza, pneumococcus, and hepatitis B (and those required by individual states)

- assessment of any other condition that may impair a staff member's ability to perform the job (AAP et al., 2011).

Unless licensing regulations require more frequent updating of staff health records, it is recommended this be done every two years. After many years of decreasing numbers of cases, tuberculosis seems to be on the rise again, so it is wise to consult your local health authorities to determine the frequency of repeat TB testing.

Currently, there are no screening or self-appraisal tools to identify specific health conditions that may seriously impair a caregiver's ability to provide safe and healthy experiences for children. However, there are some obvious things that a director can assess, including the ability or willingness to do the following:

- move quickly to supervise and assist the children

- lift children, equipment, and supplies

- sit on the floor and on child-size chairs

- respond quickly in case of an emergency

- practice frequent hand washing

- eat the same food served to the children

- hear and see at a distance for playground supervision

- not be absent from work due to illness more frequently than the typical adult, in order to provide continuity of care for young children (AAP et al., 2011)

## 12-2b Communicable Disease

Cases of communicable diseases at the child care center must be reported to all center families and to the local health authorities. The usual children's diseases, as well as cases of meningitis, scarlet fever, infectious hepatitis, and head lice, must be reported so that necessary precautions can be taken immediately. It is important that pregnant staff members consult their physician about precautions related to exposure to communicable diseases at the workplace.

Directors and some of the teaching staff should have training in communicable diseases to enable them to recognize symptoms and make decisions about exclusion of children from the group. Communicable disease training is available in most communities through the Red Cross or the local health department. Licensing usually requires updated communicable disease training for classroom staff. Every center should provide easy access to a communicable disease chart to help staff recognize symptoms and make exclusion decisions. Additionally,

**▶‖ TeachSource Video Vignette**

### The Daily Health Check

The daily evaluation of a child's health status takes very little time but can yield numerous benefits. View the video vignette entitled, *Infants & Toddlers: Daily Health Checks*. The "&" is in the title. Reflect on the following questions:

**1.** You are the director of an early childhood program who has just hired a new toddler teacher. What information would you provide to this new employee regarding the benefits of the daily health check in your center?

**2.** What information should be included in a form that teachers might use as they conduct daily health checks?

communicable disease apps (applications) are now available for mobile devices. Many states require that teachers conduct a daily health check as each child arrives to identify potential health issues.

The most important measure in preventing the spread of disease in child care centers is hand washing, not only after toileting or diapering but also after nose blowing or helping a child with a runny nose or cough, and before handling dishes or serving food (Figure 12-2). There are other occasions when hand washing should be considered. For example, some states mandate hand washing following outdoor play. You may also want to encourage the practice before and after water play or following the handling of class pets. Sanitizing surfaces after diapering or on tables before using for eating also will help cut down on the spread of disease. Cleanliness is the major contributing factor to effective disease control in child care environments.

Staff members responsible for giving first aid to children and those likely to come in contact with blood or body fluids should have special training in dealing with blood-borne pathogens such as HIV or hepatitis B. Child care programs are required to offer free hepatitis B immunizations to employees when hired or within 24 hours following exposure to blood or body fluids containing blood (Marotz, 2015).

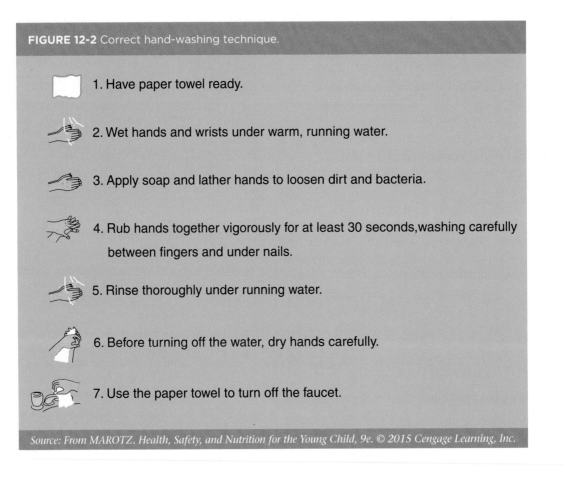

**FIGURE 12-2** Correct hand-washing technique.

1. Have paper towel ready.

2. Wet hands and wrists under warm, running water.

3. Apply soap and lather hands to loosen dirt and bacteria.

4. Rub hands together vigorously for at least 30 seconds, washing carefully between fingers and under nails.

5. Rinse thoroughly under running water.

6. Before turning off the water, dry hands carefully.

7. Use the paper towel to turn off the faucet.

*Source: From MAROTZ. Health, Safety, and Nutrition for the Young Child, 9e. © 2015 Cengage Learning, Inc.*

The spread of disease also is minimized through precautionary measures for handling situations when children become ill during the day and when children are ill on arrival. A written policy regarding management of sick children must be conveyed to parents when children are enrolled. Very few centers have facilities to care for a sick child who must be separated from the other children, so the usual practice is to call the parent or a designated adult to come for the child. In the meantime, the child usually is removed from the classroom and rests or plays quietly under adult supervision. Often, the director is the only staff person who has a schedule flexible enough to allow for time to stay with the sick child. An extra cot and a few toys for use while children are waiting to be picked up by a parent is standard equipment in many directors' offices.

## Exclusion Policy

Exclusion policies must be made clear to parents and to the child care staff. If the purpose of excluding an ill child is to prevent the spread of infection to others in the group, it is important to specify which types of illnesses require exclusion and under what circumstances children will be sent home. This list may include conditions such as the following:

- diarrhea

- vomiting three or more times within the 24-hour period prior to attending the center

- fever above 101°F (oral), 102°F (rectal), or 100°F (axillary) with changes in behavior or other symptoms such as lethargy, sore throat, vomiting, or rash (Note that a rise in body temperature is common in young children and may or may not be a symptom of a contagious or serious illness. Nonetheless, most centers have strict policies about exclusion of children with a fever. Infants younger than 4 months should be evaluated by medical personnel if they have an unexplained temperature above 100°F (axillary) or 101°F (rectal).)

- abdominal discomfort present for more than two hours or intermittent pain accompanied by other symptoms such as fever

- rash accompanied by fever or behavior changes

- mouth sores accompanied by drooling

- chickenpox (until lesions have crusted)

- head lice (until after the first treatment has been received)

- scabies (until after first treatment has been received)

- impetigo (until 24 hours after treatment has begun)

- strep throat (until 24 hours after treatment has begun)

- rubella, pertussis, mumps, measles, hepatitis A (each has a specific exclusion period and criteria for exclusion) (Aronson & Shope, 2009)

In many cases, the child's physician will provide information relative to the child's readiness to return to the center.

When the exclusion policy is clear, it helps both parents and staff make decisions about when to exclude children from the group and can reduce stress for all concerned (Button, 2008). Programs that have staffed facilities to care for mildly ill children can have more liberal exclusion policies than those without staff or space for these children to receive the extra rest and supervision they require. For working parents, finding alternative care arrangements for sick children is often a real problem. If parents don't have family leave time to use, it is helpful to provide resources for finding alternate care for an ill or recuperating child. Referring them to community agencies such as "sitters on call" or nanny services may be an answer for some families. If you locate alternative services in your community, they could be posted on the center website or published in a newsletter as a way of letting parents know that you will try to help as much as possible when their sick child is temporarily excluded from the classroom.

Although there is an ever-increasing amount 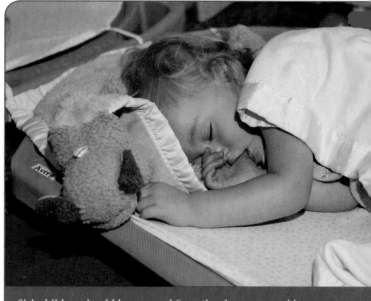 of information on the risks posed by children infected with HIV (a viral infection that can lead to AIDS) attending child care programs, evidence is inconclusive at this time. Because new information about HIV and AIDS is being generated constantly, stay in touch with local health authorities or the Centers for Disease Control and Prevention (CDC) for updated information and guidance. If a child infected with HIV applies for admission, the public health department and the child's physician can help determine if it is safe for the child to be in a group situation. They also will provide help in determining whether the presence of this child exposes other children and adults to undue risk. It should be noted that it is illegal to ask about a child's HIV/AIDS status at admission.

The number of children in group care infected with HIV may increase because newer medications and treatments are making it possible for infected children to live longer. These HIV-positive children are protected under the Americans with Disabilities Act and, therefore, cannot be denied access to educational programs. The overwhelming majority of children who are infected acquired the HIV virus from their mother during pregnancy, labor and delivery, or breastfeeding (UNAIDS, 2013). A major risk of admitting children with HIV/AIDS is that these children run a greater risk of contracting illnesses and infections from the other children because their immune systems are not functioning properly (Centers for Disease Control and Prevention et al., 2009), and these infections can pose a serious threat to the child's life. The current information regarding HIV and the hepatitis B virus (similar to HIV but more infectious) is that neither is easily transmitted in school or child care environments, nor

*Sick children should be removed from the classroom and be made comfortable under adult supervision.*

through casual contact such as touching, hugging, eating together, or sharing bathrooms. However, many centers are choosing to have a written policy on HIV and hepatitis B to protect the rights of an infected child and the other children in the center.

It is recommended that children with HIV be excluded from the group *only* if they have open sores or bleeding that would put other children at risk from exposure to the infected child's body fluids (Marotz, 2015). Whether or not there are known cases of HIV/AIDS among enrolled children, it is essential that staff follow standard precautions to prevent transmission of disease through bodily fluids such as blood, saliva, vomit, nasal/eye discharges, and human waste (urine, feces). Specific recommendations include the following:

- Use single-use disposable gloves when handling or cleaning up bodily fluids and human waste and when staff members have cuts or breaks in the skin. Utility gloves can be used, but they must be sanitized with soap and water and then dipped in a disinfectant solution up to the wrist and air dried. Disposable gloves should be discarded without being handled.

- Sanitize diaper-changing surfaces, toys, floors, walls, bathrooms, tables, and other surfaces that come into contact with bodily fluids, including human milk and human waste.

- Wash hands after coming into contact with infected surfaces/materials even if gloves are worn.

- Place contaminated materials in a plastic bag that is then securely tied and disposed of away from the children (AAP et al., 2011).

To obtain updated information on this question or others involving infectious diseases, contact your local health department or the CDC.

## Sick Child Care

As more children under 5 require some type of care outside the home, there is the consequent increase in the need for sick child care. The first alternative is to have the child at home with a caring parent whose employer allows time off for that purpose. Being at home may be the best alternative, but it is not always the most realistic. That means child care professionals, with the help of health professionals, are beginning to develop alternative sick child care models. For example, sick children might be accommodated in the following:

- a sick bay at the center (a "Get Well" room)

- a center in a separate building that might be the cooperative venture of several child care programs

- a center in a wing of a hospital or on hospital grounds that is available to the general public

- a "satellite" system of family child care homes linked to a child care center

- the child's own home under the supervision of a trained person sent from the center or local health agency

Because children with AIDS are extremely vulnerable to infection from other children, it may be unwise to have them in a sick child care facility where they would be exposed to other sick children.

# 12-3 PLANNING FOR DISASTERS AND EMERGENCIES

One of the most critical responsibilities of directors is to consider how potential disasters and emergencies might affect the lives of program staff, children, and families. Written policies should be developed that specify how such events are to be managed and should be shared regularly with all those associated with the center.

## 12-3a Disaster Planning

Although licensing regulations may not always require disaster plans, it is important to plan for building evacuation in the event of fire and to detail additional measures to be taken during tornadoes, earthquakes, smog alerts, floods, sudden loss of heat or air conditioning, or any other major emergency or national disaster. The director must instruct all staff members on the best ways to evacuate the premises and the safe places to shelter children in weather or other emergencies. It is important to practice all emergency procedures with staff so they are conditioned to respond and less likely to panic. An evacuation plan should be posted in every classroom (Figure 12-3). Fire emergency plans show alternative exit routes, and evacuation drills should be held regularly so children become familiar with this routine. Parents must be informed in advance about alternative shelters so they know the whereabouts of their children during emergencies.

Daily attendance records and information needed to reach parents must be maintained in a convenient location and removed from the building by the designated adults as part of the evacuation procedure. The "chain of command" regarding who will call for emergency fire or police help, who will secure the building and make a final check that everyone is out, how the building will be secured, and who will contact the parents all must be arranged in advance and communicated to staff by the director. Fire alarms, fire extinguishers, and emergency exit lights should be checked regularly to ensure that they are in working order. Charged cell phones should be available as well.

Supplies stored in emergency evacuation areas and to be taken to the alternative shelter include the following:

- first aid kit

- blankets

- food and water

- battery-operated radio

- flashlight

- children's books, crayons, paper, and so on

Fire, earthquake, tornado, and national emergency plans and drills are important, but keep in mind that there are many other disasters that can impact the child care center in addition to those that require building evacuation. Rehearsals for building evacuation are a necessity, but how will the staff respond when a sleeping child stops breathing, when an angry noncustodial parent appears with a gun, or when an inebriated person harasses departing parents and children? How will the staff deal with a warning of a terrorist threat? There are resources in most communities to call on for help as you develop emergency plans for a vast array of possible emergencies and as you train the staff to deal

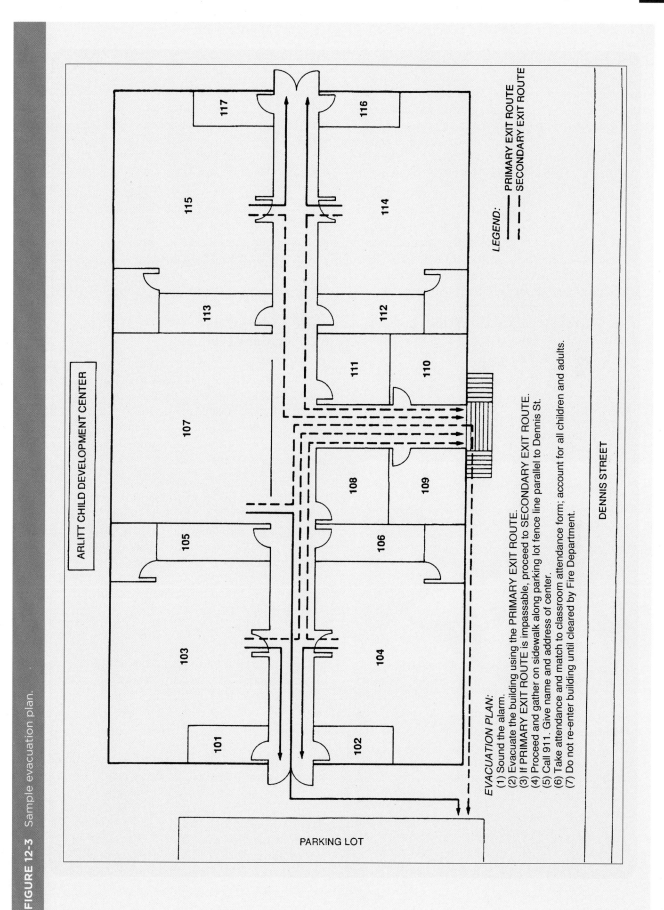

ARLITT CHILD DEVELOPMENT CENTER

*LEGEND:*
—————— PRIMARY EXIT ROUTE
– – – – – – SECONDARY EXIT ROUTE

*EVACUATION PLAN:*
(1) Sound the alarm.
(2) Evacuate the building using the PRIMARY EXIT ROUTE.
(3) If PRIMARY EXIT ROUTE is impassable, proceed to SECONDARY EXIT ROUTE.
(4) Proceed and gather on sidewalk along parking lot fence line parallel to Dennis St.
(5) Call 911. Give name and address of center.
(6) Take attendance and match to classroom attendance form; account for all children and adults.
(7) Do not re-enter building until cleared by Fire Department.

DENNIS STREET

PARKING LOT

**FIGURE 12-3** Sample evacuation plan.

with unexpected events. Invite local law enforcement personnel, health professionals, Red Cross, legal aid, and social service people to assist you with developing procedures and doing staff training. Additionally, Child Care Aware (2010) provides several resources to assist early childhood programs in preparing for disasters as does the U.S. Federal Emergency Management Agency (n.d.). You may also find the series of articles addressing development of disaster plans by Myers and Mendel (2013, 2014) to be helpful.

Directors' responsibilities do not end with plan development, training and rehearsing staff on procedures, and carrying out the plan when a real disaster strikes. They also must handle the follow-up for parents and children and deal with the press. After a crisis such as a fire, a shooting, the death of a child at the center, an allegation of child abuse or neglect, or a national disaster, it is critical that accurate information be presented to families and to the public through the press. Although this responsibility usually falls to the director, it is wise to consider who else might serve as a spokesperson. A carefully selected, knowledgeable spokesperson who is savvy about handling the press can help protect the center and its families when serious emergencies or damaging allegations such as those related to child abuse or injury arise. Choices for spokesperson may be the program's administrator or director or the center's lawyer (Bruno & Copeland, 2012). In cases where the program is an employer-sponsored center, the director of public relations or other designated individual may be selected as spokesperson. No matter who is chosen, your center's confidentiality policy precludes discussion of center staff and families. All staff must be trained to deflect media questions to the spokesperson or director and to answer informal questions from parents and others by quoting center written policy or by referring these inquiries to the director.

To obtain more information on the best methods to provide protection in particular areas, directors can contact local health and fire department and national security officials, building inspectors, the Environmental Protection Agency, or the Occupational Safety and Health Administration. Also, make sure *all foreseeable issues* are covered by various insurance policies.

## 12-3b Emergency Safety, Health, and Accident Planning

The twenty-first century presents those who care for children with new challenges relative to planning not only for children's health, injury and accidents, and natural disasters but also for the possibility of terrorist attacks. All of these plans are usually developed by the director with input from parents, staff, the board, and community groups responsible for homeland security.

Some centers may have disaster plans that are in place in case of hurricanes, tornadoes, or other weather-related events. In some cases, they will suffice for possible national security alerts as well. However, these plans need to be reviewed to make sure they are broad enough to cover bomb threats, exposure to hazardous material, and various potentially violent situations. Many states and licensing agencies prescribe forms that must be used for emergency plans (Figure 12-4).

An emergency health plan is also developed by the director. It includes the step-by-step procedures to be followed when a child is injured at the center. The purpose of this plan is to provide the center staff with a detailed set of instructions to follow when giving an injured or sick child the best and quickest treatment, notifying the family, and filling out the necessary papers for maximum liability and insurance protection for both staff and family. Many states require that centers have a medical treatment consent or authorization form on file for every child in the program (Figure 12- 5). This form, when properly completed, will give the center the authority to obtain medical treatment in an emergency situation. It usually contains specific information related to the child, such as the child's name, date of birth, address, known allergies, the child's physician, and medical insurance information. Often, there is a requirement to have this form notarized. A good resource for information on what is required for this form is your child care licensing agency.

## ▶❙❙ TeachSource Video Vignette

### Creating a Safe Physical Environment for Toddlers

This video provides an overview of the considerations in maintaining a space that is safe for young children. As you view the video, reflect on the following questions:

1.  What safety factors must be considered when planning the physical space for young children?

2.  Review the *Monitoring the Classroom for Safety Issues* video clip that appears on the same page as the video viewed above. What strategies can be used to ensure that staff members are using procedures to ensure children's safety?

**FIGURE 12-4** Medical, dental, and general emergency plan for a child care center.

Ohio Department of Job and Family Services
## MEDICAL, DENTAL AND GENERAL EMERGENCY PLAN
### For Type A Homes and Child Care Centers

| Center Name | Center Address |
|---|---|
| Campus Children's Learning Center | 555 Any Street |
| **Center Telephone Number** | |
| (XXX)XXX-XXXX | |

| EMERGENCY TELEPHONE NUMBERS | |
|---|---|
| Including 7-digit back up number as well as area code if area code must be dialed to complete the call. | |
| **Emergency Squad** | **Hospital** |
| 911 or (XXX)XXX-XXXX | 911 or (XXX)XXX-XXXX |
| **Police Department** | **Fire Department** |
| 911 or (XXX)XXX-XXXX | 911 or (XXX)XXX-XXXX |
| **Poison Control** | **Public Childrens' Service Agency** |
| (XXX)XXX-XXXX) | (XXX)XXX-XXXX |

| LOCATION OF: |
|---|
| **First Aid Kit(s)** |
| Each classroom, gyms, and closet located in main hallway |
| **Fire Extinguishers** |
| Each classroom and hallways |
| **Fire Alarm System/Main Panel** |
| Mechanical room west wing |
| **Fire Alarm Pull Stations** |
| Located throughout the building. |
| **Electrical Circuit Box** |
| Hallway next to kitchen and mechanical rooms |
| **Children's Records** |
| Front office |
| **Child Safety Seat (Or a statement that the center will use the emergency squad for emergency transportation of children.)** |
| Storage closet/teacher's work room |

In case of a **Dental Emergency**, stay with the child and summon help. When an additional staff member is present to assume responsibility for the rest of the group, consult the Dental First Aid Chart which should be posted in each room. Follow instructions indicated, notify the parents, and write an incident report. Remember if blood is involved, use vinyl or non latex gloves and sanitize afterwards following standard precautions.

**Names of staff with current training in First Aid/Communicable Disease:**
Identify staff members by name.

**Names of staff with current training in CPR:**
Identify staff members by name.

In case of an environmental emergency such as fire or tornado/weather alert, consult the posted evacuation plan/diagram or route to your classroom's "safe place". (Your local fire department or Emergency Management service should be able to help you determine this "safe" location ahead of time.)
**Fire**: Take attendance roster, secure the classroom, and exit the building with the children to the designated meeting place, which is Southwest corner of PS Playground/West side of Parking Lot. Account for all children and notify administrator or staff in charge whether all children are present or if any are missing. Do not return to classroom until the all clear is sounded. The administrator or designee should be responsible

**FIGURE 12-4** *(continued)*

for contacting the fire department or 911 if system is not automatic.

**Weather Alert:** Take attendance roster, secure the classroom, and lead children to the designated "safe place," which is classroom bathrooms and coat rooms. Account for all children and have them assume the safe position, covering head and neck. If blankets or protective covering are available, cover children. Notify administrator or staff in charge if all children are present or if any are missing. Stay in designated "safe place" until the all clear is sounded.

**Emergency Evacuation (bomb threat, gas leak, etc.):** Take attendance roster, first aid kit, and emergency contact information for children. Account for all children and exit building to the primary evacuation spot, which is southwest corner of PS playground/west side of parking lot. Account for all children with a name to face check off. Follow instructions from emergency personnel as to whether to stay in that spot or to proceed to your secondary evacuation location (which should be further away from your center in case the area around your facility also must be evacuated). The secondary location is Frericks Center on Campus. Always follow instructions of the emergency personnel on site. Parents should be notified as soon as possible. Continue to complete name to face attendance check offs on a regular basis to assure children are not lost. Complete an incident report and provide to the parents as soon as possible. ODJFS must be notified within 24 hours.

**Threat of Violence:** Secure children in the safest location in the building or outside. Take attendance roster and contact 911/Police. Follow instructions from authorities, account for all children with name to face attendance, notify parents as soon as possible, and complete an incident report for parents.

**Loss of Power, Water, Heat:** Contact utilities company to notify of outage and assess expected time of outage. Evaluate factors, including safety, temperature, daylight, refrigeration requirements, and ability to follow sanitary hygiene practices. Administrator or designee will make the determination whether the center needs to be closed or not. If in doubt contact your licensing specialist or your local health department for assistance in determining whether you can continue to provide child care services and meet rule requirements.

In the event of a **Serious Injury or Illness:** Stay with injured/ill child at all times and summon additional help if needed to supervise rest of children. Quickly complete an assessment: Appearance, Breathing, Circulation. Summon a staff member trained in First Aid/Communicable Disease if you are not trained, and determine whether EMS needs to be contacted. Check child's health information to determine if a Medical/Physical Health Care Plan has been completed for the child and contact parents. Provide basic first aid until EMS or parent arrives. Complete an incident report for parents. If child is ill, isolate away from other children; reference the ODH Communicable Disease Chart and follow instructions. Determine whether illness needs to be reported to ODH. Post exposure sign or written notice for parents. Complete an incident report for child's parent and sanitize cot/blanket if used. If blood or bodily fluids are involved, remember to wear vinyl or non-latex gloves and follow standard precautions for cleanup.

**If situation requires medical attention, ODJFS must be notified within 24 hours of the incident and report submitted within three days.**

**Supervision: Children must be supervised at all times. Children in the group must be kept within sight and hearing until additional staff are available to take control of children. Staff shall stay with children until the parent arrives.**

This plan should be posted in every room used by children and by every telephone. Every room should also have posted: written instructions for fire and weather alert, diagrams showing evacuation route and "safe place", and a Dental First Aid Chart.

Additional instructions for this facility:

*Source: Ohio Department of Job and Family Services.*

**FIGURE 12-5** Sample emergency contact information form.

## EMERGENCY CONTACT INFORMATION

Child's Name _____ Date of Birth _____

Address _____ Home Phone _____

Mother's Name _____ Business Phone _____

Father's Name _____ Business Phone _____

Name of other person to be contacted in case of an emergency:

1. _____ Address _____

   Relationship (sitter, relative, friend, etc.) _____ Phone _____

2. _____ Address _____

   Relationship (sitter, relative, friend, etc.) _____ Phone _____

Authorization is hereby given for the Child Development Center Staff to release the above named child to the following persons, provided proper identification is first established (list all names of authorized persons, including immediate family):

1. _____ Relation: _____

2. _____ Relation: _____

3. _____ Relation: _____

Physician to be called in an emergency:

1. _____ Phone _____ or _____

2. _____ Phone _____ or _____

Dentist to be called in an emergency:

1. _____ Phone _____ or _____

I, the undersigned, authorize the staff of the Child Development Center to take what emergency medical measures are deemed necessary for the care and protection of my child enrolled in the Child Development Center program.

_____
(Signature of Parent or Guardian/date)

_____
Signature witnessed by:
(Notary)

_____
(Signature of Parent or Guardian/date)

The above statement sworn before me on:

_____

_____

Source: From MAROTZ. Health, Safety, and Nutrition for the Young Child, 9e. © 2015 Cengage Learning, Inc

If the child must be taken away from the center for emergency care, the caregiver must stay with that child until the parent arrives or accompanies the child to the hospital. A signed consent form from parents that gives detailed information on where the child should be taken for emergency treatment and permission to transport the child for emergency treatment should be in each child's folder (Figure 12-5). Because the parent cannot give informed consent in advance for emergency treatment (the nature of the injury being unknown), it is essential that parents understand that the center must know their whereabouts or that of another responsible adult at all times. It is suggested that the telephone numbers on the child's emergency record, including those for the child's usual source of health care, be updated several times a year.

The director, as well as some members of the teaching staff, must be trained in administering first aid, including

**FIGURE 12-6** Sample injury report form.

**Injury Report Form**

Name of Child _____ Birth Date _____

Parent Name _____

Address _____ Phone Number _____

Usual Source of Health Care _____

Date of Injury _____ Time _____ Age _____ Sex _____

Type of Injury (circle) Bite Broken Bone Bruise Burn Choking Cut Eye Injury Foreign
Body Head Injury Poisoning Scrape Sliver Sprain Sting
Other _____

Location Where Injury Occurred _____
e.g., child care room, bathroom, hall, playground, large-muscle
room, bus, car, walk

Type of Equipment Involved _____

How Injury Happened (details of who, what, when, how): _____

_____

_____

_____

_____

Type of Treatment Required _____
e.g., first aid only in day care, visit to doctor's office or clinic,
emergency room, hospitalized, sutures, cast, bandage, medication
given

Signature of Person Filling Out the Report _____

Signatures of Witnesses _____

Name of Medical Professional Consulted _____

Date _____ Time _____ Advice _____

*Source: © Cengage Learning®*

cardiopulmonary resuscitation (CPR), so preliminary emergency treatment can begin before professional help arrives and so minor injuries will be handled correctly. An injury report must be filled out any time a child is hurt, and it should be filed in a central location with a copy in the child's file (Figure 12-6). It is essential to follow the accident plans, have staff properly trained to deal with injuries, and fill out injury reports, both for the safety and well-being of children and for the protection of staff. Directors and board members must understand that taking all these precautions may not protect the staff from liability completely. Therefore, the center should carry accident insurance on the children and have liability coverage for the staff as additional precautionary measures. It is wise to consult both an attorney and an insurance agent about what constitutes adequate coverage.

# 12-4 CHILD ABUSE AND NEGLECT

Directors must be vigilant and take steps to prevent the possibility of abuse on the premises, recognize signs of abuse on children who come to the program, and make certain that suspected cases of abuse are properly reported.

## 12-4a Prevention on the Premises

Precautions must be taken to prevent both physical and sexual abuse on the premises. Physical abuse occurs most often when adults are stressed; further, the abusive act is unplanned and explosive and usually occurs when other adults are not around. Sexual abuse, on the other hand, is frequently planned ahead (although it also occurs when other adults are not around). Pedophiles may seek employment in child care centers to gain access to children. In the latter case, careful preemployment screening and use of criminal record checks and fingerprinting may provide helpful information.

Because abuse of all types usually occurs when other adults are not around, the preventive measures mentioned in connection with staffing patterns (Chapter 9) and developing the facility (Chapter 7) and making it clear to everyone that parents may visit at any time should help eliminate the possibility of abuse occurring in your center.

## 12-4b Recognizing and Reporting Abuse and Neglect

All directors and members of the teaching staff in child care programs should have some training in recognizing the physical and behavioral signs of abuse and neglect, whether or not licensing requires it. A good resource for centers is the U.S. Department of Health and Human Services document entitled *The Role of Professional Child Care Providers in Preventing and Responding to Child Abuse and Neglect* (Karageorge & Kendall, 2008). In most states, professionals involved with children are required to report suspected cases of abuse. When mandated to report suspicion of abuse or neglect, those reporting are not required to prove their allegations. Nonetheless, reports should be made carefully because much harm can come to children and families when the accusations are unfounded. The director should be notified of all suspected cases of abuse and review the case with the staff member who has found evidence of abuse before the case is reported to the authorities. In most states, information is given to law enforcement agencies or child protective agencies. Familiarity with state laws and local rules for reporting is essential for all child care directors.

## 12-5 LEGAL ISSUES: HEALTH AND SAFETY

Lawsuits by parents resulting from injury to a child in playground accidents, exposure to serious illnesses such as HIV or AIDS, injuries inflicted by other children, or alleged child abuse are a major concern of all center staff, administrators, and board members. Lawsuits are to be avoided, not only for reasons of wanting children in our care to be kept safe and healthy but also because the suits can be won by plaintiffs even when the center staff is right. These unfortunate results can occur as a consequence of the sympathies engendered in the courts and in the press. Centers risk losing insurance coverage and suffering irreparable damage to their reputations.

The possibility of being sued for any reason, whether for an accident, a suspicion of child abuse, or alleged wrongful exclusion of a child, can be minimized by building preventive steps into your day-to-day practices.

1. Promote open, trusting communication with parents from the time they walk in the door. When parents trust center staff, they are less likely to sue when things go wrong. The positive regard they hold for the staff encourages them to talk it through and make more rational decisions before calling in their lawyers.

2. Honor the civil rights of all people with whom you work and those whom you serve. The Civil Rights Act of 1964 forbids discrimination based on sex, color, religion, race, disability, and national origin. Additionally, the Americans with Disabilities Act of 1990 prohibits discrimination against children and adults with disabilities. Beyond the legal requirements are the ethical principles that promote acceptance of diversity (NAEYC, 2011a).

3. Maintain a well-trained staff in adequate numbers to ensure proper supervision and appropriate health and safety procedures throughout each day. Make sure that staff members are aware of adults who are approved to pick up children from the center. Train staff to inspect all toys and equipment for safety hazards, report all problems in writing, and carefully fill out detailed accident reports.

4. Purchase adequate liability insurance and accident insurance on all the children, even when parents have health insurance. It promotes goodwill and means some parents will not have to cover a deductible or co-pay requirement. You will also want to work closely with insurance agents to promote principles of risk management at the center.

5. Check all applicants' references carefully and question any gaps in their employment history. Document that references have been checked under the applicant's current name as well as all previous names.

6. Keep records of all board meetings, staff meetings, licensing monitoring reports, and staff training sessions. A plaintiff's attorney can subpoena copies of any or all of these documents, in addition to other related materials such as personnel files, memos, and appointment books.

7. Have your lawyer review all promotional and marketing materials for information that might be viewed as "deceptive" under your state's consumer protection legislation.

8. Choose an attorney who is very familiar with both liability and child care laws in your state, and periodically check with your legal advisers. Make sure you discuss the idea of "due diligence" with your attorney regarding the health and safety of children and adults in your program. It is also essential to ensure that all members of your staff understand the behaviors that constitute due diligence and that they are expected to practice those behaviors.

Keep in mind that individual staff members are rarely held personally responsible for claims against the center. It is the employer who is held responsible, provided the act in question occurred within the scope of employment. Staff members may be held individually responsible only when they cause harm outside their legitimate scope of authority.

Centers are especially vulnerable to legal actions over issues of playground equipment safety and supervision and of performance of specialized health procedures to children with special needs. Additionally, programs are also vulnerable over issues related to transportation safety.

While the information in this section provides you with guidelines regarding appropriate practice, it should not be viewed as legal advice. As stated previously, administrators or directors should obtain an experienced attorney who can provide regular counsel related to owning and operating a successful, high-quality child care program.

*(Material in this section is taken from Bruno and Copeland, 2012; Child Care Law Center, 2012; and Cohen, 1998.)*

## SUMMARY

Directors are responsible for overseeing the food service and the health and safety programs in the child care center. This significant responsibility includes the following:

- Understanding how to plan menus and prepare meals with safe, nutritious food while at the same time considering cost and waste factors.

- Being aware of the responsibilities related to maintaining health and safety regulations, addressing liability issues, preventing and managing communicable disease, and providing sick child care.

- Ensuring that disaster and emergency plans are written and implemented and that staff understand the plans.

- Being familiar with child abuse and neglect laws and reporting procedures, and making sure that staff members have received training.

- Recognizing that important legal issues exist related to health and safety in a program for young children and that professional legal guidance may help forestall potential lawsuits.

## TRY IT OUT!

1. Before class, obtain the current reimbursement rates for both free and reduced-rate meals for eligible children on the USDA Child and Adult Food Program website (http://www.fns.usda.gov/cacfp/reimbursement-rates). In class, follow these steps:

    a. Using Director's Resource 12-1, record reimbursement allowances in the spaces provided.

    b. Using information from Director's Resource 12-1 and the information given in the chart "Number of Meals Served" (Director's Resource 12-2), complete the Director's Resource by calculating the amount to be reimbursed for meals served during the month.

    c. Share your results with a classmate. If your results differ, review your calculations together. If you are unable to resolve the discrepancy, share your results with another student pair.

    d. Discuss the potential administrative challenges in maintaining accurate records related to the food program.

    e. Discuss how the use of technology would facilitate the process of determining reimbursement rates for your program.

2. Work with another student and role-play a conference between a director and a cook, assuming the two roles as follows:

**Director:** As a director, you are responsible for monitoring food preparation and serving methods. You have read numerous government publications on the best way to prepare vegetables to retain nutrients. You know that cooking time should be short, that the amount of water used should be small, and that the vegetables should be prepared only minutes before eating. Furthermore, you know that children's foods should be cut in bite-size portions, that is, stew meat in half-inch cubes, bread slices in quarters, fish sticks halved, and so forth. Your cook prepares all vegetables early in the day and keeps them over low heat until serving time. Even though the recipes indicate that meat should be served in bite-size pieces and portions should be small, the meat comes from the kitchen in the same sizes in which it was delivered from the meat market.

**Cook:** You were hired for this job in the child care center after being an assistant cook in a restaurant for five years. You have looked forward to having your own kitchen, and you are proud of your previous experience and what you know about preparation of food in quantity.

As director, you must call the conference and deal with the problem. Keep in mind that you are committed to maintaining open communication and to promoting the personal and professional growth of your staff.

3. You are a new director who is interested in purchasing locally grown foods for your center. Visit the Farm to School Network website (http://www.farmtoschool. org/our-network), and check to see if your state has a Farm to School program. (If your state does not have resources available, you may want to view the materials provided for California, Massachusetts, or Ohio.) What types of programming are available in your state related to F2S? How might you go about planning to use the resources that are available in your state? What strategies would you use to convince the owner of your center, as well as the families, of the benefits provided by an F2S program?

4. As a group, discuss the evacuation plan for the room in which you are now having class. Do you see exit signs or evacuation directions in this room or in the adjacent hallways?

   a. If you were responsible for this building, what steps would you take to develop a building evacuation plan and inform the staff about it?

   b. If you had to use this room for a children's classroom, how would you evacuate the children, and how would you prepare the children for an emergency evacuation procedure without creating anxiety and fear?

   c. What issues would you need to consider in order to evacuate children or staff with medical or mobility concerns?

5. Your local chapter of the NAEYC has asked you to give a presentation to its New Director Discussion Group regarding the development of an emergency preparedness plan. Discuss what needs to be included in such a plan, and develop an outline for your presentation. What resources would you share with the group?

6. Working with two classmates, review the three sets of standards that you will find in Appendices B, C, and D at the end of the textbook. Identify those standards and competencies that relate to the health, safety, and nutrition of young children. What are early childhood professionals expected to know and be able to do related to these three areas? Discuss your findings with the class.

# Director's Resource 12-1

## FOOD REIMBURSEMENT ALLOWANCES

(for use with Try It Out! 12-1a)

|  | *Free* | *Reduced* |
|---|---|---|
| Breakfast | _____ per child | _____ per child |
| Lunch/dinner | _____ per child | _____ per child |
| Snack (supplements) | _____ per child | _____ per child |

**Fill in the above chart with information from the USDA Child and Adult Food Program website. Use this information to complete the assignment on Director's Resource 12-2.**

TeachSource Digital Download

# DIRECTOR'S RESOURCE 12-2

## NUMBER OF MEALS SERVED

**(for use with Try It Out! 12-1b)**

| Date | Breakfast | | Lunch/Dinner | | Snack | |
|------|-----------|---------|--------------|---------|-------|---------|
| | Free | Reduced | Free | Reduced | Free | Reduced |
| 3 | 12 | 2 | 21 | 3 | 21 | 3 |
| 4 | 13 | 2 | 20 | 3 | 20 | 3 |
| 5 | 11 | 1 | 18 | 2 | 19 | 2 |
| 6 | 15 | 1 | 18 | 2 | 19 | 2 |
| 7 | 15 | 2 | 18 | 1 | 18 | 1 |
| 10 | 12 | 1 | 17 | 1 | 18 | 1 |
| 11 | 14 | 2 | 21 | 1 | 20 | 1 |
| 12 | 15 | 1 | 20 | 2 | 20 | 2 |
| 13 | 15 | 2 | 18 | 3 | 18 | 3 |
| 14 | 13 | 2 | 18 | 3 | 18 | 3 |
| 17 | 12 | 2 | 19 | 2 | 19 | 2 |
| 18 | 11 | 2 | 19 | 1 | 19 | 2 |
| 19 | 13 | 1 | 18 | 3 | 19 | 3 |
| 20 | 13 | 1 | 17 | 3 | 19 | 3 |
| 21 | 14 | 2 | 19 | 3 | 18 | 3 |
| 24 | 13 | 2 | 19 | 2 | 19 | 2 |
| 25 | 14 | 1 | 18 | 3 | 18 | 3 |
| 26 | 15 | 1 | 18 | 2 | 18 | 2 |
| 27 | 16 | 0 | 19 | 3 | 19 | 3 |
| 28 | 14 | 2 | 18 | 3 | 18 | 3 |
| 31 | 14 | 2 | 20 | 3 | 20 | 2 |
| TOTAL | | | | | | |

**Using the information from Director's Resource 12-1 on reimbursement amounts for free and reduced-rate meals and the information from the chart "Number of Meals Served," fill in the following table:**

Breakfast      Number of free meals × Free rate =       _____

                     Number of reduced meals × Reduced rate =       _____

Lunch/dinner      Number of free meals × Free rate =       _____

                     Number of reduced meals × Reduced rate =       _____

Snack (supplement)      Number of free meals × Free rate =       _____

                     Number of reduced meals × Reduced rate =       _____

                     Total claim for reimbursement       _____

# REFERENCES

American Academy of Pediatrics, American Public Health Association, and National Resource Center for Health and Safety in Child Care and Early Education. (2011). *Caring for our children: National health and safety performance standards: Guidelines for out-of-home child care programs* (3rd ed.). Elk Grove Village, IL: American Academy of Pediatrics; Washington, DC: American Public Health Association; and Aurora, CO: National Resource Center for Health and Safety in Child Care and Early Education.

Aronson, S., & Shope, T. (2009). *Managing infectious diseases in child care and schools: A quick reference guide* (2nd ed.). Elk Grove Village, IL: American Academy of Pediatrics.

Bruno, H. E., & Copeland, T. (2012). *Managing legal risks in early childhood programs.* New York: Teachers College Press.

Button, L. (2008). When is a child too sick? Devising a "sick child" policy for your center. *Child Care Information Exchange, 183,* 88–91.

Centers for Disease Control and Prevention, National Institutes of Health, HIV Medicine Association of the Infectious Diseases Society of America, Pediatric Infectious Diseases Society, & American Academy of Pediatrics. (2009). *Guidelines for the prevention and treatment of opportunistic infections among HIV-exposed and HIV-infected children.* Retrieved from http://aidsinfo.nih.gov/contentfiles /lvguidelines/oi_guidelines_pediatrics.pdf.

Chapin, M. M., Rochette, L. M., Annest, J. L., Haileyesus, T., Conner, K. A., & Smith, G. A. (2013). *Nonfatal choking on food among children 14 years or younger in the United States.* Retrieved from http://pediatrics.aappublications.org /content/132/2/275.

Child Care Aware of America. (2010). *Protecting children in child care during emergencies.* Retrieved from http:// childcareaware.org/child-care-providers/resources.

Child Care Law Center. (2012). *Questions and answers about the Americans with Disabilities Act: A quick reference update for child care providers.* Retrieved from http://www .childcarelaw.org/documents/ADAQ_A-October2012.pdf.

Cohen, A. J. (1998). Bettering the odds of not getting sued. In R. Neugebauer and B. Neugebauer (Eds.), *The art of leadership: Managing early childhood organizations.* Redmond, WA: CCIE.

Committee on Injury, Violence and Poison Prevention, American Academy of Pediatrics. (2010). Policy statement— prevention of choking among children. *Pediatrics, 125*(3), 601–607.

Farm to School Network. (n.d.). *Our vision.* Retrieved from http://www.farmtoschool.org/about.

Ho, S. H., Schoenberg, D., Richards, D., & Morath, M. (2009). Using technology to control costs. *Child Care Exchange, 187,* 74–77.

Karageorge, K., & Kendall, R. (2008). *The role of professional child care providers in preventing and responding to child abuse and neglect.* Retrieved from https://www.childwelfare.gov /pubs/usermanuals/childcare/childcare.pdf.

Marotz, L. R. (2015). *Health, safety, and nutrition for the young child* (9th ed.). Stamford, CT: Cengage Learning.

Myers, P., & Mendel, M. (2013). Emergency preparedness: When disaster strikes, will the children in your care be safe? *Child Care Exchange, 213,* 20–23.

Myers, P., & Mendel, M. (2014). When disaster strikes: What to do when you have children in your care. *Child Care Exchange, 215,* 80–82.

National Association for the Education of Young Children. (2011a). NAEYC code of ethical conduct and statement of commitment. Retrieved from https://www.naeyc.org /positionstatements/ethical_conduct.

National Association for the Education of Young Children. (2011b). *Playing with food by Peter John.* Retrieved from http://www.naeyc.org/files/naeyc/file/newsroom/TYC _Nancy_Gerber_Interview.pdf.

Simon, F. (2012). Technology tools for the tough tasks: Plug in for great outcomes. *Child Care Exchange, 205,* 84–97.

Swim, T. J., & Freeman, R. (2004). Time to reflect: Using food in early childhood classrooms. *Young Children, 59*(6), 18–22.

The Ohio State University Extension. (2013). *Make a difference in the cafeteria, classroom, & community: Ohio Farm to School toolkit.* Retrieved from http://farmtoschool.osu.edu /downloads/pdf/FarmToSchoolEducatorToolkit.pdf.

UNAIDS. (2013). *Global report: UNAIDS report on the global AIDS epidemic 2013.* Retrieved from http://www.unaids.org/en /media/unaids/contentassets/documents/epidemiology /2013/gr2013/UNAIDS_Global_Report_2013_en.pdf.

U.S. Department of Agriculture, Food and Nutrition Service. (n.d.a). *Farm to school.* Retrieved from http://www.fns .usda.gov/farmtoschool/farm-school.

U.S. Department of Agriculture, Food and Nutrition Services. (n.d.b). *Income eligibility guidelines.* Retrieved from http:// www.fns.usda.gov/cnd/Governance/notices/iegs/IEGs .htm.

U.S. Federal Emergency Management Agency. (n.d.). *Coping with disaster.* Retrieved from http://www.fema.gov /coping-disaster.

U.S. Food and Drug Administration. (n.d.). *What are major food allergens?* Retrieved from http://www.fda.gov/food /resourcesforyou/consumers/ucm079311.htm.

## Learning Objectives

After reading this chapter, you should be able to:

**13-1** Identify strategies that support and engage families.

**13-2** List items to be included in written communication for families.

**13-3** Describe the components of an effective volunteer program.

**13-4** Identify local, state, and national professional organizations that can support professional growth.

**13-5** Explain why community involvement is important to early childhood programs.

*Family and community partnerships can enrich the curriculum, making learning more meaningful for children.*

## Standards Addressed in this Chapter

Accreditation Standard 7 – Families

Accreditation Standard 8 – Community Relationships

Administrator Competencies – Management Knowledge and Skills 6, 7, 8, 9, 10

Administrator Competencies – Early Childhood Knowledge and Skill 6

Professional Preparation Standards 2 – Building Family and Community Relationships

Professional Preparation Standards 3 – Observing, Documenting, and Assessing to Support Young Children and Families

In her classic 1984 article, Ellen Galinsky states, "The job of the child care center director is one that calls for enormous skill, particularly in working with parents. It is being a professional who simultaneously creates a friendly atmosphere yet retains an appropriate distance; an expert who builds competence in others, who is understanding, empathetic, yet at times firm. Most important is the role of the model—whose words or way of handling a sad, tired, or exuberant child are inspiring to parents" (p. 4). Developing a first-class program for children is the goal of the child care center administrator, and having a high-quality program cannot happen without involving families and tending to their needs. Working with volunteers and community organizations or agencies also is an integral part of the total center program that falls within the director's purview. Creating a positive climate based on good communication and demonstrating cross-cultural competence is essential for the success of this part of the program.

# 13-1 SUPPORTING AND ENGAGING FAMILIES

Center directors have a unique role in helping to establish a program that is respectful of families while also meeting the needs of children and staff. Sometimes conflicting needs of these stakeholder groups arise, and the director needs to be intentional about creating a system of policies and procedures as well as opportunities for relationship building that promote a positive outcome for all. Although classroom staff members or someone designated as a family coordinator may assume some responsibility for family involvement strategies, directors are ultimately responsible for monitoring these efforts, providing an effective role model, and serving as a resource for both staff and families.

With the recent revision of the *NAEYC Position Statement on Developmentally Appropriate Practices* (National Association for the Education of Young Children, 2009), expectations regarding family support and involvement have increased and are clearly stated in the fifth guideline, shown in Figure 13-1.

---

## MAKING THE CASE FOR *A COMPREHENSIVE COMMUNICATION SYSTEM*

Highly effective directors understand the importance of a comprehensive system of communication. Communication strategies vary greatly from traditional paper fliers placed in children's mailboxes to Facebook notices and electronic portfolios. Meeting the communication needs of families requires that directors are aware of the technologies available and also the preferences of the families being served. Directors who are effective communicators develop a communication system that includes a combination of paper and digital platforms. Communication should be both two way and ongoing. Families are bombarded with information, so directors should be selective in what they send out and should be prepared to communicate important messages three ways to increase the likelihood that the materials is read.

---

**FIGURE 13-1** Establishing reciprocal relationships with families.

Developmentally appropriate practices derive from deep knowledge of child development principles and of the program's children in particular, as well as the context within which each of them is living. The younger the child, the more necessary it is for practitioners to acquire this particular knowledge through relationships with children's families. Practice is not developmentally appropriate if the program limits "parent involvement" to scheduled events (valuable though these may be) or if the program/family relationship has a strong "parent education" orientation. Parents do not feel like partners in the relationship when staff members see themselves as having all the knowledge and insight about children and view parents as lacking such knowledge.

Such approaches do not adequately convey the complexity of the partnership between teachers and families that is a fundamental element of good practice. The following describe the kind of relationships that are developmentally appropriate for children (from birth through the primary grades), in which family members and practitioners work together as members of the learning community.

1. In reciprocal relationships between practitioners and families, there is mutual respect, cooperation, shared responsibility, and negotiation of conflicts toward achievement of shared goals. (Also see guideline 1, "Creating a Caring Community of Learners.")

2. Practitioners work in collaborative partnerships with families, establishing and maintaining regular, frequent two-way communication with them. (With families who do not speak English, teachers should use the language of the home if they are able or try to enlist the help of bilingual volunteers.)

3. Family members are welcome in the setting, and there are multiple opportunities for family participation. Families participate in program decisions about their children's care and education.

4. Teachers acknowledge a family's choices and goals for the child and respond with sensitivity and respect to those preferences and concerns, but without abdicating the responsibility that early childhood practitioners have to support children's learning and development through developmentally appropriate practices.

5. Teachers and the family share with each other their knowledge of the particular child and understanding of child development and learning as part of day-to-day communication and in planned conferences. Teachers support families in ways that maximally promote family decision-making capabilities and competence.

6. Practitioners involve families as a source of information about the child (before program entry and on an ongoing basis) and engage them in the planning for their child.

7. The program links families with a range of services, based on identified resources, priorities, and concerns.

## ▶❙ TeachSource Video Vignette

### Infants and Toddlers: Family Interactions, School, and Community

View the video vignette entitled, *Infants and Toddlers: Family Interactions, School, and Community.*

As part of the newly revised guidelines for developmentally appropriate practice, the NAEYC explains the importance of "establishing reciprocal relationships with families" (National Association for the Education of Young Children, 2009, p. 23). Read the excerpt from the position statement in Figure 13-1, and consider how well the teachers in this video met this guideline. How did the teachers in this video strive to involve families as partners in the care and education of the toddlers?

## 13-1a Reciprocal Relationships with Families from Diverse Backgrounds

The director must demonstrate a positive attitude toward families and what they can contribute to the center program. As is stated in the NAEYC Position Statement, the success of these efforts is dependent on a reciprocal relationship with families based on mutual respect. Establishing and maintaining this kind of relationship with families is challenging because of the different cultures that make up today's society and the resulting diverse views on parenting and education. The recent U.S. census reports that 20.5 percent of families use a language other than English at home (U.S. Census Bureau, 2013). This diversification of the U.S. population is impacted not only by language differences but also by varied values, beliefs, traditions, and customs related to childrearing, parenting, education, health, and a myriad of other topics that can lead to miscommunication, mistrust, and discord. It is important to recognize that differing opinions will exist, conflicts will arise, and an open exchange of ideas, goals, and needs is required among families, staff, and the director.

Interactions between center staff and families must be respectful; staff members must demonstrate intercultural competence. With the significant alterations in the American family, the changing complexion of center families requires a multicultural mindset that values diversity

(Gordon & Browne, 2010). As U.S. society becomes more heterogeneous, intercultural competence is an essential skill set for all service providers who work with young children and their families. The need to be interculturally competent is critical for all who work with young children and their families (Hanson, 2011).

## ▶❙ TeachSource Video Vignette

### Preschool: IEP and Transition Planning for a Young Child with Special Needs

View the video vignette entitled, *Preschool: IEP and Transition Planning for a Young Child with Special Needs.*

Communicating with families can be a challenging part of the job for many early childhood teachers and directors. When working with families who have a special needs child, the communication demands become even more complex. This video shows a preschool IEP and Transition Planning meeting. As you watch the video, jot down the different strategies that the teacher uses to welcome the family and help them be part of the meeting.

## 13-1b Challenges to Communicating with Parents

In addition to language and cultural differences, parents may be hesitant about communicating with the center director or staff for a number of reasons. Parenting is a challenging endeavor in even the most optimal of circumstances. Parents who are successful in other areas of their lives may have great difficulty dealing with the unpredictability of or lack of control associated with having young children. Many parents are amazed by the skill that early childhood practitioners demonstrate in getting young children to cooperate. These same parents often report feeling incompetent when they struggle to transition their crying or uncooperative children into the classroom. Add in additional factors such as poverty or a lack of school success, and many parents feel inhibited in their ability to communicate their needs to center staff (Freeman, Decker, & Decker, 2012). Feeling fully included in the center's community may also be difficult for parents who face challenges such as being a single parent, having a child with a disability, being a victim of domestic violence, having limited competence in English, or struggling with literacy.

Teachers tend to interface most easily with families who are most like their family of origin. It is important to recognize this tendency and to strive to create environments that are welcoming to all families. "A critical element in such an environment is a teacher who has taken the time to identify personal biases and has the courage to go beyond bias to reach for real understanding and appreciation of differences. Biases are mostly the result of fear, ignorance, and misinformation. It is vital that teachers make the effort to become comfortable and informed about the kinds of life experiences, values, and behaviors of diverse cultural groups and develop nonjudgmental dispositions toward working with the diversity of individual families" (Gestwicki, 2013, p. 11).

### ▶❙❙ TeachSource Video Vignette

### Communicating with Families: Best Practices in an Early Childhood Setting

After watching *Communicating with Families: Best Practices in an Early Childhood Setting*, reflect on the following questions:

1. What strategies did the teacher implement that made families feel welcome in her classroom?

2. What communication strategies could be applied to other early childhood settings?

The actions of staff and the atmosphere at the center must communicate to family members that each is valued as an individual and that each is highly regarded as the child's first teachers and as those who know a great deal about the child. All parents should be aware that they are welcome to come as frequently (or as infrequently) as they wish.

Any number of things can communicate a feeling of acceptance and trust to family members, although some are more tangible than others. A parent receiving area is the place where parents establish their first impressions of the center. Take time to look at this transition space from the perspective of a rushed parent who is late for work or a tired grandmother or uncle who enters the building to drop off or pick up a child. Is it welcoming and aesthetically pleasing, softly lit, freshly painted,

carpeted, and clean? It can be made to feel "homey" and more pleasant if there is comfortable adult seating with a collection of items for children to handle and explore. A fish tank or collection of musical instruments can draw both parents and children into the center, helping to facilitate more calm and pleasant transitions.

Parent information folders in this space sometimes contain information about the center, highlight interesting articles, and display a calendar of coming events. Pamphlets and journals on parenting, child development, toy selection, nutrition, and other resources for families can be made available in the parent receiving area. A parent and child book lending library or toy lending library might be located nearby. Sometimes, interested family members are asked to manage the entire lending program.

Some centers choose to offer additional family friendly supports such as take-out meals or dry cleaning pickup. When James Hymes originally presented this idea, he was responding to a need during World War II when mothers worked seven days a week, and many did not drive or had a limited gasoline supply if they did drive. Although few present-day parents work day or night shifts seven days a week, many find themselves using time-saving, affordable measures that help them meet their family's needs. These offerings can help ease some of the nagging stresses on young families. If you choose to offer these "extras" to your families, you must consider the space and staffing requirements, as well as costs to you and your staff in time and energy. All related expenses then should be factored into your cost per child.

The less tangible things that make family members feel welcome include the manner in which their calls are handled by the staff member who answers the telephone or the greeting they receive from the van driver who picks up their child each day. Parents' feelings about the center program and staff also are substantially influenced by their first contact with their child's teacher or the center director. It is very difficult to perceive what is having the most significant impact on the parents' reactions to a center program, so directors have to be alert to any number of subtle factors that may be influencing parental attitudes and feelings.

The building of reciprocal relationships with families depends on the feelings of trust that are established among the center staff, the children, and the families who use the center. Such trust begins to develop at the first contact and will continue to grow as it is nurtured by center staff.

The family program can be divided into three major categories:

1. family interactions

2. family support

3. family involvement

Clearly, these three aspects of the program overlap; however, they are separated here for the purpose of discussion.

## Working Smart with Technology

*Web-Based Portfolio Systems*

The parents of young children are often digital natives having grown up using technology as an important communication tool. Web-based portfolio systems appeal to many parents and offer teachers many new options for communicating with families. It is now possible for early childhood programs to provide families with access to secure web-based portfolios that include photographs, video streams, and teacher notes. Teachers can share assessment data and documentation as well as daily records that include daily routines such as diaper changes, feeding, and naps while also highlighting the rich and engaging curriculum that children experience throughout the day. Web-based portfolios can be accessed anywhere and anytime, making it possible to maintain an ongoing dialogue with family members. In contrast to the classroom cameras that parents can access in real time, web-based portfolios can provide meaning to what the parent is seeing. Because the teacher chooses what to add to the portfolio and also provides an explanation, parents are better able to understand what they are seeing. Another benefit to a web-based portfolio over a video stream is that what parents see is limited to their own child to maintain confidentiality for all the children.

Photograph by Tara Koenig

*Family members can enjoy seeing what their children are doing in school by logging onto a web-based portfolio system that can share photographs, video, and teachers' notes using a password-protected website.*

### REFLECTION

Think about a common situation in a toddler classroom where one child bites another. The fact that biting is developmentally typical for toddlers does not calm the parent who is watching a live video stream as another children takes a bite out of their son or daughter's arm. The parent of the victim is aware of who bit their child. This knowledge can lead to altercations between parents. Many see web-based portfolios as a means of sharing up-to-date information about what is happening at school while being intentional about what is shared. Confidentiality can be better maintained, and misconceptions can be avoided.

Photograph by Nicholas Dworsack

*Web-based portfolios allow families to review the child's day from the comfort of home using a variety of technology devices, including smartphones, and tablets in addition to computers.*

## 13-1c Family Interactions

Family interactions range from the most informal arrival or departure greetings, phone calls, email, and Facebook postings to formal interviews, regularly scheduled conferences, and special meetings when problems are encountered. Whatever the occasion, interactions with family members can be the basis for establishing trusting relationships. Through these contacts, the center staff members communicate to parents that they have important information to share with one another and that they have a very special mutual concern for a child whom they both value. Information that is not shared during enrollment or orientation will often be shared when trust has been established, so it is important to provide ongoing opportunities to talk. Viewing parents as partners rather than as "we" versus "they" enhances the family/center staff relationship. Chapter 10 discusses details of initial interviews and intake procedures. When staff members are not fully prepared to handle initial contacts with families, in-service training time should be devoted to discussion or role-play of parent interviews and intake procedures. (See Chapter 14 for the discussion of in-service training.)

Contacts with families range from the daily drop-off and separation in the early morning and occasional phone calls and exchange of information during the day, to the late-day reunion that can be emotional and rushed. In addition to these daily casual contacts, have a system in place for daily written communication to parents through a report form or a parent journaling plan so teachers can share something special each day about each child. All of these occasions provide opportunities to greet, welcome, and exchange information with parents but are inappropriate times to address a child's progress or to bring up more substantial problems or issues that require focused attention and discussion. It is best for teachers, families, and, ultimately, the child if these discussions are left for a planned phone conference or a scheduled parent conference.

Regularly scheduled parent conferences provide an opportunity for parents and teachers to meet at a mutually agreed-upon time and place to discuss the child. It may take several scheduled conferences and unscheduled calls or casual contacts before a teacher is successful in creating a totally relaxed environment in which both parent and teacher can discuss the child comfortably. When a good relationship exists, the scheduled conference is a time when parents and teachers can discuss the child's progress, present their concerns and their satisfaction about the child's progress, and develop a plan to follow both at home and at school that will help the child grow to full potential. In the interval between scheduled conferences, casual telephone calls and informal contacts at the center are both ways to quickly comment and update how the plan for the child and the family is working.

---

### DIRECTOR'S CORNER

"I make it clear at my very first meeting with a prospective family that we are open to parents visiting at any time. Our parents understand that even before admission to the program, they can come by to observe in our classrooms as they are weighing the pros and cons of sending their child to this center. It's the first step on the road to building a trusting relationship between the staff at the center and the families that we serve."

—*Director and owner, for-profit center*

*Transition times can provide a unique opportunity for informal but important conversations.*

---

> **FIGURE 13-2** Sample preconference planning sheet.
>
> Child's Name: _____
>
> Parent(s) Name: _____
>
> Date and Time of Conference: _____
>
> Above is the date and time of your parent/teacher conference. Please call the office and reschedule if the assigned time is not convenient.
>
> I look forward to talking with you about your child. Some of the things I have planned to share with you are:
>
> I am specifically interested in finding out about the areas of interest or concern that you would like to discuss with me. Please use the space below to tell me what those things are.
>
> Please return this to my box in the office at least a week before the scheduled conference.
>
> Thank you very much.
>
> *Source: © Cengage Learning, 2013.*

TeachSource Digital Download

Preconference planning sheets can be a useful tool in planning some parent conferences. Depending on the parent population being served, you, as a director, may have both the parents and the teachers complete a preconference planning sheet (Figure 13-2). Those parents who may have limited writing or reading skills may feel uncomfortable filling out a form with open-ended questions like those in the sample. In cases like this, teachers can call or chat with the parents when children are brought to the classroom. When dates and times are set in these casual conversations, it probably is wise for the teacher to remind families when their scheduled conference time draws near. Experienced teachers can plan the conference based on information from their notes and observations of the child, the information supplied by the family, and their knowledge of the characteristics of an effective parent conference. The director can model and provide some coaching for inexperienced staff before they conference with parents. Role-playing works well when coaching teachers.

After the preconference planning sheet has been developed, it can be used as a basis for outlining the conference itself. Items on the conference outline might include the following:

- greeting and stating the plan for this conference

- sharing a positive experience the child had within the past couple of days

- asking parents how things are at home and actively listening to their responses

- showing work samples from the child's portfolio and discussing developmental expectations in various areas represented in the samples (e.g., art, writing, etc.)

- sharing anecdotes that will focus discussion on the child's strengths as well as on those areas for potential growth (e.g., math concepts, social interactions, self-help and independence, self-control, etc.)

- asking the parents to share what they would like to see happening for their child in the classroom during the ensuing months

- developing a plan that will facilitate the child's progress toward the agreed-upon goals and expectations discussed during this conference

- closing with consensus on when the next conference should be held, while making sure the door is left open for ongoing dialogue

It is important that parent conferences start and end on a positive note and that incidents or samples of work be used to make specific points about the child's progress. Parents must be given time to express concerns while teachers practice their best listening skills. During the conference, attention to differences in communication skills, beliefs, values, and childrearing practices, all of which reflect growing up in a particular region or culture, will shape the tone and direction of the conversation. Just as early childhood professionals build trust with children by listening to concerns and reflecting those feelings, so they build trust with parents by practicing those same listening skills. Putting parents at ease and avoiding arousing anxiety enhances the quality of the relationship during the conference and carries over to the daily interactions with parents as well.

Special conferences sometimes are necessary when either parents or teachers have a need to discuss particular concerns about a child or the center program. The special conferences are likely to produce anxiety for everyone because they are called most often when a problem arises. Sometimes, the director is asked to sit in on a special conference to give support to both teacher and the family and to help clarify what is being said and heard. The teacher may have a conference with the director prior to a particularly difficult parent conference so that they both have a clear understanding of the problem to be discussed. The teacher also may ask the director to recommend the best way to present a problem and to offer some suggestions on how to handle the parents' questions and reactions during the conference. Sometimes, these special conferences include other specialists or consultants from other agencies, such as a mental health specialist or a speech and hearing professional. Both the teacher and the director should be well prepared for special conferences because they will be expected to make a knowledgeable contribution to the discussion about the child. In some cases, when outside specialists are called

in, they will have to provide support for the parent, who may feel tense and threatened.

Uninterrupted time and a comfortable space are essential for successful parent conferences. Timing is important; the time of day or evening that is chosen must suit both the staff members and the family so that no one feels pressured or rushed. The time allotted must be long enough to discuss matters thoroughly, but not so long that the discussion becomes tedious. Consider allowing at least 30 minutes of uninterrupted conversation time for a conference. Usually both parents are encouraged to attend conferences, but in cases of divorce or separation, teachers may be expected to arrange a separate conference with each parent. Both teacher and family members leave a successful conference feeling they have accomplished their goals. In addition, parents should go away with the awareness that their child is valued and appreciated. Finally, it is *critical* that parents have complete confidence that confidentiality will be maintained. The parent-teacher trust relationship will be seriously damaged if a parent learns from some outside source that shared information about the family or the child was not kept confidential.

A postconference review will help teachers evaluate the quality of their participation. It is especially important for the director to meet with inexperienced teachers after they have had a conference with a center family, even if the director participated in the conference planning or the conference itself. It is an excellent way to support new teachers and provides a time to encourage them to reflect on how they are feeling about the conference as well as what may help them in their subsequent interactions with the family. The following checklist will help them focus on their responses during the conference. Directors may want to review the following questions with their teachers after their encounters with parents:

- Did you give the parents plenty of time to talk about their concerns?

- Did you remain an accepting listener?

- Were you able to restrain yourself from giving advice? Did you ask rather than tell?

- Did you remember that suggestions usually are nothing more than advice under a different guise?

- Did the parents do most of the talking?

- Were you able to restate to the parent the feelings just expressed, always using your best active listening skills?

- Do you feel comfortable that the parent left feeling that you really cared?

## 13-1d Family Support

In recent years, the field has moved away from the parent education model that tends to focus on deficits and toward a family support approach designed to build on their strengths and foster resiliency. One such effort is the *Strengthening Families* program developed by the Center for the Study of Social Policy (CSSP). This free and open-access program is research-based and incorporates an approach to build five protective factors in families. Originally the program was designed to "reduce the incidence of child abuse and neglect by providing parents with what they need to parent effectively, even under stress" (Center for the Study of Social Policy, n.d.). It is noted, however, that many of the strategies in this program have been useful for families who have not been identified as at risk. *Strengthening Families* has been adopted by many states as the framework for state-sponsored family support programs for child care and other programs for young children and families.

One popular strategy from the *Strengthening Families* program is the "Parent Cafe," which is an approach that has been used in many programs for young children nationally. The "Parent Cafe" concept brings families together to discuss topics that they feel are important. This program capitalizes on the skills and strengths of families through a series of informal but structured small group conversations that are facilitated by trained parent leaders. The goal is to directly engage parents in building the protective factors needed to prevent maltreatment and promote healthy outcomes for their children.

The Center for the Study of Social Policy has learned that this approach is especially effective in engaging parents due to the following:

- The intimacy of the conversation and parent leadership help to create a level of candor that might not be achieved in a standard focus group or other feedback or input process.

- The careful structuring of the questions helps synthesize knowledge across a range of individual experience.

- Parents trained as cafe hosts feel that they have an area of expertise and skill base for other leadership roles (CSSP, n.d.).

Directors who seek to strengthen families look for opportunities to meet needs that are specific to the population they serve. For example, a center that serves many immigrant families may consider offering a program for English language learners. Some centers provide vocational education programs or special remedial classes to help parents complete high school or take the General Education Development test (GED). (A successful score on the GED leads to a high school equivalency certificate.) One center that served many busy professional families offered parent support resources online and chose to moderate an ongoing blog in which parents could ask questions and participate in conversations from their home or office computer. Regardless of the format and content of the parent support program, they must be built on mutual trust and strive to foster a reciprocal relationship with families.

---

### DIRECTOR'S CORNER

"A group of parents came to me with a request for a workshop on parenting skills. We had held workshops like this in the past that were not very well attended and one that ended with several parents arguing about an approach that was recommended by one of our staff members. I have to say I was a little gun-shy about offering a workshop. We then learned about the 'Parent Cafe' through our local child care resource and referral agency. Because the 'Parent Cafe' was sponsored and facilitated by families, it was well attended. Parents talked about topics important to them, and a support network was created."

—*Director, suburban for-profit center*

---

Planning parent support programs is the responsibility of the director, but the planning group should include parent and staff representatives. Format and content must reflect the needs and interests of the parents and be adjusted to the level of education and previous training of the parent population. Centers that serve families from diverse educational, cultural, and socioeconomic backgrounds should present a wide variety of choices from which the parents can select programs that are best suited to their needs.

Activities in the parent support program may be as informal as casual classroom observations followed by one-to-one or small-group discussions with a staff member or as formal as a planned lecture, workshop, panel discussion, or seminar. The planned activities should meet the parents' needs in terms of timing, content, and presentation strategy. Casual classroom observations are particularly helpful to parents who are curious about how their child's behavior compares with that of peers. For example, a mother who feels great concern about the explosive yelling and unacceptable language of her preschool son may feel reassured when she observes other 4-year-olds who also are noisy and explosive. It is then helpful for that mother to discuss these erratic outbursts with the director or a staff member who can interpret the behavior in terms of expected behaviors at this developmental stage. Group discussions, lectures, films, videotapes, DVDs, or workshops that are offered by center staff members or by outside consultants can be useful tools for providing parents with information on parenting, child development, or topics related to parental problems and concerns. Including a social time along with information sharing creates a nonthreatening, relaxed, learning atmosphere.

Topics of interest and concern to parents range from specific questions like, "What do I do about my child who awakens at 4:30 a.m. every day and wants to get up?" to broader issues facing employed parents who struggle with the stresses of job, home, and family. Programs should build on family strengths that increase parents' sense of expertise. In planning parent support programs, consider emphasis on empowering parents to explore ways to cope with their concerns and issues around parenting.

Directors are responsible for ensuring that parent support programs and parent meetings are both timely and responsive to the parents' interests and concerns. A designated parent educator may select some of the topics for parent meetings, but when parents are involved in planning parent meetings, the topics are more likely to be relevant to parents' interests (Hildebrand & Hearron, 2010).

Parent meetings usually are considered part of the total parent support program. The frequency of scheduled parent meetings varies widely from program to program. Some programs offer monthly meetings, while others have as few as one or two meetings a year. The first meeting of the year for a preschool on the typical public school calendar often is devoted to introducing the staff and taking parents through a typical day at school by using slides, videos, DVDs, or classroom visitation. The format for all parent meetings should include time for questions and for informal socialization. Regular parent meetings are a good way to create a parent support group that can be mobilized to act as a strong political force when threats to child care programs arise in your community.

Low parent turnout is a chronic issue and often very discouraging for center directors and staff who plan for parent visits to the classroom, prepare refreshments, and look forward to meeting and sharing with parents. It requires creative planning, taking time to determine the best timing for meetings, and exploring what might interest this particular population of parents. Maybe they want to learn about using the Internet or have a tasting party of Thai foods. Shifting from an exclusive focus on parenting sometimes can encourage more families to attend center functions. As center gatherings become popular, parents may begin to ask for more meetings that focus on parenting issues or child development.

## 13-1e Engaging Parents

Parent conferences and parent support programs are, indeed, parent engagement, but the parent involvement concept implies a more extensive parental commitment than participation in parent conferences or in selected parts of the parent education program. Although parents should be encouraged to become involved, they also should have the option to remain uninvolved. It is an imposition on the parents' right to choose if they are made to feel that they must become involved in the center program. Of course, if the program is a co-op, then by definition it requires full parent participation.

The NAEYC has incorporated family and community culture as an important influence in designing quality developmentally appropriate practice for young children (National Association for the Education of Young Children, 2009). One purpose of parent involvement is to get parents active in planning, implementing, and evaluating the total program. In some comprehensive child care programs such as Head Start, parents may serve on advisory and policy boards, participate in all aspects of program planning and classroom activity, take part in the evaluation of staff and program, participate in budget and personnel decisions, and come to understand their role as advocates for their children.

Parents sometimes enjoy working regularly in the classroom or helping with children's parties or field trips, and some center programs depend on the help that parents can provide. Before parents participate in any aspect of the children's program, they should know something about classroom ground rules, routines, and what to expect of the children. The mother who comes to read to the children may need some help on how to include children other than her own in a small, informal, shared reading experience. The father who takes a morning off to come and read to the children may be disappointed when only three or four children are interested enough to stay for more than one book. He must be helped to understand that children have choices and that they are free to choose not to participate. It also is helpful if he knows the ground rules about deciding who chooses books to be read and techniques for helping children wait to have their choice read. Parents who work in the classroom on a regular basis should be expected to participate in a more extensive orientation program before being assigned specific tasks when they come to the center. Both parents and volunteers can attend the same orientation sessions.

There are innumerable ways for parents to be involved in the center program other than direct classroom participation. They can do clerical work, repair or make equipment, take responsibility for the lending library, babysit during conference periods or committee meetings, drive carpools, and participate in advocacy endeavors with help from staff. If they have special talents or interests in fund-raising, they can serve as a resource for the center board or the director. If they have special language skills, they can provide priceless service in bilingual programs. There also are many opportunities for parents to serve in a variety of ways on the board, on advisory committees, or on any number of standing or ad hoc committees. (See Chapter 4 for the discussion of the composition of the center board and of the committee structure.)

Clearly, when the director is committed to parent involvement and that attitude prevails throughout the center, it is possible to find a special place for every parent to participate, provided the parent has the time and interest to become involved. However, the director must be sensitive to individual family situations. Employed parents who are unable to be involved with center activities must be reassured that they are free to choose not to

*Parent volunteers can inspire children to look at an existing activity as new and novel.*

participate. Successful parent involvement does require some management; therefore, the center staff must make a commitment to give that program the time and attention it requires.

## 13-1f  Working with Demanding Parents

The best centers work to empower parents. Administrators and teachers develop partnerships over time with parents who gradually come to feel they are a valued participant in their child's care at the center. There always will be angry parents and some "high maintenance" parents who will challenge the staff. Staff members will have to remember and practice their best communication, conflict resolution, and problem-solving skills when faced with these parents.

There are situations in which staff feelings and perceptions work against forming partnerships with parents. Parents can become "they" when these staff members get together for staff meetings. "They don't tell us what is happening at home." "They don't follow through at home." "They don't set any limits at home." Or "They are too restrictive at home." Staff might comment, "They don't care" when referring to a parent who seems to have

no interest in discussing child-related issues. On the other side of that coin, a staff member may comment, "She will not leave me alone—she questions me about everything he did or said while he was here at school and wants to know exactly what I did in response to his actions." Helping staff value diversity in family lifestyles and attitudes, as well as how various parents choose to communicate or not communicate with staff about their concerns, is something directors can plan to discuss at staff meetings and staff retreats and can model in their interactions with families (adapted from Greenman, 2003). It is helpful if staff can manage to view parents as partners and find ways to see situations from the parents' point of view.

Every program, sooner or later, will have to deal with angry and/or "high maintenance," demanding parents. Directors can encourage all staff to make encounters and exchanges with these parents, as well as all other parents, as customer friendly as possible. Child care staff may not view families and children as customers, but a review of what customers are may clarify for all that the center clients are its customers.

- Customers are people who buy products or services from you.

- Customers are not dependent on you; you are dependent on them.

- Customers are not interruptions to your work; they are the purpose of your work.

- Customers are not people you argue with; they are people you value and serve (adapted from Phipps, 2003).

Directors and all center staff are obliged to work on building positive relationships with children and center families (customers). When confronted with the angry parent's tirade or the needy "high maintenance" parent's demands on their time, it is an opportunity for center staff to make effective conflict resolution part of their customer service plan strategies (see Figure 13-3). Customer interests and needs must be dealt with in a helpful and respectful manner, even when they are extreme and unrealistic in terms of center policy or developmentally best practices or violate privacy and confidentiality rights of the director, teachers, or families.

Responses to parent demands will depend on the nature of the concern and availability of resources to meet those demands. Many demands will be best served by talking with the parents; inviting them to observe; or encouraging them to attend parent meetings that focus on topics such as child development, early childhood practice, or center policies regarding transitions, fees and admissions, referrals, and so forth. Parents who demand that toddler teachers use whatever procedures necessary to toilet train their child or insist the "biter" in the classroom be removed from the program may respond to reading materials about toddler development or a discussion group with other toddler families, after discussing

**FIGURE 13-3** Sample conflict-resolution policy in a parent handbook.

**Conflict Resolution Policy: Conflict between Adults**

While every effort is made to meet the needs of children, parents, and staff, we realize that from time to time a conflict may occur between parents, staff, and administrators. The following process is followed should a conflict occur:

- Step One–A respectful discussion is held between the persons directly involved at a time and place that assures privacy and sufficient time for a thorough resolution to take place.

- Step Two–If resolution is not found at the first meeting, a second meeting is held with the director for the purpose of creating a plan for resolution and a timeline for expected success.

- Step Three–If the conflict is not resolved according to the timeline, adjustments may be made to the plan, and an additional timeline be established, or:

- Step Four–If at any time the director determines that resolution is not possible, s/he will consider one of the following for immediate action:

1. Removal of the child from the classroom
2. Withdrawal of services from the center
3. Suspension of the staff member until disciplinary steps can be taken
4. Involvement of the Assistant Dean of the School of Education and Health Science

- Grounds for determining that a resolution is not possible include but are not exclusive of the following:

1. any person involved displays inappropriate behavior such as shouting, accusing, name-calling, swearing, or physical assault
2. any person involved refuses to follow the prescribed process
3. any person involved jeopardizes the process by spreading information concerning the conflict to those outside the immediate conflict or those involved in the resolution of the process.

*Source: Reprinted with permission from the Bombeck Family Learning Center of the University of Dayton.*

the issue with the director. Preschool parents who insist that their child be taught the alphabet through drill and practice or finish all the food on the plate before leaving the table may need to better understand center curriculum and be willing to look over a copy of the center's Curriculum Framework and discuss it with the director, or attend a meeting with other preschool parents to hear the staff talk about best practices for this age group. When there are issues regarding meals, a parent might be interested in observing mealtime in one of the preschool classrooms followed by a conversation with the director and the teacher about developmental expectations that relate to eating and appetite for this age group. Working with demanding parents is time-consuming and difficult but essential for center morale, center community building, and letting families know that their needs and concerns are taken seriously and will be heard.

## 13-1g Parent Feedback

Parents' viewpoints and suggestions can be solicited with rating scales or questionnaires. Some method of gathering evidence about family satisfaction with the parent program or parent involvement opportunities should be done annually. The information gathered is then summarized and evaluated so adjustments can be made to best meet parents' needs. Much information can also be gleaned from parent-teacher conferences, when teachers can make family-specific inquiries such as "Are your needs for information on Alley's daily experiences and interests being met?" or "How would you prefer we communicate

during your maternity leave about how Ben is handling the arrival of the new baby?" However, written evaluations or rating scales that draw attention to particular features of the total parent program, like the daily reports that are prepared for parents or the specialists brought in to discuss issues relevant to kindergarten readiness or infant "tummy time," offer respondents time to ponder and reflect on the attention given to the program. As families have time to consider what is offered, they will not only realize the breadth and depth of the parent program but also may choose to communicate ideas about how it might be improved. Directors must continue to let parents know that they are eager to hear from them and to partner with them to provide the best possible experiences for all members of the center community.

**DIRECTOR'S CORNER**

"I realize now that I really have to keep in touch with what parents are thinking about our program and how they see us. Last year we had two or three families leave our program, and I wasn't really sure why they were making a move. When I contacted several of them, I realized they were feeling that the quality of our program was not what they had come to expect from us. Of course, I acted on that immediately, but I also developed a rating scale for parents to complete so they could let us know how we're doing."

*—Director, suburban for-profit center*

## 13-2 WRITTEN COMMUNICATION MATERIALS FOR FAMILIES

A handbook for families is a convenient way **naeyc** to communicate basic program information and should be distributed to all families at some point in the enrollment procedure. The contents may change from year to year and vary from program to program, so directors will have to use some general guidelines for developing a handbook, and then adapt those to their specific program. Some items, such as program philosophy or grouping children, may or may not be part of the marketing brochure but could be repeated in the handbook. As a director, you will have to decide what information parents need to know and the best way to convey it to them. If a handbook seems too overwhelming for the particular parent population in your program, consider putting an item or two on colorful single sheets to be handed out over a period of several weeks after admission to the program.

The suggested list of items that follows is not exhaustive but provides broad guidelines for developing a parent handbook (see sample handbook for families in Director's Resource 13-1). Directors often choose to avoid including items likely to change, such as names of staff and fees. One option is to have a pocket in the back cover where single pages can be added and removed as updates are needed.

Suggested items for a parent handbook include the following:

- brief statement of the program philosophy
- outline of the daily program and an explanation of how it fits into the program philosophy
- fees and arrangements for payment, including details about reimbursement possibilities and credit for absences
- car pool and/or transportation arrangements; if transportation is not provided, indicate that fact and state what information you need to have about the family's transportation arrangements for the child
- expected arrival and pickup times and procedures
- center policy on health and safety precautions to be taken by the family and the center staff to ensure the health and safety of children; state your policy about bringing medication to the center and children coming to the center when symptoms of illness are apparent, cover the procedures used by the center staff when a child becomes ill at school, and so on
- explanation of liability and medical insurance carried by and/or available through the center
- sample menus for snacks and/or meals and any expectations the staff may have about eating
- services the center staff will offer to children and families, such as opportunities for having conferences, special medical or psychological services or referrals, discussion groups, group meetings, and so on
- center discipline policy
- requests for help from parents such as for time spent in the classroom, help on field trips, clerical help, making materials for the classroom, and so on
- summary of scheduled events at the center and what families may do at the center to celebrate holidays and birthdays; make the policies in this regard reflect the program philosophy by including what to send, what to expect the child to bring home, which holidays will be celebrated, and so on
- expectations about the child's use of transition objects while getting adjusted to the center and policies about bringing other items or food from home, making clear how these policies are developed to meet the needs of children and to reflect the program philosophy
- description of the legal obligations of center staff to report any evidence of child abuse

This list provides guidelines for developing a handbook that ultimately must be fashioned to fit your program and your parent population. In writing material for a handbook, consider content, format, length, and, most important, style of writing. Should the style be scholarly or chatty, formal or informal, general or detailed? Answers to these questions can be found by giving careful consideration to the families being served by the program.

The family handbook is a useful tool to acquaint parents with the center program initially and to help them understand what to expect. However, it must be supplemented with other written and verbal communications to keep them abreast of center events and the progress of their children. Other details concerning your program can be listed on your website. In some communities, it will be necessary to publish not only the handbook but all written materials in another language in addition to English.

Some directors send parents a newsletter describing special events that are being planned for children or families. It is important for parents to know that one family brought their new baby to visit the classroom or that a musician from a symphony orchestra came to show the children a slide trombone. Such information will help parents understand a child's questions and any ideas that are expressed at home. Newsletters can keep parents informed about the center's progress, program philosophy, special programs, and future plans. It can include a monthly calendar, information about fund-raisers, updates on staff changes, and activities. Including a profile of a staff person, another parent, or a center volunteer is a sure way to generate readership and enthusiasm about your newsletter. News items from each classroom are always welcome, especially if children's names are mentioned. Parents will search the pages to find a mention of their child or their child's teacher. Best of all, parents are eager to read the "Director's Message," which is a must for each issue. Remember, the director sets the "feeling tone" for the center, and the tone of a "Director's Message" communicates that to parents (Jones, 1996).

Other ways to communicate with families include meetings, regularly scheduled parent conferences, use of email, a center website, and telephone calls to tell parents about happy experiences their children had at school. Center staff must take advantage of every opportunity to communicate with the family to learn more about them and their child, to share ideas about the child, and to strengthen the basic trust in the relationship.

## 13-3  VOLUNTEER PROGRAM

Volunteers are welcomed in most early childhood education centers, and the volunteer program usually is managed by the center director. Occasionally, a member of the center staff other than the director or a volunteer who is willing to undertake the coordinating responsibilities manages the volunteer activities. The coordinating function includes recruiting, orienting, and scheduling the volunteers. Other aspects of the volunteer program, such as planning activities for the volunteers and handling the supervision and record-keeping responsibilities connected with a volunteer program, either must be delegated or performed by the director. Volunteers are often interested in ways to advocate for children.

### 13-3a  Volunteer Recruitment

Recruiting volunteers is time-consuming, but there are individuals in every community who are potential volunteers. Finding those people who have both the time and the interest in serving a child care center may present a problem at the outset; however, a program that provides both challenge and appropriate incentives soon will build up a roster of available volunteers who come regularly.

Available sources for recruiting volunteers will vary, depending on the size of the community and the demands of other agencies in the community. Larger cities have organized volunteer bureaus, Junior Leagues, universities with student volunteer programs, child advocacy groups, and any number of philanthropic groups that can supply volunteers. Church groups, high schools, senior citizen groups, and business groups are other sources that can be found and approached in both large urban communities and small rural areas. The volunteers must feel that they are welcome and needed; in addition, they must feel a sense of personal regard for their efforts.

*Parent handbooks can be made available as a hard-copy booklet or online as part of the program's website.*

After volunteers are recruited, screening them is essential to the success of the program. Meeting with each one personally will enable the director or volunteer coordinator to find a good fit between the volunteer's interests and abilities and program needs. Volunteers must understand that they will be supervised by the volunteer coordinator, who will apply essentially the same principles of supervision that are used for regular staff.

### 13-3b  Volunteer Orientation

Participation in the volunteer orientation program should be a requirement for every person who chooses to give time to the center program. Although it may seem presumptuous to insist that volunteers participate in an orientation, it is essential that they become completely familiar with the operation of the center and that they have a clear understanding of how their services fit into the total service offered by the center program. Furthermore, the volunteers usually recognize that a center staff person who will take the time to plan and carry through a meaningful and helpful orientation program for them also will value their involvement in the center program.

Orientation meetings should provide volunteers with a staff directory and introduction to as many staff members as possible. The director should talk about the organizational structure of the agency, the goals and objectives of the center program, and the importance of volunteer help in meeting those goals and objectives. Further, licensing standards and health requirements for volunteers must be explained. That will clarify what is expected of them regarding immunizations, health examination, and classroom health and safety procedures, as well as help them understand the rationale for restrictions on their participation. For example, in most places, a volunteer may not be alone at any time with a group of children because of licensing and insurance requirements. When the rationale for that ruling is understood, volunteers are less likely to be offended when told they may not take the children on a walk or drive them the few blocks to the park.

Confidentiality is an issue for everyone at the center, including the volunteers. It is wonderful to have volunteers who become ambassadors for the program in the community, but it is essential that they adhere to a strict policy of absolute confidentiality. Volunteers who share their general enthusiasm about working with the children or doing other work for the center can be a great asset, but talking about specific children, families, or teachers can be very damaging to your program.

Other details that should be covered at the orientation meeting include sign-in and sign-out procedures for volunteers, and where they should call if they expect to be absent. Record keeping is necessary because many publicly funded centers must report volunteer hours, and some private agencies often choose to keep records and reward volunteers based on their hours of service. Evidence of a strong commitment to a program by volunteers is useful when applying for grant money.

*Volunteers are sometimes asked to participate in setting up classroom activities.*

## 13-3c Volunteer Activities

Volunteers can do most things that family members do in a center program, and they often have more free time than working parents or parents with young families. Volunteers, like parents, must be made to feel welcome, and, like parents, they must leave with a sense of satisfaction and a feeling that their services are needed and appreciated. Because they do not have the reward of seeing the joy their own children experience by having them participate in the program, it is doubly important for the center staff to make them feel welcome, to define their task for them, and to let them know how highly their service is regarded. Volunteers will continue to serve only in situations in which they feel needed.

---

**REFLECTION**

Think about your own volunteer activities. Perhaps you tutor younger students or work in a program for children with disabilities. What motivates you to be there at the scheduled time? Do you look for excuses not to go? If not, why not? How do you feel about yourself after you spend time volunteering? What rewards do you receive?

---

# 13-4 ORGANIZATIONS AND AGENCIES

In addition to working with parents and volunteers, the director is responsible for involvement with professional organizations, referral agencies, and the community in which the center is located. In each case, the amount of time and degree of involvement vary according to the type of center and the director's individual style. Involvement in professional organizations and community outreach are both addressed in NAEYC Accreditation Standards and the Program Assessment Scale (PAS).

## 13-4a Professional Organizations

Directors frequently join one or more local, regional, and national professional organizations. Sometimes, the board encourages and assists them by paying their dues (a list of professional organizations is presented in Appendix F). Through these memberships, directors can accomplish several goals.

First, directors can obtain information and make contacts that may be personally and professionally helpful. Therefore, they may select organizations that focus on development of administrative skills, presentation of research data, and provision of information about legislation and funding. Through contacts at group meetings, the director may meet potential staff members, although "pirating" staff from other centers certainly should be avoided. Directors also may see professional organizations as providing a forum for their ideas, a place where they can speak before a group and discuss their concerns with other professionals. They may volunteer to hold meetings at their centers, thereby providing opportunities for others in the field to see different early childhood education facilities.

When directors join a professional organization, the organization is enhanced because the directors have had a number of years of education and experience and carry some influence in the community. As a result of their having belonged to these organizations or similar groups for a time, they have expertise that can help move the group forward, and they can give guidance to newer, less experienced members.

Directors may join professional organizations to become part of a group that effects change. The professional groups offer many advocacy opportunities. Legislators who will not listen to an individual's recommendations on teacher-to-child ratios or low-wage issues may be persuaded by an organization's stand, and directors can have input through their membership in the organization.

In some communities, directors form support groups because they need a forum to discuss problems unique to their particular position. They can share information and ideas and work out cooperative plans for staff training. With the increased, widespread focus on child care, national support groups are forming to provide hotlines, websites, consultation services, and management retreats.

When they join organizations, directors serve as models for staff members. In some cases, the staff profits more directly from the organization than the director, but staff members put off joining or may even be hesitant about attending meetings if they do not know other members. Directors can provide an incentive by offering to accompany teachers to the first meeting and by notifying staff members of upcoming meetings. Directors may work out a plan for released time from center duties that staff members can use to participate in the work of professional organizations. They also may provide staff meeting time for members who have attended sessions to share their information.

For similar reasons, directors should attend (and facilitate staff members' attending) lectures, courses, and conferences that are related to early childhood education. Directors also have the responsibility for reading current books, periodicals, and resources on the Internet and passing relevant materials on to staff members. Most staff members will respond positively to an article from the director that is marked to indicate a personal application such as, "This article addresses an interest of yours, new ways of teaching math concepts." Or, "Have you seen the reviews of these new multicultural books? Which ones should we order?" This personal touch encourages the staff member to read the article and perhaps discuss it further with the director. When the director has provided a model of this behavior, staff members may begin to circulate articles or books that they have found to be worthwhile.

## 13-4b Referral Agencies

Directors contact referral agencies and advise staff members to use special services when that is appropriate. Directors also help staff members delineate the boundaries of their own professional expertise and recognize those circumstances under which an opinion obtained from another type of professional could be useful.

The job of relating to referral agencies begins with the collection of a list of services that are available in the surrounding community. In some areas, a booklet is published that contains the names of all the social service agencies, their addresses, telephone numbers, fax numbers, websites, hours, charges, what services are provided and to whom, and whether a referral from a physician or case worker is required. Some communities add other kinds of information, such as lists of recreation centers, churches, schools, and government agencies and officials. If this type of directory is not available, a center director can develop a referral list. Writing the data on file cards or putting the information into a computer file provides a convenient reference that can be updated easily.

After determining which agencies provide services related to the clients' needs, directors should attempt to make personal contact with as many of these agencies as possible. This contact can be accomplished by visiting the agency, attending programs sponsored by the agency, and meeting its staff members at professional meetings. Later, when the need arises for services from such an organization, it will be easier for the director to make contacts with the people whom he already knows. The director also is in a good position to explain the nature of the services provided by these agencies to the center staff and to parents when necessary.

In addition to working with the staff in referring children and families for care and treatment, directors make use of agencies in other ways. For example, agencies usually have personnel and material resources available for in-service training or parent meetings. Some agencies in the community, such as Community Coordinated Child Care (4Cs) or child care resource and referral agencies, provide consultation and technical assistance. A range of services may be available from other types of agencies such as the public library, which usually offers storytellers, films, and teachers' collections of books.

**DIRECTOR'S CORNER**

"When I first became a director, one of the things I had trouble finding out about was the whole referral network, and I realize that takes time and comes with experience. You have to know the agencies, how they work, and the particular people to contact before you can help your teachers or your families with referrals. I always feel better when I can call a specific person whom I have already met. In addition to growing my network over time, I started with two key resources available in most counties—our referral hotline that could direct me to services across a variety of needs and our Child Care Resource and Referral agency, which was a one-stop shop for information related to young children, families, and child care services."

—*Director, YMCA-sponsored center*

If the center's program includes the provision of medical, dental, and mental health services to children, the director may be able to provide these services at low cost and with convenient scheduling through agency contacts. For example, arrangements can be made for a physician to come to the center to do routine physical checkups so that children do not have to endure long trips; boring waiting rooms; and strange, frightening buildings. The director, who is well acquainted with physicians, psychologists, speech therapists, and social workers, is able to depend on their services but is sensitive to the needs and limitations under which they operate. It is important that directors establish reciprocal relationships with these professionals by being open to accepting children referred to the center by them and their agencies.

## 13-5  COMMUNITY INVOLVEMENT

The director explains the center to the com-   **naeyc**
munity and, in turn, explains the community
to the staff. This function requires familiarity with the community in which the center is located. If some or all of the children who attend the center live in other communities, the director should become informed about those areas as well.

In marketing and publicizing the center to the community, the director uses public relations and communications techniques that were covered in Chapter 10, including news releases, open houses, and tours of the center. The effective use of the interpersonal skills that were discussed in Chapter 9 is particularly appropriate when working with the community. The appearance and maintenance of the center's building and grounds also can have an influence on the relationship with the community.

Sometimes, individual members of the community become interested in the center and its work through the director's efforts. For example, the owner of a lumber yard may agree to provide scrap lumber for the children's woodworking projects, or a printer will offer to save all the paper ends from print jobs for the children's use. If the director and staff have met the local grocer and other shopkeepers, these businesspeople may be far more responsive to the children when they visit on field trips or when they walk by as they explore the area with classmates. A university in the area may be interested in sending architecture or product design students or may come to do research. In addition, child advocacy groups in the community may offer information and support to center staff and families.

Directors help their staff members understand the community by encouraging involvement in community activity and by providing information about life in the community. Having knowledge of the historical background of the area and the cultural or ethnic groups that live there will increase staff awareness of the needs of families who come to the center. The director is responsible for making center staff members sensitive to the customs, language, and values of the people they serve. Frequently, staff members live in other communities and represent different cultural or ethnic groups. It is impossible for staff members to work effectively with children and parents from a culture about which they have no knowledge.

When the director has done a good job of understanding the community, and when all the pertinent information is conveyed to the staff, everyone at the center gains a greater appreciation of the community, and a strong working relationship can emerge. The center's team of staff, parents, and children working together can be expanded to incorporate community members as well.

## SUMMARY

The director works with or is accountable for establishing a reciprocal relationship with families. A major aspect of this role is helping staff members establish effective relationships with parents. Attention needs to be paid to family interaction, family support, and family involvement.

The director needs to emphasize the participation of individual parents to the degree that is appropriate and comfortable for them. Directors also are involved in recruiting and orienting volunteers and in providing recognition for their services. In addition, they work closely with professional organizations, referral agencies, and members of the community. Part of their role involves setting an example of an appropriate amount of professional involvement for staff members and training them in the techniques of working with a variety of resources. Directors also provide information to staff members and give them opportunities to make use of the services that professional organizations, referral agencies, and the community have to offer. To be able to collaborate with families, volunteers and the community, directors must do the following:

- Identify strategies that support and engage families.
- List items to be included in written communication for families.
- Describe the components of an effective volunteer program.
- Identify local, state, and national professional organizations that can support professional growth.
- Explain why community involvement is important to early childhood programs.

# TRY IT OUT!

1. Consider an early childhood program where you work or had a practicum experience. Use Director's Resource 13-1 to evaluate the components of the communication system being used in this program. Start the evaluation by reading the principles and strategies listed in column II and evaluate the current level of performance using the following ratings:

   N = not yet addressed
   E = emerging
   P = proficient

   Then, from the list of principles and strategies that were rated "not yet addressed" or "emerging," select a target for improvement, and complete the *Action Plan*.

2. Divide into groups of three for the purpose of role-playing a parent conference. In this situation, a young mother has requested a conference about her 3-year-old son who spends a great deal of time in the housekeeping area in the classroom. He also plays with dolls, washes dishes, and dresses up in a skirt and high heels at home. The father is very upset and annoyed by this behavior and has pressured the mother into calling for a conference. The father is unable to attend the conference. The roles are as follows:

   - male teacher
   - mother
   - female director

   Using the checklist shown in Director's Resource 13-2, discuss each item listed. If you were the director or the mother in the role-play, give your perception of how well the teacher handled the questions asked.

3. Using the "Volunteer Tasks Form" in Director's Resource 13-30, develop a list of specific tasks a volunteer could do in the specified classroom areas.

# DIRECTOR'S RESOURCE 13-1

## FAMILY ENGAGEMENT SYSTEM SELF-EVALUATION

Person/s completing this form: _____ Date: _____

Strong family engagement emerges from an intentionally developed system that engages families in meaningful ways While a system may include activities, experiences and programs, effective family engagement is broader and more inclusive than models that view family engagement as an event. This tool is designed to assist professionals as they develop and facilitate family engagement systems and strive to reflect research based practice. This tool can be used to communicate these practices to others who may not be familiar with the research on family engagement. The process of self-evaluation starts by asking the user to read the principles and strategies listed in column II and evaluate the current level of performance using the rankings provided below. Then, from the list of selected principles and strategies, users select a target for improvement and complete the *Action Plan* on page 4. Those interested in learning more about effective family engagement systems should visit the Family Engagement Collaborative of the Miami Valley at www.familyengagementcollaborative.com.

### NOTES:

1. For the purposes in this document, "culture" Is broadly defined and refers to family characteristics related to ethnicity, heritage or history, race. religion, socio economic status, education level, sexual orientation, region of origin, language and communication style, family configuration, and other factors that comprise aspects of the family's identity.

2. SOA refers to School, Organization, or Agency

   Program **Current Level** Rankings N = not yet addressed. E = emerging. P = proficient

| 1. Program current level | II. Principles and Strategies | III. Examples of Practice that Support the Principles and Strategies | Prioritize |
|---|---|---|---|
| | **A. Effective family engagement programs build relationships between the school/organization/agency (SOA) and families.** | | |
| | 1. **Establish and maintain partnerships** between the family, teachers and SOAs that reflect the belief that families, teachers, administrators and community members jointly share responsibility for school readiness and success.<br><br>■ *Ready Communities + Ready families + Ready Schools = Ready Children* | ■ Programs are generally interactive with opportunities for all parties to contribute to the agenda and participate in programming.<br><br>■ Information is communicated respectfully in a manner that shows regard for the contributions of both families and SOAs to support children as they learn and develop. | |
| | 2. **Establish a family engagement team** that includes families and representative members of SOAs to design, implement, and monitor the family engagement plan. | ■ SOAs include families from the very beginning of the design process.<br><br>■ SOAs include families in the design, implementation and evaluation of the family engagement plan in meaningful ways. | |
| | 3. Conduct a family survey to learn about how the family engagement system can meet the needs of families. | ■ SOAs get family input in the design of the survey.<br><br>■ The survey utilizes family friendly language.<br><br>■ The survey garners valuable information without being intrusive. | |

# DIRECTOR'S RESOURCE 13-1 *(continued)*

| 1. Program current level | II. Principles and Strategies | III. Examples of Practice that Support the Principles and Strategies | Prioritize |
|---|---|---|---|
| | 4. **Use data about families to plan**, implement and reevaluate a comprehensive family engagement program. | ■ The program reflects the data collected from families through the survey. ■ Data is collected from families and re-evaluated on an ongoing basis. | |
| | 5. **Incorporate many roles** for the SOAs including but not limited to that of facilitator, co-trainer, learner, advisor, host, cook, convener, advocate, business broker, cultural interpreter, instructional leader and others as appropriate. | ■ SOAs are not limited by the traditional view of professional roles. ■ SOAs acquire new knowledge, develop new skills and expand their roles to meet the needs of families. | |
| | **B. Effective family engagement programs appropriately meet the needs of families and children.** | | |
| | 1. **Empower families by focusing on strengths** and avoiding a deficit model. | ■ SOAs demonstrate a broad understanding of the complexities of family life and seek out and support areas of strength. ■ SOAs avoid assigning blame and seek out strategies to support families toward success. ■ SOAs avoid expert-novice role assignments in which the role of the SOA is that of expert while families are uninformed novices. Instead, use information sharing models that value strengths. | |
| | 2. **Address children and families' basic needs** before higher learning skills. | ■ Programs attend to physical needs such as food and comfort. Efforts are made to make children and families feel welcome and safe. | |
| | 3. **Recognize that many factors act together** to influence the development of a child. | ■ Programs balance the needs of SOAs to communicate information, policies and procedures with the needs of families to be engaged in meaningful ways. ■ Programs are both relationship and task oriented. | |
| | 4. **Provide information about community resources** available to support families and educators. | ■ Community resources are shared through a variety of mediums (print, web-based, verbally). ■ Where and how to find resources is communicated effectively overtime. ■ The resources provided are up-to-date with working links and accurate contact information. | |
| | 5. **Incorporate the Six Protective Factors** associated with Strengthening Families as described by the Child Welfare Information Gateway (U.S. Department of Health & Human Services) https://www.childwelfare.gov/preventing/preventionmonth/factors.cfm. | ■ The program fosters and addresses the importance of the following factors: 1. Nurturing and Attachment 2. Knowledge of Parenting and Child Development 3. Parental Resilience 4. Social Connections 5. Concrete Supports for Parents 6. Social and Emotional Competence of Children. | |

# DIRECTOR'S RESOURCE 13-1 *(continued)*

| 1. Program current level | II.  Principles and Strategies | III.  Examples of Practice that Support the Principles and Strategies | Prioritize |
|---|---|---|---|
| | **C.  Effective family engagement programs establish a comprehensive system of communication.** | | |
| | 1.  **Work with families to create a clear mission statement** for family engagement systems in order to establish, communicate and accomplish goals. | ■  Families are actively engaged in creating a clear mission statement. <br> ■  The goals for the family engagement program are clearly stated and regularly communicated. | |
| | 2.  **Include a two-way home and SOA's communication system** consisting of multiple opportunities for families to receive and provide information orally, in writing, and/or through the use of technology. | ■  Information is communicated multiple times using a variety of communication vehicles both formal and informal <br> ■  Vehicles for communication utilize new media (Facebook, Pinterest, Tumblr) when appropriate and reflect how families access Information. | |
| | 3.  **Include both formal and Informal meetings and/or home visits** with families in which both SOA's and families can contribute to the agenda. | ■  SOAs plan opportunities for informal interaction with families. <br> ■  SOAs schedule formal meetings or conferences during which families can participate and contribute to the agenda. | |
| | **D.  Effective family engagement programs embrace and respect the cultural background of all families.** | | |
| | 1.  **Include activities that have a clear cultural connection** to the community and the participants. | ■  Family engagement activities respect and, when appropriate, celebrate the traditions and culture of families. | |
| | 2.  **Involve SOA facilitators who are familiar with the culture** of the school and community. | ■  In addition to obvious cultural traditions, the family engagement system reflects an understanding of subtle cultural tendencies. <br> ■  SOA facilitators make use of culture guides who interpret and provide access to culture understandings of the families. | |

*Family Engagement System Continuous improvement*

## ACTION PLAN

Select a strategy or strategies from column II as a target goal or goals for improvement. Develop a plan of action including the activities, timeline and the person/s responsible for completing all aspects of the plan. Activities should be observable and measureable and evaluated regularly.

| Target/s for Improvement <br> State in observable, measurable terms | Activities <br> Observable and measureable tasks that relate directly to target goals | Timeline <br> Start and end dates | Person/s Responsible | Check when complete |
|---|---|---|---|---|
| *Principle/Strategy:* <br> *Goal/s:* | | | | |
| *Principle/Strategy:* <br> *Goal/s:* | | | | |

*Source: Reprinted with permission from the author S. M. Adams, Family Engagement Collaborative of the Miami Valley, 2014.*

# DIRECTOR'S RESOURCE 13-2

## ROLE-PLAY CHECKLIST

**(For use with Try It Out! 13-2)**

After the role-play is completed, discuss the items in this checklist. If your role was that of director or parent, respond to the questions in terms of your perception of how well the teacher handled the conference. You are expected to give more than yes or no answers. Document your answers with examples from the conference.

Did you give the parent time to talk about her concerns?

Were you a receptive listener?

When you made comments, did you talk in terms of the parent's feelings?

Were you able to restrain yourself from giving advice?

Did the parent do most of the talking?

What was accomplished during the conference?

# Director's Resource 13-3

## VOLUNTEER TASKS FORM

**(For use with Try It Out! 13-3)**

List specific tasks a volunteer could be assigned to do in each of the classroom areas or activities listed below. Think beyond supervising children. Consider care and development of materials, enriching the area, or making it more aesthetically pleasing.

Dramatic play (expand beyond house-type play)

Carpentry

Literature/library area

Writing center

Lunchtime

Nap time

# REFERENCES

Adams, S. M. (2014). *Family engagement system self-evaluation.* Dayton, OH: Family Engagement Collaborative of the Miami Valley. Retrieved from http://www.family engagementcollaborative.com/family-engagement -system-self-evaluation.html.

Center for the Study of Social Policy. (n.d.). *Strengthening families: A protection factors framework.* New York: Author. Retrieved from http://www.cssp.org/reform/strengthening-families.

Freeman, N. K., Decker, C. A., & Decker, J. R. (2012). *Planning and administering early childhood programs* (10th ed.). Upper Saddle River, NJ: Prentice Hall.

Galinsky, E. (1984, July). How to work with working parents. *Child Care Information Exchange.* p. 1–4.

Gestwicki, C. (2013). *Home, school & community relations* (7th ed.). Belmont, CA: Cengage Wadsworth.

Gordon, A. M., & Browne, K. W. (2010). *Beginnings and beyond: Foundations in early education* (6th ed.). Clifton Park, NY: Thomson Delmar Learning.

Greenman, J. (2003). Places for childhood includes parents, too. In R. Neugebauer & B. Neugebauer (Eds.), *The art of leadership: Managing early childhood organizations* (rev. ed.). Redmond, WA: Child Care Information Exchange.

Hanson, M. J. (2011). Diversity in service settings. In E. W. Lynch & M. J. Hanson (Eds.), *Developing cross-cultural competence: A guide for working with children and their families.* (4th ed.). Baltimore, MD: Brookes.

Hildebrand, V., & Hearron, P. F. (2010). *Management of child development centers* (5th ed.). Columbus, OH: Merrill.

Jones, R. (1996). Producing a school newsletter parents will read. *Child Care Information Exchange,* 91–93.

National Association for the Education of Young Children. (2009). *Developmentally Appropriate Practice in Early Childhood Programs Serving Children from Birth through Age 8.* Washington DC: Author.

Phipps, P. A. (2003). Working with angry parents: Taking the customer service approach. In R. Neugebauer & B. Neugebauer (Eds.), *The art of leadership: Managing early childhood organizations* (rev. ed.). Redmond, WA: Child Care Information Exchange.

U.S. Census Bureau. (2013). *American FactFinder.* Author: Washington, DC. Retrieved from http://factfinder2 .census.gov/faces/nav/jsf/pages/newsandnotes_listing .xhtml?_nnitem5.

*Professional development is most effective when it is job-embedded and interactive, and follow-through is expected.*

## Learning Objectives

After reading this chapter, you should be able to:

**14-1** Describe the role of staff meetings as an important professional development tool.

**14-2** Identify the elements of an effective staff development system.

**14-3** Describe effective supervision and coaching strategies.

## Standards Addressed in this Chapter

**naeyc**

Accreditation Standards 10 – Leadership and Management

Administrator Competencies – Management Knowledge and Skills 1, 3, 8, 9, 10

Administrator Competencies – Early Childhood Knowledge and Skill 10

Professional Preparation Standard 6 – Becoming a Professional

The center director is responsible for the personal and professional development of the staff. In very large centers or in corporate systems, the business and fiscal maintenance functions may be separated from the educational program maintenance, in which case, the education director is accountable for the educational program and the accompanying staff development programs. However, in most centers, one person is responsible for both the business and educational program components.

The basic assumptions underlying staff development programs are that learning is a lifelong process and that adults have the capacity to change and grow. This capacity is, in a sense, analogous to that manifested by children in their growth processes. The director's responsibility as it relates to the center staff parallels that of the classroom teacher: to create a favorable environment for optimum growth and development of all the people in the environment. When the director serves as a model of professionalism in handling staff meetings, staff training or coaching programs, and staff supervision, as well as assessing staff problems, the personal and professional development of the center staff is facilitated and enhanced.

The core of the staff development system is staff training and professional development, both of which are supported and promoted through staff supervision and coaching. The specific content or the specific strategy employed in any aspect of the staff development program depends on group composition. In the same way that classroom teachers assess the needs of children in planning appropriate learning environments, directors evaluate staff needs and plan staff development programs accordingly.

In place of the "career ladder" common to many professions, the field of early care and education has adopted the metaphor of the "career lattice." It represents the multiple entry points for and the expertise of those in our field who have years of experience and job-embedded professional development but may be pursuing a degree by stacking credentials and degrees incrementally. Others in our field may have relatively new degrees in early childhood but lack the experience of the veteran teacher. To meet the needs of both groups of teachers, the field must provide multiple opportunities for growth and development. Early childhood professionals often need to advance the career lattice horizontally, vertically, or even diagonally to meet their goals. (See Figure 14-1.)

## 14-1 PLANNING MEETINGS TO SUPPORT DEVELOPMENT

One vehicle for providing ongoing and job-embedded professional development is the staff meeting. The director is responsible for planning and conducting meaningful and relevant staff meetings. Bloom states that meetings are very important. In fact, she says meetings are "the glue that holds the organization together" (Bloom, 2002, p. 1). Although conducting a staff meeting may seem to be a routine and relatively easy task, holding meetings that are satisfying and worthwhile for both the director and the staff requires careful planning and preparation. Effective implementation of the planned agenda is dependent, largely, on the director's ability to maintain open communication among those attending the meeting.

### 14-1a Purpose of Staff Meetings

Communication is the main purpose of staff meetings. Although much can be communicated through email, newsletters, posting bulletin board

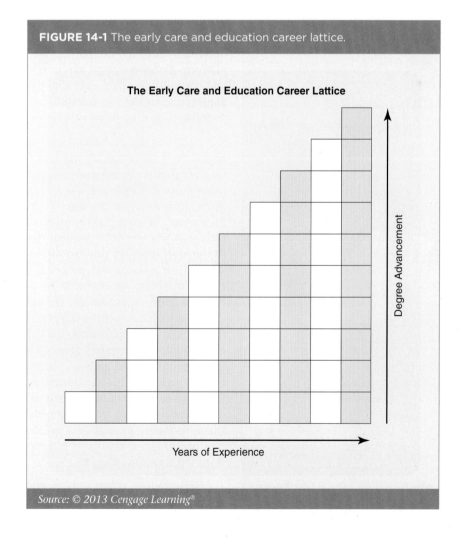

**FIGURE 14-1** The early care and education career lattice.

**The Early Care and Education Career Lattice**

Degree Advancement

Years of Experience

notices, and exchanging information on a casual one-to-one basis, many issues and problems are resolved most effectively in a meeting. Communication should be two-way, with opportunities for staff to solve problems, share ideas, engage in team discussion, and complete important tasks.

Two-way communication in a meeting permits an interchange of ideas and feelings and provides a forum for thoughtful discussion and clarification of problems and issues. The final outcome for each individual should be a better understanding of problems and issues and of self and others. When staff members are involved in discussing program issues or problems, when their opinions have been heard, and when they have had some voice in decision making, they feel a greater sense of self-worth and consider themselves a more integral part of the total center community. To be comfortable for everyone, staff meetings must provide a safe environment where staff members can ask questions, challenge others by presenting alternative ideas, and share feelings with the group.

To prevent the meeting from deteriorating into a "gripe session," the director can take an active role in channeling the complaints and concerns toward improvement

*Staff meetings can be good times for training if the amount of time needed is short and the task at hand would benefit from peer or director support.*

strategies. Open communication during staff meetings is one way to develop cooperation and harmony and to encourage the "we" feeling among staff members. This is further advanced when staff members are encouraged to suggest staff meeting agenda items. A sense of community is fundamental for the creation of a favorable environment for the personal growth of staff members, children, and families who participate in the center program.

When the director becomes aware that there is an undercurrent of discontent among the staff, a staff meeting discussion focused on concerns and issues may be useful, but only after talking informally with several staff to see if the problem can be remedied, thereby leaving staff meeting time for other agenda items. If, however, staff unrest persists, it may be necessary to assess staff morale through the use of a *climate survey*. A well-designed survey tool that includes items related to motivation, commitment, satisfaction-dissatisfaction, and other concerns can yield useful information that directors then can use to provide a framework for a staff meeting discussion. The climate survey becomes a means to an end because it helps staff focus on their most urgent issues, and it helps the director bring the staff meeting discussion toward problem resolution. Bloom, Sheerer, and Britz (2005) suggests that the climate of the organization is akin to the personality of the center. Both the director and staff can have input into the design of the survey tool, which can be developed easily through such online tools as Survey Monkey, a platform for surveys that can be completed anonymously and compiles the data into easy-to-read charts. It may be appropriate to share the results of the survey at the next staff meeting, presenting new action items as appropriate.

Staff meeting discussions may involve specific questions, such as which piece of outdoor equipment to buy, or whether to buy tricycles or books with the equipment money available at the end of the year. Sometimes, discussions focus on the use of available building or outdoor space, or on the appropriateness of timing the meal service or the monthly fire drill. The director may decide to use staff meeting time to discuss more general philosophical or educational program issues such as, "What changes should we consider in our program planning to focus more attention on emerging literacy?" A question that logically follows is, "How do we, as a staff, learn more about the application of a balanced and interactive early literacy approach?" Discussions about both educational program and general program philosophies often lead to group decisions about the focus and content of future in-service training sessions. If the group makes decisions about the training needs of the teaching staff, there undoubtedly will be a greater commitment to the training program than if the director makes those decisions without group input.

Nonetheless, when staff meeting discussions are not of particular relevance to those in attendance, boredom and restlessness become apparent, and members feel that the time is wasted. To maintain interest and open communication, try to select agenda items that are of concern to most of the staff members who are expected to attend the regular staff meetings. Remember to use icebreakers and various problem-solving strategies that will help maintain interest and keep staff focused. Make certain that the purpose of the meeting, whatever it may be, is clearly stated and understood by everyone at the meeting (Bloom, 2002). The agenda items that pertain only to the work of a few can be reserved for special meetings or assigned to small committees for discussion and subsequent decision making.

## 14-1b Timing of Staff Meetings

The frequency and timing of staff meetings vary, depending on the amount of business typically transacted and the amount of time devoted to each meeting. Weekly or biweekly meetings that are well planned and brief may be more productive than long sessions that are held less frequently. Although staff members usually prefer daytime meetings because they need evenings and weekends to rest and take care of personal matters, evenings may be the only time everyone can meet together.

> ### DIRECTOR'S CORNER
>
> "Our staff scheduling problems are so complex, there is no way I can plan a staff meeting during the day. We have evening meetings, and everyone is expected to attend. Each new employee is advised of that expectation and assured that she will receive overtime pay or hours for work will be adjusted."
>
> —*Director, employer-sponsored child care center in hospital setting*

In half-day programs, staff meetings can be scheduled after the children leave at noon, or in centers with double sessions, either early in the morning or late in the afternoon. However, full-day programs present special problems because the centers are open from early morning until very late afternoon, and the center staff usually works a staggered schedule. Nap time is often the time set aside for meetings because most staff members are present in the middle of the day; however, sleeping children must be supervised. Use of volunteers or parents for nap time supervision is an alternative but one that licensing disallows in some places. In smaller centers, hiring substitutes to cover nap rooms may be a better solution.

The center staff and the director decide which staff members, in addition to classroom staff, should be encouraged to attend staff meetings. It may be beneficial to have the bus driver, the cook, or the receptionist at staff meetings because the kind of contact these staff members have with the children and families enables them to make a unique contribution to staff meeting discussions. Directors also may find it useful to ask the consulting psychologist, the special education resource teacher, or other professionals who are involved in the program to attend staff meetings. Anyone who can profit from, or contribute to, the discussions should be encouraged to come to the meetings.

## 14-1c Preparation for Staff Meetings

Both the director and the staff members must prepare for a staff meeting so that the meeting will be productive for everyone. The director is responsible for obtaining staff input on agenda items, preparing and posting the agenda, and distributing any material that should be read by the staff before the meeting. Even though the director holds final responsibility for planning the agenda, all staff members should be invited to suggest agenda items either before or after the agenda is posted. The posted agenda might include a brief description of each item and the action to be taken. (See Figure 14-2.)

> ### DIRECTOR'S CORNER
>
> "I reserve one half-hour at the end of each monthly staff meeting and have one staff member take over the meeting. Last month a teacher talked about a workshop she had attended on dealing with stress. It was great! We all participated in some of the stress-relieving exercises she had learned."
>
> —*Director, church-sponsored early education program*

For example, if the agenda item about the use of outdoor space is to cover the timing for its use, the responsibility for setting up and cleaning up, and the equipment needs, then all these subjects for discussion would be listed. The agenda also should state clearly which items are open for discussion *and* group decision and which items are open only for discussion. In the latter case, the director hears the discussion, considers the ideas and feelings of the staff, and subsequently makes the decision. In the case of the outdoor space questions, the classroom staff probably should decide about the timing for the use of outdoor space; the total staff, including the janitor or housekeeper, should be involved in the discussion and decision about setting up and cleaning up the space; and the final decision about equipment purchase is made by the director after hearing the preferences of the entire staff. When all these expectations are spelled out clearly on the posted agenda, there is little room for confusion or misunderstanding about what will occur during the meeting.

Each item on the posted agenda includes the name of the person responsible for presenting the item and leading the discussion and a rough time estimate for adequate

**FIGURE 14-2** Sample staff meeting agenda.

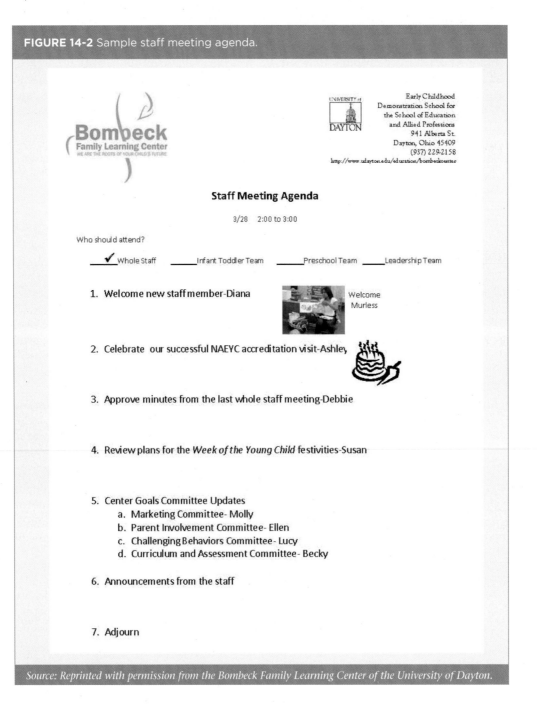

coverage of the item (see Figure 14-2). This procedure notifies staff members about their responsibility during the meeting and ensures coverage of the entire agenda within a specified meeting time. Giving staff members' responsibility for selected agenda items is an excellent way to encourage interest in center operations. Reserving part of each meeting to have a staff member present on a topic of interest also contributes to the feeling of collegiality.

The director should distribute copies of readings, minutes from previous staff or board meetings, and any other information that will provide a common basis for discussion to enhance the quality of the dialogue during the meeting. For example, if curriculum planning will be discussed as it relates to authentic assessment, research studies and program ideas on this topic could be duplicated and given to staff members several days before the meeting. Individual staff members can also be encouraged to search out additional information on the topic so the time spent during the meeting is productive and informative for everyone. Occasionally, a specialist from the community can be invited to a staff meeting to contribute to a discussion that requires particular expertise, such as services provided by the local children's protective agency or new information on infectious diseases in child care centers. When the director prepares the agenda carefully, and both the director and the staff members come well informed, the outcome is more likely to be satisfying for everyone.

## 14-1d Staff Meeting Procedure

The director usually serves as the convener and assumes the responsibility for moving the group through the agenda by facilitating, but not dominating, the discussion and helping the group maintain a balance between dealing with tasks and dealing with interpersonal processes.

At the outset, it is important that the meeting begin at the stated time and end on schedule. When the convener does not call the meeting to order on time and moves immediately to the first agenda item, group members are inclined to come late because they assume the meeting will not start on time. When the discussion of an agenda item extends beyond the time assigned, the convener should call attention to that fact and have the group decide whether more time should be spent on that item.

Time management is important. Time is finite, and you and your staff must develop good time-management skills to accomplish as much as you can within a specified time frame. The staff meeting is an excellent place for you, as a director, to demonstrate good time management.

Clearly, conducting an effective staff meeting takes careful planning and requires special skills on the part of the director. However, when meetings are satisfying and productive for the staff, they serve as a vehicle for communication and promote cooperation and good feelings among staff. Furthermore, staff meetings give the director a chance to model interpersonal communication skills that serve as the basis for all interactions with children, parents, and other staff members.

> ### REFLECTION
>
> Think about your class and study schedule and your other responsibilities. When a class is scheduled to convene at 4:00 p.m. and end at 5:30 p.m., you feel very frustrated if you rush to arrive on time only to find that the instructor is 15 minutes late. Furthermore, you may have to get home to family or prepare dinner, and you become restless and inattentive if the class goes beyond 5:30 p.m. The only way you are able to manage your time well is to have others with whom you must interact regularly maintain their time commitments to you. The same is true for you and your colleagues at the workplace.

## 14-2 EFFECTIVE STAFF DEVELOPMENT

The staff training and professional development program begins with the orientation of new staff members and includes all aspects of in-service training. Planning the total staff professional development program depends on the composition of the center staff. Just as the classroom teacher individualizes approaches to specific children, the director recognizes the developmental level of each teacher and plans training accordingly. The staff professional development must be adjusted to the experience level and career stage, as well as to the specific concerns, capabilities, and perspectives of each person, and it should focus on long-term growth and change in individuals' thinking skills (Bloom, Sheerer, & Britz, 2005).

It is the director's job to work with staff to construct a professional development program that meets the needs of the staff in a manner consistent with the center's mission. Comprehensive, job-embedded professional development is required for teachers to advance through what Tanner and Tanner (2007) describe as the three levels of teacher competency. In a field where many teachers have limited training, it is common to find early childhood programs with teachers who are at Tanner and Tanner's "first level," in which teachers rely on materials made by others (e.g., kits, worksheets, and prepackaged curricula) and do not engage in critical evaluation of materials or instructional activities. Frequently, teachers at Level I implement a series of disconnected activities that fill the day but lack the capacity to reflect on what children know and are able to do in order to design curriculum that incorporates the children's interest and meets the children's individual needs. Teachers in this stage require professional development that recognizes where the teachers are and supports their progress to the next level.

As teachers receive higher levels of professional development and support, they develop competencies at Tanner and Tanner's "second level," which requires them to recognize that instruction should reflect the emerging issues of the classroom and should also integrate content areas and developmental skills. A teacher at this level may understand that effective classrooms respond to individual needs but may be unsuccessful in knowing how to put their understanding into action. For example, Tanner and Tanner (1995) describe one Level II teacher who tried to focus on a letter of the week and connect it with each new theme because she knew that good programs support emergent literacy and connected learning. Her lack of understanding of how to implement this understanding led to simplistic connections, such as choosing the letter "d" for the farm unit, singing "BINGO" (because it was about a dog), and also signing the "Farmer in the Dell" (because dell begins with "d") (p. 10). Level II teachers may be more aware of what young children should know and be able to do, but they often lack the skills to design instructional environments that fully integrate curriculum content into learning experiences that challenge and inspire young children. Directors who have a lot of teachers at Level II will need to be very intentional in providing professional development that moves the staff from where they are to Level III.

Teachers at Level III are able to exercise independent judgment and adapt curriculum to meet children's individual needs (Tanner & Tanner, 2007). Tanner and Tanner describe a Level III teacher's ability to make curricular decisions in an example where the teacher had planned to teach a theme about living things and began the theme with a class visit to a pet store. Although the teacher had planned to focus on pets in general, she adapted her curriculum when she saw the children's excitement about the snake that was fed a live mouse, which led to a more specific focus on snakes and their prey (1995). In this example, the teacher had a sound understanding of what children should know and be able to do and had sufficient understanding of related content knowledge. The teacher also demonstrated a sense of efficacy in that she had confidence in her skill to design a learning environment that capitalized on the interest of the children and facilitated an extended investigation of a topic worthy of study.

According to Tanner and Tanner (2007), no matter what a teacher's background, he or she cannot implement a curriculum well without initial training and ongoing professional development. To be effective, such training should be provided by individuals who are familiar not only with adult learning principles but also with the realities of teachers' classrooms. Tanner and Tanner (2007) advocate for the use of comprehensive professional development plans.

### ▶❚❚ TeachSource Video Vignette

### Teaching as a Profession: An Early Childhood Teacher's Responsibilities and Development

View the video vignette entitled, *Teaching as a Profession: An Early Childhood Teacher's Responsibilities and Development.*

In this video, you will see Samantha, an early childhood teacher who is very skilled at articulating her practice. Being able to talk about what she is doing and why makes her an excellent mentor for other teachers. In the video, Samantha talks about her experience as a mentor. She also describes her own professional development, which includes examples of job-embedded professional development. Listen carefully and list all of the types of professional development that Samantha mentions. Be sure to include both formal and informal examples.

## 14-2a Professional Development Plans

Professional development plans should  be comprehensive in terms of the staff's professional level and in terms of the length of time that the staff member has been at the center. Fully trained and qualified classroom teaching staff members should have basic child development information and should be able to plan curriculum and classroom management strategies with minimal additional training. However, they may be ready for some help on working with the special education resource teacher who comes to consult with them about the children with disabilities in the center. Because special classroom strategies must be employed to truly include children with disabilities into a noncategorical classroom, training in techniques and strategies to accomplish that integration also will be helpful to the experienced teacher. The interdisciplinary classroom team of early childhood and special educators must work together to provide quality programming for all children in an inclusive environment. An interdisciplinary team building and staff development approach for both the special educators and the early childhood staff is to provide mutual training so these professionals together develop their own professional skills, as well as come to appreciate more fully the knowledge and skills of other members of the team. As team members come to accept and extend the skills and knowledge of fellow professionals, mutual respect and camaraderie are reinforced.

Teachers at Tanner and Tanner's (2007) first level, assistants, aides, and other paraprofessional classroom staff may need coaching in preparing classroom materials, in understanding growth and development, or in developing basic management skills. The classroom teacher is responsible for ensuring that all adults working or volunteering in the classroom understand the program's philosophy as well as the curriculum being implemented. Those who work in the field of early care and education are commonly more comfortable working with young children than supervising adults. The center director needs to ensure that staff members have the knowledge, skills, and time to collaborate with the other adults working in the classroom. Likewise, the custodians, food service staff, and clerical staff will need different levels and types of assistance.

When planning a staff training program, the director will have to assess the training needs of everyone, and then make decisions about time, content, and training methods for the sessions. An experienced director can assess training needs by observing staff as they carry out their job responsibilities and by having conferences with them to discover more about their own analysis of needs and their interest in professional advancement. Assessment of staff training needs and professional development should flow from staff self-evaluation as well as from directors' formal evaluation procedures and discussions from staff meetings. As directors glean insights into individual staff needs and interests, they can search for appropriate and challenging staff training and educational opportunities.

## 14-2b Time for Training

Finding a suitable time for training meetings is even more difficult than finding a suitable time for staff meetings. In the case of regularly scheduled staff meetings, the staff can plan ahead for the full year and schedule their other duties and commitments around the meeting times. However, training sessions that usually occur with less regularity often require a larger block of time than a staff meeting and have to be planned to coincide with the schedules of consultants or outside experts whose services are needed. If the director and center staff members are the only people involved in the training, scheduling difficulties are alleviated somewhat. Nonetheless, the issues of late afternoon or evening fatigue, and the inability of the staff to leave the classroom during the day, create special problems for the training of child care staff, unless the sessions can be planned for nap time or incorporated into the staff meetings. Because most training requires larger time blocks, it may be necessary to discuss the possibility of a Saturday meeting or a weekend retreat. Half-day preschool programs that usually meet during the public school academic year often have training meetings in the early autumn before school begins or in the spring after school closes. In any case, if in-service training attendance is mandatory, this point must be included in the employee's job description and spelled out during orientation of new employees.

## 14-2c Mandatory Training

Decisions about whether attendance at training sessions should be mandatory or optional used to be decided by the director at the center level. Now licensing, state quality rating systems, and reimbursement policies often require a given number of hours of training each year. Individual teachers may be responsible for keeping track of and completing required training to maintain their teaching credential or eligibility. Because the stakes are very high (i.e., centers can lose funding, a quality rating, or accreditation if staff lack required training), the director needs to establish a process for tracking mandatory training and a vehicle for staff to be able to go to training during work hours when possible.

Training may be required by the center to maintain consistent programming or to address new challenges, opportunities, and program goals. This kind of training can be exciting to plan because it reflects what makes the program unique. Directors and interested staff can work together to create professional development opportunities that reflect the program's unique culture and goals. This training is important and requires whole staff involvement to gain buy in.

---

**REFLECTION**

Think about your personal feelings when you were told that you had to attend some function such as a meeting, a party, or a class, as opposed to the times when you were given a choice. When it was a matter of choice, what were the factors that motivated you to attend? Was it curiosity about who would be there or what would take place? Was it interest in what you expected would take place? Was it to please the person who requested you attend or who told you about the event? Can you analyze your feelings and reactions when you went someplace to please someone else as opposed to the times when you went because you were intrinsically motivated?

---

## 14-2d Place for Training

When there is a comfortable lounge or conference room at the center, the staff may prefer to stay in the building for the training sessions. The comfort and familiarity of the center will help create a feeling of openness, which could be very important if the success of the training is dependent on dialogue and exchanging ideas among staff members. If the training is a cooperative effort involving several centers, a space in a centrally located community building may be more convenient for the trainees. Sometimes, getting away from the center can be helpful. Regardless of the venue, the space should be comfortable, with adult-sized furniture, including tables that provide a writing surface, and an opportunity for interacting with colleagues.

## 14-2e Training Methods and Resources

The methods or strategies employed in the in-service training program will depend on the amount of time

---

**MAKING THE CASE FOR *JOB-EMBEDDED PROFESSIONAL DEVELOPMENT***    **naeyc**

The paradigm for professional development has shifted from one-shot inspirational training to a model in which professional development is job embedded and follow-up is included. Teaching teams need to feel accountable for implementing what they have learned, and they also need to have support and feedback. Research shows that effective professional development is job embedded and is integrated into the workday. Professional development that is most likely to impact change focuses on improving classroom practice and consists of teachers finding solutions for authentic and immediate problems (National Staff Development Council, 2010). Directors who want to get the biggest impact invest in job-embedded professional development.

provided, the resources available, and the nature of the content selected. For example, if one hour of a staff meeting is set aside for a refresher course in first aid, the best way to present that information may be in a lecture given by an approved trainer from the health department. If, on the other hand, there is more time to spend on the topic of first aid, it may be desirable to plan a full-day session with a Red Cross specialist. Enrolling some staff members who do not have first aid certificates in a Red Cross course that extends over several weeks and is available evenings or on Saturday is yet another alternative. First aid training can be expanded to include health, nutrition, and safety. The expansion of the program creates new training strategy possibilities. Group discussion led by the director is an appropriate method to use in making the staff more aware of safety issues in the center. The program could include discussions about safety when using outdoor equipment, when planning cooking experiences, or when organizing field trips. The health or nutrition questions might be handled best by a nurse, physician, or dietitian who would come for a seminar. A special educator might come to discuss health and safety issues as these relate to special-needs children. When outside consultants are brought in, the director's role is to sit in on the training to be able to do follow-up with the staff, thereby extending the new information to specific situations that each teacher encounters in the classroom. Directors can choose from many possible methods, each one requiring different amounts of time and different resources and all individualized to meet the needs of the trainee. A list of training resources in the community as well as national opportunities should be available in the director's library at the center.

*Providing a comfortable room with tables and chairs facilitates collaboration between colleagues.*

On-site workshops are useful mechanisms for encouraging direct involvement of the staff in a special content area. Implicit in the workshop concept is the idea that those who attend participate actively in the program. Frequently, workshops are planned for a staff that expresses a need to know more about curriculum areas such as writing centers, math or science experiences for young children, or music in the classroom. Other areas, such as building skills for more effective conferences with parents or for ways to interact with volunteers, also can be handled in a workshop format that involves participants in a series of role-plays or simulation games. Workshops require active involvement from the participants and are more suitable for some training needs than are lectures, films, or seminars.

Planned follow-up should be provided for all types of training. Behavior change is not likely to follow a one-shot session or even a series of meetings unless there is follow-up by the director or supervisor at the center. Teachers need feedback and support to integrate new information into their day-to-day practice. It is helpful to follow up by periodically revisiting the ideas and information teachers have received, to discuss progress and/or problems they have had when attempting to implement new procedures or ideas, and to reaffirm each teacher's commitment to dealing with the challenges of change.

Visits to other centers are encouraged by some directors and can be a very helpful piece of the total staff training program. Watching other teachers and children is refreshing and interesting for some staff members. After such visits, they bring back program ideas, new and different ways to set up the physical environment, and sometimes a renewed interest in developing classroom materials such as math games or interactive charts. Some teachers who are able to move beyond the more obvious things such as equipment or curriculum ideas may begin to compare and contrast classroom environments and teaching strategies, relating these differences to the differences in the stated philosophies of the programs. Follow-up group discussions will help teachers refine their understanding of how theory relates to practice. Why are the children in one program encouraged to negotiate with one another about dividing up the play dough, while the teacher controls amounts for each child in another center? The two strategies clearly reflect different program goals. Group discussions also may encourage teachers to reexamine the theoretical basis for the center program in which they work and reevaluate the curriculum to ascertain how closely it reflects the stated philosophy of the center, as well as their own philosophy of early childhood education.

Professional conferences and workshops provide excellent training opportunities for staff. Directors who commit to a personal program of professional development by attending professional meetings set a standard of excellence for their teachers to emulate. It is important to encourage staff to take advantage of these opportunities and to facilitate their attending conferences by allowing time off from work and subsidizing their travel and registration expenses if at all possible. Some child care programs not only subsidize conference attendance but also pay for teachers' memberships in professional organizations such as NAEYC, which includes membership in state and local affiliates, the Council for Exceptional Children (CEC), the Association for Childhood Education International (ACEI), the National Association of Child Care Professionals (NACCP), and the National Child Care Association (NCCA).

---

**DIRECTOR'S CORNER**

"One of the most helpful things we did in my administration class at college was role-playing. I especially remember role-playing a parent conference. Now I use that technique all the time with my staff. In staff training sessions, when we are discussing an issue like dealing with a difficult parent, I ask for a specific example and immediately turn it into a role-play. 'OK—now I'm the parent and here is my concern—you are the teacher,' and we play it out. Then we often reverse roles so I take the role of the teacher. It works very well for me as a director."

—*Director, YMCA-sponsored center*

---

Staff members who express an interest in professional advancement are to be commended for their ambitious goals and encouraged to take courses toward a college degree in child development or early childhood education, or toward the Child Development Associate (CDA) or certified Child Care Professional (CCP) certificate in communities where these types of training programs are available. The availability of online courses offers easy access to educational opportunities for many. Some centers will help pay tuition for relevant courses as well as adjust work schedules to allow staff to attend daytime classes. Directors can lend further support to these part-time students by showing interest in what they are learning and guiding them to helpful resources available at the center.

More and more professional development training is expected to be credit based. In addition to not-for-credit or credit-based CDA programs, teachers are being encouraged to take course work that could lead to an associate or bachelor's degree in early childhood education or a closely related field. Some federally funded early childhood education programs, including Head Start, as well as a number of state licensing systems and NAEYC Accreditation Teachers Standards, have established criteria that require a certain minimum number of degreed staff

before a program is approved. Therefore, more center directors are encouraging staff to take college credit courses, and the colleges and universities across the country are trying to meet that demand. At this time, there are also a number of opportunities for professional development training on the Internet. In some places, students are permitted to enroll in individual classes without matriculating in a degree program. Staff development course work for continuing education credit is also available online. Committing to any type of credit-based staff development work is very intimidating for some staff members. They have had little or no experience with any type of college-level work, and they resist even the thought of taking courses because they are uneasy about their ability to do the work or have serious concerns about how time-consuming it will be. Directors can help them by being available to talk through what they are experiencing and what they feel may help them succeed. When they are taking classes, it may be useful to suggest that they meet with other staff at break time to share concerns and seek help with assignments or study skills.

To provide on-site materials to support and enhance all aspects of the staff development program, it is the job of the director to establish a professional library and a teachers' resource center. The library books should cover information on child development, curriculum, classroom management, special-needs children, diversity, and working with other professionals and with families. Books on specific curriculum areas, such as literacy, math, science, cooking, or music, will help the staff plan for the children. Recent copies of professional journals and newsletters should be available in the teachers' library, along with a collection of audiovisual materials, including tapes, slides, videotapes, DVDs, and computers, to provide a rich source of information on curriculum development and classroom management.

The teachers' resource center should be a space where teachers can make math games, charts, big books, and other teacher-made classroom materials. Supplies such as paper, tagboard, paper cutter, scissors, glue, tape, plain die, marking pens, and so forth must be available in addition to a large working surface. It is a luxury to have things like a laminating machine or an Ellison machine for stamping out letters and shapes for charts. When teachers have materials and space to work, they are more likely to develop individualized teacher-made classroom materials that will enrich the program for the children.

## 14-2f Training Content

A number of ideas for the professional development training program for staff already have been mentioned in the previous discussions on methods of training. Training needs will vary according to the previous training and experience of the center staff. Many teachers constantly are seeking new curriculum ideas and resource materials for the classroom; consequently, training in curriculum areas is usually welcomed. There is always interest in strategies for dealing with the difficult, challenging, disruptive child, or the withdrawn child. Furthermore, most teachers are interested in learning more about community resources where they can get advice about how to handle children with special needs or about where to refer children and families for additional help. Although staff will rarely request it, directors are obligated to hold at least one staff meeting per year or set aside a time at a regularly scheduled staff retreat to review the NAEYC Code of Ethical Conduct and Statement of Commitment and the Code of Ethical Conduct Supplement for Early Childhood Program Administrators (see Appendix A). Although the orientation of new employees includes mention of the NAEYC Code of Ethics, yearly review of this important document will renew staff members' awareness of their professional commitment to ethical practice.

The director should determine whether staff members need special coaching in conducting a home visit or a parent conference. These duties are taxing, produce anxiety, and require very special culturally sensitive communication skills that are suitable for the particular parent population being served. It is important to know that some families may be slow to accept a stranger and will draw back from someone they perceive as too intrusive. Attitudes about accepting newcomers, about education, and about childrearing vary among cultural, ethnic, and socioeconomic groups, and it is essential for staff to know what those differences are when they work with children and families. Staff members also find it helpful to have special guidance from the director in effective interpersonal communications.

There is a pressing need to assist staff in dealing with diversity in the classroom. Including children with disabilities and children from diverse cultural and ethnic groups into early childhood education programs means there must be training programs that focus on providing information about ways to meet the individual needs of children and families from these groups. Teachers may also need help handling issues regarding children of divorce, single-parent families, hospitalization of a parent or sibling, children who have been abused, and so forth.

When the staff is experienced and fully capable of coping with the day-to-day, here-and-now events in the

## Working Smart with Technology

*Online Professional Development*

It can be difficult not only to find the time for everyone to attend training but also to find training that meets the needs of individual staff members. Online professional development is becoming more common and offers some unique advantages. Because online training is not limited to a specific locality, state, or national region, the offerings can provide your staff with a wide range of topics. Many workshops are asynchronous, meaning that staff can log on and participate at times that work best for them and for the center. Staff members can take the training as individuals or with a teaching partner or team. They can take it during assigned times at work or in the comfort of their own homes. As directors consider adding online training to their professional development offerings, they need to consider the following in the selection process.

**1.** Choose online training that is facilitated. Facilitated training typically includes opportunities for interaction with an instructor and also is more likely to include moderated peer discussions. The level of accountability and the quality of the work produced tends to increase dramatically when training is facilitated.

**2.** Look for training that asks participants to apply what they have learned to their work environment. Some online training provides new information and then asks participants to try out what they have learned and bring their experiences back to the online discussion for feedback and reflection. Job-embedded professional development has been shown to have better long-term outcomes.

*Online professional development allows participants to engage in training in the comfort of their own home.*

classroom, staff development efforts can move on to the questions that challenge us in the twenty-first century. What do children need to know to survive in the twenty-first century? How will life change in the next 50 years, and what personality characteristics and thinking dispositions will be essential to function competently during those 50 years? The job of staff training is never complete because there are always new challenges.

## 14-3 STAFF SUPERVISION AND COACHING

The director, or the educational director in the case of large centers or some corporate chains, is responsible for supervision of classroom staff. (The director will be referred to as supervisor for the purposes of this discussion.) By observing, doing one-to-one mentoring and coaching, plus working in the classroom with the children and the staff, the supervisor gives support and guidance to each staff member and establishes a trusting relationship with each one. As a coach, the supervisor's job is to "encourage and provide opportunities for defining and solving problems and for self-reflection and collaboration. It is important that you (the director) model the kind of behavior you want staff to use with children—providing for self-initiated learning, risk taking, and exploration" (Carter & Curtis, 2010, p. 122). The trust and mutual respect that develop between coach and teacher provide the basis for building a teaching-learning relationship that parallels the relationship between adult and child. Then the supervisor is able to create a favorable environment in which each staff member can gain new understandings of children, of self, and of the supervisor's expectations.

An experienced supervisor knows that sometimes growth and change take place slowly. Working together, talking together, and planning together will promote personal and professional competence on the part of classroom staff members, provided the supervisor is supportive and encouraging and is not perceived as being critical or threatening.

### 14-3a Principles of Supervision

You should keep in mind a number of basic principles or assumptions as you think about the director as staff supervisor. The same principles apply to the supervisory role, whether you are working with a new, inexperienced staff member or a mature, qualified, experienced teacher or are a new director moving into a fully staffed center.

- Supervision is a dynamic, evolutionary process that is based on trust.
- Supervision is individualized and adapted to the personality and teaching style of each staff member.

- Supervision provides a support system for each staff member.
- Supervision provides a framework within which the supervisor demonstrates professional skills for the entire staff.

However, an individualized model of staff development means you must use a developmental approach to supervision, and teachers who are at different stages in their careers will require qualitatively different supervisory strategies.

### 14-3b Supervisory Process

As classroom staff members grow and change, the thrust and focus of the supervisory process shifts accordingly. The process begins by providing support and guidance for a new staff member, who is integrating past learning experiences into a personal teaching style that is compatible with the center philosophy. The process changes as the staff member adjusts and develops into an accomplished teacher, who will, in turn, supervise assistants, aides, and student teachers, or be paired with a new teacher and become a mentor. If you think of this supervisory process on a continuum, it moves from a very directive approach for new teachers where the control is in the hands of the supervisor, to a collaborative model where an accomplished teacher and the supervisor share control of the process.

One-to-one coaching is the essential ingredient of the supervisory process, whether working with the beginning teacher or the accomplished professional who, in turn, will coach others in the center. Coaching includes encouraging, modeling, observing, and giving specific feedback. A coach is a cheerleader who watches, listens, and shares skills, resources, and experience. Communicating with staff after an observation usually is handled in a conference, but when time is short, a brief note with some specific feedback may have to suffice.

The director must ensure that staff members engage in high-quality practices at all times. When there are questions and concerns about teacher performance, it is always a challenge to communicate those concerns in a way that addresses the issues but maintains program quality and does not compromise staff morale. Depending on the level of training and experience of the staff, you, as the director, will have to deal with questions and concerns about classroom practices on a regular basis. There may be issues about curriculum, classroom management, staff relationships, or interactions with parents. On any given day, you will see and hear things that must be addressed. Following are some examples:

- How should I approach Estella, who continues to call across the room to set limits for children who are not doing what she thinks they should be doing?
- I must talk with Consuelo about using positive redirection instead of the constant, "Stop running in the room" or "Don't spill your milk."

- Colin's group times are not rich or challenging these days. I must call him in and talk about that.

- What is the best way to tell Betsy that she and her assistant should be sitting with the children at lunch and eating what children eat? I also will have to tell them that they must wait until they are on break to have coffee or a Coke.

Dealing with questionable practices is especially distasteful for directors who prefer to avoid conflict and confrontations, but it is an important part of the supervisory process and goes to the core of what it takes to maintain the integrity of the program. Keep in mind that when you are responsible for supervision of staff, you will inevitably have to spend time and energy dealing with conflict (Sciarra & Dorsey, 2002).

---

### REFLECTION

How do you feel about confrontation and conflict? Do you withdraw and avoid it like a turtle? Do you approach and attack like a shark? Do you wait and watch like an owl? What is your style of dealing with conflict and confrontation? How might that affect your performance as a supervisor? (Sciarra & Dorsey, 2002, p. 147)

---

## 14-3c Supervisory Cycle

The two pieces of the supervisory cycle, formative supervisory cycle and summative supervisory cycle, each include a discovery step, a conference step, and a planning and goal-setting step (Table 14-1). Ideally the director/supervisor and the teacher/supervisee begin to build a relationship based on trust and mutual respect during the initial orientation sessions because that provides the foundation for a collaborative, ongoing supervisor/supervisee relationship.

The first step in the supervisory cycle is the discovery step for both the formative and summative segments of the cycle. The discovery step begins with a scheduled classroom observation that is followed by a scheduled conference with the teacher. Although making time and covering classrooms for regularly scheduled observations and conferences is not easy, it contributes significantly to the success of the teacher assessment/evaluation process. During the formative time period of the cycle, the emphasis for the observation and conference is reflection, discussion, and sharing of information and concerns about classroom events and practice. At the conference following the observation, the director and the teacher review and discuss events and actions observed. The formative conference is helpful for both participants if the director listens carefully and encourages the teacher to reflect, analyze, vent if needed, and evaluate events or issues that arose during the observation. A checklist for classroom observations is sometimes used to help supervisors focus

on specific aspects of a teacher's performance. Sometimes asking open-ended questions will generate discussion that will be helpful for both the teacher and the director. For example, the director may ask the following:

- What was on your mind as you asked Tully what she was thinking about when she was repeatedly stabbing the play dough with the tongue blade?

- Did you have a sense of what Farah was upset about in the bathroom before his "meltdown"?

- Did you realize that Perot had grabbed Lissa's doll baby away from her earlier in that dramatic play sequence—and that later she took his cowboy hat away from him and that is when you intervened?

The coaching and mentoring segment of the conference might include references to the center curriculum framework and books that are useful to support that framework, the NAEYC Accreditation Standards, the PAS, or licensing expectations. There may be times when sections of the job description or the performance appraisal can be used to support both the positive notations in the observation notes as well as those items that may require special attention. The conference always ends with agreed-upon goals and plans to think about and act upon before the next scheduled observation. If it is time for the teacher to be evaluated, the planning time can be used to describe the summative steps in the process. It is an ideal time for the teacher and the director to review the performance appraisal tool so the teacher understands that the next steps will be related to performance appraisal, and both the teacher and the director will be prepared for that step in the cycle. With this planning in place, the supervisory cycle continues.

The pattern of observation and conferencing for the summative segment of the supervisory cycle is also a scheduled observation followed by a scheduled conference. Programs differ in how and when summative evaluations are done. They may be done annually or semiannually or scheduled individually, based on hiring date. For the summative observation, the director uses the performance appraisal tool, summarizes the findings, and prepares to present these to the teacher at the conference. At this conference, the director takes the lead and presents the observation findings, which were based on the performance appraisal. It is important to remember that this meeting comes after many casual contacts, a number of scheduled observations and conferences, and frequent communication between the director and teacher. Therefore, there are usually no surprises for the teacher at this time. If the information shared is critical or negative, the teacher may object or argue but that has to be expected. However, if the director has coached, offered help, provided opportunities for training, and been up front about expectations during previous conferences, and if that has all been carefully documented with notes from conferences and previous encounters, the teacher should see that the results of the performance appraisal are fairly accurate. After discussion

**TABLE 14-1** Supervisory process

| Summative Supervisory Cycle | Formative Supervisory Cycle |
|---|---|
| **Discovery Step** | |
| Supervisor observes supervisee<br><br>Evaluation tool<br><br>Performance appraisal | Supervisor observes supervisee<br><br>Anecdotal records<br><br>Narrative records<br><br>Checklists<br><br>Casual notes and comments |
| **Conference Step** | |
| Supervisor reviews previously set goals<br><br>Supervisor presents findings based on the performance appraisal<br><br>Supervisor and supervisee discuss results of the performance appraisal | Supervisor empowers supervisee<br><br>Nurturing and coaching<br><br>Sharing information and concerns |
| **Planning and Goal-Setting Step** | |
| Supervisor states the decisions based on the performance appraisal<br><br>■ Raise<br>■ Promotion<br>■ No change in status<br>■ Probation<br>■ Dismissal<br><br>Develop the action plan and put it in writing<br><br>■ Training<br>■ Course work<br>■ Reading<br>■ Conditions of the probationary period<br>■ Steps to finalize dismissal<br><br>Set the time for the next summative conference | Supervisor and supervisee set mutually agreed-upon goals<br><br><br><br><br><br><br><br><br>Develop the action plan and put it in writing<br><br>■ Readings<br>■ Training or course work<br>■ Observing peers or teachers in other programs<br><br>Set the time for the next formative conference |

*Source: From Sciarra/Dorsey. Leaders and Supervisors in Child Care Programs, 1E. © 2002 Wadsworth, a part of Cengage Learning, Inc. Reproduced by permission. www.cengage.com/permissions.*

and clearly stated decisions based on the appraisal have been communicated, the conference ends with plans for the next step in the cycle, which is scheduling the coming series of formative observations and conferences to repeat the cycle (Sciarra & Dorsey, 2002).

## Supervising New Teachers

New teachers need daily or even hourly support; therefore, the director/supervisor must plan to spend some time each day observing and teaching with the new teacher. If a new teacher is recently trained, that teacher will be developing a personal teaching style and will profit from the example that is set by an experienced supervisor. It is very important for a supervisor to work beside a new teacher with the children in the classroom. This supervisory procedure creates a rich learning environment for the new teacher and often provides a more favorable transition for the children and families who know the supervisor but are not yet well acquainted with the new teacher. As a supervisor, you must make sure to remove yourself gradually so that the new teacher can build a relationship with the children and families and begin to manage the classroom without your constant support. What you are doing, in effect, is providing hourly or daily support during the initial trust-building period but stepping back when the new teacher can function independently. You are scaffolding the experience for the teacher just as you would for a child in the classroom, gradually increasing the challenge as you stay nearby because your ongoing support is still important when things do not go well.

### DIRECTOR'S CORNER

"Since I am new here, I haven't developed a schedule for regular observations as yet, but I make the rounds at least twice a day, if only to let my teachers know I am available. Of course, I have a chance to catch things going on in each room—maybe a new chart or a teacher reading a book to a sleepy child. I make sure I leave a short note in each teacher's box, mentioning some little thing I noticed when I came by. If I see an activity or a procedure that concerns me, I mention it. 'I noticed you had the toddlers finger painting with chocolate pudding today. Drop by when you have a chance—I have some ideas about that that I would like to share with you.' It seems to work well for me."

—*Director, community-agency-sponsored center*

*Staff is used to informal drop-in visits where they are more likely to hear something good about what they are doing than a complaint. Having established a trusting relationship between staff and director is important when there is a need for constructive criticism.*

## Supervising Experienced Teachers

As teachers develop their skills and become more competent, they continue to profit from the supervisor's support. Positive reinforcement and constructive criticism from supervisors are excellent motivating factors. But experienced teachers also are ready for expansion and growth in new directions. They still are integrating and reorganizing what they have learned in the past, but they are now able to reach out for new learning opportunities. These teachers now are comfortable with their teaching style and can direct more attention to curriculum development. They are ready for the intellectual stimulation they can draw from taking course work, reading new publications, and attending professional meetings. Therefore, although the supervisor continues to observe these teachers and have conferences with them on a regular basis, emphasis now is placed on the supervisor as a resource person. The supervisor can supply new program ideas, new theoretical information, articles from professional journals and websites, research materials, and as many opportunities as possible for teachers to participate actively in professional organizations and conferences.

While experienced teachers are perfecting their teaching skills under the guidance of the supervisor, they also should be developing self-evaluation skills. With encouragement and help from a supervisor, experienced teachers feel secure enough to step back and evaluate their teaching. They can begin to ask themselves some of the questions a supervisor has been asking them and engage in some self-searching about their methodology. For example, one teacher might make the inquiry, "How could I have better handled the situation between those two children who had a conflict over the sand bucket? What I did was really not productive. I must find alternative ways of handling those two children." Another teacher might ask, "How can I adjust my questioning techniques for all the children to help them become better problem solvers? I heard you mention Rheta deVries. Maybe you could give me something she has written on that topic that will help me."

## Supervising the Accomplished Teacher

The accomplished, long-term teacher still is perfecting teaching and self-evaluation skills and revising curriculum. However, having reached a new level of mastery, this teacher is ready to develop supervisory skills. While working with the teachers, the director/supervisor has not only exemplified teaching and self-evaluation skills but also supervisory skills. In working with accomplished teachers, the director/supervisor now turns to coaching them in supervisory skills. This teacher is preparing to assume responsibility for the supervision of assistants, aides, and, in some situations, student teachers. To serve in this capacity, the teacher will need instruction and support to develop the necessary skills for fulfilling supervisory responsibilities. The director/supervisor still is observing and having conferences on a regular basis, giving attention to teaching strategies and self-evaluation.

However, the new thrust is directed to this teacher's interaction with, and supervision of, other adults in the classroom.

Involving accomplished teachers with novice teachers in a mentoring program is an ideal way to offer the benefit of job enrichment for both. The director's role becomes one of modeling for the mentor by engaging in reflective practices and helping this teacher, who is very skilled at working with young children, learn more about the characteristics of the adult learner. The director models ways to use many of the same skills that teachers use when caring for young children, and now explores ways to "care for a fellow caregiver." Pairing mentors with novices is a challenge for the director who must observe, reflect, and confer with staff to ensure a "good fit" in each pairing. A successful peer mentoring program contributes to the well-being of staff and children alike. It is connected to both staff development and supervision but, at the same time, is separate. It provides unique opportunities for both mentors and novices to learn from each other and grow professionally.

Supervision is one of the most difficult and anxiety-producing aspects of the director's job. It draws on every bit of professional skill the director has because it demands expertise in interpersonal communication, children's programming, teaching strategies, and self-evaluation. It also helps the director focus on the importance of being a model for the staff by making positive suggestions to coach and motivate and by using supportive, caring gestures and voice tone. This sets the tone for staff, who, in turn, are more likely to follow a similar pattern in their interactions with children and families.

Accomplished practitioners, like successful CEOs, give thoughtful attention to grooming their successors. Through ongoing encouragement and coaching that is fashioned to the talents and abilities of each accomplished teacher, the director guides them toward optimal professional growth. This prepares them to take on more responsibility and to advance their own professional careers. It is the talented and visionary center directors who can best bring along and groom the future leaders in the field.

---

### REFLECTION

Think about the cooperating teacher who supervised your practicum. Did you receive support and constructive criticism? Did that person serve as a model of good supervisory skills for you? Think about how your cooperating teacher might have been more helpful. What do you feel you need before you can become a supervisor of a center classroom staff?

---

## 14-3d Identifying Topics for Supervision and Coaching

Staff members' areas of strength and need can provide the basis for designing the staff development program and focusing individualized supervision activities. Teacher input is essential, and after you have identified what teachers believe their needs to be, you can take the first steps toward helping them solve those problems (Bloom, Sheerer, & Britz, 2005). The expressed needs of staff can be addressed directly. If a teacher has problems handling the aggressive behaviors of a child, the director can respond in a variety of ways, including offering relevant readings, observing or participating in the classroom, discussing various management strategies, calling in a consultant to observe and conference with the classroom staff, or discussing the general problem of dealing with aggression in a staff meeting. This direct response to an expressed need may motivate the staff member to become involved in a training plan offered by the director.

On the other hand, when the selection of staff development activities is based on those issues the director views as problems, motivating staff interest will be more difficult. For example, if a new director finds the long-term staff using punitive and age inappropriate techniques in response to unacceptable classroom behaviors, but the teachers are comfortable with their management methods, those teachers will resist making a commitment to any training designed to encourage them to use more positive management strategies. The new director will have to spend time establishing a trusting working relationship with the professional staff before training related to the classroom management question will be accepted. Because the use of punitive management techniques can be hard on children, the new director may choose to bring in a consultant to work with individual staff members or may even consider making staff changes. A new director is well advised to design the initial staff development activities in response to the teachers' expressed needs.

Selection of staff development activities is often based on expressed needs of staff or is in response to new requirements that come down from funders, licensing, or government agencies, but it also emerges from the interests and goals of a visionary director. The staff development program is often designed to guide the staff to make changes in what they think and in what they do. Response to change differs from one person to another—some are exhilarated and motivated by the opportunity to work with change, while others are anxious and immobilized. As individuals on the staff begin to respond to expectations or requirements presented to them, they need the director's support and encouragement. It is now critical that responsible directors keep a watchful eye on those who fail to progress. Documentation and regular observing and conferencing throughout the process are helpful to all staff but are essential for those whose failure to progress could be a problem that will require action on the part of the director in the future.

## 14-3e Expressed Teacher Concerns

Expressed teacher concerns often cluster around a number of problem areas (Bloom, Sheerer, & Britz, 2005). The director's task is to identify and then respond to these concerns. The areas of greatest concern include those points discussed in the following paragraphs.

### Supporting Teaching Teams

A teaching team may be having problems getting all members of the team to follow through on assigned responsibilities and to work as a member of a cooperative team. In response to this problem, team decision making, communication strategies, and giving feedback are appropriate areas to address in the staff training program for the teams. The best way for the director to help teachers with this problem is to model exemplary supervisory and communication skills.

### Managing the Classroom

Teachers report problems with managing children's challenging behaviors. Behaviors on their list include aggression and violence, not picking up, not sharing, and not cooperating. In addressing the problem of working with these children, the director first might focus on developmental expectations for the specific age group in question, followed by ways to encourage prosocial behaviors. This is a sensitive problem area because the perceived problem sometimes results from teachers' unrealistic expectations. Directors must model developmentally appropriate responses to children's behaviors whenever they have encounters with children in the center. Managing children who present extremely oppositional or violent behaviors often requires the help of a mental health specialist.

### Helping Children with Special Needs and Their Families

Teachers report that they do not know enough about how to deal appropriately with children with special needs. This becomes a serious problem when children with previously unidentified social-emotional problems join the group. Teachers suddenly realize that this child is, indeed, disturbed and in need of special help, but they are not prepared for the disruption and management challenges this new child presents. They want help on how to provide rich environments for these children as well as ways to work effectively with the family. Providing reading materials and planning special meetings on this topic will be helpful to teachers who are searching for better ways to help these special children. Directors also must watch for upcoming conferences and meetings on the topic and encourage staff to attend.

Because teachers and directors are seeing an increase in the number of children who exhibit challenging behaviors, some center directors are seeking funding for more mental health services or for a mental health specialist on the staff.

The role of the mental health specialist on staff is to plan regularly scheduled classroom observations, usually taking place in the morning and lasting from two to three hours. The conference to discuss the observation, with the director and the teachers in that room, should be on the same day, if possible, so the events of the day are still clear and fresh. Conferences can often be arranged for nap time. It is essential that directors attend these meetings because they must assume responsibility for curriculum and monitor all classrooms regarding curriculum matters. The conference time is devoted to discussing events of the day and highlighting those that precipitated anxiety and tension for the children. These notable events were often those that tended to pose problems for the more fragile children.

The role of the mental health specialist in the conference is to support staff as well as coach them as they all talk about the reactions of the children, what the children may have been trying to accomplish, or what they may have been thinking. With new insights into the effects of experiences on children and their reactions to those experiences, teachers begin to feel more competent about their ability to plan, evaluate, and work with them. The major thrust of the mental health specialist is to help center staff saturate the classroom, and eventually the entire center, with refined practices that will enhance the emotional well-being of all children in the program, not just those who have been called "challenging."

For the children who continue to require additional help, the mental health specialist can arrange to meet and work with them and their families for as long as needed. Clearly this approach is a departure from the more typical procedure in which the mental health specialist is called upon to observe a specific child. The expectation, in this case, is that the specialist will observe the child; identify the problem; and then offer help to the child, the child's teachers, and members of the family. This surely benefits all who participate and work with the specialist. The plan described previously puts the focus on all children in the classroom, knowing that everyone in the classroom is entitled to have the benefit of ongoing daily practice that has at its core the emotional well-being of young children.

### Relating to Supervisors

Staff members often clash with directors. Teachers complain about not being treated fairly and not being respected as professionals. The response to this problem is clearly in the director's hands. Directors must work on their own professional development to enable them to become better staff managers.

## Maintaining Parent Cooperation

Teachers have problems with parents who send a sick child to school; who are not prompt about picking their child up after school; and who do not cooperate with the teachers' efforts, such as when teachers encourage the use of messy materials. Here, the director can reinforce center policies by reviewing the parent handbook material with the parent, as well as participate in parent conferences when necessary, to mediate and to give support to both the teacher and the parent. In-service training focused on working with parents and becoming sensitive to their needs may help teachers feel more secure about handling difficult situations with parents.

## Managing Time

Time to deal with nonteaching tasks such as cleaning, planning, making materials, or doing other paperwork is a problem for teachers. Because time management is also a major problem for directors, directors and teachers have this issue in common. Time management seminars under the guidance of an experienced trainer can be part of the staff development program. It is especially important for the director to be a part of this training and to model good time management.

Although staff concerns always are situation specific, a common core of recurring problems fall into the categories just listed. It can be reassuring to you, as a director, to know that your teachers' expressed needs are much like those of most teaching staffs.

# SUMMARY

The staff development program contributes to both the personal and professional growth of the center staff. Through the planning and implementation of effective staff meetings, staff training programs, and staff supervision, the director creates an enriched learning environment for the staff. Given the benefits of an enriched environment and a director who demonstrates good interpersonal and professional skills, the staff members have the opportunity to enjoy the inevitable personal satisfaction and excitement that result from positive, individualized, professional growth experiences. To plan and implement an effective professional development system, directors must do the following:

- Describe the role of staff meetings as an important professional development tool.

- Identify the elements of an effective staff development system.

- Describe effective supervision and coaching strategies.

# TRY IT OUT!

1. Role-play a child care center staff meeting and discuss one agenda item, "Timing for weekly staff meetings." The director has decided that the entire staff (including the cook, the janitor, and the secretary) must meet every week. The question open for discussion is the day of the week on which the staff should meet, and when and how long the meetings should be. Assign the following roles to class members:

   a. Director: works Monday through Friday 9:00 a.m. to 5:00 p.m.

   b. Teacher A: works Monday through Friday 9:00 a.m. to 5:00 p.m.

   c. Teacher B: works Monday through Friday 6:00 a.m. to 2:00 p.m.

   d. Assistant teacher C: works Monday through Friday 10:00 a.m. to 6:00 p.m.

   e. Assistant teacher D: works Monday through Friday 6:00 a.m. to 2:00 p.m.

   f. Part-time teacher E: works Monday through Friday 10:00 a.m. to 2:00 p.m.

   g. Cook: works Monday through Friday 9:00 a.m. to 3:00 p.m.

   h. Janitor: works Monday through Friday 3:00 p.m. to 8:00 p.m.

   There are 35 children in the program who arrive on a staggered schedule between 6:15 a.m. and 9:30 a.m. and leave between 2:30 p.m. and 5:30 p.m. The children occupy two classrooms and two sleeping rooms. Sleeping rooms are adjacent to one another and to the outdoor area.

   The staff meeting discussion is to be led by the director, and the group is to come to some decision about when the regular staff meeting will be held. Use the blackboard or newsprint for note taking, if you need it. Practice good listening skills; make sure that everyone participates.

2. Role-play a special staff meeting that has been called by the director to discuss and reach a decision about allocation of classroom space at the child care center. One additional classroom will be available beginning in September, and a new teacher, Mark, will be employed. The new classroom is larger than the others and opens directly to the playground.

   Sandra currently has the best classroom, which has its own bathroom. The other four rooms share a bathroom down the hall. Jean will be working with a new pilot program and will have many parents participating in her classroom. She was responsible for getting the pilot program funded, and it is a real asset for the center. Bob's classroom is far from the outside play area and from the storage room. Bob feels that this location is inconvenient. Sheila would like to keep her current classroom because she recently made curtains and painted the walls. Barbara feels that her 10 years of teaching qualify her for the new classroom.

| Name | Years at Center | Degree | Current Classroom |
|------|-----------------|--------|-------------------|
| Sandra | 6 | M.S. | Excellent |
| Barbara | 10 | B.S. | Very good |
| Sheila | 4 | B.S. | Very good |
| Bob | 6 | A.S. | Good |
| Jean | 1 | A.S. | Poor |
| Mark | 0 | B.S. | |

The staff has allocated 30 minutes for making this decision. After the group has arrived at a decision, individually rate your level of satisfaction with the decision from 1 (low) to 5 (high). Also, rate your level of participation from 1 to 5. Tally the results on the chalkboard. As a group, discuss the factors that contributed to the level of satisfaction or dissatisfaction. Was the level of participation a factor?

3. Think about a time when you were called in by a teacher or a boss for an appraisal of your performance (athletic performance, singing or dancing event, your work in a store or restaurant, etc.). Reflect on how the teacher or boss handled the situation—how you felt about what she or he said, how you felt about yourself during the conference, how you feel about yourself now as you recall the incident, and so forth. Write a few paragraphs about why you think you had the feelings about yourself then as you experienced the conference as compared with how you feel about yourself now as you remember it, and why you think those feelings differ, if they do.

# REFERENCES

Bloom, P. J. (2002). *Making the most of meetings: A practical guide.* Lake Forest, IL: New Horizons.

Bloom, P. J., Sheerer, M., & Britz, J. (2005). *Blueprint for action: Achieving center-based change through staff development.* Lake Forest, IL: New Horizons.

Carter, M., & Curtis, D. (2010). *The visionary director: A handbook for dreaming, organizing and improving.* St. Paul, MN: Redleaf Press.

National Staff Development Council. (2010). NSDC's definition of professional development [Website], http://nsdc.org/standfor/definition.cfm.

Sciarra, D. J., & Dorsey, A. G. (2002). *Leaders and supervisors in child care programs.* Clifton Park, NY: Thomson Delmar Learning.

Tanner, D., & Tanner, L. (Eds.). (2007). *Curriculum development: Theory into practice* (4th ed.). Englewood Cliffs, NJ: Merrill.

Tanner, D., & Tanner, L. (Eds.). (1995). *Curriculum development: Theory into practice* (3rd ed.). Englewood Cliffs, NJ: Merrill.

*The director and staff members work together to participate in NAEYC accreditation by becoming familiar with accreditation materials prior to beginning their self-study.*

## Standards Addressed in this Chapter

Accreditation Standard 1 – Relationships

Accreditation Standard 4 – Assessment

Accreditation Standard 7 – Families

Accreditation Standard 9 – Physical Environment

Accreditation Standard 10 – Leadership and Management

Administrator Competencies – Management Knowledge and Skills 3, 4, 5, 9, 10

Administrator Competencies – Early Childhood Knowledge and Skills 2, 3, 5, 6, 7, 9, 10

Professional Preparation Standard 3 – Observing, Documenting, and Assessing to Support Young Children and Families

Professional Preparation Standard 4 – Using Developmentally Effective Approaches

Professional Preparation Standard 6 – Becoming a Professional

Evaluation is an ongoing process. An evaluation can take the form of an analysis of a person's behavior, of an administrative policy or procedure, or of some other component of an early childhood education program or even of the whole program. Periodically, long-range planning should occur, and the mission should be examined. Such an examination should provide data about usefulness or worth. After an early childhood education program has been planned, the evaluation of that program should be designed immediately as part of the program's operational system.

Evaluation that is planned during the early stages of program development facilitates the process and notifies everyone from the start how the evaluation process will be conducted. The evaluator uses the mission statement or goals that were prepared prior to the opening of the center as the basis for making judgments about what is valuable in the program. These documents provide guidelines for assessing the center's program and the performance of individuals affiliated with that program.

Regular evaluation can indicate how successful the director and staff have been in adhering to their mission and in meeting their goals. Evaluation can help the director, board, and staff revise their goals as changes occur in the community and the world. This process also enables the director to make needed changes quickly before current practices have a negative effect on the program. Continuation of an ineffective aspect of the program is fruitless and frequently expensive. Inappropriate staff behavior may be detrimental to children's development or to staff relations. Desirable behavior, on the other hand, should be recognized, encouraged, and supported as a result of the evaluation process.

Assuming that the director has worked to create a "we" feeling rather than a "boss" approach, evaluation also will take on a collaborative tone. Rather than being threatening or punitive, evaluation will be a way to note and celebrate progress and to plan for the next stages. Then staff and director can support one another in reaching those revised or new goals.

## 15-1 PURPOSE OF EVALUATION

Early childhood center evaluation has often focused on classroom practices. However, current understandings of center effectiveness indicate that the overall administrative procedures and policies and the ways in which these are implemented ultimately relate to the quality of care and education that children receive at the center. The overriding purpose of evaluation of the center's administration is to ensure good-quality child care. Talan and Bloom (2011) have provided a tool for measuring leadership and management. Evaluation results should lead to examination of goals and their supporting policies and procedures.

Because a major purpose of evaluation is to determine whether the center's goals are being met and whether they or the program needs to be modified, the evaluators need to know what these goals are before gathering data. In effect, the evaluators must know who the clients are, what their needs are, and which of these needs the center is attempting to meet. For example, in a community where the local high school is expressing concern about the high number of dropouts due to pregnancy, a center director may decide to work with the school system to assess how many students could return to school if care were provided for their infants and toddlers. Together, the center and the school may be able to obtain funding to provide this service. In such a situation, particularly if tax dollars are to be used, community education would be important because many taxpayers may believe that the program would encourage teen pregnancy rather than prevent school dropouts.

A further purpose of evaluation is to determine how effective the program is in meeting the needs of clients and how efficient it is in terms of cost, time, and energy. Are needs met to the satisfaction of the center and the clients? Are they partially met or not met at all? More important, in our example, are significantly more teen parents returning to and staying in school when their babies receive child care? Even if needs are met, could the same job have been done for less money or by using less time or energy? Funding agencies, board members, and clients expect documentation that the center is doing what it has agreed to do. An evaluation provides the data for such documentation and possibly the basis for further funding.

A final reason for evaluation is the need to have a solid basis for future planning. The director uses the data from the current evaluation to determine the strengths and weaknesses of the program and to adapt the plan for the following year to correct any deficiencies or to respond to newly perceived needs. For example, if one of the goals of the center is to provide a parent education program for all parents, and the data show that only 10 percent of the parents participated, then the director must determine whether the goal is inappropriate or whether the method of achieving it is not meeting the needs of the clients. If a thorough evaluation has been done, the director will have information from parents regarding how they felt about the parent program and why they did or did not attend. The information then can be used to plan changes in next year's program or to ascertain that this community does not need parent education from this particular center.

It would be easy to arrive at the conclusion that parents in the preceding example do not want or need parent education. But directors have to consider other factors and perhaps ask themselves the following questions:

- Have parents been involved in the planning so that they feel as though they are part of the program?

- Is there another parent education program already established in the community that is meeting these parents' needs?

- Is the timing, format, or content inappropriate for these parents?

- Has there been a breakdown in communication so that parents do not feel welcome or comfortable about coming?

- Are there other, more pressing matters confronting the parents?

- Are there ancillary problems such as babysitting or transportation?

Because one or more of these factors may have had a major effect on parent participation, the director should certainly address them to make sure that the evaluation is accurate.

*The director must be familiar with the Program Administration Scale as well as NAEYC Early Childhood Program Standards.*

### REFLECTION

We have discussed the purpose of conducting an evaluation in early childhood centers and the people who conduct these investigations. Now think about the people who evaluate you. Who are they? Why do they evaluate you? Some of you may think of relatives or friends who evaluate your behavior on an ongoing basis. Others may immediately associate evaluation with teachers and employers. Do all these people see you in the same way? If not, why do some of them evaluate you in different ways? What is the purpose of their evaluation?

## 15-1a Evaluation Principles

Evaluation plans should be based on certain principles that reduce anxiety and increase cooperation among the individuals being evaluated.

1. The evaluation process is open; that is, the people or groups being evaluated know about the evaluation process in advance and have access to their own evaluation data. Furthermore, the people being evaluated have an opportunity to give input into their own evaluation.

2. Evaluation relates directly to program goals and objectives.

3. Each person being evaluated knows why, when, where, how, and by whom the evaluation is to be done.

4. Evaluation is conducted on an individual basis. However, for reporting purposes, the results are compiled and group data, rather than individual data, are presented.

5. The individual's evaluation is a confidential matter and is accessible only to those who need to know, such as an employee's supervisor or a child's teacher.

6. Evaluation is built into the program so that it occurs on a regular basis.

## 15-2 EVALUATION PLAN

As the director and staff work together to create an evaluation system, they consider what will be evaluated and why. They determine the intended audience for the evaluation plan. Will all or part of it be available to families, all staff, board members, funders, and the general public, or will it be available "in house" only? What does each of these groups need to know; what are they entitled to know? How will the information be used? Issues of confidentiality must be considered and must be specifically mandated in the center's policy manual. All who have access to information must agree to this overarching policy. Moreover, adopting the NAEYC Code of Ethical Conduct, its supplements, and Statement of Commitment will provide guidance when ethical dilemmas are encountered (see Appendix A).

Planners must give serious consideration to the appropriate amount of data to be collected. Keep in mind that someone has to prepare or select the evaluation tools. Someone has to see that the data are gathered and analyzed. And someone has to determine how the information will be used. Who will be responsible? Where will the information be kept and for how long? Specifying procedures to be used, including time lines, will facilitate the process and will help determine the optimum amount and type of information to be gathered.

The evaluation plan should include provisions for everyone connected with the center to participate. Staff members should be encouraged to participate in discussions about the center, its programs, policies, and procedures. The National Association for the Education of Young Children

(NAEYC), in its Accreditation Criteria for Leadership and Management Standard, has the expectation that "at least annually, administrators, families, staff and other routinely participating adults are involved in comprehensive program evaluation that measures progress toward the program's goals and objectives. Valid and reliable processes are used to gather data and evidence" (Ritchie and Willer, 2005, p. 26).

Some directors or their boards may feel that a consultant is needed to help them develop tools for collecting information to ensure that these tools will provide the type of data that will be useful. In corporate systems, a national or regional staff member may plan and conduct some or all of the evaluation. When funds are received from a governmental or private agency, an employee of that agency may be assigned to perform an evaluation. When public schools operate preschool or child care programs, the principal usually is responsible for evaluating the staff.

An early childhood education evaluation plan involves three components: staff, children, and total program evaluation. A plan for each of these components includes delineating who will evaluate what, as well as how and when the evaluation will be conducted and for what purposes a particular evaluation is being done.

## 15-3 STAFF EVALUATION

Staff evaluation is a natural outgrowth of supervision, one of the basic duties of the director. Every staff member should be evaluated on a regular basis according to the procedure included in the policies and procedures manual.

Staff evaluation is conducted to enable the director and the staff member to analyze what the staff member is doing well and in what areas growth and change are desirable or required. This type of evaluation provides information to the funding agency and the board about how employees spend their time; it also validates the work of the employees.

The first form of evaluation is *employee selection*. In assessing an applicant's ability to work well with other employees, the director must be cautious, avoiding the selection of only those people who fit a mold. A successful choice is based on a careful evaluation of credentials and behavior, rather than on an overgeneralization of positive or negative traits. For example, the candidate who answers an early question to the interviewer's liking then may be regarded as being highly qualified, although he actually may be poorly skilled in working with young children. On the other hand, the candidate with an unusual style of clothing may be considered initially as incompetent when, in reality, that person might work quite well with young children. The director should avoid hiring only those applicants who are very similar to current employees, but still must consider whether or not the qualifications of a particular candidate will combine well with those of current employees to provide the total staff strength needed to meet center goals. In any case, the most important criterion is, "Is this the best person available to do the job?" Of course, the director will check the applicants' references and will require a documented background check.

### 15-3a Process and Procedures

Ongoing evaluation of staff members begins when they accept a position. At this time, the director and the new staff member go over the job description together carefully and make adjustments as needed to fit the circumstances, writing these changes (if any) into the job description. A comprehensive evaluation is based on this job description. The director makes it clear to employees from the beginning that they will be evaluated. However, another important component to be discussed with the employee is the support that will be provided to assist new staff members as they become acclimated to a new role. This support is particularly helpful for first-year teachers. They should also be informed that all staff are guided and supported so that they continue to grow professionally (Sciarra & Dorsey, 2002).

The director informs each employee why, when, where, and by whom the evaluation will be done; outlines the basis for the evaluation; and describes the method to be used. Often, a new employee is evaluated after a two- or three-month probationary period. If the employee's work is found to be satisfactory at this time, the employee and director then plan together for further growth by writing out what the employee expects to accomplish prior to the next evaluation. In this initial step in the evaluation cycle, the employee writes out goals and brings them to a meeting with the director, at which time both must agree on their importance and reasonableness. The goals must relate to the job description, and the subsequent evaluation is based on the mutually agreed-upon objectives.

For example, if one of the teacher's goals is to maintain a more orderly classroom, that teacher's procedural plan may include teaching the children to return things to the proper shelf, rearranging the classroom, or working with the classroom aide to develop a mutually agreeable plan for keeping materials in order. Sometimes, the director gives help at this stage, either by assisting the employee in finding ways of meeting an objective or by designating areas in which specific objectives should be defined. The primary goal at this step is to draw up a workable plan that the staff member can follow and that will enhance the overall program.

Next, the director and employee decide how data will be gathered. Will the director observe? Will parents be asked for their opinions? Will the teacher be asked to engage in a self-evaluation process? Will the teachers observe each other? Will children's behavior be used as a criterion? Again, both director and staff member reach agreement on what is the best plan to use. Some centers use checklists or rating scales. These tools are most useful in large centers in which a number of staff are working on comparable skills such as fostering a comfortable classroom atmosphere or preparing appropriate classroom materials.

The objectives and evaluation format are called a *work plan*, which is the formative component of staff evaluation. After the plan has been written, the director and the staff member each receive a copy for reference as they work to achieve the objectives and to evaluate the progress that is made. They plan a specific time period for the next meeting—in a month, at the end of the semester, or whatever length of time fits their needs.

When a teacher is already doing an outstanding job, the director can support her in finding a new related interest and area for growth and development. Possibilities include offering to reschedule her hours so that she could participate in training on technology for children, or granting additional responsibilities for working with teachers new to the center and possibly even new to the field. If she is interested in administration, you may begin to involve her in work that would introduce her to that component of the early childhood field and would, at the same time, begin to prepare a successor for your role. Obviously, you will have to be able to replace her in the classroom during the time she is spending on these new endeavors, and, of course, additional funds would be needed. However, when a teacher feels that she has outgrown her job, it is likely that she will search for new opportunities with other programs.

## 15-3b The Director's Role

The director's role in staff evaluation is to observe and analyze the work of a staff person, encourage the development of that person's strengths, and look for ways to promote growth in weaker areas. If the weak areas considerably outweigh the strong, then the director must terminate the employment of that individual because the director's role (except in special cases) is to promote growth rather than to provide total on-the-job training. The staff member's role is to work out the details of meeting the agreed-upon goals and to implement these plans.

In some centers, a standard form is used to evaluate each teacher. Although this may be seen as more

*Teachers are aware that observation by the director is a regular component of the evaluation process.*

equitable, it sets the same expectations for beginners as for experienced teachers. An alternative method is to evaluate all teachers with a standard form that addresses basic requirements. In addition, the director should provide individualized planning and evaluation for each teacher.

Some directors observe each teacher weekly, biweekly, or monthly and have a conference informally after making the observation. The director may take notes during the observation or write notes afterward, but any notes should be shared with the teacher because they are useful in helping to fulfill the specific objectives that have been set. It sometimes is easy to pick out and focus on the weak spots in a teacher's style, which leaves the teacher feeling incompetent. Other directors concentrate only on the positive aspects and are unable to address problem areas. The teacher who is aware of a problem knows that the director is not providing appropriate guidance; the teacher who is unaware of a problem receives unofficial sanction of the behavior when the director ignores it. In either case, some of the center's objectives are not met, and the observation and informal conference times are nonproductive.

Some directors make video or voice recordings of teachers and review them with that teacher afterward. The advantage is that both are viewing the same situation during the conference. The disadvantage is that taping is intimidating to some staff. Of course, the tapes are confidential information, and the subject's permission must be obtained if they are to be shown to others.

When the agreed-upon observations have been completed, and other assessments have been made, the director meets with the staff member for a comprehensive evaluation of the work that is based on the work plan set up earlier. The staff member may bring a self-evaluation in a form preselected by the director to be completed by the employee, in a narrative form that is written by the employee, or in an unwritten form that the employee has planned to discuss with the director. During the conference, a work plan, including the objectives and an evaluation format, is drawn up again for the next evaluation cycle. This plan should also include opportunities for growth. The director summarizes the staff person's evaluation for the previous cycle in a written and dated form. The staff member may add written comments if desired. Together they agree upon a development plan based on the staff member's needs and interests and the program needs. Then both the staff member and the director sign the evaluation form and the new work plan. Although this process is somewhat formal, the director's evaluation role becomes businesslike, as well as personal, if it is followed.

## 15-3c Professional Approach

In all staff evaluation situations, a professional approach must be taken. Such an approach conveys to each staff member the importance of the role and of the staff member's performance. Because this may seem difficult in the rather informal child care setting, the director may want to discuss with the staff what an important professional responsibility evaluation and planning should be.

Arranging unhurried, uninterrupted time and space for evaluation sessions is essential. Such procedures may seem superfluous in the majority of situations. However, establishing the pattern sets the stage for the occasional very difficult evaluation conference and should make it easier to proceed in a professional manner in those instances. Careful and thoughtful evaluation also sends a message to all staff that their work is indeed serious and can leave them feeling quite positive about what they have accomplished and ready to work toward continued development.

A similar evaluation process is followed for the director, and the board is usually responsible for its implementation. In a multisite corporate system, a regional representative may conduct the director's evaluation. Because the staff members in a well-run center may feel very close to one another and may consider the director a personal friend, it is wise to maintain structure in the evaluation process to allow everyone to be as objective as possible. Parents' perspectives on the director's performance are also significant and may be gathered by means of a survey.

Because the director is responsible for the overall quality of the center, logically, evaluation focuses on reaching quality indicators. These include low staff turnover and equitable staff salaries, low rates of staff absenteeism, adequate time for staff planning and development, and providing sufficient classroom equipment and supplies.

Beyond that, however, managing the ever-changing needs of children, families, and staff requires tremendous

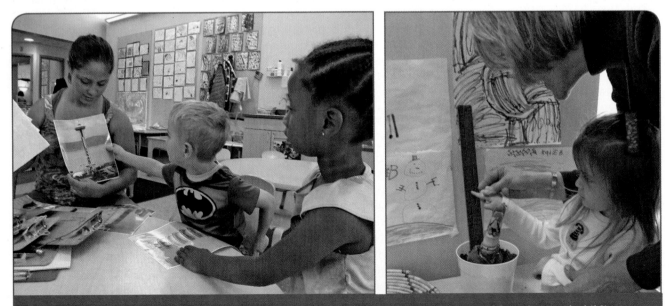

*When teachers interact with individual children, their observations become important sources of data about each child's development.*

organizational ability on the part of the director. Programs for children are complex, as evidenced by the fact that the director's day may involve developing new enrollment policies, assisting a struggling teacher in the classroom, and meeting with funders from a national organization. The complexity of the director's role reflects the unpredictable interconnectedness described by complexity theory. According to this theory, "the world is spontaneous, alive, and disorderly—in other words, complex. This results in organizations where there are no simple answers and where people and program continually interact with a constantly changing environment" (VanderVen, 2000). In evaluating directors, the complex nature of their role must be taken into account.

As director credentialing becomes more available, the board may want to require obtaining the credential as part of the evaluation. Currently, the credential is gaining in popularity as a way to improve center quality and to market the center to families. In at least one state, this credential is required. Many other states offer, or are developing, director credentials.

## 15-4 CHILD ASSESSMENT

Although the terms *assessment* and *evaluation* are often used as synonyms, Gullo (2005) offers the following definitions:

> *Assessment*: the process of gathering information about children to make educational decisions
>
> *Evaluation*: the process of making judgments about the merits, value, or worth of educational programs, projects, materials, or techniques (pp. 6–7)

As mentioned in Chapter 1, the curriculum plan is determined by the director in consultation with the teaching staff. The assessment plan is also the ultimate responsibility of the director. This plan should be designed to relate to the curriculum with emphasis on the needs and interests of each child. Because the major goals of an early childhood education center revolve around expectations about the development of children, the evaluation most commonly thought of to demonstrate the program's efficacy is child outcomes. Note that assessing young children's development has always been part of the responsibility of early childhood programs. Those assessments focus on all aspects of development.

In some cases, child assessment has been haphazard or overlooked. When directors do not take responsibility for ensuring that assessment is a regular part of the program, it may not occur, or inappropriate assessment may be done.

Child assessment may involve an individual child, all the children enrolled in an early childhood center, or all the children funded by a particular organization or agency. The director must be sure there is a valid reason for the assessment, that the assessment process will not

*Directors help teachers understand the importance of writing notes about each child's strengths and needs.*

be detrimental to the child or children, and that parents have given consent.

## 15-4a Professional Recommendations

The NAEYC and the National Association of Early Childhood Specialists in State Departments of Education (NAECS/SDE) issued an important and informative joint statement in 2003 titled, *Early Childhood Curriculum, Assessment, and Program Evaluation: Building an Effective Accountable System in Programs for Children Birth through Age 8*. This joint statement reminds us to "Make ethical, appropriate, valid, and reliable assessment a central part of all early childhood programs. To assess young children's strengths, progress, and needs, use assessment methods that are developmentally appropriate, culturally and linguistically responsive, tied to children's daily activities, supported by professional development, inclusive of families, and connected to specific, beneficial purposes" (2003, p. 1). Watch for newly developed position statements and updates of current statements on the NAEYC website.

More recently, and in response to a request from Congress, the National Research Council of the National Academies developed a report on assessment of young children. The report includes guidelines on instrument selection and implementation. For example, "Assessments should not be given without clear plans for follow-up steps that use the information productively and appropriately" (2008, p. 6) and "Assessors should be trained to meet a clearly specified level of expertise in administering assessments, should be monitored systematically, and should be reevaluated occasionally. Teachers or other program staff may administer assessments if they are carefully supervised and if reliability checks and monitoring are in place to ensure adherence to approved procedures" (2008, p. 7).

*Poppy's teacher is aware that she needs time to get comfortable at school each morning.*

*After a few minutes, Poppy peeks out.*

*She's beginning to feel safe now. Her teacher makes a note to talk with the director about how to make Poppy feel more comfortable.*

These strong, well-researched recommendations make it clear that assessment is a significant responsibility. The director's role is to ensure that the responsibility is met.

## 15-4b Relationship to Standards

The assessment issue is in the forefront today partially because every state has created academic standards for K–12 programs. Standards, known as the Common Core State Standards (National Governors Association Center for Best Practices, Council of Chief State School Officers, 2010), have also been developed for English language arts and mathematics and have been adopted by most states to date. Additionally, most states have created academic standards for prekindergarten. Assessment related to those standards has assumed a prominent position in decision making by politicians, funders, families, the media, and by early childhood educators.

A joint position statement of NAEYC and NAECS/SDE *Early Learning Standards: Creating the Conditions for Success* (2002), re iterates the long-held belief that early childhood programs must provide appropriate opportunities for *all* children to develop in all areas. The document encourages professionals to assume responsibility for recognizing the benefits and risks of the expanded standards movement and for ensuring that essential features of effective and appropriate standards be understood and delivered.

However, assessment for children in their early years must be quite different from assessment for school-age children. The National Research Council report emphasizes that "a primary purpose of assessing children or classrooms is to improve the quality of early childhood care and education...." Noting the differences between elementary-age and younger children, the report urges "extreme caution" when dealing with very young children and their programs (2008, p. 10). Assessment results should then be used to modify, but not dictate, curriculum and teaching methods and to determine where additional resources and professional development may be needed. The goal is to improve programs for young children rather than to cast aspersions on children, families, teachers, or programs.

Center directors working with staff can help families, community members, and funders understand how the early childhood curriculum is designed to help each child learn. They can help dispel the myth that children are "just playing" by demonstrating how play contributes to broader cognitive development as well as to learning in the content areas (literacy, mathematics, science, and social studies). Directors and teachers can also focus on children's need to develop socially and emotionally. Certainly they should be aware of each child's progress in relating to one another in the classroom and beyond, and in continuing to develop as a socially, physically, and emotionally healthy human being.

To help others understand the benefits and challenges of assessing young children, it is important to first spend time determining what both you and your staff believe regarding appropriate assessment. Moreover, because there is more and more pressure today to measure children's learning, it is wise to develop an assessment policy that can be included in your family and staff handbooks. In this way, you can inform new staff and families about your philosophy and maximize the potential for general agreement about your goals and methods for assessing children. See Figure 15-1 for an example of an assessment policy.

Young children develop rapidly, so it is important that the progress they make in their normal development is not attributed solely to the center's program. Many other conditions affect the child's development, including parental behavior, cultural background, nutrition, and general health. Any one of these variables or combinations of them can affect the child's development positively or negatively, just as the center's program may have a positive or negative influence. The child's total development is a result of the interaction of many factors, which makes it difficult to evaluate the influence of one variable such as a specific child care or preschool experience.

## 15-4c Methods for Assessing Child Progress

Assessment of child progress is ongoing and is expected to inform the day-to-day curriculum, including teacher-child interactions. Professional recommendations delineate *criteria* for choosing and using assessment tools. For example, the tool must be valid and reliable, and the assessor must be using the tool in a specified manner. The recommendations call for *appropriate methods* of assessing children. Therefore, directors must know which methods are appropriate and must ensure that only appropriate methods are employed.

Because teachers gather assessment information in their day-to-day teaching, directors must evaluate the methods based on the following criteria:

1. *Developmental appropriateness of the methods.* Does the teacher use appropriate questions to help understand the child's thinking? Is the teacher aware of emerging knowledge and skills being exhibited by each child? Has a wide variety of related opportunities been provided to support children's interests? Is the level of materials appropriate so that every child's needs can be met? For a clear description of developmentally appropriate practice, see Copple and Bredekamp (2008).

2. *Cultural and linguistic responsiveness of the methods.* Is there evidence that the teachers are familiar with each child's culture and are using it as they plan curriculum? Is there at least one adult available who speaks the child's home language? If that is not possible, are teachers finding ways to communicate with each child?

**FIGURE 15-1** Assessment Policy for the Bombeck Family Learning Center.

The purpose of assessment is to inform instruction in order to support the development and learning of infants, toddlers, and preschoolers. Assessment is also used to document development and learning, including progress in the Ohio Early Learning and Development Standards.

The teachers at the Bombeck Family Center implement the *ACCESS Assessment System*, which includes intentional and authentic data collection using such tools as work samples, observational checklists, photographs and videotape with anecdotal notes, and electronic portfolios. Infant and toddler teachers focus on individual child data sets. In preschool classrooms, data is aggregated or compiled using the *ACCESS Classroom Tracking System* (ACTS), which allows teachers to see up-to-date information about the strengths and needs of individual children as well as a whole class view that can inform classroom instruction. In preschool classrooms, we use assessment to plan and implement curriculum, determine individual and whole-class progress, and to inform and initiate interventions.

Children are evaluated authentically in the naturally occurring classroom environment. Assessment is intentional, ongoing, and completed by familiar adults. Formal assessments and screenings are done as required by the State and as needed to gather diagnostic information. All assessment is completed with the consent of families and by trained, experienced professionals—i.e., teacher or consultant. Parent permission is required prior to formal testing, and results are discussed during conferences.

Assessment information is shared with families quarterly during scheduled progress report conferences. Families can request additional conferences as needed.

We follow ethical standards for maintaining confidentiality of assessments. Families may ask to view any assessment information at any time. State-required forms with confidential information and evaluation results are kept in the children's files in the office area. Daily assessments and behavioral observations are kept in confidential files within the classroom. They are used to help teachers plan both individual and whole-class activities. Electronic portfolios are updated regularly and are shared with families.

Families may contribute to assessment data in several ways. Families are consistently asked for information about children during daily discussions at drop-off and pick-up times, or during conferences and intervention team meetings.

*Source: Bombeck Family Learning Center.*

3. *Connection of the methods to children's daily activities.* Do teachers plan and implement daily activities in ways that allow them to assess what children are learning? Do they use that information to plan additional or modified daily activities?

4. *Multiple sources of data collected over time.* Are varying types of evidence documenting a child's progress collected throughout the year? Are appropriate accommodations made for children with disabilities?

5. *Support of the methods by professional development.* Has the director provided opportunities for teachers to learn about the expected standards? Has professional development been provided to help teachers plan ways to help children meet the standards in meaningful ways?

6. *Inclusion of families.* Has the director provided opportunities for families to become acquainted with program goals? Have they had opportunities to observe in the classroom and to receive information about how the program is designed to meet goals? Are parents included in providing documentation of their child's growth and development? Does the director also have opportunities to develop this understanding?

7. *Connection of the methods to specific, beneficial purposes.* Are methods of assessment, particularly those using standardized assessment tools, designed to provide information that supports teachers as they modify curriculum for each child and for the group? Will the information obtained be helpful to families? Will the information demonstrate to funders the significance of the program?

## 15-4d Tools for Assessing Child Progress

The director, in consultation with the teaching staff, decides on the tools to be used to

*Evaluating children's knowledge and skills can be accomplished appropriately as they are engaged in ongoing play.*

document each child's progress. They discuss goals, time lines, and process. The assessment should also lead to planning to meet each child's needs. In cases involving researchers or funders who want or need to collect data, the director should consider whether this data collection presents an ethical dilemma. If so, the director must determine what course of action to take.

The first question to ask regarding any child assessment tool is, "Is it ethical to use this procedure?" Early childhood educators must be aware of and follow the Code of Ethical Conduct. The principle, *We shall do no harm to children*, supersedes all other principles in the code and can be used as a first consideration. (The code can be found in Appendix A, is on the NAEYC website, and can be purchased inexpensively from the NAEYC in brochure form. Providing a copy for each staff member and family helps everyone understand what is expected. The Code of Ethical Conduct addresses a breadth of principles related to early care and education and makes an excellent starting point for staff discussions of appropriate assessment.)

Important issues include the following:

- Will children be put in a stressful situation?

- Will individual children be evaluated unfairly because the test was normed on a specific population?

- Will children have had the opportunity to learn the material being assessed?

- Will the results of the assessment help the child by enabling families, teachers, and other professionals to plan for the child's continued progress?

- Will the use of the testing program or other assessment detract significantly from other important opportunities for the children (such as physical activity, arts, and opportunity to explore a wide range of materials)?

Preschool children may be assessed with screening instruments. These relatively brief tools identify children who need additional assessment because they *may* have a disability or a learning problem. Determining whether there actually is a concern and whether there is need for remediation then leads to a plan for the child and provision of an appropriate program and support. Input from parents is important. Children often behave differently at home than in a screening situation even when a parent is encouraged to be in the screening area. Children who have the advantage of early screening benefit from access to early program modifications to meet their needs whether in a preschool classroom or in a different setting. This is particularly important for children with disabilities.

Keep in mind that screening instruments are intended to provide information about an individual child's possible need for more thorough assessment and support. They are *not* intended to be administered twice to all children in a class to demonstrate the progress that a group has made by participating in that early childhood program.

Many other tools are available to be used by teachers. These include teacher observations, checklists, rating scales, portfolios, reports from other professionals, and standardized tests. The following sections take a brief look at each of these tools. Keep in mind the relationship between appropriate curriculum and appropriate assessment, but remember that assessment should not drive curriculum.

---

**REFLECTION**

Think about your own feelings about being evaluated. Are your feelings positive? Negative? Mixed? How does the evaluator influence these feelings? What is the behavior of an evaluator who helps you feel positive? Can you recall the behavior of an evaluator who left you feeling incompetent? Describe an evaluation that helped you in some way.

---

## 15-4e Teacher Observations

Throughout the year, the teacher may keep anecdotal and running records about each  child. These notes, whether recorded on file cards, written in a small notebook, or entered into a tablet computer, are summarized by the teacher periodically. Cohen, Stern, Balaban, and Gropper (2008); Jablon, Dombrom, and Dichtelmiller (2007); Nicolson and Shipstead (2001); and Nilsen (2008) are among the authors who describe general guidelines for observing children. The teacher notes the changes in developmental level and the specific objectives that the child has met or is working to develop. Using this method, the teacher is able to make statements about each child individually, placing emphasis on what the child's needs were, based on initial observations, and how the needs were met. She may modify her approach to working with the child, develop alternate play and learning opportunities, and use her developing understanding of each child to help each child continue to develop in a range of ways. This method uses subjective data provided by the teacher and is valuable only if the teacher is a skilled observer and collects data regularly. In a center that is minimally staffed, use of this method may be difficult. Nonetheless, development of observational skills is critical. Professional teachers must know what to look for and how to recognize it. While many other persons may no longer agree with this primary reliance on systematic observations, the approach itself remains worthwhile and may uncover information not picked up by standard assessments.

## 15-4f Checklists

The director may find or create a checklist that names the behaviors toward which some of the center's objectives

---

**Working Smart with Technology**

*Technology That Supports Evaluation*

The ability to record and interpret observations of young children's behavior is considered to be one of the most important skills a teacher can possess. For many educators, notes have traditionally been written on paper and later filed away in folders or binders. Today, technology provides alternative strategies for collecting and using this important information. For example, there are numerous note-taking apps for mobile devices (smartphones, laptops, tablets) that can facilitate the process. Directors or teachers can type notes in the classroom and immediately file the observations in children's or staff members' digital folders. Speech-to-text apps such as Dragon Dictation and Speech Notes can also be used to record notes without having to type. Additionally, digital photos or audio recordings can be gathered to support the written observations. The SoundNote app allows you to take notes at the same time you are recording audio. As you might guess, these tools can be invaluable to data collection and are particularly useful when documenting children's progress toward meeting individualized education plan (IEP) goals. See Donohue (2010) and Simon and Nemeth (2012) for additional information.

*Many note-taking applications exist that can facilitate director observations of teachers and children.*

are aimed. Then teachers merely check whether or not the child exhibits the listed behavior based on their observations of that child. A question arises when the child sometimes does the task and sometimes does not, either because the task is just being learned, because the child chooses not to do it, or because no opportunity is made available. For example, an item might be "Buttons own coat." The child who does this occasionally may be in the process of learning and may not be ready to struggle with buttons on some days, or the child may be asking the teacher for help because he needs attention rather than help. Checklists generally focus on easily identifiable items, so additional assessments must also be used.

## 15-4g Rating Scales

The director may create or locate a rating scale that lists the behaviors closely paralleling the center's objectives. The rating scale alleviates the problem created by a checklist by providing a way for teachers to qualify their answers. The teacher rates each child at least at the beginning and the end of the school year and perhaps more frequently. (See Figure 15-2 for an example of a rating scale.)

The problems with rating scales are that each teacher may interpret the categories differently, and most teachers are reluctant to use the two ends of the scales (1 and 5, or never and always). Such scales, however, can be useful in pointing out general strengths and weaknesses in any child's development and in the functioning of the group. Rating scales are relatively quick to complete, and teachers can do them when the children are not present if they have been observing carefully.

Both checklists and rating scales are suitable for use if they are viewed as a particular teacher's assessment of an individual child instead of as a comparison of one child or class with another. In reporting data from checklists and rating scales, the teacher may comment on how many children recognize their names in print or play cooperatively in a group of two or more children. But this information must be placed in proper context by pointing out the children's ages and other factors that may influence the data. When space is provided on the form, the child's

*Directors may encourage teachers to add photos to the children's portfolios. This photo represents two children's beginning ability to work cooperatively.*

ratings at two or more widely spread times during a year can be included to show progress and areas in which additional support is needed.

## 15-4h Portfolios

One type of assessment that can provide valuable information about each child is the portfolio. According to Lynch (2007):

> A portfolio is a tool that can be used to collect documentation of a child's growth and development over time. However, portfolio assessment is more than a compilation of unrelated writing samples, photographs, and drawings.
>
> As teachers implement this approach to assessment, they systematically observe and document children's behavior and activities, collect work samples, reflect on the significance of what has been observed, and complete the assessment cycle by using the data for curricular adaptation and/or demonstrating achievement of specified goals. (p. 2)

Some teachers use a two-part system with one folder in a locked cabinet and a second folder in the classroom readily accessible to the child. The first folder contains forms and information from families; the teacher's written observations such as anecdotal records; notes on plans for that child; progress reports; medical reports; and reports from previous teachers, agencies, or consultants who have worked with the child. This information is confidential and should be available only to those who have a legitimate right to it. The second folder provides the child with an opportunity to save products that he has created. The teacher may add photos, videos, notes, and audiotapes, although the availability of these records depends on the center's budget and the time available to teachers to prepare these records. Periodically, the records must be sorted and decisions made about what is to be retained because the record is intended to follow the child throughout school years. The child should participate in deciding what is to be retained, and the family, too, may want to be involved. Some records, however, must be retained by school policy or by law. Additionally, portfolio assessment can be a very effective strategy for obtaining a comprehensive view of children with disabilities (Lynch, 2007). See McAfee, Leong, and Bodrova (2004) and Gronlund and James (2013) for other ideas about portfolios.

## 15-4i Other Observers

The director may observe a particular child when a teacher has concerns about that child. Sometimes, an outside observer such as the director or a consultant brings a more objective analysis or may see factors in the environment or even in the teacher's behavior that appear to be influencing the child's behavior. After collecting data, the observer confers with the teacher, and together they design a plan for working with the child. When an individual

**FIGURE 15-2** Sample Preschool Rating Scale

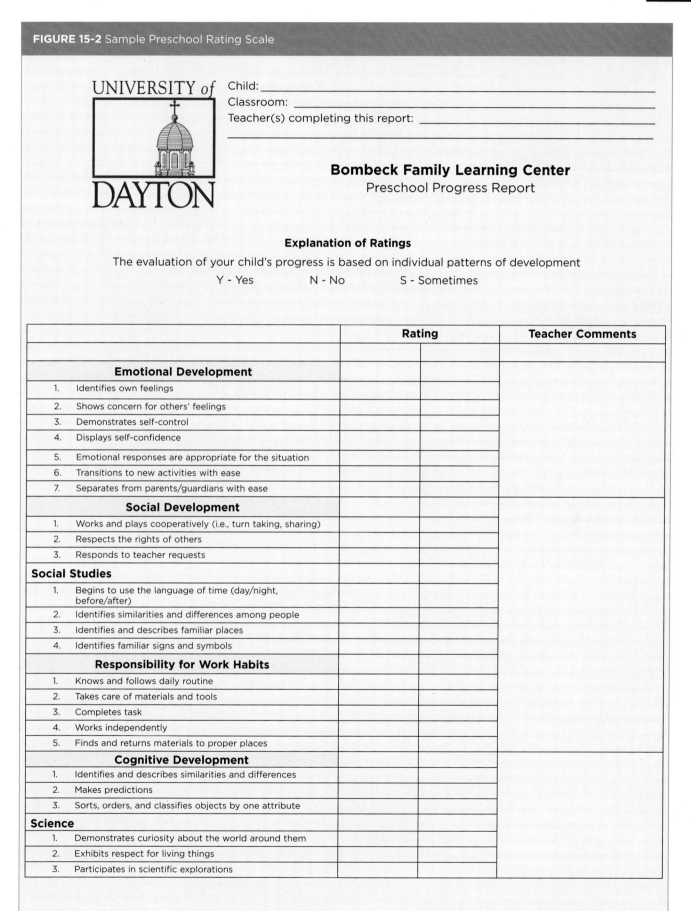

UNIVERSITY *of*

DAYTON

Child: _____

Classroom: _____

Teacher(s) completing this report: _____

_____

## Bombeck Family Learning Center
### Preschool Progress Report

**Explanation of Ratings**

The evaluation of your child's progress is based on individual patterns of development

Y - Yes          N - No          S - Sometimes

| | | Rating | | Teacher Comments |
|---|---|---|---|---|
| | | | | |
| **Emotional Development** | | | | |
| 1. | Identifies own feelings | | | |
| 2. | Shows concern for others' feelings | | | |
| 3. | Demonstrates self-control | | | |
| 4. | Displays self-confidence | | | |
| 5. | Emotional responses are appropriate for the situation | | | |
| 6. | Transitions to new activities with ease | | | |
| 7. | Separates from parents/guardians with ease | | | |
| **Social Development** | | | | |
| 1. | Works and plays cooperatively (i.e., turn taking, sharing) | | | |
| 2. | Respects the rights of others | | | |
| 3. | Responds to teacher requests | | | |
| **Social Studies** | | | | |
| 1. | Begins to use the language of time (day/night, before/after) | | | |
| 2. | Identifies similarities and differences among people | | | |
| 3. | Identifies and describes familiar places | | | |
| 4. | Identifies familiar signs and symbols | | | |
| **Responsibility for Work Habits** | | | | |
| 1. | Knows and follows daily routine | | | |
| 2. | Takes care of materials and tools | | | |
| 3. | Completes task | | | |
| 4. | Works independently | | | |
| 5. | Finds and returns materials to proper places | | | |
| **Cognitive Development** | | | | |
| 1. | Identifies and describes similarities and differences | | | |
| 2. | Makes predictions | | | |
| 3. | Sorts, orders, and classifies objects by one attribute | | | |
| **Science** | | | | |
| 1. | Demonstrates curiosity about the world around them | | | |
| 2. | Exhibits respect for living things | | | |
| 3. | Participates in scientific explorations | | | |

**FIGURE 15-2** Sample Preschool Rating Scale (*Continued*)

| | Rating | | Teachers Comments |
|---|---|---|---|
| **Math** | | | |
| 1.   Rote counts to 10 | | | |
| 2.   Demonstrates one to one correspondence to 5 | | | |
| 3.   Identifies and names numerals 0-9 | | | |
| 4.   Sequences numbers up to 5 | | | |
| 5.   Identifies common shapes | | | |
| 6.   Demonstrates an understanding of positional words | | | |
| 7.   Names pennies, nickels, dimes, and quarters | | | |
| **Motor Development** | | | |
| **Fine Motor** | | | |
| 1.   Shows hands preference—left or right | | | |
| 2.   Turns knobs, lids, etc. with ease | | | |
| 3.   Pours liquid into cup without spilling | | | |
| 4.   Fastens and unfastens zippers, buttons, and Velcro | | | |
| 5.   Can _____ dress _____ undress _____put on own shoes | | | |
| 6.   Uses scissors with control | | | |
| 7.   Uses appropriate pencil grasp | | | |
| **Large Motor** | | | |
| 1.   Walks down stairs with alternating feet | | | |
| 2.   Runs with control using opposite arms/feet-crossing midline | | | |
| 3.   Jumps _____with feet together _____on one foot | | | |
| 4.   Can _____throw _____catch _____kick  ball | | | |
| 5.   Pedals tricycle | | | |
| **Language Development** | | | |
| **Spoken Language** | | | |
| 1.   Speaks clearly to express ideas, feelings, and needs. | | | |
| 2.   Uses words to solve problems and/or negotiate with friends | | | |
| 3.   Initiates and sustains conversations | | | |
| 4.   Asks and answers questions | | | |
| **Listening** | | | |
| 1.   Listens attentively to speakers, stories, songs, and poems | | | |
| 2.   Follows simple oral directions | | | |
| **Emergent Reading** | | | |
| 1.   Identifies and reads own first name | | | |
| 2.   Identifies environmental print and/or symbols | | | |
| 3.   Identifies and/or names letters | | | |
| 4.   Knows differences between illustrations and print | | | |
| 5.   Retells stories | | | |
| **Emergent Writing** | | | |
| 1.   Pretends to write from top to bottom, left to right, in rows | | | |
| 2.   Prints letters of own name and other meaningful words using mock or real letters | | | |
| 3.   Dictates or produces "writing" to express thoughts | | | |
| **The Arts** | | | |
| 1.   Demonstrates creativity through drawing, painting, clay, and a variety of art and construction materials | | | |
| 2.   Participates in singing activities, including finger plays and dance | | | |
| 3.   Demonstrates ability to move to a beat (clap, tap, etc.) | | | |

*Source: Reprinted with permission from Shauna Adams, Bombeck Family Learning Center.*

---

## MAKING THE CASE FOR *USING ELECTRONIC PORTFOLIOS AS ASSESSMENT TOOLS*

Portfolio assessment has long been recognized as a powerful strategy for documenting children's development. Essentially, the electronic portfolio is much like the traditional version with the major difference being that the portfolio is developed in a digital format. Electronic portfolios have the benefit of being able to be shared more readily with families and of including richer documentation of children's behaviors and verbal productions. Deciding on the format of the portfolio is an important first step. PowerPoint and Evernote have been used successfully as tools to create digital portfolios (Brunette, 2013; Montgomery & Wiley, 2008).

One of the challenges of using portfolios has been the amount of time required to develop portfolios for each child. Fortunately, technology can be used to facilitate the process. For example, as mentioned in this chapter's *Working Smart with Technology feature*, many tools have been developed for helping teachers take notes, photos, and recordings, and these can be included as digital evidence of growth and development in the e-portfolio. For additional information about portfolio assessment and digital documentation, see Brunette (2013), Gronlund and James (2013), and Parnell and Bartlett (2012).

---

child is being evaluated to an extent that is beyond the center's regularly scheduled observation plan, parental permission must be obtained. Parental participation in planning is preferable and sometimes required by law.

When a child with identified special needs is enrolled, the director, with written parental permission, contacts agencies familiar with the child to obtain previous evaluations. The director, parent, and representatives of other agencies also may meet to share information that would be useful in working with the child and family.

Reporting a child's behavior to parents usually is handled in a conference. Written information may be provided, but the use of checklists and rating scales for this purpose often is misleading. Parents may misunderstand the significance of this type of written report and categorize their child as a success or a failure. A more appropriate written evaluation for parents may be a narrative that describes the child's strengths and progress at school and discusses areas in which the child has challenges. Sharing a child's portfolio with parents can also help them see how their child is developing. The teacher also may confer with parents about ways to help the child continue progressing toward future educational goals. For additional information about sharing assessment information with parents, see National Center on Parent, Family and Community Engagement (2011).

Parents have the right to review information from their child's folder at any time. In some cases, they feel that it is damaging to the child to have certain information passed along to the next teacher. In other cases, they are eager for the new teacher to understand as much as possible about their child immediately so that the child does not have to endure a time period in which the teacher is discovering a hearing loss or some other condition for which an instructional plan should be designed. In any case, the teacher and parent discuss available information about the child and together determine which data should be sent forward to the next teacher. When a child

*The director positions herself at the child's eye level so that she can talk with both child and parent.*

has an individualized family service plan (IFSP) or an individualized education plan (IEP), the new teacher should have access to that plan and participate with the IEP team in updating the plan on a regular basis. Keep in mind that the family is an essential and required part of the team.

## 15-4j Standardized Tests

Until recently, little attention was paid to using standardized tests with young children. Several reasons are apparent. First, young children can't be tested in a group because they can write only in a limited way, if at all. In a group situation, they have trouble attending to the type of test form typically used in such standardized tests. Even if their task is to draw a circle around one of three pictures for each question, they may be focused on an aspect of the question or of the pictures that is not related to the presumed correct answer.

For example, one kindergartner was asked to circle the picture of two characters from a story. The three choices were a picture of Jack and Jill falling down the hill, a picture of the three bears, and a picture of Little Red Riding Hood. After the test, the teacher talked with a child whom she was certain had well-developed concepts of twoness and threeness. She asked why he had circled the three bears. He replied, "Well, you see, there's two bears and one left over." She asked what he thought about circling Jack and Jill, and he quickly responded, "Jack and Jill is not a story; it's a poem." While that thinking may not be typical, we have no way of knowing why young children respond the way they do in a standardized testing situation. For this reason, standardized tests, if used at all with young children, must be carefully reviewed even when administered orally and individually.

When tests are administered to young children individually, results are often spurious. The answer a young child gives today may differ from the answer he provides a few days later. Children do not learn in small, isolated bits. As they examine their world, they form relationships with what they already know. Those relationships initially are not always accurate from an adult perspective but are meaningful to the child. As the child encounters additional situations, he creates new relationships, which may or may not be more realistic from an adult perspective. The information that a child learns by rote may be lost relatively quickly if it is meaningless to the child. This kind of information is often assessed on standardized tests.

Even though directors must be sure the tests used in their centers are appropriate, funders may require inappropriate assessments. Such a situation presents an ethical dilemma: Administering the test and the potential use of the results may be seen as inappropriate, while refusing to allow the testing may result in withdrawal of funds and loss of programs for children who are most in need of early education. In a critique of the Head Start National Reporting System (NRS), Meisels and Atkins-Burnett (2004) described this high-stakes achievement test for 4- and 5-year-olds as containing "items that are rife with class prejudice and are developmentally inappropriate." The authors presented a number of examples of NRS test items, explaining, in each case, the inadequacies of each. The authors concluded, "This test is not good early education practice. It is not good psychometric practice. It is not good public policy. And it is certainly not good for young children." Raver and Zigler (2004) argued that "the application of a strictly cognitive focus to assessments of school readiness runs counter to what the best developmental research tells us and what past policy experience has shown." After numerous discussions about the assessment among various constituents, the National Head Start Association reported that the NRS had been terminated and that programs were no longer required to use the NRS tests.

The director's role is to understand and use an appropriate assessment program and to work to modify or eliminate high-stakes testing. In some cases, the director's ethical decision may be to refuse to allow such testing in his center. Such a decision may involve issues such as cessation of funding based on the refusal, thus impacting many children, families, and staff. A concerted effort over time, however, with supportive position statements by professional organizations and reasoned discussions with legislators, educators, funders, and other interested parties may prove more beneficial to children in the long run.

If tests are to be administered, the director is professionally responsible for determining whether the test in question is appropriate for the children to be assessed. The director should understand what the test measures, how it is to be administered, by whom, and for what purpose. What effect will it have on the curriculum and, more important, on the children? What provisions will be made for assessing children for whom the test is culturally inappropriate based on language, other aspects of culture, or special needs? The director is expected to know or learn about terms related to testing, such as what the scores mean, what different types of tests are designed to measure, what the results mean, and how they will be used. The director is also responsible for ensuring that staff members understand these topics. A key component of the director's role is ensuring that, if standardized tests are administered, the results are not misused. A clear description of topics related to testing appears in Gullo's (2005) book on assessment and in Snow (2011).

If we find that a particular test meets the criteria described earlier in this section, the next questions include the reliability and validity of the test.

- Would the results obtained by a particular data collector be similar enough to those of another trained data collector?

- If teachers are expected to test their own classes, what preparation will they receive?

- Who will teach the class while the teacher tests one child at a time?

- Does the test measure what it purports to measure?

- How will the results be reported?

- What do the results mean to teachers? To families?

- Will the people who receive the results know how to interpret them?

- What will be done with the results? Will they be used for the purpose for which the test was designed? Are the results beneficial to the children? If not, will the benefits to someone else outweigh the impact on the children and the program?

Some misuses of standardized tests of young children include the following:

- Keeping a child from entering kindergarten when he is chronologically eligible

- Rating a program

- Evaluating teachers

- Making curricular decisions based solely on specific test content

- Giving several tests two or more times per year

- Teaching to the test

Although a wide range of opportunities for assessment of children's progress has been mentioned, the more observant preschool teachers are, the more they will learn about each child. In combining brief teacher notes, parent comments, photos of the child engaged in the classroom, and anecdotal records, the teacher has a good understanding of a child. Bringing these observations together enables teachers to create a description of the child's development over the preschool enrollment period.

The director's knowledge and ability to support staff in implementing an appropriate child assessment plan is a major factor in its success. Using the results to meet children's needs is a significant part of the program's operational system. Such a plan demonstrates that laying out a detailed curriculum for the year is not appropriate because it does not address children's particular needs and interests.

## 15-5 TOTAL PROGRAM EVALUATION

The program goals of the center, and the program itself, are designed to fulfill the particular needs that the center was established to meet. **naeyc**

*Before observing in classrooms, a program evaluator talks with the director about the procedures she will use.*

▶❚❚ **TeachSource Video Vignette**

### Goal Setting: A Center Director Sets Goals for an Early Childhood Center

This video provides an overview of issues related to evaluation of early care and education programs. As you view the video entitled, *Goal Setting: A Center Director Sets Goals for an Early Childhood Center*, reflect on the following questions:

1. What factors contribute to developing effective goals for directors? For teachers?

2. What is the value in considering a person's strengths first?

Consequently, at evaluation time, the needs, the goals, and the program are evaluated as part of the center's overall evaluation system.

At regular intervals, the community's needs must be assessed so that the center can plan for current and future populations. Because goals are closely tied to the philosophy of the center program, they change slowly. Nonetheless, they should be examined periodically, perhaps every few years, to determine whether they still are applicable. The objectives are more directly related to the individuals served at a given time. Therefore, they may change more rapidly than the goals. The objectives should be examined annually prior to the start of a new school or fiscal year.

In addition, the director or the board may prepare checklists or rating scales for the evaluation of the program. They can be distributed to staff members, parents, and community representatives; or these people may be asked to provide their evaluations in written or oral forms. Board members and funding agency representatives may contribute to the evaluation by reviewing aspects of the overall program such as the physical environment, curriculum, parent program, ancillary services, and board operations. They also may evaluate the staff performance in general, rather than individual, terms. Periodically, perhaps every few years, the policies and procedures manual, the job descriptions, and the board bylaws are reviewed. Even the evaluation plans and procedures are evaluated!

A widely used center evaluation tool is the *Early Childhood Environment Rating Scale* (Harms, Clifford, & Cryer, 2005). Seven areas are covered in separate subscales: personal care routines, furnishings and displays for children, language-reasoning experiences, fine and gross motor activities, creative activities, social development, and adult needs. After observing, the rater circles the appropriate category from 1 (inadequate) to 7 (excellent). Each subscale total rating is plotted on a profile sheet. Center staff then can decide in which areas they want to make improvements. Profiles produced at different points in time can be used to determine changes in the center's program during that time period. Similar scales have been produced for rating infant-toddler programs, school age, and family child care. Instructional guides for observers are available in print and on DVD.

Perhaps the most important evaluation a director can conduct is to look at quality of work life. Bloom points out that low morale, stress, and burnout soon affect commitment to the profession. When staff experience these tensions, it becomes very difficult for directors to maintain high-quality programs. Bloom (1996) recommends, therefore, that the director examine 10 dimensions necessary to create a professional climate. Among these are supervisor support, opportunities for professional growth, and amount of staff autonomy in decision making. She further recommends surveying the staff, and then using the resulting data to plan changes.

Staff surveys usually are anonymous, although in large centers, individuals may be asked to indicate age, job type, level of education completed, or any other category that will provide productive information. The purpose is to use the data for revising administrative practices and planning realistic changes in the center.

Items that are obviously unattainable should, of course, not be included. For instance, one would not list, "The center shall allow monthly unpaid mental health days," if such a policy would not be workable.

Many center directors and staff members are aware that they need to check the quality of their relations with parents, children, and staff members from a variety of cultures. The self-assessment documents from the National Center for Cultural Competence (2009), designed specifically for early intervention and early childhood settings, may help directors provide leadership in analyzing areas of strength and areas where improvement is needed. This publication includes sections titled, Physical Environment, Materials and Resources, Communication Styles, and Values and Attitudes.

Talan and Bloom (2011) created a publication that provides guidance related to all aspects of early childhood program assessment, focusing on the leadership and management practices of center-based early childhood organizations. The format consists of 10 categories of items, including center operations, fiscal management, program planning and evaluation, technology, and marketing and public relations. Each category is addressed on wide two-page spreads. A list of what to look for, such as needed documents, and questions to ask, appears on the left. The evaluator takes notes based on a review of the category components during the data-gathering phase. For example, when completing the section titled, Assessment in Support of Learning, evaluators would probably ask the director how curriculum is planned. They would also determine whether reliable and valid assessments are being used. Next the evaluator completes the rating scale, allowing the rater to refer back to notes made during the data-gathering phase. Using a seven-point scale for each item assessed, the evaluator can create a profile depicting the center's leadership and management strengths and areas in which improvement can be considered. When completed, these documents provide valuable planning tools for directors.

## DIRECTOR'S CORNER

"A teacher asked if she could put a notice on the bulletin board saying she has an extra ticket to a show in town and wondering whether anyone wanted to join her. Another teacher said she'd love to go. Although they knew each other slightly at that point, after spending the evening together, they decided having opportunities to relax with other staff would be a great idea. 'Join us at the outdoor rink for ice skating Saturday afternoon' and 'Is anyone interested in checking out the free concert at the college next Friday?' appeared on the board within the next few weeks. I'm noting collaboration in and across classrooms is really expanding as teachers find ways to get to know each other better."

—*Director, agency-sponsored child care center*

## 15-5a Accreditation

Accreditation in early childhood refers to a **naeyc** type of center evaluation conducted by an outside agency, usually a professional organization. Several groups currently offer some type of early childhood education accreditation. These include the NAEYC, the Association for Early Learning Leaders, and the National Child Care Association (NCCA). These organizations create descriptions of high-quality early childhood education and encourage center boards and directors to apply for accreditation. Programs such as the NAEYC's provide materials for self-study. If the center completes the self-study and decides to continue, it prepares the documents that will be reviewed and plans for a visit from trained assessors. More information can be found on the NAEYC's website and by contacting other organizations offering possible accreditation.

The Administration for Children and Families created a different type of system, the Quality Rating and Improvement System (QRIS), via the National Child Care Information and Technical Assistance Center (NCCIC). QRIS was designed to support states and communities as they work to improve the quality and availability of early care and education programs beyond the basic requirements needed for licensing. Often, Child Care and Development Funds are used for these activities. This approach provides opportunities for many programs to move at a pace that is realistic for them.

"A QRIS is not just about ratings or a stand-alone program to improve quality; it is a unique tool for system reform that has the potential to reach programs that serve a wide range of children and are financed by many public and private sources, including parent fees." Important components are related to ECE program standards as well as technical assistance and coaching (QRIS National Learning Network, n.d.). In describing efforts to support high-quality early care and education, the NCCIC recognized that many parents need assistance in selecting this type of education for their children. This belief was reinforced by a study by the National Association for Child Care Resource and Referral Agencies (NACCRRA, now called Child Care Aware of America), which found that 96 percent of parents believe that all child care providers offer learning opportunities for children, and 78 percent believe that all providers are trained in child development (2009). Understandably, many parents do not know what kinds of questions to ask.

Each state chooses standards based on research related to significant quality improvement. Although state funding is becoming more and more limited, the early childhood community works to help legislators and others understand the importance of early education. Funds are used to provide technical assistance and training to center directors and staff. As a center meets criteria and

### REFLECTION

Think about where you learned about young children, their behavior, and their interests. Maybe you have lots of older brothers and sisters, or maybe you did many hours of babysitting when you were younger. You are currently studying to be a child care administrator, so surely you must have studied child development.

Now think about parents who have not had those types of opportunities. Where might they have learned about child care and what is required in providing high-quality care for young children? Although many attempts to reach parents have been made, quite a few parents have not heard about them. They therefore choose child care based on location only or on what, from an adult perspective, looks fun. Many of us had no idea how important early childhood education, whether at home or away from home, is to a child's development.

moves to the next level (designated by stars or other symbols), it may also receive increased subsidies to be used to further staff education or to provide additional classroom equipment. The ratings symbols are becoming familiar to families and help in decisions about child care. Currently, 31 states are engaged in QRIS, and most other states are considering this program.

In some areas, it appears that centers which already lead the community in quality and are accredited by the NAEYC are joining QRIS as a model to those centers who need to start more slowly and move up bit by bit. Some of them had supported each other as they completed requirements for NAEYC accreditation and/or renewal. This type of modeling can be significant in helping more and more programs move from licensure to accreditation directly or through a series of stars. (In some states, accreditation may be considered the top level of the system, while in others, it may be a component of reaching the top step.)

The NAEYC's system for center accreditation includes lists of the values and evidence-based criteria to be used in decision making. In this system, early childhood programs are required to be in substantial compliance with all 10 standards, all of which are considered to be reliable indicators of high quality. Under this plan, the public and staff of accredited centers will know that the centers have been assessed on criteria that lead to positive outcomes for children.

The process includes four steps:

1. **Enrollment.** Engage in self-study (what you need to know in order to study what you do, what you need to think about as you study your program, and what you need to improve).

2. **Application.** Submit application. Set time frame for completing formal self-assessment report.

3. **Enter candidacy.** Submit self-assessment. Demonstrate that licensing, staffing, and health and safety requirements have been met.

4. **On-site visit.** NAEYC assessors visit and determine whether the program meets all 10 NAEYC standards and selected components related to those standards.

The NAEYC views the self-study as an important way to begin program improvement whether or not the center decides to continue with the accreditation process. Materials for the accreditation process may be obtained from the NAEYC. Most directors find that when they take the time to read through the documents, the steps they need to take are all laid out for them, and the procedures may no longer seem as intimidating. The director's role then is to obtain the support of the board and staff by letting them know what is expected, and that they will be engaging in a worthwhile team effort. Sharing the accreditation materials with confidence and being open to addressing staff members' questions and concerns will help everyone get started willingly.

Some changes will almost always be needed. Everyone involved may feel stressed as change is discussed. Here again, the director must listen to concerns and help the group decide how to address them. Making changes is less stressful when the group feels ownership. Some changes may be out of the question, often because of the finances involved. This does not necessarily mean that the center cannot become accredited, but the program report will have to describe how the staff has designed an appropriate alternate approach. In many cases, the staff will have to set priorities and create a schedule for working on various components within a certain time frame. Trying to tackle everything at once can be overwhelming and counterproductive.

Completing the accreditation self-study and the related paperwork takes time and resources. Often, successful directors find that the support of the board, parents, and colleagues makes a major difference. Preparing a time line and sticking to it also is helpful. One way to get staff involved is to begin with a discussion of the program's strengths. Encouraged by that discussion, your team will be ready to address areas that need to be improved and ways to accomplish that improvement (Eisenberg, 2000).

The board and the director must consider the cost of accreditation and the value to the children, families, and staff. In addition, the center may profit financially by being accredited as the community begins to recognize that the new process involves demonstration of quality in all aspects of the center's operation. If the decision is to move forward, the director submits the required documentation to the NAEYC Academy for Early Childhood Program Accreditation. The Academy will then review the documents and decide whether the program is ready for review.

Current information about the NAEYC accreditation process and procedures is available on the NAEYC website and in NAEYC publications.

Some directors may feel that they do not need to bother with accreditation because they have a long waiting list of children, and their programs seem to be doing well. However, directors who take a professional approach will lead their staff in a self-study periodically, whether or not they choose to participate in a particular form of accreditation.

# 15-6 SUMMARIZING DATA

No matter what center evaluation process is chosen, the director is responsible for summarizing the data that are collected from all aspects of the evaluation process, showing the progress or regression since the last evaluation rather than focusing solely on the current performance level. The summary should provide a clear data picture for the reader and should reflect accurately the facts, ideas, and opinions provided by those who participated. Usually a comment that occurs frequently should receive more weight in the summary than an item that seldom appears in the data, no matter how striking or impressive that item appears. Furthermore, no new information should appear in the summary.

The summary is written, dated, and signed by the summarizer and should include a listing of sources used in its compilation. Some data may appear in graph or chart form, particularly if this format makes it easier to understand or more likely to be read. Appropriate computer software makes this task much easier.

## 15-6a Analyzing and Using the Data

The director or a designated committee uses the summary to cull out information. For example, in analyzing enrollment records, the dropout rate of children whose transportation is provided by the school may be compared with the dropout rate of those children who get to school by some other means.

In examining this information, it is necessary to keep other factors constant. For example, if all the children receiving transportation are from low-income families, and if some or all of the other children are from middle-income families, the dropout rate might be more closely related to income level than to mode of transportation. To clarify the situation, additional data would be needed.

After the data have been analyzed, the director prepares a report for the funding agency, the board, and the other people or groups to whom the center is responsible. This type of report usually is prepared annually, although interim reports may be compiled. The report should be expressed clearly and should be easily comprehensible and professional in appearance. Current software simplifies this task and enhances the results.

Each board member receives a copy of the report, one or more copies are submitted to each funding agency that is involved, and one or more copies are filed at the center. The narrative may be enhanced and clarified by the addition of appropriate graphs, charts, or tables. A pie chart showing the use of the director's time, for example, can be more effective than a lengthy narrative that contains the same information. Graphs and charts can be computer generated and add an extra professional touch to a report. The fact that the report is read by people from a variety of backgrounds should be considered.

Usually, by the time the report for a given year is complete and is in the hands of board members, the planning process for the new year has been completed and put into operation. The report then is used primarily for future planning. The board looks at the report, which includes the director's recommendations, to determine the areas that need modification. For example, if there is a high rate of turnover among the teaching staff, the board looks further to see if the cause can be determined from the evaluation data. Perhaps the salaries at this center are much lower than those of other centers in the community, or perhaps the physical environment is poor. Decisions for change are based on available evidence that grows out of the total evaluation process.

## SUMMARY

From the center's inception, an evaluation plan is an essential component of the total program. The director should be aware of the following:

- The purpose of the plan is to determine the value of the center's operation; to evaluate the individuals within it through an analysis of the progress and functioning of the staff, the children, and the overall program; and to provide a basis for future planning for the center.

- Planning for effective evaluation of center components must be systematic and should include identifying what will be evaluated and why.

- The processes and procedures involved with evaluating staff members include collecting, summarizing, analyzing, and using data according to a prespecified plan that lets everyone involved know how, when, where, why, and by whom an evaluation is being completed.

- Certain methods and strategies are useful for conducting appropriate assessment of children's progress.

- Program evaluation and accreditation are valuable for ensuring quality.

- Analyzing and using data collected through the program evaluation process is important.

## TRY IT OUT!

1. Examine Director's Resource 15-1, which provides an example of an annual performance review document. Discuss the document contents with a classmate including the following questions:

    a. What type of information is to be included in the first section—*Planning*? How do the four sections of Planning relate to each other? (Note: SMART is an acronym for goals that are specific, measurable, attainable, realistic, and time-limited. Additional information about these goals can be found easily online.) What "professional competencies" might be addressed? If this were your own evaluation, on what competencies would you focus for the next year? (Use the NAEYC Standards for Early Childhood Professional Preparation Programs Standards in Appendix B to identify competencies.)

    b. What type of information is to be included in the *Assessing* section of the performance evaluation document?

    c. What is the value of staff members setting goals and reflecting on past performance?

    d. As a future director, what challenges might you anticipate when conducting a performance evaluation with a staff member?

2. Work with a partner and role-play a conference in which a teacher and a director set up a work plan for the next six months. If you are assuming the role as teacher, try to use your own classroom skills and areas in which you need improvement as a basis for the objectives in your work plan. If you are playing the director, use your communication skills to find out what help this teacher seems to need and where his strengths lie. After the role-play, ask your classmates for a brief evaluation of the conference. Then have two other students repeat the role-play. Is the second role-play different from the one formulated in the first role-play? Identify strategies that should be used for effective goal-setting.

3. Examine the assessment section of the NAEYC and National Association of Early Childhood Specialists in State Departments of Education Position Statement on Early Childhood Curriculum, Assessment and Program Evaluation (2003) that can be found

on the NAEYC website. Working in pairs, discuss two or three of the "indicators of effective assessment practices" identified by NAEYC and the potential challenges they would present for directors attempting to ensure appropriate assessment of young children. Be prepared to share your thoughts with the whole class.

4. With members of your class, discuss the role that ethics plays in the assessment of children and evaluation of staff. Refer to the NAEYC Code of Ethical Conduct in Appendix A and describe the way in which specific principles might apply to the evaluation and assessment process.

5. Conduct an interview with a director or administrator regarding the program's evaluation and assessment plan. Ask the following questions:

- How often are staff members evaluated? What procedures are followed?

- How are evaluations used with staff to support their development as professionals?

- How often are children assessed? What types of assessments are completed? How were the assessments chosen?

- How does the administrator feel about the appropriateness of the assessments used with children? What changes might the administrator make regarding assessment of children if permitted to do so?

- What strategies are used to ensure the confidentiality of the results?

- How often is program evaluation carried out at the center? What procedures are followed? Are changes made to the program based on the evaluation?

6. If possible, collect samples of documents used for the purpose of child, staff, and program evaluation. Following the interviews, compare and contrast your findings with those of your classmates. Using interview notes and any artifacts collected at the center, identify the similarities and differences that exist among the programs related to assessment and evaluation.

# DIRECTOR'S RESOURCE 15-1

## UNIVERSITY OF DAYTON
## PERFORMANCE MANAGEMENT ASSESSMENT
## VERSION 2

**(for use with Try It Out! 15-1)**

Employee:_____ Evaluation Period:_____

PositionTitle:_____

### Planning

I. Please attach current position description. Has the position description been reviewed for accuracy?

Yes _____ No _____

II. **Result-Based "Smart" Objectives:**

1.

2.

3.

4.

III. **Professional Competencies for Focus This Year:**

1.

2.

3.

IV. **Plans for Professional Development:**

Employee Signature _____ Date_____

Supervisor Signature_____ Date_____

# DIRECTOR'S RESOURCE 15-1 *(continued)*

## Assessing

I. **Employee Self Assessment:** Please comment on your performance in achieving each result-based objective that was included in your performance plan.

1.

2.

3.

4.

Please comment on your demonstration of the professional competencies that were listed for focus in your performance plan.

1.

2.

3.

Please comment on your progress in Professional Development and achieving the associated goals that were established in your performance plan.

II. **Supervisor Feedback:** Please comment on employee's performance in achieving each result-based objective that was included in the performance plan.

1.

2.

3.

4.

Please comment on the employee's demonstration of the professional competencies listed for focus in the performance plan.

1.

2.

3.

Please comment on the employee's progress in Professional Development and in achieving the associated goals that were established in the performance plan.

Supervisor's Overall Assessment:

Performance Summary: Consider overall performance in realizing objectives, competencies, and in accomplishing responsibilities as defined on position description. Select the appropriate descriptor from the list below.

| | |
|---|---|
| Exceptional performance. Always exceeds expectations for this position. | |
| Above average performance. Frequently exceeds expectations for this position. | |
| Expected level of performance. Consistently performs acceptably in position. | |
| Improvement is expected. Sometimes does not meet expectations for position. | |
| Major improvement required. Usually does not meet expectations for position. | |

Employee Signature _____ Date_____

Supervisor Signature_____ Date_____

*Source: University of Dayton, Office of Human Resources, Performance Management Forms. http://www.udayton.edu/hr/employee_relations/performance_management.php*

# REFERENCES

Bloom, P. J. (1996). *Improving the quality of work life in the early childhood setting*. Wheeling, IL.: The Early Childhood Professional Development Project, National Louis University.

Brunette, L. (2013). Embracing technology with e-portfolios. *Child Care Exchange, 209*, 26–29.

Cohen, D., Stern, V., Balaban, N., & Gropper, N. (2008). *Observing and recording the behavior of young children* (5th ed.). New York: Teachers College Press.

Copple, C., & Bredekamp, S. (2008, January). Getting clear about developmentally appropriate practice. *Young Children, 63*(1), 54–55.

Donohue, C. (2010). There's an app for (almost) everything: New technology tools for EC professionals – part 2. *Child Care Information Exchange, 195*, 40–44.

Eisenberg, E. (2000). Accreditation, strategies, benefits and practical tips. *Child Care Information Exchange, 131*, 70–73.

Gronlund, G., & James, M. (2013). *Focused observations: How to observe young children for assessment and curriculum planning*. St. Paul, MN: Redleaf Press.

Gullo, D. F. (2005). *Understanding assessment and evaluation in early childhood education* (2nd ed.). New York: Teachers College Press.

Harms, T., Clifford, R., & Cryer, D. (2005). *Early childhood environment rating scale* (rev. ed.). New York: Teachers College Press. (Also available in Spanish.)

Jablon, J., Dombro, A., & Dichtelmiller, M. (2007). *The power of observation for birth through eight* (2nd ed.). Independence, KY: Wadsworth-Cengage Learning.

Lynch, E. M. (2007). Authentic assessment in the inclusive classroom: Using portfolios to document change and modify curriculum. In M. Ostrosky & E. Horn (Eds.), *Linking curriculum to child and family outcomes* (pp. 55–70). Longmont, CO: Sopris West.

McAfee, O, Leong, D., & Bodrova, E. (2004). *Basics of assessment: A primer for early childhood educators*. Washington, D.C.: National Association for the Education of Young Children.

Meisels, S., & Atkins-Burnett, S. (2004). The Head Start National Reporting System: A critique. *Young Children, 59*(1), 64–66.

Montgomery, K., & Wiley, D. A. (2008). *Building e-portfolios using PowerPoint: A guide for educators*. Thousand Oaks, CA: Sage.

National Association for Child Care Resource and Referral Agencies. (2009). *Parents' perceptions of child care in the United States: NACCRRA's national parent poll* (November, 2009). Retrieved from http://www.naccrra.org/sites/default/files/publications/naccrra_publications/2012/parents_perceptionschildcareus.pdf.

National Association for the Education of Young Children and National Association of Early Childhood Specialists in State Departments of Education. (2003). *Early childhood curriculum, assessment, and program evaluation: Building an effective accountable system in programs for children birth through age 8*. Retrieved from http://www.naeyc.org/positionstatements.

National Association for the Education of Young Children and National Association of Early Childhood Specialists in State Departments of Education. (2002). *Early learning standards: Creating conditions for success*. Retrieved from http://www.naeyc.org/positionstatements.

National Center for Cultural Competence. (2009). *Promoting cultural and linguistic competency: Self-assessment checklist for personnel providing services and supports in early intervention and early childhood settings*. Retrieved from http://nccc.georgetown.edu/resources/assessments.html.

National Center on Parent, Family and Community Engagement. (2011). *Family engagement and ongoing child assessment: Responsibilities, perspectives, and strategies*. Retrieved from http://eclkc.ohs.acf.hhs.gov/hslc/tta-system/family/docs/family-engagement-and-ongoing-child-assessment-081111.pdf.

National Governors Association Center for Best Practices, Council of Chief State School Officers. (2010). Common Core state standards. Retrieved from http://www.corestandards.org/the-standards.

National Research Council. (2008). *Early childhood assessment: Why, what, and how?* Washington, DC: The National Academies Press. Retrieved from http://books.nap.edu/catalog/12446.html.

Nicolson, S., & Shipstead, S. G. (2001). *Through the looking glass: Observations in the early childhood classroom* (3rd ed.). Upper Saddle River, NJ: Pearson.

Nilsen, B. A. (2008). *Observation and assessment*. Clifton Park, NY: Thomson-Delmar Learning.

Parnell, W., & Bartlett, J. (2012). iDocument: How smartphones and tablets are changing documentation in preschool and primary classrooms. *Young Children, 67*(3), 50–59.

QRIS National Learning Network. (n.d.). Quality rating and improvement systems framework. Retrieved from http://qrisnetwork.org/our-framework.

Raver, C., & Zigler, E. (2004). Another step back? Assessing readiness in Head Start. *Young Children, 59*(1), 58–63.

Ritchie, S., & Willer, B. (Eds.). (2005). *Leadership and management: A guide to the NAEYC early childhood program standards and related accreditation criteria*. Washington, DC: National Association for the Education of Young Children.

Simon, F., & Nemeth, K. N. (2012). *Digital decisions: Choosing the right technology tools for early childhood education*. Lewisville, NC: Gryphon House.

Snow, K. (2011). *Kindergarten readiness and other large-scale assessment systems: Necessary considerations in the assessment of young children*. Retrieved from http://www.naeyc.org/files/naeyc/file/research/Assessment_Systems.pdf.

Surr, J. (2004, March). Who's accredited? What and how the states are doing on best practices in child care. *Child Care Information Exchange, 156*, 14–19.

Talan, T., & Bloom, P. (2011). *Program administrators' scale: Measuring early childhood leadership and management* (2nd ed.) New York: Teachers College Press.

Sciarra, D. J., & Dorsey, A. G. (2002). *Leaders and supervisors in child care programs*. Clifton Park, NY: Thomson Delmar Learning.

VanderVen, K. (2000). Capturing the breadth and depth of the job: The administrator as influential leader in a complex world. In M. Culkin (Ed.), *Managing quality in young children's programs: The leader's role*, 112–128. New York: Teachers College Press.

*Brand the program by consistently using a logo on promotional materials, both in print and on the web.*

## Learning Objectives

After reading this chapter, you should be able to:

**16-1** Identify the components of a well-developed marketing plan.

**16-2** Explain strategies that maximize public relations efforts.

## Standards Addressed in this Chapter

Accreditation Standard 8 – Community Relations

Administrator Competencies Management Knowledge and Skills 6, 7, 8, 9, 10

Early Childhood Knowledge and Skills 7, 10

Professional Preparation Standards 2 – Building Family and Community Relationships

Professional Preparation Standards 4 – Using Developmentally Effective Approaches

Professional Preparation Standards 6 – Becoming a Professional

An important part of the director's job in both new and ongoing programs is marketing and publicizing the center. The direction that marketing takes is based on competition in the area as well as identifying families that need to be reached in order to recruit children and promote the program. Obviously, young families are the first to come to mind because most programs are set up to serve children from infancy to 5 years of age or primary school-age children in before- and after-school programs. However, there are other considerations. If program survival depends on tuition, the target population is clearly limited to those who can afford to pay for the service.

On the other hand, if outside funding sources exist, it will be necessary to increase the scope of the publicity effort so that a greater portion of a diverse potential clientele can be reached. The marketing plan is also impacted by the program's sponsor, its location, and the geographic location in which potential families will likely live. Eligibility requirements also play a role: Sometimes program sponsors limit the population to be served to university families, families who meet poverty eligibility requirements, children of hospital personnel, children of families who are employed by a particular business, children of club or church members, and so forth.

Marketing decisions require skillful analysis of circumstances specific to the center. For example, there will be minimal gains from marketing in an area where competing programs are limited to specific populations. Similarly, marketing will have a limited effect on families who choose a preschool program offered by an exclusive private school because that guarantees the child access to this private school's elementary school. What works for one center may not for another, and the director must be knowledgeable about the factors that impact how parents make decisions about where their children will receive early care and education. Centers might promote convenience, a flexible schedule, or a prime location as selling points for potential families.

A director who is skillful with marketing his or her center must have a keen understanding of the questions, concerns, and misconceptions that parents have. Marketing efforts shouldn't focus solely on attracting new children but should also seek to retain the children who are currently enrolled. Efforts to inform potential families about the benefits of a quality program for brain development and future school success can be key selling points for certain groups of parents, but this effort can be negated if a program allows currently served families to retain misperceptions and doubts about whether a play-based curriculum can prepare young children for kindergarten. A center may be at risk of losing a family whose goal is academic readiness for school success and who has doubts about whether academic skills can be developed within an emergent and developmentally appropriate play-based program. It is the job of the director and teachers to see opportunities in the day-to-day life of the center to demonstrate how the early childhood program addresses the goals of the families, which often includes the goal of school readiness.

Good marketing strategies are proactive and look for opportunities to communicate a consistent, clear, and positive message. Effective directors understand the differences among "advertising," 'marketing," and "public relations" (see Figure 16-1) and craft a message that takes advantage of all three. Programs that identify and communicate a message consistently can avoid the misconceptions that crop up when there is a void of information. In the past, many early childhood programs have waited until the year before kindergarten to discuss school readiness. This time line misses important marketing opportunities and often portrays the purpose of the prekindergarten year as a last-ditch effort to prepare children for a kindergarten entry "event." Programs that convey an ongoing and consistent message about how children develop and learn can help parents come to understand that school readiness is a process that starts in infancy and continues through kindergarten entry and into the primary grades.

**Figure 16-1** Marketing versus advertising versus public relations.

The terms "marketing," "advertising," and "public relations" are often used interchangeably, but they are in fact unique strategies that can be implemented to communicate the assets of your program to potential users.

- *Marketing* is the broader term that includes both advertising and public relations among other activities such as product development and communication.
- *Advertising* is a process used to convey a consistent message.
- *Public relations* focuses on generating positive impressions about the program and the work that is done.

Effective marketing plans describe the program while also generating positive regard for the program and the field of early care and education.

*Source: © Cengage Learning 2014*

There are many ways to market your program, but do not underestimate the value of "word of mouth" from parents who are enthusiastic about the quality of your program. A consistently communicated message can also positively impact "word of mouth" marketing as parents talk with other parents about their child's early learning program. It is also important for staff to understand that every time parents are in the center, they gather and interpret information about the program that impacts the "word of mouth" marketing message. Directors and staff should take regular "tours" of the center and their classrooms to examine the message that is being communicated. Arranging both formal open house events and informal morning coffee conversations or afternoon snack gatherings that encourage parents to meet and chat are strategies that provide time for parents to hear a clear, consistent, and accurate message and also ask questions. But in the end, nothing sells better than offering a high-quality program worthy of accreditation and led by well-trained, qualified early childhood teachers.

# 16-1 BUILDING A MARKETING PLAN

The landscape for marketing an early childhood program has changed dramatically. Strategies that have informed marketing practices in other types of business are now being applied to early childhood settings. Likewise, social media and other technology-supported tools have changed how and where marketing efforts take place.

## 16-1a Market Research

The first step in creating an effective marketing plan is to conduct market research. After the values, beliefs, and needs of your market segment are better understood, then it is possible to identify strategies that are most likely to capture their attention and demonstrate how your program is well suited to address their needs.

Using the results of the needs assessment and strategic planning process described in Chapter 2, program administrators will have collected important data to inform the marketing plan and will have completed the first steps in marketing the program. Knowing the needs of the customer and having a clearly articulated mission will help to target the message to an audience who will be most interested in the service that is being provided. Your first step is to revisit the needs assessment data and mission and values statement from Chapter 2. This information will be helpful in developing a cost-effective and targeted marketing plan. Directors will also be able to use this information to complete a *strengths, weaknesses, opportunities,* and *threats* (SWOT) analysis for the program and proposed services.

## 16-1b SWOT Analysis

A SWOT analysis is a simple but powerful framework for analyzing the SWOT program faces. The origins of the SWOT analysis are unclear, with some identifying the 1960s work of Albert Humphrey of Stanford University and others saying that the concept emerged from Harvard. Regardless of where the concept and acronym originated, it has evolved into a framework used by marketing experts that guides the user through an evaluation of internal and external factors that can impact the success of a business or a program. Environmental factors internal to the organization can usually be classified as strengths (S) or weaknesses (W), and those external to the organization can be classified as opportunities (O) or threats (T). The SWOT analysis process helps program administrators focus on strengths, minimize weaknesses, and threats, and take the greatest possible advantage of opportunities (see Table 16-1).

### Identify Stakeholders

The first step in conducting SWOT analysis is to identify your stakeholders and data that has already been collected. A *stakeholder* is defined as someone who is impacted by your program—the most obvious stakeholders are children, families, and staff. Less obvious stakeholders include your competitors, who strive to keep up with you, and the community, which benefits from your program's services. Each program will have a slightly different list based on its mission.

**TABLE 16-1** Sample SWOT analysis chart

| Strengths | Weaknesses |
|---|---|
| Excellent staff | Staff turnover |
| Good facilities | Limited hours of operation |
| Prime location | Reduction in funding available from the county and state |
| **Opportunities** | **Threats** |
| Changing community demographics | Changing community demographics |
| New QRIS can lead to additional funding | Competitors have achieved stars on the QRIS, and your program has not |

*Source: © Cengage Learning, 2013.*

### Gather Existing Data

Stakeholders can provide important input for a well-developed marketing plan. A good place to start is to use information that has already been gathered as part of the strategic planning process. If completed within the past year or two, the needs assessment can provide important information. Think about other input from stakeholders that you might already have gathered. For example, if your program has chosen to be part of your state's Quality Rating and Improvement Systems (QRIS), has NAEYC accreditation, or has gone through a Head Start federal review, you will have already collected some information from your stakeholders. Many programs collect data about the quality of their program through such devices as the *Early Childhood Environment Rating Scale Revised* (Harms, Clifford, & Cryer, 1998; Harms, Cryer, & Clifford, 2003) or the *Program Administration Scale* (Talan & Jorde Bloom, 2004). These tools provide data that are used by supervisors, administrators, and policy makers (all of whom are stakeholders) to identify the strengths and weaknesses of aspects of a program. Child assessment data can also be used to inform your SWOT analysis.

### Determine Missing Data

After you have identified your key stakeholders and any existing data sources that you can refer to, discuss ways that you can find out more about what your stakeholders think are your program's strengths and weaknesses. What information is missing? Who do you need to hear from? How can you access that information?

### Gather Internal and External Data

Most of the data that you have collected is most likely internal data from stakeholders who are part of or directly impacted by your organization. Some of you may have collected information from or about your competitors, which would be the start of a review of the external data needed to determine the *threats* and *opportunities* in the SWOT analysis. To complete a thorough external review, you need to become well grounded in the context of early care and education, especially as it relates to quality and other trends that are impacting the market.

## Construct a SWOT Analysis Chart

To construct an accurate SWOT analysis chart, you will need to include the data that you have collected from stakeholders. You will use an internal focus to determine your program's *strengths* and *weaknesses*. To determine *threats* and *opportunities,* you will look to factors that are external to your program. See Table 16-1 for a sample SWOT analysis chart.

## Interpret the SWOT Analysis

Once completed, a SWOT analysis chart can help to identify areas where a marketing plan can have the most impact. Consider the completed sample in Table 16-1 and note how the information in the cells might be interpreted.

- **Strengths:** Note that any of the three identified strengths can become part of a marketing message that would attract new customers and retain the ones that already use the program's services.

- **Weaknesses:** It may be difficult to see how weaknesses can inform a marketing strategy until you also consider the opportunities. For example, the new QRIS that is described as an opportunity can be used to offset the reduction in funding because programs in some states can earn additional funding while improving quality. Making the connection between these two elements is an important part of the analysis of this chart. You can also deal with the perceived weakness head on by considering such moves as increasing the hours of operation after completing a careful analysis of the financial impact.

- **Opportunities:** In addition to using opportunities to address areas of weakness, they can also stand alone. For example, changing demographics can be a true opportunity to broaden the target of your marketing strategies.

- **Threats:** Note how the same item can be both an opportunity and a threat. For example, changing demographics can provide opportunities for an expanded market. It can also force change, which can be uncomfortable. It is likely to be difficult to make decisions about how to address this factor without considering it as both an opportunity and a threat.

## 16-1c Developing a Marketing Plan

After the SWOT analysis is complete and interpreted, it is time to craft a marketing plan that **naeyc**

can be communicated to others and that is in a format that can be followed by the people responsible for implementing the plan. Kalifeh (2011) suggests making a chart that includes the following when developing a marketing plan:

- Your strategies (a description of what you will do)

- A time line for when you will undertake that strategy (remembering that marketing is a year-round endeavor)

- Materials and resources needed to accomplish the strategy

- A list of who is responsible or tasked with accomplishing the work

- A description of the costs.

- *Optional:* You might also want to create a column for evaluating the strategy, determining how you will measure success. (p. 23)

The strategic planning process from Chapter 2 and the information from the SWOT analysis should provide key information about your center and the potential market that will inform the marketing plan. This information will also help to decide where, how, and to whom to promote the program.

### ▶❚❚ TeachSource Video Vignette

**Parents and Teachers Talk about Parenting in a New Culture**

To best meet the needs of children in an early childhood setting, parents and teachers must work as a team. From the start, the teacher should create a trusting and open environment with the family. The family, in turn, must feel that they have a voice in the conversation. View the video vignette entitled, *Parents and Teachers Talk about Parenting in a New Culture.*

Effective marketing strategies require the director to know the audience and identify the needs of the market, which, for a child care center, is most likely made up of parents. Watch this group of parents and teachers talk about culture to learn more about the audience. Now imagine yourself as the director of this center, and create a social media post that would be appropriate for these parents as the audience. Be sure to provide information of interest to your audience.

## Who: Generational Factors

"Not everyone sees through the same eyes or hears through the same ears" (Wassom, 2004, p. 6). The perceptions of families who may be interested in the program and their process for making decisions vary based on a wide range of factors, including the generation that they are part of. Wasson goes on to state that a closer examination of generational tendencies "reveals valuable insight into why old marketing approaches are no longer as effective, and what changes you need to make to appeal to the majority of today's early care and education buyers" (p. 6). Wassom also identifies four generational groups in America today—Matures, Boomers, Generation X-ers, and Millennials—and describes how members of each generation are linked through shared life experiences. Those shared experiences cause them to view the world in unique ways, which extends to how and when they make decisions about early care and education services. Today, the parents of young children tend to be Generation X-ers and Millennials, and their buying influences are very different from the Boomers of the past (see Table 16-2).

**TABLE 16-2** Characteristics of three generations

|  | Boomers | Generation X-ers | Millennials |
|---|---|---|---|
| **Age** | Born between 1946 and 1964 | Born between 1965 and 1979 | Born between 1980 and 2000 |
| **Early Life Experiences** | Secure economic times<br><br>Television<br><br>The start of the Peace Corps and space exploration<br><br>Civil rights assassinations of John F. Kennedy and Martin Luther King<br><br>Vietnam War | Recession and layoffs or double-digit interest and inflation<br><br>Watergate and other well-publicized scandals<br><br>Challenger exploded<br><br>Berlin Wall fell<br><br>End of the Cold War<br><br>Rise of digital technology and the World Wide Web<br><br>The Chernobyl nuclear disaster<br><br>The Exxon Valdez oil spill | A time of economic change with the longest period of economic expansion as wealth and manufacturing moved outside of the United States<br><br>Emergence of the global economy<br><br>AIDS emerges<br><br>The space shuttle program thrives<br><br>Hubble Space telescope<br><br>24-hour news networks<br><br>9–11 and the War on Terror |
| **Informed by** | Newspapers<br><br>Magazines<br><br>Radio<br><br>Network news<br><br>Technology tends to augment the traditional way of doing things | Network and cable news<br><br>Internet accessed through the personal computer<br><br>Word of mouth | Peers<br><br>Online news sources<br><br>Widespread on-demand access to the Internet via new media |
| **Group Demographics** | 80 million<br><br>Married Boomers tend to live in dual earner families<br><br>Better educated than their parents<br><br>Trusting<br><br>Impulsive buyers<br><br>Emotional decision makers | 49 million<br><br>Many parents of young children needing child care<br><br>Question authority<br><br>Grew up with uncertainty<br><br>Skeptical<br><br>Resourceful<br><br>Well educated<br><br>Less trusting | 75 million<br><br>The up and coming group of parents with young children<br><br>More optimistic and ambitious<br><br>Are realistic about what is wrong with the world but believe they can make a difference |

**TABLE 16-2** Characteristics of three generations (*continued*)

| | Boomers | Generation X-ers | Millennials |
|---|---|---|---|
| | Busy and hard working | Not easily impressed | Relationships with friends and family are highly valued |
| | Value convenience | Tend to plan and save until they can afford the best quality | Value parents' advice |
| | Grant credibility based on proven history | Take time to investigate, compare, and discuss before deciding | Value education as a means to success |
| | Few have young children but may influence how their grandchildren are raised | | Less religious |
| | | | Inclusive and value diversity |
| | | | Very active and can be stressed |
| **Childhood Technology Exposure** | Color television | Cable TV | Interactive TV and streaming video |
| | Records, 8-tracks, and cassettes | Cassettes and CDs VCRs | MP3s and iPods |
| | Landlines | Personal computers Cell phones | DVDs and TiVo |
| | | | Laptops, Netbooks, and iPads |
| | | | Smartphones |
| **Communication Preference Tendencies** | Face-to-face Phone calls | Cell phone calls Email | Text messages Facebook |
| **Buying Influencers** | Impacted by emotional benefits | Skeptical and focused on quality and value | Want to be a member of the crowd but yet stand out |
| | May not investigate thoroughly if they have good feelings | Will more likely rely on evidence and talk to others before making a decision | Hopeful about the future |
| | May want more flexible payment terms | Willing to pay top dollar but will demand the highest quality | Want to make a difference |
| | Education is important but happy children are more important | Likely to appreciate being able to use a credit card | Likely to consider recommendations from their peers and their parents |
| | Value feeling part of the center's community | Want good answers to questions about curriculum, policies, and procedures | |
| | Value convenience and ancillary services | | |
| **Advertising Approaches that Tend to Work** | Use color and emotions in photos and taglines | Third party endorsements or testimonials | Interactive digital messages |
| | Include photos that they can relate to | Use bullets to outline specifics | Includes opportunities for peers to provide feedback |
| | Use bullets to communicate a quick message | Link to professional organizations or other unbiased sources so they can verify your claims | Easily accessed at a time convenient to them |

*Source: Howell & Strauss, 2001; Marston, 2011; Wassom, 2004; Wendover, 2007.*

## Working Smart with Technology

*Social Media and the Digital Native*

Marketing efforts of the past can be time intensive and expensive. Directors who use web-based marketing strategies are often surprised that these newer methods of telling your program's story can be both cost effective and time efficient. The parents of young children tend to be digital natives who are much more likely to get their information through websites and social media than the print materials used in the past. As digital natives, most young parents grew up using technology as an important method of communication and now look to the Internet to get information about child care. With this in mind, it is important that directors do the following:

1. Make sure their center has a presence on the Internet, which means having a website. Developing websites has become surprisingly easy, and directors often find that they have a tech savvy teacher or even a parent who can help with website development and maintenance. Creating a website can be accomplished using an inexpensive drag-and-drop website-building program such as Weebly.com for as little as the cost of a domain name.

2. In addition to a website, early childhood centers need to be able to use social media to share their stories. Facebook can be a useful tool as it capitalizes on using families to promote the center when they click on "like" or "share" a post with their friends. Keep in mind that the center can have a public Facebook page that protects the children's identity and also a private Facebook page that can be limited to center family members.

*Web-based marketing strategies can be both cost effective and time efficient.*

## Characteristics of a Quality Website

As mentioned in this chapter's Working Smart with Technology feature, websites are an important component of marketing your program. For many young families, if the center doesn't have a website, it isn't even considered as a possibility. With new no-cost or low-cost software, websites can be developed in house easily and inexpensively, or directors can contract with a professional developer to create the website. Regardless of who creates the website, it is imperative that the site reflects an understanding of quality (see Table 16-3).

**Table 16-3** Characteristics of a quality child care center website

**Simplicity:** Avoid busy web page designs. Too much content on the page will frustrate the users and reduce the amount of time that they spend on the page.

**Consistency:** Effective web pages are consistent in design, navigation, writing style, and appearance throughout the pages of the website.

**Accessibility:** Web pages should be designed for the novice computer user. Avoid building websites that have complex features that are too sophisticated for the audience and their technology.

**Credibility:** For a website to become an important part of a comprehensive communication system, it must include current and relevant content. Users must be able to count on the accuracy of the information presented.

**Navigation:** Users need to be able to move throughout the web page with ease. Links to other pages should work, and the number of clicks needed to access information should be minimal.

**Appearance:** The appearance of the page should be attractive with attention paid to color, font, and the balance of text, photos, and graphics. The amount of information on a page should be able to be viewed without scrolling.

**Audience:** The audience for the web page needs to be determined at the beginning of the web-development process. The two most common audiences are current and prospective families. Prospective families are looking for slightly different information, which needs to be open access to the public. It is possible to have a section of the website that is password protected to maintain confidentially and Internet safety for children who are currently enrolled.

*Source: Adapted from Schleig 2012; Walker & Donohoue, 2007; and Wassom, 2011.*

Creating the website is one component of having an Internet presence. Equally as important is maintaining and updating the website with relevant information that keeps families and the public coming back to the site. One very common mistake is to have a high-quality website developed without considering how the page will be maintained and who will maintain it. Sometimes, it is better to select a less sophisticated web page design so that the site can be maintained in house.

## Where to Market Your Program

Traditionally, marketing a program and publicizing a center has been done through newspaper ads and radio announcements to reach a wide audience, while a more limited population is reached through direct mailing of brochures or circulars, displays of window placards, door-to-door solicitation, and advertisements in local newspapers, church bulletins, and military newsletters. In the past, telephone book advertising was also successful.

Because of the impact of technology, many of these traditional vehicles now have less of an impact. Young families today rely more on new media and the Internet for information. Consider taking advantage of Internet advertising—the Yellow Pages does not have the impact that it once did. *New media* refers to on-demand access to content anytime and anywhere using digital devices such as smartphones, iPods, iPads, and other tools. New media allows families to access just the information they need at just the time they need it. The ability to have continuous and instant access to information through search engines and social networking sites makes such platforms as Google and Facebook important marketing tools.

New media also provides opportunities for interaction, so word of mouth marketing is an even more powerful tool. The directors who develop and maintain free Facebook sites for their centers are also providing a vehicle for families to talk about centers in ways that potential families are likely to interact with and trust. These new platforms can be frightening for many directors who would like to be more in control of the message that is being sent. However, like it or not, the advent of new media has shifted control to the consumer, who can provide feedback in a forum that is open for anyone to see. A director who is aware of how the program is being presented on Facebook or where the center appears on a Google search listing can impact the marketing message. By capitalizing on the everyday opportunities to communicate a consistent message during the day-to-day operations of the center, directors can impact how current families describe the program for potential families on Facebook or on other new media vehicles.

Regardless of the vehicle used to advertise, be sure to consider the ethnic and cultural makeup of the audience, as well as reading levels and language skills, as you write and design promotional materials.

## How to Construct the Message

It is also important to construct a message that resonates with the target audience. Marston (2011) reminds us that generational differences should impact how information is presented (refer to Table 16-2):

> Understand X-ers take nothing at face value and will seek out their own information and referrals. Look at your marketing as an introduction that directs them to further information. Make sure your website is stocked with data and product specifications. Want to further your credibility with X-ers? Point them to an unbiased resource and show them you've got nothing to hide. Remember, these are the folks who were born in the Watergate era and grew up in an age of highly publicized scandals. Honesty is unexpected yet highly treasured.

Likewise, Millennials are accustomed to relying on peer feedback for credibility. If Millennials are the targeted group, then an astute director might develop a center-sponsored Facebook site and encourage current families to provide feedback on the experiences that their children are having. By being proactive and knowledgeable about the benefits and pitfalls of new media, the director can capitalize on the benefits of the tools while laying ground rules that can overcome some of the disadvantages. For example, if the Facebook site is established by the director, then he or she can provide guidance about confidentiality and respectful interactions. The owner of the site can also remove inappropriate comments and add prompts that direct the kind of feedback that is provided. New media has changed the marketing landscape; directors can choose to take advantage of these inexpensive and powerful marketing tools or not. However, ignorance of how the center is being portrayed through new media platforms can be the downfall of a center.

## 16-1d Marketing Materials

*Marketing materials* are a collection of products designed to meet established marketing goals. The marketing plan will help to determine the kinds of marketing products that will work with the target audience. In most situations a variety of materials and platforms for dissemination is the most effective approach to achieve the desired outcome. With widespread availability of easy-to-use publishing software, many directors, even those with limited computer skills, can create attractive and professional marketing materials. Many of the products designed for print materials can be adapted to digital formats,

Today, the families of young children are likely to be digital natives who rely heavily on social media to communicate and gather information. "Word of mouth" marketing is very influential with digital natives as they have immediate access to online reviews of a myriad of services. If they want to know whether a restaurant or a child care center is "good" they type their question into a search box and the reviews written by other digital natives pop up. Their understanding of "good" is not research-based but rather informed by their peers through social media. Effective directors understand how to use social media to inform the public about their services and do not leave their message to chance. They provide opportunities for an ongoing two-way stream of information using communication tools that appeal to today's parents. If a director wants families to understand what quality child care looks like, he or she provides information in short segments that can be read on a smartphone screen. Information is provided in a manner that can be "downloaded," "forwarded," and "liked" so that it can be "shared" with friends and family. Using photographs, short text segments, and video streams, the director shares information to questions that the audience many not know they had. The director is responsible for crafting the message and understanding the powerful tools that are available today to share that message.

## DIRECTOR'S CORNER

"One frustration that my teachers voiced centered on the parents' apparent lack of understanding about how an emergent and play-based curriculum could support the academic skills that children need to be ready for kindergarten. After lamenting this situation in several staff meetings, I asked my teachers what they could do to help parents better understand what their children were learning. We realized that parents didn't really want to know about the importance of play, and that our efforts to convert them were having a negative effect on their views of our program. After some brainstorming, the teachers decided to be proactive and started sharing evidence of the academic content that children learned in the context of play. While the children's experiences with a play-based and emergent curriculum remained the same, the way the program was framed for parents changed. We shifted our focus from selling the importance of play to showcasing what the children were learning during play. The weekly newsletter included examples of academic content learned. The parent communication board highlighted literacy and numeracy in the daily routine. The teachers changed the bulletin boards outside of their classrooms to documentation boards and included work samples and photographs with notations about what the children had learned. We were amazed by the impact that communicating this consistent message had on parent perceptions of what children were learning. It also had a positive effect on our word of mouth marketing."

—*Director of a university-affiliated child care program*

and cohesively. Kalifeh (2011) suggests the following as marketing resources that directors can cultivate to become part of a marketing tool kit:

- Print media (parent handbooks, business cards, brochures, press releases, advertisements, giveaways, etc.)

- Electronic media (website, social networking, email)

- Staff (an often overlooked marketing resource)

- Parents (some of your best public relations specialists)

- Events (employer partnerships, school transition partnerships, open house, Kids' Day, legislative tours, parent appreciation, etc.) (p. 23)

## Brochures and Promotional Materials

The choice of words and the photographs used in the printed materials distributed by the center should reflect a subtle message of concern, respect, and appreciation for children and should express the philosophy behind the center's program. These materials project the image of the center and should exemplify your professionalism (Tiger, 1995).

Develop marketing materials that send a distinctive and powerful message. They must define your specialties and exactly what you offer that sets you apart from your competitors. The fundamentals of "quality care," "developmentally appropriate practice," and "trained, caring staff" are descriptive but not distinctive. Brainstorm with staff, parents, board members, and consultants about how you are different, and put down some sample statements that will tell that story in the materials that you develop, such as the following:

- soft, cozy spaces in a homelike environment (use pictures if possible)

- innovative, cutting-edge social/emotional focus

- family-centered practice that treats family/child/teacher as a unit

including websites. Because of the shift to new media, which requires immediate access to information, it is even more important to be proactive and have materials available to meet a variety of marketing needs. One strategy is to create a marketing tool kit that can be used to respond to a variety of marketing opportunities quickly

Find unique ways to identify your program with a logo that appears on all business cards, stationery, ads, and so on. Use of a particular "tagline" with the logo can become your mark of distinction. In marketing circles, this is called "branding." It is something potential clients recognize and remember. Taglines give a quick and easily remembered clip of what a program is about:

- "Where Every Child Is Special"
- "We Strengthen Children Emotionally and Academically"
- "Child Care That Nurtures Our Future"

Keep in mind that you are endeavoring to attract the attention of the current generation of young parents, many of whom are Generation X-ers or Millennials. Select techniques and content for the marketing materials that appeal to and entice this target generational group. For eye appeal and influence, consider the following:

- using color and emotion in taglines and photos
- mixing pictures and graphics (a photo of a teacher and child, a parent event, your accreditation credential)
- bulleting the benefits so there is a quick and easy way to sum up *what they will get from you*—a bit different from what you have to offer
- quoting testimonials from the current parent population
- using the talents of staff and parents to do creative marketing that will help you build your enrollment

The content and appearance of brochures or fliers make a statement to parents. The words should be informative and spell out the philosophy of the center's program; the photographs or some creative, clever artwork should convey, in less obvious ways, the fact that the staff of the center is professional and creative. It is the creative design of these materials that will attract attention, and attention is the first step to generating interest. The message for parents should be clear: Any child who is sent to this center will share in the professionalism and creativity of the staff. When unsolicited letters from parents are available, using statements from those letters in brochures or publicity releases is an excellent way to get your message across. Every detail of any mailing piece to be used for initial advertising or in response to inquiries about the program should be carefully scrutinized.

The director is responsible for the preparation and the mailing of brochures, but other staff members as well as parents can contribute to the effort by providing artistic talents, access to a printer, or some other expertise. When a brochure is prepared, two major considerations are cost and content.

Costs vary depending on number, length, quality of paper, use of color, and use of photographs. Therefore, it is wise to discuss ideas for the brochure with a printer

*Effective marketing requires that a program represents what it does well. This picture might be selected for marketing materials because it shows how children are engaged in a well-planned outdoor space with strong adult-child interaction, and that this center is a university-affiliated program.*

### DIRECTOR'S CORNER

"When it was time to make our logo more current, we worked very hard to choose one that communicated what we were about while also providing some brand recognition. We contacted a local university with a graphic design program and asked the program director if there was a class that was working on logo design. We were fortunate to be able to set up a competition in this class and had teams of students interview our center staff and examine our mission statement and handbooks. Teams designed a series of eight logos, which were voted on by staff and families through a Facebook website. We had great buy-in from families and staff and ended up with a very attractive logo for the cost of the competition prize, which was a gift card to an art supply store for each member of the winning team. The process was a win for all involved."

—*Director, private not-for-profit center*

as soon as possible. Costs increase when the professionally done brochure includes photos or a logo that incorporates artwork, but it is these unique features that may be precisely what attracts the attention of prospective clients. The distinctive logo and tagline on every promotional piece becomes a familiar identifying symbol to potential customers. Money spent on an attractive brochure may be a good investment. Using a single color on heavyweight, standard-size paper will give a look of high quality yet keep the costs down. A brochure on standard-size paper in a three-fold format that can be addressed on one side is economical and efficient. Check the size and weight so that mailing costs will be within the minimal limit for first-class postage rates.

If the brochure is to be used over a long period of time, it is wise to avoid including items that are subject to change, such as the school calendar or the fee schedule. These variable items can be detailed in a short insert. The brochure itself should contain information that remains constant from year to year. The following list includes some of the more stable items typically included in a brochure:

- name, address, and telephone number of the center
- a map showing the location of the center
- description of the program
- sponsorship of the program
- enrollment procedures and children served (ages, inclusive program, diversity, etc.)
- licensing and/or accreditation status of the center

It is important to include the hours, days, and months for the program. The stability of the operational schedule will determine whether such information should go into the brochure itself or be part of the insert.

Centers sell services to families who seek solutions to concerns and have questions about quality child care. It is helpful to them when promotional materials cover all the services available at the center. Prospective customers, especially those with more than one child, will want to have information about availability of services such as before- and after-school care, summer programs for school-age children, care for the mildly ill child, and backup care for older children on school holidays or for the baby cared for at home when the regular caregiver is ill.

Other selling points to cover in promotional materials might include the following:

- accreditation by NAEYC, NACCP, NECPA, or the state's QRIS, if available
- workshops
- lending library
- web address, to help keep potential clients up to date on all center activities
- email address, to keep in touch with administrators

Keep in mind that promotional materials are designed to tell prospective families that the center offers solutions for them and is there to help and support them and their children. Brochure space is limited, so details about program operation and range of services offered to families can be described in pamphlets or booklets available for those who call for more information or visit the center. A well-planned open house provides a special opportunity to share these additional materials and publicizes the best features of the program.

## 16-2 PUBLIC RELATIONS

As a director, it behooves you to take advantage of opportunities to invite reporters to the center so that they can do newspaper or television pieces on your center. If you are affiliated with a large business or hospital, their public relations staff may help you. Television and newspaper reporters may be interested in what is new at your center. If there is a new infant room opening, or you have a new custom-designed playground, reporters and cameramen will come to you. Other newsworthy items might be a new teacher who signs for deaf children, installation of a ramp to accommodate children and adults with disabilities, or the use of senior citizen volunteers in the preschool classrooms.

Take advantage of the wave of interest that surrounds early learning and brain development in young children. When local reporters do a story on early learning, go to the reporter's web page and contribute to their blog. Sometimes it is difficult to get the attention of a busy reporter. Remember, if they have taken the time to write about a topic on their blog, they will likely read the responses that their audience makes. Be sure to identify yourself and your center. Become a regular blog contributor, and you get free publicity to an audience that is interested in the topic.

At community events that draw parents of young children, it is often useful to arrange to have a booth where a display of photos taken at the center and promotional materials will attract families who are interested in child care. Arrange for the director or a competent staff member who can answer questions and distribute admission applications to be available at these events. This is an excellent way to reach out to the community and capitalize on an opportunity to establish a personal contact with potential clients.

It is also worthwhile to get your message out to companies in the community, as well as to individuals and community groups. The first wave of companies interested in addressing the child care needs of their employees typically were attracted to setting up on-site child care centers. However, some companies are more inclined to look to existing community child care centers where they can purchase slots, buy priority status, or negotiate for corporate group rates for their employees. Developing a professional presentation that is designed for use with corporate clients and timely follow-up with appropriate contacts within the corporation will enhance your chances of attracting corporate clients (Duncan & Thornton, 1993).

The center's image is an important consideration in all aspects of the public information and public relations efforts. The appearance of the physical setting and the behavior of personnel in that setting are fundamental factors in creating good public relations and sound relationships with the children and with their parents. These factors are what convey professionalism and concern about children and families. The director serves as a model and encourages the staff to be mindful of their role as community advocates for children. Parents entering the building should see an interior prepared for use by children. Furthermore, parents should be greeted by a warm, caring person who expresses interest in them and in their children. A "Director's Coffee" once a month is a way to encourage parents to take a few minutes to chat before rushing off to work. When parents or others telephone the center, the person who answers must be pleasant, tactful, and knowledgeable.

An open house for parents who have made inquiries or have responded to your marketing efforts is a good way to expand the public relations program for the center. Remember to invite current parents, current staff members, and board members to these social events. An open house affords an opportunity for the staff to have an informal meeting with others who are interested in the center's activities. In the case of a new program, publicizing the open house can be part of the initial efforts at promotion. In the case of ongoing programs, staff and board members also will reap benefits from this kind of gathering because it provides a time for interaction and communication among adults who have common concerns and share an interest in the children attending the program.

When the center is opened to visitors, the environment should be prepared just as it would be for the children. In this way, you can demonstrate how a well-planned environment should look and also provide an opportunity for parents to participate and use available materials. What better way to give parents a feeling for what happens each day than to have them use the materials in the classrooms! In addition, slides, a scrapbook of photos, or a videotape or PowerPoint presentation of children actively participating in the classroom can give parents further insights into what a quality program can offer their children.

Planning for the open house is done by people who understand the lifestyles and expectations of the clients who are likely to show interest in the event. Careful and sensitive planning regarding the time of the event and the level of informality communicates to members of the community that the people at the center understand and care about them and their children.

## SUMMARY

The marketing plan for the program emerges from market research informed by the strategic planning process. Effective directors consider multiple factors when developing a marketing plan and can be informed by a carefully constructed SWOT analysis as well as a sound understanding of the target audience. In today's technology-enhanced society, marketing must include both traditional print strategies as well as new media. Marketing materials for the center must be drafted and directed to the population that the program is designed to serve. Successful recruitment of children and families will depend on the content and dissemination of the promotional materials about the program, as well as on the total public relations effort. While written materials advertising the center must be planned carefully to attract the families to be served, the role of word of mouth advertising cannot be overlooked. To effectively market a program, the director must do the following:

- Identify the components of a well-developed marketing plan.

- Explain strategies that maximize public relations efforts.

## TRY IT OUT!

1. Think about a center you have been in on a regular basis. You are sitting outside in the parking lot as parents arrive. Is the building inviting? Does it really welcome children and families? Now imagine yourself inside, observing the way children are greeted. Do adults stoop down and extend a friendly welcome to the children? Are parents recognized and called by name? As you walk farther into the building, how does it look? What sounds do you hear? How does it smell? The impressions you are reliving are the same impressions parents and children experience each day that they enter the center. How do the answers to these questions impact the word of mouth marketing potential for this center?

2. Work with a team to complete a SWOT analysis using Director's Resource 16-1. Consider a program that a member of the team works for or is familiar with, complete each of the four quadrants of your analysis, and describe how you would address the following:

   a. Identify strengths that you can capitalize on to promote the program.

   b. Identify weaknesses that can be addressed or turned around and used as a marketing strategy.

   c. Now look at the opportunities that you have identified. How can they be incorporated into a marketing plan?

   d. Finally examine your threats. What marketing strategies can you use to reduce the threats?

Use these answers to identify what this center might include on a Facebook page.

# Director's Resource 16-1

## SWOT ANALYSIS CHART

| STRENGTHS | WEAKNESSES |
|---|---|
| | |
| **OPPORTUNITIES** | **THREATS** |
| | |

| INTERPRETATION<br><br>Which aspects of the SWOT analysis chart should be the focus of a marketing plan? Which are top priorities or can make the most impact on the success of the program? | HOW FINDINGS ARE ADDRESSED IN THE MARKETING PLAN |
|---|---|
| **Strengths** | |
| **Weaknesses** | |
| **Opportunities** | |
| **Threats** | |

# REFERENCES

Duncan, S., & Thornton, D. (1993, January). Marketing your center's services to employers. *Child Care Information Exchange*, 53–56.

Harms, T., Clifford, R. M., & Cryer, D. (1998). *The early childhood environment rating scale* (Rev. ed.). New York: Teachers College Press.

Harms, T., Cryer, D., & Clifford, R. M. (2003). *Infant/toddler environment rating scale* (Rev. ed.). New York: Teachers College Press.

Howell, N., & Strauss, B. (2001). Millennials rising: The next great generation. New York: Vintage Books.

Kalifeh, P. (2011, March/April). Marketing: No longer an afterthought. *Child Care Information Exchange*, 22–24.

Marston, C. (2011). Marketing to different generations: Choose your message wisely. International Association of Business Communicators. Retrieved from http://www.iabc.com/cwb/archive/2007/0807/Marston.htm.

Schleig, E. (2012, November/December). Designing websites for parents. *Exchange*, 208, 62–65.

Talan, T. N., & Jorde Bloom, P. (2004). Program Administration Scale. New York: Teachers College Press.

Tiger, F. (1995, March/April). The art of brochure design. *Child Care Information Exchange*, 107, 24.

Walker, T., & Donohoue C. (2007, March/April). Decoding technology. *Exchange*, 174, 76–79.

Wassom, J. (2004, March/April). Do they see what you see? Marketing to a new generation of child care buyers. *Child Care Information Exchange*, 6–8.

Wassom, J. (2011, September/October). Making your website an effective marketing partner. *Exchange*, 201, 82-85.

Wendover, R. W. (2007). *Crossing the generational divide: From boomers to zoomers*. Shawnee Mission, KS: National Press Publications.

# APPENDIX A

## NAEYC® CODE OF ETHICAL CONDUCT AND STATEMENT OF COMMITMENT

### POSITION STATEMENT

**A position statement of the National Association for the Education of Young Children**

Revised April 2005, Reaffirmed and Updated May 2011

*Endorsed by the Association for Childhood Education International*

*Adopted by the National Association for Family Child Care*

### Preamble

NAEYC recognizes that those who work with young children face many daily decisions that have moral and ethical implications. The **NAEYC Code of Ethical Conduct** offers guidelines for responsible behavior and sets forth a common basis for resolving the principal ethical dilemmas encountered in early childhood care and education. The **Statement of Commitment** is not part of the Code but is a personal acknowledgement of an individual's willingness to embrace the distinctive values and moral obligations of the field of early childhood care and education.

The primary focus of the Code is on daily practice with children and their families in programs for children from birth through 8 years of age, such as infant/toddler programs, preschool and prekindergarten programs, child care centers, hospital and child life settings, family child care homes, kindergartens, and primary classrooms. When the issues involve young children, then these provisions also apply to specialists who do not work directly with children, including program administrators, parent educators, early childhood adult educators, and officials with responsibility for program monitoring and licensing. (Note: See also the "Code of Ethical Conduct: Supplement for Early Childhood Adult Educators," online at *www.naeyc.org/about/positions/pdf/ethics04.pdf.and* the "Code of Ethical Conduct: Supplement for Early Childhood Program Administrators," online at *http://www.naeyc.org/files/naeyc/file/positions/PSETH05_supp.pdf)*

### Core Values

Standards of ethical behavior in early childhood care and education are based on commitment to the following core values that are deeply rooted in the history of the field of early childhood care and education. We have made a commitment to

- Appreciate childhood as a unique and valuable stage of the human life cycle
- Base our work on knowledge of how children develop and learn
- Appreciate and support the bond between the child and family
- Recognize that children are best understood and supported in the context of family, culture,[1] community, and society
- Respect the dignity, worth, and uniqueness of each individual (child, family member, and colleague)
- Respect diversity in children, families, and colleagues
- Recognize that children and adults achieve their full potential in the context of relationships that are based on trust and respect

### Conceptual Framework

The Code sets forth a framework of professional responsibilities in four sections. Each section addresses an area of professional relationships: (1) with children, (2) with families, (3) among colleagues, and (4) with the community and society. Each section includes an introduction to the primary responsibilities of the early childhood practitioner in that context. The introduction is followed by a set of ideals (I) that reflect exemplary professional practice and by a set of principles (P) describing practices that are required, prohibited, or permitted.

The **ideals** reflect the aspirations of practitioners. The **principles** guide conduct and assist practitioners in resolving ethical dilemmas.[2] Both ideals and principles are intended to direct practitioners to those questions which, when responsibly answered, can provide the basis for conscientious decision making. While the Code provides

---

[1] The term *culture* includes ethnicity, racial identity, economic level, family structure, language, and religious and political beliefs, which profoundly influence each child's development and relationship to the world.

[2] There is not necessarily a corresponding principle for each ideal.

specific direction for addressing some ethical dilemmas, many others will require the practitioner to combine the guidance of the Code with professional judgment.

The ideals and principles in this Code present a shared framework of professional responsibility that affirms our commitment to the core values of our field. The Code publicly acknowledges the responsibilities that we in the field have assumed, and in so doing supports ethical behavior in our work. Practitioners who face situations with ethical dimensions are urged to seek guidance in the applicable parts of this Code and in the spirit that informs the whole.

Often "the right answer"—the best ethical course of action to take—is not obvious. There may be no readily apparent, positive way to handle a situation. When one important value contradicts another, we face an ethical dilemma. When we face a dilemma, it is our professional responsibility to consult the Code and all relevant parties to find the most ethical resolution.

# SECTION I: ETHICAL RESPONSIBILITIES TO CHILDREN

Childhood is a unique and valuable stage in the human life cycle. Our paramount responsibility is to provide care and education in settings that are safe, healthy, nurturing, and responsive for each child. We are committed to supporting children's development and learning; respecting individual differences; and helping children learn to live, play, and work cooperatively. We are also committed to promoting children's self-awareness, competence, self-worth, resiliency, and physical well-being.

## Ideals

I-1.1    To be familiar with the knowledge base of early childhood care and education and to stay informed through continuing education and training.

I-1.2    To base program practices upon current knowledge and research in the field of early childhood education, child development, and related disciplines, as well as on particular knowledge of each child.

I-1.3    To recognize and respect the unique qualities, abilities, and potential of each child.

I-1.4    To appreciate the vulnerability of children and their dependence on adults.

I-1.5    To create and maintain safe and healthy settings that foster children's social, emotional, cognitive, and physical development and that respect their dignity and their contributions.

I-1.6    To use assessment instruments and strategies that are appropriate for the children to be assessed, that are used only for the purposes for which they were designed, and that have the potential to benefit children.

I-1.7    To use assessment information to understand and support children's development and learning, to support instruction, and to identify children who may need additional services.

I-1.8    To support the right of each child to play and learn in an inclusive environment that meets the needs of children with and without disabilities.

I-1.9    To advocate for and ensure that all children, including those with special needs, have access to the support services needed to be successful.

I-1.10    To ensure that each child's culture, language, ethnicity, and family structure are recognized and valued in the program.

I-1.11    To provide all children with experiences in a language that they know, as well as support children in maintaining the use of their home language and in learning English.

I-1.12    To work with families to provide a safe and smooth transition as children and families move from one program to the next.

## Principles

P-1.1    **Above all, we shall not harm children. We shall not participate in practices that are emotionally damaging, physically harmful, disrespectful, degrading, dangerous, exploitative, or intimidating to children. *This principle has precedence over all others in this Code.***

P-1.2    We shall care for and educate children in positive emotional and social environments that are cognitively stimulating and that support each child's culture, language, ethnicity, and family structure.

P-1.3    We shall not participate in practices that discriminate against children by denying benefits, giving special advantages, or excluding them from programs or activities on the basis of their sex, race, national origin, immigration status, preferred home language, religious beliefs, medical condition, disability, or the marital status/family structure, sexual orientation, or religious beliefs or other affiliations of their families. (Aspects of this principle do not apply in programs that have a lawful mandate to provide services to a particular population of children.)

P-1.4    We shall use two-way communications to involve all those with relevant knowledge (including families and staff) in decisions concerning a child, as appropriate, ensuring confidentiality of sensitive information. (See also P-2.4.)

P-1.5    We shall use appropriate assessment systems, which include multiple sources of information, to provide information on children's learning and development.

P-1.6    We shall strive to ensure that decisions such as those related to enrollment, retention, or assignment to special education services, will be based on multiple sources of information and will never be based on a single assessment, such as a test score or a single observation.

P-1.7    We shall strive to build individual relationships with each child; make individualized adaptations in teaching strategies, learning environments, and curricula; and consult with the family so that each child benefits from the program. If after such efforts have been exhausted, the current placement does not meet a child's needs, or the child is seriously jeopardizing the ability of other children to benefit from the program, we shall collaborate with the child's family and appropriate specialists to determine the additional services needed and/or the placement option(s) most likely to ensure the child's success. (Aspects of this principle may not apply in programs that have a lawful mandate to provide services to a particular population of children.)

P-1.8    We shall be familiar with the risk factors for and symptoms of child abuse and neglect, including physical, sexual, verbal, and emotional abuse and physical, emotional, educational, and medical neglect. We shall know and follow state laws and community procedures that protect children against abuse and neglect.

P-1.9    When we have reasonable cause to suspect child abuse or neglect, we shall report it to the appropriate community agency and follow up to ensure that appropriate action has been taken. When appropriate, parents or guardians will be informed that the referral will be or has been made.

P-1.10    When another person tells us of his or her suspicion that a child is being abused or neglected, we shall assist that person in taking appropriate action in order to protect the child.

P-1.11    When we become aware of a practice or situation that endangers the health, safety, or well-being of children, we have an ethical responsibility to protect children or inform parents and/or others who can.

# SECTION II: ETHICAL RESPONSIBILITIES TO FAMILIES

Families[3] are of primary importance in children's development. Because the family and the early childhood practitioner have a common interest in the child's well-being, we acknowledge a primary responsibility to bring about communication, cooperation, and collaboration between the home and early childhood program in ways that enhance the child's development.

## Ideals

I-2.1    To be familiar with the knowledge base related to working effectively with families and to stay informed through continuing education and training.

I-2.2    To develop relationships of mutual trust and create partnerships with the families we serve.

I-2.3    To welcome all family members and encourage them to participate in the program, including involvement in shared decision making.

I-2.4    To listen to families, acknowledge and build upon their strengths and competencies, and learn from families as we support them in their task of nurturing children.

I-2.5    To respect the dignity and preferences of each family and to make an effort to learn about its structure, culture, language, customs, and beliefs to ensure a culturally consistent environment for all children and families.

I-2.6    To acknowledge families' childrearing values and their right to make decisions for their children.

I-2.7    To share information about each child's education and development with families and to help them understand and appreciate the current knowledge base of the early childhood profession.

I-2.8    To help family members enhance their understanding of their children, as staff are enhancing their understanding of each child through communications with families, and support family members in the continuing development of their skills as parents.

I-2.9    To foster families' efforts to build support networks and, when needed, participate in

---

[3] The term *family* may include those adults, besides parents, with the responsibility of being involved in educating, nurturing, and advocating for the child.

building networks for families by providing them with opportunities to interact with program staff, other families, community resources, and professional services.

## Principles

P-2.1    We shall not deny family members access to their child's classroom or program setting unless access is denied by court order or other legal restriction.

P-2.2    We shall inform families of program philosophy, policies, curriculum, assessment system, cultural practices, and personnel qualifications, and explain why we teach as we do—which should be in accordance with our ethical responsibilities to children (see Section I).

P-2.3    We shall inform families of and, when appropriate, involve them in policy decisions. (See also I-2.3.)

P-2.4    We shall ensure that the family is involved in significant decisions affecting their child. (See also P-1.4.)

P-2.5    We shall make every effort to communicate effectively with all families in a language that they understand. We shall use community resources for translation and interpretation when we do not have sufficient resources in our own programs.

P-2.6    As families share information with us about their children and families, we shall ensure that families' input is an important contribution to the planning and implementation of the program.

P-2.7    We shall inform families about the nature and purpose of the program's child assessments and how data about their child will be used.

P-2.8    We shall treat child assessment information confidentially and share this information only when there is a legitimate need for it.

P-2.9    We shall inform the family of injuries and incidents involving their child, of risks such as exposures to communicable diseases that might result in infection, and of occurrences that might result in emotional stress.

P-2.10    Families shall be fully informed of any proposed research projects involving their children and shall have the opportunity to give or withhold consent without penalty. We shall not permit or participate in research that could in any way hinder the education, development, or well-being of children.

P-2.11    We shall not engage in or support exploitation of families. We shall not use our relationship with a family for private advantage or personal gain, or enter into relationships with family members that might impair our effectiveness working with their children.

P-2.12    We shall develop written policies for the protection of confidentiality and the disclosure of children's records. These policy documents shall be made available to all program personnel and families. Disclosure of children's records beyond family members, program personnel, and consultants having an obligation of confidentiality shall require familial consent (except in cases of abuse or neglect).

P-2.13    We shall maintain confidentiality and shall respect the family's right to privacy, refraining from disclosure of confidential information and intrusion into family life. However, when we have reason to believe that a child's welfare is at risk, it is permissible to share confidential information with agencies, as well as with individuals who have legal responsibility for intervening in the child's interest.

P-2.14    In cases where family members are in conflict with one another, we shall work openly, sharing our observations of the child, to help all parties involved make informed decisions. We shall refrain from becoming an advocate for one party.

P-2.15    We shall be familiar with and appropriately refer families to community resources and professional support services. After a referral has been made, we shall follow up to ensure that services have been appropriately provided.

# SECTION III: ETHICAL RESPONSIBILITIES TO COLLEAGUES

In a caring, cooperative workplace, human dignity is respected, professional satisfaction is promoted, and positive relationships are developed and sustained. Based upon our core values, our primary responsibility to colleagues is to establish and maintain settings and relationships that support productive work and meet professional needs. The same ideals that apply to children also apply as we interact with adults in the workplace. (Note: Section III includes responsibilities to co-workers and to employers. See the "Code of Ethical Conduct: Supplement for Early Childhood Program Administrators" for responsibilities to personnel (*employees* in the original 2005 Code revision), online at *http://www.naeyc.org/files/naeyc/file /positions/PSETH05_supp.pdf*.)

## A—Responsibilities to co-workers

### Ideals

I-3A.1    To establish and maintain relationships of respect, trust, confidentiality, collaboration, and cooperation with co-workers.

I-3A.2    To share resources with co-workers, collaborating to ensure that the best possible early childhood care and education program is provided.

I-3A.3    To support co-workers in meeting their professional needs and in their professional development.

I-3A.4    To accord co-workers due recognition of professional achievement.

### Principles

P-3A.1    We shall recognize the contributions of colleagues to our program and not participate in practices that diminish their reputations or impair their effectiveness in working with children and families.

P-3A.2    When we have concerns about the professional behavior of a co-worker, we shall first let that person know of our concern in a way that shows respect for personal dignity and for the diversity to be found among staff members, and then attempt to resolve the matter collegially and in a confidential manner.

P-3A.3    We shall exercise care in expressing views regarding the personal attributes or professional conduct of co-workers. Statements should be based on firsthand knowledge, not hearsay, and relevant to the interests of children and programs.

P-3A.4    We shall not participate in practices that discriminate against a co-worker because of sex, race, national origin, religious beliefs or other affiliations, age, marital status/family structure, disability, or sexual orientation.

## B—Responsibilities to employers

### Ideals

I-3B.1    To assist the program in providing the highest quality of service.

I-3B.2    To do nothing that diminishes the reputation of the program in which we work unless it is violating laws and regulations designed to protect children or is violating the provisions of this Code.

### Principles

P-3B.1    We shall follow all program policies. When we do not agree with program policies, we shall attempt to effect change through constructive action within the organization.

P-3B.2    We shall speak or act on behalf of an organization only when authorized. We shall take care to acknowledge when we are speaking for the organization and when we are expressing a personal judgment.

P-3B.3    We shall not violate laws or regulations designed to protect children and shall take appropriate action consistent with this Code when aware of such violations.

P-3B.4    If we have concerns about a colleague's behavior, and children's well-being is not at risk, we may address the concern with that individual. If children are at risk or the situation does not improve after it has been brought to the colleague's attention, we shall report the colleague's unethical or incompetent behavior to an appropriate authority.

P-3B.5    When we have a concern about circumstances or conditions that impact the quality of care and education within the program, we shall inform the program's administration or, when necessary, other appropriate authorities.

# SECTION IV: ETHICAL RESPONSIBILITIES TO COMMUNITY AND SOCIETY

Early childhood programs operate within the context of their immediate community made up of families and other institutions concerned with children's welfare. Our responsibilities to the community are to provide programs that meet the diverse needs of families, to cooperate with agencies and professions that share the responsibility for children, to assist families in gaining access to those agencies and allied professionals, and to assist in the development of community programs that are needed but not currently available.

As individuals, we acknowledge our responsibility to provide the best possible programs of care and education for children and to conduct ourselves with honesty and integrity. Because of our specialized expertise in early childhood development and education and because the larger society shares responsibility for the welfare and protection of young children, we acknowledge a collective obligation to advocate for the best interests of children within early childhood programs and in the larger community and to serve as a voice for young children everywhere.

The ideals and principles in this section are presented to distinguish between those that pertain to the work of the individual early childhood educator and those that more typically are engaged in collectively on behalf of the best interests of children—with the understanding that individual early childhood educators have a shared responsibility for addressing the ideals and principles that are identified as "collective."

## Ideal (Individual)

I-4.1    To provide the community with high-quality early childhood care and education programs and services.

## Ideals (Collective)

I-4.2    To promote cooperation among professionals and agencies and interdisciplinary collaboration among professions concerned with addressing issues in the health, education, and well-being of young children, their families, and their early childhood educators.

I-4.3    To work through education, research, and advocacy toward an environmentally safe world in which all children receive health care, food, and shelter; are nurtured; and live free from violence in their home and their communities.

I-4.4    To work through education, research, and advocacy toward a society in which all young children have access to high-quality early care and education programs.

I-4.5    To work to ensure that appropriate assessment systems, which include multiple sources of information, are used for purposes that benefit children.

I-4.6    To promote knowledge and understanding of young children and their needs. To work toward greater societal acknowledgment of children's rights and greater social acceptance of responsibility for the well-being of all children.

I-4.7    To support policies and laws that promote the well-being of children and families, and to work to change those that impair their well-being. To participate in developing policies and laws that are needed, and to cooperate with families and other individuals and groups in these efforts.

I-4.8    To further the professional development of the field of early childhood care and education and to strengthen its commitment to realizing its core values as reflected in this Code.

## Principles (Individual)

P-4.1    We shall communicate openly and truthfully about the nature and extent of services that we provide.

P-4.2    We shall apply for, accept, and work in positions for which we are personally well-suited and professionally qualified. We shall not offer services that we do not have the competence, qualifications, or resources to provide.

---

### Glossary of Terms Related to Ethics

**Code of Ethics.** Defines the core values of the field and provides guidance for what professionals should do when they encounter conflicting obligations or responsibilities in their work.

**Values.** Qualities or principles that individuals believe to be desirable or worthwhile and that they prize for themselves, for others, and for the world in which they live.

**Core Values.** Commitments held by a profession that are consciously and knowingly embraced by its practitioners because they make a contribution to society. There is a difference between personal values and the core values of a profession.

**Morality.** Peoples' views of what is good, right, and proper; their beliefs about their obligations; and their ideas about how they should behave.

**Ethics.** The study of right and wrong, or duty and obligation, that involves critical reflection on morality and the ability to make choices between values and the examination of the moral dimensions of relationships.

**Professional Ethics.** The moral commitments of a profession that involve moral reflection that extends and enhances the personal morality practitioners bring to their work, that concern actions of right and wrong in the workplace, and that help individuals resolve moral dilemmas they encounter in their work.

**Ethical Responsibilities.** Behaviors that one must or must not engage in. Ethical responsibilities are clear-cut and are spelled out in the Code of Ethical Conduct (for example, early childhood educators should never share confidential information about a child or family with a person who has no legitimate need for knowing).

**Ethical Dilemma.** A moral conflict that involves determining appropriate conduct when an individual faces conflicting professional values and responsibilities.

#### Sources for glossary terms and definitions

Feeney, S., & N. Freeman. 2005. *Ethics and the early childhood educator: Using the NAEYC code.* Washington, DC: NAEYC.

Kidder, R.M. 1995. *How good people make tough choices: Resolving the dilemmas of ethical living.* New York: Fireside.

Kipnis, K. 1987. How to discuss professional ethics. *Young Children* 42 (4): 26–30.

P-4.3 We shall carefully check references and shall not hire or recommend for employment any person whose competence, qualifications, or character makes him or her unsuited for the position.

P-4.4 We shall be objective and accurate in reporting the knowledge upon which we base our program practices.

P-4.5 We shall be knowledgeable about the appropriate use of assessment strategies and instruments and interpret results accurately to families.

P-4.6 We shall be familiar with laws and regulations that serve to protect the children in our programs and be vigilant in ensuring that these laws and regulations are followed.

P-4.7 When we become aware of a practice or situation that endangers the health, safety, or well-being of children, we have an ethical responsibility to protect children or inform parents and/or others who can.

P-4.8 We shall not participate in practices that are in violation of laws and regulations that protect the children in our programs.

P-4.9 When we have evidence that an early childhood program is violating laws or regulations protecting children, we shall report the violation to appropriate authorities who can be expected to remedy the situation.

P-4.10 When a program violates or requires its employees to violate this Code, it is permissible, after fair assessment of the evidence, to disclose the identity of that program.

## Principles (Collective)

P-4.11 When policies are enacted for purposes that do not benefit children, we have a collective responsibility to work to change these policies.

P-4.12 When we have evidence that an agency that provides services intended to ensure children's well-being is failing to meet its obligations, we acknowledge a collective ethical responsibility to report the problem to appropriate authorities or to the public. We shall be vigilant in our follow-up until the situation is resolved.

P-4.13 When a child protection agency fails to provide adequate protection for abused or neglected children, we acknowledge a collective ethical responsibility to work toward the improvement of these services.

The National Association for the Education of Young Children (NAEYC) is a nonprofit corporation, tax exempt under Section 501(c)(3) of the Internal Revenue Code, dedicated to acting on behalf of the needs and interests of young children. The NAEYC Code of Ethical Conduct (Code) has been developed in furtherance of NAEYC's nonprofit and tax exempt purposes. The information contained in the Code is intended to provide early childhood educators with guidelines for working with children from birth through age 8.

An individual's or program's use, reference to, or review of the Code does not guarantee compliance with NAEYC

---

### Statement of Commitment*

As an individual who works with young children, I commit myself to furthering the values of early childhood education as they are reflected in the ideals and principles of the NAEYC Code of Ethical Conduct. To the best of my ability I will

- Never harm children.

- Ensure that programs for young children are based on current knowledge and research of child development and early childhood education.

- Respect and support families in their task of nurturing children.

- Respect colleagues in early childhood care and education and support them in maintaining the NAEYC Code of Ethical Conduct.

- Serve as an advocate for children, their families, and their teachers in community and society.

- Stay informed of and maintain high standards of professional conduct.

- Engage in an ongoing process of self-reflection, realizing that personal characteristics, biases, and beliefs have an impact on children and families.

- Be open to new ideas and be willing to learn from the suggestions of others.

- Continue to learn, grow, and contribute as a professional.

- Honor the ideals and principles of the NAEYC Code of Ethical Conduct.

* This Statement of Commitment is not part of the Code but is a personal acknowledgment of the individual's willingness to embrace the distinctive values and moral obligations of the field of early childhood care and education. It is recognition of the moral obligations that lead to an individual becoming part of the profession.

Early Childhood Program Standards and Accreditation Performance Criteria and program accreditation procedures. It is recommended that the Code be used as guidance in connection with implementation of the NAEYC Program Standards, but such use is not a substitute for diligent review and application of the NAEYC Program Standards.

NAEYC has taken reasonable measures to develop the Code in a fair, reasonable, open, unbiased, and objective manner, based on currently available data. However, further research or developments may change the current state of knowledge. Neither NAEYC nor its officers, directors, members, employees, or agents will be liable for any loss, damage, or claim with respect to any liabilities, including direct, special, indirect, or consequential damages incurred in connection with the Code or reliance on the information presented.

---

**NAEYC Code of Ethical Conduct 2005
Revisions Workgroup**

Mary Ambery, Ruth Ann Ball, James Clay, Julie Olsen Edwards, Harriet Egertson, Anthony Fair, Stephanie Feeney, Jana Fleming, Nancy Freeman, Marla Israel, Allison McKinnon, Evelyn Wright Moore, Eva Moravcik, Christina Lopez Morgan, Sarah Mulligan, Nila Rinehart, Betty Holston Smith, and Peter Pizzolongo (*NAEYC Staff*)

---

# CODE OF ETHICAL CONDUCT

# SUPPLEMENT FOR EARLY CHILDHOOD PROGRAM ADMINISTRATORS

Adopted July 2006, **Reaffirmed and Updated May 2011**

## A Position Statement Supplement of the National Association for the Education of Young Children

*Adopted by the National Association for Family Child Care*

Administrators of programs for young children are responsible for overseeing all program operations, serving as leaders in their programs, and representing the field to the community. Early childhood program administrators are called upon to sustain relationships with a wide variety of clients. They interact with and have responsibilities to children, families, program personnel, governing boards and sponsoring agencies, funders, regulatory agencies, their community, and the profession.

Program administrators deal with unique responsibilities and ethical challenges in the course of managing and guiding their programs and assume leadership roles within and beyond their programs. As managers and leaders, they are called upon to share their professional knowledge and expertise with families, personnel, governing boards, and others; demonstrate empathy for the families and children they serve; and communicate respect for the skills, knowledge, and expertise of teaching staff, other personnel, and families. Administrators accept primary responsibility for executing the program's mission as well as developing and carrying out program policies and procedures that support that mission. They also make a commitment to continue their own professional development and the continuing education of the personnel in the program they lead. Administrators also may be advocates for all children being able to gain access to quality programming. Some of the challenges faced by administrators involve balancing their obligations to support and nurture children with their responsibility to address the needs and safeguard the rights of families and personnel and respond to the requirements of their boards and sponsoring agencies.

## Purpose of the Supplement

Like those in the field who work directly with young children, program administrators are regularly called upon to make decisions of a moral and ethical nature. The NAEYC Code of Ethical Conduct (revised 2005, reaffirmed and updated 2011) is a foundational document that maps the ethical dimensions of early childhood educators' work in early care and education programs. Program administrators share the ethical obligations assumed by all early childhood educators—obligations that are reflected in the core values, ideals, and principles set forth in the Code. Administrators embrace the central commitment of the early care and education field—and the Codeto ensure the well-being and support the healthy development of young children.

---

**NOTE**

This Supplement was reaffirmed by the NAEYC Governing Board in May 2011 and changes were made to Ideals and Principles that regard responsibilities to families to ensure alignment with current family engagement best practices in the field. In addition, references to the Code of Ethical Conduct, Section III, Part C: Responsibilities to Employees were deleted, as Section III, Part C was deleted in the May 2011 update of the Code.

---

Given the nature of their responsibilities, however, administrators face some additional ethical challenges. Conflicts often surface in the areas of enrollment policies;

dealings with personnel; and relationships with families, licensors, governing boards, sponsoring agencies, and others in the community. The existing Code is a valuable resource that addresses many of the ethical issues encountered by administrators. However, it does not provide all of the guidance that they need to address the unique ethical issues that arise in their work. This Supplement offers additional core values, ideals, and principles related to the frequently recurring ethical issues encountered by administrators.

## Core Values

In addition to the core values spelled out in the NAEYC Code of Ethical Conduct, early childhood program administrators commit themselves to the following additional core values.

We make a commitment to

- Recognize that we have many responsibilities—to children, families, personnel, governing boards, sponsoring agencies, funders, regulatory agencies, the community, and the profession—and that the well-being of the children in our care is our primary responsibility, above our obligations to other constituencies.

- Recognize the importance of and maintain a humane and fulfilling work environment for personnel and volunteers.

- Be committed to the professional development of staff.

## Conceptual Framework

This document sets forth a conception of early childhood program administrators' professional responsibilities in five areas, some of which differ from those identified in the NAEYC Code. Each section addresses an area of professional relationships: (1) with children, (2) with families, (3) with personnel, (4) with sponsoring agencies and governing boards, and (5) with the community and society. The items in each section address the unique ethical responsibilities of administrators in early care and education settings.

## Ideals and Principles

This Supplement identifies additional **ideals** that reflect exemplary practice (our aspirations) and **principles** describing practices that are required, prohibited, or permitted. The principles guide conduct and assist practitioners in resolving ethical dilemmas. Together, the ideals and principles are intended to direct practitioners to questions that, when responsibly answered, provide the basis for conscientious decision making. While the Code and this Supplement provide specific direction for addressing some ethical dilemmas, many others will require early childhood program administrators to combine the guidance of the Code and/or this Supplement with their best professional judgment.

The ideals and principles in the Code and this Supplement present a shared framework of professional responsibility that affirms our commitment to the core values of our field. The Code and the Supplement publicly acknowledge the responsibilities that early childhood professionals assume and, in so doing, support ethical behavior in our work. Practitioners who face situations with ethical dimensions are urged to seek guidance in the applicable parts of the Code/Supplement and in the spirit that informs the whole.

The ideals and principles in this Supplement are based on early childhood program administrators' descriptions of ethical dilemmas they have encountered in their work. They are designed to inspire and guide administrators toward actions that reflect the field's current understanding of ethical responsibility.

---

### DEFINITIONS

*Administrator*

The individual responsible for planning, implementing, and evaluating a child care, pre-school, kindergarten, or primary grade program. The administrator's title may vary, depending on the program type or sponsorship of the program. Common titles include director, site manager, administrator, program manager, early childhood coordinator, and principal. (*Note:* The definition of *administrator* and other relevant text in this Supplement are consistent with the Leadership and Management standard of the NAEYC Early Childhood Program Standards and Accreditation Criteria.)

*Personnel*

Staff members employed, directed, or supervised by an administrator. Here, unless otherwise noted, *personnel* includes all program staff and volunteers providing services to children and/or families. (*Note:* Because program administrators may be supervisors and not employers, we have adopted the terms *personnel* and *staff* in lieu of *employees* for this Supplement to the Code.)

---

The Supplement also includes items from the NAEYC Code that directly relate to the work of administrators—some are duplicates of Code ideals or principles, and some are adaptations. Items from the Code that are repeated or adapted for this Supplement are cross-referenced with their corresponding ideals and principles, with the Code references indicated in parentheses. Other items that expand and extend the NAEYC Code were written specifically for this Supplement. (*Note:* There is **not** necessarily a corresponding principle for each ideal.)

## 1. Ethical responsibilities to children

The early childhood program administrator's paramount responsibility is to ensure that programs for children provide settings that are safe, healthy, nurturing, and responsive for each child. Administrators are committed to establishing and maintaining programs that support children's development and learning; promote respect for individual differences; and help children learn to live, play, and work cooperatively. Administrators are also committed to ensuring that the program promotes children's self-awareness, competence, self-worth, resiliency, and physical well-being.

## Ideals

I-1.1  To ensure that children's needs are the first priority in administrative decision making, recognizing that a child's well-being cannot be separated from that of his/her family.

I-1.2  To provide a high-quality program based on current knowledge of child development and best practices in early care and education.

## Principles

P-1.1  We shall place the welfare and safety of children above other obligations (for example, to families, program personnel, employing agency, community).

**This item takes precedence over all others in this Supplement.**

P-1.2  We shall ensure that the programs we administer are safe and developmentally appropriate in accordance with standards of the field, including those developed and endorsed by NAEYC and other professional associations.

P-1.3  We shall have clearly stated policies for the respectful treatment of children and adults in all contacts made by staff, parents, volunteers, student teachers, and other adults. We shall appropriately address incidents that are not consistent with our policies.

P-1.4  We shall support children's well-being by encouraging the development of strong bonds between children and their families and between children and their teachers.

P-1.5  We shall support children's well-being by promoting connections with their culture and collaborating with communities to ensure cultural consistency between the program and families' childrearing practices.

P-1.6  We shall make every effort to provide the necessary resources (staff, consultation, other human resources, equipment, and so on) to ensure that all children, including those with special needs, can benefit from the program.

P-1.7  We shall ensure that there is a plan for appropriate transitions for children when they enter our program, move from one classroom to another within our program, and when they leave.

P-1.8  We shall apply all policies regarding our obligations to children consistently and fairly.

P-1.9  We shall review all program policies set forth by sponsoring agencies and governing bodies to ensure that they are in the best interest of the children.

P-1.10  We shall express our professional concerns about directives from the sponsoring agency or governing body when we believe that a mandated practice is not in the best interest of children.

P-1.11  If we determine that a policy does not benefit children, we shall work to change it. If we determine that a program policy is harmful to children, we shall suspend its implementation while working to honor the intent of the policy in ways that are not harmful to children.

## 2. Ethical responsibilities to families

The administrator sets the tone for the program in establishing and supporting an understanding of the family's role in their children's development. Administrators strive to promote communication, cooperation, and collaboration between the home and the program in ways that enhance each child's development. Because administrators provide the link between the family and direct services for children, they often encounter ethical issues in this area of responsibility.

## Ideals

I-2.1  To design programs and policies inclusive of and responsive to diverse families.

I-2.2  To serve as a resource for families by providing information and referrals to services in the larger community.

I-2.3  To advocate for the needs and rights of families in the program and the larger community.

I-2.4  To support families in their role as advocate for their children and themselves.

I-2.5  To create and maintain a climate of trust and candor that fosters two-way communication and enables parents/guardians to speak and act in the best interest of their children.

## Principles

P-2.1  We shall work to create a respectful environment for and a working relationship with all families, regardless of family members' sex, race, national origin, immigration status, preferred home language, religious belief or affiliation, age, marital status/family structure, disability, or sexual orientation.

P-2.2  We shall provide families with complete and honest information concerning program philosophy, educational practices, and the services provided.

P-2.3    We shall make every attempt to use two-way communication to convey information in ways that are accessible by every family served.

P-2.4    We shall establish clear operating policies and make them available to families in advance of their child entering the program.

P-2.5    We shall develop enrollment policies that clearly describe admission policies and priorities.

P-2.6    We shall develop policies that clearly state the circumstances under which a child or family may be asked to leave the program. We shall refuse to provide services for children only if the program will not benefit them or if their presence jeopardizes the ability of other children to benefit from the program or prevents personnel from doing their jobs.

P-2.7    We shall assist families in finding appropriate alternatives when we believe their children cannot benefit from the program or when their presence jeopardizes the ability of other children to benefit from the program or prevents personnel from doing their jobs.

P-2.8    We shall apply all policies regarding obligations to families consistently and fairly.

P-2.9    In decisions concerning children and programs, we shall draw upon our relationships with families as well as each family's knowledge of their child. (See also P-3.7 in this Supplement.)

P-2.10    We shall respond to families' requests to the extent that the requests are congruent with program philosophy, standards of good practice, and the resources of the program. We shall not honor any request that puts a child in a situation that would create physical or emotional harm. In such instances, we shall communicate with the family the reason(s) why the request was not honored and work toward an alternative solution.

P-2.11    We shall work to achieve shared understanding between families and staff members. In disagreements, we shall help all parties express their particular needs and perspectives. (*Note:* This is repeated in Section 3 [P-3.16] to emphasize the responsibility to both staff and family members.)

## 3. Ethical responsibilities to personnel

Early childhood program administrators are managers with the responsibility for providing oversight for all program operations, as well as serving as leaders in early care and education programs. They are responsible for creating and maintaining a caring, cooperative workplace that respects human dignity, promotes professional satisfaction, and models positive relationships. Administrators must exemplify the highest possible standards of professional practice both within and beyond the program. Ethical responsibilities to personnel include those that are related to working with staff they supervise and/or employ as well as the unions or groups that represent these staff. (*Note:* Administrators' ethical responsibilities to co-workers and employers are included in the Code of Ethical Conduct, Section III, Part A and Part B.)

### Ideals

I-3.1    To create and promote policies and working conditions that are physically and emotionally safe and foster mutual respect, cooperation, collaboration, competence, well-being, confidentiality, and self-esteem.

I-3.2    To create and maintain a climate of trust and candor that enables staff to speak and act in the best interest of children, families, and the field of early care and education.

I-3.3    To coach and mentor staff, helping them realize their potential within the field of early care and education.

I-3.4    To strive to secure adequate and equitable compensation (salary and benefits) for those who work with or on behalf of young children.

I-3.5    To encourage and support continual development of staff in becoming more skilled and knowledgeable practitioners.

### Principles

P-3.1    We shall provide staff members with safe and supportive working conditions that respect human dignity, honor confidences, and permit them to carry out their responsibilities through performance evaluation, written grievance procedures, constructive feedback, and opportunities for continuing professional development and advancement.

P-3.2    We shall develop and maintain comprehensive written personnel policies that define program standards. These policies shall be given to new staff members and shall be easily accessible and available for review by all staff members.

P-3.3    We shall apply all policies regarding our work with personnel consistently and fairly.

P-3.4    We shall be familiar with and abide by the rules and regulations developed by unions or other groups representing the interests or rights of personnel in our programs.

P-3.5 We shall support and encourage personnel in their efforts to implement programming that enhances the development and learning of the children served.

P-3.6 We shall act immediately to prevent staff from implementing activities or practices that put any child in a situation that creates physical or emotional harm.

P-3.7 In decisions concerning children and programs, we shall draw upon the education, training, experience, and expertise of staff members. (See also P-2.9 in this Supplement.)

P-3.8 We shall work to ensure that ongoing training is available and accessible, represents current understandings of best practice, and is relevant to staff members' responsibilities.

P-3.9 We shall inform staff whose performance does not meet program expectations of areas of concern and, when possible, assist in improving their performance.

P-3.10 We shall provide guidance, additional professional development, and coaching for staff whose practices are not appropriate. In instances in which a staff member cannot satisfy reasonable expectations for practice, we shall counsel the staff member to pursue a more appropriate position.

P-3.11 We shall conduct personnel dismissals, when necessary, in accordance with all applicable laws and regulations. We shall inform staff who are dismissed of the reasons for termination. When a dismissal is for cause, justification must be based on evidence of inadequate or inappropriate behavior that is accurately documented, current, and available for the staff member to review.

P-3.12 In making personnel evaluations and recommendations, we shall make judgments based on fact and relevant to the interests of children and programs.

P-3.13 We shall make hiring, retention, termination, and promotion decisions based solely on a person's competence, record of accomplishment, ability to carry out the responsibilities of the position, and professional preparation specific to the developmental levels of children in his/her care.

P-3.14 We shall not make hiring, retention, termination, and promotion decisions based on an individual's sex, race, national origin, religious beliefs or other affiliations, age, marital status/family structure, disability, or sexual orientation. We shall be familiar with and observe laws and regulations that pertain to employment discrimination. (Aspects of this principle do not apply to programs that have a lawful mandate to determine eligibility based on one or more of the criteria identified above.)

P-3.15 We shall maintain confidentiality in dealing with issues related to an employee's job performance and shall respect an employee's right to privacy regarding personal issues.

P-3.16 We shall work to achieve shared understandings between families and staff members. In disagreements, we shall help all parties express their particular needs and perspectives. (*Note:* This is repeated from Section 2 [P-2.11] to emphasize the responsibility to both staff and family members.)

## 4. Ethical responsibilities to sponsoring agencies and governing bodies

Programs providing early care and education operate under a variety of public and private auspices with diverse governing structures and missions. All early childhood program administrators are responsible to their governing and funding bodies. Administrators ensure the program's stability and reputation by recruiting, selecting, orienting, and supervising personnel; following sound fiscal practices; and securing and maintaining licensure and accreditation. Administrators are also responsible for overseeing day-to-day program operations and fostering positive relationships among children, families, staff, and the community.

Administrators' responsibilities to sponsoring agencies and governing bodies are optimally met in a collaborative manner. Administrators establish and maintain partnerships with sponsoring agency representatives, board members, and other stakeholders to design and improve services for children and their families.

### Ideals

I-4.1 To ensure to the best of our ability that the program pursues its stated mission.

I-4.2 To provide program leadership that reflects best practices in early care and education and program administration.

I-4.3 To plan and institute ongoing program improvements.

I-4.4 To be ambassadors within the community, creating goodwill for program sponsors as well as for the program itself.

I-4.5 To advocate on behalf of children and families in interactions with sponsoring agency staff and governing body members for high-quality early care and education programs and services for children.

## Principles

P-4.1    We shall ensure compliance with all relevant regulations and standards.

P-4.2    We shall do our jobs conscientiously, attending to all areas that fall within the scope of our responsibility.

P-4.3    We shall manage resources responsibly and accurately account for their use.

P-4.4    To ensure that the program's sponsoring agency and governing body are prepared to make wise decisions, we shall thoroughly and honestly communicate necessary information.

P-4.5    We shall evaluate our programs using agreed-upon standards and report our findings to the appropriate authority.

P-4.6    In presenting information to governing bodies we shall make every effort to preserve confidentiality regarding children, families, and staff unless there is a compelling reason for divulging the information.

## 5. Ethical responsibilities to community, society, and the field of early childhood education

Like those of all early childhood educators, administrators' responsibilities to the community include cooperating with agencies and professionals that share the responsibility for children, supporting families in gaining access to services provided by those agencies and professionals, and assisting in the development of community programs and services.

Early childhood program administrators often have the knowledge, expertise, and education to assume leadership roles. For this reason, they are responsible to the community, society, and the field of early childhood education for promoting the education and well-being of young children and their families.

### Ideals

I-5.1    To provide the community with high-quality early care and education programs and services. (I-4.1)

I-5.2    To serve as a community resource, spokesperson, and advocate for quality programming for young children. To serve as a conduit between the community and programs by coordinating and collaborating with key community representatives.

I-5.3    To uphold the spirit as well as the specific provisions of applicable regulations and standards.

I-5.4    To increase the awareness of the public and policy makers about the importance of the early years and the positive impact of high-quality early care and education programs on society.

I-5.5    To advocate on behalf of children and families for high-quality programs and services for children and for professional development for the early childhood workforce.

I-5.6    To join with other early childhood educators in speaking with a clear and unified voice for the values of our profession on behalf of children, families, and early childhood educators.

I-5.7    To be an involved and supportive member of the early childhood profession.

I-5.8    To further the professional development of the field of early childhood education and to strengthen its commitment to realizing its core values as reflected in NAEYC's Code of Ethical Conduct and this Supplement. (I-4.8)

I-5.9    To ensure that adequate resources are provided so that all provisions of the Code of Ethical Conduct and this Supplement can be implemented.

## Principles

P-5.1    We shall communicate openly and truthfully about the nature and extent of services that we provide. (P-4.1)

P-5.2    We shall apply for, accept, and work in positions for which we are personally well-suited and professionally qualified. We shall not offer services that we do not have the competence, qualifications, or resources to provide. (P-4.2)

P-5.3    We shall carefully check references and not hire or recommend for employment any person whose competence, qualifications, or character makes him or her unsuited for the position. (P-4.3)

P-5.4    When we make a personnel recommendation or serve as a reference, we shall be accurate and truthful.

P-5.5    We shall be objective and accurate in reporting the knowledge upon which we base our program practices. (P-4.4)

P-5.6    We shall be knowledgeable about the appropriate use of assessment strategies and instruments and interpret results accurately to families. (P-4.5)

P-5.7    We shall be familiar with laws and regulations that serve to protect the children in our programs and be vigilant in ensuring that these laws and regulations are followed. (P-4.6)

P-5.8 We shall hold program staff accountable for knowing and following all relevant standards and regulations.

P-5.9 When we become aware of a practice or situation that endangers the health, safety, or well-being of children, we have an ethical responsibility to protect children or inform parents and/ or others who can. (P-4.7)

P-5.10 We shall not participate in practices in violation of laws and regulations that protect the children in our programs. (P-4.8)

P-5.11 When we have evidence that an early childhood program is violating laws or regulations protecting children, we shall report the violation to appropriate authorities who can be expected to remedy the situation. (P-4.9)

P-5.12 We shall be honest and forthright in communications with the public and with agencies responsible for regulation and accreditation.

P-5.13 When a program violates or requires its employees to violate NAEYC's Code of Ethical Conduct, it is permissible, after fair assessment of the evidence, to disclose the identity of that program. (P-4.10)

P-5.14 When asked to provide an informed opinion on issues, practices, products, or programs, we shall base our opinions on relevant experience, knowledge of child development, and standards of best practice.

The core NAEYC Code of Ethical Conduct is online at **www.naeyc.org/files/naeyc/file/positions/ PSETH05_supp.pdf**

National Association for the Education of Young Children 1313 L Street, NW, Washington, DC 20005-4101

*Source: From the National Association for the Education of Young Children (NAEYC). Full text of all NAEYC position statements is available at www.naeyc.org/positionstatements.*

---

**Workgroup for the Development of the 2006 NAEYC Code of Ethical Conduct Supplement for Program Administrators**

Mary Ambery, Paula Jorde Bloom, Richard Cohen, Anne Dorsey, Stephanie Feeney, Nancy Freeman, Marla Israel, Ellie Kaucher, Eva Moravcik, Beatriz Otero, Julie Powers, Martha Staker, Todd Boressoff (NAEYC Board Liaison), Peter Pizzolongo (NAEYC Staff)

# APPENDIX B

## NAEYC STANDARDS FOR EARLY CHILDHOOD PROFESSIONAL PREPARATION PROGRAMS®

The NAEYC Standards identify what early childhood educators are expected to know and do and establish criteria for determining excellence among teacher education candidates.

### Standard 1. Promoting Child Development and Learning

Students prepared in early childhood degree programs are grounded in a child development knowledge base. They use their understanding of young children's characteristics and needs and of the multiple interacting influences on children's development and learning to create environments that are healthy, respectful, supportive, and challenging for each child.

**Key elements:**

1a: Knowing and understanding young children's characteristics and needs, from birth through age 8.

1b: Knowing and understanding the multiple influences on early development and learning.

1c: Using developmental knowledge to create healthy, respectful, supportive, and challenging learning environments for young children.

### Standard 2. Building Family and Community Relationships

Students prepared in early childhood degree programs understand that successful early childhood education depends upon partnerships with children's families and communities. They know about, understand, and value the importance and complex characteristics of children's families and communities. They use this understanding to create respectful, reciprocal relationships that support and empower families and to involve all families in their children's development and learning.

**Key elements:**

2a: Knowing about and understanding diverse family and community characteristics.

2b: Supporting and engaging families and communities through respectful, reciprocal relationships.

2c: Involving families and communities in young children's development and learning.

### Standard 3. Observing, Documenting, and Assessing to Support Young Children and Families

Students prepared in early childhood degree programs understand that child observation, documentation, and other forms of assessment are central to the practice of all early childhood professionals. They know about and understand the goals, benefits, and uses of assessment. They know about and use systematic observations, documentation, and other effective assessment strategies in a responsible way, in partnership with families and other professionals, to positively influence the development of every child.

**Key elements:**

3a: Understanding the goals, benefits, and uses of assessment – including its use in development of appropriate goals, curriculum, and teaching strategies for young children.

3b: Knowing about assessment partnerships with families and with professional colleagues to build effective learning environments.

3c: Knowing about and using observation, documentation, and other appropriate assessment tools and approaches, including the use of technology in documentation, assessment and data collection.

3d: Understanding and practicing responsible assessment to promote positive outcomes for each child, including the use of assistive technology for children with disabilities.

### Standard 4. Using Developmentally Effective Approaches

Students prepared in early childhood degree programs understand that teaching and learning with young children is a complex enterprise, and its details vary depending on children's ages, characteristics, and the settings within which teaching and learning occur. They understand and use positive relationships and supportive interactions as the foundation for their work with young children and families. Students know, understand, and use a wide array of developmentally appropriate approaches, instructional strategies, and tools to connect with children and families and positively influence each child's development and learning.

## Key elements:

4a: Understanding positive relationships and supportive interactions as the foundation of their work with young children.

4b: Knowing and understanding effective strategies and tools for early education, including appropriate uses of technology.

4c: Using a broad repertoire of developmentally appropriate teaching/learning approaches.

4d: Reflecting on own practice to promote positive outcomes for each child.

## Standard 5. Using Content Knowledge to Build Meaningful Curriculum

Students prepared in early childhood degree programs use their knowledge of academic disciplines to design, implement, and evaluate experiences that promote positive development and learning for each and every young child. Students understand the importance of developmental domains and academic (or content) disciplines in an early childhood curriculum. They know the essential concepts, inquiry tools, and structure of content areas, including academic subjects, and can identify resources to deepen their understanding. Students use their own knowledge and other resources to design, implement, and evaluate meaningful, challenging curricula that promote comprehensive developmental and learning outcomes for every young child.

## Key elements:

5a: Understanding content knowledge and resources in academic disciplines: language and literacy; the arts–music, creative movement, dance, drama, visual arts; mathematics; science, physical activity, physical education, health and safety; and social studies.

5b: Knowing and using the central concepts, inquiry tools, and structures of content areas or academic disciplines.

5c: Using own knowledge, appropriate early learning standards, and other resources to design, implement, and evaluate developmentally meaningful and challenging curriculum for each child.

## Standard 6. Becoming a Professional

Students prepared in early childhood degree programs identify and conduct themselves as members of the early childhood profession. They know and use ethical guidelines and other professional standards related to early childhood practice. They are continuous, collaborative learners who demonstrate knowledgeable, reflective, and critical perspectives on their work, making informed decisions that integrate knowledge from a variety of sources. They are informed advocates for sound educational practices and policies.

## Key elements:

6a: Identifying and involving oneself with the early childhood field.

6b: Knowing about and upholding ethical standards and other early childhood professional guidelines.

6c: Engaging in continuous, collaborative learning to inform practice; using technology effectively with young children, with peers, and as a professional resource.

6d: Integrating knowledgeable, reflective, and critical perspectives on early education.

6e: Engaging in informed advocacy for young children and the early childhood profession.

## Standard 7. Early Childhood Field Experiences

Field experiences and clinical practice are planned and sequenced so that candidates develop the knowledge, skills, and professional dispositions necessary to promote the development and learning of young children across the entire developmental period of early childhood—in at least two of the three early childhood age groups (birth–age 3, 3 through 5, 5 through 8 years) and in the variety of settings that offer early education (early school grades, child care centers and homes, Head Start programs).

## Key elements:

7a: Opportunities to observe and practice in at least two of the three early childhood age groups (birth–age 3, 3–5, 5–8).

7b: Opportunities to observe and practice in at least two of the three main types of early education settings (early school grades, child care centers and homes, Head Start programs).

*Source: From the National Association for the Education of Young Children (NAEYC).*

# APPENDIX C

## NAEYC PROGRAM ADMINISTRATOR DEFINITION AND COMPETENCIES®

### I. PROGRAM ADMINISTRATOR DEFINITION

The program administrator is the individual responsible for planning, implementing, and evaluating a child care, preschool, or kindergarten program. The role of the administrator covers both leadership and management functions. Leadership functions relate to the broad plan of helping an organization clarify and affirm values, set goals, articulate a vision, and chart a course of action to achieve that vision. Managerial functions relate to the actual orchestration of tasks and the setting up of systems to carry out the organization's mission.

### Functions of the program administrator include the following:

- *Pedagogy*—Creating a learning community of children and adults that promotes optimal child development and healthy families.

- *Organizational development and systems*—Establishing systems for smooth program functioning and managing staff to carry out the mission of the program; planning and budgeting the program's fiscal resources; managing organizational change and establishing systems to monitor and evaluate organizational performance.

- *Human resources*—Recruiting, selecting, and orienting personnel; overseeing systems for the supervision, retention, and professional development of staff that affirm program values and promote a shared vision.

- *Collaboration*—Establishing partnerships with program staff, family members, board members, community representatives, civic leaders, and other stakeholders to design and improve services for children and their families.

- *Advocacy*—Taking action and encouraging others to work on behalf of high quality services that meet the needs of children and their families. The administrator may have different role titles depending on the program type or sponsorship of the program. Common titles include director, site manager, administrator, program manager, early childhood coordinator, and principal.

### II. CORE COMPETENCIES: RELEVANT INFORMATION FOR SELECTING ANNUAL PROFESSIONAL DEVELOPMENT OPTIONS

(Adapted with permission from the Illinois Director Credential)

The core competencies needed for effective early childhood program administration fall into two broad categories: management knowledge and skills and early childhood knowledge and skills. These are not discrete categories; they overlap conceptually and practically.

### Management Knowledge and Skills

Administrators need a solid foundation in the principles of organizational management, including how to establish systems for smooth program functioning and how to manage staff to carry out the mission of the program.

1. Personal and professional self-awareness

- Knowledge and application of adult and career development, personality typologies, dispositions, and learning styles

- Knowledge of one's own beliefs, values, and philosophical stance

- The ability to evaluate ethical and moral dilemmas based on a professional code of ethics

- The ability to be a reflective practitioner and apply a repertoire of techniques to improve the level of personal fulfillment and professional job satisfaction

2. Legal and fiscal management

- Knowledge and application of the advantages and disadvantages of different legal structures

- Knowledge of different codes and regulations as they relate to the delivery of early childhood program services

- Knowledge of child custody, child abuse, special education, confidentiality, antidiscrimination, insurance liability, and contract and labor laws pertaining to program management

- Knowledge of various federal, state, and local revenue sources
- Knowledge of bookkeeping methods and accounting terminology
- Skill in budgeting, cash flow management, grant writing, and fund-raising

3.  Staff management and human relations

- Knowledge and application of group dynamics, communication styles, and techniques for conflict resolution
- Knowledge of different supervisory and group facilitation styles
- The ability to relate to staff and board members of diverse racial, cultural, and ethnic backgrounds
- The ability to hire, supervise, and motivate staff to high levels of performance
- Skill in consensus building, team development, and staff performance appraisal

4.  Educational programming

- Knowledge and application of different curriculum models, standards for high-quality programming, and child assessment practices
- The ability to develop and implement a program to meet the needs of young children at different ages and developmental levels (infant–toddler, preschool, kindergarten)
- Knowledge of administrative practices that promote the inclusion of children with special needs

5.  Program operations and facilities management

- Knowledge and application of policies and procedures that meet state and local regulations as well as professional standards pertaining to the health and safety of young children
- Knowledge of nutritional and health requirements for food service
- The ability to design and plan the effective use of space based on principles of environmental psychology and child development
- Knowledge of playground safety design and practice

6.  Family support

- Knowledge and application of family systems and different parenting styles
- Knowledge of community resources to support family wellness
- The ability to implement program practices that support families of diverse cultural, ethnic, linguistic, and socioeconomic backgrounds
- The ability to support families as valued partners in the educational process

7.  Marketing and public relations

- Knowledge of the fundamentals of effective marketing, public relations, and community outreach

- The ability to evaluate the cost benefit of different marketing and promotional strategies
- The ability to communicate the program's philosophy and promote a positive public image to families, business leaders, public officials, and prospective funders
- The ability to promote linkages with local schools
- Skill in developing a business plan and effective promotional literature, handbooks, newsletters, and press releases

8.  Leadership and advocacy

- Knowledge of organizational theory and leadership styles as they relate to early childhood work environments
- Knowledge of the legislative processes, social issues, and public policy affecting young children and their families
- The ability to articulate a vision, clarify and affirm values, and create a culture built on norms of continuous improvement and ethical conduct
- The ability to evaluate program effectiveness
- The ability to define organizational problems, gather data to generate alternative solutions, and effectively apply analytical skills in its solution
- The ability to advocate on behalf of young children, their families, and the profession

9.  Oral and written communication

- Knowledge of the mechanics of writing, including organizing ideas, grammar, punctuation, and spelling
- The ability to use written communication to effectively express one's thoughts
- Knowledge of oral communication techniques, including establishing rapport, preparing the environment, active listening, and voice control
- The ability to communicate ideas effectively in a formal presentation

10. Technology

- Knowledge of basic computer hardware and software applications
- The ability to use the computer for program administrative functions

## Early Childhood Knowledge and Skills

Administrators need a strong foundation in the fundamentals of child development and early childhood education to guide the instructional practices of teachers and support staff.

1.  Historical and philosophical foundations

- Knowledge of the historical roots and philosophical foundations of early childhood care and education
- Knowledge of different types of early childhood programs, roles, funding, and regulatory structures

- Knowledge of current trends and important influences impacting program quality

- Knowledge of research methodologies

2. Child growth and development

- Knowledge of different theoretical positions in child development

- Knowledge of the biological, environmental, cultural, and social influences affecting children's growth and development from prenatal through early adolescence

- Knowledge of developmental milestones in children's physical, cognitive, language, aesthetic, social, and emotional development

- Knowledge of current research in neuroscience and its application to the field of early childhood education

3. Child observation and assessment

- Knowledge and application of developmentally appropriate child observation and assessment methods

- Knowledge of the purposes, characteristics, and limitations of different assessment tools and techniques

- Ability to use different observation techniques, including formal and informal observation, behavior sampling, and developmental checklists

- Knowledge of ethical practice as it relates to the use of assessment information

- The ability to apply child observation and assessment data to planning and structuring developmentally appropriate instructional strategies

4. Curriculum and instructional methods

- Knowledge of different curriculum models; appropriate curriculum goals; and different instructional strategies for infants, toddlers, preschoolers, and kindergarten children

- Ability to plan and implement a curriculum based on knowledge of individual children's developmental patterns, family and community goals, institutional and cultural context, and state standards

- Ability to design integrated and meaningful curricular experiences in the content areas of language and literacy, mathematics, science, social studies, art, music, drama, movement, and technology

- Ability to implement antibias instructional strategies that take into account culturally valued content and children's home experiences

- Ability to evaluate outcomes of different curricular approaches

5. Children with special needs

- Knowledge of atypical development, including mild and severe disabilities in physical, health, cognitive, social-emotional, communication, and sensory functioning

- Knowledge of licensing standards as well as state and federal laws (e.g., ADA, IDEA) as they relate to services and accommodations for children with special needs

- Knowledge of the characteristics of giftedness and how educational environments can support children with exceptional capabilities

- The ability to work collaboratively as part of a family-professional team in planning and implementing appropriate services for children with special needs

- Knowledge of special education resources and services

6. Family and community relationships

- Knowledge of the diversity of family systems; traditional, nontraditional, and alternative family structures as well as family life styles; and the dynamics of family life on the development of young children

- Knowledge of sociocultural factors influencing contemporary families, including the effect of language, religion, poverty, race, technology, and the media

- Knowledge of different community resources, assistance, and support available to children and families

- Knowledge of different strategies to promote reciprocal partnerships between home and center

- Ability to communicate effectively with parents through written and oral communication

- Ability to demonstrate awareness and appreciation of different cultural and familial practices and customs

- Knowledge of child rearing patterns in other countries

7. Health, safety, and nutrition

- Knowledge and application of practices that promote good nutrition, dental health, physical health, mental health, and safety of infants–toddlers, preschool, and kindergarten children

- Ability to implement practices indoors and outdoors that help prevent, prepare for, and respond to emergencies

- Ability to model healthful lifestyle choices

8. Individual and group guidance

- Knowledge of the rationale for and research supporting different models of child guidance and classroom management

- Ability to apply different techniques that promote positive and supportive relationships with children and among children

- Ability to reflect on teaching behavior and modify guidance techniques based on the developmental and special needs of children

9. Learning environments

- Knowledge of the effect of the physical environment on children's learning and development

- The ability to use space, color, sound, texture, light, and other design elements to create indoor and outdoor learning environments that are aesthetically pleasing, intellectually stimulating, psychologically safe, and nurturing

- The ability to select age-appropriate equipment and materials that achieve curricular goals and encourage positive social interaction

10. Professionalism

- Knowledge of laws, regulations, and policies that affect professional conduct with children and families

- Knowledge of different professional organizations, resources, and issues affecting the welfare of early childhood practitioners

- Knowledge of center accreditation criteria

- Ability to make professional judgments based on the NAEYC "Code of Ethical Conduct and Statement of Commitment"

- Ability to reflect on one's professional growth and development and make goals for personal improvement

- Ability to work as part of a professional team and supervise support staff or volunteers

*Source: From the National Association for the Education of Young Children (NAEYC).*

# APPENDIX D

## NAEYC ACCREDITATION STANDARDS FOR EARLY CHILDHOOD PROGRAMS®

### Standard 1 – Relationships

Topic 1.A: Building Positive Relationships Among Teachers and Families

Topic 1.B: Building Positive Relationships Among Teachers and Children

Topic 1.C: Helping Children Make Friends

Topic 1.D: Creating a Predictable, Consistent, and Harmonious Classroom

Topic 1.E: Addressing Challenging Behaviors

Topic 1.F: Promoting Self-Regulation

### Standard 2 – Curriculum

Topic 2.A: Curriculum: Essential Characteristics

Topic 2.B: Areas of Development: Social-Emotional Development

Topic 2.C: Areas of Development: Physical Development

Topic 2.D: Areas of Development: Language Development

Topic 2.E: Curriculum Content Area for Cognitive Development: Early Literacy

Topic 2.F: Curriculum Content Area for Cognitive Development: Early Mathematics

Topic 2.G: Curriculum Content Area for Cognitive Development: Science

Topic 2.H: Curriculum Content Area for Cognitive Development: Technology *To avoid confusion in the numbering system, there are no criteria labeled 2.I.*

Topic 2.J: Creative Expression and Appreciation for the Arts

Topic 2.K: Curriculum Content Area for Cognitive Development: Health and Safety

Topic 2.L: Curriculum Content Area for Cognitive Development: Social Studies

### Standard 3 – Teaching

Topic 3.A: Designing Enriched Learning Environments

Topic 3.B: Creating Caring Communities for Learning

Topic 3.C: Supervising Children

Topic 3.D: Using Time, Grouping, and Routine to Achieve Learning Goals

Topic 3.E: Responding to Children's Interests and Needs

Topic 3.F: Making Learning Meaningful for All Children

Topic 3.G: Using Instruction to Deepen Children's Understanding and Build Their Skills and Knowledge

### Standard 4 – Assessment

Topic 4.A: Creating an Assessment Plan

Topic 4.B: Using Appropriate Assessment Methods

Topic 4.C: Identifying Children's Interests and Needs and Describing Children's Progress

Topic 4.D: Adapting Curriculum, Individualizing Teaching, and Informing Program Development

Topic 4.E: Communicating with Families and Involving Families in the Assessment Process

### Standard 5 – Health

Topic 5.A: Promoting and Protecting Children's Health and Controlling Infectious Disease

Topic 5.B: Ensuring Children's Nutritional Well-being

Topic 5.C: Maintaining a Healthful Environment

### Standard 6 – Teachers

Topic 6.A: Preparation, Knowledge, and Skills of Teaching Staff

Topic 6.B: Teachers' Dispositions and Professional Commitment

### Standard 7 – Families

Topic 7.A: Knowing and Understanding the Program's Families

Topic 7.B: Sharing Information between Staff and Families

Topic 7.C: Nurturing Families as Advocates for Their Children

## Standard 8 – Community Relationships

Topic 8.A:  Linking with the Community

Topic 8.B:  Accessing Community Resources

Topic 8.C:  Acting as a Citizen in the Neighborhood and the Early Childhood Community

## Standard 9 – Physical Environment

Topic 9.A:  Indoor and Outdoor Equipment, Materials, and Furnishings

Topic 9.B:  Outdoor Environment Design

Topic 9.C:  Building and Physical Design

Topic 9.D:  Environment Health

## Standard 10 – Leadership And Management

Topic 10.A: Leadership Topic

Topic 10.B: Management Policies and Procedures

Topic 10.C: Fiscal Accountability Policies and Procedures

Topic 10.D: Health, Nutrition, and Safety Policies and Procedures

Topic 10.E: Personnel Policies

Topic 10.F: Program Evaluation, Accountability, and Continuous Improvement

*Source: From the National Association for the Education of Young Children (NAEYC).*

## SOURCES OF EARLY CHILDHOOD MATERIALS, EQUIPMENT, AND SUPPLIES

### Achievement Products for Special Needs

P.O. Box 7636

Spreckels, CA 93962-7636

(800) 373-4699

*http://www.achievement-products.com*

### Albert Whitman & Company

250 South Northwest Highway, Suite 320

Park Ridge, IL 60068

(800) 255-7675

*http://www.albertwhitman.com*

### Angeles Corporation

9 Capper Drive

Daily Industrial Park

Pacific, MO 63069

(800) 346-6313

*http://www.angelesstore.com*

### Becker's School Supplies

1500 Melrose Highway

Pennsauken, NJ 08110-1410

(800) 523-1490

*http://www.shopbecker.com*

### Broderbund Software

Navarre Corporation

7400 49th Avenue North

Minneapolis, MN 55428

Broderbund Ordering:

(800) 395-0277

*http://www.broderbund.com*

### Busy Kids LLC

937 139th Avenue NW

Andover, MN 55304-4124

(763) 757-0512

*http://busy-kids.com*

### Candlewick Press

99 Dover Street

Somerville, MA02144

(617) 661-3330

*http://www.candlewick.com*

### Cengage Learning, Inc.

10650 Toebben Drive

Independence, KY 41051

(800) 354-9706

*http://www.cengage.com*

### Child Care Manager

Personalized Software

118 S. Main Street

Phoenix, OR 97535-0359

(800) 553-2312

*http://www.childcaremanager.com*

### Childforms

110 Charleston Drive, Suite 106

Mooresville, NC 28117

(800) 447-3349

*http://www.childforms.com*

### Child Plus Software

Two Ravinia Drive, Suite 1300

Atlanta, GA 30346

(800) 888-6674

*http://www.childplus.net*

### Clarion Books

Houghton Mifflin Harcourt

215 Park Avenue South

New York, NY 10003

(212) 420-5800

*http://www.houghtonmifflinbooks.com/hmh/site/hmhbooks /home/kids*

## Community Playthings

2032 Route 213

Rifton, NY 12471

(800) 777-4244

*http://www.communityplaythings.com*

## Custom Recreation

2190 North Cullen Avenue

Evansville, IN 47715

(888) 987-4477

*http://www.customrecreation.com*

## Dick Blick Art Materials

P.O. Box 1267

Galesburg, IL 61402-1267

(800) 828-4548

*http://www.dickblick.com*

## Didax Educational Resources Inc.

395 Main Street

Rowley, MA 01969

(800) 458-0024

*http://www.didax.com*

## Discount School Supply

P.O. Box 6013

Carol Stream, IL 60197-6013

(800) 627-2829

*http://www.discountschoolsupply.com*

## The Discovery Channel

One Discovery Place

Silver Spring, MD 20910

(240) 662-2000

*http://www.discovery.com*

## Don Johnston Inc.

26799 West Commerce Drive

Volo, IL 60073

(800) 999-4660

*http://www.donjohnston.com*

## Environments Inc.

P.O. Box 1348

Beaufort, SC 29901-1348

(800) 342-4453

*http://www.environments.com*

## Flagship Carpet

P.O. Box 1779

Calhoun, GA 30701

(800) 848-4055

*http://www.flagshipcarpets.com*

## Growing Tree Toys

202 South Allen Street

State College, PA 16801

(800) 993-8697

*http://www.growingtreetoys.com*

## Gryphon House Inc.

P.O. Box 10

6858 Leon's Way

Lewisville, NC 27023

(800) 638-0928

*http://www.gryphonhouse.com*

## Hachette Book Group

237 Park Avenue

New York, NY 10017

(800) 759-0190

*http://www.hachettebookgroup.com*

## HarperCollins Children's Books

10 East 53rd Street

New York, NY 10022

(212) 207-7000

*http://www.harpercollinschildrens.com*

## Houghton Mifflin Harcourt Publishers

School Division (Pre-K through 8)

9205 South Park Center Loop

Orlando, FL 32819

(800) 269-5232

*http://www.hmhco.com*

## Insect Lore

P.O. Box 1535

Shafter, CA 93263

(800) 548-3284

*http://www.insectlore.com*

## International Playthings Inc.

75D Lackawanna Avenue

Parsippany, NJ 07054

(800) 631-1272

*http://www.intplay.com*

**John R. Green**

411 West 6th Street

Covington, KY 41011

(800) 354-9737

*http://www.johnrgreenco.com*

**Jonti-Craft Inc.**

P.O. Box 30

171 Highway 68

Wabasso, MN 56293

(800) 543-4149

*http://www.jonti-craft.com*

**Kaplan Early Learning Company**

1310 Lewisville-Clemmons Road

Lewisville, NC 27023

(800) 334-2014

*http://www.kaplanco.com*

**Kohburg Early Childhood Educational Furniture**

1926 West Holt Avenue

Pomona CA, 91768

(888) 718-8880

*http://www.kohburg.com/*

**Lakeshore Learning Materials**

2695 East Dominguez Street

P.O. Box 6261

Carson, CA 90895

(800) 778-4456

*http://www.lakeshorelearning.com*

**Landscape Structures Inc.**

601 7th Street South

Delano, MN 55328-0198

(800) 438-6574

*http://www.playlsi.com*

**Learning Resources Inc.**

380 North Fairway Drive

Vernon Hills, IL 60061

(800) 333-8281

*http://www.learningresources.com*

**Learning Station**

315 Highway 314, Suite B

Fayetteville, GA 30214

(678) 610-3129

*http://www.learningstationonline.com*

**The Little Tikes Co.**

2180 Barlow Road

Hudson, OH 44236-9984

(866) 855-4650

*http://www.littletikes.com*

**Music Together LLC**

66 Witherspoon Street

Princeton, NJ 05842

(800) 728-2692

*http://www.musictogether.com*

**Playtime Equipment and School Supply Inc.**

5310 North 99th Street

Omaha, NE 68134

(402) 571-1717

*http://www.playtimeschoolsupply.com*

**Private Advantage**

Child Care Management Software

Mt. Taylor Programs

716 College Avenue, Suite B

Santa Rosa, CA 95404

(800) 238-7015

*http://www.privateadv.com*

**Procare Software**

3581 Excel Drive

Medford, OR 97504

(800) 338-3884

*http://www.procaresoftware.com*

**Redleaf Press**

10 Yorkton Court

St. Paul, MN 55117-1065

(800) 423-8309

*http://www.redleafpress.org*

**Rhythm Band Instruments Inc.**

P.O. Box 126

Fort Worth, TX 76102

(800) 424-4724

http://www.rhythmband.com

**S+S Worldwide**

75 Mill Street

Colchester, CT 06415

(800) 566-6678

http://www.ssww.com

**Scholastic, Inc.**

557 Broadway

New York, NY 10012

(800) 724-6527

http://www.scholastic.com

**School Specialty**

(888) 388-3224

http://www.schoolspecialty.com

**Seedlings Braille Books for Children**

P.O. Box 51924

Livonia, MI 48151-5924

(800) 777-8552

http://www.seedlings.org

**SofterWare Inc.**

132 Welsh Road, Suite 140

Horsham, PA 19044-2217

(215) 628-0400

http://www.softerware.com

**Stress Free Kids**

2561 Chimney Springs

Marietta, GA30062

(800) 841-4204

http://www.stressfreekids.com

**Sunburst Technology**

3150 W Higgins Road, Suite 140

Hoffman Estates, IL 60619

(800) 321-7511

http://www.sunburst.com

**Teachers College Press**

P.O. Box 20

Williston, VT 05495-0020

(800) 575-6566

http://www.teacherscollegepress.com

**Terrapin Software**

955 Massachusetts Avenue #365

Cambridge, MA 02139-3233

(800) 774-5646

http://www.terrapinlogo.com

**Tom Snyder Productions**

100 Talcott Avenue

Watertown, MA 02472-5703

(800) 342-0236

http://www.tomsnyder.com

**Toys to Grow On**

2695 East Dominguez Street

Carson, CA 90895

(800) 987-4454

http://www.ttgo.com

**Tree Blocks**

(800) 873-4960

http://www.treeblocks.com

**Triarco Arts & Crafts**

9909 South Shore Drive, Suite 1015

Plymouth, MN 55441-5037

(800) 328-3360

http://www.triarcoarts.com

**Turn the Page Press Inc.**

213 Vernon Street

Roseville, CA 95678

(800) 959-5549

http://www.turnthepage.com

**U.S. Toy Company**

13201 Arrington Road

Grandview, MO 64030-1117

(800) 832-0224

http://www.ustoy.com

# APPENDIX F

## EARLY CHILDHOOD PROFESSIONAL ORGANIZATIONS AND INFORMATION SOURCES

**Administration for Children and Families**

370 L'Enfant Promenade, SW

Washington, DC 20447

(202) 401-9200

*http://www.acf.hhs.gov*

**American Academy of Pediatrics**

141 Northwest Point Boulevard

Elk Grove Village, IL 60007-1098

(847) 434-4000

*http://www.aap.org*

**American Association of Family & Consumer Sciences**

400 North Columbus Street, Suite 202

Alexandria, VA 22314

(703) 706-4600

*http://www.aafcs.org*

**American Association of School Administrators**

801 North Quincy Street, Suite 700

Arlington, VA 22203

(800) 424-8080

*http://www.aasa.org*

**American Council on Education (ACE)**

One Dupont Circle, NW, Suite 800

Washington, DC 20036

(202) 939-9300

*http://www.acenet.edu*

**American Educational Research Association (AERA)**

1430 K Street, NW

Washington, DC 20005

(202) 238-3200

*http://www.aera.net*

**American Federation of Teachers (AFT)**

555 New Jersey Avenue, NW

Washington, DC 20001

(202) 879-4400

*http://www.aft.org*

**American Medical Association**

330 North Wabash

Chicago, IL 60611-5885

(800) 621-8335

*http://www.ama-assn.org*

**American Montessori Society (AMS)**

116 East 16th Street

New York, NY 10003

(212) 358-1250

*http://www.amshq.org*

**American Speech-Language-Hearing Association**

2200 Research Boulevard

Rockville, MD 20850-3289

(301) 296-5700

*http://www.asha.org*

**The Annie E. Casey Foundation**

701 Saint Paul Street

Baltimore, MD 21202

(410) 547-6600

*http://www.aecf.org*

**Appalachian Regional Commission**

1666 Connecticut Avenue, NW, Suite 700

Washington, DC 20009-1068

(202) 884-7700

*http://www.arc.gov*

## Association for Childhood Education International (ACEI)

1101 16th Street, NW, Suite 300

Washington, DC 20036

(800) 423-3563

*http://www.acei.org/*

## Association for Early Learning Leaders

8000 Centre Park Drive, Suite 170

Austin, TX 78754

(800) 537-1118

*http://www.earlylearningleaders.org*

## Association for Library Service to Children-American Library Association

50 E. Huron

Chicago, IL 60611

(800) 545-2433

*http://www.ala.org/alsc*

## Association for Supervision and Curriculum Development (ASCD)

1703 North Beauregard Street

Alexandria, VA 22311-1714

(800) 933-2723

*http://www.ascd.org*

## Association Montessori Internationale/USA

410 Alexander Street

Rochester, NY 14607

(585) 461-5920

*http://amiusa.org/*

## California Child Care Resource and Referral Agency

111 New Montgomery

San Francisco, CA 94105

(415) 882-0234

*http://www.rrnetwork.org*

## Center for Child Care Workforce

555 New Jersey Avenue, NW

Washington, DC 20001

(202) 662-8005

*http://www.ccw.org*

## Center for Nutrition Policy and Promotion

3101 Park Center Drive

Alexandria, VA 23202-1594

(703) 305-7600

*http://www.cnpp.usda.gov*

## Centers for Disease Control and Prevention

1600 Clifton Road N.E.

Atlanta, GA 30333

(800) 232-4636

*http://www.cdc.gov*

## ChildCare Aware of America

1515 North Courthouse Road, 11th Floor

Arlington, VA 22201

(703) 341-4100

*http://www.naccrra.org*

## Child Care Bureau

U.S. Department of Health and Human Services

Administration for Children and Families

Office of Family Assistance

370 L'Enfant Promenade, SW

5th Floor East

Washington, DC 20447

(202) 690-6782

*http://www.acf.hhs.gov/programs/occ/*

## Child Care Education Institute

3059 Peachtree Industrial Boulevard, NW, Suite 100

Duluth, GA 30097

(800) 499-9907

*http://www.cceionline.com*

## Child Care Information Exchange

17725 NE 65th Street, B-275

Redmond, WA 98052

(800) 221-2864

*http://www.childcareexchange.com*

## Child Care Law Center

445 Church Street

San Francisco, CA 94114

(415) 558-8005

*http://www.childcarelaw.org*

**Child Care Services Association**

1829 East Franklin Street, Building 1000

P.O. Box 901

Chapel Hill, NC 27514

(919) 967-3272

*http://www.childcareservices.org*

**Child Trauma Academy**

5161 San Felipe, Suite 320

Houston, TX 77056

(866) 943-9779

*http://www.childtrauma.org*

**Child Welfare League of America (CWLA)**

1726 M Street, NW, Suite 500

Washington, DC 20036

(202) 688-4200

*http://www.cwla.org*

**Children's Book Council Inc.**

54 West 39th Street, 14th Floor

New York, NY 10018

(212) 966-1990

*http://www.cbcbooks.org*

**Children's Defense Fund**

25 E Street, NW

Washington, DC 20001

(800) 233-1200

*http://www.childrensdefense.org*

**Children's Foundation**

P.O. Box 1443

Loveland, CO 80539-1443

(888) 934-3733

*http://www.childrensfoundationinc.com*

**Common Core State Standards Initiative**

c/o National Governors Association

Hall of the States

444 N. Capitol Street, Suite 267

Washington, DC 20001-1512

(202) 624-5300

*http://www.nga.org/cms/home.html (NGA)*

*http://www.corestandards.org/ (Standards)*

**Council for Early Childhood Professional Recognition (CDA)**

2640 16th Street, NW

Washington, DC 20009-3547

(800) 424-4310

*http://www.cdacouncil.org*

**Council for Exceptional Children (CEC)**

2900 Crystal Drive, Suite 1000

Arlington, VA 22202-3557

(888) 232-7733

*http://www.cec.sped.org*

**Council of Chief State School Officers**

One Massachusetts Avenue, NW, Suite 700

Washington, DC 20001-1431

(202) 336-7000

*http://www.ccsso.org*

**Division for Early Childhood—Council for Exceptional Children**

3415 South Sepulveda Blvd.

Suite 1100, Unit 1127

Los Angeles, CA 90034

(310) 428-7209

*http://www.dec-sped.org*

**Early Childhood Leadership Program**

Bank Street College of Education

610 West 112th Street

New York, NY 10025

(212) 875-4400

*http://www.bnkst.edu/graduate-school/academics/programs/leadership-programs-overview/early-childhood-leadership/*

**Education Development Center (EDC)**

43 Foundry Avenue

Waltham, MA 02453-8313

(617) 969-7100

*http://www.edc.org*

**Families and Work Institute**

267 Fifth Avenue, 2nd Floor

New York, NY 10006

(212) 465-2044

*http://www.familiesandwork.org*

## The Foundation Center

79 Fifth Avenue/16th Street

New York, NY 10003-3076

(212) 620-4230

*http://foundationcenter.org*

## Foundation for Child Development

295 Madison Avenue, 40th Floor

New York, NY 10017

(212) 867-5777

*http://www.fcd-us.org*

## Head Start-Johnson & Johnson Management Fellows Program

UCLA Anderson School of Management

110 Westwood Plaza, Suite B307

Los Angeles, CA 90095-1481

(310) 825-6306

*http://www.anderson.ucla.edu/price/jnj/headstart*

## Head Start State Collaborative Project Center for Schools and Communities

275 Grandview Avenue, Suite 200

Camp Hill, PA 17011

(717) 763-1661

*http://www.center-school.org*

## High/Scope Educational Research Foundation

600 North River Street

Ypsilanti, MI 48198-2898

(800) 587-5639

*http://www.highscope.org*

## International Child Resource Institute

125 University Avenue2nd Floor, Southwest Suite

Berkeley, CA 94710

(510) 644-1000

*http://www.icrichild.org*

## International Reading Association

P.O. Box 8139

800 Barksdale Rd.

Newark, DE 19714-8139

(800) 336-7323

*http://www.reading.org*

## McCormick Center for Early Childhood Leadership

National-Louis University

6200 Capitol Drive

Wheeling, IL 60090

(847) 947-5063

*http://mccormickcenter.nl.edu/*

## National AfterSchool Association

2961A Hunter Mill Rd., #626

Oakton, VA 22124

(504) 903-9930

*http://www.naaweb.org/*

## National Association for Bilingual Education

8701 Georgia Avenue, Suite 700

Silver Spring, MD 20910

(240) 450-3700

*http://www.nabe.org*

## National Association for Family Child Care

1743 W. Alexander Street

Salt Lake City, Utah 84119

(801) 886-2322

*http://nafcc.org*

## National Association for Gifted Children

1331 H Street NW, Suite 1001

Washington, DC 20005

(202) 785-4268

*http://www.nagc.org*

## National Association for the Education of Young Children (NAEYC)

1313 L Street, NW, Suite 500

Washington, DC 20005

(800) 424-2460

*http://www.naeyc.org*

## National Association for the Education of Young Children

Accreditation of Programs for Young Children

1313 L Street, NW, Suite 500

Washington, DC 20005

(800) 424-2460

*http://www.naeyc.org/academy*

**National Association of Elementary School Principals**

1615 Duke Street

Alexandria, VA 22314-3483

(800) 386-2377

*http://www.naesp.org*

**National Association of State Boards of Education**

2121 Crystal Drive, Suite 350

Arlington, VA 22202

(800) 368-5023

*http://www.nasbe.org*

**National Association of State Directors of Special Education (NASDSE)**

225 Reinekers Lane, Suite 420

Alexandria, VA 22314

(703) 519-3800

*http://www.nasdse.org*

**National Black Child Development Institute (NBCDI)**

1313 L Street, NW, Suite 110

Washington, DC 20005-4110

(800) 556-2234

*http://www.nbcdi.org*

**National Board for Professional Teaching Standards**

1525 Wilson Blvd., Ste 500

Arlington, VA 22209

(800) 228-3224

*http://www.nbpts.org*

**National Center for Children in Poverty**

215 West 125th Street, 3rd Floor

New York, NY 10027

(646) 284-9600

*http://www.nccp.org*

**National Center for Education in Maternal and Child Health**

Georgetown University

Box 571272

Washington, DC 20057-1272

(877) 624-1935

*http://www.ncemch.org*

**National Child Care Association (NCCA)**

1325 G Street NW, Suite 500

Washington, DC 20005

(800) 543-7161

*http://www.nccanet.org*

**National Coalition for Campus Children's Centers**

2036 Larkhall Circle

Folsom, CA 95630

916-790-8261

*http://campuschildren.org*

**National Early Childhood Program Accreditation (NECPA)**

c/o NECPA Commission Inc.

887 Johnnie Dodds Boulevard, Suite 212

Mount Pleasant, SC 29464

(800) 505-9878

*http://www.necpa.net*

**National Early Childhood Technical Assistance Center**

Campus Box 8040, UNC-CH

Chapel Hill, NC 27599-8040

(919) 962-2001

*http://www.nectac.org*

**National Education Association (NEA)**

1201 16th Street, NW

Washington, DC 20036-3290

(202) 833-4000

*http://www.nea.org*

**National Food Service Management Institute (NFSMI)**

The University of Mississippi

6 Jeanette Phillips Drive

P.O. Drawer 188

University, MS 38677-0188

(622) 915-7658

*http://www.nfsmi.org*

**National Head Start Association**

1651 Prince Street

Alexandria, VA 22314

(703) 739-0875

*http://www.nhsa.org*

## National Institute of Child Health and Human Development (NICHD)

*Eunice Kennedy Shriver* National Institute of Child Health and Human Development (NICHD)

31 Center Drive

Building 31, Room 2A32

Bethesda, MD 20892-2425

(800) 370-2943

http://www.nichd.nih.gov

## National Institute on Out-of-School Time

Wellesley Centers for Women, Wellesley College

106 Central Street

Wellesley, MA 02481

(781) 283-2547

http://www.niost.org

## National Latino Children's Institute

118 Broadway St, Suite 615

San Antonio, Texas 78205

(210) 228-9997

http://www.nlci.org

## National Parent Teacher Association

1250 North Pitt Street

Alexandria, VA 22314

(800) 307-4781

http://www.pta.org

## National Resource Center for Health and Safety in Child Care and Early Education

National Resource Center for Health and Safety in Child Care and Early Education

13120 E. 19th Ave., Mail Stop F541

P.O. Box 6511

Aurora, CO 80045

(800) 598-5437

http://nrckids.org

## National Women's Law Center

11 Dupont Circle, NW, Suite 800

Washington, DC 20036

(202) 588-5180

http://www.nwlc.org

## North American Montessori Teachers Association (NAMTA)

13693 Butternut Road

Burton, OH 44021

(440) 834-4011

http://www.montessori-namta.org

## Office of Child Care's Child Care Technical Assistance Network (CCTAN)

c/o Administration for Children and Families

370 L'Enfant Promenade, SW

Washington, DC 20447

(202) 401-9200

http://www.acf.hhs.gov

## Office of Indian Education

c/o Office of Elementary and Secondary Education

400 Maryland Avenue, SW

(202) 401-0113

http://www2.ed.gov/about/offices/list/oese/oie/index.html

## Office of Minority Health

U.S. Department of Health and Human Services

The Tower Building

1101 Wootton Parkway, Suite 600

Rockville, MD 20852

(240) 453-2882

http://minorityhealth.hhs.gov

## Office of Special Education and Rehabilitation Services (OSERS)

U.S. Department of Education

400 Maryland Avenue, SW

Washington, DC 20202-7100

(202) 245-7459

http://www2.ed.gov/about/offices/list/osers/osep/index.html

## Parent Cooperative Preschools International (PCPI)

National Cooperative Business Center

1401 New York Avenue, NW, Suite 1100

Washington, DC 20005

(800) 636-6222

http://www.preschools.coop

**Race to the Top Early Learning Challenge**

c/o Office of Elementary and Secondary Education

400 Maryland Avenue, SW

Washington, DC 20202-7100

(202) 401-0113

*http://www2.ed.gov/programs/racetothetop/index.html*

**Save the Children Federation**

54 Wilton Road

Westport, CT 06880

(800) 728-3843

*http://www.savethechildren.org*

**Society for Research in Child Development (SRCD)**

2950 St. State Street, Suite 401

Ann Arbor, MI 48104

(734) 926-0600

*http://www.srcd.org*

**Southern Early Childhood Association (SECA)**

P.O. Box 55930

Little Rock, AR 72215-5930

(800) 305-7322

*http://www.southernearlychildhood.org*

**Southern Institute on Children and Families**

90-F Glenda Trace, Suite 326

Newnan, GA 30265

(803) 779-2607

*http://www.thesoutherninstitute.org*

**United Way of America**

701 North Fairfax Street

Alexandria, VA 22314

(703) 836-7100

*http://www.unitedway.org*

**U.S. Consumer Product Safety Commission**

4330 East West Highway

Bethesda, MD 20814

(800) 638-2772

*http://www.cpsc.gov*

**U.S. Department of Agriculture**

1400 Independence Avenue, SW

Washington, DC 20250

(202) 720-2791

*http://www.usda.gov*

**USDA Food and Nutrition Service**

3101 Park Center Drive, Room 926

Alexandria, VA 22302

(703) 305-2276

*http://www.usda.gov*

**U.S. Department of Education**

400 Maryland Avenue, SW

Washington, DC 20202

(800) 872-5327

*http://www.ed.gov*

**U.S. National Committee of OMEP**

World Organisation for Early Childhood Education

14804 Cloverdale Road

Dale City, VA 22193

(703) 878-7416

*http://www.worldomep.org/en/*

**Zero to Three National Center for Infants, Toddlers and Families**

1255 23rd Street, NW, Suite 350

Washington, DC 20037

(202) 638-1144

*http://www.zerotothree.org*

# APPENDIX G

## EARLY CHILDHOOD PERIODICALS AND MEDIA

### PERIODICALS

**Beginnings Exchange Press Inc.**

17725 NE 65th Street, B-275

Redmond, WA 98052

(800) 221-2864

http://www.childcareexchange.com

(Published as *part of Child Care Information Exchange*)

**CDF Monthly Newsletter**

Children's Defense Fund

25 E Street, NW

Washington, DC 20001

(800) 233-1200

http://www.childrensdefense.org

**Child Care Information Exchange**

17725 NE 65th Street, B-275

Redmond, WA 98052

(800) 221-2864

http://www.childcareexchange.com

**Child Development**

Monographs of the Society for Research in Child Development

Published by Wiley-Blackwell

10475 Crosspoint Boulevard

Indianapolis, IN 45256

(877)752-2974

http://www.wiley.com/bw/journal.asp?ref=0009-3920

**Childhood Education**

Association of Childhood Education International

1101 16th Street, NW, Suite 300

Washington, DC 20036

(800) 423-3563

http://www.acei.org/childhood-education

**Research Blast**

National Head Start Association

1651 Prince Street

Alexandria, VA 22314

(866) 677-8724

http://www.nhsa.org/research/research_blast_archive

**Children Now**

1404 Franklin Street, Suite 700

Oakland, CA 94612

(510) 763-2444

http://www.childrennow.org

**Children's Voice Online**

Child Welfare League of America

1726 M Street, NW, Suite 500

Washington, DC 20036

(202) 688-4200

http://www.cwla.org/voice/default.htm

**Dimensions of Early Childhood**

Southern Early Childhood Association

1123 S. University Ave., Suite 255

Little Rock, AR 72204

http://www.southernearlychildhood.org/publications.php

**Early Childhood Education Journal**

Published by Springer

233 Spring Street

New York, NY 10013

(800) 777-4643

http://www.springer.com/education+%26+language/learning+%26+instruction/journal/10643

**Early Childhood Research Quarterly**

Elsevier Publishing

225 Wyman Street, Waltham, MA 02144

(781) 663-5200

http://www.journals.elsevier.com/early-childhood-research-quarterly/

**Early Developments**

Frank Porter Graham Child Development Institute

University of North Carolina at Chapel Hill

105 Smith Level Rd

Chapel Hill, NC 27516

*http://www.fpg.unc.edu/resources/early-developments-archive*

**Education Week**

Editorial Projects in Education Inc.

6935 Arlington Road

Bethesda, MD 20814

(800) 346-1834

*http://www.edweek.org/ew/index.html?intc=thed*

**Eric Project**

c/o Computer Science Corporation

655 15th Street, NW, Suite 500

Washington, DC 20005

(800) 538-3742

*http://www.eric.ed.gov*

**Exceptional Children**

Council for Exceptional Children

2900 Crystal Drive, Suite 1000

Arlington, VA 22202

(888) 232-7733

*http://www.cec.sped.org*

**Growing Child**

P.O. Box 2505

Lafayette, IN 47996

(800) 927-7289

*http://www.growingchild.com*

**ExtendED Notes**

P.O. Box 10

6848 Leon's Way

Lewisville, NC 27023

(888) 977-7955

*http://www.extendednotes.com*

**InfoWorld**

501 Second Street

San Francisco, CA 94107

(415) 572-7341

*http://www.infoworld.com*

**Journal of Research in Childhood Education**

Association of Childhood Education International

Published by Taylor & Francis

*http://www.tandf.co.uk/journals/UJRC*

**MacWorld**

501 2nd Street

San Francisco, CA 94107

*http://www.macworld.com*

**PC Magazine**

Ziff-Davis Media Inc.

28 East 28th Street, 11th Floor

New York, NY 10016

(800) 289-0429

*http://www.pcmag.com*

**PC World**

PCW Communications Inc.

501 2nd Street

San Francisco, CA 94107

*http://www.pcworld.com*

**Reading Today and Reading Teacher**

International Reading Association Inc.

800 Barksdale Road

P.O. Box 8139

Newark, DE 19714-8139

(800) 336-7323

*http://www.reading.org*

**ReSource**

High-Scope Educational Research Foundation

600 North River Street

Ypsilanti, MI 48198-2898

(800) 587-5639

*http://www.highscope.org*

**Teaching Young Children**

National Association for the Education of Young Children

1313 L Street, NW, Suite 500

Washington, DC 20005

(800) 424-2460

*http://www.naeyc.org/tyc*

### Texas Child Care Quarterly

P.O. Box 162881

Austin, TX 78716

(512) 441-6633

*http://www.childcarequarterly.com*

### Young Children

National Association for the Education of Young Children

1313 L Street, NW, Suite 500

Washington, DC 20005

(800) 424-2460

*http://www.naeyc.org/yc/*

### Young Exceptional Children

Division for Early Childhood/Council for Exceptional Children

3415 S. Sepulveda Blvd., Suite 1100, Unit 1127

Los Angeles, CA 90034

(310) 428-7209

*http://www.dec-sped.org*

### Zero to Three

Zero to Three—National Center for Infants, Toddlers, and Families

1255 23rd Street, NW, Suite 350

Washington, DC 20037

(202) 638-1144

*http://www.zerotothree.org*

## MEDIA

### Arlitt Instructional Media

c/o Purdy Productions

6851 Steger Drive Cincinnati, OH 45237

(513) 821-1785

*http://cech.uc.edu/centers/arlitt/arlitt_instructional_media.html*

These videos from the Arlitt Child & Family Research and Education Center at the University of Cincinnati provide numerous clips of evidence-based practices and curriculum being implemented in the classroom.

### Center on the Developing Child at Harvard University

50 Church Street, 4th Floor

Cambridge, MA 02138

(617) 496-0578

*http://developingchild.harvard.edu/*

The Center on the Developing Child provides numerous online videos related to various aspects of development and learning

### Child Development Media, Inc.

5632 Van Nuys Boulevard, Suite 286

Van Nuys, CA 91401

(800) 405-8942

*http://www.childdevelopmentmedia.com*

Child Development Media offers a wide selection of videos related to child development, early childhood education, and early intervention.

### Child Trauma Academy

5161 San Felipe, Suite 320

Houston, TX 77056

(281) 816-5604

*http://childtrauma.org*

The Child Trauma Academy is a nonprofit research, service, and education collaborative addressing the needs of children who have experienced or who are at risk for maltreatment. They make available both print and visual media, including many free resources, related to this issue.

### Davidson Films Inc.

P.O. Box 664

Santa Margarita, CA 93453

(888) 437-4200

*http://www.davidsonfilms.com*

Davidson Films supplies videos and DVDs featuring many of the most well-known thinkers who have influenced early childhood education. Its "Giants" series includes Piaget, Elkind, Montessori, Ainsworth, and Bandura.

**National Association for the Education of Young Children**

1313 L Street, NW, Suite 500

Washington, DC 20005

(800) 424-2460

*http://www.naeyc.org*

NAEYC offers many videos, some in DVD format, that address nearly every aspect of early childhood education, including curriculum, developmentally appropriate practice, diversity, literacy, children with disabilities, play, and child development.

**Program Development Associates**

32 Court Street, 21st Floor

Brooklyn, NY 11201

(800) 876-1710

*http://www.disabilitytraining.com*

This company supplies multimedia training and educational resources on numerous disability-related topics.

# APPENDIX H

## DIRECTOR'S LIBRARY

### ADVOCACY

Children's Defense Fund. (n.d.). Take action. Available online at *http://www.childrensdefense.org/take-action/*.

> This web page provides links to various resources that can inform advocacy efforts on behalf of young children and their families.

Kieff, J. (2009). *Informed advocacy in early childhood care and education: Making a difference for young children and families*. Upper Saddle River, NJ: Pearson/Merrill.

> This guide discusses the need for advocacy in early childhood and presents information on how to develop an advocacy plan. Six contexts for conducting advocacy are identified: individual child and family, the profession, program-based, the private sector, and the political and global arenas.

NAEYC. (2010). *Position statement on a call for vigilance and action by all policymakers on behalf of children and families*. Available online at *http://www.naeyc.org/positionstatements/vigilance*.

> This document presents NAEYC's position regarding the need to be mindful of the impact that legislation, laws, and regulations may have on young children's learning and development.

Robinson, A., & Stark, D. R. (2005). *Advocates in action: Making a difference for young children* (rev. ed.). Washington, DC: NAEYC.

> This book provides specific strategies for making change on behalf of young children and families. Included is information on the legislative process as well as examples of advocacy efforts throughout the country.

Washington, V., & Andrews, J. D. (Eds.). (2010). *Children of 2020: Creating a better tomorrow*. Washington, DC: Council for Professional Recognition.

> This book challenges readers to advance the field of early care and education through "smart improvisation." National leaders present analyses of progress as well as issues that must be addressed in the future. Discussion questions are provided that encourage discussion and taking action.

### CHILD DEVELOPMENT

Charlesworth, R. (2014). *Understanding child development* (9th ed.). Independence, KY: CengageLearning.

> This book introduces the reader to the unique qualities of the young child as distinguished from older children and demonstrates how to work with young children in ways that match their developmental level. The author also includes critical social and emotional factors that relate to and have an effect on development.

Wittmer, D. S., Petersen, D. H., & Puckett, M. B. (2013). *The young child: Development from prebirth through age eight* (6th ed.). Upper Saddle River, NJ: Pearson.

> A comprehensive coverage of child development written on a level appropriate for CDA programs and beyond.

### CHILDREN WITH DISABILITIES

Allen, K. E., & Cowdery, G. E. (2015). *The exceptional child: Inclusion in early childhood education* (8th ed.). Clifton Park, NY: Cengage Learning.

> This text on inclusion in the early childhood environment emphasizes the fact that teachers of children with disabilities must have a thorough knowledge of typical growth and development. When teachers see developmental variations, they are able to judge where and how to work with each child and identify when there is a need for clinical evaluations and referrals. This book offers a comprehensive overview of early intervention and public policy, types and causes of developmental disabilities, working with parents, and "how to" strategies for classroom teachers.

Child Care Law Center. (2009). *ADA and out-of-school providers*. Available online at *http://www.childcarelaw.org/pubs-audience.shtml*.

Child Care Law Center. (2012). *Questions & answers about the Americans with Disabilities Act: A quick reference for child care providers*. Available online at *http://www.childcarelaw.org/documents/ADAQ_A-October2012.pdf*.

These regularly updated documents provide an excellent overview of the requirements of the Americans with Disabilities Act. Written in question-and-answer format, information specific to child care providers is presented.

Deiner, P. L. (2013 ). *Inclusive early childhood education: Development, resources, and practice* (5th ed.). Independence, KY: Cengage Learning.

> This comprehensive resource contains information related to working with children with diverse abilities. It can be used as a reference book, but it also contains guidelines, vignettes, and hands-on program planning ideas to prepare educators to successfully integrate all children into the early childhood program. Particularly useful for inexperienced teachers is the information related to translating IFSP/IEP goals into day-to-day classroom programming.

Division for Early Childhood/Council for Exceptional Children. *Young exceptional children monograph series.* Available online at *http://bookstore.dec-sped.org/category-s /1513.htm*.

This series of monographs provides collections of articles on all aspects of educating children with disabilities. Topics include challenging behavior, natural environments, teaching strategies, assessment, family-based practices, collaborative teaming, early literacy, social-emotional development, and linking curriculum to child and family outcomes.Division for Early Childhood of the Council for Exceptional Children, National Association for the Education of Young Children, & National Head Start Association. (2013). Frameworks for response-to-intervention in early childhood: Description and implications. Available online at *http://www.naeyc.org/content/frameworks-response -intervention-paperwww.naeyc.org/*.

> The goal of this document is to present various perspectives on the philosophy, design, and implementation of response-to-intervention models in the early childhood setting.

Gruenberg, A. M., & Miller, R. (2011). *A practical guide to early childhood inclusion: Effective reflection.* Upper Saddle River, NJ: Pearson.

> This text presents a developmental approach to including children with disabilities in the general early childhood classroom. A distinctive feature of this book includes the incorporation of a reflective decision-making model for practitioners.

Milbourne, S. A., & Campbell, P. H. (2007). *Cara's kit: Creating adaptations for routines and activities.* Arlington, VA: Council for Exceptional Children.

> This kit provides guidance for adapting activities and routines in order to integrate young children with diverse abilities. The teacher version contains a booklet about adaptations and a CD-ROM with additional resources.

Noonan, M. J., & McCormick, L. (2014). *Teaching young children with disabilities in natural environments* (2nd ed.). Baltimore, MD: Paul H. Brookes.

This volume presents specific evidence-based strategies for teaching young children with disabilities during the naturally occurring activities of the classroom.

Roffman, L., & Wanerman, T. (2011). *Including one, including all: A guide to relationship-based early childhood inclusion.* St. Paul, MN: Redleaf Press.

> This volume provides theoretical, conceptual, and practical information on inclusive early childhood programming. The authors present blueprints for organizing work with children and their families and addresses the challenges and rewards of inclusive environments for all children.

Watson, A., & McCathren, R. (2009). Including children with special needs: Are you and your early childhood program ready? *Young Children, 64*(2), 20–26.

> This article presents information to help preschool and kindergarten administrators and teachers develop confidence in teaching children with disabilities.

Wolery, R. A., & Odom, S. (2000). An *administrator's guide to preschool inclusion.* Chapel Hill, NC: Frank Porter Graham Child Development Institute.

> For many administrators working in early childhood programs, inclusion is filled with complex and puzzling issues. Administrators hold a powerful role in creating and maintaining inclusive classrooms for young children. This text provides insight into the administrative challenges and successes of inclusion. The document can be downloaded free of charge at *http://www.fpg.unc.edu/sites/fpg.unc.edu/files /resources/reports-and-policy-briefs/ECRII_Administrators _Guide_2000.pdf*.

## COMPUTERS AND TECHNOLOGY

Campaign for a Commercial-Free Childhood, Alliance for Childhood & Teachers Resisting Unhealthy Children's Entertainment. (2012). *Facing the screen dilemma: Young children, technology and early education.* Boston, MA: Campaign for a Commercial-Free Childhood; New York, NY: Alliance for Childhood. Available online at *http://www .truceteachers.org/docs/facing_the_screen_dilemma.pdf*.

> This document highlights issues related to screen technologies that should concern members of the early childhood community, including the use of technology in classrooms and child care settings.

Carter, M. (2010). Helping teachers think about technology. *Exchange, 32*(1), 30–33.

> In this article, the author discusses Information and Communication Technology (ICT) as a tool for

supporting and facilitating learning in early childhood environments. When selecting technologies for use with young children, readers are challenged to consider their values and philosophical beliefs and to reflect on how their choices can enhance or undermine learning.

Levin, D. E. (2013). *Beyond remote-controlled childhood: Teaching young children in the media age*. Washington, DC: NAEYC.

> This volume provides teachers with information about how screen time and media culture are affecting the lives of young children and their families. Suggestions for the appropriate use of media in the curriculum are offered.

NAEYC. (2012). *Technology and interactive media as tools in early childhood programs serving children from birth through age 8: A joint position statement issued by the National Association for the Education of Young Children and the Fred Rogers Center for Early Learning and Children's Media at Saint Vincent College*. Available online at *http://www.naeyc .org/positionstatements*.

> This document presents the position of two highly respected organizations related to the appropriate use of technology with young children.

Parrette, H., & Blum, C. (2013). *Instructional technology in early childhood: Teaching in the digital age*. Baltimore, MD: Paul H. Brookes.

> This volume provides an overview of the use of technology in pre-K and kindergarten and how it can be used to support learning for both those with and without disabilities.

## DIVERSITY/ANTI-BIAS CURRICULUM

Copple, E. (Ed.). (2003). *A world of difference*. Washington, DC: NAEYC.

> This collection of readings provides a knowledge base and a thought-provoking discussion of issues relative to culture, language, religion, inclusion, and socioeconomic status. Emphasis is on building mutual respect and understanding between and among child care staff, children, and families.

Derman-Sparks, L., & Edwards, J. O. (2010). *Anti-bias education for young children and ourselves*. Washington, DC: NAEYC.

> This volume, the successor to Derman-Sparks' classic *Anti-bias Curriculum*, provides updated information about creating early childhood environments that meet the needs of all children and their families. Tips are provided to help staff and children respect each other, themselves, and those who have diverse backgrounds, experiences, families, abilities, cultures, and language.

Espinosa, L. (2009). *Getting it RIGHT for young children from diverse backgrounds: Applying research to improve practice*. Upper Saddle River, NJ: Pearson.

> This book provides research-based strategies that can be used to meet the challenges of teaching diverse children including those who are learning English and/or living in poverty.

Gonzalez-Mena, J. (2011). *Foundations of early childhood education: Teaching children in a diverse society*. Columbus, OH: McGraw-Hill.

> This text provides an introduction to planning appropriate programming for young children with real-life examples, case studies, stories, and anecdotes. It incorporates discussions of cultural influences and identifies what staff members can do to meet every child's needs.

Gonzalez-Mena, J. (2008). *Diversity in early care and education programs: Honoring differences* (5th ed.). New York: McGraw-Hill.

> This author describes an anti-bias approach to preschool curriculum through discussion of culture, adult relations, and conflicts in goals, values, expectations, and childrearing practices.

Parlakian, R. (2004). *How culture shapes social-emotional development: Implications for practice in infant-family programs*. Washington, DC: Zero to Three Press.

> Intended for leaders and practitioners, this book examines how culture shapes children's fundamental learning about themselves and their world and provides a framework for resolving cultural dilemmas.

## ETHICS

Feeney, S., & Freeman, N. K. (2012). *Ethics and the early childhood educator: Using the NAEYC Code*. Washington, DC: NAEYC.

> This companion to the NAEYC Code of Ethics presents a framework that can be used to help clarify key aspects of the position statement and to encourage discussion on these important issues.

Feeney, S., Freeman, N., & Moravcik, E. (2008). *Teaching the NAEYC code of ethical conduct: Activity sourcebook* (2005 Code ed.). Washington, DC: NAEYC.

> This book provides tools and techniques that can be used in college courses or staff trainings to introduce the use of the NAEYC Code of Ethical Conduct.

NAEYC. (2006, Reaffirmed and Updated 2011). *Code of Ethical Conduct: Supplement for early childhood program administrators*. Available online at *http://www.naeyc.org /files/naeyc/file/positions/Supplement%20PS2011.pdf*

> This important document presents guidelines that can be used by program administrators as they face

ethical challenges that are unique to their positions as leaders.

# EVALUATION AND ASSESSMENT

*The evaluation and assessment tools identified in this section represent no official endorsement of any practice, publication, or program by the authors.*

## Children

Berke, K., Bickart, T., & Heroman, C. (2010). *Teaching Strategies Gold® birth through kindergarten assessment toolkit.* Bethesda, MD: Teaching Strategies, LLC.

> This observational assessment system enables teachers to conduct evaluations during everyday routines and activities (available in both English and Spanish).

Grisham-Brown, J., & Frontczak, K. P. (2011). *Assessing young children in inclusive settings: The blended practices approach.* Baltimore, MD: P. H. Brookes.

> This text presents a comprehensive model for the authentic assessment of young children, with and without disabilities, that can be used to inform planning and to ensure that program practices are aligned with both NAEYC and DEC guidelines. Classroom vignettes and examples are included along with other practical resources such as checklists and excerpts from selected assessment tools.

Johnson-Martin, N. M., Attermeier, S. M., & Hacker, B. J. (2004). *The Carolina curriculum for infants and toddlers with special needs* (2nd ed., 3rd ed.). Baltimore: Brookes Publishing.

> Both editions of this material provide an integrated assessment and intervention program for young children with mild to severe disabilities. This criterion-referenced system permits observation of children in their natural environments playing with familiar materials, and supports collaboration among teachers, families, and service providers.

Linder, T. W. (2007). *Transdisciplinary play-based assessment* (2nd ed.). Baltimore: Brookes Publishing.

> These materials provide an integrated assessment and intervention program for children ages birth to 6 years. Children engage in natural play with a parent while four developmental domains are evaluated by a professional: sensorimotor, social and emotional, communication and language, and cognition. Interventions are based on results of the assessment.

Lynch, E. (2007). Authentic assessment in the inclusive classroom: Using portfolios to document change and modify curriculum. In E. Horn, C. Peterson, & L. Fox (Eds.), *Linking curriculum to child and family outcomes.* Longmont, CO: Sopris West.

> This article provides an overview of a developmentally appropriate assessment process that can be used with all children. Specific details on the benefits of the process as well as how to plan and implement portfolio assessment are included.

McLean, M., Hemmeter, M. L., & Snyder, P. (2014). *Essential elements for assessing infants and preschoolers with special needs.* Upper Saddle River, NJ: Pearson.

> This text provides an overview of evidence-based practices that can be used to assess infant and preschoolers with disabilities ages birth to five.

Puckett, M. B., & Black, J. K. (2008). *Meaningful assessments of the young child: Celebrating development and learning* (3rd ed.). Upper Saddle River, NJ: Pearson.

> This text, based on the premise that curriculum, assessment, and teaching are intertwined, provides information on conducting informal and formal assessments and on developing an assessment system that draws information from a variety of sources.

## Environment

Harms, T., Cryer, D., & Clifford, R. (2005). *Early Childhood Environment Rating Scale.* New York: Teachers College Press.

> There are four Harms, Cryer, and Clifford Rating Scales:

- Infant/Toddler Environment Rating Scale, Revised Edition (ITERS-R)
- Early Childhood Environment Rating Scale, Revised Edition (ECERS-R)
- Family Child Care Environment Rating Scale, Revised Edition (FCCERS-R)
- School-Age Care Environment Rating Scale, Revised Edition (SACERS-R)

> These easy-to-use evaluation instruments answer many questions about the adequacy of early childhood settings. The ratings cover issues such as space, care routines, language, reasoning skills, social development, and adult needs.

## Staff and Program

Bloom, P. J. (1996). *The early childhood work environment survey.* Wheeling, IL: National-Louis University.

> This tool assesses staff perceptions and attitudes about staff relations, administrative support, goal consensus, and the physical setting of the program.

Bloom, P. J. (2010). *Measuring work attitudes in the early childhood setting: Technical manual for the Early Childhood Job Satisfaction Survey and the Early Childhood Work Environment Survey.* Wheeling, IL: McCormick Center for Early Childhood Leadership, National-Louis University.

This technical guide and resource manual describes 10 dimensions of organizational climate and provides many ideas for increasing job satisfaction and professionalism in early childhood programs.

North Carolina Institute for Early Childhood Professional Development. (n.d.). *Self-assessment for administrators of child care programs*. Available online at *http://www.ncicdp.org/documents/assess.pdf*.

This self-assessment document challenges directors to evaluate their philosophies and skills related to managing a program for young children.

Sylva, K., Srai-Batchford, I., & Taggarat, B. (2006). *Assessing quality in the early years: Early childhood environment rating scale – extension (ECERS-E)* (rev. ed.). Stoke on Trent, United Kingdom: Trentham Books. (Available through Stylus Publishing in the United States.)

The ECERS-E has been developed to measure program quality in literacy, math, science and environment, and diversity. This revised edition clarifies and builds on the previous text, enabling programs to improve pedagogy and curriculum in preschool settings.

Talan, T. N., & Bloom, P. J. (2011). *The Program Administration Scale: Measuring leadership and management in early childhood*. (2nd ed.). New York, NY: Teachers College Press.

The instrument examines the following 10 categories: human resources development, personnel cost and allocation, center operations, child assessment, fiscal management, program planning and evaluation, family partnerships, marketing and public relations, technology, and staff qualifications.

## FINANCIAL MANAGEMENT, FUND-RAISING, AND MARKETING

Bray, I. (2008). *Effective fundraising for nonprofits: Real-world strategies that work*. Berkeley, CA: Nolo.

This volume presents information about working with individual donors, getting media coverage, soliciting grants from foundations and corporations, planning special events and using the Internet effectively. It addresses IRS rules and regulations and provides numerous planning worksheets.

Gross, M., Warshauer, W., & Shelmon, N. E. (2010). *Financial and accounting guide for not-for-profit organizations*. New York: Wiley.

This book provides detailed advice on cash, accrual, and fund accounting; financial statements; budgeting; internal control; tax requirements; and bookkeeping.

Jack, G. (2005). *The business of child care: Management and financial strategies*. Clifton Park, NY: Thomson Delmar Learning.

This volume focuses on managing enrollment, recruiting and retaining staff, budgeting, financial record keeping, and decision making. The accompanying CD-ROM provides financial spreadsheets that can be implemented in child care settings.

## FUNDING

Bergman, R. (2010). *Not just small change: Fund development for early childhood programs*. Redmond, WA: Child Care Information Exchange.

This book, written specifically for those involved with early childhood programming, covers numerous strategies related to fund-raising and grant writing.

McDonough, B., & Bazikian, D. (Eds.). (2013). *Annual register of grant support 2014: A directory of funding sources*. Medford, NJ: Information Today, Inc.

A comprehensive guide to various types of grant support, both governmental and private.

USDA National Agriculture Library Rural Information Center. (2013). Starting a child care center. Available online at *http://www.nal.usda.gov/ric/ricpubs/rural_child_care.htm*.

This guide provides information related to each step in the planning and operating of an early childhood program. Included are links to sources that provide information on funding sources for child care programs.

U.S. Small Business Association. (n.d.). Starting a child care business? Government tools and resources that can help. Available online at *http://www.sba.gov/community/blogs/community-blogs/small-business-matters/starting-child-care-business-government-tools#*.

## GUIDANCE

Gartrell, D. J. (2004). *The power of guidance: Teaching social-emotional skills in early childhood classrooms*. Clifton Park, NY: Thomson Delmar Learning.

This book is well titled because it is, indeed, a powerful book as it explores age-appropriate and developmentally appropriate ways to teach social-emotional skills in the classroom through the use of thoughtful guidance practices. Gartrell has an informal, friendly writing style, and he uses many anecdotes to help the reader reflect on and apply his suggested approaches that promote the emotional well-being of young children.

Gartrell, D. J. (2014). *A guidance approach for the encouraging classroom* (5th ed.). Independence, KY: Cengage Learning.

The first part of this excellent text explores the foundation of guidance and addresses issues such as conventional discipline versus guidance, mistaken behavior, the guidance tradition, and innovative theories about child development with guidance. Part two focuses on building an encouraging classroom. Of particular interest is the author's discussion of leadership communication that focuses on the importance of effective interaction with staff and parents.

Miller, D. F. (2010). *Positive child guidance* (7th ed.). Independence, KY: Cengage Learning.

> Child guidance is a challenging process of finding ways to help children become responsible, cooperative members of their group. This book is for caregivers who spend a great deal of time helping children become self-disciplined members of society. It is intended as a road map to guide adults as they work to meet the individual needs of children from infancy through early childhood.

## HEALTH, SAFETY, AND SICK CHILD CARE

American Academy of Pediatrics, American Public Health Association, & Maternal and Child Health Bureau. (2011). *Caring for our children: National health and safety performance standards: Guidelines for out-of-home child care programs* (3rd ed.). Denver, CO: National Resource for Health and Safety in Child Care.

> This edition offers nine comprehensive chapters of the latest information and program activities for child care providers, licensors, and policy makers in the early child care field. It covers healthy development, safe play facilities, supplies and equipment, infectious diseases, principles for including and caring for children with special needs, and much more. Updates to this volume can be found at: *http://cfoc.nrckids.org*.

American Academy of Pediatrics, American Public Health Association, & National Resource Center for Health and Safety in Child Care and Early Education. (2010). *Preventing childhood obesity in early care and education programs*. Denver, CO: National Resource for Health and Safety in Child Care.

This booklet presents national standards that describe best practices in nutrition and physical activity for all types of early childhood programs. The document is available online at *http://cfoc.nrckids.org/StandardView/SpcCol/Preventing_Childhood_Obesity.Aronson, S. (2012).* Healthy young children: A manual for programs. Washington, DC: NAEYC.

> This manual contains a new chapter on promoting children's health through physical activity as well as updated standards, procedures, and resources, including sample forms and checklists.

Aronson, S., & Shope, T. (2009). *Managing infectious diseases in child care and schools: A quick reference guide* (2nd ed.). Elk Grove Village, IL: American Academy of Pediatrics.

> This is a convenient, easy-to-reference guide specifically designed for use by child care teachers. It offers a quick resource to industry standards and proven policies for protecting the children in your care, the center staff, and the organization's liability.

Boise, P. (2009). *Go green rating scale for early childhood settings*. St. Paul, MN: Redleaf Press.

> This research-based rating scale helps early childhood staff determine the level of environmental health and safety in their program and explains why particular scores are earned.

Marotz, L. R. (2015). *Health, safety and nutrition for the young child* (9th ed.). Independence, KY: Cengage Learning.

> This up-to-date, comprehensive text covers the essential aspects of health, safety, and nutrition for young children. It includes material on infant nutrition, AIDS, and sanitary procedures in group care facilities.

## INFANT/TODDLER CARE

Copple, C., Bredekamp, S., Koralek, D., & Charner, K. (2013). *Developmentally appropriate practice: Focus on infants and toddlers*. Washington, DC: NAEYC.

Copple, C., Bredekamp, S., Koralek, D. & Charner, K. (2013). *Developmentally appropriate practice: Focus on preschoolers*. Washington, DC: NAEYC.

> These companion volumes provide teachers and administrators with information about developmentally appropriate practice for young learners. Additionally, the authors include practical suggestions for implementing developmentally appropriate practice in the classroom.

Gonzalez-Mena, J., & Widmeyer Eyer, D. (2012). *Infants, toddlers, and caregivers: A curriculum of respective, responsive care and education* (9th ed.). Columbus, OH: McGraw-Hill.

> This book offers excellent coverage of infant/toddler development. It serves as a complete resource on attachment as well as infant and toddler care in group settings.

Greenman, J., Stonehouse, A., & Schweikert, G. (2007). *Prime times: A handbook for excellence in infant and toddler programs* (2nd ed.). St. Paul, MN: Redleaf Press.

> The authors explore the topic of what makes for quality in infant and toddler programs, emphasizing the need for primary caregivers; small groups; responsive interactions; and environments that are safe, secure, and "filled with learning." This is a hands-on guide for practitioners.

Lally, D. (2008). *Caring for infants and toddlers in groups: Developmentally appropriate practice* (2nd ed.). Washington, DC: Zero to Three Press.

This book identifies research-based elements of quality care that support optimal development and learning of infants and toddlers in group care. Family- and center-based providers will learn research-based strategies to impact the lives of the children and the families they serve.

Raikes, H. H., & Edwards, C. P. (2009). *Extending the dance in infant and toddler caregiving: Enhancing attachment and relationships.* Baltimore, MD: Paul H. Brookes.

The authors provide a comprehensive blueprint for establishing and maintaining an early childhood program based on the formation of nurturing relationships and strengthening parent-child attachment.

# LEADERSHIP

Bloom, P. J. (2002). *Making the most of meetings: A practical guide.* Lake Forest, IL: New Horizons.

A rich resource for guiding the planning and preparation of meetings, with helpful strategies for carrying out a successful meeting plus ways one can enhance effectiveness of meetings. This book will help directors preside over stimulating and inspiring staff and parent meetings.

Bloom, P. J. (2003). *Leadership in action: How effective directors get things done.* Lake Forest, IL: New Horizons.

This book includes discussion of many facets of leadership, including leadership roles, leadership as a way of thinking, knowing thyself, and becoming a facilitative leader. Bloom discusses the essential functions of a leader in early childhood education—to inspire, to inform, to motivate, and to serve as a symbol for the collective identity of the group.

Bruno, H. E. (2012). *What you need to lead an early childhood program: Emotional intelligence in practice.* Washington, DC: NAEYC.

This volume serves as a guide to building respectful, dynamic relationships with families and staff members. Topics include financial management, marketing and development, and the use of emotional intelligence in effective leadership.

Collins, J. C. (2001). *Good to great: Why some companies make the leap … and others don't.* New York: Harper Collins.

While not a book written specifically for early childhood educators, this volume is considered to be an excellent discussion of how companies remain successful over time and how administrators and managers can attain sustained performance.

Collins, J. C. (2005). *Good to great and the social sectors: A monograph to accompany good to great.* New York: Harper Collins.

Collins applies the principles described in *Good to Great* to the not-for-profit sector. He calls himself a student of the social sector and explores the challenges facing social-sector leaders. Directors will discover ideas and inspiration from this interesting author.

Gordon, T. (2001). *Leadership effectiveness training (LET).* E. Rutherford, NJ: The Penguin Group.

The basic skills for effective interpersonal communication, including active listening, "I" messages, and no-lose problem solving, are covered. These skills are analogues to those covered in Gordon's *Teacher Effectiveness Training* and *Parent Effectiveness Training.*

Neugebauer, B., & Neugebauer, R. (Eds.). (2003). *The art of leadership: Managing early childhood organizations* (Rev. ed.). Redmond, WA: Child Care Information Exchange.

The Neugebauers have carefully selected articles covering a wide range of topics of interest to directors. This is a collection of more than 90 articles written by respected specialists and covering leadership, organizational management, financial management, personnel management, program development, and community relations. Those directors who find *Child Care Information Exchange: A Magazine for Directors* helpful will find this compilation of informative articles assembled by the Neugebauers an excellent resource.

Sciarra, D. J., & Dorsey, A. G. (2002). *Leaders and supervisors in child care programs.* Clifton Park, NY: Thomson Delmar Learning.

The book is about leadership and supervision in the field of early child care and education. It is divided into three sections. Section I, Describing the Leader, draws on principles from business that leaders in early childhood can apply to the business of child care. Section II, Supervision 101, offers an in-depth discussion of supervision that will guide directors through the specific steps of an effective supervisory program. Section III considers other aspects of the leader's role. It addresses the issues faced by leaders as change agents and the leader's role as a professional in the field. This textbook has features similar to Sciarra and Dorsey's *Developing and Administering a Child Care Center* that make it a suitable companion for use in a college-level course as well as for working directors.

Winton, P. J., McCollum, J. A., & Catlett, C. (2007). *Practical approaches to early childhood professional development: Evidence, strategies, and resources.* Washington, DC: Zero to Three Press.

This book provides an organized format for building quality into professional development experiences. A CD-ROM includes handouts and activities as well as additional resources.

## NEUROSCIENCE AND EARLY CHILDHOOD

Fox, N., & Shonkoff, J. P. (2011, June). How persistent fear and anxiety can affect young children's learning, behaviour, and health. *Early Childhood Matters*, 116, 8–14.

This article emphasizes that policies and programs must consider the impact of abuse, maltreatment, and violence on the developing brain.

Marshall, J. (2011). Neurosensory development: Considerations for infant child care. *Early Childhood Education Journal*, 39, 175–181.

This article provides recommendations for the infant child care environment based on research about early neurological development.

Rushton, S. P., Rushton, A. J., & Larkin, E. (2010). Neuroscience, play and early childhood education: Connections, implications and assessment. *Early Childhood Education Journal*, 37, 351–361.

This article emphasizes the importance of play for "brain-compatible" individual learning and describes what constitutes a "brain-enriched" environment for young children.

Twardosz, S. (2012). Effects of experience on the brain: The role of neuroscience in early development and education. *Early Education and Development*, 23, 96–119.

This article presents an overview of the effects of experience on brain development.

## PLANNING SPACES

Curtis, D., & Carter, M. (2002). *Designs for living and learning: Transforming early childhood environments*. St. Paul, MN: Redleaf Press.

This book will inspire directors and teachers to create wonderful environments that are comfortable and inviting for children, families, and staff.

DeViney, J., Duncan, S., Harris, S., Rody, M. A., & Rosenberry, L (2010). *Inspiring spaces for young children*. Lewisville, NC: Gryphon House.

This volume presents step-by-step guidance and associated photographs for administrators and teachers interested in transforming their classrooms into learning spaces that support growth and development.

Greenman, J. (2005). *Caring spaces, learning places: Children's environments that work*. Redmond, WA: Exchange Press.

This is a helpful guide to planning spaces for young children. It is full of ideas and observations, as well as problems and solutions for those responsible for planning spaces for child care.

## PROGRAM DEVELOPMENT AND CURRICULUM APPROACHES AND PACKAGES

*The curricula identified in this section represent no official endorsement of any practice, publication, or program by the authors.*

Albrecht, K., & Miller, L. G. (2000). *Innovations: The comprehensive infant curriculum: A complete interactive curriculum for infants from birth to 18 months*. Beltsville, MD: Gryphon House.

Albrecht, K., & Miller, L. G. (2001). *Innovations: The comprehensive toddler curriculum: A complete interactive curriculum for toddlers from 18 months to 36 months*. Beltsville, MD: Gryphon House.

Albrecht, K., & Miller, L. G. (2004). *Innovations: The comprehensive preschool curriculum*. Beltsville, MD: Gryphon House.

These three volumes by Albrecht and Miller offer a complete review of child development for each age group followed by sections on interactions, relationships, communicating, making friends, and age-appropriate activities. It is a very comprehensive series that presents a convincing position that curriculum is much more than well-arranged rooms and interesting activities.

Copple, C., & Bredekamp, S. (Eds.). (2009). *Developmentally appropriate practice in early childhood programs: Serving children from birth through age 8* (3rd ed.). Washington, DC: NAEYC.

This updated version of the contemporary early childhood education classic is accompanied by a supplementary CD containing readings on key topics plus video vignettes showing developmentally appropriate practice in action. Based on research, this volume helps teachers, directors, parents, and board members better understand sound practice that should reverse the current trend toward a narrow focus on academics for young children.

Curtis, D., & Carter, M. (2007). *Learning together with young children: A curriculum framework for reflective teachers*. St. Paul, MN: Redleaf Press.

This text presents a collaborative framework for thinking about curriculum. Teachers are challenged to consider their values and to explore how they can teach through observation, reflection, inquiry, and action. In addition, a discussion of how teachers can encourage children to represent their learning in multiple ways is provided.

Dodge, D. T., Colker, L. J., & Heroman, C. (2010 ). *The creative curriculum for pre-school* (5th ed.). Washington, DC: Teaching Strategies.

Dodge, D. T., Rudick, S., & Berke, K. (2006). *The creative curriculum for infants, toddlers and twos* (2nd ed.). Washington, DC: Teaching Strategies.

The Creative Curriculum™ materials present an environment-based approach to curriculum but also clearly define the teacher's role in connecting content, teaching, and learning. They apply recent research to the practice and strategies that help meet the needs of all children, including those with special needs as well as those who are second language learners.

Edwards, C., Gandini, L., & Forman, G. (Eds.). (1998). *The hundred languages of children: The Reggio Emilia approach—Advanced reflections* (2nd ed.). Stamford, CT: Ablex Publishing.

This classic book is a comprehensive overview of the Reggio Emilia approach to education, including its history and philosophy, teaching methods, parent perspectives, school organization, and attention to the planning of physical environments. The volume also discusses the role of adults in planning and implementing the curriculum as well as the inclusion of children with disabilities.

Epstein, A., & Hohmann, A. (2012). *The HighScope preschool curriculum*. Ypsilanti, MI: HighScope Press.

This book provides the details of the revised HighScope™ curriculum for preschoolers. This approach to curriculum is based on the HighScope Educational Research Foundation's longitudinal research on educating children in environments that support active and participatory learning.

Gordon, A. M., & Williams Browne, K. (2013). *Beginnings and beyond: Foundations in early childhood* (9th ed.). Independence, KY: Cengage Learning.

A comprehensive text covering many of the traditional questions that are of interest to early childhood educators, including the following: What is the field of early childhood? Who is the young child? Who are the teachers of the young child? What is the setting? What is being taught? How do we teach for tomorrow?

Jackman, H. (2012 ). *Early education curriculum: A child's connection to the world* (5th ed.). Independence, KY: Cengage Learning.

The fifth edition focuses on curriculum planning and implementation as well as on designing inclusive environments that meet all children's needs.

Montessori, M. (1986). *The discovery of the child*. New York: Ballantine Books.

Montessori, M. (2002). *The Montessori method*. Mineola, NY: Dover Publications.

Before educators explore the materials and methods of Montessori, they should first understand her basic philosophies, and these volumes provide a valuable introduction to the topic. In Montessori's own words, these books provide an overview of her approach to and theoretical basis for educating children as well as her understanding of the nature of the child.

Moomaw, S. (2002). *More than singing: Discovering music in preschool*. St. Paul, MN: Redleaf Press.

This book, which includes a CD, offers a wealth of wonderful musical experiences that teachers can plan, even though they may not be trained musicians. Teachers will learn to make resonant, inexpensive instruments as well as gain knowledge about how to select songs and rhythm activities and coordinate these with their whole language curriculum.

Moomaw, S., & Hieronymous, B. (2002). *Much more than counting: Whole math activities for preschool and kindergarten*. St. Paul, MN: Redleaf Press.

An excellent resource for use by teachers and parents as they come to understand the "whole math" curriculum based on the constructivist model of cognitive development. The math games and materials described here in detail are not just additions to enrich the curriculum, they are the math curriculum for preschool and kindergarten.

Moomaw, S., & Hieronymous, B. (1997). *More than magnets: Exploring the wonder of science in preschool and kindergarten*. St. Paul, MN: Redleaf Press.

The science curriculum in early childhood classrooms has typically consisted of a classroom "display," usually with a plant/animal focus or teacher-directed experiments. This book offers a comprehensive, developmentally appropriate approach to science education with young children, with special attention to physics and math. It has more than a hundred activities that engage children in interactive science explorations in many areas of the classroom.

Moomaw, S., & Hieronymous, B. (2002). *More than letters: Literacy activities for pre-school, kindergarten and first grade*. St. Paul, MN: Redleaf Press.

This excellent book is an extensive compilation of emergent-literacy materials and activities that translate theory and research into a dynamic, effective literacy program for young children. The curriculum evolved following the emergence of the whole language movement and took shape as the authors explored their interest in how children construct literacy concepts.

Sandall, S., Hemmeter, M. L., Smith, B. J., & McLean, M. E. (Eds.). (2005). *DEC recommended practices: A comprehensive guide for practical application in early intervention/early childhood special education.* Longmont, CO: Sopris West.

This collection of readings provides specific guidelines for early childhood programs that serve children with disabilities. Included are suggestions related to curriculum, child and program assessment, family-based practices, interdisciplinary teaming, and technology.

## PROGRAM MANAGEMENT

Bloom, P. J., Hentschel, A., & Bella, J. (2010). *A great place to work: Creating a healthy organizational climate.* Lake Forest, IL: New Horizons

This text helps directors identify how 10 dimensions of a center impact the work life for staff. These important dimensions include collegiality, opportunities for professional growth, supervisor support, reward systems, and goal consensus.

Bruno, H. E., & Copeland, T. (2012). *Managing legal risks in early childhood programs: How to prevent flare-ups from becoming lawsuits.* New York, NY: Teachers College Press.

This text, written by two attorneys, addresses the complex legal issues that must be considered when owning or managing an early childhood program. Topics covered include privacy issues, employee hiring practices, insurance coverage, and reducing the risk of lawsuits.

Jack, G. (2005). *The business of child care: Management and financial strategies.* Clifton Park, NY: Thomson Delmar Learning.

This volume focuses on managing enrollment, recruiting and retaining staff, budgeting, financial record keeping, and decision making. The accompanying CD-ROM provides financial spreadsheets that can be implemented in child care settings.

## WORKING WITH STAFF, BOARD, COMMUNITY, AND PARENTS

Baker, A. C., & Manfredi/Petitt, L. A. (2004). *Relationships, the heart of quality care: Creating community among adults in early care settings.* Washington, DC: NAEYC.

This volume describes the concept of relationship-based child care, what attitudes support such care, and the policies required to implement this important approach to staff interaction and teaching.

Bloom, P. J. (2000). *Circle of influence: Implementing shared decision making and participative management.* Lake Forest, IL: New Horizons.

In this book, you learn that participative management is both a philosophy and a set of behaviors that define your interactions with people. You will explore techniques for managing the daily business of your center. If you implement these strategies and expand your staff's circle of influence over decision making, you will have true collaboration and commitment to shared goals.

Bloom, P. J. (2005). *Blueprint for action: Achieving center-based change through staff development* (2nd ed.). Lake Forest, IL: New Horizons.

This book is based on two basic assumptions, namely, that high-quality programs are distinguished by their willingness to deal with their imperfections and that organizational change can come about only through change in individuals. The blueprint Bloom presents in this excellent book serves as a guide for enhancing the professional development of all who work together to achieve changes that will move them toward their shared vision of excellence.

Bloom, P. J. (2007). *From the inside out: The power of reflection and self-awareness.* Lake Forest, IL: New Horizons.

Bloom speaks to personhood of early childhood educators in this book—ideas like self-mentoring, self-awareness, and being a self-reflective practitioner are just a few of her provocative words for those of us who spend our lives working with and thinking about the care of young children.

Carter, M., & Curtis, D. (2009). *The visionary director: A handbook for dreaming, organizing and improvising in your center* (2nd ed.). St. Paul, MN: Redleaf Press.

The major thrust of this book is to help administrators develop their potential as leaders. Each principle presented in this book is accompanied by practical strategies that can guide the professional development of the administrator.

Gonzalez-Mena, J. (2013). *50 strategies for communicating and working with diverse families* (3rd ed.). Upper Saddle River, NJ: Pearson.

This book presents culturally relevant ideas for working with families in today's diverse society. Included are strategies related to advocacy, nonverbal and written communication, handling conferences, transitions in the child's education, working with immigrant families, working with families of children with special needs, working with families referred for abuse or neglect, and many others.

Keyser, J. (2006). *From parents to partners: Building a family-centered early childhood program.* St. Paul, MN: Redleaf Press.

This volume describes how directors can encourage parents to become involved in early childhood programs through the use of effective communication, newsletters, conferences, and special events. It also explores the reasons and methods for partnering with family members.

# INDEX

*Note: Page numbers referencing figures are italicized and followed by an "f". Page numbers referencing tables are italicized and followed by a "t"*